AF817963

Foundations of Criminal Forensic Neuropsychology

K. Jayasankara Reddy

Foundations of Criminal Forensic Neuropsychology

Bridging Mind, Law, and Criminal Justice

Springer

K. Jayasankara Reddy
Department of Psychology
Christ University
Bangalore, Karnataka, India

ISBN 978-3-031-83770-8 ISBN 978-3-031-83771-5 (eBook)
https://doi.org/10.1007/978-3-031-83771-5

© The Editor(s) (if applicable) and The Author(s), under exclusive license to Springer Nature Switzerland AG 2025

This work is subject to copyright. All rights are solely and exclusively licensed by the Publisher, whether the whole or part of the material is concerned, specifically the rights of translation, reprinting, reuse of illustrations, recitation, broadcasting, reproduction on microfilms or in any other physical way, and transmission or information storage and retrieval, electronic adaptation, computer software, or by similar or dissimilar methodology now known or hereafter developed.
The use of general descriptive names, registered names, trademarks, service marks, etc. in this publication does not imply, even in the absence of a specific statement, that such names are exempt from the relevant protective laws and regulations and therefore free for general use.
The publisher, the authors and the editors are safe to assume that the advice and information in this book are believed to be true and accurate at the date of publication. Neither the publisher nor the authors or the editors give a warranty, expressed or implied, with respect to the material contained herein or for any errors or omissions that may have been made. The publisher remains neutral with regard to jurisdictional claims in published maps and institutional affiliations.

This Springer imprint is published by the registered company Springer Nature Switzerland AG
The registered company address is: Gewerbestrasse 11, 6330 Cham, Switzerland

If disposing of this product, please recycle the paper.

Preface

The intricate interplay between the mind, the law, and the criminal justice system forms a compelling and complex domain of study, one that has far-reaching implications for society at large. *Foundations of Criminal Forensic Neuropsychology: Bridging Mind, Law, and Criminal Justice* seeks to explore this intersection, offering readers an in-depth understanding of how advances in neuropsychology illuminate the cognitive, emotional, and behavioral underpinnings of criminal behavior. This book provides a foundational framework for students, practitioners, and scholars navigating this rapidly evolving field while addressing the ethical, scientific, and practical challenges accompanying such interdisciplinary endeavors.

The origins of forensic neuropsychology can be traced back to efforts to understand the link between brain dysfunction and criminal behavior. As neuroimaging techniques, cognitive assessments, and neuropsychological theories advanced, so too did our ability to investigate the neural substrates of behaviors that contribute to criminality. These developments have opened up new opportunities to evaluate criminal responsibility, competence to stand trial, and the risk of recidivism. However, they also bring forth critical questions about the limitations of neuroscience in the courtroom, protecting individuals' rights, and the potential for misusing or overinterpreting neuropsychological data.

This book is born from a need to address these questions systematically. Its goal is not only to educate but also to foster a sense of responsibility among those involved in criminal forensic neuropsychology. The reader is encouraged to consider both the promise and the perils of using neuropsychological evidence in legal contexts. This book aims to establish best practices for integrating neuropsychological knowledge into the criminal justice system by emphasizing rigorous scientific methodology, ethical considerations, and the need for cultural competence.

The structure of the book reflects the interdisciplinary nature of the field, beginning with a historical and conceptual overview. The opening chapters trace the evolution of criminal forensic neuropsychology, highlighting key theoretical advancements and landmark legal cases that have shaped the discipline. These chapters set the stage for discussions about the brain-behavior relationship, focusing on how abnormalities in brain function—whether due to traumatic brain injury, neurodegenerative conditions, or developmental disorders—can influence decision-making, impulse control, and moral reasoning.

Subsequent chapters delve into the practical aspects of forensic neuropsychological assessments. These chapters provide a step-by-step guide to conducting evaluations in legal contexts, addressing critical issues such as malingering, cultural sensitivity, and the integration of neuroimaging findings. Particular attention is paid to the challenges of assessing individuals with complex comorbidities, such as substance abuse disorders or severe mental illness, who frequently intersect with the criminal justice system. Case studies are used to illustrate how theoretical concepts are applied in practice, offering readers a window into the real-world complexities of forensic neuropsychological work.

A significant portion of the book is dedicated to the ethical and legal considerations surrounding the use of neuropsychological evidence in court. These chapters explore contentious topics, such as the role of neuroscience in determining criminal responsibility, the admissibility of neuropsychological findings as evidence, and the implications of neuroscientific advancements for sentencing and rehabilitation. The discussion is grounded in analyzing relevant legal precedents and ethical frameworks, ensuring that readers understand both the potential benefits and the inherent risks of this intersectional work.

One of the unique contributions of this book is its emphasis on cultural and contextual factors. Criminal behavior and its interpretations are deeply influenced by sociocultural norms, systemic biases, and individual lived experiences. The book highlights the need for culturally informed neuropsychological assessments and calls for an interdisciplinary approach that includes perspectives from anthropology, sociology, and law. By doing so, it aims to address the inequities that often permeate the criminal justice system and to advocate for more holistic and equitable practices.

Another central theme of the book is the integration of neuropsychology into broader criminal justice reform efforts. By elucidating the neural underpinnings of behaviors such as aggression, impulsivity, and empathy deficits, neuropsychology offers valuable insights for designing evidence-based interventions and policies. The book discusses how these insights can inform rehabilitation programs, diversion initiatives, and preventative measures, ultimately contributing to a more effective and humane justice system.

As the field of criminal forensic neuropsychology continues to grow, so does the need for ongoing research and dialogue. This book concludes with a forward-looking perspective, identifying emerging trends and pressing questions that will shape the discipline in the years to come. Topics such as artificial intelligence in neuropsychological assessment, advances in neurogenetics, and the ethical implications of predictive analytics are explored, underscoring the dynamic and evolving nature of the field.

This book is intended to serve as both a foundational text for newcomers to the field and a comprehensive resource for experienced practitioners seeking to deepen their knowledge. Whether you are a student aspiring to work in forensic neuropsychology, a legal professional seeking to understand the scientific basis of neuropsychological evidence, or a researcher exploring the frontiers of this interdisciplinary field, we hope that this book will provide you with valuable insights and practical tools.

In conclusion, *Foundations of Criminal Forensic Neuropsychology: Bridging Mind, Law, and Criminal Justice* is more than a textbook; it is a call to action. It challenges readers to think critically about the intersection of neuroscience and law, to embrace the complexities of human behavior, and to work toward a justice system that is informed by science and guided by ethics. We invite you to embark on this journey with us as we explore the profound connections between the mind, the law, and the pursuit of justice.

Bangalore, India K. Jayasankara Reddy

Acknowledgments

This book, *Foundations of Criminal Forensic Neuropsychology: Bridging Mind, Law, and Criminal Justice*, is the culmination of collaborative efforts, thoughtful guidance, and steadfast support from several individuals and institutions to whom I am deeply indebted.

I extend my heartfelt gratitude to the Centre for Research Projects at Christ (Deemed to be University), Bangalore, for their generous funding and invaluable assistance throughout the writing process. Their unwavering support was instrumental in bringing this project to fruition.

I am profoundly grateful to our esteemed Vice-Chancellor for their encouragement and insightful guidance, which have inspired me throughout this journey.

I also acknowledge the tireless efforts of the book editors, whose meticulous reviews and constructive criticism enriched this work and ensured its academic rigor. Their dedication to excellence is deeply appreciated.

A special note of thanks goes to my research assistant, Aparna Prashanth. This book would not have been possible without her exceptional contributions to research, her relentless hard work, and her unwavering dedication. Her efforts were pivotal in shaping the scope and depth of this project.

To all who supported this endeavor, I am profoundly grateful for your belief in this work and its significance.

Contents

Introduction to Forensic Neuropsychology

1 Overview of Forensic Neuropsychology

Forensic neuropsychology is a specialized field that integrates the principles of clinical neuropsychology with the legal system (*Clinical Neuropsychology*, n.d.). It involves the application of neuropsychological knowledge and expertise to understand and evaluate the relationship between brain function and behavior in legal contexts. Forensic neuropsychologists assess individuals with suspected neurological or psychiatric conditions to determine the potential impact of these conditions on their cognitive, emotional, and behavioral functioning, which can have significant implications for legal proceedings (Harvey, 2012).

The field of forensic neuropsychology has its roots in the early nineteenth century, with the recognition of the link between brain injuries and changes in behavior (Kim, 2016). However, it was not until the mid-twentieth century that forensic neuropsychology emerged as a distinct subfield within clinical neuropsychology. The development of neuropsychological assessment techniques and the increased understanding of brain–behavior relationships contributed to the growth of this field.

Neuropsychological insights are increasingly sought in various legal contexts, including criminal, civil, and family law cases. In criminal cases, neuropsychological evaluations can help determine whether an individual has a mental disorder that may affect their criminal culpability or competency to stand trial (Patiz & Bayraktar, 2023). In civil cases, neuropsychological assessments may be used to evaluate the extent of cognitive and emotional impairments resulting from traumatic brain injuries (TBIs) or other neurological conditions, which can have implications for personal injury claims (Patiz & Bayraktar, 2023). In family law cases, neuropsychological evaluations can help assess the parenting capacity of individuals with neurological or psychiatric conditions (Norlin & Randell, 2022).

Forensic neuropsychologists utilize a variety of assessment techniques to evaluate individuals involved in legal proceedings. These techniques may include

© The Author(s), under exclusive license to Springer Nature Switzerland AG 2025

K. J. Reddy, *Foundations of Criminal Forensic Neuropsychology*,
https://doi.org/10.1007/978-3-031-83771-5_1

neuropsychological tests, interviews, and collateral information from family members, friends, or medical professionals. The information gathered from these assessments is then interpreted within the context of the legal issues at hand. Forensic neuropsychologists may provide expert testimony in court, explaining their findings and their relevance to the case (Van Es et al., 2020).

Forensic neuropsychology bridges the gap between neuroscience and the legal system, providing a framework for understanding how brain function can influence behavior and decision-making. This field has contributed to the development of legal standards related to mental health, criminal responsibility, and civil liability. As neuroscience continues to advance, forensic neuropsychologists will play a crucial role in interpreting and applying new scientific findings to legal cases.

2 Relationship Between the Brain and Behavior

The role of neuropsychologists as expert witnesses is becoming increasingly prevalent. These professionals provide judges with insights into brain injuries' behavioral, emotional, and cognitive consequences and the significance of psychosocial factors in influencing brain function and dysfunction (Hom, 2003). The integration of neuropsychology and law has been shaped by the convergence of several related factors that have driven the professionalization of this field. Key aspects include the quantitative study of brain–behavior relationships, interpretive strategies for inferring the presence, location, and nature of neuropathology, decision-making regarding legal issues such as the determination of disability, the characterization of cognitive-behavioral profiles associated with neurological disorders, the influence of psychosocial factors, and the selection of appropriate intervention (Guinea, 2001).

The relationship between the brain and behavior is a foundational concept in neuroscience, psychology, and neuropsychology. Understanding how the brain's structure and function influence behavior and cognition is essential for deciphering the complexities of human actions, emotions, and thoughts. We will delve into basic neuroscience concepts, exploring the brain's structures and functions and how they shape behavior. Additionally, it examines the role of neuropsychology in explaining criminal behavior and provides case examples illustrating brain–behavior links.

The brain, a complex organ composed of billions of neurons, is the body's command center, governing everything from essential physiological functions to complex cognitive processes. Understanding the brain's structure and function is crucial for comprehending how it influences behavior. The brain's outermost layer, the cerebral cortex, is responsible for higher-order functions, including thought, perception, and voluntary movement. The frontal lobe involves decision-making, problem-solving, planning, and voluntary movement. It also plays a crucial role in controlling behavior and emotions (Thau et al., 2022).

The limbic system is a group of interconnected structures involved in emotion, motivation, and memory. There are multiple key components in the limbic system that play a role in emotions and emotion regulation. The amygdala is involved in emotional processing, particularly fear and aggression (Šimić et al., 2021). Another important component of the limbic system is the hippocampus. The hippocampus is important in the formation of new memories. One of the primary challenges in forensic psychology is the inability to reliably distinguish between genuine and false memories when the sole evidence presented by the prosecution relies on the recollection of a witness or victim (Pérez-Mata & Diges, 2024). Given the challenge of reliably distinguishing between true and false memories at a functional level of analysis, there has been growing interest in identifying the neurological foundations for this distinction. The goal is to determine whether brain responses can achieve what has been elusive through behavioral, cognitive, or phenomenological approaches—namely, the reliable differentiation between true and false memories (Pérez-Mata & Diges, 2024). Damage to the hippocampus can have profound effects on memory. One of the most well-documented consequences is anterograde amnesia, the inability to form new memories. Individuals with hippocampal damage may be able to recall events from their past (prior to the damage) but struggle to remember new information, events, or experiences after the injury (Allen, 2018).

The brain's function is intricately linked to behavior and cognition. Neurons, the brain's building blocks, communicate through electrical and chemical signals, enabling various brain regions to work together to produce thoughts, emotions, and actions. The prefrontal cortex, located in the frontal lobe, is critical for executive functions like decision-making, impulse control, and social behavior. It acts as a regulatory center, helping individuals to evaluate situations, consider potential consequences, and make informed decisions. This region is also involved in managing emotions and controlling impulses, which are essential for adaptive behavior in social and personal contexts (Pirau & Lui, 2023). Damage or dysfunction in the prefrontal cortex can have profound effects on an individual's behavior and personality. Individuals with prefrontal cortex injuries may exhibit significant changes in personality, such as becoming more impulsive, making poor decisions, or engaging in socially inappropriate behaviors. These changes occur because the prefrontal cortex is no longer able to effectively regulate and control the cognitive and emotional processes that guide behavior. As a result, affected individuals may struggle with tasks that require planning, delayed gratification, or consideration of long-term consequences (Barrash et al., 2018). Moreover, the prefrontal cortex's role in social behavior underscores its importance in maintaining interpersonal relationships and adhering to social norms. When this area is compromised, individuals may lose the ability to understand social cues, empathize with others, or inhibit inappropriate responses, leading to difficulties in social interactions and potentially contributing to antisocial behavior (Mohapatra & Wagner, 2023).

The anterior cingulate cortex (ACC) plays a crucial role in cognitive functions such as error detection, conflict monitoring, emotional regulation, and decision-making, particularly in situations that require the resolution of conflicting information. In the context of deception, decision-making becomes a complex process, often involving a need to manage conflicting internal and external motivations. When an individual engages in deceptive behavior, they must weigh the benefits of deceit against the potential consequences of being discovered, creating cognitive conflict (Newman et al., 2014). The ACC is particularly active during such scenarios because it is responsible for monitoring conflicts and errors. Studies using functional neuroimaging techniques have demonstrated increased ACC activation during deceptive tasks, suggesting its involvement in detecting inconsistencies between one's true knowledge and the fabricated information being conveyed. This conflict monitoring function of the ACC is vital in decision-making during deception, as it helps the individual navigate the tension between lying and maintaining a consistent narrative. Additionally, the ACC has been linked to the regulation of emotions, which is often necessary during deception to avoid revealing cues that might betray the lie (Apps et al., 2016).

In summary, the ACC's role in deception extends to managing cognitive conflict, regulating emotional responses, and contributing to decision-making processes where the individual must balance truth and fabrication.

The limbic system, particularly the amygdala, plays a significant role in emotional responses. The amygdala is a small, almond-shaped structure that plays a central role in processing and interpreting emotional stimuli (Šimić et al., 2021). It is particularly involved in the generation of emotions such as fear, anger, and pleasure. The amygdala acts as an emotional processing hub, rapidly assessing sensory input and triggering appropriate emotional responses, often before conscious awareness of the stimulus. This rapid processing is essential for survival, as it allows for quick reactions to potential threats in the environment (AbuHasan et al., 2023).

However, the amygdala's activity is not limited to threat detection. It is also involved in emotional learning, such as associating certain stimuli with positive or negative experiences. This associative learning is crucial for forming memories of emotionally significant events, which can influence future behavior. For example, a person who has experienced a traumatic event may develop a heightened sensitivity to similar stimuli in the future, leading to anxiety or avoidance behaviors—a process heavily influenced by amygdala activity.

Overactivity in the amygdala has been linked to anxiety and aggression. When the amygdala is overactive, it can lead to exaggerated emotional responses, particularly anxiety and aggression. In conditions such as generalized anxiety disorder or posttraumatic stress disorder (PTSD), the amygdala is often hyperactive, leading to persistent feelings of fear or stress even in the absence of immediate threats. This heightened amygdala activity can result in an individual perceiving benign situations as threatening, contributing to chronic anxiety and heightened stress levels (Mitchell & Beech, 2018). Similarly, overactivity in the amygdala has been linked to aggressive behaviors, as the individual may be more prone to interpret social cues as hostile or threatening (Bremner, 2006).

Conversely, underactivity in the amygdala can impair emotional processing and social bonding. Individuals with reduced amygdala function may exhibit blunted emotional responses, which can affect their ability to form strong social connections or respond appropriately to social cues. This underactivity has been observed in certain psychiatric conditions, such as psychopathy, where there is a diminished capacity for empathy and emotional engagement. In such cases, the lack of a robust emotional response can lead to difficulties in forming meaningful relationships and a reduced ability to understand or care about the emotional experiences of others (Saghir et al., 2018).

The amygdala and hippocampus do not function in isolation; they are closely interconnected and often work together in the processing of emotionally charged memories. For instance, the amygdala can enhance the consolidation of memories in the hippocampus, particularly for events that carry significant emotional weight. This is why emotionally intense experiences, whether positive or negative, tend to be more vividly remembered than neutral ones (Tyng et al., 2017). In cases where both the amygdala and hippocampus are affected, such as in certain neurodegenerative diseases or following TBI, individuals may experience profound disturbances in both emotional regulation and memory. This can lead to complex clinical presentations where the individual may struggle with emotional volatility, memory deficits, and difficulties in social interactions (Tyng et al., 2017).

Neurotransmitters play a pivotal role in regulating various aspects of behavior, emotion, and cognition by transmitting signals across the synaptic gaps between neurons. These chemical messengers are essential for the proper functioning of the nervous system, as they modulate the activity of neural circuits and influence how we perceive the world, experience emotions, and react to stimuli. Two of the most extensively studied neurotransmitters, dopamine and serotonin, are particularly important in understanding the biological underpinnings of behavior and mental health.

Dopamine is a neurotransmitter that plays a central role in the brain's reward system, influencing how individuals experience pleasure, motivation, and reinforcement of behaviors. It is also involved in regulating movement, attention, and learning. Abnormalities in dopamine levels can lead to significant behavioral changes that may be relevant in forensic evaluations.

Dopamine's influence on behavior extends beyond pleasure and reward. It is also involved in motor control, attention, and decision-making. The mesolimbic pathway, a key dopaminergic pathway in the brain, is closely associated with the reinforcement of behaviors that are essential for survival, such as eating and reproduction. However, this pathway can also be hijacked by addictive substances, such as drugs and alcohol, leading to the development of substance use disorders. These substances artificially elevate dopamine levels, creating intense feelings of pleasure and leading to repeated use and, ultimately, addiction (Olguín et al., 2016).

In conditions such as schizophrenia, which is characterized by distorted thinking, hallucinations, and delusions, dopamine dysregulation is a key factor. Overactivity of dopamine in certain brain pathways, particularly in the mesolimbic pathway, is believed to contribute to the positive symptoms of schizophrenia, such as hallucinations and delusions. From a forensic perspective, this is significant because individuals with schizophrenia may commit crimes under the influence of these psychotic symptoms, believing that their actions are justified or necessary due to their delusional beliefs. For example, a person with schizophrenia might act violently because they believe they are defending themselves against a perceived threat that does not actually exist (Luvsannyam et al., 2022).

In legal contexts, forensic neuropsychologists may be called upon to assess whether an individual's criminal behavior was influenced by a psychotic disorder like schizophrenia. If it can be demonstrated that the defendant's actions were driven by dopamine-induced delusions, this may affect determinations of criminal responsibility and could lead to a verdict of not guilty by reason of insanity. The defendant might then be directed toward psychiatric treatment rather than traditional incarceration (Tsimploulis et al., 2018). Dopamine also plays a role in impulse control disorders, such as pathological gambling, kleptomania, and substance use disorders. These conditions are characterized by an inability to resist impulses that may be harmful to oneself or others. Dysregulation in dopamine pathways can lead to heightened sensitivity to rewards and a diminished ability to evaluate the long-term consequences of actions, which can drive compulsive behaviors. Forensic neuropsychologists might evaluate individuals with these disorders to determine the extent to which their behavior was influenced by impaired dopamine function (Brewer & Potenza, 2008).

Serotonin is another key neurotransmitter involved in regulating mood, anxiety, and aggression. It modulates various emotional and behavioral processes, and imbalances in serotonin levels have been implicated in a range of psychiatric conditions, including depression, anxiety disorders, and impulsive aggression (Seo et al., 2008). Low levels of serotonin have been consistently associated with increased aggression and impulsive behavior. This connection is particularly relevant in forensic cases involving violent crimes. Individuals with reduced serotonin activity may struggle to control aggressive impulses, leading to behaviors that are out of proportion to the provocation. Research has shown that individuals with a history of violent offenses often have lower levels of serotonin or dysregulated serotonin functioning (Seo et al., 2008).

In a forensic evaluation, a neuropsychologist might assess whether low serotonin levels could have contributed to the defendant's inability to control aggressive impulses during the commission of a crime. This information can be critical in determining the degree of intent and the likelihood of future violent behavior, influencing both sentencing and decisions about rehabilitation. In some cases, treatment options that target serotonin levels, such as selective serotonin reuptake inhibitors (SSRIs), might be recommended as part of a comprehensive approach to reducing recidivism (Van Der Gronde et al., 2014).

The forensic application of neuropsychology often involves a detailed examination of how neurotransmitter imbalances may contribute to criminal behavior. Forensic neuropsychologists use this knowledge to provide courts with insights into the biological factors that may have impaired an individual's capacity for self-control, rational decision-making, and adherence to social norms (Forensic Neuropsychology: Principal Issues and Applications, 2001).

In some cases, the presence of a neurotransmitter imbalance may be used as part of an insanity defense, where the argument is made that the defendant's behavior was a direct result of a neurobiological condition that rendered them unable to understand the nature of their actions or distinguish right from wrong. In other situations, understanding these neurochemical influences might lead to recommendations for alternative sentencing, focusing on treatment rather than punishment, especially if the behavior is linked to a treatable disorder.

Moreover, neurotransmitter imbalances are often explored in the context of risk assessment. For instance, individuals with certain neurochemical profiles may be more prone to recidivism due to ongoing issues with impulse control or aggression. Forensic neuropsychologists might recommend specific interventions, such as medication or therapy, to address these issues and reduce the risk of future offenses (Seo et al., 2008).

Neuropsychology has made significant contributions to understanding criminal behavior by examining how brain dysfunction can influence actions that deviate from social norms. Research has shown that individuals with damage or abnormalities in certain brain areas, such as the prefrontal cortex, may be more prone to impulsive and antisocial behavior. The prefrontal cortex is responsible for executive functions, including impulse control, decision-making, and social behavior. Impairments in this area can lead to a lack of foresight, poor judgment, and difficulty in controlling aggressive impulses, all of which can contribute to criminal behavior. Individuals with TBI that affect the frontal lobes may exhibit personality changes, increased aggression, and impulsivity. These changes can predispose them to engage in criminal activities that they might not have considered prior to the injury.

The case of Phineas Gage remains one of the most pivotal in the history of neuroscience and psychology, serving as an early and dramatic illustration of the relationship between brain injury and changes in personality and behavior. The case is often cited in both clinical and forensic neuropsychology to explain the significant impact that damage to specific brain regions can have on an individual's behavior, decision-making, and social interactions. Phineas Gage was a 25-year-old railroad construction foreman working in Vermont in 1848. He was known among his peers as a competent, reliable, and well-liked individual, displaying a strong work ethic and being responsible in his duties. However, on September 13, 1848, Gage's life changed dramatically when an accidental explosion drove a large iron tamping rod—measuring over three feet in length and weighing about 13 pounds—through his skull. The rod entered his left cheek, passed behind his left eye, and exited through the top of his skull, damaging a significant portion of his brain, particularly the prefrontal cortex. Remarkably, Gage survived the incident and was conscious immediately after the accident, even speaking with those around him. He was quickly attended to by Dr. John Martyn Harlow, who managed his care during the critical postinjury period. Gage recovered physically, but the impact of the brain injury on his behavior and personality was profound. Before the accident, Gage was described as a model employee—efficient, capable, and socially well-adjusted. However, the damage to his prefrontal cortex, an area of the brain associated with executive functions such as decision-making, social behavior, and impulse control, resulted in dramatic changes to his personality. He became impulsive, irreverent, and unable to adhere to social norms and expectations. Gage's once responsible and balanced temperament gave way to a more erratic, unpredictable, and inappropriate demeanor. He began to exhibit behaviors that were socially unacceptable, such as using profane language, making poor decisions, and displaying a lack of respect for others. His ability to plan, make sound judgments, and control his impulses was severely compromised. As a result, Gage was no longer able to maintain his position as a foreman, and his relationships with those around him deteriorated. Phineas Gage's case is often referenced in neuropsychology as it highlights the importance of the prefrontal cortex in executive functions, which include decision-making, planning, social behavior, and self-control. The prefrontal cortex is critical for maintaining appropriate social interactions and for adhering to societal norms. When this area is damaged, as in Gage's case, individuals may struggle to control their impulses, make reasoned decisions, or behave in socially acceptable ways.

In the field of forensic neuropsychology, Gage's case is frequently used as a foundational example of how brain injuries can alter behavior and decision-making processes, potentially leading to criminal behavior. In legal cases where a defendant has a history of brain injury, forensic neuropsychologists may assess whether damage to areas like the prefrontal cortex could have contributed to the defendant's actions, reducing their ability to control impulses or understand the consequences of their behavior. Furthermore, the Gage case is instructive for developing rehabilitation strategies for individuals with brain injuries. Understanding the specific behavioral and cognitive impairments associated with prefrontal cortex damage can guide the creation of targeted interventions aimed at improving impulse control, decision-making, and social functioning. Such interventions are crucial for reducing the likelihood of criminal behavior and enhancing the quality of life for individuals with similar injuries.

3 Cognitive Evaluation Techniques

Cognitive evaluation techniques are essential tools used by neuropsychologists to assess an individual's cognitive functioning, particularly in the context of forensic settings. These techniques provide valuable insights into various cognitive domains, such as memory, attention, executive function, language, and visuospatial skills. In forensic contexts, cognitive assessments are crucial for understanding how cognitive deficits may impact behavior, decision-making, and legal responsibility. We will explore the methods of cognitive assessment, the procedures for conducting these evaluations in forensic settings, and how the results are interpreted to inform legal decisions.

Cognitive assessments typically involve a combination of standardized neuropsychological tests, clinical interviews, and observational methods. Cognitive evaluations in forensic settings follow a systematic approach to ensure that the assessment is thorough, objective, and relevant to the legal questions at hand.

The neuropsychologist conducts a clinical interview with the individual being assessed. This interview gathers information about the individual's medical history, cognitive complaints, educational background, work history, and social functioning. In a forensic setting, the interview may also explore the individual's understanding of legal concepts and their role in the legal process. Based on the information gathered during the case review and clinical interview, the neuropsychologist selects appropriate neuropsychological tests to administer. These tests are conducted in a controlled environment to minimize distractions and ensure that the results accurately reflect the individual's cognitive abilities. During the testing process, the neuropsychologist observes the individual's behavior, noting factors such as effort, motivation, and response style. In forensic settings, it is particularly important to assess whether the individual is providing their best effort, as malingering (feigning or exaggerating cognitive deficits) can be a concern. After the tests are administered, the neuropsychologist scores the results and interprets them in the context of the individual's history, the clinical interview, and behavioral observations. The interpretation considers both the individual's strengths and weaknesses across different cognitive domains.

Cognitive assessments typically involve a combination of standardized neuropsychological tests, clinical interviews, and observational methods. These tools are designed to measure different aspects of cognitive functioning and help neuropsychologists identify potential deficits or abnormalities. The Wechsler Adult Intelligence Scale IV (WAIS-IV) is one of the most widely used tests to assess general cognitive ability or intelligence. It measures various cognitive domains, including verbal comprehension, perceptual reasoning, working memory, and processing speed. In forensic settings, the WAIS-IV can be used to determine whether an individual has cognitive impairments that might affect their competency to stand trial or understand legal proceedings. The Mini Mental Status Examination (MMSE) is a brief screening tool used to assess cognitive function, particularly in older adults. It evaluates orientation, attention, memory, language, and visuospatial skills. While not as comprehensive as other neuropsychological tests, the MMSE can be useful in forensic evaluations to quickly determine the presence of cognitive impairments that might impact an individual's legal capacity. The Wisconsin Card Sorting Test (WCST) is used to assess executive functions, including cognitive flexibility, problem-solving, and the ability to shift strategies in response to changing conditions. Executive functions are often critical in forensic assessments, as impairments in this domain can affect decision-making, impulse control, and judgment, which are relevant to criminal behavior and legal responsibility (Marcopulos et al., 2024).

Neuroimaging techniques are powerful tools that allow researchers and clinicians to visualize and assess changes in brain structures, providing insights into how these changes relate to behavior. These techniques have become increasingly important in both clinical and forensic settings, where understanding the brain–behavior relationship is crucial. MRI uses strong magnetic fields and radio waves to create detailed images of the brain's anatomy. It is particularly useful for detecting structural abnormalities, such as lesions, tumors, or atrophy, which can be associated with changes in behavior and cognitive function. PET scans use radioactive tracers to measure metabolic activity in the brain. This technique can reveal areas of the brain that are underactive or overactive, which may correspond to specific behavioral or cognitive symptoms (Yen et al., 2023).

Neuroimaging techniques are employed to detect and monitor changes in brain structures that may be associated with various conditions, such as TBI, neurodegenerative diseases, and mental health disorders (Mayer & Quinn, 2022). These changes can manifest in several ways. Neurodegenerative diseases like Alzheimer's or Parkinson's disease often lead to atrophy or shrinking of brain tissue. MRI can measure the extent of atrophy, which is typically associated with cognitive decline, memory loss, and changes in personality or behavior. TBIs or strokes can result in lesions, or areas of damaged tissue, visible on MRI or CT scans. The location and extent of these lesions can predict specific behavioral outcomes, such as difficulties with language, motor skills, or impulse control. DTI can reveal disruptions in the brain's white matter tracts, which are responsible for communication between different brain regions. Changes in connectivity can lead to cognitive and emotional impairments, such as problems with executive function, emotional regulation, or social behavior (*Alzheimer's Disease Fact Sheet*, 2023).

The relationship between brain structure and behavior is complex, and neuroimaging provides a way to explore this relationship in detail. Neuroimaging allows researchers to identify which brain regions are involved in specific cognitive and behavioral functions. Damage to the prefrontal cortex, often detected through MRI, is associated with impairments in decision-making, impulse control, and executive functions (Yen et al., 2023). Understanding the role of specific brain regions helps in explaining behavioral changes observed in individuals with brain injuries or neurological disorders. By comparing neuroimaging data with behavioral assessments, clinicians can identify correlations between structural changes in the brain and observed behaviors. For instance, a reduction in hippocampal volume, as seen in MRI scans of individuals with PTSD, is often linked to memory problems and emotional dysregulation. These correlations are critical in forensic settings, where they may be used to explain behavior that is relevant to legal proceedings (Siddiqi et al., 2022). Neuroimaging data can be used to develop predictive models that estimate the likelihood of certain behaviors based on brain structure. For example, fMRI studies have shown that reduced activity in the amygdala, a region associated with emotion regulation, may predict a higher risk of aggressive or antisocial behavior. Such models can inform risk assessments in forensic cases (Ahmed et al., 2015).

The interpretation of cognitive test results in forensic settings goes beyond simply identifying cognitive deficits; it involves understanding how these deficits may impact the individual's behavior, decision-making, and legal responsibilities. One of the primary legal concerns in forensic neuropsychology is determining whether an individual is competent to stand trial (Woods et al., 2012). Cognitive assessments can identify impairments in understanding, reasoning, and communication that may render an individual unable to participate meaningfully in their defense. Significant deficits in memory, attention, or executive function might impair an individual's ability to understand legal proceedings, communicate with their attorney, or make informed decisions.

In cases where a defendant's mental state at the time of the crime is in question, neuroimaging can provide evidence of brain abnormalities that impair judgment or impulse control, supporting an insanity defense. For example, abnormalities in the prefrontal cortex and amygdala, detected through fMRI, have been linked to impaired decision-making and emotional regulation, which are relevant in assessing criminal responsibility. Neuroimaging can also be used to assess whether an individual has the cognitive capacity to understand legal proceedings and participate in their defense. For instance, structural MRI might reveal atrophy or lesions in brain areas associated with language or memory, indicating that the individual may not be competent to stand trial. Neuroimaging evidence can be presented during sentencing to argue for mitigating circumstances. Evidence of brain damage from a traumatic injury could be used to explain impulsive or violent behavior, potentially leading to a reduced sentence or alternative sentencing options focused on rehabilitation (Woods et al., 2012).

Cognitive evaluations can also inform decisions about criminal responsibility, particularly in cases where cognitive impairments may have contributed to the criminal behavior. For instance, impairments in executive function might lead to poor impulse control or an inability to foresee the consequences of one's actions, which could be relevant in determining the degree of culpability or the appropriateness of an insanity defense (Norman et al., 2022). Neuropsychological assessments can be used to evaluate the risk of future criminal behavior. Cognitive deficits, particularly in areas such as executive function and impulse control, are often associated with an increased risk of recidivism. Understanding these deficits can guide recommendations for sentencing, rehabilitation, and the management of individuals within the criminal justice system (Harvey, 2012). In some cases, cognitive impairments may be considered as mitigating factors during sentencing. If an individual has a documented history of brain injury or a neurodevelopmental disorder that affects their cognitive functioning, this information might be used to argue for a reduced sentence or alternative forms of punishment, such as treatment or rehabilitation programs.

4 Use of Neuropsychological Evidence in Court

Neuropsychological evidence has become increasingly important in legal proceedings, offering insights into how brain function and cognitive deficits may influence behavior, decision-making, and culpability. The use of such evidence in court has evolved, with legal standards and criteria being established to determine its admissibility. We will explore the admissibility of neuropsychological evidence, present case studies, and discuss the practical applications of this evidence in landmark legal cases.

The admissibility of neuropsychological evidence in court is governed by specific legal standards that ensure the reliability and relevance of the evidence presented. These standards are critical in determining whether neuropsychological findings can be used to support or challenge the claims made in a legal case.

The Frye standard, also known as the "general acceptance" test, was one of the earliest legal standards used to determine the admissibility of scientific evidence. According to the Frye standard, scientific evidence is admissible only if the methodology or scientific principle on which the evidence is based has gained general acceptance in the relevant scientific community. This standard was applied to neuropsychological evidence in its early use in courts, where the acceptance of neuropsychology as a field and its methods were critical for admissibility.

The Daubert standard, established in *Daubert v. Merrell Dow Pharmaceuticals, Inc.*, replaced the Frye standard in federal courts and many state courts. The Daubert standard requires that scientific evidence must be based on reliable principles and methods, and that the expert witness presenting the evidence must apply these methods reliably to the facts of the case. Under this standard, judges serve as gatekeepers, evaluating the relevance and reliability of neuropsychological evidence before it can be admitted in court. The Daubert standard considers factors such as whether the theory or technique has been tested, whether it has been subject to peer review and publication, the known or potential error rate, and the degree of acceptance within the scientific community (*Daubert V. Merrell Dow Pharmaceuticals, Inc., 509 U.S. 579 (1993)*, n.d.).

Neuropsychological evidence has been utilized in various legal cases, ranging from criminal defense to personal injury claims.

In *Indiana v. Edwards* (2008), the issue of competency to stand trial was central to the case. Ahmad Edwards, who was accused of attempted murder, theft, and other charges, had a documented history of schizophrenia. Neuropsychological evaluations were conducted to assess Edwards' cognitive abilities, particularly his understanding of legal proceedings and his ability to participate in his defense. The neuropsychological evidence suggested that while Edwards understood the nature of the charges against him, his mental illness impaired his ability to represent himself effectively. The US Supreme Court ruled that states could insist on representation by counsel for defendants deemed mentally ill, even if they are competent to stand trial. This case highlights how neuropsychological evidence can be crucial in determining a defendant's competency and legal rights (*Indiana V. Edwards, 554 U.S. 164 (2008)*, n.d.).

In the case of *People v. Weinstein* (1992), neuropsychological evidence played a critical role in the defense's argument that the defendant, Herbert Weinstein, was not criminally responsible for the murder of his wife due to a brain abnormality. Weinstein, who had no prior history of violence, was found to have a cyst in the arachnoid membrane of his brain, which his defense argued impaired his ability to control his behavior. The defense presented neuropsychological assessments and neuroimaging studies to support the claim that Weinstein's brain abnormality contributed to his actions. Although the court allowed the neuropsychological evidence, the case ultimately resulted in a plea deal, with Weinstein pleading guilty to a lesser charge. This case is significant because it demonstrated the potential for neuropsychological evidence to influence the outcome of a criminal trial, particularly in cases involving the insanity defense (Aono et al., 2019).

5 Interdisciplinary Collaboration

The intersection of law and neuropsychology has given rise to an interdisciplinary collaboration that is increasingly vital in addressing complex legal issues. Neuropsychologists bring a deep understanding of brain–behavior relationships, while lawyers possess the expertise to navigate the legal system. When these two disciplines work together, they can significantly enhance justice outcomes by providing more informed, scientifically grounded perspectives in legal decision-making. We will explore the role of neuropsychologists in legal settings, how they collaborate with legal professionals, and strategies for improving the integration of neuropsychological insights into the legal process.

Forensic neuropsychologists often serve as expert witnesses in legal cases, where their primary role is to provide objective, scientifically based opinions about an individual's cognitive, emotional, and behavioral functioning. These experts are typically called upon in cases where brain injury, neurological disorders, or mental health issues are central to the legal questions at hand. Their assessments can influence various aspects of a case, including the determination of competency, the evaluation of criminal responsibility, and the assessment of damages in personal injury claims.

One of the critical functions of a forensic neuropsychologist is to assess whether an individual is competent to stand trial. This involves evaluating the person's cognitive abilities, understanding of legal proceedings, and ability to participate in their defense (Marcopulos et al., 2024). Neuropsychologists use standardized tests and neuroimaging techniques (as discussed earlier) to provide a comprehensive picture of the individual's mental state. In criminal cases, neuropsychologists may be asked to assess whether a defendant's mental state at the time of the crime was impaired due to a neurological condition or brain injury. This can play a significant role in determining criminal responsibility, particularly in cases involving insanity defenses or diminished capacity arguments. In civil litigation, neuropsychologists assess the extent of cognitive and emotional impairments resulting from injuries such as TBI. Their evaluations can help quantify the impact of the injury on the individual's daily life and earning capacity, which is crucial for determining appropriate compensation (Math et al., 2015).

The collaboration between neuropsychologists and legal professionals extends beyond the courtroom. In many cases, these experts work closely with attorneys during the preparation of cases, providing insights that can shape legal strategies and decisions (Kaufmann, 2009).

Attorneys often seek the expertise of neuropsychologists to help them understand the neurocognitive aspects of their cases. This collaboration can involve interpreting medical records, suggesting lines of questioning for witnesses, or identifying relevant neuropsychological issues that may not be immediately apparent (Kaufmann, 2013). Neuropsychologists may conduct assessments before a trial begins to provide attorneys with a clearer understanding of their client's cognitive and psychological state. This information can be critical for plea negotiations, settlement discussions, or determining the need for accommodations during the trial. One of the less formal but equally important roles of neuropsychologists in legal settings is educating the legal team about the implications of neuropsychological findings. This involves translating complex scientific concepts into language that lawyers, judges, and jurors can understand, ensuring that the neuropsychological evidence is appropriately integrated into the legal arguments (Kaufmann, 2013).

The integration of neuropsychological insights into legal decision-making can significantly enhance justice outcomes. By providing a scientifically grounded understanding of a defendant's or plaintiff's cognitive and emotional state, neuropsychologists can help ensure that legal decisions are based on a comprehensive assessment of all relevant factors.

Neuropsychological evaluations can inform sentencing decisions by providing evidence of mitigating factors, such as cognitive impairments or mental health issues that may have contributed to the defendant's behavior. This can lead to more tailored sentencing that takes into account the individual's neuropsychological profile, potentially reducing the likelihood of recidivism (Harvey, 2012). Ensuring that defendants are competent to stand trial is fundamental to the fairness of the legal process. Neuropsychologists play a crucial role in safeguarding this fairness by providing accurate assessments of competency, which are essential for upholding the legal rights of individuals with cognitive or mental health impairments. In civil cases, neuropsychological evidence can be critical in ensuring that plaintiffs receive appropriate compensation for their injuries. By providing a detailed assessment of the cognitive and emotional impact of an injury, neuropsychologists help courts determine the extent of damages and the appropriate level of compensation (Harvey, 2012).

Interdisciplinary approaches that combine the expertise of neuropsychologists and legal professionals offer significant potential for addressing complex legal issues. As the legal system increasingly recognizes the importance of understanding the neurocognitive and psychological factors that influence behavior, the collaboration between these disciplines becomes more critical. In criminal cases involving questions of intent, competency, or mental state, interdisciplinary collaboration can provide a more nuanced understanding of the defendant's behavior (Matros, 2022). By combining legal expertise with neuropsychological insights, courts can make more informed decisions that consider both the legal and psychological dimensions of the case. As neuroscience and neuropsychology continue to advance, new legal challenges will arise. As our understanding of the neurobiological underpinnings of behavior deepens, questions about free will, responsibility, and the implications of neuropsychological evidence for sentencing and rehabilitation will become increasingly relevant. Interdisciplinary collaboration will be essential in navigating these challenges and ensuring that legal decisions are informed by the latest scientific knowledge.

6 Conclusion

While neuroscientific insights are increasingly integrated into clinical mental health practices, they have been somewhat overlooked in forensic mental healthcare. Recent advancements in neuroscience have not only expanded our understanding of the etiology of psychopathology but have also heightened awareness of the potential applications of neuroscience in forensic psychiatry and psychology. In India, there is a notable absence of formal graduate programs in forensic psychiatry, and the availability of Forensic Psychiatric Training Centers and clinical services is limited across the country. The establishment of Forensic Psychiatry Training Centers at the state level to provide specialized training for mental health professionals, judicial personnel, human rights advocates, and correctional officers. The initiation of prison mental health services in all central prisons. There is an urgent need to train psychiatrists in district hospitals and medical colleges in assessing insanity defenses and evaluating fitness to stand trial, to ensure that forensic psychiatric services are immediately accessible and minimizing delays in obtaining expert opinions. A reevaluation of criminal responsibility and the systematic conduct of research in the areas of criminal and diminished responsibility. To fully realize the potential of interdisciplinary collaboration between neuropsychologists and lawyers, several strategies can be employed. Enhancing collaboration starts with education. Lawyers need a foundational understanding of neuropsychology to appreciate the relevance of neuropsychological evidence fully (Brown et al., 2023). Likewise, neuropsychologists should be familiar with legal standards and procedures to present their findings effectively in court. Educational programs that bridge these two fields can foster better communication and understanding between professionals. Establishing interdisciplinary teams that include both legal professionals and neuropsychologists can improve case outcomes. These teams can work together from the outset of a case, ensuring that neuropsychological insights are integrated into the legal strategy from the beginning. This approach can be particularly effective in complex cases where neuropsychological issues are central to the legal questions (Brown et al., 2023). Developing clear guidelines and standards for the use of neuropsychological evidence in legal settings can enhance its integration. These guidelines should address the ethical considerations of using neuropsychological evidence, the standards for expert testimony, and the procedures for presenting and interpreting neuropsychological data in court. By standardizing these practices, the legal system can better utilize neuropsychological insights to achieve fairer outcomes.

References

AbuHasan, Q., Reddy, V., & Siddiqui, W. (2023, July 17). *Neuroanatomy, amygdala*. StatPearls - NCBI Bookshelf. https://www.ncbi.nlm.nih.gov/books/NBK537102/

Ahmed, S. P., Bittencourt-Hewitt, A., & Sebastian, C. L. (2015). Neurocognitive bases of emotion regulation development in adolescence. *Developmental Cognitive Neuroscience, 15*, 11–25. https://doi.org/10.1016/j.dcn.2015.07.006

Allen, R. J. (2018). Classic and recent advances in understanding amnesia. *F1000Research, 7*, 331. https://doi.org/10.12688/f1000research.13737.1

Alzheimer's Disease Fact Sheet. (2023, April 5). National Institute on Aging. https://www.nia.nih.gov/health/alzheimers-and-dementia/alzheimers-disease-fact-sheet

Aono, D., Yaffe, G., & Kober, H. (2019). Neuroscientific evidence in the courtroom: A review. *Cognitive Research Principles and Implications, 4*(1). https://doi.org/10.1186/s41235-019-0179-y

Apps, M. A., Rushworth, M. F., & Chang, S. W. (2016). The anterior cingulate gyrus and social cognition: Tracking the motivation of others. *Neuron, 90*(4), 692–707. https://doi.org/10.1016/j.neuron.2016.04.018

Barrash, J., Stuss, D. T., Aksan, N., Anderson, S. W., Jones, R. D., Manzel, K., & Tranel, D. (2018). "Frontal lobe syndrome"? Subtypes of acquired personality disturbances in patients with focal brain damage. *Cortex, 106*, 65–80. https://doi.org/10.1016/j.cortex.2018.05.007

Bremner, J. D. (2006). Traumatic stress: Effects on the brain. *Dialogues in Clinical Neuroscience, 8*(4), 445–461. https://doi.org/10.31887/dcns.2006.8.4/jbremner

Brewer, J. A., & Potenza, M. N. (2008). The neurobiology and genetics of impulse control disorders: Relationships to drug addictions. *Biochemical Pharmacology, 75*(1), 63–75. https://doi.org/10.1016/j.bcp.2007.06.043

Brown, S., Sparapani, R., Osinski, K., Zhang, J., Blessing, J., Cheng, F., Hamid, A., MohamadiPour, M. B., Lal, J. C., Kothari, A. N., Caraballo, P., Noseworthy, P., Johnson, R. H., Hansen, K., Sun, L. Y., Crotty, B., Cheng, Y. C., Echefu, G., Doshi, K., & Olson, J. (2023). Team principles for successful interdisciplinary research teams. *American Heart Journal Plus Cardiology Research and Practice, 32*, 100306. https://doi.org/10.1016/j.ahjo.2023.100306

Clinical Neuropsychology. (n.d.). https://www.apa.org. https://www.apa.org/ed/graduate/specialize/neuropsychology

Daubert v. Merrell Dow Pharmaceuticals, Inc., 509 U.S. 579 (1993). (n.d.). *Justia Law*. https://supreme.justia.com/cases/federal/us/509/579/

Fernández Guinea, S. (2001). La neuropsicología forense: consideraciones básicas y campos de aplicación [Forensic neuropsychology: Principal issues and applications]. *Revista de neurologia, 32*(8), 783–787.

[Forensic Neuropsychology: Principal Issues and Applications]. (2001, April 1). PubMed. https://pubmed.ncbi.nlm.nih.gov/11391518/

Harvey, P. D. (2012). Clinical applications of neuropsychological assessment. *Dialogues in Clinical Neuroscience, 14*(1), 91–99. https://doi.org/10.31887/dcns.2012.14.1/pharvey

Hom, J. (2003). Forensic Neuropsychology: Are we there yet? *Archives of Clinical Neuropsychology, 18*(8), 827–845. https://doi.org/10.1016/s0887-6177(03)00076-3

Indiana v. Edwards, 554 U.S. 164 (2008). (n.d.). *Justia Law*. https://supreme.justia.com/cases/federal/us/554/164/

Kaufmann, P. M. (2009). Protecting raw data and psychological tests from wrongful disclosure: A primer on the law and other persuasive strategies. *The Clinical Neuropsychologist, 23*(7), 1130–1159. https://doi.org/10.1080/13854040903107809

Kaufmann, P. M. (2013). Neuropsychologist experts and neurolaw: Cases, controversies, and admissibility challenges. *Behavioral Sciences & the Law, 31*(6), 739–755. https://doi.org/10.1002/bsl.2085

Kim, A. (2016, September 10). *Wilhelm Maximilian Wundt*. https://plato.stanford.edu/archives/fall2016/entries/wilhelm-wundt/

Luvsannyam, E., Jain, M. S., Pormento, M. K. L., Siddiqui, H., Balagtas, A. R. A., Emuze, B. O., & Poprawski, T. (2022). Neurobiology of schizophrenia: A comprehensive review. *Cureus*. https://doi.org/10.7759/cureus.23959

Marcopulos, B. A., Kaufmann, P., & Patel, A. C. (2024). Forensic neuropsychological assessment. *Behavioral Sciences & the Law*. https://doi.org/10.1002/bsl.2656

Math, S. B., Kumar, C. N., & Moirangthem, S. (2015). Insanity defense: Past, present, and future. *Indian Journal of Psychological Medicine, 37*(4), 381–387. https://doi.org/10.4103/0253-7176.168559

Matros, D. (2022, February 19). Neuropsychology and the possibilities of free will - Daniel Matros – Medium. *Medium*. https://medium.com/@danielmatros1/neuropsychology-and-the-possibilities-of-free-will-a2dd8b38a80c

Mayer, A. R., & Quinn, D. K. (2022). Neuroimaging biomarkers of new-onset psychiatric disorders following traumatic brain injury. *Biological Psychiatry, 91*(5), 459–469. https://doi.org/10.1016/j.biopsych.2021.06.005

Mitchell, I. J., & Beech, A. R. (2018). Neurobiology for forensic psychologists. *Psychology Crime and Law, 24*(3), 210–227. https://doi.org/10.1080/1068316x.2017.1421186

Mohapatra, A. N., & Wagner, S. (2023). The role of the prefrontal cortex in social interactions of animal models and the implications for autism spectrum disorder. *Frontiers in Psychiatry, 14*. https://doi.org/10.3389/fpsyt.2023.1205199

Newman, L. A., Creer, D. J., & McGaughy, J. A. (2014). Cognitive control and the anterior cingulate cortex: How conflicting stimuli affect attentional control in the rat. *Journal of Physiology-Paris, 109*(1–3), 95–103. https://doi.org/10.1016/j.jphysparis.2014.06.004

Norlin, J., & Randell, E. (2022). Social workers' perceptions of assessing the parental capacity of parents with intellectual disabilities in child protection investigations. *Journal of Intellectual Disabilities, 27*(4), 976–993. https://doi.org/10.1177/17446295221113717

Norman, E. M., Polaschek, D. L. L., & Starkey, N. J. (2022). Executive function in individuals who are compliant and non-compliant with the conditions of a community-based sentence. *Psychiatry Psychology and Law, 30*(2), 161–176. https://doi.org/10.1080/13218719.2021.2003268

Olguín, H. J., Guzmán, D. C., García, E. H., & Mejía, G. B. (2016). The role of dopamine and its dysfunction as a consequence of oxidative stress. *Oxidative Medicine and Cellular Longevity, 2016*, 1–13. https://doi.org/10.1155/2016/9730467

Patiz, B., & Bayraktar, S. (2023). Evaluation of neuropsychological characteristics and attention bias in juvenile offenders, juvenile victims, and juveniles who have not participated in the criminal justice system. *Frontiers in Psychology, 14*. https://doi.org/10.3389/fpsyg.2023.1229044

Pérez-Mata, N., & Diges, M. (2024). False memories in forensic psychology: Do cognition and brain activity tell the same story? *Frontiers in Psychology, 15*. https://doi.org/10.3389/fpsyg.2024.1327196

Pirau, L., & Lui, F. (2023, July 17). *Frontal lobe syndrome*. StatPearls - NCBI Bookshelf. https://www.ncbi.nlm.nih.gov/books/NBK532981/

Saghir, Z., Syeda, J. N., Muhammad, A. S., & Abdalla, T. H. B. (2018). The amygdala, sleep debt, sleep deprivation, and the emotion of anger: A possible connection? *Cureus*. https://doi.org/10.7759/cureus.2912

Seo, D., Patrick, C. J., & Kennealy, P. J. (2008). Role of serotonin and dopamine system interactions in the neurobiology of impulsive aggression and its comorbidity with other clinical disorders. *Aggression and Violent Behavior, 13*(5), 383–395. https://doi.org/10.1016/j.avb.2008.06.003

Siddiqi, S. H., Kording, K. P., Parvizi, J., & Fox, M. D. (2022). Causal mapping of human brain function. *Nature Reviews. Neuroscience, 23*(6), 361–375. https://doi.org/10.1038/s41583-022-00583-8

Šimić, G., Tkalčić, M., Vukić, V., Mulc, D., Španić, E., Šagud, M., Olucha-Bordonau, F. E., Vukšić, M., & Hof, P. R. (2021). Understanding emotions: Origins and roles of the amygdala. *Biomolecules, 11*(6), 823. https://doi.org/10.3390/biom11060823

Thau, L., Reddy, V., & Singh, P. (2022, October 10). *Anatomy, central nervous system*. StatPearls - NCBI Bookshelf. https://www.ncbi.nlm.nih.gov/books/NBK542179/

Tsimploulis, G., Niveau, G., Eytan, A., Giannakopoulos, P., & Sentissi, O. (2018). Schizophrenia and criminal responsibility. *The Journal of Nervous and Mental Disease, 206*(5), 370–377. https://doi.org/10.1097/nmd.0000000000000805

Tyng, C. M., Amin, H. U., Saad, M. N. M., & Malik, A. S. (2017). The influences of emotion on learning and memory. *Frontiers in Psychology, 8*. https://doi.org/10.3389/fpsyg.2017.01454

Van Der Gronde, T., Kempes, M., Van El, C., Rinne, T., & Pieters, T. (2014). Neurobiological correlates in forensic assessment: A systematic review. *PLoS ONE, 9*(10), e110672. https://doi.org/10.1371/journal.pone.0110672

Van Es, R., Kunst, M., & De Keijser, J. (2020). Forensic mental health expert testimony and judicial decision-making: A systematic literature review. *Aggression and Violent Behavior, 51*, 101387. https://doi.org/10.1016/j.avb.2020.101387

Woods, G. W., Freedman, D., & Greenspan, S. (2012). Neurobehavioral assessment in forensic practice. *International Journal of Law and Psychiatry, 35*(5–6), 432–439. https://doi.org/10.1016/j.ijlp.2012.09.014

Yen, C., Lin, C., & Chiang, M. (2023). Exploring the frontiers of neuroimaging: A review of recent advances in understanding brain functioning and disorders. *Life, 13*(7), 1472. https://doi.org/10.3390/life13071472

Understanding Neuropsychology of Crime

1 Introduction

The intersection of neuropsychology and criminal behavior offers a profound avenue for understanding the underlying mechanisms that influence criminal actions. This chapter delves into the core principles of brain architecture and function, providing an essential foundation for exploring neuropsychological phenomena in forensic contexts. By examining the intricate relationship between brain structure, neural networks, and behavior, we aim to uncover how alterations in brain morphology can lead to behavioral and cognitive outcomes that are particularly relevant in criminal cases.

The primary purpose of this chapter is to bridge the gap between neuropsychological theory and its application in forensic settings. Through a detailed exploration of brain structures and neural networks, we seek to elucidate how neuropsychological assessments can inform our understanding of criminal behavior. The chapter is designed to equip readers with a comprehensive understanding of how changes in the brain's architecture can manifest as cognitive and behavioral anomalies, which are often observed in individuals involved in legal proceedings. By integrating traditional assessment methodologies with advanced neuroimaging techniques, the chapter demonstrates how a multifaceted approach to neuropsychological testing can provide a more complete and accurate evaluation of individuals in forensic contexts.

The significance of this chapter lies in its ability to connect neuropsychological concepts with real-world applications in the criminal justice system. As the legal field increasingly recognizes the importance of understanding the neurological underpinnings of behavior, neuropsychology emerges as a critical tool in evaluating cognitive functioning, decision-making competence, and potential neurological abnormalities in offenders. This chapter underscores the relevance of

© The Author(s), under exclusive license to Springer Nature Switzerland AG 2025

K. J. Reddy, *Foundations of Criminal Forensic Neuropsychology*,
https://doi.org/10.1007/978-3-031-83771-5_2

neuropsychological assessments in legal settings, offering practical insights through case studies that illustrate how these assessments can influence legal outcomes.

Neuropsychology plays a pivotal role in unraveling the complexities of criminal behavior. By examining the brain's structure and function, neuropsychologists can identify neurological impairments or dysfunctions that may contribute to criminal actions. For instance, damage to the prefrontal cortex—a region responsible for executive functions such as impulse control, decision-making, and social behavior—has been linked to increased aggression and antisocial behavior (Siever, 2008). Similarly, abnormalities in neural networks, particularly those involved in emotion regulation and moral reasoning, can predispose individuals to engage in criminal activities.

Understanding the neuropsychological aspects of crime not only aids in identifying potential neurological contributors to criminal behavior but also enhances the ability to assess an individual's cognitive capacity and decision-making competence within legal proceedings. This is particularly important in cases where mental health defenses, such as insanity pleas, are considered (Ghiasi et al., 2023). By providing a thorough analysis of the brain-behavior relationship, neuropsychology offers a scientifically grounded framework for evaluating the cognitive and behavioral aspects of crime, thereby contributing to more informed legal decisions (*Introduction, Definition and Description of Neuropsychology*, n.d.).

This chapter aims to provide readers with a comprehensive understanding of how neuropsychological principles can be applied to the study of criminal behavior. Through a detailed examination of brain structures, neural networks, and assessment methodologies, we explore the practical implications of neuropsychology in forensic contexts, ultimately highlighting its critical role in the criminal justice system.

2 Fundamental Concepts of Brain Architecture and Function

The human brain is a complex and highly organized structure, composed of various regions that work in concert to produce thought, behavior, and emotions. Understanding the major brain structures is crucial for grasping how different areas contribute to cognitive and behavioral processes. This section provides an overview of the key brain structures—the cortex, limbic system, and brainstem—and their respective functions and roles.

The cerebral cortex is the outermost layer of the brain and is often referred to as the "gray matter" due to its appearance. It is divided into two hemispheres, each of which is further subdivided into four lobes: the frontal, parietal, temporal, and occipital lobes. Each of these lobes plays a distinct role in processing information and guiding behavior. At the core of the frontal lobe's responsibilities are higher cognitive functions (Mercadante & Tadi, 2023). These include reasoning, which allows individuals to make logical connections between ideas, and planning, which involves the ability to think ahead, set goals, and develop strategies to achieve them. Problem-solving is another critical function of the frontal lobe, enabling individuals to identify challenges, evaluate potential solutions, and implement effective responses. These cognitive abilities are fundamental to daily life and are often compromised in individuals with frontal lobe damage, leading to difficulties in managing tasks that require forethought and organization (Pirau & Lui, 2023).

The frontal lobe is also home to the brain's executive functions, which are crucial for regulating behavior and emotions. These functions include working memory (the ability to hold and manipulate information over short periods), cognitive flexibility (the capacity to shift thinking and adapt to new situations), and inhibitory control (the ability to suppress inappropriate impulses and responses). These executive functions are essential for goal-directed behavior, enabling individuals to focus their attention, resist distractions, and make deliberate decisions (Diamond, 2013).

One of the most significant areas within the frontal lobe related to executive functions is the prefrontal cortex (PFC). The PFC is involved in the management of complex behaviors and social interactions, playing a vital role in decision-making, impulse control, and moral reasoning. In forensic neuropsychology, the prefrontal cortex is of particular interest because impairments in this area can lead to difficulties in controlling impulses, making sound decisions, and understanding the consequences of one's actions. Such impairments are often observed in individuals with a history of antisocial behavior or criminal activity (Goyal et al., 2008).

In addition to its role in cognitive functions, the frontal lobe is critical for motor control. The primary motor cortex, located in the posterior part of the frontal lobe, is responsible for the initiation and coordination of voluntary movements. It sends signals to muscles throughout the body, allowing for precise and purposeful actions. Damage to the motor cortex can result in motor deficits, such as weakness or paralysis on the opposite side of the body (El-Baba & Schury, 2023).

The frontal lobe is also crucial for speech production, a function primarily governed by Broca's area, located in the left hemisphere of the frontal lobe. Broca's area is responsible for the motor aspects of speech, enabling the articulation of words and the construction of coherent sentences. Damage to this area, as seen in conditions such as Broca's aphasia, can lead to difficulties in speech production, where an individual may understand language but struggle to speak fluently or produce grammatically correct sentences (The Editors of Encyclopaedia Britannica, 2024).

The prefrontal cortex is a region of immense importance in forensic neuropsychology due to its role in social behavior, impulse control, and decision-making. The PFC is involved in evaluating risks and rewards, understanding the long-term consequences of actions, and regulating emotions. These functions are essential for making ethical decisions and conforming to social norms (Kim & Lee, 2011).

In forensic contexts, abnormalities or damage to the prefrontal cortex can have profound implications. For instance, individuals with prefrontal cortex dysfunction may exhibit poor impulse control, leading to impulsive and potentially criminal behavior. They may also struggle with moral reasoning, making it difficult for them to distinguish right from wrong or to understand the impact of their actions on others. These deficits can contribute to behaviors such as aggression, theft, or other forms of antisocial conduct (Sener et al., 2015).

Moreover, the prefrontal cortex is involved in the ability to empathize with others and anticipate their reactions, which are crucial for social interactions and moral judgments. Impairments in these areas can result in a lack of empathy or remorse, traits often associated with psychopathy and other personality disorders that are frequently examined in forensic settings (Koenigs, 2012).

In legal contexts, understanding the functioning of the prefrontal cortex can be crucial for assessing an individual's criminal responsibility, decision-making competence, and the potential for rehabilitation. Neuropsychological assessments that evaluate prefrontal cortex function can provide valuable insights into whether an individual's criminal behavior is related to neurological impairments, which may influence legal outcomes, such as sentencing or the application of mental health defenses (Egbenya & Adjorlolo, 2021).

The limbic system is a group of interconnected structures that lie deep within the brain and are primarily associated with emotions, memory, and motivation. Key components of the limbic system include the amygdala, hippocampus, hypothalamus, and cingulate gyrus.

The amygdala is crucial for processing emotions, particularly fear and aggression. It plays a role in emotional learning, such as forming memories of traumatic events, and influences how we respond to threats. The hippocampus is essential for the formation and retrieval of long-term memories. It also contributes to spatial navigation and context-dependent learning. Damage to the hippocampus can result in memory impairments, which can have significant implications for behavior. The hypothalamus is responsible for regulating many autonomic functions, such as hunger, thirst, temperature control, and circadian rhythms. It also plays a role in the regulation of emotions and drives, influencing behaviors related to survival, such as eating and reproduction. The cingulate gyrus is involved in emotion regulation and cognitive processing. It helps integrate emotional responses with cognitive functions, such as decision-making and attention.

The brainstem is the oldest and most primitive part of the brain, located at the base where the brain connects to the spinal cord. It is responsible for controlling basic life-sustaining functions such as heart rate, breathing, and arousal (Basinger & Hogg, 2023).

The midbrain acts as a relay station for auditory and visual information and is involved in motor control. It contains structures like the substantia nigra, which is involved in movement and is affected in disorders such as Parkinson's disease. The pons is involved in regulating sleep, respiration, and facial expressions. It serves as a bridge connecting the cerebellum with the rest of the brain. The medulla controls vital functions such as heart rate, blood pressure, and digestion. It also coordinates reflex actions like swallowing and coughing (Ackerman, 1992).

Beyond individual brain structures, understanding how these areas communicate and work together is crucial. Neural networks are systems of interconnected neurons that collaborate to perform complex functions. Two key networks that play pivotal roles in behavior and cognition are the default mode network (DMN) and the executive network.

2.1 *Default Mode Network (DMN)*

The default mode network (DMN) is a group of brain regions that are active when a person is at rest and not focused on the external environment. The DMN includes the medial prefrontal cortex, posterior cingulate cortex, and the angular gyrus, among other areas. It is associated with self-referential thoughts, such as daydreaming, reflecting on the past, and imagining the future. The DMN plays a role in internalized thinking, including autobiographical memory and social cognition. Dysregulation of the DMN has been implicated in various psychiatric conditions, such as depression and anxiety, where individuals may become overly focused on negative internal states.

2.2 *Executive Network*

The executive network, also known as the central executive network, is involved in goal-directed behaviors and cognitive control. It includes the dorsolateral prefrontal cortex and the anterior cingulate cortex. This network is crucial for tasks that require planning, decision-making, problem-solving, and the regulation of attention. The executive network is also involved in inhibitory control, which is essential for managing impulses and delaying gratification—functions that are often compromised in criminal behavior. Dysfunction in this network can lead to difficulties in maintaining attention, controlling impulses, and making rational decisions, all of which can contribute to antisocial or criminal behavior (Friedman & Robbins, 2021).

2.3 *Neural Networks and Behavior*

Neural networks are not isolated systems; they interact with one another to produce coordinated behavior and cognition. For instance, while the DMN is more active during rest, the executive network is activated when attention is directed toward a specific task. The dynamic interplay between these networks allows for flexibility in thought and behavior, enabling individuals to switch between internal reflection and external focus as needed (Gandelman et al., 2018).

Disruptions in these networks can lead to various cognitive and behavioral issues. An overactive DMN or an underactive executive network might result in excessive rumination and impaired decision-making, both of which are factors that could contribute to maladaptive behaviors, including those seen in criminal contexts. Understanding these networks and their functions provides insight into the neural basis of complex behaviors, offering a framework for interpreting how brain dysfunction might lead to criminal actions (Mowinckel et al., 2017).

3 Brain Morphology and Behavioral Outcomes

The human brain is a dynamic organ whose structure plays a pivotal role in regulating cognition and behavior. In forensic neuropsychology, understanding how changes in brain morphology can affect behavior is crucial for explaining deviant or criminal actions. This section explores the types of structural brain changes commonly observed in forensic contexts and the cognitive and behavioral outcomes associated with these changes. By examining the correlation between brain morphology and behavior, we gain insights into how neurological impairments may contribute to criminal behavior.

Changes in brain morphology refer to alterations in the structure of the brain that can emerge due to various causes, including injury, disease, genetic abnormalities, and even environmental influences such as prolonged substance abuse. These structural changes are especially important in forensic contexts because they can have a direct impact on behavior, potentially leading to deviant or criminal actions. Understanding how these morphological changes affect brain function and behavior is critical for neuropsychologists working in legal settings, as these insights can help explain why some individuals engage in impulsive, violent, or socially inappropriate behavior (Montana et al., 2024).

One of the most common types of structural changes observed in forensic settings is brain atrophy, which refers to the loss of neurons and neural connections. This reduction in brain volume can occur across the entire brain or be localized to specific areas, depending on the underlying cause. Atrophy is commonly seen in neurodegenerative diseases such as Alzheimer's and Parkinson's, but it is also prevalent in individuals with a history of traumatic brain injury (TBI), stroke, or chronic alcohol and drug use (Sungura et al., 2020).

In forensic neuropsychology, the link between brain atrophy and criminal behavior is of particular interest, especially when the frontal or temporal lobes are affected. The frontal lobes are responsible for executive functions, including decision-making, impulse control, and social behavior. Atrophy in this area can lead to impulsive, disinhibited, and aggressive behaviors, which are common in some criminal cases. The temporal lobes, on the other hand, are involved in memory, emotion, and social cognition. Damage to this region, particularly in areas like the amygdala and hippocampus, can result in emotional instability, heightened aggression, and difficulties in forming appropriate social responses.

Research has shown that individuals with significant frontal lobe atrophy, such as those with frontotemporal dementia, may engage in behaviors that are socially inappropriate or even criminal, such as theft or physical assault, despite having no prior history of such actions. These behaviors often arise because the affected individual lacks the capacity to regulate impulses or consider the consequences of their actions.

Lesions are another significant type of morphological change that can have profound effects on behavior. A lesion is any abnormal area of tissue in the brain, typically resulting from injury, stroke, or infection. Lesions can be focal, affecting a specific area of the brain, or diffuse, impacting multiple areas.

In forensic cases, the location of the lesion is key to understanding its behavioral outcomes. Lesions in the prefrontal cortex, for instance, are often associated with poor impulse control, lack of foresight, and antisocial behavior, while lesions in the limbic system—which includes structures such as the amygdala and hippocampus—can lead to emotional dysregulation, aggression, and violent outbursts. Lesions affecting these regions can impair an individual's ability to empathize with others or recognize social boundaries, increasing the likelihood of criminal actions.

One of the most famous examples of the relationship between brain lesions and behavior is the case of Phineas Gage, a railroad worker who suffered a traumatic brain injury when an iron rod penetrated his frontal lobe. Before the injury, Gage was known to be responsible and socially adept, but after the incident, his behavior became erratic, impulsive, and aggressive. This case has been widely studied as a demonstration of how damage to specific brain regions can radically alter personality and behavior (Filho & Vieira, 2020).

In modern forensic settings, neuroimaging techniques such as magnetic resonance imaging (MRI) and computed tomography (CT) scans are used to identify lesions in individuals who have committed crimes, helping to determine whether their behavior may be linked to brain damage (Filho & Vieira, 2020).

3.1 Structural Abnormalities

Beyond atrophy and lesions, forensic neuropsychologists also encounter structural abnormalities that are either congenital or arise from developmental disorders. Conditions such as ventriculomegaly (enlargement of the brain's ventricles) or cortical dysplasia (abnormal brain development) are examples of such abnormalities that can impact cognition and behavior. In the context of criminal behavior, individuals with these abnormalities may exhibit difficulties in regulating emotions, controlling impulses, or understanding social norms. Structural abnormalities that affect the frontal lobe, for instance, can impair decision-making and problem-solving abilities, increasing the risk of engaging in criminal activities due to poor judgment or failure to consider the consequences of one's actions (Severino et al., 2020).

3.2 Correlation Between Morphological Changes and Behavioral Outcomes

The connection between brain morphology and behavior is a central topic in forensic neuropsychology. Numerous studies have established that changes in brain structure—whether due to injury, disease, or developmental abnormalities—can lead to impairments in cognition and behavior. These impairments often manifest in ways that are directly relevant to criminal justice, such as difficulties with impulse control, heightened aggression, and emotional dysregulation.

3.3 Frontal Lobe Damage and Behavioral Outcomes

Damage to the frontal lobes, especially the prefrontal cortex, is often associated with criminal behavior. The prefrontal cortex is essential for executive functions like decision-making, impulse control, and moral reasoning. When this area is damaged—whether due to atrophy, lesions, or developmental abnormalities—an individual's ability to regulate their behavior and emotions is significantly compromised. Individuals with frontal lobe damage often struggle with impulsivity and poor judgment, making them more likely to engage in risky or socially inappropriate behaviors. They may also have difficulty planning ahead, considering the consequences of their actions, or empathizing with others. These deficits can lead to behaviors such as theft, physical assault, or substance abuse, all of which are common in forensic cases (Pirau & Lui, 2023).

The amygdala, located in the temporal lobe, plays a critical role in processing emotions, particularly fear and aggression. Structural abnormalities or lesions in the amygdala are strongly associated with violent or aggressive behaviors. Individuals with amygdala damage may have difficulty controlling their anger or responding appropriately to emotional stimuli, leading to impulsive acts of violence. In cases involving psychopathy or antisocial personality disorder, abnormalities in the amygdala are often implicated. These individuals may exhibit a lack of empathy, heightened aggression, and difficulty forming emotional connections with others. Neuroimaging studies have shown that psychopaths often have reduced amygdala volume or abnormal amygdala activity, which may help explain their emotional detachment and propensity for violence (AbuHasan et al., 2023).

Changes in brain morphology do not affect behavior in isolation; they also impact cognitive functions, which, in turn, influence behavior. Cognitive impairments resulting from structural changes in the brain can affect memory, attention, decision-making, and emotional regulation, all of which are critical for normal social functioning. Individuals with hippocampal damage may experience memory deficits, leading to confusion or difficulty recalling important information. This can be particularly problematic in legal settings, where accurate memory recall is crucial for providing testimony or understanding the sequence of events related to a crime (Dhakal & Bobrin, 2023).

Similarly, individuals with damage to the prefrontal cortex may exhibit poor decision-making and risk-taking behaviors. This is because the prefrontal cortex is responsible for evaluating risks and rewards, making it essential for making sound decisions. When this area is compromised, individuals may make impulsive, risky choices without fully considering the consequences, increasing the likelihood of engaging in criminal activities (National Academies Press (US), 2011).

Changes in brain morphology do not affect behavior in isolation; they also impact cognitive functions, which, in turn, influence behavior. Cognitive impairments resulting from structural changes in the brain can affect memory, attention, decision-making, and emotional regulation, all of which are critical for normal social functioning (Dhakal & Bobrin, 2023). Individuals with hippocampal damage may experience memory deficits, leading to confusion or difficulty recalling important information. This can be particularly problematic in legal settings, where accurate memory recall is crucial for providing testimony or understanding the sequence of events related to a crime (Dhakal & Bobrin, 2023).

Similarly, individuals with damage to the prefrontal cortex may exhibit poor decision-making and risk-taking behaviors. This is because the prefrontal cortex is responsible for evaluating risks and rewards, making it essential for making sound decisions. When this area is compromised, individuals may make impulsive, risky choices without fully considering the consequences, increasing the likelihood of engaging in criminal activities (Kim & Lee, 2011).

4 Approaches to Neuropsychological Assessment

In forensic neuropsychology, accurate assessment of brain function and behavior is critical for understanding the role of neurological impairments in criminal behavior, decision-making competence, and cognitive functioning. The field employs both traditional and advanced assessment methods to gather comprehensive data on individuals involved in legal proceedings. This section provides an in-depth look at these methods, their applications, and their relevance in forensic contexts.

Traditional neuropsychological assessments rely on paper-and-pencil tests and standardized clinical measures that evaluate various aspects of cognitive functioning, including memory, attention, executive functions, language, and visuospatial skills. These tests have been widely used for decades in both clinical and forensic settings, providing a foundation for understanding cognitive impairments that may result from brain injury, disease, or developmental disorders.

Wechsler Adult Intelligence Scale (WAIS): One of the most widely used intelligence tests, the WAIS assesses a range of cognitive abilities, including verbal comprehension, perceptual reasoning, working memory, and processing speed. It is often used to evaluate cognitive impairments that may impact decision-making competence or criminal responsibility.

Rey-Osterrieth Complex Figure Test: This test assesses visuospatial abilities and executive functioning by requiring individuals to copy a complex geometric figure from memory. It can reveal deficits in planning, organization, and memory, which are relevant in forensic cases involving traumatic brain injury (TBI).

Wisconsin Card Sorting Test (WCST): The WCST is used to measure executive functioning, particularly cognitive flexibility and problem-solving ability. It is commonly used in forensic contexts to assess individuals with frontal lobe damage, as impairments in this area are linked to impulsivity and poor decision-making.

Trail Making Test: This test measures attention, processing speed, and mental flexibility by requiring individuals to connect numbered or lettered circles in a specific sequence. It is useful in detecting cognitive slowing and difficulties with multitasking, which are often seen in individuals with neurological impairments.

In forensic neuropsychology, traditional paper-and-pencil tests are often used to assess cognitive impairments that may be linked to criminal behavior. These tests provide valuable information on an individual's cognitive abilities, helping to determine whether they are competent to stand trial, understand the consequences of their actions, or have cognitive deficits that could mitigate their legal responsibility. Individuals with frontal lobe damage may perform poorly on tests of executive functioning, such as the Wisconsin Card Sorting Test, indicating that they struggle with impulse control and decision-making. This information can be used to argue that the individual's neurological impairments contributed to their criminal behavior.

Similarly, memory tests like the California Verbal Learning Test (CVLT) can reveal whether an individual has memory deficits that affect their ability to accurately recall events. This can be crucial in cases where the individual's recollection of a crime is central to the legal proceedings.

While traditional neuropsychological assessments are valuable, they also have limitations, particularly in forensic contexts. Traditional tests often rely on the individual's effort and cooperation, which can be problematic in forensic settings where there may be concerns about malingering (feigning cognitive impairment) or lack of motivation. Paper-and-pencil tests primarily measure cognitive abilities but may not capture the full extent of neurological impairments, particularly those related to emotional regulation, aggression, or social cognition. These areas are often crucial in understanding criminal behavior. Traditional tests provide a snapshot of cognitive functioning at a single point in time, making it difficult to assess changes over time or in response to interventions (Harvey, 2012). Because of these limitations, forensic neuropsychologists often supplement traditional assessments with advanced neuroimaging techniques, which provide a more comprehensive view of brain function.

In recent years, neuroimaging has become an indispensable tool in forensic neuropsychology. These techniques allow for the direct visualization of brain structure and function, offering insights into how neurological abnormalities may contribute to cognitive and behavioral impairments.

Magnetic resonance imaging (MRI) provides detailed images of brain structure, allowing neuropsychologists to detect abnormalities such as lesions, atrophy, and structural asymmetries. This technique is particularly useful in forensic cases involving traumatic brain injury (TBI) or neurodegenerative conditions. For example, MRI can reveal damage to the prefrontal cortex, which is associated with impulsivity and poor decision-making in criminal cases (Shenton et al., 2012).

While traditional MRI captures static images of brain structure, functional MRI (fMRI) measures brain activity by detecting changes in blood flow. This allows neuropsychologists to assess how different regions of the brain function during specific tasks. fMRI has been used in forensic settings to study brain activity related to decision-making, impulse control, and emotional processing. For instance, individuals with reduced activation in the prefrontal cortex during decision-making tasks may be more prone to impulsive behavior (Glover, 2011).

Positron emission tomography (PET) scans measure metabolic activity in the brain by tracking the uptake of radioactive tracers. This technique is often used to assess brain function in individuals with neurodegenerative diseases, such as Alzheimer's or Parkinson's, which may impair cognitive functioning. In forensic contexts, PET scans can reveal abnormalities in brain regions related to aggression or emotional regulation, helping to explain violent behavior (Kapoor & Kasi, 2022).

Neuroimaging techniques provide critical insights into the relationship between brain structure and behavior, which is particularly relevant in forensic neuropsychology. By identifying structural and functional abnormalities, neuroimaging can help explain why certain individuals. Individuals with prefrontal cortex damage, as seen in MRI or fMRI scans, may have reduced capacity for impulse control and moral reasoning, which can lead to criminal actions such as theft, assault, or fraud. Similarly, abnormalities in the amygdala, detected through PET or fMRI scans, can result in heightened aggression or emotional dysregulation, which are common in individuals who commit violent crimes (Yen et al., 2023).

In forensic settings, neuroimaging is also used to assess competency to stand trial. By examining brain function, neuropsychologists can determine whether an individual has the cognitive capacity to understand the legal proceedings and assist in their own defense. For instance, individuals with significant brain atrophy, as detected through MRI, may have impairments in memory and reasoning that affect their ability to participate in their defense (Treadway & Buckholtz, 2011).

Neuroimaging also plays a key role in distinguishing between organic brain damage and malingering. In cases where an individual claims cognitive impairment to avoid legal responsibility, neuroimaging can provide objective evidence of whether there are actual neurological abnormalities. For example, if an MRI or fMRI scan shows no signs of brain damage in an individual claiming severe cognitive deficits, this may suggest malingering.

Neuroimaging offers several advantages in forensic neuropsychology. Unlike traditional tests, neuroimaging provides objective, quantifiable data on brain structure and function, reducing the risk of malingering or deception. Neuroimaging allows for a more comprehensive assessment of brain function, capturing both structural abnormalities and functional impairments that may contribute to criminal behavior.

However, there are also limitations. Neuroimaging techniques are expensive and not always accessible, particularly in legal cases with limited resources. While neuroimaging provides detailed data, interpreting the results in the context of behavior and legal responsibility can be complex. Abnormalities in brain function do not always lead to criminal behavior, and it can be difficult to establish a direct causal link.

5 Practical Application of Assessment Methods in Forensic Neuropsychology

The practical application of neuropsychological assessment methods is essential in forensic neuropsychology for evaluating cognitive impairments, understanding criminal behavior, and determining legal competence. These assessments help establish whether an individual's neurological or cognitive deficits have impacted their ability to make decisions, control impulses, or understand legal proceedings. This section explores the practical applications of assessment methods, focusing on assessing neurological abnormalities, measuring cognitive functioning, and determining decision-making competence.

Identifying neurological abnormalities is a fundamental aspect of forensic neuropsychology. The methods used in this process range from traditional paper-and-pencil assessments to advanced neuroimaging techniques that provide detailed information about brain structure and function. One of the most commonly used techniques for identifying brain abnormalities is neuroimaging, which includes tools like magnetic resonance imaging (MRI), functional MRI (fMRI), and positron emission tomography (PET). These methods offer a noninvasive way to visualize structural and functional abnormalities in the brain.

MRI provides high-resolution images of brain structures and is particularly effective in identifying lesions, atrophy, and other abnormalities. MRI scans can show damage to the prefrontal cortex, which is associated with impulsivity and poor decision-making, traits often seen in individuals involved in criminal activities. fMRI tracks blood flow in the brain, giving insights into which areas are active during specific cognitive tasks. This can help in forensic cases by revealing whether a defendant has impaired functioning in areas responsible for emotional regulation, impulse control, or moral reasoning. PET scans measure metabolic activity, which can highlight dysfunctional areas of the brain, such as reduced activity in the amygdala, a structure associated with aggression and emotional regulation (Professional, 2024).

The case study below will aid us in understanding the connection between the brain abnormalities and their correlated change in behavior.

The defendant, a 24-year-old woman identified as JF, faced charges of murder after smothering her newborn child immediately following delivery. She concealed the infant's body by wrapping it in a towel and placing it inside a suitcase (Rigoni et al., 2010). Subsequently, the defendant claimed that the infant had been stillborn due to drug abstinence syndrome. Anamnestic information revealed that JF began smoking heavily at the age of eleven and had a long-standing history of substance abuse, including alcohol and multiple illicit drugs, starting from the age of thirteen. The pregnancy occurred during a party, and she continued using drugs throughout its course (Rigoni et al., 2010).

A forensic psychiatric examination revealed a personality profile characterized by significant antisocial traits. These included a history of illegal behavior, sensation seeking, familial conflict, emotional insensitivity, rejection of conventional societal norms, poor responses to threatening situations, and a tendency to act without careful consideration of alternative solutions. The neuropsychological assessment further identified marked impulsivity, demonstrated by an inability to inhibit dominant responses, as measured by the Hayling Sentence Completion Test. Additionally, deficits in planning were observed through the Tower of London task, along with impairments in emotional attribution and difficulties in recognizing violations of social norms, as assessed by the Emotion Attribution Task and the Social Situation Task. The structural MRI of the defendant was analyzed in comparison to the MRIs of healthy female controls using voxel-based morphometry (VBM), a neuroimaging technique designed to detect subtle structural anatomical differences. The analysis indicated a reduction in gray matter volume in the left prefrontal cortex of JF (refer to Fig. 1) compared to the control group (Rigoni et al., 2010).

The reference paper specifies that the gray matter loss is localized within the middle frontal gyrus. According to the defense consultant, the sNI data were crucial in elucidating the constellation of symptoms observed in the defendant's history. Specifically, the identified brain alteration in the frontal lobe correlates strongly

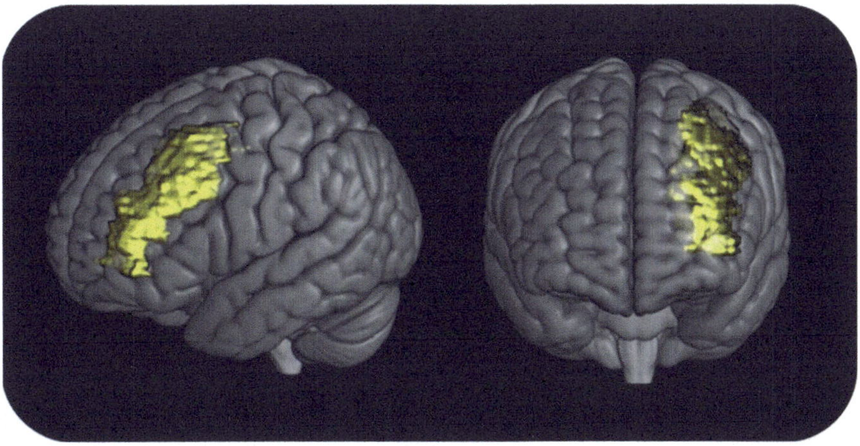

Fig. 1 Location of the gray matter reduction in JF (Scarpazza et al., 2018)

with the clinical presentation of frontal syndrome. This syndrome encompasses symptoms such as impulsivity, deficits in planning and automatic response inhibition, and difficulties in emotional attribution. Additionally, the defendant exhibited alterations in personality, with high scores on the borderline, depression, and substance abuse subscales. The false-positive distribution map indicates that the observed reduction in gray matter in the dorsolateral prefrontal cortex (DLPFC) in this individual compared to the control group has a probability of only 0.5–5% of being a false-positive. From a criminodynamic perspective, the presence of frontal lobe abnormalities is significant. The symptoms observed in JF suggested a diminished capacity to control her behavior, which is highly relevant to evaluating the prosecutor's hypothesis that JF acted impulsively in smothering the newborn. The pathological features identified clinically are causally linked to the crime, thereby providing a basis for an insanity defense (Laumann et al., 2015). The combination of JF's behavioral reports and the neuroimaging findings offered substantial biological evidence supporting the defense's argument. In conclusion, the defense consultants determined that the behavioral and neuropsychological symptoms exhibited by JF were strongly correlated with the identified brain abnormalities and were causally related to the criminal act. They argued that JF should be deemed not responsible for her actions due to her inability to inhibit her impulses.

Measuring cognitive functioning is a core element of forensic neuropsychological assessments. These methods are used to evaluate various cognitive domains, including memory, attention, language, executive function, and visuospatial skills. The results are often crucial in forensic cases to determine whether cognitive deficits contributed to criminal behavior or impaired the individual's competence.

The Wechsler Adult Intelligence Scale (WAIS) test assesses general intellectual ability, including verbal comprehension, perceptual reasoning, working memory, and processing speed. In forensic contexts, the WAIS can reveal deficits in problem-solving, reasoning, and judgment, which are relevant in determining whether cognitive impairments influence criminal behavior. The California Verbal Learning Test (CVLT) test assesses verbal memory and recall abilities. In forensic cases, individuals with memory deficits may struggle to accurately remember the events surrounding a crime, which could affect the credibility of their testimony or statements. The Wisconsin Card Sorting Test (WCST) measures executive functions, including cognitive flexibility and problem-solving. It is often used to assess individuals with frontal lobe damage, who may struggle with impulsive decision-making and fail to anticipate the consequences of their actions. The Trail Making Test evaluates processing speed and attention by requiring individuals to connect numbers and letters in sequence. It is particularly useful in cases where cognitive slowing or attention deficits are suspected (Abdelhamid et al., 2021).

In forensic settings, cognitive assessments can help establish whether an individual has the mental capacity to understand legal proceedings, provide accurate testimony, or even comprehend the moral implications of their actions. For example, a defendant with significant deficits in executive functioning, as measured by the WCST, may not have been able to control impulsive behaviors or foresee the consequences of their actions. This type of assessment can play a critical role in determining criminal responsibility or establishing a defense based on diminished capacity (Woods et al., 2012).

Decision-making competence is a key issue in many forensic cases, especially when determining whether an individual is capable of standing trial or making informed legal decisions. Neuropsychological assessments can provide insights into an individual's capacity to understand legal proceedings, communicate with their attorney, and make rational decisions regarding their defense. Evaluating decision-making competence involves assessing cognitive functions such as reasoning, judgment, impulse control, and moral reasoning (Van Es et al., 2020).

The Competency to Stand Trial Evaluations assess whether an individual has the cognitive ability to understand the legal process and participate in their defense. The evaluation includes assessing the individual's ability to understand the charges, the roles of various courtroom participants, and the potential consequences of the trial. As mentioned earlier, tests like the WCST and Trail Making Test assess cognitive flexibility, planning, and impulse control, all of which are essential for competent decision-making. In forensic contexts, individuals who perform poorly on the Executive Function Tests may lack the ability to weigh legal options, such as accepting a plea deal or testifying in court. The moral reasoning assessments evaluate an individual's ability to understand right from wrong and foresee the moral implications of their actions. Defendants with impaired moral reasoning may not fully comprehend the gravity of their crimes, affecting their criminal responsibility (Wall & Lee, 2020).

There have been multiple cases where forensic neuropsychology assessments have been used to examine the competency of the patient on trial. One such case involves John Hinckley and his assassination attempt of President Ronald Reagan. In 1981, the attempted assassination of President Ronald Reagan by John Hinckley became one of the most prominent cases to incorporate neuroscience into a criminal trial. Hinckley's defense presented a computed tomography (CT) scan of his brain to support their claim that he was suffering from schizophrenia and thus should be acquitted under the defense of not guilty by reason of insanity (NGRI). Although the prosecution contested the admissibility of the CT scans, the presiding district court judge ruled in favor of their inclusion. Hinckley was ultimately found not guilty by reason of insanity (Aono et al., 2019).

Another case involved Weinstein was charged with second-degree murder for strangling his wife and throwing her from the 12th floor of their Manhattan apartment, a charge he readily admitted to. His attorneys considered it suspicious that Weinstein would show so little remorse for his actions, and ordered positron emission tomography (PET) scans. At trial, Weinstein's defense team presented his PET scans to support their claim that, due to an arachnoid cyst, his brain function was disrupted. Thus, they claimed that the defendant did not have the requisite mental state to be found criminally responsible. Weinstein was later allowed to plead guilty to the lesser charge of manslaughter.

6 Importance of a Multi-Method Approach

In forensic neuropsychology, the assessment of cognitive functioning and brain abnormalities is critical for understanding how neurological deficits may influence behavior, decision-making, and legal responsibility. A multi-method approach—combining both traditional assessment methods and advanced neuroimaging techniques—offers a comprehensive, reliable, and scientifically sound way to evaluate individuals involved in legal proceedings. This approach enhances the accuracy and validity of evaluations, which are crucial in forensic settings where the stakes are high, such as determining criminal responsibility or competence to stand trial. This section discusses the importance of a multi-method approach, focusing on two key aspects: comprehensive testing and enhancing accuracy in legal contexts (Woods et al., 2012).

Comprehensive testing involves using a combination of traditional neuropsychological tests and advanced neuroimaging techniques to assess cognitive functioning and neurological abnormalities. Each method has its strengths and limitations, but when used together, they offer a more holistic and accurate understanding of the individual's cognitive abilities and brain structure. Traditional neuropsychological tests, such as paper-and-pencil tasks and standardized cognitive assessments, are widely used to evaluate various cognitive functions, including memory, attention, executive function, language, and visuospatial abilities. Some of the most common tests include the **Wechsler Adult Intelligence Scale (WAIS)**, the **Wisconsin Card Sorting Test (WCST)**, and the **California Verbal Learning Test (CVLT)**. These tests provide valuable insights into cognitive deficits that may result from brain injury, neurodegenerative diseases, or developmental disorders (Harvey, 2012).

Traditional tests allow for the measurement of specific cognitive domains. For example, the WAIS provides a comprehensive overview of verbal comprehension, perceptual reasoning, working memory, and processing speed, which are essential in understanding cognitive impairments in legal cases. These tests have been standardized across large populations, which means they offer normative data for comparison. This makes it easier for neuropsychologists to determine the extent of an individual's impairments relative to the general population. Traditional assessments are generally more affordable and accessible compared to advanced techniques like neuroimaging. This makes them a practical choice in many forensic cases (Harvey, 2019).

While traditional methods provide valuable insights into cognitive functioning, they do not offer direct information about the brain's structure or function. This is where advanced neuroimaging techniques like magnetic resonance imaging (MRI), functional MRI (fMRI), and positron emission tomography (PET) become essential. These techniques allow for the visualization of brain structures and the measurement of brain activity, which can provide crucial evidence in forensic contexts. MRI scans can reveal structural abnormalities, such as lesions or atrophy, which may not be apparent through cognitive testing alone. For instance, damage to the prefrontal cortex—a region associated with impulse control and decision-making—can be clearly visualized using MRI. fMRI and PET scans offer insights into how different areas of the brain function during specific cognitive tasks. This is particularly useful in forensic cases where the defendant's ability to regulate emotions or control impulses is in question. For example, reduced activity in the amygdala, a brain region associated with aggression and emotional regulation, can be linked to violent behavior. In forensic settings, there is often concern about malingering, or feigning cognitive impairments to avoid legal responsibility. Neuroimaging provides objective evidence of brain function, making it more difficult for individuals to fake neurological deficits (Xue et al., 2010).

The real strength of a multi-method approach lies in combining the detailed cognitive profile provided by traditional tests with the objective data obtained through neuroimaging. For example, an individual may perform poorly on the WCST, indicating executive function deficits. Neuroimaging can then be used to confirm whether these deficits are linked to structural abnormalities in the prefrontal cortex. Together, these methods offer a comprehensive view of the individual's cognitive and neurological status, making it easier to determine the extent to which their impairments influenced their behavior.

6.1 Enhancing Accuracy in Legal Contexts

In legal contexts, the accuracy and reliability of neuropsychological evaluations are paramount. These evaluations often play a key role in determining whether an individual is competent to stand trial, criminally responsible for their actions, or capable of making informed decisions. A multi-method approach enhances the accuracy of these evaluations by providing a more nuanced and reliable understanding of cognitive and neurological impairments.

One of the main challenges in forensic neuropsychology is ensuring the reliability of assessments. Traditional tests can be subjective, relying on the individual's effort and cooperation. This is particularly problematic in forensic cases, where individuals may attempt to exaggerate or understate their impairments. By combining traditional tests with neuroimaging techniques, neuropsychologists can cross-validate their findings and reduce the risk of false results (Woods et al., 2012).

Neuroimaging can be used to confirm the findings of traditional tests. For example, if an individual shows memory deficits on the CVLT, neuroimaging may reveal atrophy in the hippocampus, a brain region critical for memory. This cross-validation strengthens the reliability of the assessment. As mentioned earlier, neuroimaging provides objective evidence of brain function, making it more difficult for individuals to feign cognitive impairments. For instance, if an individual claims to have significant memory deficits but neuroimaging shows no abnormalities in the hippocampus or other memory-related structures, this may indicate malingering. Traditional tests can be influenced by cultural, educational, or socioeconomic factors, which may affect an individual's performance. Neuroimaging, however, provides objective data that is less influenced by these variables, reducing the potential for bias in forensic evaluations (Xue et al., 2010).

7 Conclusion

The field of forensic neuropsychology offers critical insights into the complex relationship between brain structure, function, and behavior, particularly in legal contexts. A comprehensive understanding of brain architecture and function lays the foundation for analyzing how alterations in brain morphology can result in significant behavioral and cognitive changes. These fundamental concepts are crucial when considering individuals involved in the legal system, as they offer a scientific basis for understanding impairments that may influence criminal behavior, decision-making competence, and culpability. The discussion on brain morphology and behavioral outcomes underscores the importance of recognizing how structural changes, such as lesions, atrophy, or damage to specific brain regions, directly correlate with cognitive and behavioral deficits. For instance, damage to the prefrontal cortex may impair impulse control and decision-making, while abnormalities in the limbic system might affect emotional regulation and aggression. Understanding these relationships helps neuropsychologists and legal professionals make informed decisions about an individual's mental state and potential criminal responsibility. In forensic contexts, these findings can influence the outcome of trials, sentencing, and rehabilitation efforts. Approaches to neuropsychological assessment in forensic settings emphasize the need for robust and scientifically validated tools. Traditional paper-and-pencil tests remain vital in assessing various cognitive domains such as memory, attention, and executive functioning. However, these tests have limitations, particularly in detecting subtle neurological abnormalities. To address these gaps, advanced neuroimaging techniques like MRI, fMRI, and PET scans have been introduced, providing direct insights into the brain's structure and function. By combining these traditional and modern methods, forensic neuropsychologists can achieve a more thorough understanding of the individual's cognitive and neurological status. The practical application of assessment methods is another essential aspect of forensic neuropsychology. Through case studies, this chapter demonstrates how neuropsychological assessments help identify neurological abnormalities, measure cognitive functioning, and determine decision-making competence. These applications are crucial in legal settings, where decisions often hinge on the individual's mental capacity, ability to understand legal proceedings, and criminal responsibility.

References

Abdelhamid, G. S. M., Bassiouni, M. G. A., & Gómez-Benito, J. (2021). Assessing cognitive abilities using the WAIS-IV: An item response theory approach. *International Journal of Environmental Research and Public Health, 18*(13), 6835. https://doi.org/10.3390/ijerph18136835

AbuHasan, Q., Reddy, V., & Siddiqui, W. (2023, July 17). *Neuroanatomy, amygdala*. StatPearls - NCBI Bookshelf. https://www.ncbi.nlm.nih.gov/books/NBK537102/

Ackerman, S. (1992). *Major structures and functions of the brain*. Discovering the Brain - NCBI Bookshelf. https://www.ncbi.nlm.nih.gov/books/NBK234157/

Aono, D., Yaffe, G., & Kober, H. (2019). Neuroscientific evidence in the courtroom: A review. *Cognitive Research Principles and Implications, 4*(1). https://doi.org/10.1186/s41235-019-0179-y

Basinger, H., & Hogg, J. P. (2023, July 4). *Neuroanatomy, brainstem*. StatPearls - NCBI Bookshelf. https://www.ncbi.nlm.nih.gov/books/NBK544297/

Dhakal, A., & Bobrin, B. D. (2023, February 14). *Cognitive deficits*. StatPearls - NCBI Bookshelf. https://www.ncbi.nlm.nih.gov/books/NBK559052/

Diamond, A. (2013). Executive functions. *Annual Review of Psychology, 64*(1), 135–168. https://doi.org/10.1146/annurev-psych-113011-143750

Egbenya, D. L., & Adjorlolo, S. (2021). Advancement of neuroscience and the assessment of mental state at the time of offense. *Forensic Science International Mind and Law, 2*, 100046. https://doi.org/10.1016/j.fsiml.2021.100046

El-Baba, R. M., & Schury, M. P. (2023, May 29). *Neuroanatomy, frontal cortex*. StatPearls - NCBI Bookshelf. https://www.ncbi.nlm.nih.gov/books/NBK554483/

Filho, T., & Vieira, R. (2020). Phineas Gage's great legacy. *Dementia & Neuropsychologia, 14*(4), 419–421. https://doi.org/10.1590/1980-57642020dn14-040013

Friedman, N. P., & Robbins, T. W. (2021). The role of prefrontal cortex in cognitive control and executive function. *Neuropsychopharmacology, 47*(1), 72–89. https://doi.org/10.1038/s41386-021-01132-0

Gandelman, J. A., Newhouse, P., & Taylor, W. D. (2018). Nicotine and networks: Potential for enhancement of mood and cognition in late-life depression. *Neuroscience & Biobehavioral Reviews, 84*, 289–298. https://doi.org/10.1016/j.neubiorev.2017.08.018

Ghiasi, N., Azhar, Y., & Singh, J. (2023, March 30). *Psychiatric illness and criminality*. StatPearls - NCBI Bookshelf. https://www.ncbi.nlm.nih.gov/books/NBK537064/

Glover, G. H. (2011). Overview of functional magnetic resonance imaging. *Neurosurgery Clinics of North America, 22*(2), 133–139. https://doi.org/10.1016/j.nec.2010.11.001

Goyal, N., Siddiqui, S., Chatterjee, U., Kumar, D., & Siddiqui, A. (2008). Neuropsychology of prefrontal cortex. *Indian Journal of Psychiatry, 50*(3), 202. https://doi.org/10.4103/0019-5545.43634

Harvey, P. D. (2012). Clinical applications of neuropsychological assessment. *Dialogues in Clinical Neuroscience, 14*(1), 91–99. https://doi.org/10.31887/dcns.2012.14.1/pharvey

Harvey, P. D. (2019). Domains of cognition and their assessment. *Dialogues in Clinical Neuroscience, 21*(3), 227–237. https://doi.org/10.31887/dcns.2019.21.3/pharvey

Introduction, Definiton and Description of Neuropsychology. (n.d.). https://profilelogin.admissione.online/UploadFiles/Documents/ProfileLgoin/Subtitle/NColge_1372_Neuropsychology.pdf

Kapoor, M., & Kasi, A. (2022, October 3). *PET scanning*. StatPearls - NCBI Bookshelf. https://www.ncbi.nlm.nih.gov/books/NBK559089/

Kim, S., & Lee, D. (2011). Prefrontal cortex and impulsive decision making. *Biological Psychiatry, 69*(12), 1140–1146. https://doi.org/10.1016/j.biopsych.2010.07.005

Koenigs, M. (2012). The role of prefrontal cortex in psychopathy. *Reviews in the Neurosciences, 23*(3). https://doi.org/10.1515/revneuro-2012-0036

Laumann, T. O., Gordon, E. M., Adeyemo, B., Snyder, A. Z., Joo, S. J., Chen, M., Gilmore, A. W., McDermott, K. B., Nelson, S. M., Dosenbach, N. U., Schlaggar, B. L., Mumford, J. A., Poldrack, R. A., & Petersen, S. E. (2015). Functional system and areal organization of a highly sampled individual human brain. *Neuron, 87*(3), 657–670. https://doi.org/10.1016/j.neuron.2015.06.037

Mercadante, A. A., & Tadi, P. (2023, July 24). *Neuroanatomy, gray matter*. StatPearls - NCBI Bookshelf. https://www.ncbi.nlm.nih.gov/books/NBK553239/

Montana, A., Alfieri, L., Neri, M., Piano, D., Renier, E., Marti, M., Palpacelli, M., Basile, G., Tossetta, G., & Busardò, F. P. (2024). Macroscopic and microscopic cerebral findings in drug and alcohol abusers: The point of view of the forensic pathologist. *Biomedicines, 12*(3), 681. https://doi.org/10.3390/biomedicines12030681

Mowinckel, A. M., Alnæs, D., Pedersen, M. L., Ziegler, S., Fredriksen, M., Kaufmann, T., Sonuga-Barke, E., Endestad, T., Westlye, L. T., & Biele, G. (2017). Increased default-mode variability is related to reduced task-performance and is evident in adults with ADHD. *NeuroImage Clinical, 16*, 369–382. https://doi.org/10.1016/j.nicl.2017.03.008

National Academies Press (US). (2011). *Biobehavioral processes*. The Science of Adolescent Risk-Taking: Workshop Report - NCBI Bookshelf. https://www.ncbi.nlm.nih.gov/books/NBK53414/

Pirau, L., & Lui, F. (2023, July 17). *Frontal lobe syndrome*. StatPearls - NCBI Bookshelf. https://www.ncbi.nlm.nih.gov/books/NBK532981/

Professional, C. C. M. (2024, May 1). *Brain MRI*. Cleveland Clinic. https://my.clevelandclinic.org/health/diagnostics/22966-brain-mri

Rigoni, D., Pellegrini, S., Mariotti, V., Cozza, A., Mechelli, A., Ferrara, S. D., Pietrini, P., & Sartori, G. (2010). How neuroscience and behavioral genetics improve psychiatric assessment: Report on a violent murder case. *Frontiers in Behavioral Neuroscience, 4*. https://doi.org/10.3389/fnbeh.2010.00160

Scarpazza, C., Ferracuti, S., Miolla, A., & Sartori, G. (2018). The charm of structural neuroimaging in insanity evaluations: guidelines to avoid misinterpretation of the findings. *Translational Psychiatry, 8*(1). https://doi.org/10.1038/s41398-018-0274-8

Sener, M. T., Ozcan, H., Sahingoz, S., & Ogul, H. (2015). Criminal responsibility of the frontal lobe syndrome. *Eurasian Journal of Medicine, 47*(3), 218–222. https://doi.org/10.5152/eurasianjmed.2015.69

Severino, M., Geraldo, A. F., Utz, N., Tortora, D., Pogledic, I., Klonowski, W., Triulzi, F., Arrigoni, F., Mankad, K., Leventer, R. J., Mancini, G. M. S., Barkovich, J. A., Lequin, M. H., & Rossi, A. (2020). Definitions and classification of malformations of cortical development: Practical guidelines. *Brain, 143*(10), 2874–2894. https://doi.org/10.1093/brain/awaa174

Shenton, M. E., Hamoda, H. M., Schneiderman, J. S., Bouix, S., Pasternak, O., Rathi, Y., Vu, M., Purohit, M. P., Helmer, K., Koerte, I., Lin, A. P., Westin, C., Kikinis, R., Kubicki, M., Stern, R. A., & Zafonte, R. (2012). A review of magnetic resonance imaging and diffusion tensor imaging findings in mild traumatic brain injury. *Brain Imaging and Behavior, 6*(2), 137–192. https://doi.org/10.1007/s11682-012-9156-5

Siever, L. J. (2008). Neurobiology of aggression and violence. *American Journal of Psychiatry, 165*(4), 429–442. https://doi.org/10.1176/appi.ajp.2008.07111774

Sungura, R. E., Spitsbergen, J. M., Mpolya, E. A., Sauli, E., & Vianney, J. (2020). The neuroimaging magnitude of pediatric brain atrophy in northern Tanzania. *Pan African Medical Journal, 36*. https://doi.org/10.11604/pamj.2020.36.25.22515

The Editors of Encyclopaedia Britannica. (2024, September 2). *Broca area | Definition, Function, & Facts*. Encyclopedia Britannica. https://www.britannica.com/science/Broca-area

Treadway, M., & Buckholtz, J. W. (2011). On the use and misuse of genomic and neuroimaging science in forensic psychiatry: current roles and future directions. *Child and Adolescent Psychiatric Clinics of North America, 20*(3), 533–546. https://doi.org/10.1016/j.chc.2011.03.012

Van Es, R., Kunst, M., & De Keijser, J. (2020). Forensic mental health expert testimony and judicial decision-making: A systematic literature review. *Aggression and Violent Behavior, 51*, 101387. https://doi.org/10.1016/j.avb.2020.101387

Wall, B., Lee, R (2020, October 30). Assessing competency to stand trial. *Psychiatric Times*. https://www.psychiatrictimes.com/view/assessing-competency-to-stand-trial

Woods, G. W., Freedman, D., & Greenspan, S. (2012). Neurobehavioral assessment in forensic practice. *International Journal of Law and Psychiatry, 35*(5–6), 432–439. https://doi.org/10.1016/j.ijlp.2012.09.014

Xue, G., Chen, C., Lu, Z., & Dong, Q. (2010). Brain imaging techniques and their applications in decision-making research. *Acta Psychologica Sinica, 42*(1), 120–137. https://doi.org/10.3724/sp.j.1041.2010.00120

Yen, C., Lin, C., & Chiang, M. (2023). Exploring the frontiers of neuroimaging: A review of recent advances in understanding brain functioning and disorders. *Life, 13*(7), 1472. https://doi.org/10.3390/life13071472

The Role of Neuropsychology in Legal Contexts

1 Introduction

Neuropsychology, as a field bridging neuroscience and psychology, plays an increasingly pivotal role in legal contexts. The complex relationship between brain function, cognition, behavior, and law is being explored in ways that can fundamentally impact both the administration of justice and the understanding of individual responsibility (Harvey, 2012). The legal system often grapples with issues surrounding competency, criminal responsibility, and the assessment of cognitive and psychological impairments, all of which fall within the domain of neuropsychology (Pandey et al., 2021).

Neuropsychologists provide essential insights into how brain injuries, developmental disorders, or neurodegenerative conditions affect behavior and decision-making, which, in turn, have significant implications for legal cases. From criminal proceedings to civil litigation and family law, neuropsychological assessments can influence decisions on competency to stand trial, criminal responsibility, sentencing, custody disputes, and disability claims. This section explores the importance of neuropsychology in legal contexts, examining the scope of neuropsychological assessments, the ethical considerations involved, and the growing intersection of neuropsychology with legal frameworks (Wegierek et al., 2019).

Neuropsychological assessments are designed to evaluate a wide range of cognitive functions, including memory, attention, executive functioning, language abilities, and emotional regulation. In legal cases, these assessments can clarify the extent of cognitive impairment, the cause of abnormal behavior, or the likelihood of a defendant being able to participate meaningfully in their defense. Neuropsychologists employ various standardized tests and clinical interviews to assess an individual's cognitive and psychological profile, often in cases where brain damage or psychiatric disorders are suspected to have affected behavior or decision-making (Determinations, 2015).

© The Author(s), under exclusive license to Springer Nature Switzerland AG 2025

K. J. Reddy, *Foundations of Criminal Forensic Neuropsychology*,
https://doi.org/10.1007/978-3-031-83771-5_3

One of the most frequent applications of neuropsychology in the legal context is in determining a defendant's competency to stand trial. In many legal systems, competency refers to the individual's ability to understand the nature of the charges against them, engage in a rational defense, and work cooperatively with their attorney. Neuropsychological assessments help determine whether cognitive deficits—such as those stemming from traumatic brain injuries (TBI), intellectual disabilities, or psychiatric conditions—may impair a defendant's competency. This can lead to alternative legal proceedings, such as mental health treatment, rather than traditional criminal prosecution (Nestor et al., 1999).

Neuropsychology also plays a critical role in evaluating criminal responsibility, particularly in cases where defendants argue that a mental or neurological condition impaired their ability to understand the wrongfulness of their actions (Math et al., 2015). This intersects with the legal concept of the insanity defense. Neuropsychologists assess whether brain dysfunctions or psychiatric illnesses, such as schizophrenia, bipolar disorder, or frontal lobe damage, influenced the individual's behavior at the time of the offense. For instance, damage to the frontal lobe, which is responsible for executive functions like impulse control, can result in disinhibited, socially inappropriate, or even criminal behaviors. Such evaluations can shape judicial outcomes by determining whether the defendant can be held fully accountable for their actions (Gkintoni, 2023).

During sentencing, neuropsychological evaluations can provide mitigating evidence, particularly in capital cases. For example, individuals with documented brain damage or neurodevelopmental disorders may receive lighter sentences if it can be demonstrated that their condition compromised their judgment or behavioral regulation. This aspect of neuropsychology supports more nuanced sentencing practices, aiming to balance societal safety with a fair and individualized response to criminal behavior (Groscup & Wood, n.d.).

In civil and family law, neuropsychologists are often called upon to assess the cognitive and emotional functioning of individuals involved in legal disputes. Common cases include personal injury lawsuits, where plaintiffs may claim that a brain injury sustained during an accident has resulted in long-term cognitive impairments, emotional distress, or disability (Foote et al., 2020). Neuropsychological evaluations provide objective evidence of the extent of the injury and its impact on the individual's daily life, which can influence the size of settlements or the awarding of damages.

Neuropsychologists are integral in evaluating the cognitive consequences of brain injuries resulting from accidents, workplace incidents, or medical malpractice (Torregrossa et al., 2023). These assessments inform the court of the degree of cognitive, emotional, or functional impairment, which is essential in determining compensation. For instance, after a motor vehicle accident, an individual may claim post-concussive syndrome, manifesting in memory problems, concentration difficulties, and emotional instability. A neuropsychologist's evaluation can confirm the presence and severity of such impairments, thereby influencing the outcome of the lawsuit.

In family law, neuropsychological assessments may be used to determine parental competency in child custody cases (Law4u, n.d.). Parents with cognitive impairments, brain injuries, or mental health issues may undergo evaluations to assess their ability to provide care and make responsible decisions for their children. These assessments are crucial in cases where a parent's mental health or neurological condition may compromise the welfare of the child.

Neuropsychologists working within legal contexts face unique ethical challenges, particularly in balancing the demands of their role as objective assessors with the adversarial nature of the legal system. They must ensure that their evaluations are scientifically valid, unbiased, and reliable while considering the profound consequences their findings may have on an individual's liberty or financial standing.

One significant ethical issue is maintaining confidentiality and obtaining informed consent from individuals undergoing assessment. In legal cases, neuropsychological evaluations are often requested by the court, and the findings may be disclosed to multiple parties, including legal teams and judges. Neuropsychologists must navigate these situations carefully, ensuring that their clients are fully aware of how the information gathered will be used (National Academy of Neuropsychology et al., 2003). Another challenge is ensuring objectivity in evaluations. Given the adversarial nature of the legal system, there may be pressure from attorneys or clients to emphasize certain findings over others. Neuropsychologists must resist such pressures to maintain the integrity of their assessments and the fairness of the legal process (National Academy of Neuropsychology et al., 2003).

The role of neuropsychology in the legal context is both profound and expanding. By providing critical insights into how cognitive impairments, brain injuries, and mental health conditions affect behavior, neuropsychologists play an essential role in ensuring justice is administered in a fair and scientifically informed manner. Their contributions to assessing competency, criminal responsibility, and the impact of cognitive impairments in civil and family law cases have had a significant impact on legal outcomes. As neuropsychological research continues to advance, its integration into the legal field will likely deepen, leading to more refined and equitable legal processes.

2 Historical Development

The history of forensic neuropsychology can be traced back to early inquiries into the relationship between brain function and behavior. The nineteenth century was a period of significant advancement in the understanding of brain-behavior relationships, particularly with the work of pioneers such as Paul Broca and Carl Wernicke. Broca's discovery in 1861 that damage to a specific area of the brain's frontal lobe could impair speech production was one of the earliest demonstrations that cognitive abilities are localized in specific brain regions. Similarly, Wernicke's identification of a brain region responsible for language comprehension further reinforced the idea that different brain areas are specialized for different cognitive functions

(Verona, n.d.). These early findings laid the groundwork for neuropsychology by illustrating how damage to distinct brain regions could lead to predictable impairments in cognitive and behavioral functioning. However, the application of these concepts in legal contexts was still in its infancy during the late 19th and early 20th centuries (Harvey, 2012). In this period, the field of neurology, rather than psychology, was more directly involved in the legal system. Physicians were called upon to assess individuals accused of crimes, with particular attention to brain injuries, seizures, or other neurological disorders that could potentially influence criminal behavior (Bigenwald & Chambon, 2019).

The concept of mental illness and its relationship to criminal responsibility began to take shape in the late nineteenth century, especially with the development of the insanity defense. The M'Naghten Rule, established in 1843, was one of the first legal standards for determining whether an individual could be held criminally responsible for their actions based on their mental state. Although this standard primarily focused on mental illness, it laid the foundation for future discussions about cognitive impairments and their impact on criminal behavior (Johnston & Vincent T. Leahey, 2021). The twentieth century marked a period of significant growth and professionalization for the field of neuropsychology, leading to its eventual integration into the legal system. Several key milestones stand out as turning points in the development of forensic neuropsychology (Prakash & Prakash B, 2023).

The mid-twentieth century saw the development of standardized neuropsychological assessment tools, which allowed for more precise evaluations of cognitive functions. Pioneering work by Alexander Luria, who developed a systematic approach to neuropsychological testing, was influential in understanding how brain injuries impacted cognitive functions like memory, attention, and executive functioning. Luria's work, along with that of others, contributed to the refinement of neuropsychological assessments that would later become essential in forensic contexts, particularly in assessing brain injury, cognitive decline, and developmental disorders in individuals involved in legal cases (Casaletto & Heaton, 2017).

The aftermath of World War II was another critical turning point for the field, as large numbers of veterans returned with traumatic brain injuries (TBI). The war provided an opportunity for neuropsychologists to study the long-term effects of brain trauma on behavior, cognition, and emotional regulation. These studies contributed significantly to the understanding of how specific brain injuries could result in changes in cognitive and behavioral functioning, further establishing the link between brain damage and behavioral impairments—a crucial factor in legal cases involving injury, criminal behavior, and competency assessments (Mckee & Daneshvar, 2015). The formal integration of neuropsychology into the legal system began to take shape in the latter half of the twentieth century. In the 1970s and 1980s, forensic neuropsychology began to emerge as a distinct subfield, with practitioners increasingly called upon to provide expert testimony in legal cases. Early cases that involved neuropsychological testimony often centered on brain injuries in personal injury lawsuits, where plaintiffs sought compensation for cognitive impairments resulting from accidents. Over time, neuropsychologists began to play a more prominent role in criminal cases as well, particularly in assessing competency to stand trial and criminal responsibility.

The evolution of neuropsychology in legal settings has been driven by advances in neuroscience, neuroimaging technology, and an increasing recognition of the importance of brain-behavior relationships in legal proceedings. The advent of neuroimaging techniques, such as computed tomography (CT) scans, magnetic resonance imaging (MRI), and functional MRI (fMRI), has revolutionized the field by allowing for direct visualization of brain structures and functions. These technologies provide objective evidence of brain damage or dysfunction, which can be used in court to support claims of cognitive impairment or diminished responsibility (Roalf & Gur, 2017).

One of the major areas where forensic neuropsychology has had a significant impact is in the assessment of criminal responsibility and competency to stand trial. The legal system's interest in whether an individual has the cognitive ability to understand legal proceedings and participate meaningfully in their defense has led to the widespread use of neuropsychological assessments in these contexts. In capital cases, where the death penalty is a possibility, neuropsychological evaluations are often used to assess whether brain damage or intellectual disabilities might warrant a lesser sentence (Egbenya & Adjorlolo, 2021). Forensic neuropsychology also plays a critical role in civil litigation, particularly in cases involving personal injury, where plaintiffs claim brain damage as a result of accidents, medical malpractice, or other incidents. Neuropsychologists provide expert testimony on the extent of cognitive impairment and its impact on the individual's life, often influencing the outcome of settlements and compensation awards (Hom, 2003).

Forensic neuropsychology has developed from its early roots in understanding brain-behavior relationships into a vital component of the legal system. With key milestones such as the case of Phineas Gage, the development of standardized neuropsychological assessments, and advances in neuroimaging technology, the field has grown significantly. Today, forensic neuropsychologists play a crucial role in evaluating criminal responsibility, competency, and cognitive impairments in both criminal and civil cases, shaping legal outcomes with scientifically grounded insights into brain function. As neuroscience continues to advance, the role of forensic neuropsychology in legal settings is likely to expand, offering increasingly sophisticated tools for understanding the complex interplay between brain function and behavior in the courtroom.

3 Neuropsychology and the Legal System

Forensic neuropsychologists play a crucial role in providing expert testimony, assessing cognitive and emotional impairments, and informing legal decisions. This section explores the role of neuropsychology in court cases, the relationship between neuroscience and legal practice, and influential cases that have shaped the field of forensic neuropsychology.

Neuropsychologists contribute to the legal system in several key ways, often serving as expert witnesses who provide insights into how cognitive and neurological conditions affect behavior. Their involvement typically revolves around assessing mental states, cognitive functions, and brain injuries in both criminal and civil cases.

One of the primary roles of forensic neuropsychologists is to evaluate a defendant's competency to stand trial. This assessment determines whether an individual has the cognitive and psychological capacity to understand the legal proceedings and assist in their defense. Neuropsychologists use various tests to evaluate memory, attention, language, and executive functioning, as well as to assess whether cognitive impairments—such as those resulting from brain injuries, intellectual disabilities, or psychiatric conditions—compromise the defendant's ability to participate meaningfully in their trial. For example, individuals with severe cognitive impairments or certain mental health disorders might be deemed incompetent to stand trial, which can lead to alternative legal proceedings, such as mental health treatment instead of criminal prosecution (Marcopulos et al., 2024).

Neuropsychologists also play a critical role in determining criminal responsibility, particularly in cases involving the insanity defense. They assess whether a defendant's cognitive or neurological impairments were severe enough to impact their ability to understand the nature and wrongfulness of their actions at the time of the crime. This involves evaluating whether mental illness, brain injury, or developmental disorders influenced the defendant's behavior. Neuropsychologists provide crucial insights into whether such impairments can be linked directly to the criminal behavior in question, which can impact the verdict and sentencing (Math et al., 2015).

In criminal cases, neuropsychological evaluations can provide mitigating evidence that influences sentencing. For instance, if a defendant has a documented neurological condition that affects impulse control or decision-making, this information can be used to argue for a reduced sentence or alternative sentencing options. Neuropsychologists may assess the extent to which cognitive impairments or brain injuries contributed to criminal behavior, which can lead to more individualized and nuanced sentencing decisions (Aono et al., 2019).

In civil cases, neuropsychologists are often called upon to assess the impact of brain injuries or psychological conditions on an individual's quality of life. For instance, in personal injury lawsuits, neuropsychologists evaluate the cognitive and emotional consequences of injuries sustained in accidents or medical malpractice cases. Their assessments can provide objective evidence of impairment and help determine appropriate compensation for damages (Harvey, 2012).

The relationship between neuroscience and legal practice has evolved significantly over the past few decades, reflecting advancements in our understanding of brain function and its implications for behavior.

Advances in neuroimaging technologies, such as MRI and fMRI, have provided new ways to visualize and understand brain structures and functions. These techniques allow forensic neuropsychologists to provide objective evidence of brain damage or dysfunction, which can be critical in legal cases. For example, neuroimaging can reveal abnormalities in brain regions associated with impulse control, decision-making, or memory, offering insights into how these abnormalities might influence behavior and legal responsibility. As neuroscience has advanced, it has influenced legal standards and practices. The growing understanding of brain development and neuroplasticity has led to revisions in legal standards related to criminal responsibility and sentencing. For instance, research on adolescent brain development has informed legal decisions regarding the treatment of juvenile offenders, recognizing that adolescents may have less mature cognitive control and decision-making abilities compared to adults. This has led to reforms in sentencing practices and the implementation of age-specific legal considerations (Johnson et al., 2009).

The integration of neuroscience into legal practice also presents challenges and ethical considerations. Forensic neuropsychologists must navigate issues such as the potential misuse of neuroimaging evidence, the risk of overstating the significance of neurological findings, and the need to balance scientific objectivity with the adversarial nature of legal proceedings. Ensuring that neuropsychological assessments and testimony are accurate, reliable, and presented in a manner that is comprehensible to legal professionals and juries is crucial for maintaining the integrity of the legal process (Manupatra, 2021).

Several landmark cases have had a significant impact on the development and application of forensic neuropsychology, shaping how the field is integrated into legal contexts.

Roper v. Simmons (2005) In this landmark U.S. Supreme Court case, the Court ruled that the death penalty cannot be imposed on individuals who were under 18 at the time of their crime. The decision was influenced by research on adolescent brain development, which demonstrated that adolescents have less mature impulse control and decision-making abilities compared to adults. This case highlighted the importance of considering neuroscientific evidence in legal decisions, particularly regarding the capacity for criminal responsibility and the appropriateness of severe penalties for juvenile offenders (Roper V. Simmons, n.d.).

Atkins v. Virginia (2002) This U.S. Supreme Court case held that executing individuals with intellectual disabilities constitutes cruel and unusual punishment, in violation of the Eighth Amendment. The Court's decision was based in part on evidence from neuropsychological assessments demonstrating that individuals with intellectual disabilities have diminished capacities for understanding and reasoning. This case underscored the role of neuropsychological evaluations in determining the appropriateness of capital punishment and other severe penalties for individuals with cognitive impairments (Atkins V. Virginia, n.d.).

4 Neuropsychological Assessments in Legal Contexts

Neuropsychological assessments utilize a range of methods and tools to evaluate cognitive functions and behavioral characteristics. These assessments are designed to provide objective and reliable information about an individual's cognitive and emotional state, which can be crucial in legal contexts.

Standardized Neuropsychological Tests Standardized tests are fundamental in neuropsychological assessments. They provide a consistent method for evaluating various cognitive domains, including memory, attention, language, and executive functioning. Commonly used tests include the Wechsler Adult Intelligence Scale (WAIS), which assesses general intelligence and cognitive abilities, and the Wisconsin Card Sorting Test (WCST), which evaluates executive functions such as cognitive flexibility and problem-solving. These tests offer benchmarks for comparing an individual's performance to normative data, aiding in the identification of cognitive impairments or deficits (Determinations, 2015).

Neuroimaging Techniques Neuroimaging technologies, such as computed tomography (CT), magnetic resonance imaging (MRI), and functional MRI (fMRI), are increasingly used in forensic neuropsychology. CT and MRI provide structural images of the brain, allowing for the detection of abnormalities such as tumors, lesions, or traumatic injuries. fMRI, on the other hand, measures brain activity by detecting changes in blood flow, offering insights into functional brain processes. These imaging techniques can corroborate neuropsychological test results and provide objective evidence of brain damage or dysfunction (Glover, 2011).

Clinical Interviews and Observations In addition to standardized tests and neuroimaging, clinical interviews and behavioral observations are essential components of neuropsychological assessments. Interviews help gather information about an individual's medical history, cognitive and emotional functioning, and daily life activities. Observations of behavior and interactions can provide context for understanding how cognitive impairments manifest in real-world situations, which is particularly relevant in legal settings where functional abilities are often scrutinized (Harvey, 2012).

Cognitive Functioning: Assessment and Interpretation Assessing and interpreting cognitive functioning is a central aspect of neuropsychological evaluations. These assessments aim to identify cognitive strengths and weaknesses and to understand how these may impact behavior and legal responsibility.

Domains of Cognitive Functioning Neuropsychologists evaluate multiple domains of cognitive functioning, including memory, attention, language, executive functions, and visuospatial abilities. Memory assessments might involve tasks such as recalling a list of words or stories, while attention is evaluated through tasks requiring sustained or selective focus. Language assessments include evaluating comprehension and expressive language abilities, and executive functions are assessed through tasks that require planning, organization, and problem-solving (Harvey, 2019).

Interpretation of Results Interpreting the results of neuropsychological assessments involves comparing an individual's performance to normative data and considering the context of their cognitive and emotional functioning. Forensic neuropsychologists must differentiate between cognitive impairments resulting from neurological conditions and those due to psychological factors, such as malingering or feigning symptoms. Accurate interpretation requires an understanding of the specific brain regions and networks involved in different cognitive functions and how impairments in these areas might affect behavior and legal decisions (Schaefer et al., 2023).

Contextual Factors Interpretation of cognitive assessments also involves considering contextual factors that might influence an individual's performance. For example, an individual's educational background, cultural differences, and psychological state can impact their test performance and should be taken into account when interpreting results. In legal contexts, neuropsychologists must ensure that their assessments are not biased by external factors and that their conclusions are based on a comprehensive evaluation of the individual's cognitive and behavioral functioning (Kelso & Tadi, 2022).

Establishing mental capacity and competency is a critical function of forensic neuropsychology, particularly in legal cases involving criminal responsibility and civil litigation.

Mental Capacity Mental capacity refers to an individual's ability to understand and make decisions about specific aspects of their life. In legal contexts, this often involves determining whether an individual can make informed decisions regarding their legal rights, such as consenting to medical treatment or participating in legal proceedings. Neuropsychologists assess mental capacity by evaluating cognitive abilities such as understanding, reasoning, and decision-making. Their findings can inform legal decisions regarding an individual's ability to manage their affairs or participate in legal processes (Leo, 1999).

Competency to Stand Trial Competency to stand trial is a legal determination of whether a defendant has the cognitive and psychological capacity to understand the charges against them, participate in their defense, and comprehend the legal proceedings. Neuropsychologists assess various cognitive functions, including memory, attention, and understanding of legal concepts, to determine if the defendant can participate meaningfully in their trial. If a defendant is found incompetent, legal proceedings may be postponed or altered, and the individual may receive mental health treatment or other interventions instead (Adjorlolo & Chan, 2016).

5 Impact of Neurological Conditions on Behavior

Neurological conditions can significantly impact behavior, cognition, and legal responsibility. Understanding how these conditions affect an individual's behavior is crucial for forensic neuropsychologists.

Brain Injuries Traumatic brain injuries (TBI) and acquired brain injuries, such as those resulting from strokes or infections, can lead to various cognitive and behavioral impairments. Depending on the location and severity of the injury, individuals may experience difficulties with memory, attention, executive functions, or emotional regulation. Forensic neuropsychologists assess these impairments to determine how they might influence behavior and legal responsibility, particularly in cases involving criminal behavior or personal injury claims (Galgano et al., 2017).

Neurodegenerative Disorders Neurodegenerative conditions, such as Alzheimer's disease, Parkinson's disease, and frontotemporal dementia, can progressively impair cognitive functioning and behavior. These conditions often lead to difficulties with memory, judgment, and daily functioning. Neuropsychologists assess the extent of cognitive decline and its impact on the individual's ability to engage in legal proceedings or manage personal affairs. Their evaluations help inform decisions regarding competency, guardianship, and legal responsibility (Kumar et al., 2024).

Developmental Disorders Developmental disorders, such as intellectual disabilities and autism spectrum disorders, can affect cognitive and adaptive functioning from an early age. Neuropsychologists assess how these conditions influence behavior and legal decisions, including competency to stand trial and criminal responsibility. Understanding the impact of developmental disorders is essential for ensuring fair and appropriate legal outcomes for individuals with these conditions (Zwick, 2017).

6 Challenges and Controversies

Ethical issues are at the forefront of forensic neuropsychology due to the high stakes of legal proceedings and the potential for neuropsychological assessments to significantly impact legal outcomes. Forensic neuropsychologists must navigate several ethical dilemmas as they work within the adversarial nature of the legal system.

Confidentiality and Dual Relationships One of the primary ethical challenges in forensic neuropsychology is managing confidentiality and the potential for dual relationships. Unlike in clinical settings, where the neuropsychologist's role is to assist the patient, in forensic contexts, the neuropsychologist is often working for a third party, such as a court or legal team. This can lead to conflicts of interest, as the neuropsychologist's findings may not always benefit the individual being evaluated.

Maintaining objectivity while adhering to ethical guidelines about confidentiality can be difficult, especially when the neuropsychologist's findings may influence the outcome of a trial or sentencing (Yadav, 2017).

Informed Consent and Voluntary Participation Ensuring informed consent is another ethical concern. In some cases, individuals being evaluated may not fully understand the purpose of the assessment or the potential consequences of the findings. Neuropsychologists must ensure that individuals are aware of the nature of the assessment and the potential legal implications, but this can be challenging when dealing with individuals who have cognitive impairments or mental health issues. Additionally, questions of voluntariness arise in cases where individuals are court-ordered to undergo neuropsychological assessments, raising concerns about coercion and the ethical implications of non-voluntary participation (Yadav, 2017).

Malingering and Feigned Symptoms Another ethical challenge is the detection of malingering, where individuals intentionally exaggerate or feign cognitive impairments to avoid legal consequences. Forensic neuropsychologists are often called upon to differentiate between genuine cognitive deficits and malingering, which can be difficult given the complexity of cognitive assessments. Failing to detect malingering can lead to unjust legal outcomes, while falsely identifying malingering may result in unfair treatment of individuals with legitimate cognitive impairments. Ethical practice requires careful evaluation and the use of objective measures to ensure that neuropsychologists do not misinterpret an individual's symptoms (Yadav, 2017).

The reliability and validity of neuropsychological evidence are critical issues in forensic neuropsychology, particularly given the legal system's reliance on objective and scientifically sound data. Questions about the accuracy and consistency of neuropsychological assessments can influence the weight given to these findings in court.

Standardization and Test Norms One challenge to the reliability of neuropsychological assessments lies in the standardization of tests and the applicability of normative data. Many neuropsychological tests are standardized on specific populations, often based on factors such as age, education, and cultural background. When these tests are used in diverse legal populations, there is a risk that the results may not accurately reflect an individual's cognitive abilities. For example, individuals from different cultural backgrounds may perform differently on standardized tests due to language barriers or differences in educational experience, leading to potential misinterpretation of their cognitive functioning. Ensuring that tests are appropriately standardized and that normative data is relevant to the individual being assessed is crucial for maintaining reliability (Nielsen et al., 2024).

External Validity in Legal Settings Another issue with the validity of neuropsychological evidence is whether the tests and assessments used accurately predict real-world behavior, particularly in the high-stakes environment of legal proceedings. While neuropsychological tests are designed to measure cognitive functions such as memory, attention, and executive functioning, there is often a gap between test performance and how these functions manifest in everyday behavior. In legal cases, this gap can create difficulties in applying neuropsychological findings to questions of criminal responsibility or competency to stand trial. Ensuring that assessments have external validity—meaning that the results are applicable to the specific legal question at hand—is a challenge for forensic neuropsychologists (Malik, n.d.).

Subjectivity in Interpretation While neuropsychological assessments rely on standardized tests, the interpretation of these results is often subjective. Two neuropsychologists might interpret the same data differently, especially when dealing with complex cases involving cognitive impairments or mental health issues. This subjectivity can lead to conflicting opinions in court, raising questions about the reliability of neuropsychological evidence. To mitigate this issue, neuropsychologists must use multiple tests and data sources, apply consistent interpretive frameworks, and provide transparent explanations of their reasoning when presenting findings in court (Harvey, 2012).

Forensic neuropsychologists face unique challenges in interpreting and applying their findings in court settings, where legal standards and scientific evidence must align. Bridging the gap between the scientific rigor of neuropsychological assessments and the legal requirements of the courtroom is a complex task.

Communication with Legal Professionals One of the biggest challenges forensic neuropsychologists face is effectively communicating their findings to judges, attorneys, and juries, many of whom may not have a background in neuroscience or psychology. Neuropsychological assessments involve complex scientific data, and translating this information into terms that are understandable to non-experts is essential. Misunderstandings can lead to the misapplication of neuropsychological evidence, resulting in unjust legal outcomes. To address this, neuropsychologists must be skilled in presenting their findings in a clear, concise, and accessible manner, ensuring that the scientific evidence is accurately understood and appropriately applied in legal contexts.

Legal Standards Versus Scientific Standards Another challenge is reconciling the different standards of evidence used in the legal and scientific fields. In court, the legal system operates under standards such as the "preponderance of evidence" in civil cases or "beyond a reasonable doubt" in criminal cases. In contrast, neuropsychology relies on statistical significance and empirical validation. The subjective nature of legal decision-making, which involves moral and ethical judgments, can sometimes conflict with the objective, data-driven nature of neuropsychological findings. This creates a challenge for neuropsychologists, who must present their evidence in a way that is scientifically sound but also meets the legal standards of proof (Ho, 2008).

The Risk of Over-Reliance on Neuropsychological Evidence While neuropsychological evidence can be a powerful tool in legal cases, there is a risk of over-reliance on this evidence by legal professionals. For instance, neuroimaging techniques, such as MRI or fMRI scans, can provide compelling visual evidence of brain abnormalities. However, the presence of brain damage on an imaging scan does not necessarily correlate with cognitive or behavioral impairments. There is a danger that judges and juries may give undue weight to neuropsychological evidence without fully understanding its limitations. Forensic neuropsychologists must take care to present a balanced view of the evidence, emphasizing both its strengths and its limitations (*Scanning for Justice: Using Neuroscience to Create a More Inclusive Legal System—Columbia Human Rights Law Review*, n.d.).

7 Future Directions

Technological advancements are rapidly transforming the landscape of forensic neuropsychology, offering new tools and methodologies for understanding brain function and its impact on behavior. These emerging trends promise to enhance the accuracy and reliability of neuropsychological assessments, while also raising new ethical and legal challenges.

1. **Advanced Neuroimaging Techniques:** One of the most significant trends in forensic neuropsychology is the increasing use of advanced neuroimaging techniques, such as functional magnetic resonance imaging (fMRI), diffusion tensor imaging (DTI), and positron emission tomography (PET). These imaging tools allow neuropsychologists to visualize brain activity and structure with unprecedented precision. For instance, fMRI can identify specific brain regions involved in decision-making, impulse control, and emotional regulation, which are often relevant in legal cases. DTI can map white matter tracts to assess brain connectivity, which is crucial in understanding the impact of traumatic brain injuries. These technologies provide objective data that can be used in court to support claims of brain dysfunction or impairment (Roalf & Gur, 2017).
2. **Biomarkers and Genetic Testing:** Another emerging trend is the identification of biomarkers and genetic factors associated with neurological conditions. Biomarkers, such as specific proteins in the blood or cerebrospinal fluid, can provide early indications of neurodegenerative diseases like Alzheimer's or Parkinson's. Genetic testing may reveal predispositions to certain neurological disorders, which could be relevant in cases involving questions of diminished responsibility or criminal behavior. For example, individuals with genetic mutations linked to impulsivity or aggression might be more likely to engage in criminal behavior under certain conditions. As the science of biomarkers and genetics advances, this information could be used to inform legal decisions about criminal responsibility, sentencing, and rehabilitation (Toader et al., 2023).

3. **Artificial Intelligence and Machine Learning:** Artificial intelligence (AI) and machine learning are becoming increasingly important in the field of forensic neuropsychology. AI can analyze large datasets from neuropsychological assessments and neuroimaging studies to identify patterns that might not be immediately apparent to human evaluators. This can help improve the accuracy of cognitive assessments, reduce bias, and provide more standardized evaluations across different populations. AI-driven tools may also be used to predict future behavior based on neuropsychological data, such as the likelihood of recidivism or cognitive decline. However, the use of AI in legal contexts raises important ethical questions about transparency, accountability, and the potential for overreliance on algorithmic predictions.
4. **Virtual Reality and Simulated Environments:** Virtual reality (VR) is emerging as a novel tool for cognitive assessments in forensic neuropsychology. VR technology allows individuals to interact with simulated environments that mimic real-world situations, providing a more ecologically valid assessment of cognitive functioning. For example, VR-based assessments could simulate complex decision-making scenarios or social interactions, offering insights into how cognitive impairments affect behavior in real-world contexts. This could be particularly useful in cases involving competency evaluations or assessments of functional abilities, where traditional neuropsychological tests may not fully capture the complexities of daily life (Pieri et al., 2023).

The integration of these emerging trends and technologies into forensic neuropsychology has the potential to significantly impact legal practice and policy. As the field continues to evolve, it is likely to influence how courts handle cases involving cognitive impairments, criminal responsibility, and mental competency.

One of the most immediate impacts of technological advances in forensic neuropsychology is the potential to provide more objective and reliable evidence in court. Neuroimaging data, biomarker analysis, and AI-driven assessments offer scientifically grounded evidence that can support or refute claims about an individual's cognitive functioning. For example, in cases involving traumatic brain injury, neuroimaging can provide concrete evidence of brain damage that may not be apparent through traditional psychological assessments. This objective data can help reduce reliance on subjective interpretations of behavior and increase the credibility of neuropsychological evidence in legal proceedings (Treadway & Buckholtz, 2011).

As neuropsychological assessments become more precise, they may play a larger role in tailoring sentencing and rehabilitation programs to individual needs. Courts could increasingly use neuropsychological data to determine the most appropriate course of action for individuals with cognitive impairments. For instance, individuals with severe brain injuries or neurodegenerative diseases may be diverted to specialized treatment programs rather than traditional incarceration. Neuroimaging and biomarker analysis could also be used to track an individual's progress in rehabilitation, allowing for more personalized and adaptive treatment plans based on objective data (Harvey, 2012).

The growing use of neuropsychological and neuroimaging evidence in court cases is likely to lead to new legal precedents and policy changes. For example, courts may need to establish guidelines for the admissibility of neuroimaging data and genetic testing in criminal and civil cases. Policymakers may also need to develop regulations governing the use of AI in forensic assessments, ensuring that these technologies are used ethically and transparently. Additionally, as neuropsychological evidence becomes more widely accepted, legal definitions of competency, responsibility, and mental health may need to be revised to reflect new scientific insights (Aono et al., 2019).

Forensic neuropsychology is poised to play a critical role in shaping future legal standards, particularly in areas involving mental competency, criminal responsibility, and the relationship between brain dysfunction and behavior. As the field continues to evolve, it is likely to influence how courts define and apply legal concepts related to cognitive impairments. As neuropsychological assessments become more sophisticated, they may lead to a redefinition of legal standards for mental competency and criminal responsibility. Courts may adopt new criteria for determining whether an individual is competent to stand trial, enter into legal agreements, or make decisions about their own care. For example, neuropsychological evidence might be used to establish that an individual with early-stage dementia is no longer capable of making informed decisions about their finances or legal matters. Similarly, individuals with brain injuries or neurodevelopmental disorders may be found to have diminished responsibility for their actions, leading to more lenient sentencing or alternative forms of punishment.

As forensic neuropsychology continues to advance, it may contribute to the expansion of legal protections for vulnerable populations, such as individuals with cognitive impairments or mental health disorders. For example, neuropsychological evidence could be used to argue for more lenient sentencing or alternative treatment options for individuals with traumatic brain injuries, intellectual disabilities, or neurodegenerative diseases. Legal standards may evolve to better reflect the complexities of cognitive functioning and its impact on behavior, leading to more nuanced approaches to justice that take into account individual differences in brain function (Torregrossa et al., 2023).

Finally, forensic neuropsychology is likely to influence broader mental health and criminal justice policy. As our understanding of the brain and behavior continues to grow, policymakers may revise laws related to the treatment of individuals with cognitive impairments in the criminal justice system. For instance, laws governing the involuntary commitment of individuals with severe mental illness or cognitive impairments may be updated to reflect new insights from neuropsychology and neuroscience. Additionally, advances in neuroimaging and biomarker analysis could lead to the development of new standards for assessing mental health in legal contexts, ensuring that individuals receive appropriate care and treatment based on objective evidence (Arboleda-Flórez, 2006).

8 Conclusion

The integration of neuropsychology within legal contexts has evolved significantly, providing crucial insights into cognitive functioning and behavior in ways that directly impact legal decision-making. Neuropsychological assessments play an essential role in the courtroom, offering evidence related to mental capacity, competency, and the effects of neurological conditions on behavior. These assessments not only provide a scientific basis for understanding individual cases but also help shape broader legal standards concerning criminal responsibility, cognitive impairment, and mental health.

Historically, the field of neuropsychology began with foundational theories focusing on the relationship between brain function and behavior. Over time, key milestones—such as advances in neuroimaging and diagnostic tools—have revolutionized the application of neuropsychology in legal settings. Influential cases, especially those involving traumatic brain injuries and criminal culpability, have established a precedent for the use of neuropsychological evidence in determining legal outcomes.

In modern legal contexts, neuropsychological assessments are used to evaluate cognitive functioning, determine competency, and assess the influence of neurological conditions on behavior. The methods and tools used for these evaluations are highly specialized, focusing on both cognitive and behavioral outcomes. The relationship between neuroscience and legal practice continues to deepen, especially as courts increasingly rely on scientific evidence to make informed decisions. This relationship is exemplified by the use of neuropsychology in cases ranging from criminal culpability to civil suits involving brain injuries.

Despite its growing importance, forensic neuropsychology faces challenges and controversies. Ethical considerations around the use of neuropsychological data, questions regarding the reliability and validity of this evidence, and the difficulties of interpreting complex brain-behavior relationships in court all present ongoing issues. Practitioners must navigate these challenges while maintaining scientific rigor and ethical standards.

Looking to the future, the field of forensic neuropsychology is poised for further expansion. Emerging trends, such as advances in neuroimaging, biomarkers, artificial intelligence, and virtual reality, promise to enhance the accuracy and reliability of neuropsychological evaluations. These advancements will likely have a profound impact on legal practice and policy, shaping future legal standards and further integrating neuroscience into the justice system.

For practitioners and legal professionals, the ongoing developments in forensic neuropsychology highlight the need for interdisciplinary collaboration, continual professional education, and adherence to ethical principles. As neuropsychological evidence becomes more central to legal decisions, the field will play a pivotal role in ensuring that the legal system is both scientifically informed and just.

References

Adjorlolo, S., & Chan, H. C. (2016). Determination of competency to stand trial (fitness to plead): An exploratory study in Hong Kong. *Psychiatry Psychology and Law, 24*(2), 205–222. https://doi.org/10.1080/13218719.2016.1247417

Aono, D., Yaffe, G., & Kober, H. (2019). Neuroscientific evidence in the courtroom: a review. *Cognitive Research Principles and Implications, 4*(1). https://doi.org/10.1186/s41235-019-0179-y

Arboleda-Flórez, J. (2006, June 1). Forensic psychiatry: Contemporary scope, challenges and controversies. PubMed Central (PMC). https://www.ncbi.nlm.nih.gov/pmc/articles/PMC1525122/

Atkins v. Virginia. (n.d.). Oyez. https://www.oyez.org/cases/2001/00-8452.

Bigenwald, A., & Chambon, V. (2019). Criminal responsibility and neuroscience: No revolution yet. *Frontiers in Psychology, 10*. https://doi.org/10.3389/fpsyg.2019.01406

Casaletto, K. B., & Heaton, R. K. (2017). Neuropsychological assessment: Past and future. *Journal of the International Neuropsychological Society, 23*(9–10), 778–790. https://doi.org/10.1017/s1355617717001060

Determinations, C. O. P. T. I. V. T. F. S. S. a. D (2015, June 29). Cognitive tests and performance validity tests. Psychological Testing in the Service of Disability Determination - NCBI Bookshelf. https://www.ncbi.nlm.nih.gov/books/NBK305230/.

Egbenya, D. L., & Adjorlolo, S. (2021). Advancement of neuroscience and the assessment of mental state at the time of offense. *Forensic Science International Mind and Law, 2*, 100046. https://doi.org/10.1016/j.fsiml.2021.100046

Foote, W. E., Goodman-Delahunty, J., & Young, G. (2020). Civil Forensic evaluation in psychological injury and law: Legal, professional, and ethical considerations. *Psychological Injury and Law, 13*(4), 327–353. https://doi.org/10.1007/s12207-020-09398-3

Galgano, M., Toshkezi, G., Qiu, X., Russell, T., Chin, L., & Zhao, L. (2017). Traumatic brain injury. *Cell Transplantation, 26*(7), 1118–1130. https://doi.org/10.1177/0963689717714102

Glover, G. H. (2011). Overview of functional magnetic resonance imaging. *Neurosurgery Clinics of North America, 22*(2), 133–139. https://doi.org/10.1016/j.nec.2010.11.001

Gkintoni, E. (2023). Clinical neuropsychological characteristics of bipolar disorder, with a focus on cognitive and linguistic pattern: a conceptual analysis. *F1000Research, 12*, 1235. https://doi.org/10.12688/f1000research.141599.1

Groscup, J. L., & Wood, S. (n.d.). *Neuropsychology's role in capital mitigation*. https://www.apa.org. https://www.apa.org/monitor/2010/12/jn.

Harvey, P. D. (2012). Clinical applications of neuropsychological assessment. *Dialogues in Clinical Neuroscience, 14*(1), 91–99. https://doi.org/10.31887/dcns.2012.14.1/pharvey

Harvey, P. D. (2019). Domains of cognition and their assessment. *Dialogues in Clinical Neuroscience, 21*(3), 227–237. https://doi.org/10.31887/dcns.2019.21.3/pharvey

Ho, H. L. (2008). Standard of proof. In *Oxford University Press eBooks* (pp. 173–230). https://doi.org/10.1093/acprof:oso/9780199228300.003.0004

Hom, J. (2003). Forensic neuropsychology: Are we there yet? *Archives of Clinical Neuropsychology, 18*(8), 827–845. https://doi.org/10.1016/s0887-6177(03)00076-3

Johnson, S. B., Blum, R. W., & Giedd, J. N. (2009). Adolescent maturity and the brain: The promise and pitfalls of neuroscience research in adolescent health policy. *Journal of Adolescent Health, 45*(3), 216–221. https://doi.org/10.1016/j.jadohealth.2009.05.016

Johnston, E. L., & Leahey, V. T. (2021). *The Status and Legitimacy of M'Naghten's Insane Delusion Rule* (Vol. 54, pp. 1777–1778). University of California. https://lawreview.sf.ucdavis.edu/sites/g/files/dgvnsk15026/files/media/documents/54-4_Johnston_Leahey.pdf

Kelso, I. G., & Tadi, P. (2022, November 7). Cognitive assessment. StatPearls - NCBI Bookshelf. https://www.ncbi.nlm.nih.gov/books/NBK556049/.

Kumar, A., Sidhu, J., Lui, F., & Tsao, J. W. (2024, February 12). Alzheimer disease. StatPearls - NCBI Bookshelf. https://www.ncbi.nlm.nih.gov/books/NBK499922/.

Leo, R. J. (1999). Competency and the capacity to make treatment decisions. *The Primary Care Companion for CNS Disorders, 1*(5). https://doi.org/10.4088/pcc.v01n0501

Law4u. (n.d.). *Can a parent's mental health condition affect child custody determinations in India? | Law4u.* https://law4u.in/answer/5570/can-a-parents-mental-health-condition-affect-child-custody-determinations-in-india.

Malik, A. B.. (n.d.). *Medscape registration.* https://emedicine.medscape.com/article/317596-overview?form=fpf.

Manupatra. (2021, May 17). The intersection of law and neuroscience: Implications on law of evidence. https://articles.manupatra.com/article-details/The-Intersection-of-Law-and-Neuroscience-Implications-On-Law-of-Evidence.

Marcopulos, B. A., Kaufmann, P., & Patel, A. C. (2024). Forensic neuropsychological assessment. *Behavioral Sciences & the Law*. https://doi.org/10.1002/bsl.2656

Math, S. B., Kumar, C. N., & Moirangthem, S. (2015). Insanity defense: Past, present, and future. *Indian Journal of Psychological Medicine, 37*(4), 381–387. https://doi.org/10.4103/0253-7176.168559

Mckee, A. C., & Daneshvar, D. H. (2015). The neuropathology of traumatic brain injury. *Handbook of Clinical Neurology*, 45–66. https://doi.org/10.1016/b978-0-444-52892-6.00004-0

National Academy of Neuropsychology, Johnson-Greene, D., & APA, A. P. A. (2003). *Informed consent in clinical neuropsychology practice.* https://www.nanonline.org/docs/paic/pdfs/naninformedconsent.pdf.

Nestor, P. G., Daggett, D., Haycock, J., & Price, M. (1999). Competence to stand trial: A neuropsychological inquiry. *Law and Human Behavior, 23*(4), 397–412. https://doi.org/10.1023/a:1022339130582

Nielsen, T. R., Franzen, S., Watermeyer, T., Jiang, J., Calia, C., Kjærgaard, D., Bothe, S., & Mukadam, N. (2024). Interpreter-mediated neuropsychological assessment: Clinical considerations and recommendations from the European Consortium on Cross-Cultural Neuropsychology (ECCroN). *The Clinical Neuropsychologist*, 1–31. https://doi.org/10.1080/13854046.2024.2335113

Pandey, P., Varshney, P., Gajera, G. V., Nirisha, P. L., Malathesh, B. C., Manjunatha, N., Sivakumar, P. T., Kumar, C. N., & Math, S. B. (2021). Criminal responsibility in Geropsychiatry: Competence, culpability, and care. *Indian Journal of Psychological Medicine, 43*(5_suppl), S97–S106. https://doi.org/10.1177/02537176211030993

Pieri, L., Tosi, G., & Romano, D. (2023). Virtual reality technology in neuropsychological testing: A systematic review. *Journal of Neuropsychology, 17*(2), 382–399. https://doi.org/10.1111/jnp.12304

Prakash, B., Jr., & Prakash, B. (2023). Forensic psychology and its impact on the legal system. *Journal of Criminology and Forensic Studies, 5*(1), 180056. Journal-article. https://academicstrive.com/JOCFS/JOCFS180056.pdf

Roper v. Simmons. (n.d.). https://www.apa.org. https://www.apa.org/about/offices/ogc/amicus/roper.

Roalf, D. R., & Gur, R. C. (2017). Functional brain imaging in neuropsychology over the past 25 years. *Neuropsychology, 31*(8), 954–971. https://doi.org/10.1037/neu0000426

Scanning for justice: Using neuroscience to create a more inclusive legal system—Columbia Human Rights Law Review (n.d.). https://hrlr.law.columbia.edu/hrlr/scanning-for-justice-using-neuroscience-to-create-a-more-inclusive-legal-system/.

Schaefer, L. A., Thakur, T., & Meager, M. R. (2023, May 16). Neuropsychological assessment. StatPearls - NCBI Bookshelf. https://www.ncbi.nlm.nih.gov/books/NBK513310/.

Toader, C., Dobrin, N., Brehar, F., Popa, C., Covache-Busuioc, R., Glavan, L. A., Costin, H. P., Bratu, B., Corlatescu, A. D., Popa, A. A., & Ciurea, A. V. (2023). From recognition to remedy: The significance of biomarkers in neurodegenerative disease pathology. *International Journal of Molecular Sciences, 24*(22), 16119. https://doi.org/10.3390/ijms242216119

Torregrossa, W., Torrisi, M., De Luca, R., Casella, C., Rifici, C., Bonanno, M., & Calabrò, R. S. (2023). Neuropsychological assessment in patients with traumatic brain injury: A comprehensive review with clinical recommendations. *Biomedicine, 11*(7), 1991. https://doi.org/10.3390/biomedicines11071991

Treadway, M., & Buckholtz, J. W. (2011). On the use and misuse of genomic and neuroimaging science in Forensic psychiatry: Current roles and future directions. *Child and Adolescent Psychiatric Clinics of North America, 20*(3), 533–546. https://doi.org/10.1016/j.chc.2011.03.012

Verona, W. (n.d.). Neuropsychology and other Unit 3 historical perspective of disciplines. In *Neuropsychology* (pp. 43–45) .

Wegierek, A. M. J., Lesniak, K., Patel, S., & Bogdanovskaya, Y. (2019). A collaborative approach to treatment of Alzheimer's disease from a psychological Perspective. In *Codon publications eBooks* (pp. 237–250). https://doi.org/10.15586/alzheimersdisease.2019.ch15

Yadav, P. K. (2017). Ethical issues across different fields of forensic science. *Egyptian Journal of Forensic Sciences, 7*(1). https://doi.org/10.1186/s41935-017-0010-1

Zwick, G. P. (2017). Neuropsychological assessment in autism spectrum disorder and related conditions. *Dialogues in Clinical Neuroscience, 19*(4), 373–379. https://doi.org/10.31887/dcns.2017.19.4/gzwick

Neurodevelopmental Disorders and Criminal Behavior

1 Introduction

The intersection of neurodevelopmental disorders and criminal behavior is an area of increasing interest and complexity within the fields of psychology, neuroscience, and criminal justice. Neurodevelopmental disorders, such as autism spectrum disorder (ASD) and attention deficit hyperactivity disorder (ADHD), are characterized by atypical brain development that affects cognitive, social, and behavioral functioning. In recent years, there has been a growing body of research exploring the links between these disorders and an individual's propensity for engaging in criminal behavior. Understanding these connections is crucial not only for accurate assessments within the criminal justice system but also for developing intervention strategies that reduce reoffending and promote rehabilitation.

This chapter delves into the intricate relationship between neurodevelopmental disorders and criminal behavior, focusing on the mechanisms through which these disorders influence behavioral outcomes. The chapter synthesizes empirical research, theoretical models, and case studies to offer a comprehensive view of how conditions like ASD and ADHD can contribute to criminal conduct. Through this exploration, the chapter aims to highlight the unique challenges faced by individuals with neurodevelopmental disorders in the criminal justice system, as well as the broader implications for legal decision-making and intervention strategies.

Neurodevelopmental disorders are typically diagnosed in childhood, though their effects persist into adolescence and adulthood. These disorders affect a range of cognitive and behavioral processes, including impulse control, emotional regulation, and social functioning, which are all key factors in understanding criminal behavior. ASD, for example, is often associated with difficulties in social communication and interaction, as well as restricted and repetitive patterns of behavior. Individuals with ASD may struggle with interpreting social cues, which can lead to misunderstandings in social situations, sometimes escalating into legal

© The Author(s), under exclusive license to Springer Nature Switzerland AG 2025

K. J. Reddy, *Foundations of Criminal Forensic Neuropsychology*,
https://doi.org/10.1007/978-3-031-83771-5_4

confrontations. On the other hand, ADHD is characterized by hyperactivity, impulsivity, and difficulties with attention, all of which can increase the likelihood of engaging in risky or unlawful behavior, especially when compounded by external stressors such as peer pressure or adverse environmental conditions.

A central focus of this chapter is how the specific characteristics of neurodevelopmental disorders may predispose individuals to engage in behaviors that are criminalized, despite these behaviors often being the result of impaired cognitive or emotional functioning rather than malicious intent. For example, individuals with ADHD may engage in impulsive acts without fully considering the consequences, while those with ASD may unknowingly violate social or legal norms due to deficits in social understanding.

One of the critical areas this chapter addresses is the impact of neurodevelopmental disorders on cognitive processes, particularly those related to impulse control and decision-making. Impulse control is a major factor in criminal behavior, and individuals with neurodevelopmental disorders often exhibit deficits in this area. ADHD, for example, is strongly associated with impulsivity, which may lead individuals to act without considering long-term consequences. This lack of foresight can result in offenses such as theft, assault, or other impulsive criminal acts. Similarly, the executive functioning deficits associated with both ASD and ADHD—such as difficulties with planning, problem-solving, and emotional regulation—can further impair an individual's ability to make rational decisions in high-pressure situations, increasing the likelihood of criminal involvement.

The chapter examines how these cognitive deficits are not only a hallmark of neurodevelopmental disorders but are also influenced by early brain development. Disruptions in the development of brain regions such as the prefrontal cortex, which is responsible for regulating impulse control, decision-making, and social behavior, are commonly observed in individuals with neurodevelopmental disorders. This neurobiological foundation provides insight into why individuals with these conditions may struggle with behaviors that are considered criminal, as their brain development affects their capacity to regulate actions in socially appropriate ways.

Understanding the role of early brain development in neurodevelopmental disorders is critical for comprehending the broader implications of these conditions on behavior, particularly in a legal context. This chapter explores how disruptions in early neural development, often influenced by genetic and environmental factors, contribute to the cognitive and behavioral challenges faced by individuals with ASD, ADHD, and related disorders. These disruptions can manifest in difficulties with impulse control, emotional regulation, and moral reasoning—factors that are often implicated in criminal behavior.

In addition to the neurobiological underpinnings, the chapter explores the environmental influences that can exacerbate the behavioral challenges associated with neurodevelopmental disorders. Adverse environmental factors such as childhood trauma, poverty, and exposure to violence are known to interact with pre-existing neurological vulnerabilities, further increasing the risk of criminal behavior. For example, children with ADHD who are exposed to chaotic or abusive environments may be more likely to engage in delinquent behavior as a coping mechanism or as a result of impaired emotional regulation. The chapter emphasizes the importance of considering these environmental factors when evaluating individuals with neurodevelopmental disorders in the criminal justice system.

The chapter also discusses the critical role of accurate and thorough neuropsychological assessments in identifying neurodevelopmental disorders within the criminal justice system. These assessments are essential for distinguishing between intentional criminal acts and behaviors that may stem from underlying cognitive impairments. For individuals with ASD or ADHD, traditional legal proceedings may fail to account for their unique cognitive and behavioral challenges, leading to inappropriate sentencing or punishment. By conducting comprehensive evaluations, forensic neuropsychologists can provide courts with crucial information regarding an individual's mental capacity, competency, and potential for rehabilitation.

Intervention strategies tailored to the needs of individuals with neurodevelopmental disorders are another central theme of the chapter. Early intervention, particularly during childhood and adolescence, is essential for preventing criminal behavior later in life. The chapter outlines evidence-based strategies aimed at improving impulse control, social functioning, and emotional regulation, all of which are crucial for reducing the risk of criminal involvement. Additionally, the chapter emphasizes the importance of providing support systems within the criminal justice system, such as diversion programs and specialized rehabilitation services, to ensure that individuals with neurodevelopmental disorders receive the appropriate care and intervention rather than punitive measures that may exacerbate their challenges.

The complex relationship between neurodevelopmental disorders and criminal behavior underscores the need for a more nuanced understanding of how these conditions influence behavior and decision-making. This chapter offers a comprehensive examination of the neurobiological, cognitive, and environmental factors that contribute to criminal conduct among individuals with ASD, ADHD, and related disorders. By exploring the unique challenges these individuals face in the criminal justice system, the chapter highlights the importance of early intervention, accurate assessment, and targeted rehabilitation strategies. Through a synthesis of research and case studies, this chapter provides valuable insights into how neurodevelopmental disorders intersect with criminal behavior, offering pathways for more compassionate and effective legal responses.

2 Understanding Neurodevelopmental Disorders

Neurodevelopmental disorders are a category of psychiatric conditions characterized by developmental impairments in the brain that result in difficulties with behavior, cognition, or motor functioning. These disorders typically emerge during early childhood and persist throughout an individual's life, although their manifestations may evolve over time. What sets neurodevelopmental disorders apart is the underlying dysfunction in the brain's development, which impacts cognitive, emotional, and social functioning in profound and lasting ways.

Some of the most well-known neurodevelopmental disorders include autism spectrum disorder (ASD) and attention deficit hyperactivity disorder (ADHD). ASD is characterized by challenges with social communication, repetitive behaviors, and restricted interests. Individuals with ASD may struggle to interpret social cues, engage in typical social interactions, or exhibit behaviors that seem rigid or overly focused on specific interests. The spectrum nature of ASD means symptoms can vary widely, from subtle social difficulties to more severe impairments in communication and daily functioning. ADHD, on the other hand, is primarily associated with patterns of inattention, hyperactivity, and impulsivity. Children and adults with ADHD often find it difficult to sustain attention, follow through on tasks, or regulate their impulses, which can lead to struggles in academic, social, and professional settings.

Beyond ASD and ADHD, other neurodevelopmental disorders include intellectual disabilities, communication disorders, specific learning disorders, and motor disorders such as developmental coordination disorders and tic disorders. While each of these conditions presents unique challenges, they all share a common foundation in early disruptions to brain development.

To be diagnosed with ADHD, inattention and/or hyperactivity-impulsivity must be present for at least 6 months, inconsistent with developmental level, and negatively impacting social, academic, or occupational functioning.

A. Inattention

Six (or more) of the following symptoms for at least 6 months (for adults, 17 and older, five symptoms are enough):

1. Often fails to give close attention to details or makes careless mistakes.
2. Often has difficulty sustaining attention in tasks or play activities.
3. Often does not seem to listen when spoken to directly.
4. Often does not follow through on instructions and fails to finish tasks.
5. Often has difficulty organizing tasks and activities.
6. Often avoids or is reluctant to engage in tasks requiring sustained mental effort.
7. Often loses things necessary for tasks or activities.
8. Is often easily distracted by extraneous stimuli.
9. Is often forgetful in daily activities.

B. Hyperactivity and Impulsivity

Six (or more) of the following symptoms for at least 6 months (for adults, 17 and older, five symptoms are enough):

1. Often fidgets with or taps hands or feet or squirms in seat.
2. Often leaves seat in situations when remaining seated is expected.
3. Often runs about or climbs in inappropriate situations (for adults, may feel restless).

4. Often unable to play or engage in leisure activities quietly.
5. Is often "on the go," acting as if "driven by a motor."
6. Often talks excessively.
7. Often blurts out an answer before a question has been completed.
8. Often has difficulty waiting their turn.
9. Often interrupts or intrudes on others.

C. Symptoms must be present before age 12.
D. Several symptoms must be present in two or more settings (e.g., home, school, work).
E. There must be clear evidence that the symptoms interfere with or reduce the quality of social, academic, or occupational functioning.
F. Symptoms do not occur exclusively during the course of schizophrenia or another psychotic disorder, and are not better explained by another mental disorder (e.g., anxiety, mood disorder, personality disorder).

ASD is characterized by persistent deficits in social communication and social interaction, as well as restricted, repetitive patterns of behavior.

A. Persistent deficits in social communication and social interaction across multiple contexts, as manifested by the following:

   1. Deficits in social-emotional reciprocity (e.g., abnormal social approach, failure to initiate/respond to social interactions).
   2. Deficits in nonverbal communicative behaviors used for social interaction (e.g., poorly integrated verbal and nonverbal communication, abnormalities in eye contact, body language, or deficits in understanding gestures).
   3. Deficits in developing, maintaining, and understanding relationships (e.g., difficulties adjusting behavior to suit different social contexts, difficulty in making friends, lack of interest in peers).

B. Restricted, repetitive patterns of behavior, interests, or activities, as manifested by at least two of the following:

   1. Stereotyped or repetitive motor movements, use of objects, or speech (e.g., simple motor stereotypes, lining up toys).
   2. Insistence on sameness, inflexible adherence to routines, or ritualized patterns of verbal or nonverbal behavior (e.g., extreme distress at small changes).
   3. Highly restricted, fixated interests that are abnormal in intensity or focus.
   4. Hyper- or hyporeactivity to sensory input or unusual interest in sensory aspects of the environment (e.g., apparent indifference to pain/temperature, excessive smelling/touching of objects).

C. Symptoms must be present in the early developmental period (but may not fully manifest until social demands exceed limited capacities or may be masked by learned strategies later in life).
D. Symptoms cause clinically significant impairment in social, occupational, or other important areas of current functioning.

E. These disturbances are not better explained by intellectual disability (intellectual developmental disorder) or global developmental delay. Intellectual disability and ASD frequently co-occur, but social communication should be below expected levels based on the individual's developmental level.

Understanding the neurobiological foundations of neurodevelopmental disorders requires a focus on the structures and functions of the brain that are most commonly implicated in these conditions. In ASD, research has identified abnormalities in several brain regions, including the prefrontal cortex, amygdala, and the mirror neuron system. The prefrontal cortex, which plays a critical role in executive functioning, social cognition, and emotional regulation, tends to show atypical patterns of connectivity in individuals with ASD. This may contribute to the difficulties they experience in planning, problem-solving, and understanding the intentions or emotions of others. The amygdala, which is central to emotional processing, has also been found to function differently in individuals with ASD, possibly explaining their challenges in emotional regulation and social interactions (Ha et al., 2015).

Similarly, ADHD is associated with dysfunctions in the prefrontal cortex, basal ganglia, and the dopaminergic system. The prefrontal cortex's role in attention, impulse control, and working memory is often impaired in individuals with ADHD, leading to difficulties in maintaining focus, regulating behavior, and controlling impulsive responses. The basal ganglia, which helps coordinate motor activity and cognitive control, is also implicated in ADHD, and abnormalities in this structure may contribute to the hyperactive and restless behaviors characteristic of the disorder. Additionally, dopamine, a neurotransmitter essential for regulating mood, reward, and attention, is thought to be dysregulated in ADHD, further contributing to deficits in motivation, focus, and impulse control (Arnsten, 2009).

These neurobiological differences not only affect specific behaviors but also have broader implications for cognitive processes. For example, the impairments in executive functioning observed in individuals with ASD and ADHD can hinder their ability to organize information, shift attention between tasks, and inhibit inappropriate responses. In both conditions, these cognitive deficits can lead to difficulties in navigating social environments, controlling impulsive behaviors, and succeeding in structured settings such as school or work (Schachar et al., 2022).

The origins of neurodevelopmental disorders are closely linked to early brain development. Critical periods in early development—particularly the prenatal and early postnatal stages—are times when the brain undergoes rapid growth and specialization. During these stages, neural connections are formed, synaptic pruning occurs, and key brain structures become established. Any disruptions to these processes, whether through genetic mutations, environmental influences, or a combination of both, can lead to the development of neurodevelopmental disorders.

In the case of ASD, research has suggested that atypical brain development may begin as early as the prenatal stage. Studies using neuroimaging have shown that children with ASD often exhibit differences in brain volume, connectivity, and cortical thickness early in life. For example, infants who go on to develop ASD may show accelerated growth in brain volume during the first year of life, followed by a plateau or deceleration in later years. These early differences in brain structure can set the stage for the cognitive and behavioral challenges observed in ASD, such as difficulties with social communication and repetitive behaviors (Shen & Piven, 2017).

Similarly, ADHD is believed to stem from both genetic and environmental factors that affect early brain development. One theory suggests that delayed maturation of brain structures like the prefrontal cortex is a contributing factor to ADHD. Children with ADHD often show a lag in the development of key brain regions responsible for regulating attention, behavior, and executive functions. This delay in maturation can result in impulsive and inattentive behaviors that are characteristic of the disorder. Additionally, prenatal exposure to environmental toxins, maternal stress, and other adverse factors may further disrupt normal brain development, increasing the risk for ADHD (Arnsten, 2009).

The importance of early brain development in neurodevelopmental disorders underscores the need for early diagnosis and intervention. Detecting these disorders in their early stages, during critical periods of brain plasticity, offers the best chance for mitigating their impact on behavior and cognitive functioning. Early interventions, such as behavioral therapy, social skills training, and educational support, can help children with ASD, ADHD, and other neurodevelopmental disorders develop better-coping strategies, improve social functioning, and reduce the likelihood of negative outcomes later in life.

3 Neurodevelopmental Disorders and Impulse Control

Impulse control, a key aspect of behavioral regulation, refers to the ability to resist or delay immediate reactions, urges, or behaviors that might be inappropriate or harmful. For individuals with neurodevelopmental disorders, this function is often impaired due to underlying brain abnormalities and dysfunctions in cognitive processes. Disorders such as autism spectrum disorder (ASD) and attention deficit hyperactivity disorder (ADHD) are frequently associated with deficits in impulse control, leading to challenges in managing behavior in social, academic, and occupational settings (Wang et al., 2023). This section explores how neurodevelopmental disorders affect impulse control, presents key empirical research findings on the topic, and examines case studies to illustrate the real-world impact of impulse control issues in individuals with these disorders.

Impulse control is an essential component of executive functioning, a set of cognitive processes that enable individuals to plan, focus attention, and regulate behavior. Impulsivity refers to the tendency to act without adequate forethought, leading to spontaneous and sometimes inappropriate or risky actions (Fig. 1). For individuals with neurodevelopmental disorders like ASD and ADHD, impulsivity is a hallmark feature, affecting their capacity to behave in socially acceptable ways or to avoid behaviors that may lead to negative consequences (Bakhshani, 2014).

In ADHD, impulsivity is one of the core symptoms, alongside inattention and hyperactivity. Individuals with ADHD often struggle to pause and think before

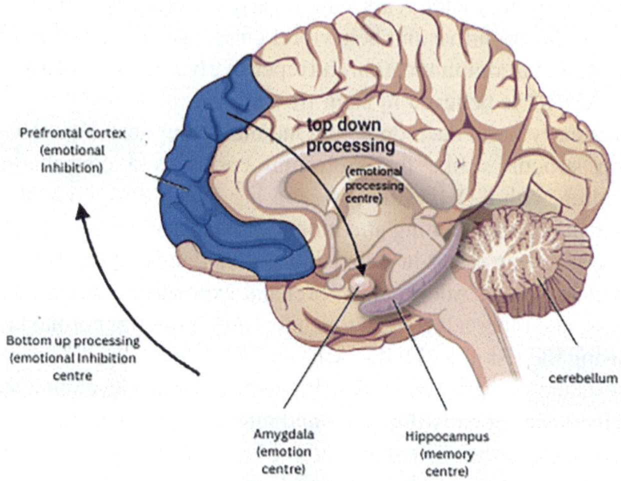

Fig. 1 Shows the various brain areas that are involved in emotional regulation and impulsivity (Godet et al., 2022)

acting, which can result in behaviors such as interrupting others, making hasty decisions, and engaging in risky activities without considering potential dangers. The inability to inhibit impulses stems from dysfunctions in the prefrontal cortex, the area of the brain responsible for executive functioning. The prefrontal cortex in individuals with ADHD often exhibits delayed maturation, which may contribute to their persistent difficulties in regulating impulsive behavior (Magnus et al., 2023).

ASD, though not primarily characterized by impulsivity, also presents significant challenges related to behavioral regulation. Individuals with ASD may experience difficulties in emotional regulation and controlling their responses to sensory stimuli or social cues. While some individuals with ASD may exhibit impulsive behaviors, these actions often result from difficulties in processing environmental stimuli or managing emotional responses rather than an innate tendency toward impulsivity. In ASD, the atypical development of the amygdala, prefrontal cortex, and other brain regions involved in emotion regulation and executive functioning may contribute to impulsivity and difficulties with behavioral control (Mazefsky et al., 2013).

Impaired impulse control can manifest in various ways in individuals with neurodevelopmental disorders. In social settings, individuals with ASD may respond impulsively when they are overwhelmed by sensory input or social interactions, while individuals with ADHD may have difficulty adhering to rules, waiting their turn, or refraining from disruptive behavior. These behaviors can lead to challenges in forming and maintaining social relationships, succeeding in structured environments, and avoiding negative interactions with authority figures (Dougnon & Matsui, 2022).

A growing body of empirical research has explored the relationship between neurodevelopmental disorders and impulse control deficits, with many studies focusing on ADHD and ASD. Key findings have revealed patterns of brain activity and cognitive processing that help explain why individuals with these disorders struggle with behavioral regulation.

One prominent study by Barkley (1997) introduced a model of ADHD that places a strong emphasis on the role of executive functioning deficits in explaining impulsivity. According to Barkley, individuals with ADHD exhibit dysfunction in the prefrontal cortex (Fig. 2), leading to impaired response inhibition, delayed gratification, and difficulties with emotional self-regulation. These executive function deficits make it difficult for individuals with ADHD to suppress inappropriate behaviors, plan for the future, and manage their emotional responses to stimuli. Subsequent research has supported Barkley's model, linking ADHD-related impulsivity to structural and functional abnormalities in brain regions responsible for executive functioning, including the prefrontal cortex and basal ganglia (Barkley, 1997).

Research on ASD and impulsivity has taken a slightly different focus, often examining how emotional dysregulation and sensory processing issues contribute to impulsive behaviors. A study by Samson et al. (2012) found that individuals with ASD showed significant impairments in emotional regulation, which correlated with impulsive behaviors in social and sensory contexts. The study suggested that difficulties in processing emotions and regulating responses to sensory stimuli could lead individuals with ASD to react impulsively, particularly when they are overwhelmed by their environment. These findings point to a unique mechanism for impulsivity in ASD, one that is more related to emotional regulation than to cognitive deficits in executive functioning (Samson et al., 2012).

Additional studies have highlighted the importance of early brain development in the manifestation of impulse control deficits in neurodevelopmental disorders.

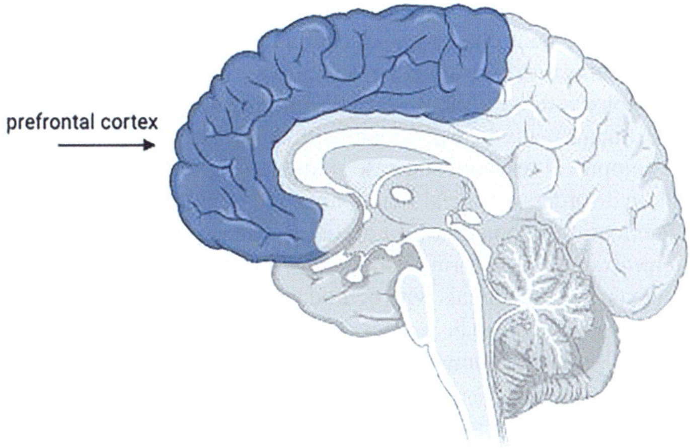

Fig. 2 Shows the prefrontal cortex, an important brain region involved in response inhibition, delayed gratification, and difficulties with emotional self-regulation (McGraw, 2012)

Structural MRI studies have consistently shown that individuals with ADHD exhibit reduced volume in the prefrontal cortex and delayed cortical maturation, both of which are linked to impulsive behaviors (Shaw et al., 2007). In contrast, individuals with ASD show atypical connectivity between the prefrontal cortex and other brain regions involved in emotional processing, such as the amygdala (Kennedy & Courchesne, 2008). These neural differences provide a biological basis for understanding the unique patterns of impulsivity in these two disorders.

Impulse control is a significant challenge for individuals with neurodevelopmental disorders such as ADHD and ASD. While impulsivity in ADHD is often linked to executive functioning deficits and delayed brain maturation, impulsivity in ASD is more commonly associated with difficulties in emotional regulation and sensory processing. Empirical research has provided valuable insights into the brain mechanisms underlying these impulse control deficits, with studies highlighting structural and functional abnormalities in key brain regions such as the prefrontal cortex and amygdala. Case studies further demonstrate how these impulsivity issues manifest in real-world settings, affecting social interactions, academic performance, and safety. Understanding these mechanisms and their impact is critical for developing effective interventions and support strategies for individuals with neurodevelopmental disorders.

4 Social Functioning and Cognitive Processes

Neurodevelopmental disorders, including autism spectrum disorder (ASD) and attention deficit hyperactivity disorder (ADHD), profoundly affect individuals in various ways, particularly in the realms of social functioning and cognitive processes. These disorders alter how people interact with others, perceive social cues, and process information. As a result, individuals with neurodevelopmental disorders often face significant challenges in communication, social engagement, and cognitive functioning, such as attention, executive function, and problem-solving. This section explores these difficulties by examining social interaction challenges and cognitive impairments in individuals with ASD and ADHD. It also provides insights from empirical research and case studies to highlight the real-world implications of these disorders on social functioning and cognitive processes.

Social functioning encompasses the ability to engage effectively in social interactions, interpret social cues, form relationships, and maintain appropriate behavior in social contexts. For individuals with neurodevelopmental disorders like ASD and ADHD, social functioning can be severely impaired, manifesting in difficulties with communication, understanding social norms, and forming meaningful relationships.

4.1 Social Challenges in ASD

One of the hallmark features of ASD is significant difficulty in social interaction. Individuals with ASD often struggle to understand and respond to social cues, such as facial expressions, body language, and tone of voice. These challenges can lead to misunderstandings in social situations and make it difficult for individuals to engage in typical social exchanges. Additionally, individuals with ASD may have trouble with reciprocal social interactions, meaning they might not naturally take turns in conversation, maintain eye contact, or express empathy in ways that are expected in typical social interactions (Autism Spectrum Disorder: Communication Problems in Children, 2020).

To expand on the communication challenges prevalent in autism spectrum disorder (ASD), it is important to note the wide spectrum of abilities and impairments that individuals with ASD can exhibit. For instance, some individuals may be entirely nonverbal, which means they rely on alternative methods of communication, such as picture exchange communication systems (PECS), sign language, or assistive communication devices. For these individuals, social interactions are often hindered by the absence of spoken language, making it challenging to express their needs, desires, or emotions effectively. This inability to communicate verbally can lead to significant frustration, which may manifest in behavioral issues such as tantrums, withdrawal, or aggression, particularly when they feel misunderstood (Kasari et al., 2013).

At the other end of the spectrum are individuals with ASD who have typical or even advanced language skills in terms of vocabulary and grammar. However, despite their fluency, they may struggle with the pragmatics of language—how language is used in social contexts. These individuals often have difficulty understanding non-literal language, such as idioms, metaphors, and sarcasm, which are frequently used in everyday conversation. For example, a phrase like "it's raining cats and dogs" may be interpreted literally, leading to confusion or misinterpretation of the speaker's intent. This can make it difficult for individuals with ASD to follow conversations or engage in playful banter, further distancing them from their peers (Schaeffer et al., 2023).

Additionally, individuals with ASD may exhibit what is known as echolalia, which involves repeating words or phrases that they have heard previously, often without understanding their meaning. While echolalia can sometimes be functional (for example, repeating a question to help process it), in many cases, it may serve as a coping mechanism or an attempt to engage in communication without the necessary understanding of how to respond appropriately. This behavior can be confusing or off-putting to neurotypical individuals, leading to further social isolation for the person with ASD (Patra & De Jesus, 2023).

Social isolation is a common outcome of these communication difficulties. Because individuals with ASD often struggle to engage in typical social exchanges or misunderstand social cues, they may be excluded from social activities or withdraw voluntarily due to the anxiety or confusion that social situations can provoke.

Over time, this social withdrawal can lead to feelings of loneliness, depression, or low self-esteem, further complicating the individual's ability to form meaningful relationships (Orsmond et al., 2013).

Furthermore, difficulty in understanding others' intentions or emotions is another significant challenge for individuals with ASD. This impairment is often linked to deficits in the theory of mind, which refers to the ability to attribute mental states—such as beliefs, desires, and intentions—to oneself and others. Without a well-developed theory of mind, individuals with ASD may struggle to predict or interpret the behavior of others, making social interactions feel unpredictable and overwhelming. For example, they may not recognize when someone is joking or teasing, or they might misinterpret a friendly gesture as a threat. These misunderstandings can lead to conflict, rejection, or avoidance of social situations altogether (Rosello et al., 2020).

In educational or professional settings, communication challenges in individuals with ASD can also impact their ability to succeed. In the classroom, students with ASD may find it difficult to understand group dynamics, follow verbal instructions, or engage in collaborative activities, leading to frustration for both the student and the teacher. Similarly, in the workplace, individuals with ASD may struggle with understanding unwritten rules, such as office politics or appropriate social behavior during meetings, which can hinder their career advancement or job satisfaction (Autism Spectrum Disorder: Communication Problems in Children, 2020).

Communication challenges are also prevalent in ASD, and they can vary widely across the spectrum. Some individuals with ASD may be nonverbal or have limited speech, while others may speak fluently but struggle with the pragmatics of language, such as understanding idioms, metaphors, or sarcasm. These difficulties in social communication often contribute to isolation, as individuals with ASD may find it hard to form and maintain friendships or other social relationships. Social withdrawal and difficulty in understanding others' intentions further exacerbate these challenges (Vogindroukas et al., 2022).

4.2 Social Challenges in ADHD

While individuals with ADHD do not typically face the same level of social communication difficulties as those with ASD, they often experience significant challenges in social functioning due to impulsivity, inattention, and hyperactivity. Children and adults with ADHD may interrupt conversations, struggle to wait their turn, and have difficulty following social rules, such as maintaining appropriate personal space. These behaviors can lead to social rejection or conflict with peers, as others may perceive individuals with ADHD as disruptive or inattentive (Rich et al., 2009).

Inattention in ADHD also impacts social functioning by making it difficult for individuals to stay engaged in conversations or remember important social details. For instance, they may forget a friend's birthday or overlook social cues that signal a change in mood or behavior. This lack of attention to social subtleties can strain relationships and make it difficult to build lasting friendships (Magnus et al., 2023).

Inattention, another core feature of ADHD, plays a significant role in the social difficulties experienced by individuals with the disorder. People with ADHD often have trouble focusing on social interactions, particularly in group settings where there are multiple conversations happening simultaneously. This can make it challenging for them to keep track of what is being said, follow the flow of conversation, or stay engaged in long discussions. As a result, they may appear distracted or uninterested in the people they are interacting with, leading to feelings of exclusion or frustration among their peers (Magnus et al., 2023).

In addition to these difficulties, inattention can cause individuals with ADHD to miss important social cues. These cues, such as changes in tone of voice, facial expressions, or body language, are critical for understanding the emotions and intentions of others. For instance, someone with ADHD may not notice when a friend is upset or when a conversation has shifted from playful banter to a more serious topic. This lack of awareness can result in social misunderstandings, as the person with ADHD may continue to behave inappropriately for the situation, further alienating them from others (Magnus et al., 2023).

The forgetfulness associated with inattention also impacts social functioning. People with ADHD may forget important details about their friends' lives, such as upcoming events, personal preferences, or past conversations. This can make it difficult for them to show the level of attentiveness and care needed to nurture close relationships, causing their friends or partners to feel neglected or undervalued (Langmaid, 2022).

Hyperactivity, particularly in children with ADHD, can be another source of social difficulties. Hyperactive individuals often have excess energy that leads them to fidget, pace, or engage in physical activity at inappropriate times. In a social context, this restlessness can be disruptive. For example, a child with ADHD may have difficulty sitting still during a group activity, constantly getting up or moving around, which can annoy others and result in social isolation (Gawrilow et al., 2014).

In adults, hyperactivity often manifests as an inner sense of restlessness or a need to always be on the go. This can make it challenging for them to engage in quieter, more introspective social activities, such as having a deep conversation or simply relaxing with friends. The need for constant stimulation may drive them to seek out more high-energy environments, such as parties or events, which may not always align with the preferences of their social circle. This mismatch in social preferences can create friction in relationships, as friends or partners may feel overwhelmed by the constant need for activity (Attention-Deficit/Hyperactivity Disorder in Adults: What You Need to Know, n.d.).

The combination of impulsivity, inattention, and hyperactivity can lead to social rejection, particularly in childhood. Children with ADHD are more likely to be perceived by their peers as disruptive or difficult to get along with. Their impulsive behaviors, such as interrupting or failing to wait their turn, can make them unpopular in group settings, where social norms around politeness and cooperation are expected. As a result, they may be excluded from group activities or become the target of bullying, further exacerbating their social isolation (Rich et al., 2009). Research has shown that children with ADHD often experience higher levels of peer rejection compared to their neurotypical peers. This rejection can have long-term consequences on their emotional well-being, leading to low self-esteem, depression, or anxiety. In adulthood, the social difficulties associated with ADHD can persist, affecting not only friendships but also romantic relationships and professional interactions (Mrug et al., 2012).

Research on social functioning in ASD has consistently demonstrated impairments in social cognition and communication. A study by Chevallier et al. (2012) found that individuals with ASD exhibit deficits in social motivation, which refers to the drive to seek out and engage in social interactions. This lack of social motivation, combined with difficulties in interpreting social cues, contributes to the social isolation often experienced by individuals with ASD. In ADHD, social functioning impairments are often linked to impulsivity and inattention. A study by Hoza et al. (2005) found that children with ADHD are more likely to experience peer rejection due to their disruptive and inattentive behaviors. The study also highlighted that social difficulties in ADHD are exacerbated by the disorder's impact on attention and impulse control, which can interfere with the development of social skills and relationships.

Case studies provide real-world examples of how social functioning and cognitive impairments impact individuals with neurodevelopmental disorders.

Arun, a four-year-old and the second child of his parents, was referred for consultation. As he entered the room, his loud wailing was immediately noticeable. It took a while for him to calm down, and once he did, it became clear that he was extremely restless. Arun ran around the room, pulling down cushions and creating a general mess, while his mother struggled to manage him. He was diagnosed with autism spectrum disorder (ASD). His parents were concerned about his tendency to put objects like paper, cloth, and wall plaster in his mouth. Arun would become very upset if his demands were not met, and he showed limited emotional connection with his parents. He struggled to follow simple commands, making it increasingly difficult for his parents to handle him. Although therapy helped improve his eye contact slightly and he began to follow a few simple commands, progress was slow. Arun was a picky eater who preferred crunchy foods and suffered from constipation. He had not yet been toilet trained.

Arun's limited emotional connection with his parents reflects a common challenge in social cognition related to ASD. Social cognition involves understanding and responding to the emotions and intentions of others. Arun's reduced emotional engagement suggests difficulties in recognizing and forming emotional bonds, which is a key component of social cognition. Arun's behavior, such as his tendency to put objects in his mouth and his restlessness, indicates challenges in interpreting and responding to social and environmental cues. Social cognition includes the ability to make sense of social interactions and adjust behavior accordingly. Arun's difficulty in following simple commands and his unpredictable behavior highlight his struggle with processing and responding to social instructions. His struggle with eye contact and following commands are aspects of social communication, which is a subset of social cognition. Effective social communication requires understanding nonverbal cues (like eye contact) and responding appropriately to verbal commands. Arun's slow progress in these areas points to challenges in these cognitive processes. The case study mentions Arun's tendency to become very upset if his demands are not met. This behavior can be linked to difficulties in self-regulation and understanding social expectations. Social cognition involves not only interpreting others' behavior but also regulating one's own responses in social contexts. Arun's preference for specific textures and his issues with constipation may relate to sensory processing differences, which can impact social cognition. People with ASD often have heightened or diminished sensory responses, which can influence how they interact with their environment and with others.

Overall, the case study highlights how social cognition encompasses various abilities related to understanding and interacting with others, including emotional connectivity, response to social cues, communication skills, and behavioral regulation. Arun's symptoms and behaviors illustrate the challenges faced in these areas within the context of ASD.

Another case study looks into Ethan, an 8-year-old boy diagnosed with ASD, who struggles with social interaction and communication. He has difficulty making eye contact and interpreting the emotions of others, which often leads to misunderstandings with his peers. In school, Ethan prefers to play alone, as he finds group activities overwhelming and confusing. His teachers report that Ethan struggles to follow social rules, such as taking turns in conversation or sharing toys. Additionally, Ethan exhibits rigidity in his thinking, becoming upset when routines are disrupted or when he is asked to switch tasks. These social and cognitive challenges have led to social isolation and frustration for Ethan, as he finds it difficult to connect with others and adapt to changes in his environment.

Sarah, a 15-year-old girl with ADHD, experiences significant challenges with attention and impulse control. In school, Sarah has difficulty focusing on her assignments and often forgets to complete her homework. Her teachers report that Sarah frequently interrupts class discussions, blurting out answers without raising her hand. At home, Sarah struggles with time management and organization, often leaving tasks unfinished or forgetting important deadlines. Her impulsivity has also led to risky behaviors, such as skipping class and engaging in dangerous activities without considering the consequences. These cognitive impairments have affected Sarah's academic performance and social relationships, as her peers find her behavior unpredictable and disruptive.

Social functioning and cognitive processes are significantly impacted in individuals with neurodevelopmental disorders such as ASD and ADHD. Social interaction challenges in ASD stem from difficulties in communication, interpreting social cues, and understanding others' perspectives, while ADHD-related social challenges often result from impulsivity, inattention, and difficulty adhering to social norms. Cognitive impairments in both disorders, including deficits in executive function, attention, and impulse control, further complicate the ability to navigate social environments and manage daily tasks. Empirical research has provided valuable insights into the neural mechanisms underlying these deficits, while case studies highlight the real-world implications for individuals with neurodevelopmental disorders. Understanding these challenges is crucial for developing effective interventions that can support individuals in improving their social functioning and cognitive processes, ultimately enhancing their quality of life.

5 The Intersection of Neurodevelopmental Disorders and Criminal Behavior

Criminal behavior has long been a subject of interest in psychology, criminology, and sociology. While various factors contribute to an individual's likelihood of engaging in criminal activity, recent research has increasingly focused on the intersection of neurodevelopmental disorders (NDDs) and criminal behavior. Neurodevelopmental disorders, such as autism spectrum disorder (ASD), attention deficit hyperactivity disorder (ADHD), and intellectual disabilities, can affect cognitive, emotional, and social functioning, potentially contributing to deviant or criminal behaviors. Understanding the risk factors that make individuals with NDDs more susceptible to criminal involvement, as well as the environmental influences that may exacerbate or mitigate this susceptibility, is critical for effective prevention and intervention strategies. This section will explore the relationship between neurodevelopmental disorders and criminal behavior, examining risk factors such as impulse control issues, social dysfunction, and cognitive impairments. It will also delve into the role of environmental factors, such as socioeconomic status, familial influences, and community support systems, in shaping the behavior of individuals with NDDs. Furthermore, case studies will be presented to illustrate how neurodevelopmental disorders can contribute to criminal activity, and the broader implications of these cases will be discussed in the context of prevention, intervention, and the criminal justice system.

5.1 Risk Factors for Criminal Behavior

Impulse control is a critical factor in regulating behavior, and individuals with neurodevelopmental disorders often struggle with managing their impulses. For example, ADHD is characterized by impulsivity, hyperactivity, and inattention, all of which can lead to difficulty adhering to social norms and legal boundaries. People with ADHD may act without fully considering the consequences of their actions, which increases the risk of engaging in behaviors that could be deemed criminal. This impulsivity can manifest in various ways, such as theft, physical altercations, or substance abuse, all of which may land an individual in legal trouble (Magnus et al., 2023).

Research indicates that children and adolescents with ADHD are at an increased risk of engaging in antisocial behavior, including aggression and delinquency. The lack of impulse control can lead to spontaneous decisions to engage in criminal acts, especially when the individual is placed in a stressful or high-pressure environment (Saylor & Amann, 2016). In addition, co-occurring disorders like conduct disorder, which often accompanies ADHD, further increase the likelihood of engaging in criminal behavior due to a combination of impulsivity, aggression, and a disregard for rules and social norms (Fletcher & Wolfe, 2009).

5.2 Social Dysfunction

Social dysfunction is another key risk factor for criminal behavior in individuals with neurodevelopmental disorders. NDDs like ASD are marked by difficulties in social communication and interaction, which can result in misunderstandings, social isolation, and inappropriate behavior in social settings (Wang et al., 2023). Individuals with ASD often struggle to interpret social cues and may engage in actions that are perceived as aggressive, non-compliant, or criminal, even when they do not intend harm (Fitzpatrick et al., 2016). For example, someone with ASD may be unable to recognize the personal boundaries of others, leading to behaviors such as inappropriate touching or trespassing, which could be interpreted as criminal.

Moreover, social dysfunction can make individuals with NDDs more vulnerable to negative peer influence. In an attempt to fit in or gain acceptance, individuals with social impairments may be more easily manipulated or coerced into participating in criminal activities. Their difficulties with understanding social dynamics and consequences can make it challenging to resist peer pressure or recognize when they are being exploited by others for illegal purposes (Laursen & Veenstra, 2021).

5.3 Cognitive Impairments

Cognitive impairments associated with neurodevelopmental disorders can also play a significant role in criminal behavior. Intellectual disabilities, for example, often involve deficits in reasoning, problem-solving, and judgment, making it difficult for individuals to understand the legality and morality of their actions (Guina et al., 2022). Cognitive impairments can affect an individual's ability to assess risks and anticipate the outcomes of their behavior, leading to poor decision-making that may result in criminal activity (Dhakal & Bobrin, 2023).

For instance, individuals with intellectual disabilities may not fully comprehend the consequences of stealing or trespassing, and they may lack the cognitive ability to navigate complex social and legal situations. This can result in encounters with the criminal justice system, even when the individual's intent was not malicious

(Davis & The Arc, n.d.). Furthermore, cognitive impairments may limit an individual's ability to engage in meaningful employment or education, potentially increasing their reliance on illegal activities for financial gain (Dhakal & Bobrin, 2023).

5.4 *Environmental Influences*

While neurodevelopmental disorders create inherent vulnerabilities, environmental factors also play a crucial role in either exacerbating or mitigating the risk of criminal behavior. These factors include socioeconomic status, family dynamics, and community support systems.

5.4.1 Socioeconomic Factors

Individuals with neurodevelopmental disorders are often disproportionately affected by poverty and low socioeconomic status, which are well-established risk factors for criminal behavior. Families with limited financial resources may struggle to access appropriate healthcare, educational opportunities, and therapeutic interventions for their children with NDDs, leading to unmet developmental and social needs. The lack of adequate support can exacerbate behavioral problems, increasing the likelihood of criminal behavior (Wang et al., 2023).

Moreover, socioeconomic stressors, such as financial instability and inadequate housing, can create environments that are conducive to criminal activity. In low-income communities, individuals with NDDs may be exposed to higher levels of crime and violence, which can influence their behavior and increase the risk of criminal involvement. The absence of positive role models and structured activities further compounds this risk (Ejlskov et al., 2023).

5.4.2 Familial Influences

Family dynamics are critical in shaping the behavior of individuals with neurodevelopmental disorders. Supportive and nurturing family environments can provide individuals with the tools they need to manage their symptoms and avoid criminal behavior. However, dysfunctional family relationships, characterized by neglect, abuse, or lack of understanding of the individual's needs, can contribute to behavioral problems (Jabbari et al., 2023).

Parents of children with NDDs often face significant challenges in managing their child's behavior, especially when resources and support are lacking. In some cases, parents may resort to punitive or inconsistent discipline methods, which can worsen the child's behavioral problems and increase the risk of criminal behavior. Additionally, family members may struggle to recognize the signs of neurodevelopmental disorders and may attribute the child's behavior to intentional defiance or misconduct, rather than a result of the disorder (Sanvictores & Mendez, 2022).

5.4.3 Community Support and Intervention

The presence or absence of community support systems can also influence the likelihood of criminal behavior in individuals with neurodevelopmental disorders. Communities that offer access to specialized educational programs, mental health services, and social support groups can help mitigate the risk of criminal behavior by providing individuals with the tools they need to manage their symptoms and develop positive social connections (Kirkbride et al., 2024).

Conversely, communities that lack these resources may leave individuals with NDDs without the necessary support to navigate their social and emotional challenges. This can lead to increased frustration, social isolation, and engagement in criminal behavior as a means of coping with unmet needs. In addition, individuals with NDDs may be more vulnerable to exploitation by criminal networks in environments where community support is lacking (Novotney, n.d.).

6 Case Studies and Real-World Implications

6.1 Case Study 1: ASD and Criminal Behavior

A notable case involved a young man diagnosed with autism spectrum disorder who was arrested for what was perceived as stalking behavior. The individual had developed a fixation on a female acquaintance and sent her repeated messages, despite her clear requests for him to stop. The young man did not understand the boundaries of appropriate social behavior and was unable to comprehend that his actions were causing distress. His behavior escalated to showing up at her workplace unannounced, which led to legal action being taken against him (Rawdon et al., 2024).

In this case, the individual's social impairments, characteristic of ASD, contributed to behavior that was interpreted as criminal. The criminal justice system, however, initially failed to recognize the role of his neurodevelopmental disorder in his actions, leading to harsh legal consequences. This case underscores the need for increased awareness and education about neurodevelopmental disorders within the criminal justice system, as well as the importance of early intervention and support to prevent such outcomes (Rawdon et al., 2024).

6.2 Case Study 2: ADHD and Juvenile Delinquency

Another case involves a teenager diagnosed with ADHD who was repeatedly arrested for petty theft and vandalism. His impulsive nature, combined with a lack of appropriate supervision and support at home, contributed to his engagement in delinquent behavior. The young man struggled with impulse control and was easily influenced by peers who encouraged him to participate in illegal activities. Despite several arrests, he received minimal intervention from the juvenile justice system, which focused on punitive measures rather than addressing the underlying issues related to his ADHD. This case highlights the importance of understanding the role of neurodevelopmental disorders in criminal behavior and the need for rehabilitative approaches rather than purely punitive responses. Early identification and treatment of ADHD, along with supportive family and community environments, could have mitigated the young man's involvement in criminal activities (Sibley et al., 2010).

7 Implications for Understanding and Preventing Criminal Behavior

These case studies illustrate the complex relationship between neurodevelopmental disorders and criminal behavior. Individuals with NDDs often struggle to navigate social and legal norms due to their cognitive, emotional, and social impairments. Without appropriate intervention, support, and understanding from the criminal justice system, they are at an increased risk of becoming involved in criminal activities, often unintentionally (Sibley et al., 2010).

To better address this issue, several key strategies should be considered. Early diagnosis and treatment of neurodevelopmental disorders are crucial for preventing criminal behavior. By addressing cognitive, social, and emotional impairments through therapy, education, and support services, individuals can develop the skills needed to manage their behavior and avoid legal trouble (Morris-Rosendahl & Crocq, 2020). Increased awareness and training for law enforcement, judges, and attorneys on the unique needs and challenges of individuals with neurodevelopmental disorders are essential. This would enable the criminal justice system to respond more appropriately to individuals with NDDs, focusing on rehabilitation rather than punishment (Clasby et al., 2022). Families and communities play a vital role in shaping the behavior of individuals with NDDs. Access to educational programs, therapy, and social support systems (Cavonius-Rintahaka et al., 2019).

8 Assessment and Intervention in Neurodevelopmental Disorders and Criminal Behavior

The relationship between neurodevelopmental disorders (NDDs) and criminal behavior has gained increasing attention in recent years, given the growing awareness of how cognitive, emotional, and social impairments can contribute to deviant behaviors. For professionals in the criminal justice system and mental health sectors, this understanding emphasizes the critical need for thorough assessment and effective intervention to better support individuals with NDDs and reduce the likelihood of criminal activity. Individuals with neurodevelopmental disorders, such as autism spectrum disorder (ASD), attention deficit hyperactivity disorder (ADHD), and intellectual disabilities, are often at greater risk of involvement in criminal behavior due to deficits in impulse control, social cognition, and judgment.

In this section, we will explore the importance of comprehensive assessment for individuals with NDDs who may be involved in the criminal justice system. Accurate diagnosis is essential to understanding the individual's specific challenges and developing targeted intervention strategies aimed at reducing criminal behavior. We will also discuss intervention programs that have shown success in mitigating criminal behavior in this population. Finally, we will provide recommendations for professionals working with individuals with NDDs in the criminal justice system, focusing on strategies to improve outcomes and prevent reoffending.

A comprehensive and accurate assessment is the foundation of any effective intervention for individuals with neurodevelopmental disorders, especially in the context of criminal behavior. Given the complexity of NDDs, which often involve a range of cognitive, social, and emotional impairments, it is critical to identify the specific nature and extent of the disorder to inform appropriate interventions. Without a thorough assessment, misdiagnosis or underdiagnosis can occur, leading to inappropriate or ineffective responses that may exacerbate rather than mitigate criminal behavior.

Individuals with neurodevelopmental disorders often present with a range of symptoms that can overlap with other psychological or behavioral issues, such as conduct disorder, mood disorders, or substance abuse (Antolini & Colizzi, 2023). This overlap makes it essential for practitioners to differentiate between criminal behavior that stems from cognitive or developmental impairments and behavior that is more typical of individuals without such disorders. For instance, impulsivity and poor decision-making are common in both ADHD and conduct disorder, but the underlying causes and treatment approaches differ significantly (Engelhardt et al., 2019).

An accurate diagnosis also ensures that individuals receive the appropriate legal protections under the law, including the possibility of diversion from traditional criminal justice pathways into treatment-oriented alternatives (Young et al., 2017). Individuals with intellectual disabilities may not fully understand the legal proceedings against them or the consequences of their actions, making them more vulnerable to harsh sentencing if their disorder is not properly diagnosed.

Several assessment tools and methods are utilized to evaluate neurodevelopmental disorders in individuals involved in the criminal justice system. These assessments typically focus on cognitive functioning, social skills, emotional regulation, and adaptive behavior. The use of standardized tests and observational methods ensures that assessments are comprehensive and capture the full range of impairments that may be contributing to criminal behavior.

Tools such as the Wechsler Intelligence Scales (WAIS or WISC) are commonly used to assess cognitive functioning, including intelligence, memory, attention, and executive function. Individuals with NDDs, particularly intellectual disabilities or ADHD, may demonstrate impairments in these areas that contribute to poor decision-making and impulsivity, which can lead to criminal behavior (Marinopoulou et al., 2024). For individuals with ASD or other social impairments, tools such as the Vineland Adaptive Behavior Scales or the Autism Diagnostic Observation Schedule (ADOS) can assess social communication skills, daily living skills, and interpersonal relationships (Yu et al., 2023). These assessments help identify difficulties in social cognition, such as understanding social norms or recognizing the emotions of others, which may lead to criminal misbehavior. Instruments like the Behavior Assessment System for Children (BASC) or the Conners' Rating Scales can be used to evaluate emotional regulation, impulsivity, and behavioral problems in individuals with ADHD or similar disorders. Understanding emotional and behavioral dysregulation is key to developing interventions that address aggressive or impulsive criminal behavior (Bradstreet et al., 2016).

In addition to these standardized tools, professionals should also consider the individual's life history, including family dynamics, educational background, trauma exposure, and prior involvement with the criminal justice system. A multidisciplinary approach that includes input from psychologists, social workers, teachers, and family members ensures that the assessment is holistic and provides a clear picture of the individual's needs (Russell et al., 2015).

Once a thorough assessment has been conducted, targeted intervention strategies can be developed to address the specific challenges faced by individuals with neurodevelopmental disorders who are at risk of engaging in criminal behavior. Effective interventions aim not only to reduce criminal activity but also to improve the individual's overall quality of life by enhancing social skills, emotional regulation, and cognitive functioning (Merlo et al., 2023).

One of the most widely used approaches for reducing criminal behavior in individuals with NDDs is cognitive behavioral therapy (CBT). CBT is particularly effective for individuals with ADHD and ASD, as it focuses on teaching individuals to identify and change maladaptive thought patterns that lead to problematic behavior (Chand et al., 2023). By addressing cognitive distortions—such as impulsive thinking, misinterpretation of social cues, and poor problem-solving skills—CBT can help individuals develop better-coping mechanisms and decision-making skills. For individuals with ADHD, CBT can be combined with behavioral interventions such as reinforcement strategies that reward positive behavior and reduce negative behavior (Nakao et al., 2021). In criminal justice settings, these interventions can be delivered through structured programs that focus on impulse control, emotional regulation, and moral reasoning. Social skills training is another critical intervention for individuals with neurodevelopmental disorders, especially those with ASD or intellectual disabilities. Many individuals with these disorders struggle to navigate social interactions, which can lead to misunderstandings, frustration, and ultimately, criminal behavior (Yizengaw, 2021). Social skills training helps individuals develop the ability to recognize social cues, understand others' emotions, and engage in appropriate communication and behavior. Programs such as the PEERS® (Program for the Education and Enrichment of Relational Skills) curriculum have shown success in improving social functioning in individuals with ASD. These programs focus on teaching individuals how to form and maintain friendships, resolve conflicts, and manage social anxiety. In the context of criminal behavior, improved social functioning reduces the likelihood of negative interactions that could escalate into criminal acts.

For individuals who struggle with aggression or emotional dysregulation, anger management programs are essential. These programs teach individuals how to recognize the early signs of anger and develop strategies for managing their emotions before they escalate into violent or criminal behavior ("Control Anger Before It Controls You," 2023). Techniques such as deep breathing, mindfulness, and problem-solving are commonly used to help individuals manage their emotions more effectively. Programs like the Aggression Replacement Training (ART) have been successfully used with individuals who have a history of violent behavior. ART focuses on teaching social skills, anger control, and moral reasoning, and has been adapted for individuals with neurodevelopmental disorders. By addressing the root causes of aggressive behavior, such programs can significantly reduce the likelihood of reoffending (Sharma et al., 2016).

For some individuals with neurodevelopmental disorders, medication may be an important component of their intervention plan. For example, stimulant medications such as methylphenidate (Ritalin) are commonly prescribed to individuals with ADHD to help improve attention, impulse control, and overall behavior (Verghese & Abdijadid, 2023). Similarly, individuals with ASD may benefit from medications that target anxiety, aggression, or repetitive behaviors. However, medication should always be used in conjunction with behavioral interventions, as it alone cannot address the social and cognitive challenges that contribute to criminal behavior. Ongoing monitoring of medication effectiveness and side effects is also essential to ensure that the individual's needs are being met (Lopez et al., 2018).

9 Recommendations for Practice

Professionals working with individuals with neurodevelopmental disorders in the criminal justice system play a crucial role in ensuring that these individuals receive appropriate care and intervention (Woodhouse et al., 2024). Given the unique challenges faced by this population, it is essential to adopt practices that are sensitive to their cognitive, emotional, and social impairments while promoting rehabilitation and preventing reoffending (Young et al., 2017).

One of the key recommendations is the creation of specialized assessment and intervention teams within the criminal justice system. These teams should include professionals with expertise in neurodevelopmental disorders, such as psychologists, psychiatrists, and social workers, who can conduct comprehensive assessments and design individualized intervention plans. This multidisciplinary approach ensures that individuals with NDDs receive the support they need and that their behavior is understood within the context of their disorder (Rutherford et al., 2021).

Diversion programs that focus on rehabilitation rather than punishment are particularly important for individuals with neurodevelopmental disorders. These programs allow individuals to receive treatment and support instead of incarceration, which may exacerbate their cognitive and emotional challenges (Dammer & Weise-Pengelly, 2014). For example, mental health courts and specialized juvenile courts have been successful in diverting individuals with NDDs into community-based treatment programs that address the root causes of their behavior.

Increased training for law enforcement officers, judges, and attorneys is essential to ensure that they are equipped to recognize and respond to individuals with neurodevelopmental disorders. Law enforcement officers are often the first point of contact for individuals with NDDs, and their understanding of the disorder can make a significant difference in how the situation is handled (Lorey & Fegert, 2021). Training on de-escalation techniques, communication strategies, and the importance of referring individuals for mental health assessments can improve outcomes and reduce the likelihood of unnecessary arrests. Similarly, legal professionals should receive training on how neurodevelopmental disorders may impact an individual's understanding of legal proceedings, decision-making abilities, and culpability (Goodman et al., 2020). This knowledge can inform more compassionate and just sentencing decisions that prioritize rehabilitation over punishment.

Finally, early intervention is critical for preventing criminal behavior in individuals with neurodevelopmental disorders. Identifying and addressing NDDs during childhood and adolescence can significantly reduce the risk of criminal involvement later in life. Schools, healthcare providers, and community organizations should work together to provide early screening, diagnosis, and intervention services for at-risk youth (Aldharman et al., 2023). By addressing the underlying cognitive and social impairments, early intervention can improve long-term outcomes and reduce the likelihood of criminal behavior.

The intersection of neurodevelopmental disorders and criminal behavior is complex and multifaceted, requiring a thorough and nuanced approach to assessment and intervention (Mullin et al., 2013). Accurate and comprehensive assessments are essential for identifying the specific challenges faced by individuals with NDDs, while targeted interventions can help reduce the risk of criminal behavior and improve overall functioning (Holland et al., 2021). Professionals working in the criminal justice system must adopt practices that prioritize rehabilitation and support, ensuring that individuals with NDDs receive the care they need to thrive. By implementing specialized assessment teams, diversion programs, and training for legal professionals, the criminal justice system can better address the unique needs of individuals with neurodevelopmental disorders (Chandler et al., 2009). Early intervention remains a key factor in preventing criminal behavior, highlighting the importance of collaboration between healthcare, education, and community sectors. Through these strategies, it is possible to improve outcomes for individuals with NDDs and reduce the overall impact of criminal behavior on society.

10 Conclusion

The intersection of neurodevelopmental disorders (NDDs) and criminal behavior is a complex and multifaceted issue that requires a nuanced approach to understanding, legal judgment, and intervention. As we have explored throughout this discussion, neurodevelopmental disorders like autism spectrum disorder (ASD), attention deficit hyperactivity disorder (ADHD), and intellectual disabilities significantly influence the way individuals perceive, interpret, and respond to social and environmental cues. This cognitive and emotional framework can, in some cases, contribute to behaviors that fall under criminal definitions, although the underlying causes are often rooted in neurodevelopmental impairments rather than intentional delinquency.

One of the main findings is the crucial role that neurodevelopmental disorders play in contributing to criminal behavior through deficits in impulse control, social cognition, emotional regulation, and decision-making. Individuals with NDDs often experience difficulties in understanding social norms, recognizing others' emotions, and interpreting ambiguous social situations. These impairments can lead to unintentional violations of the law or impulsive actions that result in criminal charges. For instance, those with ADHD may engage in risky behaviors due to poor impulse control, while individuals with ASD may have trouble interpreting social rules, leading to problematic behaviors.

Furthermore, it is essential to recognize the variety of neurodevelopmental disorders and the diverse range of challenges they present. Each disorder affects cognition and behavior differently, which complicates both assessment and intervention strategies. The overlap between symptoms of different NDDs and other mental health conditions—such as mood disorders or conduct disorder—underscores the importance of accurate diagnosis to ensure appropriate interventions are implemented. Through thorough assessments involving tools like cognitive evaluations, behavioral assessments, and social skill testing, professionals can better understand the unique challenges an individual faces and provide tailored support. The interventions designed for individuals with NDDs who engage in criminal behavior must be carefully targeted to their specific cognitive and emotional needs. Cognitive behavioral therapy (CBT), social skills training, anger management programs, and, in some cases, medication, have shown to be effective in addressing behaviors that may lead to criminal activity. However, without a solid understanding of the root neurodevelopmental impairments driving these behaviors, interventions risk being superficial and insufficient. The insights from this exploration hold significant implications for the criminal justice system. Legal judgments must account for the neurological underpinnings of criminal behavior in individuals with NDDs, as traditional interpretations of intent and culpability may not apply. Courts need to be sensitive to the cognitive and emotional limitations that individuals with NDDs experience. For example, understanding that someone with an intellectual disability may not fully grasp the consequences of their actions or that an individual with ASD may struggle to interpret social norms is critical when determining appropriate sentencing and intervention measures. The integration of neurological perspectives into the criminal justice system can shift how individuals with NDDs are treated. In some cases, diversion programs that prioritize treatment and rehabilitation over punishment are more effective and humane. These individuals may not benefit from incarceration, which often exacerbates their symptoms and leads to recidivism. Instead, treatment-oriented programs that address their specific neurodevelopmental challenges are more likely to yield positive outcomes and reduce the likelihood of reoffending. Moreover, the importance of specialized training for legal and law enforcement professionals cannot be overstated. Officers and legal professionals must be equipped to recognize the signs of NDDs and understand how these disorders may influence behavior. This knowledge can inform more compassionate and just approaches to handling criminal cases involving individuals with NDDs, promoting rehabilitation over retribution.

The exploration of neurodevelopmental disorders and criminal behavior is still a developing field, and there are several areas where further research is necessary to enhance our understanding and improve intervention outcomes. Future research should aim to better understand the nuanced ways in which different NDDs contribute to criminal behavior. While current research often groups disorders together under broad categories, it is crucial to explore how each specific disorder—whether ADHD, ASD, or intellectual disabilities—uniquely influences behavior in a criminal context. Another promising avenue for future research is the examination of how environmental factors, such as socioeconomic status, trauma, and family dynamics, interact with neurodevelopmental disorders to influence criminal behavior. By understanding these interactions, professionals can develop more holistic interventions that address both the neurological and environmental factors contributing to criminality. Additionally, ongoing research into neuroimaging techniques and other neurobiological tools could enhance the accuracy of diagnosis and provide more detailed insights into how brain abnormalities contribute to behavior. Advances in technology, such as functional MRI, could help identify specific brain structures or networks that are impaired in individuals with NDDs who engage in criminal behavior. This information could then be used to tailor interventions even more precisely, targeting the neurological pathways involved in poor impulse control, social dysfunction, or emotional dysregulation.

In terms of practical applications, future efforts should focus on improving early identification and intervention strategies for children and adolescents with NDDs. By providing support at an earlier age, it may be possible to reduce the likelihood of future criminal behavior and improve long-term outcomes. Schools, healthcare providers, and community organizations play a pivotal role in identifying at-risk youth and connecting them with the appropriate services. Lastly, there is a need for more longitudinal studies that track individuals with NDDs over time to better understand the trajectory of criminal behavior in this population. These studies can provide valuable data on the effectiveness of different interventions and help refine approaches to treatment and prevention.

In conclusion, the relationship between neurodevelopmental disorders and criminal behavior is intricate and requires an approach that integrates psychological, social, and neurological perspectives. Through comprehensive assessments and targeted interventions, individuals with NDDs can receive the support they need to navigate challenges, reducing their likelihood of engaging in criminal behavior. The criminal justice system must adapt to these insights by incorporating specialized training for professionals and prioritizing rehabilitative programs over punitive measures. Looking forward, ongoing research into the neurobiological, environmental, and developmental aspects of NDDs will further enhance our understanding and ability to support individuals with these disorders, ultimately improving outcomes for both individuals and society as a whole.

References

Aldharman, S. S., Al-Jabr, K. H., Alharbi, Y. S., Alnajar, N. K., Alkhanani, J. J., Alghamdi, A., Abdellatif, R. A., Allouzi, A., Almallah, A. M., & Jamil, S. F. (2023). Implications of early diagnosis and intervention in the management of neurodevelopmental delay (NDD) in children: A systematic review and meta-analysis. *Cureus*. https://doi.org/10.7759/cureus.38745

Antolini, G., & Colizzi, M. (2023). Where do neurodevelopmental disorders go? Casting the eye away from childhood towards adulthood. *Healthcare, 11*(7), 1015. https://doi.org/10.3390/healthcare11071015

Arnsten, A. F. (2009). ADHD and the prefrontal cortex. *The Journal of Pediatrics, 154*(5), I-S43. https://doi.org/10.1016/j.jpeds.2009.01.018

Attention-Deficit/Hyperactivity Disorder in Adults: What You Need to Know. (n.d.). National Institute of Mental Health (NIMH). https://www.nimh.nih.gov/health/publications/adhd-what-you-need-to-know.

Autism Spectrum Disorder: Communication Problems in Children. (2020, April 13). NIDCD. https://www.nidcd.nih.gov/health/autism-spectrum-disorder-communication-problems-children.

Bakhshani, N. (2014). Impulsivity: A predisposition toward risky behaviors. *International Journal High Risk Behaviors & Addiction, 3*(2). https://doi.org/10.5812/ijhrba.20428

Barkley, R. A. (1997). Behavioral inhibition, sustained attention, and executive functions: Constructing a unifying theory of ADHD. *Psychological Bulletin, 121*(1), 65–94. https://doi.org/10.1037/0033-2909.121.1.65

Bradstreet, L. E., Juechter, J. I., Kamphaus, R. W., Kerns, C. M., & Robins, D. L. (2016). Using the BASC-2 parent rating scales to screen for autism spectrum disorder in toddlers and preschool-aged children. *Journal of Abnormal Child Psychology, 45*(2), 359–370. https://doi.org/10.1007/s10802-016-0167-3

Cavonius-Rintahaka, D., Aho, A. L., Voutilainen, A., Billstedt, E., & Gillberg, C. (2019). Health, functionality, and social support in families with a child with a neurodevelopmental disorder - a pilot study. *Neuropsychiatric Disease and Treatment, 15*, 1151–1161. https://doi.org/10.2147/ndt.s195722

Chand, S. P., Kuckel, D. P., & Huecker, M. R. (2023, May 23). Cognitive behavior therapy. StatPearls - NCBI Bookshelf. https://www.ncbi.nlm.nih.gov/books/NBK470241/.

Chandler, R. K., Fletcher, B. W., & Volkow, N. D. (2009). Treating drug abuse and addiction in the criminal justice system. *JAMA, 301*(2), 183. https://doi.org/10.1001/jama.2008.976

Chevallier, C., Kohls, G., Troiani, V., Brodkin, E. S., & Schultz, R. T. (2012). The social motivation theory of autism. *Trends in Cognitive Sciences, 16*(4), 231–239. https://doi.org/10.1016/j.tics.2012.02.007

Clasby, B., Mirfin-Veitch, B., Blackett, R., Kedge, S., & Whitehead, E. (2022). Responding to neurodiversity in the courtroom: A brief evaluation of environmental accommodations to increase procedural fairness. *Criminal Behaviour and Mental Health, 32*(3), 197–211. https://doi.org/10.1002/cbm.2239

Control Anger Before It Controls You. (2023, November 3). https://www.apa.org. https://www.apa.org/topics/anger/control.

Dammer, H. R., & Weise-Pengelly, C. A. (2014, April 8). Diversion | Criminal Justice Reform & Alternatives. Encyclopedia Britannica. https://www.britannica.com/topic/diversion.

Davis, L. A. & The Arc. (n.d.). People with intellectual disabilities in the criminal Justice Systems: Victims & Suspects. https://thearc.org/wp-content/uploads/forchapters/Criminal%20Justice%20System.pdf.

Dhakal, A., & Bobrin, B. D. (2023, February 14). Cognitive deficits. StatPearls - NCBI Bookshelf. https://www.ncbi.nlm.nih.gov/books/NBK559052/.

Dougnon, G., & Matsui, H. (2022). Modelling autism Spectrum disorder (ASD) and attention-deficit/hyperactivity disorder (ADHD) using mice and Zebrafish. *International Journal of Molecular Sciences, 23*(14), 7550. https://doi.org/10.3390/ijms23147550

Ejlskov, L., Antonsen, S., Wulff, J. N., Agerbo, E., Plana-Ripoll, O., Sabel, C. E., Fan, C. C., Thompson, W. K., Mok, P. L. H., Pedersen, C. B., & Webb, R. T. (2023). Multilevel interactions between family and neighbourhood socioeconomic indices in childhood and later risks of self-harm and violent criminality in Denmark: A national cohort study. *The Lancet Public Health, 8*(2), e99–e108. https://doi.org/10.1016/s2468-2667(22)00292-4

Engelhardt, P. E., Nobes, G., & Pischedda, S. (2019). The relationship between adult symptoms of attention-deficit/hyperactivity disorder and criminogenic cognitions. *Brain Sciences, 9*(6), 128. https://doi.org/10.3390/brainsci9060128

Fitzpatrick, S., Srivorakiat, L., Wink, L., Pedapati, E., & Erickson, C. (2016). Aggression in autism spectrum disorder: Presentation and treatment options. *Neuropsychiatric Disease and Treatment, 12*, 1525–1538. https://doi.org/10.2147/ndt.s84585

Fletcher, J., & Wolfe, B. (2009, September 1). Long-term consequences of childhood ADHD on criminal activities. PubMed Central (PMC). https://www.ncbi.nlm.nih.gov/pmc/articles/PMC3398051/.

Gawrilow, C., KÃhnhausen, J., Schmid, J., & Stadler, G. (2014). Hyperactivity and motoric activity in ADHD: Characterization, assessment, and intervention. *Frontiers in Psychiatry, 5*. https://doi.org/10.3389/fpsyt.2014.00171

Godet, A., Fortier, A., Bannier, E., Coquery, N., & Val-Laillet, D. (2022). Interactions between emotions and eating behaviors: Main issues, neuroimaging contributions, and innovative preventive or corrective strategies. *Reviews in Endocrine and Metabolic Disorders, 23*(4), 807–831. https://doi.org/10.1007/s11154-021-09700-x

Goodman, H., Brooks, C. P., Price, O., & Barley, E. A. (2020). Barriers and facilitators to the effective de-escalation of conflict behaviours in forensic high-secure settings: A qualitative study. *International Journal of Mental Health Systems, 14*(1). https://doi.org/10.1186/s13033-020-00392-5

Guina, J., Hernandez, C., Witherell, J., Cowan, A., Dixon, D., King, I., & Gentile, J. P. (2022). Neurodevelopmental disorders, criminality, and criminal responsibility. *PubMed, 50*(3), 358–368. https://doi.org/10.29158/jaapl.210103-21

Ha, S., Sohn, I., Kim, N., Sim, H. J., & Cheon, K. (2015). Characteristics of brains in autism spectrum disorder: Structure, function and connectivity across the lifespan. *Experimental Neurobiology, 24*(4), 273–284. https://doi.org/10.5607/en.2015.24.4.273

Holland, L., Reid, N., & Smirnov, A. (2021). Neurodevelopmental disorders in youth justice: A systematic review of screening, assessment and interventions. *Journal of Experimental Criminology, 19*(1), 31–70. https://doi.org/10.1007/s11292-021-09475-w

Hoza, B., Mrug, S., Gerdes, A. C., Hinshaw, S. P., Bukowski, W. M., Gold, J. A., Kraemer, H. C., Pelham, W. E., Wigal, T., & Arnold, L. E. (2005). What aspects of peer relationships are impaired in children with attention-deficit/hyperactivity disorder? *Journal of Consulting and Clinical Psychology, 73*(3), 411–423. https://doi.org/10.1037/0022-006x.73.3.411

Jabbari, B., Schoo, C., & Rouster, A. S. (2023, September 16). Family dynamics. StatPearls - NCBI Bookshelf. https://www.ncbi.nlm.nih.gov/books/NBK560487/.

Kasari, C., Brady, N., Lord, C., & Tager-Flusberg, H. (2013). Assessing the minimally verbal school-aged child with autism spectrum disorder. *Autism Research, 6*(6), 479–493. https://doi.org/10.1002/aur.1334

Kennedy, D. P., & Courchesne, E. (2008). Functional abnormalities of the default network during self- and other-reflection in autism. *Social Cognitive and Affective Neuroscience, 3*(2), 177–190. https://doi.org/10.1093/scan/nsn011

Kirkbride, J. B., Anglin, D. M., Colman, I., Dykxhoorn, J., Jones, P. B., Patalay, P., Pitman, A., Soneson, E., Steare, T., Wright, T., & Griffiths, S. L. (2024). The social determinants of mental health and disorder: Evidence, prevention and recommendations. *World Psychiatry, 23*(1), 58–90. https://doi.org/10.1002/wps.21160

Langmaid, S. (2022, July 14). Is memory loss ADHD, or something else? WebMD. https://www.webmd.com/add-adhd/adult-adhd-memory-loss.

Laursen, B., & Veenstra, R. (2021). Toward understanding the functions of peer influence: A summary and synthesis of recent empirical research. *Journal of Research on Adolescence, 31*(4), 889–907. https://doi.org/10.1111/jora.12606

Lopez, P. L., Torrente, F. M., Ciapponi, A., Lischinsky, A. G., Cetkovich-Bakmas, M., Rojas, J. I., Romano, M., & Manes, F. F. (2018). Cognitive-behavioural interventions for attention deficit hyperactivity disorder (ADHD) in adults. *Cochrane Library, 2018*(3). https://doi.org/10.1002/14651858.cd010840.pub2

Lorey, K., & Fegert, J. M. (2021). Increasing mental health literacy in law enforcement to improve best practices in policing—introduction of an empirically derived, modular, differentiated, and end-user driven training design. *Frontiers in Psychiatry, 12*. https://doi.org/10.3389/fpsyt.2021.706587

Magnus, W., Nazir, S., Anilkumar, A. C., & Shaban, K. (2023, August 8). Attention deficit hyperactivity disorder. StatPearls - NCBI Bookshelf. https://www.ncbi.nlm.nih.gov/books/NBK441838/.

Marinopoulou, M., Johnels, J. Å., Bornehag, C., Hallerbäck, M. U., & Billstedt, E. (2024). Do Wechsler intelligence scales predict academic achievement in children with ADHD or autism? A systematic review and meta-analysis. *Applied Neuropsychology Child*, 1–15. https://doi.org/10.1080/21622965.2024.2361022

Mazefsky, C. A., Herrington, J., Siegel, M., Scarpa, A., Maddox, B. B., Scahill, L., & White, S. W. (2013). The role of emotion regulation in autism spectrum disorder. *Journal of the American Academy of Child & Adolescent Psychiatry, 52*(7), 679–688. https://doi.org/10.1016/j.jaac.2013.05.006

McGraw, J. J. (2012). Tongues of men and angels: Assessing the neural correlates of glossolalia. In *BRILL eBooks* (pp. 57–79). https://doi.org/10.1163/9789004225343_005

Merlo, G., Chifari, A., Chiazzese, G., Denaro, P., Firrera, N., Lo Savio, N., Patti, S., Palmegiano, L., Taibi, D., & Seta, L. (2023). The BEHAVE application as a tool to monitor inclusive interventions for subjects with neurodevelopmental disorders. *Frontiers in Psychology, 13*. https://doi.org/10.3389/fpsyg.2022.943370

Morris-Rosendahl, D. J., & Crocq, M. (2020). Neurodevelopmental disorders—the history and future of a diagnostic concept. *Dialogues in Clinical Neuroscience, 22*(1), 65–72. https://doi.org/10.31887/dcns.2020.22.1/macrocq

Mrug, S., Molina, B. S. G., Hoza, B., Gerdes, A. C., Hinshaw, S. P., Hechtman, L., & Arnold, L. E. (2012). Peer rejection and friendships in children with attention-deficit/hyperactivity disorder: Contributions to long-term outcomes. *Journal of Abnormal Child Psychology, 40*(6), 1013–1026. https://doi.org/10.1007/s10802-012-9610-2

Mullin, A., Gokhale, A. S., Moreno-De-Luca, A., Sanyal, S., Waddington, J. L., & Faundez, V. (2013). Neurodevelopmental disorders: Mechanisms and boundary definitions from genomes, interactomes and proteomes. *Translational Psychiatry, 3*(12), e329. https://doi.org/10.1038/tp.2013.108

Nakao, M., Shirotsuki, K., & Sugaya, N. (2021). Cognitive–behavioral therapy for management of mental health and stress-related disorders: Recent advances in techniques and technologies. *BioPsychoSocial Medicine, 15*(1). https://doi.org/10.1186/s13030-021-00219-w

Novotney, A. (n.d.). *The risks of social isolation*. https://www.apa.org. https://www.apa.org/monitor/2019/05/ce-corner-isolation.

Orsmond, G. I., Shattuck, P. T., Cooper, B. P., Sterzing, P. R., & Anderson, K. A. (2013). Social participation among young adults with an autism spectrum disorder. *Journal of Autism and Developmental Disorders, 43*(11), 2710–2719. https://doi.org/10.1007/s10803-013-1833-8

Patra, K. P., & De Jesus, O. (2023, August 23). Echolalia. StatPearls - NCBI Bookshelf. https://www.ncbi.nlm.nih.gov/books/NBK565908/.

Rawdon, N., Vinter, L. P., Allely, C., & Wheatley, R. (2024). Exploring the experiences of an autistic male convicted of stalking. *Journal of Forensic Psychiatry and Psychology*, 1–34. https://doi.org/10.1080/14789949.2024.2339537

Rich, E. C., Loo, S. K., Yang, M., Dang, J., & Smalley, S. L. (2009). Social functioning difficulties in ADHD: Association with PDD risk. *Clinical Child Psychology and Psychiatry, 14*(3), 329–344. https://doi.org/10.1177/1359104508100890

Rosello, B., Berenguer, C., Baixauli, I., García, R., & Miranda, A. (2020). Theory of mind profiles in children with autism Spectrum disorder: Adaptive/social skills and pragmatic competence. *Frontiers in Psychology, 11*. https://doi.org/10.3389/fpsyg.2020.567401

Russell, H. F., Richardson, E. J., Bombardier, C. H., Dixon, T. M., Huston, T. A., Rose, J., Sheaffer, D., Smith, S. A., & Ullrich, P. M. (2015). Professional standards of practice for psychologists, social workers, and counselors in SCI rehabilitation. *Journal of Spinal Cord Medicine, 39*(2), 127–145. https://doi.org/10.1080/10790268.2015.1119966

Rutherford, M., Maciver, D., Johnston, L., Prior, S., & Forsyth, K. (2021). Development of a pathway for multidisciplinary neurodevelopmental assessment and diagnosis in children and young people. *Children, 8*(11), 1033. https://doi.org/10.3390/children8111033

Samson, A. C., Huber, O., & Gross, J. J. (2012). Emotion regulation in Asperger's syndrome and high-functioning autism. *Emotion, 12*(4), 659–665. https://doi.org/10.1037/a0027975

Sanvictores, T., & Mendez, M. D. (2022, September 18). Types of parenting styles and effects on children. StatPearls - NCBI Bookshelf. https://www.ncbi.nlm.nih.gov/books/NBK568743/.

Saylor, K. E., & Amann, B. H. (2016). Impulsive aggression as a comorbidity of attention-deficit/hyperactivity disorder in children and adolescents. *Journal of Child and Adolescent Psychopharmacology, 26*(1), 19–25. https://doi.org/10.1089/cap.2015.0126

Schachar, R. J., Dupuis, A., Arnold, P. D., Anagnostou, E., Kelley, E., Georgiades, S., Nicolson, R., Townes, P., Burton, C. L., & Crosbie, J. (2022). Autism spectrum disorder and attention-deficit/hyperactivity disorder: Shared or unique neurocognitive profiles? *Research on Child and Adolescent Psychopathology, 51*(1), 17–31. https://doi.org/10.1007/s10802-022-00958-6

Schaeffer, J., El-Raziq, M. A., Castroviejo, E., Durrleman, S., Ferré, S., Grama, I., Hendriks, P., Kissine, M., Manenti, M., Marinis, T., Meir, N., Novogrodsky, R., Perovic, A., Panzeri, F., Silleresi, S., Sukenik, N., Vicente, A., Zebib, R., Prévost, P., & Tuller, L. (2023). Language in autism: Domains, profiles and co-occurring conditions. *Journal of Neural Transmission, 130*(3), 433–457. https://doi.org/10.1007/s00702-023-02592-y

Sharma, M. K., Sharma, M. P., & Marimuthu, P. (2016). Mindfulness-based program for management of aggression among youth: A follow-up study. *Indian Journal of Psychological Medicine, 38*(3), 213–216. https://doi.org/10.4103/0253-7176.183087

Shaw, P., Eckstrand, K., Sharp, W., Blumenthal, J., Lerch, J. P., Greenstein, D., Clasen, L., Evans, A., Giedd, J., & Rapoport, J. L. (2007). Attention-deficit/hyperactivity disorder is characterized by a delay in cortical maturation. *Proceedings of the National Academy of Sciences, 104*(49), 19649–19654. https://doi.org/10.1073/pnas.0707741104

Shen, M. D., & Piven, J. (2017). Brain and behavior development in autism from birth through infancy. *Dialogues in Clinical Neuroscience, 19*(4), 325–333. https://doi.org/10.31887/dcns.2017.19.4/mshen

Sibley, M. H., Pelham, W. E., Molina, B. S. G., Gnagy, E. M., Waschbusch, D. A., Biswas, A., MacLean, M. G., Babinski, D. E., & Karch, K. M. (2010). The delinquency outcomes of boys with ADHD with and without comorbidity. *Journal of Abnormal Child Psychology, 39*(1), 21–32. https://doi.org/10.1007/s10802-010-9443-9

Verghese, C., & Abdijadid, S. (2023, January 2). Methylphenidate. StatPearls - NCBI Bookshelf. https://www.ncbi.nlm.nih.gov/books/NBK482451/.

Vogindroukas, I., Stankova, M., Chelas, E., & Proedrou, A. (2022). Language and speech characteristics in autism. *Neuropsychiatric Disease and Treatment, 18*, 2367–2377. https://doi.org/10.2147/ndt.s331987

Wang, L., Wang, B., Wu, C., Wang, J., & Sun, M. (2023). Autism Spectrum disorder: Neurodevelopmental risk factors, biological mechanism, and precision therapy. *International Journal of Molecular Sciences, 24*(3), 1819. https://doi.org/10.3390/ijms24031819

Woodhouse, E., Hollingdale, J., Davies, L., Al-Attar, Z., Young, S., Vinter, L. P., Agyemang, K., Bartlett, C., Berryessa, C., Chaplin, E., Deeley, Q., Freckelton, I., Gerry, F., Gudjonsson, G., Maras, K., Mattison, M., McCarthy, J., Mills, R., Misch, P., et al. (2024). Identification and support of autistic individuals within the UK criminal justice system: A practical approach based upon professional consensus with input from lived experience. *BMC Medicine, 22*(1). https://doi.org/10.1186/s12916-024-03320-3

Yizengaw, S. S. (2021). Effect of social skills training on interpersonal interactions of children with autism: An interventional research. *International Journal of Developmental Disabilities, 68*(6), 858–866. https://doi.org/10.1080/20473869.2021.1902730

Young, S., Greer, B., & Church, R. (2017). Juvenile delinquency, welfare, justice and therapeutic interventions: A global perspective. *BJPsych Bulletin, 41*(1), 21–29. https://doi.org/10.1192/pb.bp.115.052274

Yu, Y., Ozonoff, S., & Miller, M. (2023). Assessment of autism spectrum disorder. *Assessment, 31*(1), 24–41. https://doi.org/10.1177/10731911231173089

Neuropsychology of Criminal Responsibility

1 Introduction

The intersection of neuropsychology and criminal law presents a profound and complex landscape, where the intricacies of brain function meet the foundational principles of justice. Understanding criminal responsibility through a neuropsychological lens involves delving into the ways in which brain activity influences a person's capacity to comprehend their actions and the societal laws that govern them. As our understanding of the human brain has expanded through advancements in neuroscience, it has become increasingly clear that neurological conditions—ranging from traumatic brain injuries (TBIs) to chronic neurodegenerative diseases—can significantly affect an individual's cognition, behavior, and moral reasoning. This chapter aims to explore these connections, providing insights into how such brain disorders impact legal determinations of culpability.

At the heart of criminal responsibility lies the principle that individuals must possess a certain level of understanding and intent regarding their actions to be held accountable for them. Traditional legal frameworks often hinge on concepts of intent and moral agency, suggesting that a rational, autonomous individual must understand the nature and consequences of their actions to be deemed criminally liable. However, when neurological impairments are present, this foundational assumption can be called into question. For instance, individuals suffering from conditions like schizophrenia, severe epilepsy, or traumatic brain injuries may experience altered perceptions of reality or diminished cognitive capacities, complicating assessments of their intent and culpability during criminal proceedings.

Recent empirical research highlights the need for a more nuanced understanding of how specific brain disorders can distort cognitive functions essential for maintaining criminal responsibility. Studies indicate that brain injuries can impair judgment, inhibit impulse control, and disrupt emotional regulation, factors that can lead to behaviors that fall outside the typical expectations of societal norms. For

© The Author(s), under exclusive license to Springer Nature Switzerland AG 2025

K. J. Reddy, *Foundations of Criminal Forensic Neuropsychology*,
https://doi.org/10.1007/978-3-031-83771-5_5

example, individuals with damage to the prefrontal cortex may exhibit impulsivity and a reduced ability to foresee the consequences of their actions. This raises critical questions about the fairness of applying conventional legal standards to individuals whose neurological conditions have fundamentally altered their ability to navigate moral and legal obligations.

As this chapter examines various case laws and empirical findings, it will become evident that the standards of criminal responsibility are not static; they are evolving in response to emerging neuropsychological evidence. Courts increasingly consider neuropsychological evaluations in culpability decisions, acknowledging that an individual's brain condition can significantly impact their criminal actions. This shift necessitates an ongoing dialogue between legal professionals and neuroscientists to ensure that the judicial system accurately interprets and integrates neuropsychological evidence within legal frameworks.

Through detailed case studies, this chapter will illustrate the challenges faced by the legal system in adjudicating cases involving individuals with neurological disabilities. For instance, cases where defendants exhibit clear evidence of neurological impairments, yet are nonetheless prosecuted under traditional legal standards, reveal the complex interplay between neurobiological factors and the judicial concepts of intent and moral responsibility. These case studies serve not only to highlight the limitations of current legal paradigms but also to underscore the ethical imperatives of adapting legal standards to accommodate the realities of neurological impairments.

One of the critical lessons from this exploration is the necessity for a sophisticated understanding of the factors that contribute to criminal guilt, particularly in individuals with brain dysfunctions. The implications extend beyond individual cases; they challenge existing sentencing guidelines and underscore the need for tailored approaches that account for the unique circumstances surrounding each defendant. As the judicial system grapples with these questions, it becomes increasingly clear that the integration of neuropsychological insights is essential for fostering a fair and just legal process.

In conclusion, the neuropsychology of criminal responsibility represents a vital area of inquiry that demands the attention of both legal and psychological professionals. As we advance in our understanding of the brain and its impact on behavior, it is imperative to consider how these insights can inform our legal standards and practices. This chapter aims to illuminate these intersections, fostering a deeper appreciation of the complexities surrounding criminal responsibility and the potential for reform in how we approach culpability in light of neurological impairments. As we navigate this evolving terrain, we must remain vigilant in ensuring that justice is both served and equitable, reflecting the intricate realities of human cognition and behavior.

2 Objectives

The field of neuropsychology offers critical insights into the complexities of human behavior, particularly in the context of criminality and legal responsibility. Understanding the interplay between brain function and criminal behavior is essential for both the legal system and mental health professionals. This chapter aims to articulate the objectives of examining neuropsychology in relation to criminal behavior, specifically focusing on how brain disorders, injuries, and diseases affect an individual's legal responsibility, as well as analyzing the influence of neuropsychological evidence on courtroom decisions and sentencing.

2.1 Examining the Impact of Brain Disorders on Legal Responsibility

One of the primary objectives of this chapter is to explore how various brain disorders and injuries influence an individual's understanding of their actions and their ability to conform to societal norms. The legal concept of criminal responsibility is predicated on the assumption that individuals have the capacity to comprehend the nature of their actions and the consequences thereof. However, when neurological impairments are present, this assumption becomes problematic.

Brain disorders, such as traumatic brain injury (TBI), schizophrenia, and certain neurodegenerative diseases, can significantly impair cognitive functions essential for rational decision-making and moral reasoning. For instance, individuals with TBI may experience deficits in impulse control, judgment, and emotional regulation, leading to behavior that deviates from societal expectations (Kocka & Gagnon, 2014). By examining case studies and empirical research, this chapter seeks to illustrate how these impairments can undermine an individual's legal responsibility, challenging the conventional notions of guilt and intent.

The objective is to foster a deeper understanding of how specific brain dysfunctions manifest in behavior, potentially absolving or mitigating legal culpability. By exploring the nuances of mental states affected by neurological conditions, the chapter highlights the importance of integrating neuropsychological evaluations into legal proceedings. This can ensure that individuals with significant cognitive impairments are not unjustly punished under a framework that fails to account for their diminished capacity for moral reasoning.

2.2 Analyzing Neuropsychological Evidence in Courtroom Decisions

Another crucial objective of this chapter is to analyze how neuropsychological evidence influences courtroom decisions and sentencing. As the legal landscape evolves, there is a growing recognition of the importance of considering neurological factors in determining culpability. Neuropsychological evaluations provide valuable insights into an individual's mental state at the time of the offense, which can significantly impact the court's perception of their responsibility.

Neuropsychological evidence can take various forms, including brain imaging results, cognitive assessments, and expert testimony regarding the effects of brain disorders on behavior. Courts increasingly rely on this evidence to understand the defendant's mental condition, which can lead to more informed and equitable decisions. For example, if a defendant is found to have a significant cognitive impairment that affected their understanding of the crime they committed, this may lead to a verdict of not guilty by reason of insanity or reduced sentencing (Insanity Defense, 2020).

The chapter will analyze specific cases where neuropsychological evidence played a pivotal role in courtroom outcomes. These analyses aim to demonstrate how such evidence can influence jury perceptions, judicial reasoning, and ultimately, the legal consequences faced by individuals with neurological impairments. The objective is to elucidate the complex dynamics at play in legal contexts and underscore the importance of a multidisciplinary approach that includes insights from neuroscience.

2.3 Implications for Sentencing and the Justice System

An important objective of this chapter is to examine the implications of neuropsychological findings for sentencing practices and the broader justice system. Understanding how brain disorders affect behavior is not only crucial for legal determinations of guilt but also for shaping fair and appropriate sentencing guidelines. The chapter will discuss how traditional punitive approaches may fail to account for the underlying neurological issues that contribute to criminal behavior.

As the chapter explores the evolving standards of criminal responsibility, it will highlight the need for reform in sentencing practices that consider the individual's cognitive capacities and the potential for rehabilitation. Individuals with neurological impairments may benefit more from therapeutic interventions than from incarceration, suggesting a need for alternative sentencing models that emphasize rehabilitation over punishment. This objective aims to provoke critical discussions about the ethics of punishment and the role of the justice system in addressing the complexities of criminal behavior.

In summary, the objectives of the chapter on neuropsychology and criminal behavior are multifaceted, focusing on the impact of brain disorders on legal responsibility and the influence of neuropsychological evidence on courtroom decisions. By examining how neurological impairments can complicate traditional notions of culpability, the chapter seeks to provide a nuanced understanding of criminal behavior that accounts for the intricacies of human cognition. Additionally, by analyzing the role of neuropsychological evidence in shaping legal outcomes, the chapter aims to promote a more informed and equitable judicial process.

Ultimately, the insights gained from this exploration have significant implications for the justice system, urging a reconsideration of how we define criminal responsibility and the appropriate responses to individuals affected by brain disorders. As the fields of neuropsychology and law continue to intersect, it is essential to advocate for a legal framework that reflects the complexities of human behavior, fostering a system that is both just and compassionate.

3 Theoretical Foundations of Criminal Behavior

The intricate relationship between neuropsychology and criminal responsibility is a compelling area of study that illuminates how brain function can significantly influence behavior and cognitive processes. As neuropsychology investigates the connections between brain activity and psychological functioning, it becomes an essential lens through which to examine the complexities of criminal behavior. Understanding the theoretical foundations of criminal responsibility through this lens not only enhances our comprehension of human actions but also prompts critical discussions about justice, accountability, and the implications of neurological impairments.

Neuropsychology is fundamentally concerned with how brain function affects behavior and cognitive processes. This field seeks to understand how various brain regions contribute to different aspects of cognition, emotion, and behavior. When applied to criminal behavior, neuropsychology offers insights into how specific neurological impairments—such as traumatic brain injuries, developmental disorders, and neurodegenerative diseases—can influence an individual's capacity to comprehend their actions and the consequences thereof.

Understanding these impairments is crucial for evaluating criminal responsibility. Traditional legal frameworks often assume that individuals possess the cognitive capacity to understand the nature of their actions and the laws they are expected to follow. However, when brain function is compromised, this assumption can become problematic. For example, a person with a significant impairment in impulse control due to a frontal lobe injury may act impulsively, lacking the ability to foresee the consequences of their actions. This raises important questions about the fairness of applying conventional standards of culpability to individuals whose neurological conditions fundamentally alter their decision-making processes.

Theoretical foundations of criminal responsibility often draw from various disciplines, including philosophy, psychology, and law. Several key theories attempt to define the criteria for establishing an individual's legal culpability. The most prominent of these include the concepts of intent, knowledge, and volition.

1. **Intent**: Legal systems typically require that a person possesses intent to commit a crime for them to be held criminally responsible. This notion is rooted in the belief that individuals must understand what they are doing and have the capacity to choose their actions (Keiler et al., 2014). Neuropsychological research complicates this notion by highlighting cases where individuals may lack the cognitive ability to form intent due to neurological impairments. For example, a person experiencing severe psychosis may not fully grasp the nature of their actions, thereby complicating legal determinations of intent (Calabrese & Khalili, 2023).
2. **Knowledge**: The requirement of knowledge is closely tied to the concept of intent. It posits that individuals must be aware of the nature and consequences of their actions to be held accountable. Neuropsychology provides valuable insights into how conditions such as dementia or severe mental illness can impair an individual's knowledge of their actions. In such cases, the cognitive distortions caused by neurological conditions can lead to behaviors that are criminal yet not reflective of a clear understanding of their wrongful nature (Rnic et al., 2016).
3. **Volition**: Volition refers to the capacity to make choices and control one's actions. This concept is crucial in the evaluation of criminal responsibility, as it underscores the importance of free will in determining culpability. Neuropsychological disorders, particularly those affecting impulse control and emotional regulation, can significantly undermine an individual's volitional capacity (Frith, 2013). For instance, individuals with certain personality disorders may exhibit behaviors driven by pathological urges, raising questions about their ability to exercise free will in a legal context.

3.1 The Role of Neurological Impairments in Criminal Behavior

Neurological impairments are pivotal in understanding criminal behavior and its complexities. Research has shown that various brain conditions can lead to changes in personality, judgment, and moral reasoning, thereby influencing an individual's propensity for criminality.

1. **Traumatic Brain Injury (TBI)**: Individuals with TBI often experience cognitive deficits, including impaired judgment and reduced impulse control. Studies have demonstrated that such impairments can lead to an increased likelihood of engaging in criminal behavior (Maresca et al., 2023). Understanding these rela-

tionships is vital for developing appropriate interventions and legal considerations for individuals who have sustained brain injuries.
2. **Neurodevelopmental Disorders**: Conditions such as attention-deficit hyperactivity disorder (ADHD) and autism spectrum disorder (ASD) can also play a role in criminal behavior. Individuals with ADHD, for example, may struggle with impulse control and executive functioning, leading to behaviors that may be deemed criminal (George, 2022). An understanding of these disorders within the context of neuropsychology highlights the need for tailored approaches to both prevention and intervention in the criminal justice system.
3. **Mental Illness**: The interplay between mental illness and criminal behavior is well-documented. Many mental health disorders can affect an individual's ability to comprehend their actions fully. The recognition of this relationship has led to a growing emphasis on mental health assessments in legal contexts, as well as the need for alternative sentencing options that consider an individual's psychological state.

The theoretical foundations of criminal responsibility, when viewed through the lens of neuropsychology, underscore the need for a nuanced understanding of how brain function affects behavior and cognitive processes. As we explore the impact of neurological impairments on criminal behavior, it becomes clear that traditional notions of intent, knowledge, and volition must be reconsidered to accommodate the realities of brain function.

This exploration not only challenges the legal system to adapt its standards of culpability but also advocates for a more compassionate and informed approach to justice. By integrating neuropsychological insights into discussions of criminal responsibility, we can foster a legal framework that is both just and responsive to the complexities of human behavior, ultimately leading to more equitable outcomes for individuals impacted by neurological disorders.

4 Impact of Brain Disorders

4.1 Schizophrenia and Psychotic Disorders

The intersection of neuropsychology and criminal responsibility is particularly complex in cases involving schizophrenia and other psychotic disorders. Schizophrenia, characterized by disturbances in thought processes, perceptions, and emotions, can significantly impair an individual's grasp of reality, judgment, and ability to control their actions. Understanding these effects is crucial for assessing legal culpability, as psychotic episodes can lead to behaviors that are criminal yet not necessarily reflective of a person's moral agency. This section explores the neuropsychological underpinnings of schizophrenia, its impact on behavior, and the legal implications of these effects, supported by empirical research and relevant case studies.

4.2 Impairments in Reality Perception and Judgment

Schizophrenia is often marked by symptoms such as hallucinations, delusions, disorganized thinking, and impaired insight (Schizophrenia, n.d.). These symptoms can drastically alter an individual's perception of reality and influence their judgment. For instance, hallucinations—perceptual experiences without external stimuli—can lead individuals to act on commands or threats that do not exist in reality. Delusions, defined as strongly held false beliefs, may cause a person to misinterpret social cues or perceive benign situations as threatening.

Research indicates that individuals with schizophrenia often exhibit impaired executive functioning, which includes difficulties with planning, decision-making, and impulse control. A study by Green et al. (2000) highlighted that cognitive deficits in schizophrenia significantly correlated with functional outcomes, including social behavior and legal encounters (Green et al., 2000). Individuals with impaired judgment may fail to foresee the consequences of their actions, raising critical questions about their capacity to understand the nature of their behavior in legal contexts.

4.3 Case Studies Illustrating the Impact of Schizophrenia on Criminal Behavior

Several case studies exemplify how schizophrenia can lead to criminal behavior under circumstances that challenge conventional notions of culpability. One notable case involved a man diagnosed with schizophrenia who committed a violent act during a psychotic episode (Understanding Psychosis, n.d.). During the incident, he experienced auditory hallucinations that commanded him to harm another individual. When apprehended, the defendant's lack of insight into his condition and inability to perceive reality were pivotal in determining his culpability.

In another case, a woman with a long history of schizophrenia committed theft while in a delusional state, believing she was acting under divine instruction. Expert testimonies regarding her mental state were crucial in the trial, ultimately leading to a verdict of not guilty by reason of insanity (Appelbaum, 2006). These cases illustrate the challenges faced by the legal system in navigating the complexities of criminal responsibility when mental illness is involved (Appelbaum, 2006).

4.4 Legal Implications of Psychotic Episodes on Culpability

The legal implications of psychotic episodes on culpability are significant and continue to evolve. Most legal systems operate on the assumption that individuals possess the ability to understand their actions and control their behaviors. However, when a person is in the throes of a psychotic episode, this assumption can be deeply flawed. The M'Naghten Rule, which is a legal standard used to determine criminal insanity, states that a defendant may be excused from liability if, at the time of the offense, they were suffering from a severe mental illness that impaired their ability to understand the nature of their actions or distinguish right from wrong (Busby, 2023).

Empirical research supports the notion that individuals with schizophrenia may lack the necessary cognitive and emotional capacities to be held fully accountable for their actions. A study by Del Pinal & Nathan (2013) found that individuals with psychotic disorders often have diminished capacities for rational thought and decision-making during episodes. This research suggests that the intersection of neuropsychology and law must account for the cognitive impairments associated with schizophrenia when determining culpability.

4.5 The Role of Neuropsychological Evaluations in Legal Contexts

Neuropsychological evaluations play a crucial role in assessing the impact of schizophrenia on criminal behavior. These assessments can provide insights into an individual's cognitive functioning, including their capacity for impulse control, judgment, and insight. By employing standardized tests and expert evaluations, legal professionals can better understand how a defendant's mental state may have influenced their actions during a crime.

Neuropsychological assessments may reveal deficits in executive functioning, helping to elucidate how these impairments affected the defendant's ability to conform to legal standards. Such evaluations can be instrumental in cases where a defendant's mental health history is a critical factor in determining legal outcomes and guiding decisions regarding insanity defenses or alternative sentencing options (Math et al., 2015).

5 Mood Disorders

Mood disorders, particularly bipolar disorder and major depressive disorder (MDD), are characterized by significant fluctuations in mood, energy, and activity levels that impair everyday functioning. Bipolar disorder involves alternating episodes of mania and depression, each with distinct cognitive and behavioral symptoms. Manic episodes are marked by elevated mood, impulsivity, and hyperactivity, while depressive episodes involve feelings of hopelessness, lethargy, and impaired decision-making.

In contrast, severe depression, as seen in MDD, presents prolonged periods of low mood, loss of interest in activities, and significant cognitive impairments. These impairments can affect judgment, concentration, and impulse control, making it difficult for individuals to understand or manage their behavior effectively. Given the profound impact these mood disorders have on cognition and behavior, understanding their role in criminal behavior is crucial for assessing culpability and appropriate legal responses.

5.1 *Bipolar Disorder: Manic Episodes and Impulsive Behavior*

Bipolar disorder is a mood disorder that can have a dramatic effect on an individual's behavior, particularly during manic episodes. Mania is characterized by elevated or irritable mood, increased energy, and a decreased need for sleep. While individuals in a manic state may experience heightened creativity and productivity, they are also prone to impulsivity, poor decision-making, and reckless behavior, which can sometimes lead to criminal actions.

5.2 *Impulsivity and Irrational Behavior in Mania*

During manic episodes, individuals often engage in risky or impulsive activities without fully considering the consequences of their actions. This can manifest in behaviors such as reckless driving, excessive spending, substance abuse, or even violent actions. Impulsivity in mania stems from dysfunctions in the brain's prefrontal cortex, which is responsible for executive functions such as planning, decision-making, and impulse control. Studies have shown that individuals experiencing mania exhibit impaired activity in the prefrontal cortex, leading to reduced inhibition and difficulty in regulating behavior.

In legal contexts, impulsivity during manic episodes raises questions about criminal responsibility. If a person's behavior is driven by impaired judgment and loss of self-control due to mania, traditional standards of legal culpability, which assume rational decision-making, may not be entirely applicable. For instance, a person in a manic state who engages in criminal activity, such as theft or assault, may not fully comprehend the gravity of their actions or foresee the legal consequences, complicating the assessment of intent and responsibility.

5.3 *Case Studies of Mania and Criminal Behavior*

Several case studies highlight the legal challenges of dealing with criminal behavior resulting from manic episodes.

Mr. T, a 38-year-old man, was charged with assault and vandalism after a violent altercation at a local market. According to witnesses, Mr. T displayed erratic and aggressive behavior, shouting incoherently and damaging property before physically attacking a vendor. Upon arrest, he was visibly agitated, displaying elevated mood, pressured speech, and grandiose delusions, consistent with symptoms of mania. Mr. T had a known history of bipolar I disorder, characterized by episodes of severe mania and depression. At the time of the offense, he was reportedly off his medication and had been experiencing increasing manic symptoms for several weeks. His defense team argued that his actions were a direct result of his mental illness, requesting a forensic neuropsychological assessment to evaluate his cognitive and emotional state, as well as his capacity to understand his actions during the crime. The primary goal of the assessment was to determine whether Mr. T's manic episode influenced his criminal behavior and to assess his current cognitive functioning, including impulse control, judgment, and the ability to distinguish right from wrong.

The assessment revealed that Mr. T was experiencing severe cognitive and emotional dysregulation consistent with an acute manic episode. The neuropsychological tests indicated significant impairments in executive functioning, including poor impulse control, impaired judgment, and a diminished capacity to evaluate the consequences of his actions. His thought processes were characterized by grandiosity and delusional thinking, further compromising his decision-making abilities. Collateral information from family members corroborated that Mr. T's behavior had become increasingly erratic in the weeks leading up to the crime, with marked sleep disturbances, hyperactivity, and excessive spending—common symptoms of mania. These findings supported the conclusion that his criminal behavior was directly linked to his manic state rather than deliberate or malicious intent. Additionally, Mr. T's poor insight into his mental illness and lack of adherence to his treatment regimen were identified as significant risk factors contributing to his behavior. The assessment highlighted the importance of consistent medication compliance and psychiatric follow-up to manage his symptoms effectively.

The neuropsychological assessment played a crucial role in informing the court's understanding of Mr. T's mental state at the time of the crime. The findings were presented in court, emphasizing that Mr. T's actions were significantly influenced by his manic episode and impaired cognitive functioning. Based on the neuropsychologist's report, the court acknowledged that Mr. T was not fully responsible for his actions due to his mental illness. He was found guilty but was granted a reduced sentence with mandated psychiatric treatment, including inpatient stabilization and a structured treatment plan involving medication management, psychotherapy, and close monitoring by mental health professionals. The case underscored the need for tailored management plans for individuals with severe mental illnesses in the criminal justice system, prioritizing treatment over punishment when mental health significantly impairs judgment and behavior.

These case studies underscore the need for the legal system to account for the neuropsychological effects of mania when assessing criminal responsibility. Individuals experiencing manic episodes may lack the capacity to understand or control their behavior, warranting a more nuanced approach to legal culpability that considers mental health as a significant factor.

5.4 *Bipolar Disorder: Depressive Episodes and Impaired Decision-Making*

While manic episodes in bipolar disorder are associated with impulsive and reckless behavior, depressive episodes present a different set of challenges. During periods of severe depression, individuals often experience profound emotional and cognitive impairments that can affect their decision-making, motivation, and ability to function. These impairments can also lead to criminal behavior, particularly when depression manifests as hopelessness, apathy, or self-destructive actions (Chand & Arif, 2023).

5.5 *Impaired Decision-Making in Depression*

Severe depression is characterized by deficits in cognitive processes such as attention, memory, and decision-making. Research has shown that individuals with major depressive disorder often exhibit impaired functioning in the prefrontal cortex and the anterior cingulate cortex, regions of the brain involved in decision-making, planning, and impulse control. These impairments can result in difficulty assessing the consequences of actions, leading to poor judgment and a lack of self-regulation.

One of the most troubling aspects of depression is its ability to distort an individual's perception of reality. People with severe depression may believe that their situation is hopeless, leading to impaired decision-making and behaviors that are irrational or self-destructive. This can manifest in actions such as theft, substance abuse, or even violence, as the person struggles to cope with their overwhelming emotional pain (What Is Depression?, n.d.).

In legal settings, the cognitive impairments associated with depression can affect determinations of criminal responsibility. For example, a person with severe depression who engages in criminal behavior may do so out of desperation or an inability to think clearly, rather than with malicious intent. These factors complicate traditional notions of culpability, which are based on the assumption that individuals are capable of making rational decisions.

5.6 *Case Studies of Depression and Criminal Behavior*

A notable case involving depression and criminal responsibility occurred when a man suffering from major depressive disorder committed arson after losing his job and experiencing significant financial stress. His legal team argued that his depression had impaired his judgment and led him to believe that destroying his property was a rational solution to his problems. The court considered his mental state at the time of the offense and issued a reduced sentence, coupled with mandatory psychiatric treatment.

In another case, a woman with severe depression shoplifted during a period of emotional distress. Her defense emphasized that her depressive episode had affected her ability to make rational decisions and that her actions were not motivated by criminal intent. The court took her mental health condition into account, leading to a more lenient sentence focused on rehabilitation rather than punishment.

Defendant D, a 42-year-old man, was charged with arson after setting fire to his own home. At the time of the incident, Defendant D was alone, and the fire was quickly contained, resulting in no physical harm to others but significant property damage. Witnesses, including neighbors and family members, reported that Defendant D had been increasingly withdrawn, expressing feelings of hopelessness, guilt, and worthlessness in the weeks leading up to the crime. A clinical review of his history revealed that Defendant D had been diagnosed with major depressive disorder, severe psychotic features, characterized by pervasive low mood, suicidal ideation, and episodes of severe guilt delusions. He had been prescribed antidepressants and antipsychotics but was not consistently adhering to his medication regimen, and his mental state had deteriorated significantly. The defense argued that Defendant D's actions were a direct result of his severe depression and psychotic symptoms, leading to impaired judgment and decision-making. The primary goal of the forensic neuropsychological assessment was to evaluate Defendant D's cognitive functioning, determine the impact of his severe depression on his behavior, and assess his capacity to understand the nature and consequences of his actions during the incident.

The forensic neuropsychologist conducted a comprehensive evaluation, including a detailed clinical interview, review of medical and psychiatric records, and administration of a battery of neuropsychological tests designed to assess cognitive functioning, emotional state, and insight into his actions. The neuropsychological assessment revealed significant impairments in Defendant D's cognitive functioning, particularly in executive functioning, decision-making, and problem-solving abilities. Tests showed that Defendant D had marked difficulties with attention, processing speed, and working memory, which are commonly affected in severe depression. His performance suggested that his cognitive impairments were closely linked to his depressive state, which severely impacted his ability to make rational decisions. During the assessment, Defendant D expressed overwhelming guilt and delusional beliefs that setting the fire was a form of self-punishment and a way to rid himself of his perceived failures. His cognitive distortions were directly tied to his depressive and psychotic symptoms, demonstrating a diminished capacity to appreciate the wrongfulness of his actions at the time of the crime. Collateral interviews with family members and a review of psychiatric records confirmed that Defendant D's depressive symptoms had been worsening for months, with escalating suicidal ideation and impaired daily functioning. The neuropsychologist concluded that Defendant D's actions were not driven by malice or intent to harm others but were instead the result of severe cognitive and emotional dysregulation caused by his mental illness.

This case study highlights how depressive episodes can lead to irrational or impulsive behavior that may be criminal but is not necessarily indicative of moral culpability. By considering the neuropsychological effects of depression, courts can make more informed decisions that balance the need for justice with the recognition of mental health issues.

5.7 *Severe Depression and the Loss of Self-Control*

One of the most significant aspects of severe depression is the profound loss of self-control that individuals may experience. Unlike mania, which is characterized by heightened energy and impulsivity, depression often involves lethargy, hopelessness, and a lack of motivation. However, this emotional state can still lead to criminal behavior, particularly when individuals feel they have no other options or when their impaired judgment leads to poor decision-making.

The loss of self-control in depression is closely tied to dysfunction in brain areas responsible for regulating behavior. Studies have shown that the prefrontal cortex, which is involved in decision-making and self-regulation, is often hypoactive in individuals with severe depression (Drevets et al., 1997). This lack of activity can result in an inability to inhibit negative thoughts or impulses, leading to actions that are irrational or destructive.

5.8 *Legal Implications of Mood Disorders in Criminal Responsibility*

The legal implications of mood disorders, particularly bipolar disorder and severe depression, are significant when considering criminal responsibility. Traditional legal frameworks often assume that individuals have the capacity to make rational decisions and understand the consequences of their actions. However, the neuropsychological effects of mood disorders challenge this assumption, as individuals in manic or depressive states may lack the cognitive and emotional capacities necessary for rational decision-making (Ghiasi et al., 2023).

5.9 *Insanity Defense and Mood Disorders*

One of the key legal defenses used in cases involving mood disorders is the insanity defense, which argues that the defendant was not capable of understanding the nature of their actions due to a mental illness. This defense is often employed in cases where individuals with bipolar disorder or severe depression engage in criminal behavior during manic or depressive episodes. The insanity defense hinges on the idea that the individual's mental state at the time of the offense impaired their ability to differentiate right from wrong or control their actions.

Empirical research supports the notion that individuals with mood disorders may lack the necessary mental faculties to be held fully accountable for their actions. For instance, studies have shown that individuals with bipolar disorder exhibit significant cognitive deficits during manic and depressive episodes, which can affect their decision-making and impulse control (Robinson et al., 2006). Similarly, individuals with severe depression may experience impaired judgment and decision-making abilities, leading to irrational or self-destructive behavior.

5.10 *Alternative Sentencing and Treatment*

In light of the neuropsychological impairments associated with mood disorders, some legal systems have adopted alternative sentencing options for individuals with mental health conditions. Rather than imposing traditional punishments, such as incarceration, courts may mandate psychiatric treatment or rehabilitation programs designed to address the underlying mental health issues (Rössler, 2006). This approach recognizes that individuals with mood disorders may benefit more from mental health interventions than from punitive measures, particularly when their criminal behavior is driven by psychiatric symptoms.

6 Neurodevelopmental Disorders

Neurodevelopmental disorders (NDDs), such as autism spectrum disorder (ASD), attention deficit hyperactivity disorder (ADHD), and intellectual disabilities, significantly impact cognitive, social, and behavioral development. These disorders often present unique challenges in the legal context, particularly when it comes to understanding criminal behavior and determining legal culpability (Ghiasi et al., 2023). Given the cognitive and behavioral impairments associated with NDDs, individuals diagnosed with these disorders may struggle with impulse control, social understanding, and moral reasoning, which can lead to criminal actions that deviate from societal norms. This section explores the effects of NDDs on criminal behavior, focusing on their impact within the legal system.

Individuals with neurodevelopmental disorders frequently exhibit cognitive impairments that affect their ability to reason, make decisions, and control impulses. For example, individuals with ADHD often experience difficulties with executive functioning, which includes planning, impulse control, and the ability to foresee the consequences of their actions. This can lead to impulsive or reckless behavior, such as theft or assault, that may be interpreted as criminal in a legal setting. Similarly, individuals with ASD may struggle with social communication, empathy, and understanding social norms, leading to behaviors that could be perceived as inappropriate or even criminal (Lee et al., 2021). For instance, someone with ASD might engage in actions that infringe on others' personal space without understanding the social boundaries they are violating. This can result in legal consequences, despite the individual's lack of intent to harm or break the law. Intellectual disabilities present another challenge in the legal context, as individuals with significant cognitive impairments may have limited understanding of legal proceedings and the consequences of their actions (Lee et al., 2021). These individuals may be more susceptible to manipulation or coercion by others, leading them to engage in criminal behavior without fully comprehending the ramifications.

The presence of a neurodevelopmental disorder complicates traditional legal assessments of criminal responsibility. In most legal systems, criminal responsibility hinges on the assumption that individuals have the capacity to understand the nature of their actions and the ability to distinguish between right and wrong. However, individuals with NDDs may not meet these criteria due to their cognitive and social deficits, raising questions about their legal culpability. The concept of mens rea, or the intent to commit a crime, is a key element in determining criminal responsibility. Individuals with NDDs may lack the ability to form mens rea due to their impaired judgment or understanding of social norms. For instance, a person with an intellectual disability might engage in a criminal act without fully understanding that their behavior is illegal or morally wrong. In such cases, the legal system must carefully evaluate the individual's mental state and cognitive functioning to determine whether they can be held fully accountable for their actions.

Neuropsychological assessments play a critical role in evaluating individuals with neurodevelopmental disorders within the legal context (Harvey, 2012). These assessments can provide insights into the cognitive, emotional, and social impairments associated with the disorder, helping legal professionals understand how these factors may have contributed to the individual's criminal behavior. In some cases, these evaluations may support an insanity defense or lead to alternative sentencing options, such as mental health treatment or rehabilitation programs, instead of traditional incarceration.

Neurodevelopmental disorders present significant challenges in the legal context when assessing criminal behavior and responsibility. The cognitive and behavioral impairments associated with these disorders often complicate traditional notions of mens rea and legal culpability. By understanding the impact of NDDs on behavior and utilizing neuropsychological assessments, the legal system can make more informed decisions that consider the unique challenges faced by individuals with neurodevelopmental disorders, ultimately fostering a more just and compassionate approach to criminal justice (Guina et al., 2022).

6.1 Case Example: Autism Spectrum Disorder

Mr. C.T. was diagnosed with autism spectrum disorder when he was 43 years of age. In one of Mr. C.T.'s psychological reports, it stated that: "adept and intelligent use of expressive language would not allow an unsuspecting observer to consider the presence of some of these more subtle qualities in his neurocognitive functioning. We believe this has been a significant stumbling block in more general recognition of the fact that [Mr C.T.] has an underlying disability, namely, Asperger's Syndrome."

Mr. C.T., a British citizen, is currently serving a life sentence (discretionary). Mr. C.T. has spent more than 10 years in prison. At the time of completing the questionnaire for the present study, Mr. C.T. was 51 years of age. Pled guilty to charges of (1) lewd, indecent, and libidinous practices and behavior; (2) making an indecent photograph contrary to s52(1)(a) of the Civic Government (Scotland) Act 1982; and (3) possession of indecent photographs contrary to s52(A)(1) of the Civic Government (Scotland) Act 1982. Mr. C.T. was convicted of Lewd, Indecent and Libidinous Practices and Behaviour and 2 x Civic Government (Scotland) Act, Section 52 (1) (a) and was sentenced to life imprisonment with a punishment part of 6 years. The victim was a girl aged between 7 and 8 years old at the time of the offenses and was known to Mr. C.T. Mr. C.T. was 37 years old at the time of the offense. As mentioned above, the Civic Government charges relate to Mr. C.T.'s having indecent photographs or pseudo-photographs of children in his possession. This also included the same victim when she was 8 years old. Mr. C.T. pled guilty to these charges, although he stated that he had not done many of the behaviors they included but had wanted to prevent his victim from being put through the trauma of trial. He said that he had not been in possession of IIOC. In a more recent communication in 2022, Mr. C.T. has stated that he admitted taking photos of his victim "but emphatically denied the images that were recovered from a zip disk that was brand new and still sealed in its security cellophane wrapping when police seized it." Also, he states that "he did not find any pornographic images arousing regardless of their nature." Given the charges (such as the taking indecent photos of a minor, which Mr. C.T.), exploring how certain features of ASD may provide the context of vulnerability to engaging in indecent images of children is important in understanding psychopathology from a criminal context.

7 Neurodegenerative Disorders

Neurodegenerative diseases, such as Alzheimer's disease, Parkinson's disease, frontotemporal dementia (FTD), and Huntington's disease, are characterized by progressive damage to the nervous system, leading to a gradual decline in cognitive, behavioral, and motor functions. These diseases can have profound effects on an individual's ability to control impulses, understand social norms, and make decisions, sometimes resulting in criminal behavior. The impact of neurodegenerative diseases on criminal responsibility presents complex challenges for the legal system, as these conditions affect cognitive processes that are crucial for determining culpability. This section explores how neurodegenerative diseases influence criminal behavior and examines the legal implications of such cases.

Neurodegenerative diseases are often associated with impairments in cognitive functions such as memory, attention, decision-making, and executive control. These impairments arise from the progressive loss of neurons and synaptic connections in regions of the brain responsible for higher-order cognitive functions.

Alzheimer's disease primarily affects memory, spatial awareness, and later, decision-making, resulting in confusion and disorientation. As the disease progresses, patients may lose the ability to understand social norms, increasing the likelihood of engaging in behavior that could be interpreted as criminal, such as theft or trespassing. Frontotemporal dementia (FTD), a less common but equally devastating condition, involves significant atrophy of the frontal and temporal lobes of the brain (Kumar et al., 2024). The frontal lobes are essential for regulating social behavior, impulse control, and moral reasoning. Damage to these areas can lead to dramatic changes in personality and behavior, including impulsivity, aggression, and inappropriate social conduct, all of which may result in criminal charges (Waltmann et al., 2021).

As neurodegenerative diseases erode cognitive and behavioral control, individuals may commit acts that are considered criminal, despite a lack of malicious intent or awareness. Common types of criminal behavior associated with neurodegenerative diseases include shoplifting or theft (Lamptey et al., 2022). Individuals with Alzheimer's disease or FTD may engage in shoplifting or theft, not out of desire to commit a crime but due to memory loss, confusion, or a failure to recognize the moral implications of their actions. Some individuals with FTD or advanced Alzheimer's may exhibit aggressive behavior toward others, including family members or caregivers, as part of the disease's progression. This aggression can result in assault charges, despite the person's inability to control their actions (Yu et al., 2018). Neurodegenerative diseases, especially FTD, can lead to disinhibition and inappropriate sexual advances, including public indecency or harassment, even in individuals with no prior history of such behavior. Cognitive decline in diseases like Alzheimer's may cause individuals to wander or become disoriented, leading them to trespass on private property or damage property unintentionally (Emmady et al., 2022).

These behaviors raise complex legal questions, particularly regarding the capacity to form criminal intent, or mens rea. In many cases, individuals with neurodegenerative diseases may not fully understand the consequences of their actions, challenging traditional legal standards of culpability. The legal system traditionally relies on the concept of mens rea, or the intent to commit a crime, as a central element of criminal responsibility. In cases involving neurodegenerative diseases, determining whether an individual had the capacity to form mens rea is complicated by cognitive impairments that affect decision-making, moral reasoning, and impulse control (Chesney, n.d.).

In cases involving neurodegenerative diseases, neuropsychological evaluations are critical in determining the extent to which cognitive decline has impaired an individual's ability to understand their actions and conform to social and legal norms. For example, individuals with FTD may lack the ability to regulate aggressive impulses or comprehend that their actions are socially or legally unacceptable. The legal doctrine of diminished capacity can be invoked when an individual's mental impairment, such as a neurodegenerative disease, affects their ability to form intent or premeditation. Courts may consider neurodegenerative diseases as mitigating factors when determining criminal responsibility, leading to reduced charges or alternative sentencing, such as mandated mental health treatment instead of incarceration (Ghiasi et al., 2023).

In some cases, defendants with neurodegenerative diseases may assert the insanity defense, arguing that their cognitive and behavioral impairments prevented them from understanding the wrongfulness of their actions. The insanity defense is based on the principle that individuals who are incapable of distinguishing right from wrong or controlling their behavior due to mental illness should not be held fully accountable for their actions (Math et al., 2015).

7.1 Case Studies

Several legal cases involving individuals with neurodegenerative diseases illustrate the challenges of applying traditional legal standards to criminal behavior resulting from cognitive decline.

This case study focuses on Mr. John Doe (a pseudonym), a 72-year-old man diagnosed with Alzheimer's disease, who was involved in criminal activity due to cognitive decline. John had no prior history of criminal behavior, but his progressive memory loss, confusion, and impaired judgment led him to engage in unlawful activities, ultimately bringing him into the legal system. The case demonstrates the complexity of assessing criminal responsibility in individuals with neurodegenerative disorders and the legal implications of Alzheimer's disease in criminal proceedings. John had been living independently with his wife until the symptoms of Alzheimer's disease began to appear in his late 60s. Initially, his family noticed mild memory lapses and occasional confusion about everyday tasks, but over time, his condition worsened. He became increasingly disoriented, often losing his way in familiar places, forgetting names, and misplacing personal belongings. Despite his cognitive decline, John's family did not seek formal medical intervention until he started exhibiting more severe symptoms of Alzheimer's, including paranoia and aggressive outbursts. At the time of the criminal incident, John had been diagnosed with moderate-stage Alzheimer's disease. One day, John entered a local grocery store near his home. He walked through the aisles, picked up several items, and left the store without paying.

The store's security personnel approached him in the parking lot and confronted him about the unpaid items. John appeared confused and defensive, claiming that he had already paid for the items. When the security guard attempted to stop him, John became agitated and aggressive, pushing the guard and causing a minor physical altercation. He was subsequently arrested for theft and assault. John was charged with theft and assault. During the legal proceedings, his defense team raised the issue of his Alzheimer's diagnosis, arguing that his cognitive impairments prevented him from understanding the nature and consequences of his actions. They presented medical records and expert testimony from a neuropsychologist who assessed John's cognitive abilities and confirmed that his Alzheimer's disease had significantly impaired his memory, judgment, and decision-making. The neuropsychologist's testimony was crucial in establishing that John's behavior was a direct result of his Alzheimer's disease. The expert explained how the progressive degeneration of John's brain had led to deficits in his ability to form criminal intent (mens rea). The neuropsychologist emphasized that John likely forgot that he needed to pay for the items, which explained his behavior in the store. He did not act with intent to steal, but rather out of confusion caused by memory loss. John's disorientation in the grocery store, combined with his failure to understand the security guard's confrontation, showed his inability to process social situations accurately. His confusion and agitation during the altercation were likely due to his inability to comprehend what was happening around him. The expert testified that John's aggressive response to the security guard was not an intentional assault but rather a consequence of his diminished impulse control, which is common in Alzheimer's patients.

Based on the neuropsychological evidence and the severity of John's Alzheimer's disease, the court found that John lacked the capacity to form the intent to commit theft or assault. His defense team successfully argued for a dismissal of the charges, emphasizing that John's actions were not the result of criminal intent but rather a consequence of his neurodegenerative condition. The court ordered that John receive ongoing medical care and supervision, including placement in a long-term care facility where his cognitive decline could be managed more appropriately. The decision reflected an understanding of the impact of Alzheimer's disease on criminal behavior and the need for alternative approaches to justice for individuals with severe cognitive impairments. The court's decision to dismiss the charges and mandate long-term care reflects the growing recognition that traditional punitive measures may not be appropriate for individuals with severe cognitive impairments. Instead, a focus on medical care and supervision ensures that individuals with Alzheimer's receive the support they need while minimizing the risk of harm to themselves and others.

When individuals with neurodegenerative diseases are charged with criminal offenses, the legal system faces ethical and practical dilemmas regarding appropriate punishment. Incarceration may not be the most suitable response, as individuals with neurodegenerative diseases often require specialized care and treatment that cannot be adequately provided in a prison setting. Instead, courts may consider alternatives.

Mandating psychiatric or neurological treatment, including placement in a long-term care facility, can ensure that individuals receive the care they need while protecting society from further harm. In cases where cognitive decline has resulted in criminal behavior, courts may assign guardians or supervisors to monitor the individual's behavior and ensure that they do not pose a risk to themselves or others. For individuals with neurodegenerative diseases who exhibit behavioral disturbances, rehabilitation programs focusing on impulse control and behavioral management may be more appropriate than traditional punitive measures.

Neurodegenerative diseases present unique challenges in the legal context when assessing criminal behavior and responsibility. The cognitive and behavioral impairments associated with conditions like Alzheimer's disease, FTD, Parkinson's disease, and Huntington's disease complicate traditional notions of criminal intent and culpability. As the legal system grapples with these challenges, it is essential to adopt a more nuanced understanding of how neurodegenerative diseases affect behavior and decision-making.

8 Effects of Brain Injuries

Traumatic brain injury (TBI) and acquired brain injury (ABI) are forms of brain damage that occur when a sudden trauma or external force injures the brain, resulting in a wide range of physical, cognitive, emotional, and behavioral impairments. TBIs can result from falls, car accidents, assaults, or sports injuries, while ABIs may be caused by strokes, infections, or lack of oxygen to the brain (Traumatic Brain Injury (TBI), n.d.). These injuries can have a profound impact on an individual's behavior, including increased aggression, impulsivity, and impaired judgment, which may lead to criminal activity. This section explores the relationship between TBI, ABI, and criminal behavior, focusing on the legal implications of these injuries.

TBI is typically classified as either mild, moderate, or severe, depending on the extent of damage to the brain and the associated symptoms. ABI, while similar in terms of outcomes, differs in that it is not caused by an external trauma but results from an internal event such as a stroke, infection, or oxygen deprivation (Brain Injury Association of America, 2023). Both TBI and ABI can affect various areas of the brain, including those responsible for impulse control, emotional regulation, and executive functioning. The frontal lobes, in particular, are crucial for decision-making, planning, moral reasoning, and inhibiting inappropriate behaviors. When the frontal lobes or other brain regions are damaged due to injury, the individual may struggle with impulsivity, aggression, and a diminished ability to conform to social norms (Pirau & Lui, 2023).

Following a brain injury, individuals may exhibit significant changes in behavior and personality. These changes are often linked to the areas of the brain that have been damaged and the extent of the injury. Common behavioral and cognitive changes associated with TBI and ABI include Impulsivity and Poor Judgment (Kocka & Gagnon, 2014). Damage to the frontal lobes can impair the ability to inhibit impulsive behaviors, leading to poor decision-making. Individuals with TBI may act without considering the consequences of their actions, increasing the likelihood of engaging in risky or illegal behavior (Pirau & Lui, 2023). Brain injuries can result in heightened irritability and aggression, even in individuals who were previously calm and even-tempered. This aggression can manifest in physical altercations, domestic violence, or other forms of criminal conduct. Injuries that affect the brain's memory centers, such as the hippocampus, can lead to memory problems and difficulty paying attention. In some cases, individuals may engage in criminal behavior, such as theft or trespassing, without remembering their actions or understanding the implications. Brain injuries often cause difficulties in managing emotions, leading to unpredictable mood swings, inappropriate emotional responses, or disproportionate reactions to stress. This emotional instability can contribute to criminal behavior, particularly in high-pressure situations (Model Systems Knowledge Translation Center (MSKTC), n.d.). Damage to the brain's inhibitory mechanisms can lead to socially inappropriate or unlawful behaviors, such as public indecency or sexual misconduct, as individuals may struggle to control urges or follow social norms (Chapter 2: Etiology of Adult Sexual Offending | Office of Sex Offender Sentencing, Monitoring, Apprehending, Registering, and Tracking, n.d.).

There is substantial evidence to suggest that individuals with TBIs or ABIs are more likely to engage in criminal behavior. Studies have found that people with a history of brain injury are overrepresented in the criminal justice system. For instance, research indicates that a significant proportion of incarcerated individuals have experienced a TBI, with estimates ranging from 25% to 87%, compared to 8.5% of the general population. This overrepresentation suggests a strong correlation between brain injury and criminal conduct, particularly in cases involving violent or impulsive behavior (Schneider et al., 2021).

One theory posits that brain injuries impair the neural circuits responsible for inhibiting aggressive and antisocial behaviors, leading to an increased risk of violent acts. Additionally, the cognitive deficits associated with TBI and ABI, such as memory problems and impaired judgment, may lead individuals to make poor choices or misunderstand social cues, resulting in criminal behavior (Schwarzbold et al., 2008).

8.1 Case Studies

The case of Mr. David Brown (a pseudonym) is a compelling example of how traumatic brain injury (TBI) can lead to drastic changes in behavior, ultimately resulting in criminal activity. David was a 32-year-old man with no prior criminal record or history of violent behavior. He had been employed as an electrician, was a devoted father to two children, and led a relatively stable life. However, David's life dramatically changed after a severe car accident in which he sustained a traumatic brain injury. The injury left him with permanent cognitive and emotional impairments, which gradually impacted his ability to function in his personal and professional life. The car accident occurred when David's vehicle was struck by a drunk driver. He suffered a significant blow to his head, resulting in a traumatic brain injury, specifically in the frontal lobe region, which is responsible for regulating emotions, decision-making, and impulse control. After being hospitalized for several weeks, he was discharged but continued to experience cognitive difficulties. Doctors diagnosed him with a moderate-to-severe TBI, and over time, David exhibited noticeable behavioral changes that were consistent with damage to the frontal lobe. Despite rehabilitation efforts, David's behavior became increasingly erratic. He began struggling with emotional regulation, experiencing frequent mood swings, and acting impulsively. His family noticed a sharp decline in his patience and an increase in irritability. He also began to have memory problems, often forgetting important details related to his daily responsibilities. Although David had previously been a calm and composed individual, his post-TBI symptoms included aggression and difficulty managing anger.

Two years after the accident, the turning point came during a heated argument with his brother during a family gathering. What began as a verbal disagreement escalated when David, unable to control his anger, physically assaulted his brother, causing serious injuries that required hospitalization. The family was shocked by David's outburst, as it was completely out of character for him. The police were called, and David was arrested for assault and battery. During the investigation, it became clear that David's criminal behavior was directly linked to the changes in his brain function following the TBI. Before the accident, he had been a peaceful and law-abiding citizen. However, the injury to his frontal lobe had caused deficits in his impulse control and emotional regulation, leading to his violent behavior.

As part of the legal proceedings, a neuropsychologist was brought in to assess David's cognitive and emotional functioning. The evaluation revealed several key deficits. David exhibited significant impairment in his ability to plan, organize, and control his actions. His executive functions, which are essential for regulating behavior and inhibiting inappropriate responses, had been compromised by the TBI. The neuropsychologist identified severe emotional dysregulation, including heightened irritability and difficulty managing anger. These emotional changes were directly linked to the damage in the frontal lobes, an area critical for controlling aggression and social behavior. The assessment also revealed increased impulsivity, which had been a contributing factor in the assault. David was no longer able to think through the consequences of his actions, leading to rash and harmful decisions. While not directly related to the criminal act, David's memory impairments highlighted the overall cognitive decline he had experienced after the injury. He struggled to recall important details from the day of the incident, further illustrating the impact of TBI on his cognitive functioning. The neuropsychological assessment concluded that David's criminal behavior was a direct consequence of his brain injury. His frontal lobe damage had diminished his capacity to regulate his emotions and behavior, making him more prone to aggression and impulsive actions. David's defense team argued that his actions were the result of diminished capacity due to his traumatic brain injury. They presented evidence of his pre-injury life, emphasizing that he had no history of violent or criminal behavior prior to the accident. The defense contended that the brain injury had significantly altered his personality and impaired his ability to control his impulses, which was critical in understanding the circumstances surrounding the assault.

Medical records, testimony from his neurologist, and the neuropsychologist's report were submitted as evidence, demonstrating the extent of his cognitive and emotional impairments. The defense argued that David lacked the mens rea (criminal intent) necessary to be held fully responsible for the assault, as his TBI had compromised his ability to understand and control his actions in the moment. The court recognized the impact of David's traumatic brain injury on his behavior and criminal actions. While the severity of the assault could not be overlooked, the judge acknowledged that the injury had significantly impaired David's cognitive and emotional functioning. As a result, the court reduced his criminal culpability, recognizing that his brain injury had played a pivotal role in the incident. David was ordered to undergo ongoing psychological therapy to address his emotional dysregulation and impulse control problems. This treatment was deemed essential to prevent future outbursts of aggression. He was enrolled in cognitive rehabilitation programs designed to improve his executive functioning and help him develop strategies for managing his cognitive deficits. David was placed on probation, during which time he had to regularly report to a probation officer and demonstrate progress in his rehabilitation efforts. Any further violent behavior during this period would result in harsher legal consequences.

8.2 Legal Implications

When brain injuries are found to have contributed to criminal behavior, courts may opt for alternative sentencing options, such as mandatory psychological treatment, rehabilitation programs, or placement in a mental health facility. This approach recognizes that individuals with TBIs or ABIs may benefit more from therapeutic interventions than from punitive measures like incarceration, which may not address the underlying causes of their behavior. In rare cases, individuals with severe brain injuries may invoke the insanity defense, arguing that their injury rendered them incapable of distinguishing right from wrong or controlling their behavior (Longman, 2024). This defense is most commonly used in cases where the brain injury has resulted in profound cognitive and emotional impairments, such as severe frontal lobe damage. In cases where brain injuries impair cognitive functions such as decision-making, impulse control, and moral reasoning, the defense may argue diminished capacity (Galgano et al., 2017). This legal concept suggests that the defendant's mental state was compromised at the time of the crime, reducing their ability to form intent or understand the wrongfulness of their actions. In such cases, courts may impose lesser charges or alternative sentences, such as mental health treatment or rehabilitation.

Traumatic brain injury (TBI) and acquired brain injury (ABI) can have a profound impact on an individual's behavior, leading to increased impulsivity, aggression, and poor decision-making. These changes can result in criminal activity, even in individuals with no prior history of such behavior. The legal system faces the challenge of balancing the need for justice with an understanding of how brain injuries affect behavior and intent.

9 Integration of Neurospsychological Evidence

The integration of neuropsychological evidence in criminal cases has become increasingly relevant as neuroscience offers deeper insights into how brain function influences behavior. Neuropsychological assessments play a pivotal role in understanding an individual's cognitive and behavioral capacity, especially in cases where brain dysfunction may affect criminal responsibility. This section explores the role of neuropsychological assessments in determining criminal responsibility, the methods used, the challenges in interpretation, and the impact such evidence has had on legal outcomes through case studies.

Neuropsychological assessments are crucial for evaluating how brain function impacts behavior, particularly when determining criminal responsibility. These assessments aim to uncover cognitive and emotional impairments that might explain why an individual acted in a way that deviated from societal norms or legal standards. For instance, individuals with traumatic brain injuries (TBI), neurodegenerative diseases, or psychiatric disorders may have diminished capacity to control impulses, regulate emotions, or understand the consequences of their actions (Schwarzbold et al., 2008).

The main purpose of these assessments is to identify whether brain impairments might have contributed to the criminal behavior. This evidence is used in legal proceedings to support arguments related to diminished capacity, insanity defenses, or mitigating circumstances. In cases where an individual's brain function is significantly compromised, neuropsychological evidence can demonstrate that their criminal actions were not entirely voluntary or intentional, thus affecting their legal culpability.

Neuropsychological assessments encompass various methods, each aimed at measuring different aspects of brain function. The methods are commonly used to assess brain-behavior relationships. Functional magnetic resonance imaging (fMRI), positron emission tomography (PET), and computed tomography (CT) scans are frequently used to visualize structural and functional abnormalities in the brain (Crosson et al., 2010). These techniques can reveal lesions, areas of hypoperfusion, or neurodegenerative changes that correlate with behavioral impairments. For example, damage to the prefrontal cortex can affect decision-making and impulse control, which may play a role in criminal behavior. Standardized cognitive tests such as the Wechsler Adult Intelligence Scale (WAIS) or the Wisconsin Card Sorting Test (WCST) are used to evaluate various cognitive domains, including memory, executive function, attention, and problem-solving (Stuss et al., 2000). These tests help determine whether the individual's cognitive abilities are consistent with the impairments typically associated with their brain condition. In addition to neuroimaging and cognitive tests, clinical interviews and behavioral observations are critical. These evaluations offer insight into the individual's emotional state, mood, and capacity for social functioning. They can help clinicians understand the impact of neurological impairments on everyday behavior and decision-making. By integrating these methods, neuropsychologists can provide a comprehensive understanding of an individual's brain function and its potential role in criminal acts (Lee & Suhr, 2021).

While neuropsychological evidence can be valuable in the courtroom, its interpretation is fraught with challenges. The reliability of this evidence depends on various factors, including individual differences in brain function, variability in neuropsychological test results, and potential biases in the evaluation process (Harvey, 2012). One of the key challenges in interpreting neuropsychological evidence is the variability in brain function across individuals. People with similar brain injuries or disorders can exhibit vastly different behaviors, making it difficult to generalize findings. For instance, two individuals with damage to the same area of the brain may show different levels of impulse control or emotional regulation. This variability complicates the process of linking specific brain abnormalities to specific behaviors, particularly when assessing criminal responsibility. Additionally, the results of cognitive tests and neuroimaging are influenced by a variety of factors, including the individual's educational background, pre-injury cognitive abilities, and the time elapsed since the injury. As a result, there is often a degree of uncertainty in the conclusions drawn from neuropsychological assessments. Courts must consider this uncertainty when weighing the evidence (Torregrossa et al., 2023).

Biases also present a significant challenge in the use of neuropsychological evidence. Neuropsychologists may unintentionally introduce biases when interpreting test results, especially when they are aware of the legal context. Confirmation bias, where the evaluator may overemphasize evidence that supports the defendant's argument, is one potential issue. Additionally, there may be cultural or socioeconomic biases that affect both the interpretation of test results and the weight given to neuropsychological evidence. In some cases, juries and judges may also be swayed by the perceived objectivity of neuroimaging data, particularly when presented with complex brain scans or scientific jargon (Lidén, 2018). This phenomenon, known as the "neuro-realism" effect, can lead to overreliance on brain-based explanations for behavior, potentially undermining the role of other relevant factors, such as environmental influences or personal history.

9.1 Case Studies

The use of neuropsychological evidence in court has had a profound impact on legal decisions, particularly in cases involving diminished capacity or insanity defenses. The following case studies highlight how such evidence has been used to shape outcomes in criminal trials.

The integration of neuropsychological evidence into criminal cases offers valuable insights into how brain function affects behavior and criminal responsibility. Through assessments involving neuroimaging, cognitive testing, and clinical evaluations, neuropsychologists can provide evidence that informs legal decisions about culpability and sentencing. However, the interpretation of this evidence is complicated by issues of reliability, variability in brain function, and potential biases. Despite these challenges, case studies demonstrate the significant impact that neuropsychological evidence can have in shaping court outcomes, as it raises important ethical and legal questions about the nature of free will, responsibility, and justice.

10 Legal Standards and Evolving Practices

The legal system's approach to criminal responsibility is undergoing a significant evolution, particularly on how it integrates the usage of neuropsychological evidence. The use of such evidence brings into light the effects of how brain impairments can have an effect on criminal behavior. The current section explores how legal standards are maintained along with incorporating neuropsychological evidence, looking into recent reforms, trends, and potential for future directions in the field of neuropsychology.

Different jurisdictions have developed their own approaches to how to incorporate neuropsychological assessments into the legal context while maintaining the same reliable and valid approach. Legal systems worldwide follow different models of evaluating criminal responsibility.

For instance, in the United States, the M'Naghten Rule is widely used to assess criminal responsibility by determining whether the defendant could understand the nature of their actions and differentiate right from wrong at the time of the offense. The M'Naghten Rule originates from a mid-nineteenth-century English legal case, in which a defendant argued that a mental illness absolved him of criminal responsibility. This case became foundational in shaping the M'Naghten Rule within criminal law (Strom, 2023). Under this rule, neuropsychological evidence may be presented to demonstrate that brain impairments, such as those caused by traumatic brain injuries (TBI) or psychiatric conditions, interfered with the defendant's ability to make sound judgments. However, the level of influence such evidence has on legal outcomes varies by state, leading to inconsistencies in how brain impairments are treated.

In contrast, other countries employ different standards for assessing criminal responsibility. For example, Germany uses a broader approach that emphasizes diminished capacity or partial responsibility, allowing for neuropsychological evidence to play a larger role in both determining guilt and influencing sentencing. The United Kingdom, on the other hand, has adopted the insanity defense, which involves neuropsychological assessments to determine if a defendant's mental disorder prevented them from understanding the wrongfulness of their actions (Math et al., 2015). In Canada, the legal system allows for the use of the Not Criminally

Responsible on Account of Mental Disorder (NCRMD) defense, where neuropsychological evidence can demonstrate that a mental disorder rendered the defendant incapable of understanding the nature of their criminal actions (Crocker et al., 2015). This standard allows neuropsychological evaluations to play a significant role in determining criminal responsibility and shaping legal outcomes.

These jurisdictional differences highlight the complexities in developing consistent legal standards for neuropsychological evidence in criminal cases. While some jurisdictions are more open to integrating this type of evidence, others remain more conservative in how they consider brain impairments when determining guilt or sentencing (Manupatra, 2021).

Over the past few decades, there has been a growing recognition of the impact that neuropsychological factors can have on criminal behavior. This trend reflects the increasing understanding of brain function and its role in decision-making, impulse control, and moral reasoning, all of which are crucial in determining criminal responsibility (Petoft et al., 2022). One major reform has been the increased use of neuroimaging technologies in legal proceedings. Techniques like functional magnetic resonance imaging (fMRI), positron emission tomography (PET) scans, and electroencephalograms (EEG) are being introduced in courtrooms to show brain abnormalities linked to impaired cognitive and behavioral control. For instance, research has shown that individuals with damage to the prefrontal cortex, a brain region responsible for regulating impulses and decision-making, may exhibit increased aggression or impulsivity, which can affect their culpability for certain crimes (Crosson et al., 2010).

Additionally, the rise of neuroscientific defenses, such as claims of diminished capacity due to brain injury or psychiatric disorders, has led to reforms in how courts assess criminal responsibility (Aharoni et al., 2008). Defendants are increasingly using neuropsychological evidence to argue that brain impairments diminished their ability to form intent or control their actions, leading to a shift in how courts handle cases involving neurological and psychiatric conditions. In some cases, neuropsychological assessments have resulted in reduced sentences, diversion to mental health treatment programs, or the use of alternative sentencing options that take into account the defendant's cognitive limitations (Harvey, 2012). Juvenile justice systems have also recognized the importance of neuropsychological evidence in determining responsibility. Given the developmental stage of the adolescent brain, courts are now more likely to consider neuropsychological factors when sentencing young offenders, acknowledging that brain development continues into early adulthood and that impaired executive functioning or impulse control may play a significant role in juvenile delinquency (Luna, 2012).

As neuropsychological evidence becomes more widely accepted, legal practices regarding the assessment of criminal responsibility and sentencing are evolving. One such practice is the greater reliance on multidisciplinary evaluations, where neuropsychologists, psychiatrists, and neurologists work together to provide a comprehensive understanding of how brain impairments influence behavior. These evaluations help courts make more informed decisions about whether a defendant's brain dysfunction contributed to their criminal actions.

Courts are also increasingly considering neuropsychological evidence not just during trials but also at the sentencing phase. Neuropsychological evaluations are often used to inform the type of sentence that is most appropriate, with many courts opting for sentences that incorporate treatment or rehabilitation for individuals whose criminal behavior was influenced by cognitive impairments. This represents a shift from purely punitive measures to more rehabilitative approaches that recognize the role of brain function in criminal behavior.

As neuroscience continues to evolve, future advancements in neuroimaging and cognitive assessments are likely to have a profound impact on how courts handle cases involving brain impairments. New technologies, such as diffusion tensor imaging (DTI), which maps the brain's white matter pathways, and magnetoencephalography (MEG), which records magnetic fields produced by brain activity, offer even more detailed insights into how brain function is related to behavior. These technological advancements could enhance the accuracy of neuropsychological assessments, providing clearer evidence of how specific brain abnormalities influence criminal actions. Additionally, future research into genetic predispositions for cognitive and behavioral disorders could further inform legal decisions by offering insights into the biological basis of certain behaviors. To better integrate these advancements, legal systems may need to undergo further reforms. One potential direction is the standardization of legal criteria for the use of neuropsychological evidence across jurisdictions. This could reduce the variability in how such evidence is treated in court, ensuring more consistent and equitable outcomes for defendants with brain impairments. Another area of reform could be the creation of specialized courts or diversion programs for defendants with significant neuropsychological impairments. Such courts could focus on rehabilitation and treatment, recognizing that traditional punitive measures may not be appropriate for individuals whose criminal behavior is driven by brain dysfunction. Additionally, expanded training for judges, lawyers, and juries on how to interpret neuropsychological evidence would be crucial for ensuring fair and accurate legal outcomes.

11 Ethical and Practical Considerations of Criminal Responsibility and Neuropsychology

The intersection of neuropsychology and criminal responsibility presents a complex array of ethical and practical considerations, particularly when evaluating the role of brain disorders, injuries, and cognitive impairments in criminal behavior. Advances in neuroscience have provided critical insights into how abnormalities in brain functioning can impact an individual's capacity to make decisions, regulate impulses, and conform to legal and social norms. These developments raise significant questions regarding culpability, fairness in the legal system, and the appropriate use of neuropsychological evidence in court. This section explores the key ethical and practical considerations in this area, focusing on issues such as free will, fairness in sentencing, the reliability of neuropsychological evidence, and the broader societal implications of using brain science in legal contexts.

At the heart of the debate on criminal responsibility is the concept of mens rea, or the mental intent to commit a crime. Traditionally, criminal law assumes that individuals are rational actors capable of making choices between right and wrong. However, when neuropsychological impairments such as traumatic brain injuries (TBI), mood disorders, or neurodevelopmental disorders like autism come into play, the line between voluntary actions and uncontrollable behavior becomes blurred. The central ethical question revolves around free will: Can individuals with significant brain dysfunction truly be held responsible for their actions? If neurological impairments limit a person's ability to control impulses or understand the consequences of their actions, it challenges the conventional notion that they acted with criminal intent. Holding individuals with severe brain impairments fully accountable for their actions can seem unjust, as their behavior may be driven by factors beyond their conscious control.

On the other hand, this raises the risk of excusing harmful behavior and potentially diminishing the accountability of individuals whose impairments might not entirely prevent them from exercising moral judgment. Balancing these concerns requires nuanced ethical considerations, particularly when weighing the severity of the crime against the degree of impairment.

One of the practical challenges of incorporating neuropsychological evidence into legal proceedings is ensuring fairness in sentencing. Courts must determine whether an individual's cognitive impairments should mitigate their responsibility for a crime and, if so, how this should influence the outcome of their case. For instance, individuals with severe brain injuries or disorders might receive lighter sentences or alternative forms of punishment, such as mandatory treatment, rather than incarceration. While this approach emphasizes rehabilitation, it raises concerns about consistency and equity. Should every defendant with a neuropsychological impairment be treated similarly, regardless of the nature of their crime or the extent of their impairment? There is also the potential for defendants without cognitive impairments to argue that their actions were the result of temporary psychological states, such as stress or intoxication, thereby muddying the waters of culpability. This can lead to a perception that certain individuals are receiving preferential treatment, which undermines the perceived fairness of the legal system. Further complicating this issue is the fact that access to high-quality neuropsychological evaluations can be limited by socioeconomic factors. Defendants from disadvantaged backgrounds may not have the same access to expert witnesses or comprehensive neuropsychological assessments as wealthier individuals, potentially resulting in unequal legal outcomes. This disparity presents an ethical concern regarding equal justice under the law.

The use of neuropsychological evidence in legal proceedings also presents practical challenges related to its reliability and interpretation. Neuropsychology is a rapidly advancing field, but the scientific understanding of how specific brain abnormalities affect behavior is still evolving. Not all individuals with brain injuries or disorders exhibit criminal behavior, and the relationship between brain dysfunction and culpability is not always straightforward. For example, functional magnetic resonance imaging (fMRI) and other neuroimaging techniques can reveal abnormalities in brain structures, but these findings do not always translate into clear behavioral outcomes. A brain scan showing reduced activity in areas associated with impulse control does not necessarily prove that the individual had no control over their actions at the time of the crime. Judges and juries may struggle to interpret such evidence, particularly when it is presented alongside other factors, such as the defendant's personal history and the specifics of the crime. Moreover, expert witnesses in neuropsychology can provide differing interpretations of the same data, potentially leading to confusion or bias in courtrooms. Some experts might overstate the influence of a brain injury on behavior, while others may downplay its significance. The ethical use of neuropsychological evidence requires a careful balance between acknowledging the role of brain dysfunction in behavior and ensuring that it is not used to absolve individuals of responsibility altogether.

The broader societal implications of using neuropsychological evidence in criminal cases must also be considered. If individuals with brain injuries or cognitive disorders are viewed as less culpable due to their impairments, society faces the challenge of determining how to balance the need for justice with public safety. While it may be ethically appropriate to reduce sentences or provide alternative rehabilitation for individuals with significant brain impairments, the risk of recidivism must also be addressed. For instance, if a defendant with a history of violent behavior linked to a brain injury is released or given a reduced sentence, there may be a heightened risk of reoffending. Courts and mental health professionals must work together to ensure that these individuals receive adequate treatment and monitoring to prevent future harm to society. This requires collaboration between legal systems, healthcare providers, and social services to create effective rehabilitation programs that address both the neurological and behavioral aspects of criminality. Additionally, the increased reliance on neuropsychological evidence in criminal cases could lead to a broader societal shift in how criminal behavior is perceived. If brain dysfunction is increasingly seen as a mitigating factor, this may challenge traditional notions of punishment and deterrence, leading to calls for reform in how the justice system handles individuals with cognitive impairments. While this shift may result in more compassionate and scientifically informed legal practices, it also raises concerns about the potential for overreliance on neuropsychological explanations for behavior, which could erode personal accountability in certain cases.

12 Conclusion

The exploration of the neuropsychological foundations of criminal responsibility offers profound insights into how brain function influences behavior, particularly in the context of criminal actions. Neuropsychology, as a discipline, seeks to understand the intricate relationship between brain activity and cognitive processes, highlighting how impairments in brain function can lead to behaviors that may conflict with societal and legal norms. Through examining the impact of various brain disorders—such as mood disorders, neurodevelopmental disorders, and neurodegenerative diseases—on criminal behavior, it becomes evident that these impairments can significantly affect an individual's ability to understand, control, or foresee the consequences of their actions.

In particular, mood disorders, including bipolar disorder and major depression, can lead to impulsive or irrational behaviors during manic or depressive episodes, impairing decision-making and self-control. Individuals experiencing manic episodes may engage in risky or illegal behaviors, while those suffering from severe depression may struggle with diminished capacity to comprehend the impact of their actions. Neurodevelopmental disorders, such as autism spectrum disorder (ASD) or attention-deficit/hyperactivity disorder (ADHD), further complicate the legal evaluation of responsibility. These conditions often result in cognitive deficits that affect judgment, emotional regulation, and social behavior, which can contribute to involvement in criminal activity. In neurodegenerative diseases like Alzheimer's, cognitive decline can erode an individual's ability to follow laws, as memory, judgment, and comprehension progressively deteriorate.

The ethical implications of incorporating neuropsychological evidence into legal contexts are vast. Legal systems must strike a balance between holding individuals accountable for their actions and recognizing that brain dysfunctions can severely impair one's capacity for criminal intent. Courts must navigate complex questions, such as whether individuals with significant cognitive impairments should face traditional punishment or be diverted into treatment programs. Additionally, the potential for biases in the interpretation of neuropsychological evidence raises concerns about equitable treatment across different cases and jurisdictions. Judges, lawyers, and juries require adequate training in the interpretation of neuropsychological data to ensure that decisions are both scientifically informed and ethically sound.

Looking to the future, advancements in neuroimaging and cognitive assessment techniques promise to enhance the accuracy and reliability of neuropsychological evaluations. Tools like functional magnetic resonance imaging (fMRI) and diffusion tensor imaging (DTI) offer new avenues for understanding how specific brain regions and networks contribute to criminal behavior. As technology progresses, legal systems must evolve to integrate these findings in a standardized manner, ensuring consistency in how brain impairments are considered across different jurisdictions. This evolution will require continued research into the neuroscience of criminal behavior, as well as reforms in legal practices to accommodate the complexities of neuropsychological evidence.

In conclusion, the impact of brain disorders on criminal responsibility demands a nuanced approach that combines legal, ethical, and scientific perspectives. As understanding of the brain's role in behavior deepens, the legal system must continue to adapt, ensuring that individuals are both fairly judged and appropriately treated based on the neuropsychological realities of their conditions. By advancing legal standards and improving the integration of neuropsychological evidence, future legal practices will better reflect the complexities of human behavior and the brain.

References

639. Insanity—Scope of Expert Testimony. (2020, January 22). https://www.justice.gov/archives/jm/criminal-resource-manual-639-insanity-scope-expert-testimony.

Aharoni, E., Funk, C., Sinnott-Armstrong, W., & Gazzaniga, M. (2008). Can neurological evidence help courts assess criminal responsibility? Lessons from law and neuroscience. *Annals of the New York Academy of Sciences, 1124*(1), 145–160. https://doi.org/10.1196/annals.1440.007

Appelbaum, P. S. (2006). Violence and mental disorders: Data and public policy. *American Journal of Psychiatry, 163*(8), 1319–1321. https://doi.org/10.1176/ajp.2006.163.8.1319

Brain Injury Association of America. (2023, August 28). Non-Traumatic Brain Injury - Brain Injury Association of America. https://www.biausa.org/brain-injury/about-brain-injury/what-is-a-brain-injury/non-traumatic-brain-injury.

Busby, J. C. (2023, August 4). M'naghten rule. LII / Legal Information Institute. https://www.law.cornell.edu/wex/m%27naghten_rule.

Calabrese, J., & Khalili, Y. A. (2023, May 1). Psychosis. StatPearls - NCBI Bookshelf. https://www.ncbi.nlm.nih.gov/books/NBK546579/.

Chand, S. P., & Arif, H. (2023, July 17). Depression. StatPearls - NCBI Bookshelf. https://www.ncbi.nlm.nih.gov/books/NBK430847/.

Chapter 2: Etiology of Adult Sexual Offending | Office of Sex Offender Sentencing, Monitoring, Apprehending, Registering, and Tracking. (n.d.). Office of Sex Offender Sentencing, Monitoring, Apprehending, Registering, and Tracking. https://smart.ojp.gov/somapi/chapter-2-etiology-adult-sexual-offending.

Chesney, E. J. (n.d.). Concept of Mens Rea in the criminal law. In Journal of Criminal Law and Criminology (Vol. 29, Issue 5) [Journal-article]. https://scholarlycommons.law.northwestern.edu/cgi/viewcontent.cgi?article=2828&context=jclc.

Crocker, A. G., Nicholls, T. L., Seto, M. C., & Côté, G. (2015). The National Trajectory Project of individuals found not criminally responsible on account of mental disorder in Canada. *The Canadian Journal of Psychiatry, 60*(3), 96–97. https://doi.org/10.1177/070674371506000303

Crosson, B., Ford, A., McGregor, K. M., Meinzer, M., Cheshkov, S., Li, X., Walker-Batson, D., & Briggs, R. W. (2010). Functional imaging and related techniques: An introduction for rehabilitation researchers. *The Journal of Rehabilitation Research and Development, 47*(2), vii. https://doi.org/10.1682/jrrd.2010.02.0017

Del Pinal, G., & Nathan, M. J. (2013). There and up again: On the uses and misuses of neuroimaging in psychology. *Cognitive Neuropsychology, 30*(4), 233–252. https://doi.org/10.1080/02643294.2013.846254

Drevets, W. C., Price, J. L., Simpson, J. R., Todd, R. D., Reich, T., Vannier, M., & Raichle, M. E. (1997). Subgenual prefrontal cortex abnormalities in mood disorders. *Nature, 386*(6627), 824–827. https://doi.org/10.1038/386824a0

Emmady, P. D., Schoo, C., & Tadi, P. (2022, November 19). Major neurocognitive disorder (Dementia). StatPearls - NCBI Bookshelf. https://www.ncbi.nlm.nih.gov/books/NBK557444/.

Frith, C. (2013). The psychology of volition. *Experimental Brain Research, 229*(3), 289–299. https://doi.org/10.1007/s00221-013-3407-6

Galgano, M., Toshkezi, G., Qiu, X., Russell, T., Chin, L., & Zhao, L. (2017). Traumatic brain injury. *Cell Transplantation, 26*(7), 1118–1130. https://doi.org/10.1177/0963689717714102

George, A. (2022). The connections between attention-deficit/hyperactivity disorder and levels of criminal behavior among adults. *Open Journal of Social Sciences, 10*(2), 1–45. https://doi.org/10.4236/jss.2022.102001

Ghiasi, N., Azhar, Y., & Singh, J. (2023, March 30). Psychiatric illness and criminality. StatPearls - NCBI Bookshelf. https://www.ncbi.nlm.nih.gov/books/NBK537064/.

Green, M. F., Kern, R. S., Braff, D. L., & Mintz, J. (2000). Neurocognitive deficits and functional outcome in schizophrenia: Are we measuring the "Right Stuff"? *Schizophrenia Bulletin, 26*(1), 119–136. https://doi.org/10.1093/oxfordjournals.schbul.a033430

Guina, J., Hernandez, C., Witherell, J., Cowan, A., Dixon, D., King, I., & Gentile, J. P. (2022). Neurodevelopmental disorders, criminality, and criminal responsibility. *PubMed, 50*(3), 358–368. https://doi.org/10.29158/jaapl.210103-21

Harvey, P. D. (2012). Clinical applications of neuropsychological assessment. *Dialogues in Clinical Neuroscience, 14*(1), 91–99. 10.31887/dcns.2012.14.1/pharvey *insanity defense*. (n.d.). LII / Legal Information Institute. https://www.law.cornell.edu/wex/insanity_defense

Keiler, J., Panzavolta, M., & Roef, D. (2014). Criminal law. In *Springer eBooks* (pp. 121–156). https://doi.org/10.1007/978-3-319-06910-4_7

Kocka, A., & Gagnon, J. (2014). Definition of impulsivity and related terms following traumatic brain injury: A review of the different concepts and measures used to assess impulsivity, Disinhibition and other related concepts. *Behavioral Sciences, 4*(4), 352–370. https://doi.org/10.3390/bs4040352

Kumar, A., Sidhu, J., Lui, F., & Tsao, J. W. (2024, February 12). Alzheimer disease. StatPearls - NCBI Bookshelf. https://www.ncbi.nlm.nih.gov/books/NBK499922/.

Lamptey, R. N. L., Chaulagain, B., Trivedi, R., Gothwal, A., Layek, B., & Singh, J. (2022). A review of the common neurodegenerative disorders: Current therapeutic approaches and the potential role of nanotherapeutics. *International Journal of Molecular Sciences, 23*(3), 1851. https://doi.org/10.3390/ijms23031851

Lee, G. J., & Suhr, J. A. (2021). Principles and practices of neuropsychological assessment. In *Elsevier eBooks* (pp. 167–178). https://doi.org/10.1016/b978-0-12-818697-8.00114-x

Lee, R. R., Ward, A. R., Lane, D. M., Aman, M. G., Loveland, K. A., Mansour, R., & Pearson, D. A. (2021). Executive function in autism: Association with ADHD and ASD symptoms. *Journal of Autism and Developmental Disorders, 53*(2), 688–700. https://doi.org/10.1007/s10803-020-04852-2

Lidén, M. (2018). *Confirmation bias in criminal cases* [Thesis]. Department of Law, Uppsala University. https://www.diva-portal.org/smash/get/diva2:1237959/FULLTEXT01.pdf.

Longman, J. (2024, June 4). The advantages and disadvantages of an insanity plea | Longman Jakuback. Longman Jakuback.

Luna, B. (2012, August 1). The Relevance of Immaturities in the Juvenile Brain to Culpability and Rehabilitation. PubMed Central (PMC). https://www.ncbi.nlm.nih.gov/pmc/articles/PMC5662008/.

Manupatra. (2021, May 17). *MyApp*. https://articles.manupatra.com/article-details/The-Intersection-of-Law-and-Neuroscience-Implications-On-Law-of-Evidence.

Maresca, G., Lo Buono, V., Anselmo, A., Cardile, D., Formica, C., Latella, D., Quartarone, A., & Corallo, F. (2023). Traumatic brain injury and related antisocial behavioral outcomes: A systematic review. *Medicina, 59*(8), 1377. https://doi.org/10.3390/medicina59081377

Math, S. B., Kumar, C. N., & Moirangthem, S. (2015). Insanity defense: Past, present, and future. *Indian Journal of Psychological Medicine, 37*(4), 381–387. https://doi.org/10.4103/0253-7176.168559

Model Systems Knowledge Translation Center (MSKTC). (n.d.). Emotional Problems After Traumatic Brain Injury. In *Traumatic brain injury model system consumer information* (pp. 2–4). https://msktc.org/sites/default/files/lib/docs/Factsheets/TBI_Emotional_Problems_and_TBI.pdf

Petoft, A., Abbasi, M., & Zali, A. (2022). Toward children's cognitive development from the perspective of neurolaw: Implications ofRoper v Simmons. *Psychiatry Psychology and Law, 30*(2), 144–160. https://doi.org/10.1080/13218719.2021.2003267

Pirau, L., & Lui, F. (2023, July 17). Frontal lobe syndrome. StatPearls - NCBI Bookshelf. https://www.ncbi.nlm.nih.gov/books/NBK532981/.

Rnic, K., Dozois, D. J. A., & Martin, R. A. (2016). Cognitive distortions, humor styles, and depression. *Europe's Journal of Psychology, 12*(3), 348–362. https://doi.org/10.5964/ejop.v12i3.1118

Robinson, L. J., Thompson, J. M., Gallagher, P., Goswami, U., Young, A. H., Ferrier, I. N., & Moore, P. B. (2006). A meta-analysis of cognitive deficits in euthymic patients with bipolar disorder. *Journal of Affective Disorders, 93*(1–3), 105–115. https://doi.org/10.1016/j.jad.2006.02.016

Rössler, W. (2006, October 1). Psychiatric rehabilitation today: An overview. PubMed Central (PMC).

Schizophrenia. (n.d.). National Institute of Mental Health (NIMH). https://www.nimh.nih.gov/health/statistics/schizophrenia

Schneider, B. S., Arciniegas, D. B., Harenski, C., Clarke, G. J. B., Kiehl, K. A., & Koenigs, M. (2021). The prevalence, characteristics, and psychiatric correlates of traumatic brain injury in incarcerated individuals: An examination in two independent samples. *Brain Injury, 35*(14), 1690–1701. https://doi.org/10.1080/02699052.2021.2013534

Schwarzbold, M., Diaz, A., Martins, E. T., Rufino, A., Amante, L. N., Thais, M. E., Quevedo, J., Hohl, A., Linhares, M. N., & Walz, R. (2008). Psychiatric disorders and traumatic brain injury. *Neuropsychiatric Disease and Treatment*, 797. https://doi.org/10.2147/ndt.s2653

Strom, S. (2023, November 30). The M'Naghten rule. Findlaw. https://www.findlaw.com/criminal/criminal-procedure/the-m-naghten-rule.html.

Stuss, D., Levine, B., Alexander, M., Hong, J., Palumbo, C., Hamer, L., Murphy, K., & Izukawa, D. (2000). Wisconsin card sorting test performance in patients with focal frontal and posterior brain damage: Effects of lesion location and test structure on separable cognitive processes. *Neuropsychologia, 38*(4), 388–402. https://doi.org/10.1016/s0028-3932(99)00093-7

Torregrossa, W., Torrisi, M., De Luca, R., Casella, C., Rifici, C., Bonanno, M., & Calabrò, R. S. (2023). Neuropsychological assessment in patients with traumatic brain injury: A comprehensive review with clinical recommendations. *Biomedicine, 11*(7), 1991. https://doi.org/10.3390/biomedicines11071991

Traumatic Brain Injury (TBI). (n.d.). National Institute of Neurological Disorders and Stroke. https://www.ninds.nih.gov/health-information/disorders/traumatic-brain-injury-tbi.

Understanding Psychosis. (n.d.). National Institute of Mental Health (NIMH). https://www.nimh.nih.gov/health/publications/understanding-psychosis.

Waltmann, M., Herzog, N., Horstmann, A., & Deserno, L. (2021). Loss of control over eating: A systematic review of task based research into impulsive and compulsive processes in binge eating. *Neuroscience & Biobehavioral Reviews, 129*, 330–350. https://doi.org/10.1016/j.neubiorev.2021.07.016

What Is Depression? (n.d.). https://www.psychiatry.org/patients-families/depression/what-is-depression.

Yu, R., Topiwala, A., Jacoby, R., & Fazel, S. (2018). Aggressive behaviors in Alzheimer disease and mild cognitive impairment: Systematic review and meta-analysis. *American Journal of Geriatric Psychiatry, 27*(3), 290–300. https://doi.org/10.1016/j.jagp.2018.10.008

Neuropsychological Assessment in Criminal Cases

1 Introduction

Neuropsychological assessment has become an essential component in understanding the cognitive, emotional, and behavioral functioning of individuals involved in criminal cases. With the growing recognition of how brain functioning can impact behavior, particularly in complex legal settings, neuropsychological assessments provide critical insight into issues of mental health, personality, and cognitive impairment. Such assessments are instrumental in understanding an individual's competence to stand trial, criminal responsibility, or potential risk factors associated with neurocognitive disorders. The integration of these evaluations into criminal justice systems has enhanced the capacity for more nuanced judicial decisions, allowing for a deeper understanding of the defendant's psychological and neurological profile. This introduction explores neuropsychological assessments within the legal context, focusing on the assessment steps, tools, and challenges inherent to the process. By examining the protocols for conducting such assessments, the ethical considerations involved, and the role of interdisciplinary collaboration, this section sheds light on the importance of scientifically sound and ethically appropriate assessments in criminal cases.

Neuropsychological assessments in criminal cases aim to evaluate cognitive functions, mental health conditions, and personality traits that may influence criminal behavior. This type of assessment plays a crucial role in various phases of criminal proceedings, such as evaluating competency to stand trial, determining the mental state at the time of the offense (i.e., insanity defenses), and assessing the potential for rehabilitation. Importantly, these evaluations are distinct from clinical neuropsychological assessments because they are conducted for legal rather than therapeutic purposes. A central goal of neuropsychological assessments in criminal cases is to provide objective, scientifically validated data that can aid in judicial decisions. Forensic neuropsychologists must maintain a careful balance between

© The Author(s), under exclusive license to Springer Nature Switzerland AG 2025

K. J. Reddy, *Foundations of Criminal Forensic Neuropsychology*,
https://doi.org/10.1007/978-3-031-83771-5_6

their scientific role and the legal requirements of the case. Their assessments are not only scrutinized for accuracy and reliability but are also subject to cross-examination in court, which necessitates a high degree of methodological rigor.

The neuropsychological assessment process in criminal cases involves several critical steps, starting with a comprehensive review of the individual's medical, psychological, and criminal history. This review helps in formulating hypotheses about potential cognitive or psychiatric issues that may impact the individual's behavior. Following this, neuropsychologists employ a combination of standardized tests and clinical interviews to evaluate different cognitive domains such as attention, memory, executive functioning, and language abilities. While neuropsychological assessments provide invaluable insights, several challenges arise in their application within the legal context. One significant challenge is the issue of validity and reliability. Forensic settings are unique in that individuals may be motivated to feign or exaggerate cognitive deficits, a phenomenon known as malingering. Neuropsychologists must be vigilant in detecting malingering, often using specialized tests like the Test of Memory Malingering (TOMM) to differentiate between genuine and exaggerated impairments (Zucco & Sartori, 2023). Another challenge involves cultural and linguistic differences, which can complicate the interpretation of test results. Many standardized tests are developed for specific populations, and their application to individuals from diverse cultural or linguistic backgrounds may lead to inaccurate conclusions. Forensic neuropsychologists must account for these variables to avoid biased or unfair assessments (Harvey, 2012). Ethical considerations also loom large in forensic neuropsychological assessments. Unlike clinical settings, where the primary goal is to help the client, forensic neuropsychologists are often retained by legal parties, which raises questions about confidentiality, informed consent, and potential conflicts of interest. These professionals must adhere to strict ethical guidelines to ensure that their assessments are conducted with fairness and respect for the individual's rights (What Is Ethics in Research and Why Is It Important?, n.d.).

Given the complexity of neuropsychological assessments in criminal cases, interdisciplinary collaboration is often necessary. Neuropsychologists frequently work alongside legal professionals, psychiatrists, and other experts to provide a comprehensive understanding of the defendant's cognitive and psychological state (Schaefer et al., 2023). This collaboration ensures that the assessment is thorough and considers multiple perspectives, leading to more informed and just outcomes. By incorporating insights from multiple disciplines, forensic neuropsychologists can offer a more nuanced understanding of how cognitive and mental health factors intersect with criminal behavior. This interdisciplinary approach is especially critical when assessing individuals with complex neurocognitive disorders, such as traumatic brain injury or neurodevelopmental conditions, which may require expertise from various fields to fully understand their legal implications.

In conclusion, neuropsychological assessments play a pivotal role in criminal cases, offering vital information about an individual's cognitive and psychological functioning. While these assessments are indispensable tools in the legal arena, they are also fraught with challenges, including issues of malingering, cultural sensitivity, and ethical dilemmas. Through careful attention to these challenges and by fostering interdisciplinary collaboration, neuropsychological assessments can significantly contribute to the pursuit of justice in criminal cases.

2 Objectives

Neuropsychological assessment in criminal cases has become a crucial tool for understanding an individual's cognitive functioning, mental health, and personality traits, which may influence their involvement in criminal activities. These assessments offer insight into how brain dysfunction or mental illness might contribute to criminal behavior, helping courts determine critical factors such as competency to stand trial, criminal responsibility, and appropriate sentencing or rehabilitation strategies (Van Es et al., 2020). However, these assessments also come with practical and ethical challenges. This section explores the key objectives of neuropsychological assessments in criminal cases, including the protocols used to evaluate mental health, personality, and cognitive functioning, while also addressing the ethical dilemmas and practical issues that arise in forensic assessments (De Pádua Serafim et al., 2015).

Neuropsychological assessments in criminal cases are designed to objectively evaluate a defendant's mental health, personality traits, and cognitive abilities. These assessments are structured to answer specific legal questions, such as whether the defendant was mentally competent at the time of the offense or whether they can adequately participate in their defense during trial (Barak & Buchanan, 2010). To achieve this, neuropsychologists employ a variety of standardized tests, clinical interviews, and background reviews. Mental health evaluations are critical in understanding whether a defendant suffers from psychiatric disorders that may affect their legal competency or criminal responsibility. These evaluations typically include clinical interviews and structured diagnostic tools, such as the Diagnostic and Statistical Manual of Mental Disorders (DSM-5) criteria, to assess symptoms of mental illness. In many cases, mental health evaluations focus on identifying conditions such as schizophrenia, bipolar disorder, major depressive disorder, or personality disorders, which could impair the defendant's judgment or behavior during the crime.

Personality assessments are another key component of neuropsychological evaluations in criminal cases. These assessments aim to understand enduring personality traits that may predispose an individual to engage in criminal behavior or affect their ability to engage with the legal system. Commonly used tools include the Minnesota Multiphasic Personality Inventory (MMPI) and the Millon Clinical Multiaxial Inventory (MCMI), which assess personality disorders, behavioral tendencies, and psychopathology. By evaluating personality, neuropsychologists can provide insights into patterns of behavior, such as impulsivity, aggression, or manipulative tendencies, which may be relevant to the case. Cognitive assessments are central to neuropsychological evaluations, especially in cases where the defendant's brain functioning is in question due to traumatic brain injury, neurological disease, or developmental disorders. Cognitive testing typically covers areas such as memory, attention, executive functioning, language abilities, and visuospatial skills. Tools such as the Wechsler Adult Intelligence Scale (WAIS), the Wisconsin Card Sorting Test (WCST), and the Rey Complex Figure Test are commonly used to assess these domains. Cognitive evaluations are crucial in determining whether the defendant's cognitive impairments could have contributed to poor decision-making, a lack of understanding of their actions, or an inability to communicate effectively with their legal team (Sarason, 2024).

While neuropsychological assessments provide essential information for legal decision-making, they are fraught with ethical dilemmas and practical challenges that require careful consideration. Forensic neuropsychologists must navigate these issues to ensure that their evaluations are scientifically valid, ethically sound, and fair to the defendant.

One of the most significant ethical dilemmas in forensic neuropsychological assessments arises from the dual loyalty of the neuropsychologist. Unlike traditional clinical settings, where the neuropsychologist's primary duty is to the client's well-being, forensic neuropsychologists serve the court or legal team. This shift in allegiance raises potential conflicts of interest, as the neuropsychologist must balance the rights and needs of the defendant with the demands of the legal system. For instance, a neuropsychologist may be asked to evaluate a defendant's competency to stand trial, but the findings may lead to legal consequences that are not in the defendant's best interest, such as extended incarceration or commitment to a psychiatric facility. Informed consent is another ethical issue in forensic neuropsychology. In clinical settings, patients voluntarily seek help and provide informed consent for treatment. However, in forensic assessments, defendants may not fully understand the implications of participating in the evaluation or the potential legal consequences of the results. It is the neuropsychologist's responsibility to ensure that defendants are fully aware of the purpose of the assessment, its limitations, and how the findings might be used in court. Confidentiality is also a complex issue in forensic contexts. In clinical practice, the neuropsychologist is bound to protect the patient's privacy, but in forensic cases, the findings of the assessment are often disclosed to the court, legal teams, and other parties involved in the case. Neuropsychologists must clearly explain the limits of confidentiality to defendants and ensure that their reports are factual, objective, and based on sound scientific principles (Merkt et al., 2021).

2.1 *Practical Issues in Forensic Neuropsychological Assessments*

In addition to ethical dilemmas, practical issues frequently arise during neuropsychological assessments in criminal cases. One major challenge is malingering, or the deliberate feigning or exaggeration of symptoms to achieve a legal advantage, such as avoiding criminal responsibility or receiving a reduced sentence. Defendants may have strong incentives to exaggerate cognitive deficits or mental illness, making it difficult for neuropsychologists to obtain accurate and reliable data. To address this issue, neuropsychologists use specialized tests, such as the Test of Memory Malingering (TOMM) or the Structured Inventory of Malingered Symptomatology (SIMS), to detect deception. However, detecting malingering is not always straightforward, and false positives or negatives can occur, leading to potential miscarriages of justice (Iverson, 2006).

Another practical challenge is the cultural and linguistic diversity of defendants. Standardized neuropsychological tests are often developed and normed on specific populations, typically individuals from Western, educated, industrialized, rich, and democratic (WEIRD) societies. Applying these tests to defendants from diverse cultural or linguistic backgrounds can lead to biased or inaccurate results. For instance, a non-native English speaker may perform poorly on language-based cognitive tests not due to cognitive impairment but due to language barriers. Neuropsychologists must be aware of these limitations and take steps to adapt their assessments to be culturally sensitive and fair (Manly, 2008).

Finally, interdisciplinary collaboration is a critical practical issue in forensic neuropsychological assessments. These assessments often require input from legal professionals, psychiatrists, and other experts to ensure that all relevant aspects of the defendant's case are considered. Forensic neuropsychologists must work closely with these professionals to provide comprehensive evaluations that address the legal questions while maintaining scientific rigor.

Neuropsychological assessments in criminal cases serve as invaluable tools for evaluating defendants' mental health, personality, and cognitive functioning. These evaluations help courts make informed decisions about competency, criminal responsibility, and appropriate sentencing. However, forensic neuropsychological assessments are also fraught with ethical dilemmas and practical challenges, including issues of dual loyalty, malingering, and cultural sensitivity. By carefully navigating these challenges, neuropsychologists can provide assessments that uphold justice while respecting the rights and dignity of the individuals being evaluated.

3 Assessment Protocols

Neuropsychological assessments play a critical role in criminal cases, providing the court with insights into the cognitive functioning, mental health, and personality traits of individuals involved in legal proceedings. These assessments can be pivotal in determining competency to stand trial, criminal responsibility, and potential rehabilitation pathways. To ensure that these assessments are both thorough and legally sound, they must follow specific protocols. This section explores the key steps involved in neuropsychological assessment protocols in criminal cases, including gathering background information, selecting appropriate tools, administering assessments, interpreting results, and reporting findings. Each step in this process is essential to conducting comprehensive and accurate evaluations, and ultimately guiding legal decision-making based on empirical evidence.

3.1 Initial Evaluation: Gathering Background Information and Defining Assessment Goals

The first step in the neuropsychological assessment process is the initial evaluation, which involves gathering pertinent background information and defining the goals of the assessment. This stage is essential in forming a comprehensive understanding of the individual's history, including medical, psychological, educational, and legal records. The neuropsychologist will review these records to identify relevant details about the defendant's cognitive and mental health status, prior assessments, and any prior diagnoses or treatments. Additionally, during the initial evaluation, the neuropsychologist works with legal professionals to define the goals of the assessment. In criminal cases, these goals may include evaluating the defendant's competency to stand trial, determining their mental state at the time of the offense, or assessing their potential for rehabilitation. Defining these goals ensures that the assessment focuses on the specific legal questions that need to be addressed (Professional, 2024).

3.2 Selection of Tools: Choosing Appropriate Tests and Measures

Once the background information has been gathered and the assessment goals defined, the neuropsychologist selects appropriate tests and measures to evaluate the individual's cognitive functioning, personality traits, and mental health. This step is critical because the selection of tools must be tailored to the unique characteristics of the defendant and the legal questions being posed. Neuropsychologists have a wide array of standardized tools at their disposal. Cognitive tests, such as the Wechsler Adult Intelligence Scale (WAIS) or the Wisconsin Card Sorting Test

(WCST), are commonly used to assess general intellectual functioning and executive functioning. Personality assessments, such as the Minnesota Multiphasic Personality Inventory (MMPI), are useful for evaluating psychopathology and personality traits that may influence behavior. Additionally, mental health assessments, such as the Beck Depression Inventory (BDI) or the Structured Clinical Interview for DSM-5 (SCID), can provide insight into the defendant's psychiatric state. The choice of assessment tools must also take into account factors such as the individual's cultural and linguistic background, educational level, and any physical or neurological impairments that may affect test performance. Selecting appropriate tools ensures that the assessment is both valid and reliable for the specific individual being evaluated (Professional, 2024).

3.3 Administration: Conducting Assessments Using Standardized Procedures

After selecting the appropriate tools, the next step is administering the assessments using standardized procedures. Standardization is crucial in forensic neuropsychology because it ensures that the assessments are conducted in a consistent manner, allowing for accurate comparisons with normative data and minimizing potential biases. During the administration phase, the neuropsychologist will often conduct a clinical interview with the defendant to gather qualitative information about their cognitive, emotional, and behavioral functioning. This interview helps contextualize the test results and provides insight into the defendant's subjective experiences. The neuropsychologist then administers the selected tests, carefully following standardized instructions to ensure that the results are comparable to normative samples. In forensic settings, one of the challenges during administration is the possibility of malingering, where the defendant may exaggerate or feign symptoms in an attempt to influence the legal outcome. To address this, neuropsychologists may use specific tests designed to detect malingering, such as the Test of Memory Malingering (TOMM) or the Structured Interview of Reported Symptoms (SIRS). Accurate administration of tests is critical to ensuring the integrity of the assessment process and producing reliable data (Professional, 2024).

3.4 Interpretation: Analyzing Results and Drawing Conclusions

Once the tests have been administered, the neuropsychologist analyzes the results and draws conclusions based on the data. Interpretation is a complex process that involves comparing the defendant's test scores to normative data, analyzing patterns of performance across different cognitive domains, and integrating the results with information gathered from the clinical interview and background records. During interpretation, the neuropsychologist must also consider factors such as cultural biases, language barriers, and any inconsistencies between test results and the defendant's behavior during the assessment. It is important to contextualize the results within the defendant's broader life experiences, as well as any neurological or psychiatric conditions that may influence their cognitive and emotional functioning. The conclusions drawn from the assessment must be directly related to the legal questions being asked. For example, if the assessment is intended to evaluate competency to stand trial, the neuropsychologist will assess whether the defendant has the cognitive and psychological capacity to understand the legal proceedings and effectively participate in their defense. Careful interpretation ensures that the conclusions are grounded in empirical evidence and are relevant to the legal context (Professional, 2024).

3.5 Reporting: Documenting Findings and Providing Recommendations

The final step in the neuropsychological assessment process is reporting the findings and providing recommendations to the court. The report must be clear, concise, and objective, as it will be used by judges, attorneys, and other legal professionals to make decisions about the case. In the report, the neuropsychologist summarizes the assessment results, discusses their interpretation, and offers conclusions about the defendant's cognitive and psychological functioning. The report may also include recommendations for legal decision-making, such as whether the defendant is competent to stand trial or whether they may benefit from mental health treatment or rehabilitation services. It is essential that the report is written in a manner that is accessible to non-experts, as it will be read by individuals without specialized knowledge of neuropsychology. The neuropsychologist must ensure that the findings are presented in an unbiased and fact-based manner, and that the recommendations are grounded in the scientific evidence obtained during the assessment.

Each step in the neuropsychological assessment process plays a critical role in ensuring that the evaluation is thorough, accurate, and useful in guiding legal decision-making. The initial evaluation ensures that the neuropsychologist has a comprehensive understanding of the defendant's background and the legal questions that need to be addressed. The careful selection of assessment tools ensures that the tests used are appropriate for the defendant's characteristics and the legal context. Standardized administration of the assessments ensures that the results are reliable and valid, while thoughtful interpretation of the data allows the neuropsychologist to draw conclusions that are grounded in empirical evidence. Finally, the reporting of findings ensures that the court has the information it needs to make informed decisions. By following these protocols, neuropsychological assessments in criminal cases provide valuable insights into the defendant's cognitive and psychological functioning, which can have a significant impact on legal outcomes. Each step in the process contributes to the overall accuracy and integrity of the assessment, ensuring that the findings are both scientifically sound and legally relevant. In this way, neuropsychological assessments help to ensure that justice is served by providing courts with objective, evidence-based information about defendants' mental health and cognitive abilities (Filamrush, 2024).

4 Assessment Instruments

To ensure that assessments are thorough and accurate, neuropsychologists use a variety of assessment instruments. These tools are designed to evaluate different aspects of brain functioning, behavior, and emotional states, helping to create a comprehensive profile of the defendant. This section explores the major categories of assessment instruments used in neuropsychological evaluations in criminal cases, including cognitive tests, personality inventories, and mental health assessments. The discussion will highlight common tools such as the Wechsler Adult Intelligence Scale (WAIS), the Minnesota Multiphasic Personality Inventory (MMPI), and neuropsychological test batteries, emphasizing their relevance to legal decision-making.

4.1 Cognitive Tests: Assessing Memory, Attention, and Executive Function

Cognitive tests are a cornerstone of neuropsychological assessments in criminal cases, as they help to evaluate the brain's functioning across various domains. These tests assess cognitive abilities such as memory, attention, language, problem-solving, and executive functioning. In criminal contexts, cognitive tests are often used to determine whether a defendant has impairments that might affect their capacity to understand legal proceedings or make sound decisions. Cognitive deficits, particularly in areas like executive function, may also provide insight into the defendant's behavior at the time of the offense.

Memory assessments are crucial for determining whether an individual has impairments in recalling information or learning new material. In criminal cases, memory deficits can have significant legal implications, particularly when evaluating a defendant's ability to recall events surrounding the crime. Tests like the California Verbal Learning Test (CVLT) or the Rey Auditory Verbal Learning Test (RAVLT) are often used to assess both short-term and long-term memory, providing critical data about the defendant's cognitive functioning (Arvanitakis et al., 2019).

Attention and executive functioning are often impaired in individuals with brain injuries, psychiatric conditions, or neurodevelopmental disorders. Deficits in these areas can affect a defendant's ability to focus, plan, or regulate their behavior. The Wisconsin Card Sorting Test (WCST) is frequently used to assess executive functioning, as it measures an individual's ability to shift between different tasks and think flexibly. Impairments in executive function are often linked to impulsive or poorly regulated behavior, which may be relevant in explaining criminal actions (Rabinovici et al., 2015).

The WAIS is one of the most widely used cognitive assessment tools in both clinical and forensic settings. It provides a comprehensive evaluation of an individual's general intellectual functioning, assessing cognitive domains such as verbal comprehension, perceptual reasoning, working memory, and processing speed. In criminal cases, the WAIS can help determine whether a defendant has intellectual deficits that might impair their ability to understand legal proceedings or communicate effectively with their defense team. The WAIS is particularly useful in cases where the defendant's intellectual capacity is in question, such as in determining competency to stand trial (Grabowski et al., 2023).

4.2 Personality Inventory: Evaluating Traits and Behavioral Tendencies

Personality inventories are another key component of neuropsychological assessments in criminal cases. These tools assess the enduring traits and behavioral tendencies that characterize an individual's personality, including potential psychopathology. In legal contexts, personality assessments can provide insight into whether a defendant has personality disorders or other traits that may have contributed to their criminal behavior. These assessments are also used to evaluate the defendant's ability to engage in rehabilitation or their risk of recidivism.

The MMPI is one of the most widely used personality inventories in forensic settings. It assesses a wide range of psychological conditions, including mood disorders, anxiety, and personality disorders, by asking individuals to respond to statements about their thoughts, feelings, and behaviors (Hathaway & Parsons, 2002). The MMPI provides a profile of the individual's psychological functioning, highlighting areas where they may have difficulties regulating emotions, coping with stress, or interacting with others. In criminal cases, the MMPI is particularly useful for identifying psychopathological traits that may be relevant to the individual's criminal behavior. For example, individuals with antisocial personality disorder or borderline personality disorder often exhibit impulsive or aggressive behaviors, which can contribute to criminal actions. The MMPI also includes scales designed to detect malingering or the deliberate exaggeration of symptoms, which is crucial in forensic assessments where defendants may attempt to manipulate the outcome of the evaluation (Floyd & Gupta, 2023).

The MCMI is another personality assessment commonly used in forensic contexts. Like the MMPI, the MCMI evaluates a broad range of psychological conditions, with a particular emphasis on personality disorders. It is often used to assess individuals who may have personality traits or disorders that increase their risk of engaging in criminal behavior (Moore, 2022). For instance, individuals with narcissistic or paranoid personality disorders may have distorted thinking patterns or emotional regulation difficulties that contribute to criminal behavior. The MCMI can also provide insights into the defendant's ability to engage in treatment or rehabilitation programs, helping the court make informed decisions about sentencing and rehabilitation.

4.3 Mental Health Assessments: Diagnosing Disorders and Evaluating Emotional State

Mental health assessments are an integral part of neuropsychological evaluations in criminal cases, as they help to diagnose psychiatric disorders and evaluate the emotional state of the defendant. These assessments are often used to determine whether the defendant was experiencing mental illness at the time of the offense, which may impact their legal responsibility. Mental health assessments also play a crucial role in evaluating the defendant's competency to stand trial, as individuals with severe mental illness may be unable to participate in legal proceedings.

The SCID is a commonly used tool for diagnosing psychiatric disorders based on the criteria outlined in the Diagnostic and Statistical Manual of Mental Disorders (DSM-5). It is a semi-structured interview that allows the clinician to systematically assess the presence of mood disorders, anxiety disorders, psychotic disorders, and personality disorders (*Structured Clinical Interview for DSM Disorders (SCID)*, 2018). In criminal cases, the SCID can be used to diagnose conditions such as schizophrenia, bipolar disorder, or major depressive disorder, which may have influenced the defendant's behavior at the time of the crime.

The BDI is a self-report questionnaire that assesses the severity of depressive symptoms. It is particularly useful in cases where the defendant's mental state may have contributed to their criminal behavior. For example, individuals who were suffering from severe depression at the time of the crime may have impaired judgment or diminished capacity for making rational decisions (Schrag et al., 2007). The BDI provides valuable information about the defendant's emotional state, which can be used to evaluate their mental health and inform decisions about sentencing or treatment.

4.4 *Neuropsychological Test Battery: Comprehensive Assessment of Cognitive Functioning*

Neuropsychological test batteries, such as the Halstead-Reitan Neuropsychological Test Battery, provide a comprehensive evaluation of cognitive functioning across multiple domains. These batteries are often used in criminal cases where there is a need for an in-depth assessment of the defendant's brain functioning, particularly in cases involving traumatic brain injury, neurological disease, or developmental disorders. The Halstead-Reitan Battery includes tests that assess memory, attention, language, motor skills, and executive functioning, providing a detailed profile of the defendant's cognitive strengths and weaknesses. This battery is particularly useful in cases where cognitive impairments may have contributed to the defendant's criminal behavior, such as in cases involving brain injury or neurodevelopmental disorders like fetal alcohol syndrome (Mattson et al., 2019).

Neuropsychological assessments in criminal cases rely on a range of assessment instruments, including cognitive tests, personality inventories, and mental health assessments. Tools like the Wechsler Adult Intelligence Scale, the Minnesota Multiphasic Personality Inventory, and neuropsychological test batteries play a critical role in evaluating defendants' cognitive functioning, personality traits, and mental health. By providing courts with empirical data about a defendant's cognitive abilities, psychological functioning, and emotional state, these assessments help to inform legal decisions about competency, criminal responsibility, and sentencing. Each instrument used in neuropsychological assessments offers a unique perspective on the defendant's functioning, contributing to a comprehensive understanding of the individual's behavior and its relationship to the criminal offense.

5 Challenges in Forensic Assessments

Forensic assessments are integral to legal proceedings, particularly in cases that require the evaluation of an individual's cognitive, psychological, or emotional state. These assessments can determine competency to stand trial, criminal responsibility, or risk of recidivism. However, conducting forensic assessments comes with significant challenges that can influence the quality and accuracy of the results. Three key challenges include validity issues, reliability concerns, and the need for cultural sensitivity in the assessment process. Validity refers to the extent to which a test measures what it claims to measure. In forensic assessments, validity is crucial because the conclusions drawn from the evaluation can have profound legal consequences. Ensuring the validity of the assessment tools is therefore a top priority, but achieving it is not without difficulties.

One major concern is the accuracy and relevance of the findings. For instance, certain neuropsychological tests may be designed to measure general cognitive functioning, but may not accurately reflect specific issues that are pertinent to the legal case, such as an individual's capacity to understand legal proceedings or their mental state at the time of an offense (Determinations, 2015). If the tests do not directly address the legal questions at hand, the assessment may yield results that are less relevant to the case, raising questions about the validity of the findings. Moreover, tests that are used in forensic settings often need to account for malingering, or the intentional exaggeration or fabrication of symptoms. Some defendants may attempt to manipulate the outcome of the assessment by exaggerating cognitive or psychological impairments to avoid legal responsibility. This adds another layer of complexity in ensuring that the tests are valid and the results reflect the defendant's true cognitive and psychological state.

Reliability refers to the consistency of test results over time and across different evaluators. In forensic settings, it is important that the tests produce stable and consistent results to ensure that the assessment is fair and accurate. However, maintaining reliability in forensic assessments can be challenging for several reasons. First, the consistency of test results can be affected by external factors, such as the conditions under which the assessment is conducted. Differences in the environment, the defendant's mood or attention during the assessment, or even the relationship between the defendant and the examiner can all influence the results. For instance, a defendant may perform differently on a cognitive test if they are anxious or stressed, leading to variations in test outcomes. Another significant factor affecting reliability is the expertise of the examiner. Neuropsychological assessments require specialized knowledge, and different evaluators may interpret test results differently depending on their experience and training. Variability in scoring or interpretation can result in inconsistent findings, which in turn can undermine the reliability of the assessment. This is particularly concerning in forensic cases, where the stakes are high, and inconsistencies in assessment results could impact legal decisions.

Cultural sensitivity is a critical concern in forensic assessments, as individuals from diverse cultural backgrounds may have different experiences, values, and ways of understanding behavior and cognition. If cultural differences are not accounted for, the assessment may introduce biases that unfairly affect individuals from minority or marginalized groups (Bronx Partners for Healthy Communities, n.d.). One of the key challenges in achieving cultural sensitivity is ensuring that the assessment tools are appropriate for individuals from different cultural backgrounds. Many psychological and neuropsychological tests are developed and standardized based on Western populations, and may not be valid or reliable for individuals from other cultural contexts. For example, a cognitive test that assumes familiarity with certain concepts or languages may disadvantage individuals who are not from the same cultural background as the normative sample. Additionally, cultural differences can influence how individuals express emotions, respond to authority figures, or interpret legal concepts. If these factors are not considered, the assessment may fail to accurately capture the individual's true cognitive or psychological state. To avoid such biases, examiners must adapt their approach to assessments, taking into account cultural factors and ensuring that the evaluation is fair for all individuals, regardless of their background.

Addressing these challenges is essential to ensure that forensic assessments are accurate, fair, and legally sound. By carefully considering these factors, neuropsychologists can provide courts with reliable and relevant information that contributes to just and informed decision-making.

6 Ethical Dilemmas and Ethical Requirements in Forensic Assessments

Forensic assessments often involve high-stakes situations, such as determining competency to stand trial, criminal responsibility, or appropriate sentencing. Given their impact, it is essential that these evaluations are conducted with strict adherence to ethical standards. However, forensic neuropsychologists frequently encounter ethical dilemmas that challenge their ability to maintain professional integrity and uphold the principles of justice and fairness (Yadav, 2017). Some of the most pressing ethical concerns include ensuring informed consent, maintaining confidentiality, preventing the misuse of findings, and addressing conflicts of interest. This section explores these ethical dilemmas and highlights the best practices and guidelines necessary for conducting forensic neuropsychological assessments in an ethical and impartial manner.

6.1 Informed Consent in Forensic Assessments

One of the fundamental ethical principles in any form of psychological assessment is obtaining informed consent. In forensic neuropsychology, this can be particularly challenging due to the unique context in which these evaluations are conducted. Informed consent involves ensuring that individuals understand the purpose of the assessment, the procedures involved, the potential risks and benefits, and the ways in which the findings may be used. In criminal cases, defendants may not always fully comprehend the legal or psychological implications of the assessment, raising concerns about their ability to provide truly informed consent.

In forensic settings, individuals undergoing assessment are often mandated to participate by the court. This can create confusion about their rights and autonomy. A defendant may feel compelled to agree to the assessment without fully understanding that their participation is required by law, but that they have rights regarding the use of the assessment results. Neuropsychologists must take extra care to explain the limitations of confidentiality in forensic settings, the potential impact of the assessment on legal outcomes, and the fact that the results will be shared with legal professionals, not kept confidential between the evaluator and the individual as in clinical contexts. For example, a defendant may agree to participate in a neuropsychological assessment without realizing that the findings could be used to support a legal argument against their interests, such as diminished responsibility or dangerousness. Ensuring that individuals understand these potential outcomes is a key ethical responsibility. To navigate this, forensic neuropsychologists should use clear, non-technical language to explain the process and obtain written consent that explicitly acknowledges the individual's understanding of the potential implications of the assessment.

6.2 *Confidentiality and Privacy Concerns*

Confidentiality is another cornerstone of ethical psychological practice, but it is uniquely complex in forensic settings. In clinical contexts, the results of a psychological assessment are typically kept private and shared only with the patient or relevant healthcare providers. However, in forensic assessments, the findings are often shared with attorneys, judges, and other legal professionals, which can create ethical dilemmas regarding the protection of personal information.

In forensic neuropsychological assessments, the examiner is often required to provide a report that becomes part of the legal record. This means that sensitive personal information, including details about an individual's mental health, cognitive functioning, and psychological history, may be disclosed to multiple parties involved in the legal process. This can be particularly concerning when the findings of the assessment could be damaging to the individual's legal case, such as when the evaluation reveals a diagnosis of a severe mental illness or cognitive impairment. Forensic neuropsychologists must be transparent with individuals about the limits of confidentiality in this context. They should explain that while efforts will be made to protect their privacy, the results of the assessment are likely to be shared with the court and could become public records. Furthermore, neuropsychologists should take steps to minimize the amount of personal information included in reports, disclosing only what is necessary to address the legal questions at hand.

At times, forensic neuropsychologists may face situations where legal obligations conflict with ethical responsibilities. For example, if a neuropsychologist discovers information during an assessment that suggests the individual poses a risk to themselves or others, they may be ethically and legally obligated to break confidentiality to protect public safety. Balancing these competing obligations requires careful judgment and adherence to ethical guidelines, with the primary goal of ensuring both the individual's rights and public safety (Olejarczyk & Young, 2024).

6.3 *Potential for Misuse of Neuropsychological Findings*

One of the most significant ethical concerns in forensic neuropsychological assessments is the potential for misuse of findings. Neuropsychological evaluations provide detailed insights into an individual's cognitive functioning, mental health, and personality traits, which can be highly influential in legal decisions. However, these findings are sometimes used in ways that may not align with the original intent of the assessment, or they may be misinterpreted by legal professionals who lack expertise in neuropsychology. In some cases, neuropsychological findings may be presented in a manner that exaggerates their significance or misrepresents their implications. For instance, an attorney may use the results of a cognitive test to argue that a defendant was incapable of forming intent to commit a crime, even if the findings do not support such a conclusion. Alternatively, neuropsychological findings may be cherry-picked or taken out of context to bolster a particular legal argument, potentially leading to unjust outcomes.

Neuropsychologists must be vigilant in ensuring that their findings are not misused. This involves providing clear and comprehensive reports that explain the limitations of the assessment results, as well as being available to clarify or testify about their findings in court. Additionally, neuropsychologists should avoid making legal conclusions themselves, instead focusing on providing the data and interpretations that can inform legal professionals without overstepping their professional boundaries.

6.4 Conflicts of Interest and Maintaining Objectivity

In forensic settings, neuropsychologists are often hired by one side of a legal dispute, whether by the prosecution or the defense. This creates the potential for conflicts of interest, where the neuropsychologist may feel pressure to deliver findings that support the hiring party's position. Maintaining objectivity and impartiality is essential to conducting ethical assessments, but it can be challenging in adversarial legal contexts (Andorno, 2022).

The adversarial nature of the legal system means that forensic neuropsychologists may be viewed as advocates for the side that hired them, even though their role is supposed to be impartial. Attorneys may attempt to influence the neuropsychologist's findings by framing the assessment in a way that favors their case, or by selectively using certain parts of the evaluation while ignoring others. Neuropsychologists must be careful to resist such pressures and remain objective in their evaluations. To mitigate conflicts of interest, forensic neuropsychologists should adhere to best practices that promote objectivity. This includes using standardized assessment tools, following established protocols, and ensuring that their findings are based on empirical data rather than subjective judgment. Furthermore, neuropsychologists should make it clear to attorneys and other legal professionals that their role is not to advocate for one side, but to provide an impartial evaluation that aids the court in making informed decisions (Harvey, 2012).

6.5 Ethical Requirements in Forensic Assessments

In addition to navigating specific ethical dilemmas, forensic neuropsychologists must also adhere to broader ethical requirements that ensure justice, fairness, and respect for the individuals being assessed. Upholding the principles of justice means conducting assessments in a way that is unbiased and equitable, regardless of the individual's background or the legal context.

One of the core ethical principles in forensic assessments is the obligation to ensure that evaluations are conducted impartially and without bias. This is especially important in cases where the individual being assessed comes from a marginalized or vulnerable group. Neuropsychologists must be mindful of potential biases that could affect their interpretation of the data, such as racial, cultural, or socioeconomic biases, and take steps to mitigate these influences. In ensuring fairness, neuropsychologists must also be careful to avoid over-reliance on psychological or neuropsychological data in making legal decisions. While these assessments can provide valuable insights, they should not be the sole determinant of an individual's legal fate. Neuropsychologists should emphasize the limitations of their findings and advocate for a holistic approach to legal decision-making that takes into account multiple factors beyond the results of the neuropsychological evaluation (APA PRACTICE ORGANIZATION, 2015).

6.6 Best Practices and Professional Guidelines

To address the ethical challenges discussed above, forensic neuropsychologists must adhere to established professional guidelines and best practices. These guidelines, provided by organizations such as the American Psychological Association (APA) and the National Academy of Neuropsychology (NAN), offer detailed recommendations for conducting ethical forensic assessments.

One of the most important best practices in forensic neuropsychology is the use of standardized assessment tools and procedures. Standardization ensures that the results of the assessment are reliable, valid, and comparable across different individuals and settings. Neuropsychologists should also engage in continuous professional development to stay informed about emerging ethical concerns and advances in assessment techniques. In addition to following professional guidelines, forensic neuropsychologists should actively review and improve their assessment methods. This may involve seeking peer review or consultation from colleagues to ensure that their evaluations are thorough and objective. It may also include conducting research to refine assessment tools and procedures, particularly in areas where ethical challenges are most prevalent, such as cultural sensitivity and the potential for misuse of findings (Johnson-Greene & Bechtold, 2002).

Forensic neuropsychological assessments are complex evaluations that carry significant ethical responsibilities. Ensuring informed consent, maintaining confidentiality, preventing the misuse of findings, and addressing conflicts of interest are all critical ethical dilemmas that neuropsychologists must navigate in legal contexts (Rocchio, 2020). By adhering to professional guidelines, upholding the principles of justice and fairness, and continually reviewing their assessment practices, neuropsychologists can ensure that their evaluations contribute to just and informed legal decisions. These assessments, when conducted ethically, can provide courts with valuable insights while safeguarding the rights and dignity of the individuals being assessed.

7 Case Studies on Neuropsychological Assessments in the Indian Context

Case Study 1 Defendant A's Assessment

Defendant A was a 32-year-old man facing trial for murder. He was accused of killing his neighbor during a violent altercation. His defense team argued that he was not of sound mind during the incident, and as such, should not be held criminally responsible. To support this defense, the court ordered a neuropsychological assessment to determine whether Defendant A had any cognitive or mental health impairments that could have influenced his behavior during the crime. The primary goal of the neuropsychological assessment was to evaluate Defendant A's cognitive functioning, particularly his executive function, impulse control, and decision-making abilities. The assessment also aimed to explore any possible neurological or psychological conditions that could explain his violent behavior.

7.1 Challenges Encountered

The neuropsychologist conducting the assessment faced several challenges, primarily regarding the validity and reliability of the tests used. Most standardized neuropsychological tests available in India are adaptations of Western assessments, which may not fully account for cultural and linguistic differences. Defendant A came from a rural background and had limited formal education. His native language was not Hindi or English, which posed communication difficulties during the assessment. To ensure the validity of the assessment, the neuropsychologist had to use interpreters and culturally adapted tests, which posed risks to both test standardization and the reliability of the results. Additionally, Defendant A was not cooperative during parts of the assessment, possibly due to a lack of understanding of the purpose of the tests. This non-cooperation raised concerns about the reliability of the assessment results, as inconsistent engagement can lead to skewed data.

7.2 *Impact of Assessment Results on Legal Decisions*

Despite these challenges, the neuropsychologist's findings suggested that Defendant A had significant cognitive impairments in areas related to executive functioning and impulse control. These impairments were likely exacerbated by a history of untreated mental health issues, including possible substance use disorder. The neuropsychological assessment contributed to the defense's argument that Defendant A was not fully responsible for his actions at the time of the crime due to diminished capacity. In the end, the court took the neuropsychological findings into consideration and ruled that Defendant A was guilty of manslaughter rather than murder. The assessment played a crucial role in informing the court's decision, highlighting the importance of careful and culturally sensitive assessments in criminal cases.

Case Study 2 Defendant B's Assessment

Defendant B was a 45-year-old woman charged with fraud and forgery in connection with a financial scam. Her defense claimed that she was suffering from a cognitive impairment that affected her judgment and memory, leading to unintentional involvement in the fraudulent activities. The court requested a neuropsychological assessment to determine whether Defendant B had any cognitive deficits that could explain her actions. The assessment focused on evaluating Defendant B's memory, attention, and decision-making abilities. The neuropsychologist also aimed to assess whether there were any underlying neurological conditions, such as dementia or mild cognitive impairment, that could have affected her behavior.

Defendant B belonged to a minority ethnic community in India, and her primary language was a regional dialect that had no direct translation in most standardized psychological tests. Furthermore, Defendant B had a limited understanding of the legal system and the assessment process, which made her initially resistant to participating in the tests. The neuropsychologist recognized the need to adapt the assessment to account for these cultural and linguistic differences. Instead of relying solely on standard tests like the Wechsler Adult Intelligence Scale (WAIS), the neuropsychologist incorporated culturally relevant tasks, such as memory tests that used familiar local objects and language. In addition, they worked closely with an interpreter from Defendant B's community to ensure that instructions were clear and that her responses were accurately recorded. However, adapting the tests while maintaining their validity and reliability posed significant challenges. Some aspects of the assessment, such as tasks involving abstract reasoning or complex language processing, were difficult to adapt without compromising the test's integrity. The neuropsychologist had to be cautious in interpreting the results, acknowledging the limitations of the adapted tests.

7.3 Outcome

The assessment revealed that Defendant B had mild cognitive impairments, particularly in short-term memory and attention, which may have affected her ability to fully understand the financial transactions in which she was involved. However, the neuropsychologist was careful to note that the results were influenced by cultural and linguistic factors, and that more research is needed to develop culturally appropriate assessment tools in India. The findings ultimately influenced the court's decision to impose a lighter sentence, acknowledging that Defendant B's cognitive impairments played a role in her actions. The case underscored the importance of cultural sensitivity in forensic neuropsychological assessments and highlighted the need for ongoing development of assessment tools that are relevant to India's diverse population. This case also illustrated the importance of interdisciplinary collaboration. The neuropsychologist worked closely with legal professionals, who helped frame the results in a way that the court could understand and use. Additionally, the involvement of an interpreter and input from community representatives helped ensure that the assessment was as culturally appropriate as possible.

8 Limitations of Psychological Testing in Forensic Neuropsychology

Psychological testing is a critical tool in forensic neuropsychology, providing insight into an individual's cognitive, emotional, and psychological functioning. These assessments are commonly used in legal contexts to determine a defendant's competency, mental state at the time of a crime, or potential risk of reoffending. However, while psychological testing offers valuable information, it has several limitations that can impact its efficacy and reliability in forensic settings. This section explores the drawbacks of psychological testing in forensic neuropsychology, the risks of over-reliance on these assessments, and the importance of integrating alternative approaches, such as interdisciplinary collaboration and holistic evaluation, to ensure a comprehensive understanding of an individual's psychological state (Louw, 2015).

Psychological testing, while helpful, has inherent limitations that can affect the accuracy and applicability of its findings in forensic contexts. These limitations often arise from the scope of testing and the specific challenges of applying psychological assessments to legal cases.

One of the primary limitations of psychological testing is its restricted scope. Most psychological tests are designed to measure specific cognitive or emotional functions, such as memory, attention, or personality traits. While these assessments can provide important insights into an individual's mental functioning, they often fall short of offering a comprehensive picture of an individual's psychological state (Determinations, 2015). For instance, a neuropsychological test may reveal deficits in executive functioning, but it may not fully explain why these deficits exist or how they relate to the individual's behavior in a legal context. Moreover, psychological tests are typically standardized on specific populations, meaning they may not account for individual differences in culture, socioeconomic background, or life experiences. In forensic settings, where the population is highly diverse, this limitation can result in assessments that do not accurately reflect the experiences or functioning of certain individuals. For example, a cognitive test that assumes familiarity with certain language or cultural concepts may disadvantage individuals from different backgrounds, leading to inaccurate or incomplete assessments.

Another significant drawback of psychological testing in forensic neuropsychology is the risk of over-reliance. Legal professionals, including attorneys and judges, may place undue weight on the results of psychological tests, viewing them as objective and definitive evidence of an individual's mental state. However, psychological tests are only one piece of the puzzle, and they should not be used in isolation to draw conclusions about an individual's behavior or responsibility. Over-reliance on psychological testing can lead to unjust outcomes, particularly when the results are misinterpreted or overextended beyond their intended use. For example, a low score on an intelligence test might be used to argue that an individual lacks the cognitive capacity to form criminal intent (Determinations, 2015). However, intelligence tests measure only certain aspects of cognitive functioning and may not fully capture the individual's ability to understand or control their actions in the context of a crime. Furthermore, psychological tests are subject to various forms of bias, including examiner bias, cultural bias, and the effects of situational factors such as stress or fatigue. These biases can distort the results of the assessment, leading to conclusions that do not accurately reflect the individual's true cognitive or psychological state. Over-reliance on these flawed results can result in unfair or incorrect legal judgments.

To address the limitations of psychological testing in forensic neuropsychology, it is essential to adopt alternative approaches that complement and expand upon the insights gained from assessments. Two key approaches that can enhance the accuracy and fairness of forensic evaluations are interdisciplinary collaboration and holistic evaluation. One of the most effective ways to overcome the limitations of psychological testing is through interdisciplinary collaboration. Forensic cases often involve complex questions about an individual's mental state, behavior, and legal responsibility. No single discipline can provide a complete answer to these questions, and psychological testing is only one of many tools that can contribute to the evaluation. Interdisciplinary collaboration involves combining the expertise of neuropsychologists with other professionals, such as psychiatrists, social workers, legal experts, and criminologists, to develop a more comprehensive understanding of the individual's mental state and behavior (Adcox, 2024). For example, a psychiatrist may provide valuable insight into an individual's psychiatric history and current mental health status, while a criminologist can offer context about the social and environmental factors that may have influenced the individual's behavior. By incorporating multiple perspectives and forms of evidence, interdisciplinary collaboration ensures that psychological test results are interpreted within a broader context and are supplemented with additional information that can inform legal decisions. This approach reduces the risk of over-reliance on psychological tests and helps to ensure that forensic evaluations are more accurate and nuanced.

Another important alternative to over-reliance on psychological testing is adopting a holistic approach to forensic evaluations. Psychological tests are often limited in their ability to capture the full complexity of an individual's life, experiences, and circumstances. A holistic evaluation considers the broader context in which the individual's behavior occurred, including factors such as their personal history, environmental influences, and social relationships (Determinations, 2015). For example, when evaluating a defendant's mental state at the time of a crime, a holistic approach would not only consider the results of psychological tests but also examine the individual's history of trauma, substance abuse, or mental illness. It would also take into account the situational factors that may have contributed to the crime, such as financial stress, family dynamics, or social isolation. A holistic evaluation recognizes that behavior is influenced by a wide range of factors and that psychological testing alone cannot fully capture the complexities of human behavior. By considering the individual's life in its entirety, holistic evaluations provide a more comprehensive understanding of the individual's mental state and legal responsibility, leading to more just and informed legal decisions.

Psychological testing is a valuable tool in forensic neuropsychology, providing critical insights into an individual's cognitive and psychological functioning. However, these assessments have inherent limitations, including the restricted scope of testing and the risk of over-reliance on test results in legal contexts. To ensure that forensic evaluations are accurate, fair, and comprehensive, it is essential to supplement psychological testing with alternative approaches, such as interdisciplinary collaboration and holistic evaluation. By combining psychological test results with insights from other experts and considering the broader context of the individual's behavior, forensic neuropsychologists can provide more accurate and nuanced assessments that contribute to just and informed legal outcomes.

9 Interdisciplinary Collaboration

Given the complex nature of psychological assessments, interdisciplinary collaboration has emerged as a crucial element in ensuring that forensic evaluations are accurate, fair, and comprehensive. In India, where the legal and medical systems are continually evolving, interdisciplinary collaboration is particularly vital for integrating diverse perspectives and improving the outcomes of forensic assessments. This section explores the importance of interdisciplinary collaboration in forensic neuropsychology in India, highlighting how the integration of expertise from neuropsychologists, legal professionals, and medical specialists can enhance the accuracy of assessments and ensure justice.

9.1 Combining Expertise for Comprehensive Evaluations

Forensic neuropsychology, by its nature, deals with complex issues that extend beyond the scope of psychology or neuropsychology alone. Questions about criminal responsibility, competency to stand trial, or the impact of mental disorders on behavior require a deep understanding of not only cognitive and psychological functioning but also medical conditions, legal standards, and ethical considerations. Therefore, it is crucial to combine the expertise of professionals from various fields to provide a holistic and accurate evaluation of an individual's mental state.

In the Indian legal system, where cases can involve a wide range of medical, psychological, and social factors, the collaboration between neuropsychologists, legal professionals, and other specialists is essential. Neuropsychologists bring their expertise in assessing cognitive functioning and identifying neurological deficits that may impact behavior, while legal professionals provide an understanding of the legal context, including how these assessments will be used in court. Medical professionals, such as neurologists or psychiatrists, can offer additional insights into the neurological or psychiatric conditions that may underlie an individual's actions. This combination of expertise ensures that assessments are comprehensive and take into account all relevant factors (Wahass, 2005).

9.2 Enhancing Accuracy and Fairness in Legal Decisions

One of the key advantages of interdisciplinary collaboration in forensic neuropsychology is its ability to enhance the accuracy and fairness of legal decisions. In a legal setting, the stakes are high, and incorrect or incomplete assessments can have serious consequences, including wrongful convictions or unjust sentencing. By involving multiple experts, interdisciplinary collaboration ensures that assessments are based on a broader and more nuanced understanding of the individual's condition, reducing the risk of error (Prakash & Prakash B, 2023).

For example, a neuropsychologist might assess an individual's cognitive functioning and conclude that they have significant impairments in executive functioning, such as planning or decision-making. However, without input from a medical professional, the neuropsychologist may not be aware that these impairments are caused by an underlying neurological condition, such as a traumatic brain injury or a degenerative disease. Similarly, a legal professional may not fully understand the implications of cognitive impairments for an individual's ability to form criminal intent. By working together, these professionals can provide a more accurate assessment that better informs legal decisions, ensuring that the individual receives a fair trial and that justice is served (Professional, 2024).

9.3 *Forensic Psychologists Working with Legal Teams*

One of the most common examples of interdisciplinary collaboration in forensic neuropsychology is the partnership between forensic psychologists and legal teams. In India, forensic psychologists are often called upon to provide expert testimony in criminal cases, particularly in cases involving questions of mental health or cognitive functioning. However, for their assessments to be meaningful in a legal context, forensic psychologists must work closely with legal professionals to ensure that their findings are presented in a way that is understandable and relevant to the court. For instance, in cases involving the insanity defense, a forensic psychologist may conduct a neuropsychological assessment to determine whether the defendant was suffering from a mental disorder at the time of the crime. However, for the court to accept this assessment, it must be framed in terms of legal standards, such as whether the defendant was able to distinguish right from wrong. By collaborating with attorneys and judges, forensic psychologists can ensure that their findings are interpreted correctly and used appropriately in legal decisions (Wahass, 2005).

In India, this collaboration is especially important given the complexities of the legal system and the growing recognition of mental health issues within the judicial process. Forensic psychologists can help legal professionals understand the psychological and cognitive factors that may influence an individual's behavior, while legal professionals can guide psychologists in ensuring that their assessments meet the requirements of the court. This partnership ultimately leads to more informed and fair legal decisions (*Forensic Psychology: Bridging the Gap Between Law and Human Behavior—Blog*, 2024).

9.4 *Medical Professionals Providing Neurological Insights*

Another crucial area of interdisciplinary collaboration in forensic neuropsychology involves the integration of medical professionals, particularly neurologists and psychiatrists. In many cases, individuals involved in criminal cases may have underlying medical conditions that affect their cognitive or psychological functioning. These conditions may include traumatic brain injuries, neurodegenerative diseases, or psychiatric disorders, all of which require medical expertise to diagnose and understand fully.

For example, in a case where a defendant exhibits signs of cognitive impairment, a neuropsychologist may conduct tests to assess memory, attention, and executive function. However, if the impairment is due to a neurological condition such as Alzheimer's disease or a brain injury, the input of a neurologist is critical for providing a complete diagnosis and understanding the implications for the individual's behavior. Similarly, psychiatrists can offer insights into how psychiatric disorders, such as schizophrenia or bipolar disorder, may affect an individual's mental state and capacity for responsibility.

In India, where access to specialized medical care can be limited in certain regions, collaboration between forensic neuropsychologists and medical professionals is particularly valuable. By combining neuropsychological assessments with medical evaluations, professionals can provide a more accurate and comprehensive understanding of the individual's condition, ensuring that the court receives all relevant information before making a decision (Casaletto & Heaton, 2017).

9.5 *Challenges and Future Directions*

While interdisciplinary collaboration in forensic neuropsychology offers significant benefits, it also presents challenges, particularly in the Indian context. One challenge is the lack of infrastructure and resources to support effective collaboration between professionals from different fields. In many parts of India, access to qualified neuropsychologists, neurologists, and forensic psychologists is limited, making it difficult to assemble interdisciplinary teams. Furthermore, the legal system may not always recognize the value of interdisciplinary collaboration, leading to a reliance on isolated assessments that do not provide a full picture of the individual's condition.

To address these challenges, it is essential to promote greater awareness of the importance of interdisciplinary collaboration in forensic neuropsychology and to develop systems that support this collaboration. This could include creating networks of professionals who can consult on forensic cases, offering training programs for legal professionals to understand the value of interdisciplinary assessments, and ensuring that courts are willing to consider the input of multiple experts when making decisions.

10 Conclusion

Neuropsychological assessments play a critical role in criminal cases, offering valuable insights into an individual's cognitive, emotional, and psychological functioning. These assessments help determine important legal issues such as a defendant's competency to stand trial, criminal responsibility, and potential risk for recidivism. The process of neuropsychological assessment involves a series of steps, including gathering background information, selecting appropriate tests, administering them, and interpreting results, all of which must be carried out thoroughly and ethically. Accurate assessments are vital to ensuring that legal decisions are based on a comprehensive understanding of the individual's mental state, rather than on incomplete or biased evaluations.

A key consideration in these assessments is the importance of cultural sensitivity. In a diverse country like India, where individuals come from various cultural, linguistic, and socioeconomic backgrounds, it is essential that assessments are adapted to avoid cultural bias. Using standardized tests that may not reflect the experiences or realities of certain populations can lead to inaccurate conclusions, potentially resulting in unjust outcomes in criminal cases. Thus, neuropsychologists must ensure that they use culturally appropriate tools and are aware of the influence of an individual's background on their cognitive and psychological performance.

Furthermore, the ethical dimensions of neuropsychological assessments are paramount. Neuropsychologists are tasked with maintaining the integrity of their evaluations by upholding ethical standards, such as informed consent, confidentiality, and the proper interpretation of results. The potential misuse of neuropsychological findings in legal contexts, particularly when the findings are overextended or misinterpreted, raises serious ethical concerns. Forensic neuropsychologists must remain impartial and ensure their work supports justice and fairness in legal proceedings.

10.1 Implications for Practice

For forensic neuropsychological assessments to be effective, there is a growing need for ongoing training and interdisciplinary collaboration. Continuous education ensures that neuropsychologists stay informed about the latest developments in assessment techniques, tools, and ethical guidelines. Since forensic cases often involve complex issues that span legal, medical, and psychological domains, collaboration between neuropsychologists, legal professionals, medical experts, and social workers is essential. This interdisciplinary approach enriches the evaluation process, allowing for a more holistic and accurate understanding of the individual's mental state, which in turn helps to inform legal decision-making.

Moreover, forensic neuropsychologists must also be equipped to communicate their findings clearly and effectively to legal professionals, ensuring that their assessments are understood and applied appropriately in court. By engaging with attorneys, judges, and other experts, neuropsychologists can bridge the gap between scientific findings and legal application, enhancing the fairness and accuracy of legal outcomes.

10.2 Future Directions

Looking ahead, improvements in forensic assessment practices will involve the refinement of assessment tools to better account for cultural and contextual differences, ensuring that tests are relevant and applicable to diverse populations. The integration of neuroimaging and other advanced techniques may also offer more objective insights into cognitive and neurological functioning, complementing traditional neuropsychological assessments.

Additionally, as the field continues to evolve, greater emphasis on interdisciplinary collaboration will be essential. Developing networks of experts from different fields, particularly in countries like India where resources may be limited, can improve the quality and depth of forensic evaluations. As forensic neuropsychology grows, the continued focus on ethical, thorough, and culturally sensitive evaluations will be vital for ensuring justice is served in criminal cases.

In conclusion, neuropsychological assessments in criminal cases are indispensable tools that offer critical insights into cognitive and psychological functioning. By adhering to ethical guidelines, embracing cultural sensitivity, and fostering interdisciplinary collaboration, the field of forensic neuropsychology can continue to make meaningful contributions to the legal system, ensuring fair and informed decisions in the pursuit of justice.

References

Adcox, S. (2024, June 24). What is a neuropsychologist? WebMD. https://www.webmd.com/mental-health/what-is-a-neuropsychologist.

Andorno, R. (2022, January 25). *Conflict of interest in research: What is it and why it matters?* H2020 INTEGRITY. https://h2020integrity.eu/conflict-of-interest-in-research-what-is-it-and-why-it-matters/

APA PRACTICE ORGANIZATION. (2015). Requests for test data and materials: Respond with care. In *GOOD PRACTICE: Vol. Winter–2015* (pp. 2–3). https://www.apaservices.org/practice/good-practice/test-data.pdf

Arvanitakis, Z., Shah, R. C., & Bennett, D. A. (2019). Diagnosis and management of dementia: Review. *JAMA, 322*(16), 1589. https://doi.org/10.1001/jama.2019.4782

Barak, A., & Buchanan, T. (2010). Internet-based psychological testing and assessment. In *Elsevier eBooks* (pp. 225–255). https://doi.org/10.1016/b978-0-12-378596-1.00012-5

Bronx Partners for Healthy Communities. (n.d.). *Cultural sensitivity*. https://www.nyc.gov/assets/ochia/downloads/pdf/cultural_sensitivity_wkshp.pdf.

Casaletto, K. B., & Heaton, R. K. (2017). Neuropsychological assessment: Past and future. *Journal of the International Neuropsychological Society, 23*(9–10), 778–790. https://doi.org/10.1017/s1355617717001060

De Pádua Serafim, A., Saffi, F., Da Silva, T. G. B., De Almeida, C. V., Hokama, E., De Barros, D. M., & Dias, A. M. (2015). Forensic neuropsychological assessment: a review of its scope. *Archives of Clinical Psychiatry (São Paulo), 42*(2), 63–67. https://doi.org/10.1590/0101-60830000000049

Determinations, C. O. P. T. I. V. T. F. S. S. a. D (2015, June 29). Cognitive tests and performance validity tests. Psychological Testing in the Service of Disability Determination - NCBI Bookshelf. https://www.ncbi.nlm.nih.gov/books/NBK305230/.

Filamrush. (2024, September 20). Neuropsychological Assessment Patient's Guide. Abbey Neuropsychology Clinic. https://www.abbeyneuropsychologyclinic.com/neuropsychological-assessment-patients-guide/.

Floyd, A. E., & Gupta, V. (2023, April 24). Minnesota multiphasic personality inventory. StatPearls - NCBI Bookshelf. https://www.ncbi.nlm.nih.gov/books/NBK557525/.

Forensic Psychology: Bridging the Gap Between Law and Human Behavior—Blog. (2024, May 22). https://blog.geetauniversity.edu.in/forensic-psychology-bridging-the-gap-between-law-and-human-behavior/.

Grabowski, K., Morgan, R., & Scanlon, F. (2023). Intellectual deficits and restoration to competency to stand trial: An examination of IQ cut off scores. *Journal of Intellectual Disabilities*. https://doi.org/10.1177/17446295231218782

Harvey, P. D. (2012). Clinical applications of neuropsychological assessment. *Dialogues in Clinical Neuroscience, 14*(1), 91–99. https://doi.org/10.31887/dcns.2012.14.1/pharvey

Hathaway, K. M., & Parsons, G. E. (2002). Behavioral management in patients with temporomandibular disorders. In *Elsevier eBooks* (pp. 326–336). https://doi.org/10.1016/b0-7216-7278-7/50025-3

Iverson, G. L. (2006). Ethical issues associated with the assessment of exaggeration, poor effort, and malingering. *Applied Neuropsychology, 13*(2), 77–90. https://doi.org/10.1207/s15324826an1302_3

Johnson-Greene, D., & Bechtold, K. T. (2002). Ethical considerations for peer review in forensic neuropsychology. *The Clinical Neuropsychologist, 16*(1), 97–104. https://doi.org/10.1076/clin.16.1.97.8335

Louw, D. (2015). Forensic psychology. In *Elsevier eBooks* (pp. 351–356). https://doi.org/10.1016/b978-0-08-097086-8.21074-x

Manly, J. J. (2008). Critical issues in cultural neuropsychology: Profit from diversity. *Neuropsychology Review, 18*(3), 179–183. https://doi.org/10.1007/s11065-008-9068-8

Mattson, S. N., Bernes, G. A., & Doyle, L. R. (2019). Fetal alcohol Spectrum disorders: A review of the neurobehavioral deficits associated with prenatal alcohol exposure. *Alcoholism Clinical and Experimental Research, 43*(6), 1046–1062. https://doi.org/10.1111/acer.14040

Merkt, H., Haesen, S., Eytan, A., Habermeyer, E., Aebi, M. F., Elger, B., & Wangmo, T. (2021). Forensic mental health professionals' perceptions of their dual loyalty conflict: Findings from a qualitative study. *BMC Medical Ethics, 22*(1). https://doi.org/10.1186/s12910-021-00688-2

Moore, M. (2022, November 17). What is the Millon clinical multiaxial inventory (MCMI-IV)? Psych Central. https://psychcentral.com/lib/millon-clinical-multiaxial-inventory-mcmi-iii.

Olejarczyk, J. P., & Young, M. (2024, May 6). Patient rights and ethics. StatPearls - NCBI Bookshelf. https://www.ncbi.nlm.nih.gov/books/NBK538279/.

Prakash, B., Jr., & Prakash, B. (2023). Forensic Psychology and its impact on the legal system. *Journal of Criminology and Forensic Studies, 5*(1), 180056. [Journal-article] . https://academicstrive.com/JOCFS/JOCFS180056.pdf

Professional, C. C. M. (2024, May 31). Neuropsychological testing and assessment. Cleveland Clinic. https://my.clevelandclinic.org/health/diagnostics/4893-neuropsychological-testing-and-assessment.

Rabinovici, G. D., Stephens, M. L., & Possin, K. L. (2015). Executive dysfunction. *CONTINUUM Lifelong Learning in Neurology, 21*, 646–659. https://doi.org/10.1212/01.con.0000466658.05156.54

Rocchio, L. M. (2020). Ethical and professional considerations in the forensic assessment of complex trauma and dissociation. *Psychological Injury and Law, 13*(2), 124–134. https://doi.org/10.1007/s12207-020-09384-9

Sarason, I. G. (2024, September 13). Personality assessment | definition, types, importance, uses, & facts. *Encyclopedia Britannica*. .

Schaefer, L. A., Thakur, T., & Meager, M. R. (2023, May 16). Neuropsychological assessment. StatPearls - NCBI Bookshelf. https://www.ncbi.nlm.nih.gov/books/NBK513310/.

Schrag, A., Barone, P., Brown, R. G., Leentjens, A. F., McDonald, W. M., Starkstein, S., Weintraub, D., Poewe, W., Rascol, O., Sampaio, C., Stebbins, G. T., & Goetz, C. G. (2007). Depression rating scales in Parkinson's disease: Critique and recommendations. *Movement Disorders, 22*(8), 1077–1092. https://doi.org/10.1002/mds.21333

Structured Clinical Interview for DSM Disorders (SCID). (2018, July 26). Columbia University Department of Psychiatry. https://www.columbiapsychiatry.org/research/research-areas/services-policy-and-law/structured-clinical-interview-dsm-disorders-scid.

Van Es, R., Kunst, M., & De Keijser, J. (2020). Forensic mental health expert testimony and judicial decision-making: A systematic literature review. *Aggression and Violent Behavior, 51*, 101387. https://doi.org/10.1016/j.avb.2020.101387

Wahass, S. H. (2005, August 1). The role of psychologists in health care delivery. PubMed Central (PMC). https://www.ncbi.nlm.nih.gov/pmc/articles/PMC3410123/.

What Is Ethics in Research and Why Is It Important? (n.d.). National Institute of Environmental Health Sciences. https://www.niehs.nih.gov/research/resources/bioethics/whatis

Yadav, P. K. (2017). Ethical issues across different fields of forensic science. *Egyptian Journal of Forensic Sciences, 7*(1). https://doi.org/10.1186/s41935-017-0010-1

Zucco, G. M., & Sartori, G. (2023). Sensory and cognitive malingering: Studies and tests. *Sci, 5*(3), 27. https://doi.org/10.3390/sci5030027

Neuropsychological Interventions in Forensic Settings

1 Introduction

Rehabilitative therapy for individuals with neurological impairments resulting from criminal activity represents a critical intersection of neuroscience, psychology, and criminal justice. Neurological impairments, often arising from head trauma, substance abuse, or developmental disorders, can influence criminal behavior and complicate the rehabilitation process. Addressing these impairments requires an interdisciplinary approach that combines forensic neuropsychology, rehabilitation techniques, and legal frameworks. In forensic settings, rehabilitative therapies focus on the cognitive, emotional, and behavioral rehabilitation of offenders. Various interventions, ranging from cognitive behavioral therapies (CBT) to neurorehabilitation techniques, are employed to reduce recidivism and improve behavioral outcomes. This section explores the different therapeutic techniques used in forensic settings, evaluates their effectiveness in reducing criminal behavior, and assesses their impact on recidivism.

Neurological impairments play a significant role in criminal behavior. For instance, traumatic brain injury (TBI) is linked to increased aggression, impulsivity, and difficulty in controlling behavior, which are risk factors for criminal activity. Substance abuse, particularly involving alcohol and drugs like methamphetamine, can also lead to impairments in decision-making, emotional regulation, and social cognition, further heightening the risk of engaging in criminal acts. Developmental disorders such as attention deficit hyperactivity disorder (ADHD), fetal alcohol spectrum disorder (FASD), and autism spectrum disorder (ASD) are associated with deficits in impulse control, empathy, and executive functioning, making individuals more vulnerable to involvement in the criminal justice system. Effective rehabilitation must address the neurological underpinnings of these behaviors, not only for the sake of reducing criminal tendencies but also for the overall improvement of the individual's mental and physical health.

© The Author(s), under exclusive license to Springer Nature Switzerland AG 2025

K. J. Reddy, *Foundations of Criminal Forensic Neuropsychology*,
https://doi.org/10.1007/978-3-031-83771-5_7

2 Therapeutic Techniques in Forensic Settings

1. Cognitive Behavioral Therapy (CBT)

Cognitive behavioral therapy remains one of the most widely used interventions in forensic settings. CBT focuses on altering maladaptive thought patterns and behaviors that contribute to criminal actions. In individuals with neurological impairments, such as those resulting from TBI or developmental disorders, CBT can help modify impulsive and aggressive behaviors, improving emotional regulation and problem-solving abilities. CBT is often delivered through structured programs like "Reasoning and Rehabilitation," designed to teach cognitive skills such as critical thinking, moral reasoning, and empathy.

2. Neurorehabilitation Techniques

Neurorehabilitation aims to restore lost neurological function, enhance cognitive abilities, and help individuals regain control over their behavior. Techniques such as cognitive remediation therapy (CRT) are employed to address cognitive deficits in areas like attention, memory, and executive functioning. For offenders with TBI, CRT helps improve their ability to plan, inhibit inappropriate responses, and make sound decisions. These interventions are often combined with other therapeutic approaches to address the emotional and behavioral components of criminal conduct.

Additionally, newer approaches like neurofeedback and transcranial magnetic stimulation (TMS) are being explored for their potential in improving self-regulation and cognitive control in offenders with neurological impairments. While still experimental in forensic settings, these therapies have shown promise in enhancing cognitive functions and reducing impulsivity, making them potential tools for reducing recidivism.

3. Mindfulness-Based Interventions (MBI)

Mindfulness-based interventions, such as mindfulness-based stress reduction (MBSR), have gained traction in the criminal justice system for their ability to reduce stress, enhance emotional regulation, and promote self-awareness. For individuals with neurological impairments, MBI offers a noninvasive approach to rehabilitation by helping them become more aware of their thoughts and emotions, thereby reducing impulsive behaviors and aggression. Research suggests that mindfulness can improve neural connectivity in areas of the brain related to attention and emotional regulation, which are often compromised in individuals with TBI or substance abuse histories (Keng et al., 2011).

4. Dialectical Behavior Therapy (DBT)

DBT is another effective therapeutic approach for individuals with neurological impairments, particularly those with emotional dysregulation (Vijayapriya & Tamarana, 2023). Originally developed for treating borderline personality disorder, DBT has been adapted for forensic populations to help manage extreme emotional responses, reduce self-harming behaviors, and improve interpersonal relationships. DBT teaches skills such as distress tolerance, emotional regulation, and interpersonal effectiveness, making it a suitable intervention for offenders struggling with anger, impulsivity, or violent tendencies due to neurological impairments.

5. Occupational Therapy (OT)

Occupational therapy focuses on helping individuals regain functional abilities necessary for daily life, including social and vocational skills (Jacob & Samuel, 2017). In forensic settings, OT can be particularly beneficial for offenders with cognitive impairments, offering interventions that promote independence, improve cognitive functioning, and help offenders reintegrate into society. Through a focus on life skills, OT helps address the social and practical challenges that may contribute to criminal behavior, such as poor impulse control or an inability to manage daily stressors.

3 Evaluating the Impact of Interventions on Recidivism

Recidivism, or the tendency of previously convicted individuals to re-offend, is a critical measure of the success of rehabilitative therapies in forensic settings. Research on the effectiveness of interventions such as CBT, neurorehabilitation, and mindfulness-based therapies indicates varying degrees of success in reducing recidivism (Tickell et al., 2019).

Studies have shown that CBT-based programs, when tailored to the specific cognitive deficits and behavioral challenges of individuals with neurological impairments, can lead to significant reductions in recidivism (Lardén et al., 2021). For instance, offenders with TBI or developmental disorders who participated in CBT programs exhibited improved problem-solving skills, increased empathy, and a better ability to control impulsive behavior, leading to lower rates of re-offending.

Neurorehabilitation has also shown promise in reducing recidivism by improving cognitive functions and self-regulation. Offenders who underwent cognitive remediation therapy demonstrated enhanced executive functioning and decision-making skills, reducing their likelihood of engaging in criminal activities post-release (Jones et al., 2024). However, more research is needed to determine the long-term effectiveness of neurorehabilitation in forensic settings.

Mindfulness-based interventions have been found to reduce recidivism by promoting self-awareness, emotional regulation, and empathy. By improving neural connectivity in areas of the brain responsible for emotional control, MBI helps individuals with neurological impairments develop the cognitive and emotional skills necessary to avoid future criminal behavior.

In forensic settings, the application of therapeutic interventions serves the dual purposes of rehabilitation and protection. Rehabilitation aims to correct criminal behavior by addressing psychological, cognitive, and emotional deficits, thus encouraging prosocial behaviors (Morgan et al., 2011). Various therapeutic techniques are employed in these settings, including psychotherapy, pharmaceutical therapies, and cognitive remediation programs (CRPs), all of which are tailored to meet the unique needs of the forensic population. This section explores each of these approaches, emphasizing their significance in promoting cognitive rehabilitation and reducing recidivism.

3.1 *Rehabilitative Therapies*

Rehabilitation in forensic settings is designed to correct maladaptive behaviors, enhance cognitive functioning, and foster positive social engagement. For individuals with criminal behavior, rehabilitative therapies aim to address cognitive deficits such as impulsivity, problem-solving difficulties, and emotional dysregulation. These therapies focus on increasing insight into one's behaviors and their consequences, improving impulse control, and enhancing decision-making abilities.

A fundamental goal of rehabilitation is the reduction of recidivism. Rehabilitative therapies are considered crucial for encouraging prosocial behavior by addressing underlying psychological or cognitive deficits that may contribute to criminal activity. For example, impulse control is a significant concern in many individuals within the criminal justice system, especially those convicted of violent crimes. The enhancement of cognitive abilities, including self-regulation and decision-making, is central to successful rehabilitation and reintegration into society.

3.2 *Types of Interventions in Forensic Settings*

In forensic settings, three primary therapeutic interventions are widely used to address the unique challenges posed by the forensic population: psychotherapy, pharmaceutical therapies, and cognitive remediation programs. These interventions often operate in tandem to target various facets of criminal behavior, from psychological disorders to cognitive deficits.

3.2.1 Psychotherapy

Psychotherapy is an essential tool in forensic settings and is adapted to address specific challenges faced by offenders. Psychotherapeutic approaches can range from cognitive behavioral therapy (CBT) to more specialized therapies such as dialectical behavior therapy (DBT) and trauma-focused therapy. These therapies aim to help offenders understand the root causes of their behavior, identify triggers, and develop healthier coping mechanisms.

Cognitive behavioral therapy (CBT) is one of the most widely used therapies in forensic settings. CBT is particularly effective in addressing cognitive distortions, impulsive behaviors, and emotional regulation, all of which are common issues in the forensic population. By challenging distorted thinking patterns, CBT helps offenders take responsibility for their actions and develop strategies to manage their impulses. CBT is structured, goal-oriented, and often delivered in group settings, making it suitable for correctional environments.

Dialectical behavior therapy (DBT) is another psychotherapeutic intervention tailored to individuals with high emotional dysregulation, such as those with borderline personality disorder. In forensic settings, DBT has been used to reduce self-harm, suicidal behaviors, and aggression. DBT teaches mindfulness, emotional regulation, distress tolerance, and interpersonal effectiveness, providing offenders with the tools to manage their emotions and interactions with others more effectively.

Trauma-focused therapies are increasingly recognized in forensic settings, particularly for individuals who have experienced trauma, abuse, or neglect (Cohen & Mannarino, 2015). Many offenders have histories of trauma, and untreated trauma can perpetuate criminal behavior. Trauma-informed care focuses on understanding the role of trauma in shaping behavior and offers therapeutic strategies that prioritize safety, empowerment, and healing.

3.2.2 Pharmaceutical Therapies

Pharmaceutical therapies are often used in conjunction with psychotherapy to manage mental health conditions and improve cognitive functioning. Many offenders in forensic settings suffer from psychiatric disorders such as depression, anxiety, bipolar disorder, and schizophrenia. Without proper treatment, these conditions can exacerbate criminal behavior, particularly if the individual experiences hallucinations, delusions, or mood dysregulation.

Antipsychotics, mood stabilizers, antidepressants, and anxiolytics are commonly prescribed to manage psychiatric symptoms that may contribute to maladaptive behaviors (Correll et al., 2015). For instance, antipsychotic medications are used to treat individuals with schizophrenia or schizoaffective disorders, particularly those who exhibit delusions or hallucinations. Mood stabilizers like lithium and anticonvulsants may be used to regulate mood swings, which are common in individuals with bipolar disorder or severe emotional dysregulation.

The use of psychotropic medications can help stabilize offenders, making them more responsive to psychotherapeutic interventions. However, pharmaceutical treatments must be carefully monitored, particularly in forensic settings where compliance may be an issue (Sardella et al., 2021). Integrating medication management into broader therapeutic programs ensures that offenders receive comprehensive care, addressing both the psychological and biological aspects of their behavior.

3.2.3 Cognitive Remediation Programs

Cognitive remediation is a targeted therapeutic approach designed to improve cognitive deficits often found in the forensic population, including impairments in attention, memory, executive function, and problem-solving abilities. These deficits can exacerbate impulsivity, hinder decision-making, and impair the individual's ability to plan and execute prosocial behaviors.

Cognitive remediation programs focus on enhancing cognitive skills through structured exercises, computerized tasks, and real-world applications (Joyal et al., 2016). These programs often target specific cognitive domains that are impaired in offenders, such as working memory or cognitive flexibility. Working memory training, for example, helps individuals hold and manipulate information, which is crucial for problem-solving and making informed decisions.

In forensic settings, cognitive remediation programs are often integrated with other therapeutic approaches, such as CBT. This integration ensures that offenders not only receive direct interventions to address their cognitive deficits but also learn to apply these newly acquired skills in everyday situations. For example, offenders may practice problem-solving skills in the context of managing conflicts, thus directly translating cognitive improvements into behavioral changes.

Neurofeedback is another innovative form of cognitive remediation that has shown promise in forensic settings. Neurofeedback involves training individuals to self-regulate brain activity through real-time monitoring of brain waves. This technique is particularly effective for individuals with impulse control disorders or attention deficits. By learning to modulate their brain activity, offenders can improve self-regulation, focus, and decision-making abilities.

Therapeutic techniques in forensic settings play a crucial role in addressing the complex psychological, cognitive, and emotional needs of offenders. Rehabilitative therapies aim to reduce recidivism and encourage prosocial behavior by targeting underlying cognitive and emotional deficits. Psychotherapy, pharmaceutical therapies, and cognitive remediation programs each contribute uniquely to the rehabilitation process, offering a comprehensive approach to managing criminal behavior. By addressing the root causes of maladaptive behaviors, these therapeutic interventions provide offenders with the tools they need to reintegrate into society successfully and lead prosocial lives.

4 Psychotherapy

Neuropsychological interventions in forensic settings have gained increasing recognition as effective tools for addressing the complex psychological and cognitive needs of individuals involved in the criminal justice system. These interventions encompass a range of psychotherapeutic approaches, each designed to tackle the unique challenges faced by offenders, including harmful thought patterns, emotional dysregulation, and a lack of motivation for change. Key therapeutic modalities include cognitive behavioral therapy (CBT), dialectical behavior therapy (DBT), and motivational interviewing (MI). This section will explore these psychotherapeutic approaches, their effectiveness in forensic contexts, and their roles in promoting rehabilitation and improving the quality of life for individuals with neurological impairments.

Psychotherapy is a cornerstone of neuropsychological interventions in forensic settings, providing a structured environment for individuals to explore and modify their thoughts, emotions, and behaviors. In many cases, offenders may exhibit patterns of thinking and behavior that contribute to criminal activity, often driven by underlying neurological or psychological issues. By engaging in psychotherapy, individuals can gain insight into these patterns, learn to manage their symptoms, and develop healthier coping strategies.

4.1 *Types of Psychotherapy*

Several psychotherapeutic approaches are particularly relevant in forensic settings, including cognitive behavioral therapy (CBT), dialectical behavior therapy (DBT), and motivational interviewing (MI). Each of these modalities has distinct goals and techniques tailored to address the specific needs of the forensic population.

4.1.1 Cognitive Behavioral Therapy (CBT)

Cognitive behavioral therapy (CBT) is one of the most widely used psychotherapeutic approaches in forensic settings cognitive behavioral therapy (CBT) is one of the most widely used psychotherapeutic approaches in forensic settings. CBT focuses on identifying and modifying dysfunctional thought patterns and behaviors that contribute to maladaptive actions, including criminal behavior. This approach operates on the premise that cognitive distortions—such as negative thinking, catastrophizing, or all-or-nothing thinking—can significantly impact emotional regulation and decision-making.

In CBT, individuals are taught to recognize and challenge their negative thought patterns. For example, an offender may hold the belief that "I can never change" or "I have no control over my actions." Through the therapeutic process, they learn to replace these distorted thoughts with more balanced and constructive beliefs. This cognitive restructuring empowers individuals to make more informed decisions, manage their impulses, and ultimately reduce the likelihood of re-offending.

Research has demonstrated the effectiveness of CBT in reducing recidivism rates among offenders. Studies indicate that CBT can significantly decrease criminal behavior by equipping individuals with coping strategies and enhancing their ability to think critically about their actions (Nakao et al., 2021). The structured nature of CBT, often involving homework assignments and skill-building exercises, ensures that individuals are actively engaged in their rehabilitation process.

4.1.2 Dialectical Behavior Therapy (DBT)

Dialectical behavior therapy (DBT) is another effective therapeutic approach frequently employed in forensic settings, particularly for individuals with emotional dysregulation and interpersonal difficulties (May et al., 2016). Originally developed for individuals with borderline personality disorder, DBT focuses on enhancing emotional regulation and improving interpersonal skills. This therapy emphasizes the balance between acceptance and change, encouraging individuals to accept their current emotions while also striving for personal growth.

In forensic contexts, DBT has shown promise in reducing self-destructive behaviors, impulsivity, and aggression. The skills taught in DBT—including mindfulness, distress tolerance, emotional regulation, and interpersonal effectiveness—are particularly beneficial for individuals with histories of trauma or emotional instability. By learning to manage their emotions more effectively, offenders can reduce their reliance on maladaptive coping mechanisms, such as substance abuse or violence.

DBT also incorporates group therapy sessions, where individuals can practice their skills in a supportive environment. This communal aspect fosters accountability and encourages individuals to learn from one another's experiences. Studies have indicated that DBT can lead to significant reductions in self-harm behaviors and criminal activity, making it a valuable intervention in forensic settings (Kothgassner et al., 2021).

4.1.3 Motivational Interviewing (MI)

Motivational interviewing (MI) is a client-centered approach that aims to enhance an individual's motivation for change. In forensic settings, MI is particularly relevant for individuals who may be ambivalent about engaging in treatment or making significant life changes. By fostering an open dialogue, MI helps individuals explore their motivations, values, and barriers to change, ultimately guiding them toward a commitment to self-improvement.

The MI process involves reflective listening, empathetic responses, and open-ended questions to encourage individuals to articulate their thoughts and feelings about change. This approach empowers individuals to take ownership of their recovery journey, making them more likely to engage in therapy and adhere to treatment recommendations.

Research has shown that MI can be an effective intervention for promoting change among individuals in forensic settings (Bischof et al., 2021). By enhancing intrinsic motivation, MI can lead to improved treatment adherence, increased participation in rehabilitative programs, and a reduction in criminal behavior. The collaborative nature of MI fosters a supportive therapeutic alliance, which is critical for individuals who may have experienced distrust in relationships due to their past behaviors.

4.2 *Effectiveness of Neuropsychological Interventions*

Neuropsychological interventions, including CBT, DBT, and MI, have demonstrated significant effectiveness in forensic settings. These therapeutic approaches help individuals understand and modify harmful behaviors, manage symptoms related to neurological impairments, and enhance their overall functioning. The structured nature of these therapies provides offenders with the tools they need to navigate their thoughts and emotions effectively.

Moreover, the integration of psychotherapy within a comprehensive rehabilitation program can lead to improved outcomes. By addressing underlying cognitive and emotional issues, neuropsychological interventions play a vital role in reducing recidivism and promoting successful reintegration into society. As individuals gain insight into their behaviors and develop healthier coping strategies, they become better equipped to manage their lives positively.

5 Neuropsychological Interventions on Criminal Behavior: Pharmaceutical Therapies

Criminal behavior is often the result of a complex interplay of biological, psychological, and social factors. Within this context, neuropsychological interventions play a crucial role in addressing the cognitive and behavioral patterns that may contribute to criminal activity. Among these interventions, pharmaceutical therapies are essential for managing psychiatric and neurological conditions that may exacerbate impulsivity, aggression, and other maladaptive behaviors commonly found in the criminal population. This section explores the types of medications used in neuropsychological interventions—antidepressants, antipsychotics, and stimulants—and examines their impact on behavior and cognitive function in individuals with criminal tendencies.

Pharmaceutical therapies are a vital component of neuropsychological interventions in forensic settings, particularly for individuals who present with severe mental health issues that contribute to their criminal behavior. These therapies aim to alleviate symptoms related to mood disorders, psychosis, impulsivity, and cognitive deficits that often underlie criminal actions. By stabilizing mood, enhancing cognitive functioning, and reducing aggressive tendencies, medications can significantly improve an individual's ability to engage in rehabilitative programs and decrease the likelihood of re-offending.

5.1 Medication Types in Neuropsychological Interventions

Three main categories of medications are frequently used to address the psychiatric and cognitive issues associated with criminal behavior: antidepressants, antipsychotics, and stimulants. Each of these medication types targets specific symptoms, and their use is often tailored to the individual's unique neuropsychological profile.

5.1.1 Antidepressants: Managing Mood Disorders and Impulsivity

Antidepressants are commonly prescribed to individuals with mood disorders such as depression and anxiety, which can significantly influence criminal behavior. Mood disorders, particularly when left untreated, can exacerbate impulsivity, aggression, and poor decision-making. For instance, individuals with major depressive disorder may experience persistent feelings of hopelessness or worthlessness, which can manifest in destructive behaviors or substance abuse. In other cases, anxiety disorders can lead to heightened irritability and impulsiveness, contributing to violent or erratic actions.

There are several classes of antidepressants, including selective serotonin reuptake inhibitors (SSRIs), serotonin-norepinephrine reuptake inhibitors (SNRIs), and tricyclic antidepressants (Chu & Wadhwa, 2023). SSRIs, such as fluoxetine (Prozac) and sertraline (Zoloft), are the most commonly prescribed antidepressants due to their relatively mild side-effect profile and effectiveness in improving mood regulation. SNRIs, such as venlafaxine (Effexor), are often used when SSRIs are ineffective, as they target both serotonin and norepinephrine, enhancing their efficacy in regulating mood and reducing impulsivity.

In a forensic context, the use of antidepressants can significantly reduce symptoms of depression and anxiety, leading to improved emotional regulation and impulse control. For instance, individuals with depression who experience emotional numbness or irritability may become more responsive to psychotherapy once their mood stabilizes. Similarly, those with anxiety-related criminal behavior may exhibit reduced aggression and a greater ability to think rationally in high-stress situations. By improving mood and emotional resilience, antidepressants indirectly help offenders manage the emotional triggers that may lead to criminal activity.

5.1.2 Antipsychotics: Addressing Psychosis and Severe Mental Illness

Antipsychotic medications are used to manage symptoms of psychosis, including delusions, hallucinations, and paranoia, which can be prevalent in individuals with schizophrenia, schizoaffective disorder, or bipolar disorder (Ceraso et al., 2020). These symptoms can lead to criminal behavior, particularly if an individual's perception of reality is impaired. For example, individuals experiencing delusions may believe they are acting in self-defense or under the orders of a perceived authority, leading to violent or erratic actions.

There are two main classes of antipsychotics: typical (first-generation) and atypical (second-generation) antipsychotics (Chokhawala & Stevens, 2023). Typical antipsychotics, such as haloperidol (Haldol), are effective in treating positive symptoms of psychosis, such as hallucinations and delusions, but often come with severe side effects, including extrapyramidal symptoms (motor control issues). Atypical antipsychotics, such as risperidone (Risperdal) and olanzapine (Zyprexa), are preferred in modern clinical practice due to their lower risk of motor side effects and their ability to treat both positive and negative symptoms of psychosis (such as social withdrawal and emotional flatness).

In forensic populations, antipsychotic medications play a crucial role in stabilizing individuals with severe mental illness, making them more amenable to treatment and reducing their risk of engaging in criminal behavior. By diminishing hallucinations and delusions, antipsychotics allow individuals to engage more fully with reality, thereby decreasing the likelihood of engaging in violent or illegal activities driven by distorted perceptions. Moreover, as their mood and cognitive function stabilize, individuals may become more responsive to therapeutic interventions aimed at rehabilitation.

5.1.3 Stimulants: Managing Attention Deficits and Impulsivity

Stimulant medications, such as methylphenidate (Ritalin) and amphetamines (Adderall), are primarily used to treat attention deficit hyperactivity disorder (ADHD). ADHD is characterized by symptoms such as impulsivity, hyperactivity, and inattention, all of which can contribute to criminal behavior. Individuals with ADHD may struggle to regulate their impulses, leading to poor decision-making, risk-taking behaviors, and difficulties adhering to social norms (Winstanley et al., 2006).

In forensic settings, stimulant medications are used to enhance cognitive functioning, particularly in individuals with ADHD. These medications work by increasing the levels of dopamine and norepinephrine in the brain, thereby improving attention, impulse control, and executive functioning. By enhancing an individual's ability to focus and regulate their impulses, stimulant medications can reduce the likelihood of engaging in impulsive or criminal behaviors.

Research has demonstrated that stimulant medications can significantly reduce symptoms of ADHD, leading to improved cognitive function and a reduction in criminal behavior (Chang et al., 2019). For instance, individuals who previously struggled with impulsivity may find it easier to plan and execute their actions more thoughtfully. Moreover, by improving attention and focus, stimulants can increase an individual's engagement in rehabilitative programs, further reducing the risk of recidivism.

5.2 *Impact on Criminal Behavior*

The impact of pharmaceutical therapies on criminal behavior is profound, as these medications help manage the symptoms that often contribute to maladaptive actions. By addressing underlying mood disorders, psychosis, and attention deficits, pharmaceutical therapies stabilize individuals' emotions and cognitive functioning, enabling them to engage more productively in rehabilitative efforts. For example, antidepressants help individuals manage mood swings and reduce impulsivity, making them less likely to act out in anger or frustration. Antipsychotics, by reducing psychotic symptoms, decrease the likelihood of criminal actions driven by delusions or hallucinations. Stimulants, by improving attention and impulse control, enable individuals to regulate their behaviors more effectively and adhere to societal norms. In addition to stabilizing mood and cognitive function, pharmaceutical therapies can enhance the effectiveness of other therapeutic interventions, such as psychotherapy. Individuals who are more emotionally and cognitively stable are better able to participate in therapy, process feedback, and develop prosocial behaviors that reduce the risk of future criminal activity. By using medications such as antidepressants, antipsychotics, and stimulants, clinicians in forensic settings can stabilize mood, improve cognitive functioning, and reduce impulsivity, thereby decreasing the likelihood of recidivism. These interventions, when integrated with broader rehabilitative programs, play a critical role in promoting long-term behavioral change and successful reintegration into society.

6 Cognitive Remediation Programs: A Tool for Enhancing Cognitive Function in Criminal Populations

Cognitive remediation programs (CRPs) have emerged as a powerful intervention to address cognitive deficits that often contribute to criminal behavior. These programs are designed to improve cognitive functions such as memory, attention, executive functioning, and problem-solving, all of which are essential for adaptive behavior in daily life. By enhancing these skills, CRPs aim to reduce criminal tendencies and promote rehabilitation in individuals who may struggle with cognitive impairments. This section will explore the purpose of cognitive remediation programs, the techniques used to enhance cognitive function, and the effectiveness of these interventions in reducing cognitive deficits related to criminal behavior.

The primary purpose of cognitive remediation programs is to improve cognitive functions that are often impaired in individuals who exhibit criminal behavior. Many offenders suffer from cognitive deficits that affect their ability to think rationally, regulate impulses, make decisions, and solve problems. These deficits can arise from various sources, including neurological conditions, substance abuse, trauma, or developmental issues, which are prevalent among criminal populations. In particular, cognitive impairments in areas such as executive functioning, memory, and attention can severely limit an individual's ability to make informed choices, adhere to social norms, and engage in constructive behaviors. For instance, poor executive functioning may result in impulsive decision-making, while deficits in memory and attention can hinder an individual's ability to follow through with plans or recall important information, both of which are essential for social integration and law-abiding behavior. By targeting these cognitive deficits, CRPs seek to improve an individual's overall cognitive functioning, which can, in turn, reduce the risk of criminal activity. The underlying belief is that improving cognitive abilities can foster better decision-making, increase impulse control, and enhance the ability to adapt to societal expectations, ultimately decreasing the likelihood of recidivism.

Cognitive remediation programs employ a variety of techniques to enhance cognitive functioning. These techniques are typically tailored to the specific needs of individuals and may include computer-based training, skills training, and memory rehabilitation. Each of these techniques addresses different aspects of cognitive functioning and plays a crucial role in promoting cognitive recovery and adaptive behavior.

6.1 Computer-Based Training

Computer-based training is one of the most commonly used techniques in CRPs, particularly for improving attention, memory, and executive functioning. This type of training involves a series of exercises designed to challenge and enhance cognitive abilities through repetitive tasks. The exercises are typically delivered via specialized software programs that target specific cognitive domains. For instance, computer-based training may include tasks that require participants to focus on visual or auditory stimuli for extended periods, helping to improve sustained attention. Other exercises might involve working memory tasks that require individuals to hold and manipulate information in their minds, enhancing memory retention and recall. Executive functioning exercises may involve problem-solving tasks that challenge individuals to think strategically, plan ahead, and make decisions under pressure. Research has shown that computer-based training can lead to measurable improvements in cognitive functioning, particularly in areas like attention, memory, and executive control (Yang & Kwak, 2017). The repetitive nature of these exercises allows individuals to practice and refine their cognitive skills over time, leading to lasting improvements that can enhance daily functioning and reduce the cognitive deficits associated with criminal behavior.

6.2 *Skills Training*

Skills training is another key component of cognitive remediation programs, focusing on the development of practical skills that are essential for daily functioning. This type of training is designed to help individuals improve their ability to navigate everyday tasks, such as managing time, organizing activities, solving problems, and making decisions. In forensic settings, skills training often emphasizes practical applications that are directly relevant to an individual's life, such as managing finances, maintaining employment, and adhering to legal requirements like probation conditions. These practical skills are essential for successful reintegration into society and can reduce the likelihood of re-offending. Skills training typically involves both cognitive and behavioral components. On the cognitive side, individuals learn to develop mental strategies for planning, organizing, and problem-solving. On the behavioral side, individuals practice these skills in real-world settings, often with the guidance of a therapist or coach who provides feedback and support. By combining cognitive and behavioral elements, skills training helps individuals translate their cognitive improvements into meaningful behavioral changes that can enhance their ability to function in society.

6.3 *Memory Rehabilitation*

Memory rehabilitation is a critical component of CRPs, particularly for individuals who struggle with memory deficits that affect their ability to recall information and perform everyday tasks. Memory impairments are common among individuals with neurological conditions, substance use disorders, or traumatic brain injuries, all of which are prevalent in criminal populations. Memory rehabilitation focuses on teaching individuals strategies to improve their memory retention and recall. These strategies may include mnemonic devices, visualization techniques, repetition, and the use of external aids such as calendars, checklists, or alarms. The goal is to provide individuals with tools that can help them compensate for their memory deficits and improve their ability to retain and retrieve information. For example, individuals may learn to break down complex tasks into smaller, manageable steps and use visual or verbal cues to remember each step. They may also practice recalling information under timed conditions to enhance their ability to retrieve memories quickly and accurately. By improving memory functioning, individuals are better able to manage daily tasks, adhere to schedules, and meet social and legal obligations, all of which contribute to reducing criminal behavior.

6.4 *Effectiveness of Cognitive Remediation Programs*

The effectiveness of cognitive remediation programs in forensic settings has been well-documented in research. Numerous studies have shown that CRPs can lead to significant improvements in cognitive functioning, particularly in areas such as attention, memory, and executive control (Halicka et al., 2020). These improvements are not only measurable in terms of cognitive performance but also translate into real-world benefits, such as enhanced decision-making, impulse control, and problem-solving abilities. One of the key benefits of CRPs is their ability to reduce cognitive deficits that contribute to criminal behavior. For instance, individuals who struggle with impulsivity due to poor executive functioning may be more likely to engage in criminal acts without considering the consequences. By improving executive control through cognitive exercises and skills training, CRPs help individuals develop the ability to think more rationally and make more informed decisions. Moreover, by enhancing memory and attention, CRPs improve an individual's ability to adhere to social norms and legal obligations. Individuals with better memory retention are more likely to remember important details, such as court dates, probation requirements, or treatment plans, reducing the likelihood of legal infractions. Additionally, the benefits of CRPs extend beyond cognitive functioning to include improvements in mental health and well-being. As individuals gain confidence in their cognitive abilities, they may experience reductions in stress, anxiety, and frustration, which can further contribute to their rehabilitation and reduce the risk of recidivism.

Cognitive remediation programs are a valuable tool in forensic settings, offering targeted interventions that enhance cognitive functioning and reduce cognitive deficits related to criminal behavior. Through techniques such as computer-based training, skills training, and memory rehabilitation, CRPs help individuals improve essential cognitive skills, such as memory, attention, and executive control. These improvements not only enhance cognitive performance but also contribute to better decision-making, impulse control, and daily functioning, ultimately reducing the likelihood of criminal behavior and promoting successful reintegration into society.

7 Achievements and Challenges in Forensic Interventions

Forensic interventions, particularly those aimed at addressing cognitive, behavioral, and psychological deficits, have gained prominence in efforts to rehabilitate criminal offenders. These interventions often encompass a range of therapeutic approaches, including cognitive-behavioral therapies (CBT), cognitive remediation programs (CRPs), and pharmacological treatments. Despite their potential to reduce recidivism and improve behavior, the implementation of these interventions faces several challenges. This section explores the key achievements of forensic interventions—reduced recidivism and improved behavior—while also examining the challenges that persist in their application, including implementation issues and individual differences in response to treatment.

One of the most significant achievements of forensic interventions is their ability to reduce recidivism and foster positive behavioral change. Recidivism, or the tendency of previously convicted individuals to re-offend, has long been a concern in criminal justice systems around the world. Through targeted interventions, forensic programs aim to address the underlying cognitive, psychological, and behavioral factors that contribute to criminal behavior, leading to lasting changes in an individual's propensity to engage in unlawful activities.

8 Reduced Recidivism: Evidence of Success

One of the clearest indicators of the success of forensic interventions is the reduction in recidivism rates. Research has consistently shown that therapeutic interventions, when applied appropriately, can significantly lower the likelihood of re-offending (Lamberti, 2016). Cognitive behavioral therapy (CBT), for instance, has been found to be particularly effective in reducing recidivism among offenders. CBT targets maladaptive thought patterns, teaching individuals how to replace negative cognitions with more adaptive, prosocial thinking. By changing the way offenders view themselves, others, and the world around them, CBT helps to prevent future criminal behavior.

A meta-analysis conducted by Lipsey and colleagues found that cognitive-behavioral programs reduced recidivism rates by approximately 25 to 30% among adult offenders. Similarly, cognitive remediation programs (CRPs), which focus on improving cognitive functions such as attention, memory, and executive functioning, have been shown to enhance individuals' decision-making skills and reduce impulsivity, both of which are critical factors in preventing re-offending. By improving cognitive control, individuals become better equipped to make rational decisions and manage their impulses, reducing the likelihood of engaging in criminal behavior.

In addition to traditional therapeutic approaches, pharmacological treatments targeting underlying psychiatric and cognitive disorders have also played a significant role in reducing recidivism. Medications, such as antipsychotics, antidepressants, and mood stabilizers, are used to manage symptoms of mental illnesses, which, if left untreated, can contribute to criminal behavior. Stabilizing mood, improving cognitive function, and reducing psychotic symptoms can enable offenders to participate more fully in rehabilitative programs, thereby decreasing their risk of re-offending.

9 Improved Behavior and Cognitive Functioning

In addition to reducing recidivism, forensic interventions have been successful in fostering positive behavioral changes and improving cognitive functioning in offenders. Individuals who participate in cognitive and behavioral therapy often demonstrate significant improvements in their ability to regulate emotions, manage stress, and solve problems. These behavioral changes are crucial for reintegration into society, as they enable individuals to navigate social, legal, and occupational environments more effectively.

Moreover, forensic interventions have been shown to enhance cognitive functioning in offenders, particularly in areas such as attention, memory, and executive control. Cognitive deficits, such as poor impulse control, impaired problem-solving, and deficits in memory and attention, are often associated with criminal behavior. By targeting these cognitive deficits through interventions such as cognitive remediation programs, individuals can improve their ability to process information, make decisions, and regulate their actions. These improvements in cognitive function are essential for adaptive behavior and can reduce the likelihood of engaging in criminal activities.

10 Challenges

Despite the notable achievements of forensic interventions, several challenges remain in their implementation and effectiveness. These challenges include difficulties in applying therapeutic programs effectively and the variability in individual responses to interventions based on personal and situational factors.

10.1 Implementation Issues: Difficulties in Applying Therapeutic Programs Effectively

One of the main challenges in forensic interventions is the issue of implementation. While research has shown that cognitive behavioral therapies, cognitive remediation programs, and pharmacological treatments can be effective in reducing recidivism and improving behavior, applying these programs consistently and effectively in real-world settings remains a challenge (De Ribera et al., 2024). Several factors contribute to these implementation issues, including a lack of resources, insufficient training for therapists, and the complex nature of the forensic population.

Many correctional facilities, particularly in lower-income regions, lack the financial resources and staff required to implement comprehensive therapeutic programs. Additionally, even in well-resourced systems, there may be inconsistencies in how these programs are delivered due to insufficient training or a lack of standardized protocols. For instance, a therapist may not be adequately trained in the specific cognitive-behavioral techniques that are most effective in reducing recidivism, leading to less successful outcomes.

Furthermore, the nature of the forensic population presents additional challenges to program implementation. Offenders often have complex mental health and substance abuse issues, which can complicate their participation in therapeutic programs. For example, individuals with severe psychiatric conditions or cognitive impairments may struggle to engage in traditional therapeutic interventions, necessitating specialized approaches that are not always available in forensic settings.

10.2 Individual Differences: Variability in Response to Interventions

Another major challenge in forensic interventions is the variability in individual responses to treatment. While some individuals respond well to cognitive behavioral therapy or cognitive remediation programs, others may not experience the same level of success due to personal or environmental factors. Individual differences in cognitive abilities, personality traits, motivation levels, and the severity of mental health issues all play a role in determining how effective an intervention will be for a given person.

For instance, individuals with severe cognitive impairments or psychiatric disorders may require more intensive and tailored interventions than those with less severe impairments. Similarly, offenders who are highly motivated to change their behavior may benefit more from therapeutic interventions than those who are resistant to treatment or lack insight into their behavior. The variability in response to treatment makes it difficult to predict which interventions will be most effective for a given individual, highlighting the need for personalized approaches to rehabilitation.

Additionally, environmental factors such as the availability of support systems, access to resources, and post-release conditions also influence the effectiveness of forensic interventions. For example, individuals who return to environments characterized by poverty, crime, or substance abuse may struggle to maintain the behavioral changes they achieved during rehabilitation, leading to higher rates of recidivism.

Forensic interventions have made significant strides in reducing recidivism and improving the behavior and cognitive functioning of offenders. Cognitive behavioral therapies, cognitive remediation programs, and pharmacological treatments have all contributed to positive outcomes in criminal populations, enabling individuals to make more rational decisions, regulate their impulses, and engage in prosocial behavior. However, challenges remain in the implementation of these programs, particularly in terms of resource limitations and the variability in individual responses to treatment. To maximize the effectiveness of forensic interventions, it is essential to address these challenges by developing more personalized, flexible approaches that account for the complex needs of offenders and the environments in which they are situated.

11 Interdisciplinary Collaboration in Forensic Rehabilitation

Interdisciplinary collaboration plays a pivotal role in the forensic rehabilitation setting, where the complexities of criminal behavior, mental health issues, and cognitive impairments intersect. Effective rehabilitation of offenders requires not only the expertise of a single discipline but also a coordinated effort between professionals from diverse fields. This collaboration brings together neuropsychologists, psychiatrists, social workers, legal professionals, and other specialists to address the wide range of factors contributing to criminal behavior. By working together, these experts can enhance treatment planning, improve outcomes, and provide a holistic approach to rehabilitation. This section explores the role of interdisciplinary collaboration, the professionals involved, the benefits of this collaboration, and real-world examples such as case management teams and multidisciplinary reviews.

In the context of forensic rehabilitation, the role of interdisciplinary collaboration is critical for addressing the complex and multifaceted nature of criminal behavior. Criminal offenders often present with a combination of psychological, neurological, social, and legal issues that contribute to their behavior. These factors can include mental illness, substance abuse, cognitive impairments, trauma, and environmental stressors. A single professional, no matter how skilled, may not have the expertise or resources to address all these factors effectively.

Collaboration ensures that each professional brings their specialized knowledge to the table, allowing for a more comprehensive understanding of the offender's needs. For example, a neuropsychologist can assess cognitive impairments, a psychiatrist can manage psychiatric symptoms, a social worker can address environmental and social factors, and legal professionals can ensure that interventions are aligned with legal requirements and restrictions. Together, these experts can develop a treatment plan that addresses the full spectrum of factors influencing an offender's behavior, increasing the likelihood of successful rehabilitation.

11.1 Professionals Involved

Neuropsychologists play a key role in interdisciplinary collaboration by assessing cognitive and neurological impairments that may contribute to criminal behavior. Offenders often suffer from deficits in executive functioning, attention, memory, and impulse control, which can hinder their ability to make rational decisions and regulate their behavior. Neuropsychological assessments can provide valuable insights into the cognitive profiles of offenders, helping to inform treatment plans that address these deficits.

For example, if a neuropsychologist identifies significant impairments in executive functioning, the treatment team might focus on cognitive remediation programs that aim to improve decision-making and problem-solving skills. Neuropsychologists also work closely with other professionals to ensure that cognitive interventions are integrated into broader rehabilitation efforts, such as psychotherapy and substance abuse treatment.

Psychiatrists are responsible for diagnosing and managing psychiatric conditions that may contribute to criminal behavior. Many offenders suffer from mental health disorders such as depression, schizophrenia, bipolar disorder, or anxiety, which can exacerbate impulsivity, aggression, or poor judgment. Psychiatrists play a crucial role in providing medication management, ensuring that offenders receive the pharmacological treatment needed to stabilize their mood, reduce psychotic symptoms, and manage anxiety.

Collaboration between psychiatrists and other professionals is essential for ensuring that psychiatric treatment is effectively integrated into the overall rehabilitation plan. For instance, if an offender is prescribed antipsychotic medication, the psychiatrist will work closely with the neuropsychologist and psychotherapist to monitor the impact of the medication on cognitive functioning and behavior. This collaboration ensures that psychiatric symptoms are managed without interfering with cognitive or behavioral therapies.

Social workers play a vital role in addressing the environmental and social factors that contribute to criminal behavior. Offenders often come from disadvantaged backgrounds, with histories of poverty, trauma, substance abuse, and unstable family environments. Social workers are responsible for providing case management services, connecting offenders with community resources, and helping them develop the social skills needed for reintegration into society.

In an interdisciplinary team, social workers collaborate with neuropsychologists and psychiatrists to ensure that offenders receive comprehensive care. For example, a social worker might help an offender find stable housing and employment, while the neuropsychologist and psychiatrist focus on improving cognitive functioning and managing psychiatric symptoms. This holistic approach ensures that offenders receive the support they need in all areas of their lives, increasing the chances of successful rehabilitation.

Legal professionals, including lawyers, judges, and probation officers, play a critical role in ensuring that rehabilitation efforts align with legal requirements. Offenders in the criminal justice system are often subject to court-ordered treatment plans, probation conditions, and other legal restrictions that must be taken into account when designing rehabilitation programs. Legal professionals collaborate with the treatment team to ensure that interventions comply with legal mandates while also supporting the offender's rehabilitation.

For example, if an offender is required to attend anger management classes as part of their probation, the legal professional will work with the treatment team to ensure that this requirement is integrated into the broader rehabilitation plan. Legal professionals also play a role in advocating for appropriate treatment options in court, ensuring that offenders receive the support they need to rehabilitate rather than simply being punished.

11.2 Benefits of Interdisciplinary Collaboration

11.2.1 Enhanced Treatment Planning

One of the primary benefits of interdisciplinary collaboration is the enhancement of treatment planning. By bringing together professionals from diverse fields, the treatment team can develop a more comprehensive and personalized plan for each offender. Each professional contributes their expertise to identify the offender's unique needs and challenges, ensuring that the treatment plan addresses all relevant factors.

For example, a treatment plan for an offender with a history of substance abuse, cognitive impairments, and depression might include substance abuse counseling, cognitive remediation exercises, and medication management. Without interdisciplinary collaboration, the treatment plan might overlook one or more of these critical areas, reducing the likelihood of successful rehabilitation.

11.3 Holistic Approach to Rehabilitation

Interdisciplinary collaboration also facilitates a holistic approach to rehabilitation, addressing not only the cognitive and psychological factors that contribute to criminal behavior but also the social, legal, and environmental factors. By considering the whole person rather than focusing on isolated symptoms, the treatment team can provide more comprehensive care that supports the offender's long-term success.

A holistic approach recognizes that criminal behavior is often the result of a combination of factors, including mental illness, cognitive deficits, trauma, and social disadvantage. By addressing all these factors simultaneously, interdisciplinary collaboration increases the likelihood that offenders will develop the skills and resilience needed to reintegrate into society and avoid re-offending.

11.4 Examples of Collaboration

One real-world example of interdisciplinary collaboration is the use of case management teams. In many forensic settings, case management teams are responsible for coordinating the care and interventions provided to offenders. These teams typically include neuropsychologists, psychiatrists, social workers, and legal professionals, who work together to ensure that all aspects of the offender's rehabilitation are addressed.

For example, a case management team might develop a treatment plan that includes cognitive behavioral therapy (CBT), medication management, vocational training, and legal advocacy. The team meets regularly to review the offender's progress and make adjustments to the treatment plan as needed. This collaborative approach ensures that the offender receives consistent and coordinated care, reducing the risk of gaps in treatment.

11.5 Multidisciplinary Reviews

Another example of interdisciplinary collaboration is the use of multidisciplinary reviews, which involve regular meetings to assess the progress of offenders and modify treatment plans as needed. These reviews provide an opportunity for all members of the treatment team to share their observations and insights, ensuring that treatment remains aligned with the offender's evolving needs.

For instance, if a psychiatrist observes that an offender's mood has stabilized with medication but their cognitive functioning remains impaired, the team might decide to increase the focus on cognitive remediation exercises. These regular reviews ensure that the treatment plan remains flexible and responsive, increasing the likelihood of successful rehabilitation.

Interdisciplinary collaboration is essential in forensic rehabilitation, where the complexities of criminal behavior require a coordinated approach from multiple professionals. By working together, neuropsychologists, psychiatrists, social workers, and legal professionals can develop comprehensive treatment plans that address the full range of factors contributing to criminal behavior. This collaboration enhances treatment planning, supports a holistic approach to rehabilitation, and increases the likelihood of successful outcomes for offenders. Through case management teams and multidisciplinary reviews, interdisciplinary collaboration ensures that offenders receive the personalized, coordinated care they need to rehabilitate and reintegrate into society.

12 Ethical and Practical Considerations in Forensic Rehabilitation

In forensic rehabilitation, addressing criminal behavior requires a careful balance between ethical considerations and practical challenges. Professionals involved in this process must navigate the complex interplay of individual rights, societal safety, and the effective allocation of limited resources. Ethical concerns such as informed consent and fairness in access to rehabilitation programs are fundamental in maintaining the integrity of interventions. Concurrently, practical challenges related to resource allocation and the monitoring and evaluation of treatment progress can hinder the implementation of effective rehabilitation programs. This section examines these ethical and practical issues in forensic rehabilitation, exploring how professionals can address them while ensuring that interventions remain both fair and effective.

12.1 Consent: Ensuring Informed Consent for All Interventions

One of the primary ethical concerns in forensic rehabilitation is the issue of consent. Informed consent is a cornerstone of ethical practice, requiring that individuals fully understand the nature of the interventions they are undergoing, including the potential benefits, risks, and alternatives. However, obtaining informed consent in forensic settings can be challenging for several reasons.

First, many offenders may have cognitive impairments or mental health issues that limit their capacity to fully understand the implications of treatment. Neuropsychological deficits, such as memory impairments, attention deficits, or impaired executive functioning, can make it difficult for individuals to process complex information about the treatment process. In such cases, professionals must take extra care to ensure that consent is truly informed, potentially involving the use of simplified language, visual aids, or multiple discussions to ensure comprehension.

Second, the coercive nature of the criminal justice system can complicate the concept of voluntary consent. Offenders may feel pressured to participate in rehabilitation programs, particularly if they believe that doing so will lead to reduced sentences or other legal benefits. This dynamic raises concerns about the voluntariness of their participation, as true consent should be given freely and without undue influence. To address this issue, professionals must ensure that offenders understand that participation in rehabilitation programs is voluntary and that they are free to withdraw consent at any time without negative repercussions.

Despite these challenges, ensuring informed consent remains a crucial ethical obligation. Professionals in forensic rehabilitation must strive to create an environment where individuals feel empowered to make informed decisions about their treatment, even within the constraints of the legal system.

12.2 Fairness: Providing Equitable Access to Rehabilitation Programs

Another key ethical concern in forensic rehabilitation is the issue of fairness, specifically in providing equitable access to rehabilitation programs. Offenders come from diverse backgrounds, with varying levels of access to resources, education, and social support. In many cases, those from marginalized communities may face additional barriers to accessing rehabilitation programs, including discrimination, language barriers, or a lack of culturally appropriate services.

Equitable access to rehabilitation programs means ensuring that all individuals, regardless of their background, have the opportunity to participate in interventions that can support their rehabilitation (Velez et al., 2023). This requires professionals to be aware of the potential for bias in the allocation of resources and to work actively to eliminate barriers to participation. For example, rehabilitation programs should be designed to be inclusive of individuals with different cultural, linguistic, and educational needs. Additionally, professionals should advocate for the provision of services in under-resourced communities, where individuals may have fewer opportunities to access mental health care, substance abuse treatment, or vocational training.

Failing to ensure fairness in access to rehabilitation programs can perpetuate existing inequalities and undermine the effectiveness of the criminal justice system. Therefore, professionals in forensic rehabilitation must prioritize equity in their practice, advocating for policies and programs that provide all individuals with a fair opportunity to rehabilitate and reintegrate into society.

13 Practical Challenges in Forensic Rehabilitation

13.1 Resource Allocation: Availability of Resources for Effective Interventions

One of the most significant practical challenges in forensic rehabilitation is the issue of resource allocation. Effective rehabilitation programs require significant resources, including trained professionals, specialized facilities, and access to therapeutic interventions. However, in many forensic settings, resources are limited, leading to difficult decisions about how to allocate them.

The scarcity of resources can impact the availability and quality of rehabilitation programs in several ways. First, there may be a shortage of trained professionals, such as neuropsychologists, psychiatrists, and social workers, who are essential for providing individualized care to offenders. This shortage can lead to high caseloads, reduced contact time with offenders, and a reliance on more generalized interventions that may not address the specific needs of each individual.

Second, limited resources can affect the availability of specialized treatment programs, such as cognitive remediation programs, substance abuse treatment, or vocational training (Verdejo-Garcia et al., 2022). Offenders with complex needs, such as those with co-occurring mental health and substance use disorders, may require intensive, multimodal interventions that are costly and resource-intensive to deliver. In resource-limited settings, these individuals may not receive the full spectrum of care they need to rehabilitate effectively.

To address these challenges, professionals in forensic rehabilitation must advocate for the allocation of additional resources to support rehabilitation efforts. This may involve lobbying for increased funding for mental health and substance abuse services within the criminal justice system, as well as exploring alternative funding sources, such as partnerships with community organizations or philanthropic foundations. Additionally, professionals should prioritize the most resource-intensive interventions for those individuals who stand to benefit the most, ensuring that limited resources are used as effectively as possible.

13.2 Monitoring and Evaluation: Ensuring Accurate Tracking of Progress and Outcomes

Another practical challenge in forensic rehabilitation is the need for effective monitoring and evaluation of treatment progress and outcomes. Rehabilitation programs must be carefully monitored to ensure that they are achieving their intended goals, such as reducing recidivism, improving mental health, or enhancing cognitive functioning. However, accurately tracking progress can be difficult in practice, particularly in forensic settings where individuals may be resistant to treatment or have complex, fluctuating needs.

One of the key challenges in monitoring progress is the need for valid and reliable assessment tools. Professionals must have access to appropriate instruments for measuring cognitive functioning, mental health symptoms, and behavioral changes. In some cases, existing assessment tools may not be suitable for use with forensic populations, particularly if they were designed for use in general clinical settings rather than in the context of criminal behavior. As a result, professionals may need to adapt or develop new assessment tools that are better suited to the specific needs of forensic populations.

Additionally, the evaluation of rehabilitation programs must take into account the long-term nature of rehabilitation. Behavioral change is a gradual process, and improvements may not be immediately apparent (Wade, 2020). Therefore, professionals must be patient in their evaluations, recognizing that even small gains in cognitive or emotional functioning can represent significant progress for offenders with complex needs. Regular re-assessments are critical to ensuring that treatment plans remain relevant and effective over time, and adjustments should be made as needed based on ongoing evaluation.

Finally, accurate tracking of outcomes requires effective communication and coordination between members of the interdisciplinary team. Neuropsychologists, psychiatrists, social workers, and legal professionals must share their observations and insights regularly to ensure that all aspects of the offender's progress are being monitored. This collaborative approach helps to ensure that no aspect of the offender's rehabilitation is overlooked and that the treatment plan remains comprehensive and responsive to their evolving needs.

14 Conclusion

Ethical and practical considerations are central to the successful implementation of rehabilitation programs in forensic settings. Ensuring informed consent and equitable access to interventions are essential ethical obligations that professionals must uphold to maintain the integrity of the rehabilitation process. At the same time, practical challenges such as resource allocation and the monitoring and evaluation of progress can hinder the effectiveness of rehabilitation efforts. Addressing these challenges requires a combination of advocacy for additional resources, the development of appropriate assessment tools, and a commitment to ongoing evaluation and adjustment of treatment plans. By navigating these ethical and practical issues effectively, professionals in forensic rehabilitation can help support offenders in their journey toward rehabilitation and reintegration into society.

References

Bischof, G., Bischof, A., & Rumpf, H. (2021). Motivational interviewing: An evidence-based approach for use in medical practice. *Deutsches Ärzteblatt International.* https://doi.org/10.3238/arztebl.m2021.0014

Ceraso, A., Lin, J. J., Schneider-Thoma, J., Siafis, S., Tardy, M., Komossa, K., Heres, S., Kissling, W., Davis, J. M., & Leucht, S. (2020). Maintenance treatment with antipsychotic drugs for schizophrenia. *Cochrane Library, 2020*(8). https://doi.org/10.1002/14651858.cd008016.pub3

Chang, Z., Ghirardi, L., Quinn, P. D., Asherson, P., D'Onofrio, B. M., & Larsson, H. (2019). Risks and benefits of attention-deficit/hyperactivity disorder medication on behavioral and neuropsychiatric outcomes: A qualitative review of pharmacoepidemiology studies using linked prescription databases. *Biological Psychiatry, 86*(5), 335–343. https://doi.org/10.1016/j.biopsych.2019.04.009

Chokhawala, K., & Stevens, L. (2023, February 26). Antipsychotic medications. StatPearls - NCBI Bookshelf. https://www.ncbi.nlm.nih.gov/books/NBK519503/.

Chu, A., & Wadhwa, R. (2023, May 1). Selective serotonin reuptake inhibitors. StatPearls - NCBI Bookshelf. https://www.ncbi.nlm.nih.gov/books/NBK554406/.

Cohen, J. A., & Mannarino, A. P. (2015). Trauma-focused cognitive behavior therapy for traumatized children and families. *Child and Adolescent Psychiatric Clinics of North America, 24*(3), 557–570. https://doi.org/10.1016/j.chc.2015.02.005

Correll, C. U., Detraux, J., De Lepeleire, J., & De Hert, M. (2015). Effects of antipsychotics, antidepressants and mood stabilizers on risk for physical diseases in people with schizophrenia, depression and bipolar disorder. *World Psychiatry, 14*(2), 119–136. https://doi.org/10.1002/wps.20204

De Ribera, O. S., Urzúa, V. C., & Pienaar, G. (2024). How effective is the "Reasoning and Rehabilitation" (R&R) program in changing cognitive and behavioral skills? A systematic review and meta-analysis. *Aggression and Violent Behavior, 76*, 101950. https://doi.org/10.1016/j.avb.2024.101950

Halicka, M., Vittersø, A. D., Proulx, M. J., & Bultitude, J. H. (2020). Neuropsychological changes in complex regional pain syndrome (CRPS). *Behavioural Neurology, 2020*, 1–30. https://doi.org/10.1155/2020/4561831

Jacob, K., & Samuel, R. (2017). Occupational therapy in India: Focus on functional recovery and need for empowerment. *Indian Journal of Psychiatry, 59*(2), 242. https://doi.org/10.4103/psychiatry.indianjpsychiatry_111_17

Jones, R., Malouf, P., Talbot, D., Elhindi, J., Baker, R., & Harris, A. (2024). Examining the impact of a group treatment using cognitive and social cognition remediation for young offenders: The justice health NSW school-link advantage pilot study. *Early Intervention in Psychiatry*. https://doi.org/10.1111/eip.13560

Joyal, M., Bonneau, A., & Fecteau, S. (2016). Speech and language therapies to improve pragmatics and discourse skills in patients with schizophrenia. *Psychiatry Research, 240*, 88–95. https://doi.org/10.1016/j.psychres.2016.04.010

Keng, S., Smoski, M. J., & Robins, C. J. (2011). Effects of mindfulness on psychological health: A review of empirical studies. *Clinical Psychology Review, 31*(6), 1041–1056. https://doi.org/10.1016/j.cpr.2011.04.006

Kothgassner, O. D., Goreis, A., Robinson, K., Huscsava, M. M., Schmahl, C., & Plener, P. L. (2021). Efficacy of dialectical behavior therapy for adolescent self-harm and suicidal ideation: a systematic review and meta-analysis. *Psychological Medicine, 51*(7), 1057–1067. https://doi.org/10.1017/s0033291721001355

Lamberti, J. S. (2016). Preventing criminal recidivism through mental health and criminal justice collaboration. *Psychiatric Services, 67*(11), 1206–1212. https://doi.org/10.1176/appi.ps.201500384

Lardén, M., Högström, J., & Långström, N. (2021). Effectiveness of an individual cognitive-behavioral intervention for serious, young male violent offenders: Randomized controlled study with twenty-four-month follow-up. *Frontiers in Psychiatry, 12*. https://doi.org/10.3389/fpsyt.2021.670957

May, J. M., Richardi, T. M., & Barth, K. S. (2016). Dialectical behavior therapy as treatment for borderline personality disorder. *Mental Health Clinician, 6*(2), 62–67. https://doi.org/10.9740/mhc.2016.03.62

Morgan, R. D., Flora, D. B., Kroner, D. G., Mills, J. F., Varghese, F., & Steffan, J. S. (2011). Treating offenders with mental illness: A research synthesis. *Law and Human Behavior, 36*(1), 37–50. https://doi.org/10.1037/h0093964

Nakao, M., Shirotsuki, K., & Sugaya, N. (2021). Cognitive–behavioral therapy for management of mental health and stress-related disorders: Recent advances in techniques and technologies. *BioPsychoSocial Medicine, 15*(1). https://doi.org/10.1186/s13030-021-00219-w

Sardella, M., Belcher, G., Lungu, C., Ignoni, T., Camisa, M., Stenver, D. I., Porcelli, P., D'Antuono, M., Castiglione, N. G., Adams, A., Furlan, G., Grisoni, I., Hall, S., Boga, L., Mancini, V., Ciuca, M., Chonzi, D., Edwards, B., Mangoni, A. A., et al. (2021). Monitoring the manufacturing and quality of medicines: a fundamental task of pharmacovigilance. *Therapeutic Advances in Drug Safety, 12*, 204209862110384. https://doi.org/10.1177/20420986211038436

Tickell, A., Ball, S., Bernard, P., Kuyken, W., Marx, R., Pack, S., Strauss, C., Sweeney, T., & Crane, C. (2019). The effectiveness of mindfulness-based cognitive therapy (MBCT) in real-world healthcare services. *Mindfulness, 11*(2), 279–290. https://doi.org/10.1007/s12671-018-1087-9

Velez, M., Lugo-Agudelo, L. H., Lugo, D. F. P., Glenton, C., Posada, A. M., Franco, L. F. M., Negrini, S., Kiekens, C., Brunal, M. A. S., Roberg, A. B., & Sarmiento, K. M. C. (2023). Factors that influence the provision of home-based rehabilitation services for people needing rehabilitation: a qualitative evidence synthesis. *Cochrane Library, 2023*(2). https://doi.org/10.1002/14651858.cd014823

Verdejo-Garcia, A., Rezapour, T., Giddens, E., Zonoozi, A. K., Rafei, P., Berry, J., Caracuel, A., Copersino, M. L., Field, M., Garland, E. L., Lorenzetti, V., Malloy-Diniz, L., Manning, V., Marceau, E. M., Pennington, D. L., Strickland, J. C., Wiers, R., Fairhead, R., Anderson, A., et al. (2022). Cognitive training and remediation interventions for substance use disorders: a Delphi consensus study. *Addiction, 118*(5), 935–951. https://doi.org/10.1111/add.16109

Vijayapriya, C., & Tamarana, R. (2023). Effectiveness of dialectical behavior therapy as a transdiagnostic treatment for improving cognitive functions: a systematic review. *Research in Psychotherapy Psychopathology Process and Outcome, 26*(2). https://doi.org/10.4081/ripppo.2023.662

Wade, D. T. (2020). What is rehabilitation? An empirical investigation leading to an evidence-based description. *Clinical Rehabilitation, 34*(5), 571–583. https://doi.org/10.1177/0269215520905112

Winstanley, C. A., Eagle, D. M., & Robbins, T. W. (2006). Behavioral models of impulsivity in relation to ADHD: Translation between clinical and preclinical studies. *Clinical Psychology Review, 26*(4), 379–395. https://doi.org/10.1016/j.cpr.2006.01.001

Yang, Y., & Kwak, Y. T. (2017). Improvement of cognitive function after computer-based cognitive training in early stage of Alzheimer's dementia. *Dementia and Neurocognitive Disorders, 16*(1), 7. https://doi.org/10.12779/dnd.2017.16.1.7

Ethical and Professional Considerations in Forensic Neuropsychology

1 Introduction

Forensic neuropsychology, a specialized branch of neuropsychology, lies at the intersection of brain science and the law, where the assessment of cognitive functioning is applied within legal contexts. Given the profound implications that neuropsychological assessments have on legal outcomes—such as determining competency, criminal responsibility, or the extent of injury after traumatic events—ethical and professional standards become paramount. The field, due to its hybrid nature, requires adherence to both general ethical principles from neuropsychology and the added complexity of legal regulations. Ethical and professional considerations in forensic neuropsychology are not just administrative guidelines but foundational elements guiding moral decision-making in practice, ensuring that practitioners uphold integrity, objectivity, and respect for individuals within the legal system.

2 Importance of Ethical and Professional Standards in Forensic Neuropsychology

Forensic neuropsychologists often find themselves in positions where their work has significant consequences on an individual's future, from influencing court decisions in criminal cases to affecting settlements in civil litigation. Such responsibility underscores the need for high ethical and professional standards, which act as the scaffolding that supports fair, objective, and reliable practices. The key ethical principles embedded in forensic neuropsychology are drawn from larger frameworks, including the American Psychological Association (APA) Ethical Principles of

© The Author(s), under exclusive license to Springer Nature Switzerland AG 2025

K. J. Reddy, *Foundations of Criminal Forensic Neuropsychology*,
https://doi.org/10.1007/978-3-031-83771-5_8

Psychologists and Code of Conduct and the Specialty Guidelines for Forensic Psychologists (Specialty Guidelines for Forensic Psychology, n.d.).

The integration of these ethical standards serves several crucial purposes. First, they protect the rights of the individuals involved, be it a defendant undergoing neuropsychological evaluation, a plaintiff in a personal injury case, or other relevant parties (Foote et al., 2020). The concept of autonomy, as derived from bioethics, is vital in ensuring that all individuals are treated with dignity, are informed about the procedures and outcomes, and give their informed consent when necessary. For instance, neuropsychologists must ensure that participants understand the purpose of the evaluations and the potential implications of the results for legal proceedings. Secondly, these standards promote beneficence and non-maleficence, ensuring that neuropsychologists act in the best interest of the examinees while avoiding causing harm (Varkey, 2020). This is particularly essential in forensic settings, where assessments can lead to legal actions that have significant consequences. Evaluations that are conducted poorly or with bias may result in wrongful convictions, unfair penalties, or unjust outcomes, making the ethical mandate to avoid harm particularly salient.

Further, ethical standards in forensic neuropsychology help maintain professional competence (Yadav, 2017). Neuropsychologists working within legal contexts must stay up to date with both neuropsychological methodologies and the evolving legal standards relevant to their practice. Failing to do so not only violates professional standards but may also lead to flawed assessments that cannot withstand the scrutiny of the courtroom. Continuing education, peer review, and supervision are therefore critical components of maintaining professional competence and ensuring that neuropsychologists can effectively integrate neuropsychological findings with legal requirements.

3 Analyzing Values and Standards Guiding Moral Decision-Making in Practice

Forensic neuropsychologists, in their practice, are constantly faced with morally complex situations. Ethical and professional standards provide a framework to navigate these challenges by offering guidance on how to resolve conflicts between competing values such as truth, fairness, confidentiality, and social justice. Central to this is the notion of objectivity, where forensic neuropsychologists are required to maintain impartiality, free from personal biases or pressures from retaining parties.

One of the primary challenges faced by forensic neuropsychologists is maintaining dual roles—balancing their duty to the legal system with their responsibility to the individual being assessed (Merkt et al., 2021). In clinical neuropsychology, the primary duty is typically to the patient, focusing on their well-being and recovery.

However, in forensic neuropsychology, the neuropsychologist's primary obligation shifts toward providing the legal system with an objective assessment of cognitive functioning. This shift in duty must be navigated carefully, as it can present ethical dilemmas. For example, while the clinician may want to provide a thorough explanation to the examinee, the forensic neuropsychologist must also consider the possibility of influencing the individual's responses, which could affect the validity of the assessment. Therefore, clarity of roles and maintaining transparency are essential in making moral decisions that balance these dual responsibilities. Another ethical consideration is confidentiality. In a clinical setting, maintaining the privacy of client information is one of the cardinal ethical principles. However, in forensic contexts, confidentiality can become complicated because the results of neuropsychological assessments are often shared with courts, attorneys, and other parties involved in the legal proceedings. Neuropsychologists must ensure that they clearly explain the limits of confidentiality to examinees, avoiding any potential misunderstandings that could arise during evaluations. This discussion must be thorough and must occur early in the evaluation process to prevent any confusion later on when sensitive information is disclosed in a courtroom.

The value of integrity is also central in guiding the moral decision-making process within forensic neuropsychology (Swanepoel, 2010). Neuropsychologists must ensure that their methods, reports, and testimonies are accurate and not misleading. Given the adversarial nature of legal systems, forensic neuropsychologists may face pressure from attorneys or clients to present information in a way that favors one side. Resisting this pressure and maintaining an objective stance is crucial to ensuring that justice is served. Neuropsychologists are also ethically obligated to only work within the boundaries of their expertise and to refrain from offering opinions on issues outside their competence. Lastly, the principle of justice ensures that forensic neuropsychologists strive to be fair and impartial, providing equal treatment to all individuals regardless of their background, status, or position within the legal process. This includes being aware of potential biases—whether based on race, gender, socioeconomic status, or disability—and actively working to minimize their influence on the evaluation process. Justice also implies that neuropsychologists should use standardized, reliable, and valid tests, ensuring that their assessments are not only fair but also legally defensible.

Ethical and professional standards are not just theoretical constructs in forensic neuropsychology; they are critical to the practice's integrity and success. These standards guide practitioners in making complex moral decisions, ensuring that their work is conducted with fairness, accuracy, and respect for all parties involved. By adhering to these principles, forensic neuropsychologists contribute to the broader goal of justice, offering expertise that bridges the gap between cognitive science and the legal system. In this way, they provide valuable insights while upholding the highest ethical standards, protecting the rights of individuals, and ensuring that their assessments are both scientifically and legally sound.

4 Ethical Responsibility

Ethical obligations in this domain go beyond standard clinical practice due to the legal implications of their work, making it essential for forensic neuropsychologists to adhere to rigorous ethical frameworks. Key ethical responsibilities in forensic neuropsychology include performing thorough examinations, providing accurate interpretations of findings, communicating effectively with legal stakeholders, and adhering to professional rules and ethical frameworks.

4.1 Key Ethical Obligations

One of the core ethical obligations of forensic neuropsychologists is to perform thorough examinations. The assessments they conduct must be comprehensive, employing reliable and valid measures to ensure that the results are scientifically sound and legally defensible (Sullivan, 2011). Given the high stakes in legal cases, incomplete or rushed assessments could result in flawed conclusions, potentially leading to unjust outcomes. For instance, if a neuropsychologist evaluates an individual's cognitive impairments without a thorough understanding of their medical history or using improper testing methods, the final results may not accurately reflect the person's true neuropsychological state, thereby compromising the legal process.

In addition to thorough examinations, neuropsychologists must provide an accurate interpretation of findings. Cognitive and neuropsychological tests often produce complex results that require careful analysis. The ethical responsibility lies in interpreting these findings objectively and avoiding bias. Misinterpretation can have severe consequences, such as wrongly concluding that an individual is malingering (faking cognitive impairment) or inaccurately diagnosing a cognitive deficit. To maintain ethical standards, forensic neuropsychologists must rely on current research, standardized testing protocols, and their expertise to ensure that their interpretations are based on sound scientific evidence (Guilmette & Hagan, 1997).

Another critical obligation is effective communication with legal stakeholders. Forensic neuropsychologists serve as expert witnesses and consultants, communicating their findings to attorneys, judges, and other legal professionals who may not have a scientific background (Ward, 2022). It is their ethical responsibility to present their conclusions clearly, avoiding overly technical language and ensuring that legal stakeholders understand the implications of the neuropsychological assessment. At the same time, they must remain neutral, presenting facts without advocacy for either party involved in the case. Maintaining this objectivity ensures that their role contributes to justice rather than distorting legal outcomes.

4.2 *Professional Rules and Ethical Frameworks*

To uphold these key ethical obligations, forensic neuropsychologists operate under a variety of professional rules and frameworks. The American Psychological Association's (APA) Ethical Principles of Psychologists and Code of Conduct provides broad ethical guidelines, including principles like beneficence, nonmaleficence, integrity, and respect for people's rights and dignity. These principles ensure that neuropsychologists prioritize the welfare of individuals, avoid harm, and maintain honesty in their professional dealings. In the forensic context, this framework is complemented by the Specialty Guidelines for Forensic Psychology, which offer specific recommendations for maintaining competence, impartiality, and clarity in communication when working within legal systems (Young & Kenny, 2022).

These guidelines emphasize that forensic neuropsychologists must remain within their area of expertise, consistently updating their knowledge and skills through continuing education and professional development. They also stress the importance of maintaining neutrality, particularly when hired by one party in a legal dispute. Forensic neuropsychologists must avoid any appearance of bias and ensure their work is based solely on objective data.

Ethical responsibility in forensic neuropsychology is crucial for maintaining the integrity of both the scientific and legal processes. Performing thorough examinations, providing accurate interpretations, and effectively communicating with legal stakeholders are all key ethical obligations that forensic neuropsychologists must uphold. These responsibilities are governed by comprehensive ethical frameworks, such as the APA's Code of Conduct and the Specialty Guidelines for Forensic Psychology, which ensure that neuropsychologists remain competent, impartial, and objective in their work. By adhering to these standards, forensic neuropsychologists play a vital role in delivering justice while maintaining the highest levels of professional integrity.

5 Informed Consent

Informed consent is a fundamental ethical and legal principle that ensures individuals have the right to make autonomous decisions about their participation in activities, including medical treatments, psychological assessments, and legal proceedings. It involves providing clear, understandable information about the nature, purpose, potential risks, and benefits of the procedure or assessment to allow individuals to make informed decisions about their involvement (Shah et al., 2023). Informed consent is grounded in the ethical principles of autonomy, respect for persons, and the duty to ensure individuals have the necessary information to make voluntary, informed decisions.

In forensic settings, informed consent becomes even more critical due to the unique context in which forensic evaluations take place. Unlike clinical settings, where patients seek services for their well-being, forensic evaluations are often court-ordered or conducted within legal disputes, where individuals may not fully understand the nature of the assessment or its potential consequences. Forensic neuropsychologists, for example, must ensure that individuals understand the purpose of the evaluation, its potential impact on legal decisions, and the limits of confidentiality. Failure to obtain proper informed consent in these situations can compromise the integrity of the evaluation, lead to ethical violations, and potentially harm the individual's legal standing (Kadam, 2017).

5.1 Why Is Informed Consent Critical in Forensic Settings?

In forensic settings, informed consent is not only an ethical obligation but also a safeguard to ensure fairness and protect the rights of individuals undergoing assessments. One key reason why informed consent is so important in this context is that forensic evaluations can significantly impact legal outcomes. For example, a neuropsychological assessment might influence decisions regarding a defendant's competency to stand trial, criminal responsibility, or the extent of cognitive impairment in civil cases. Given the high stakes, individuals must understand the nature of the evaluation, its potential consequences, and how the results might be used in the legal process. This ensures that they can participate knowingly and that their rights are protected throughout the evaluation process.

Informed consent is also essential for preserving the ethical integrity of forensic neuropsychologists and other professionals involved in legal cases. These professionals have a duty to remain objective and ensure that their evaluations are conducted with respect for the individual's autonomy and rights. Obtaining informed consent is a way to affirm this commitment, clarifying that the individual's participation is voluntary and that they have been fully informed of the process. Forensic practitioners risk undermining their neutrality and the ethical foundations of their work without proper informed consent (Yadav, 2017).

5.2 Process of Obtaining Consent

The process of obtaining informed consent in forensic settings involves several critical steps and considerations. It is not merely a one-time event but an ongoing dialogue between the practitioner and the individual being evaluated (Roux et al., 2022).

The first step is providing information. The forensic professional must clearly explain the purpose of the evaluation, the procedures involved, the potential risks and benefits, and how the results may be used in legal proceedings. In this phase, it is crucial to use plain language and avoid overly technical or legalistic terms that might confuse the individual. In forensic neuropsychology, for instance, the practitioner might explain that the evaluation will involve tests to measure cognitive abilities, memory, and other brain functions, and that the results could be shared with the court or legal representatives. The professional must also clarify the limits of confidentiality, as the information gathered during a forensic evaluation is often not protected in the same way it is in clinical settings and may be disclosed in court.

The second step is assessing the individual's understanding. It is not enough to simply provide the information; the practitioner must also ensure that the individual comprehends it. This is particularly important in forensic settings, where the complexity of the legal context can make it challenging for individuals to fully grasp the implications of the evaluation. The practitioner can assess understanding by asking the individual to summarize the information in their own words or by checking whether they have any questions or concerns. This step is crucial for preventing misunderstandings that could lead to ethical breaches or legal complications later in the process.

Another vital step in the informed consent process is ensuring voluntary participation. In forensic settings, individuals may feel coerced into participating in evaluations due to the involvement of the legal system. For example, a defendant might believe they have no choice but to undergo a neuropsychological evaluation if it has been ordered by the court. While court-ordered evaluations do limit an individual's ability to refuse participation, forensic practitioners must still ensure that the individual understands their right to refuse or withdraw from the evaluation at any point. The practitioner should emphasize that participation should be as voluntary as possible, given the circumstances, and that any decisions made during the evaluation are theirs to make.

Once these steps have been completed, the final part of the process is documenting informed consent. In many forensic settings, obtaining written consent is a legal requirement. The consent form should clearly outline all relevant information, including the purpose of the evaluation, the limits of confidentiality, and the potential risks and benefits. It should also confirm that the individual has had the opportunity to ask questions and that they are participating voluntarily. The practitioner and the individual both sign the consent form, providing legal documentation that informed consent has been obtained.

5.3 Ensuring Understanding and Voluntary Participation

Ensuring that individuals fully understand the nature of forensic evaluations and that their participation is voluntary is a fundamental aspect of informed consent. To do so, forensic practitioners must be sensitive to the individual's cognitive and emotional state, cultural background, and any potential language barriers that might affect their comprehension. For instance, if the individual has a cognitive impairment, the practitioner must take extra care to explain the information in a way that is accessible and clear. This might involve simplifying complex concepts, providing visual aids, or allowing more time for the individual to ask questions (Yadav, 2017).

In addition to promoting understanding, practitioners must remain vigilant in ensuring that participation is voluntary, even in situations where the evaluation is legally mandated. While individuals may not have the option to refuse a court-ordered evaluation, they should still have the freedom to ask questions, express concerns, and withdraw from specific parts of the process if they feel uncomfortable. This respect for the individual's autonomy reinforces the ethical foundation of informed consent and helps maintain trust between the practitioner and the individual being evaluated.

6 Confidentiality and Privacy

Confidentiality and privacy are foundational principles in all areas of psychology, but they take on special importance and complexity in forensic neuropsychology. Forensic neuropsychologists often work in legal contexts where their evaluations are intended to assist courts, attorneys, and other legal stakeholders in making decisions about an individual's cognitive or mental health status. This intersection of healthcare and law creates ethical and legal challenges, especially when it comes to balancing confidentiality with legal requirements. Ensuring the privacy of client information is not just an ethical duty but also a legal obligation, both in India and the USA, where confidentiality laws and regulations differ significantly. Understanding these obligations and adopting best practices is essential for forensic neuropsychologists to navigate the delicate balance between protecting privacy and fulfilling legal responsibilities.

6.1 Ethical and Legal Obligations to Protect Client Information

The principle of confidentiality is central to the professional ethics of psychologists and neuropsychologists. It refers to the obligation of professionals to protect the privacy of their clients by not disclosing personal information without the client's informed consent. Confidentiality ensures that individuals feel safe to disclose sensitive information, which is critical for the accuracy and efficacy of psychological assessments, including neuropsychological evaluations (Boone et al., 2024). Forensic neuropsychologists, therefore, have an ethical obligation to maintain the confidentiality of the information shared with them, despite the legal context in which they operate.

In the USA, the American Psychological Association (APA) Ethical Principles of Psychologists and Code of Conduct outlines specific guidelines for maintaining confidentiality (Ethical Principles of Psychologists and Code of Conduct, n.d.). The APA's standards emphasize that psychologists must take reasonable precautions to protect the confidentiality of the information they obtain. Additionally, they are required to inform clients of the limits of confidentiality, especially in forensic settings where legal mandates might override some aspects of privacy. In healthcare settings, the Health Insurance Portability and Accountability Act (HIPAA) further strengthens confidentiality protections by regulating how healthcare providers manage and disclose personal health information (Gowsika, 2024).

In India, the Indian Mental Health Act (2017) similarly protects the privacy of individuals receiving mental health services (Chadda, 2019). The act specifies that mental health professionals must not disclose any personal information without the patient's consent, except in circumstances where the law mandates reporting. Although India's regulations are less comprehensive than HIPAA in the USA, they reflect the importance of confidentiality in healthcare services. Additionally, the Ethical Guidelines for Biomedical Research on Human Participants by the Indian Council of Medical Research (ICMR) highlights the importance of privacy and confidentiality in research and clinical settings (Indian Council of Medical Research et al., 2017).

6.2 *Balancing Confidentiality with Legal Requirements*

One of the central challenges in forensic neuropsychology is balancing the ethical duty to protect confidentiality with the legal requirements that often necessitate disclosure of information. In many forensic evaluations, neuropsychologists are retained by courts, attorneys, or insurance companies to provide expert opinions. This means that their findings—whether related to cognitive impairments, malingering, or mental health conditions—are often shared with the legal system, where confidentiality can be limited.

In both the USA and India, confidentiality has clear exceptions in forensic contexts. For instance, if a neuropsychological evaluation is court-ordered, the results are typically not confidential and are expected to be shared with the court and relevant legal parties. In the USA, forensic neuropsychologists must explain these limitations to the individuals they assess. According to the APA's Specialty Guidelines for Forensic Psychology, forensic practitioners must inform individuals about the intended use of the assessment, the limits of confidentiality, and the fact that the information gathered may be disclosed in legal proceedings. This ensures transparency and allows individuals to make informed decisions about participating in the evaluation (Specialty Guidelines for Forensic Psychology, n.d.).

Similarly, in India, forensic neuropsychologists must also disclose the limits of confidentiality in legal settings. While the Indian Evidence Act (1872) (last updated in 2020) recognizes privilege between a psychologist and their client, this privilege can be waived in cases involving court orders or criminal investigations, where the public interest may outweigh the individual's right to confidentiality (Government of India, 2020). However, Indian laws provide less structured guidelines compared to the APA standards, which may lead to inconsistencies in how confidentiality is managed in forensic cases.

Balancing these competing demands requires careful judgment on the part of forensic neuropsychologists. While they must respect the individual's right to confidentiality, they are also obligated to fulfill their legal duties and provide accurate, objective information to the courts. One strategy to manage this balance is to ensure that all parties involved—clients, attorneys, and judges—are fully informed about the nature of the assessment and the limits of confidentiality from the outset.

6.3 Best Practices and Strategies for Maintaining Privacy

Given the complexity of confidentiality in forensic neuropsychology, adopting best practices to maintain privacy is crucial. These strategies help ensure that ethical standards are upheld while meeting legal requirements.

1. **Informed Consent**: One of the most important practices is obtaining informed consent. In both India and the USA, forensic neuropsychologists must inform the individual about the purpose of the evaluation, the limits of confidentiality, and how the information will be used. This consent process should be thorough, ensuring that the individual understands the implications of the evaluation. For example, individuals should be made aware that their test results, clinical impressions, and any personal history disclosed during the evaluation could be revealed in court.
2. **Data Security**: Forensic neuropsychologists must take steps to protect the physical and digital security of client data. In the USA, HIPAA requires healthcare professionals to use encrypted communications, secure data storage, and restricted access to client records. While India's regulations on digital security in healthcare are not as robust as HIPAA, professionals can still adopt best practices such as using password-protected files, encrypted emails, and secure storage for physical records to protect sensitive information (Rights, 2022).
3. **Clear Communication**: Neuropsychologists should clearly communicate with legal stakeholders, explaining the ethical boundaries of confidentiality and ensuring that the legal parties understand what information can be disclosed (Darby & Weinstock, 2018). They must also remain impartial, avoiding any pressure to disclose more information than is ethically appropriate.
4. **Ethical Consultation**: Given the ethical dilemmas that often arise in forensic settings, consulting with other professionals or ethics boards can be helpful in making difficult decisions about confidentiality. Forensic neuropsychologists should seek advice when facing challenging situations, such as when legal requirements conflict with ethical obligations to protect client privacy (Yadav, 2017).

Confidentiality and privacy are essential yet complex issues in forensic neuropsychology. Forensic neuropsychologists must navigate the delicate balance between protecting client information and fulfilling legal obligations. In both the USA and India, professionals are bound by ethical and legal requirements to safeguard privacy, but the approaches differ in their specificity and enforcement. By adopting best practices such as informed consent, data security, and clear communication, forensic neuropsychologists can maintain the highest ethical standards while working within the constraints of the legal system. Ensuring privacy in forensic evaluations is not only a matter of legal compliance but also a core ethical responsibility that helps preserve the integrity of the profession.

7 Conflict of Interest in Forensic Neuropsychology

A conflict of interest arises when a professional's judgment, objectivity, or integrity is compromised, or appears to be compromised, due to external influences such as personal, financial, or professional interests. In forensic neuropsychology, where professionals are expected to provide impartial and objective evaluations for legal proceedings, conflicts of interest can jeopardize the accuracy and credibility of their assessments. Forensic neuropsychologists serve as expert witnesses and their findings often significantly impact legal outcomes, such as rulings on competency, criminal responsibility, or the degree of impairment in civil cases. Therefore, conflicts of interest can have serious ethical, legal, and professional ramifications (Segal, 2024).

In the context of forensic neuropsychology, conflicts of interest can take various forms. One common example is when a neuropsychologist has a financial interest in the outcome of a case. If a neuropsychologist is being paid by a particular party in a legal dispute and that payment is contingent on the evaluation's findings, it can create a bias toward favoring that party. For instance, if a neuropsychologist is hired by the defense in a personal injury case, they might feel pressured—consciously or unconsciously—to downplay the plaintiff's cognitive impairments to ensure repeat business from the defense team. Such a scenario presents a clear conflict between the neuropsychologist's ethical duty to provide an impartial assessment and their financial interest in maintaining a profitable relationship with a legal client (Foote et al., 2020).

Another example is a dual relationship, where the neuropsychologist has a personal or professional relationship with one of the parties involved in the case. This can include evaluating a former patient or a colleague's family member, which can blur the boundaries between personal and professional responsibilities. In such cases, it becomes difficult for the neuropsychologist to remain fully objective, as their emotional ties or loyalty to the individual might influence the evaluation process or the interpretation of results (Harvey, 2012).

8 Implications for Practice

Conflicts of interest have significant implications for the practice of forensic neuropsychology. First and foremost, they can compromise the objectivity and accuracy of the neuropsychological evaluation (Stenclik, & University at Albany, State University of New York, 2013). Forensic neuropsychologists are tasked with providing unbiased opinions based solely on the data collected during an assessment. When conflicts of interest are present, there is a risk that the evaluation will be skewed, either intentionally or unintentionally. This can lead to inaccurate conclusions about an individual's cognitive abilities, impairments, or malingering behaviors, which in turn can result in unjust legal outcomes. For instance, in criminal cases, a neuropsychologist's biased assessment might lead to an inaccurate determination of competency to stand trial, affecting the defendant's legal rights and the fairness of the judicial process.

Conflicts of interest also undermine the credibility and reputation of the forensic neuropsychologist. The legal system relies on expert witnesses to provide trustworthy and scientifically sound opinions. If a conflict of interest is revealed during cross-examination or at any point during legal proceedings, it can cast doubt on the neuropsychologist's integrity, leading judges, attorneys, and juries to question the validity of their findings. This can weaken the impact of their testimony and, in some cases, disqualify the neuropsychologist from serving as an expert witness (Academike, 2024). Additionally, repeated conflicts of interest can damage a neuropsychologist's professional reputation, making it difficult for them to gain future opportunities to serve as an expert witness or even to continue practicing in the forensic field.

Another important implication is the potential for legal consequences. In both the USA and India, ethical violations stemming from conflicts of interest can result in disciplinary actions from professional licensing boards, legal penalties, or malpractice lawsuits. For example, if a neuropsychologist's biased evaluation leads to a wrongful conviction or unjust civil settlement, they could face legal challenges from the affected parties. In the USA, professional standards outlined by the American Psychological Association (APA) and the National Academy of Neuropsychology (NAN) emphasize the importance of avoiding conflicts of interest, and violations can result in sanctions (Ethical Principles of Psychologists and Code of Conduct, n.d.). Similarly, in India, breaches of confidentiality or unethical conduct can lead to actions under the Indian Evidence Act and other relevant legal frameworks, though regulations may not be as explicitly defined as in the USA.

9 Strategies to Avoid Conflict of Interest

To protect their objectivity and professional integrity, forensic neuropsychologists must proactively avoid situations where conflicts of interest could arise. Several strategies can help mitigate these risks and ensure that evaluations remain impartial and credible.

1. Declining Inappropriate Cases: One of the most effective ways to avoid conflicts of interest is to decline cases where a conflict might exist. Forensic neuropsychologists should refrain from accepting cases in which they have any form of personal, financial, or professional stake. For instance, if the neuropsychologist has previously treated the individual being evaluated, or if they have a business relationship with one of the parties in the case, it is best to decline the referral to avoid compromising their objectivity.
2. Maintaining Clear Boundaries: It is crucial for forensic neuropsychologists to maintain clear professional boundaries in all of their interactions. This involves avoiding dual relationships, such as treating or evaluating individuals with whom the neuropsychologist has personal ties. Furthermore, neuropsychologists should ensure that their professional fees are based on standard practices and are not contingent on the outcome of the case. Doing so prevents any appearance of bias or influence over their assessment.
3. Regular Ethical Training and Consultation: Neuropsychologists should engage in ongoing ethical training and seek consultation when necessary. Regularly reviewing ethical guidelines, such as the APA's Ethical Principles and the Specialty Guidelines for Forensic Psychology, can help forensic neuropsychologists stay aware of potential conflicts of interest and how to address them. Consulting with colleagues or ethics committees when facing challenging cases is another valuable strategy for navigating potential conflicts.

10 Transparency and Disclosure Practices

While it is important to avoid conflicts of interest whenever possible, some situations may require the forensic neuropsychologist to proceed with an evaluation despite the presence of potential conflicts. In such cases, transparency and disclosure become essential to maintaining ethical standards. Forensic neuropsychologists are ethically obligated to disclose any potential conflicts of interest to all relevant parties, including the courts, attorneys, and the individuals being evaluated. Full disclosure allows the legal stakeholders to make informed decisions about whether to proceed with the neuropsychologist's involvement or seek an alternative evaluator.

For example, if a neuropsychologist has previously worked with one of the attorneys involved in the case, they should disclose this relationship at the outset of the evaluation process. Transparency ensures that there are no hidden biases and that all parties are aware of the potential for conflicts. In some cases, the court may still permit the neuropsychologist to proceed with the evaluation, but full disclosure helps preserve the integrity of the process and mitigates any potential challenges during legal proceedings.

In addition to transparency, maintaining documentation is a critical practice for forensic neuropsychologists (Specialty Guidelines for Forensic Psychology, n.d.). Keeping detailed records of potential conflicts, decisions made regarding these conflicts, and all communications related to the evaluation can provide legal and ethical protection. This documentation demonstrates that the neuropsychologist has acted in good faith and has taken steps to address potential conflicts of interest in an ethical manner.

10.1 Ethical Dilemmas in Practice

Case of Tarasoff v. Regents of the University of California (1976)
Overview

The *Tarasoff* case is one of the most widely cited legal precedents involving ethical challenges in psychology, and it has direct implications for forensic neuropsychology, particularly regarding the balance between client confidentiality and societal safety. In 1969, Prosenjit Poddar, a student at the University of California, confided to his university psychologist that he intended to kill a fellow student, Tatiana Tarasoff. The psychologist, believing this to be a serious threat, informed campus police but did not notify Tatiana or her family. Poddar later killed Tarasoff, leading to a lawsuit by her parents (*Tarasoff V. Regents of University of California, 83 A.L.R. 3d 1166, 551 P.2d 334, 17 Cal. 3d 425, 131 Cal. Rptr. 14, 1976 Cal. LEXIS 297—CourtListener.com*, n.d.).

Ethical Challenge
The central ethical dilemma in this case involved the conflict between client confidentiality and the duty to warn third parties of impending harm. The psychologist's duty to maintain confidentiality with Poddar clashed with the need to prevent harm to a third party. The court ruled that mental health professionals have a "duty to protect" individuals who are being threatened by a client, establishing the legal obligation to breach confidentiality when there is a foreseeable risk of harm.

Key Takeaways

- This case highlights the need to balance a client's right to confidentiality with the safety of others. In forensic neuropsychology, professionals must navigate similar challenges, especially when conducting evaluations that involve potential risks to society, such as criminal cases involving violent offenders.
- The court's ruling placed a legal duty on mental health professionals, overriding the ethical duty of confidentiality. Forensic neuropsychologists must remain aware of such legal precedents and consider the broader societal implications of their assessments, particularly in cases involving threats of violence.

- The *Tarasoff* ruling led to the development of best practices, including risk assessment protocols and clear guidelines on when to breach confidentiality in the interest of public safety. Forensic neuropsychologists must remain vigilant in identifying potential risks and clearly document the reasoning behind decisions to disclose or protect client information.

Case of People V. Hawthorne (1940)
Overview

The case of *People v. Hawthorne* involved the admissibility of expert testimony by a psychologist in a criminal trial, which raised ethical and legal questions about the qualifications of mental health professionals to provide opinions on legal matters. Lester Hawthorne was convicted of murder, and his defense argued that he was insane at the time of the crime. A psychologist was brought in to testify regarding Hawthorne's mental state. The trial court, however, rejected the psychologist's testimony on the grounds that only a medical doctor (psychiatrist) could provide expert opinions on insanity (*People V. Hawthorne, 293 Mich. 15*, n.d.).

Ethical Challenge

This case highlighted the ethical and professional boundary issues surrounding the qualifications and roles of different mental health professionals in the legal system. For forensic neuropsychologists, this raised the question of how to navigate the boundaries of their expertise when offering testimony in legal cases. The trial court's decision restricted the role of psychologists, even though they had expertise in assessing mental health.

Key Takeaways

- The case demonstrated the challenge forensic neuropsychologists face when the legal system's demands clash with their professional competencies. While psychologists are often more qualified than psychiatrists to assess cognitive function, courts may limit their testimony based on legal precedents that favor medical professionals. This tension between judicial expectations and the professional capabilities of forensic neuropsychologists persists in many legal settings.
- Forensic neuropsychologists must clearly define and stay within the scope of their expertise while being transparent about their qualifications. In cases where neuropsychological assessments are critical, professionals need to assert their expertise confidently, especially when testifying on matters like cognitive impairments, competency, or mental health.
- While the trial court originally excluded the psychologist's testimony, the appellate court reversed this decision, acknowledging that psychologists have the necessary expertise to assess and testify on mental health matters. This case helped pave the way for greater recognition of psychologists in forensic contexts, demonstrating the importance of ongoing ethical advocacy in shaping the role of neuropsychologists in the legal system.

Citation

- *People v. Hawthorne*, 293 Mich. 15; 291 N.W. 205 (1940).

These two cases underscore the ethical complexities faced by forensic neuropsychologists, particularly in balancing the interests of clients, judicial demands, and societal needs. In the Tarasoff case, the ethical conflict between confidentiality and the duty to protect third parties highlighted the legal and professional responsibilities that come with risk assessment. In contrast, the Hawthorne case emphasized the challenges forensic neuropsychologists face when their professional qualifications are questioned in legal contexts, illustrating the need for clarity in defining professional boundaries. Both cases demonstrate that forensic neuropsychologists must be aware of legal precedents and maintain a strong ethical foundation in their practice. They must also navigate the demands of the legal system while adhering to their professional obligations, ensuring that their evaluations remain objective and credible. By understanding these ethical challenges and adopting best practices, forensic neuropsychologists can effectively contribute to the legal process while upholding the integrity of their profession.

11 Resolving Moral Dilemmas in Forensic Neuropsychology

As forensic neuropsychologists assess cognitive functions, brain-behavior relationships, and mental health issues within legal contexts, they face dilemmas that require careful ethical consideration. The complexity of legal proceedings, high stakes for individuals involved, and societal implications demand that forensic neuropsychologists employ robust ethical decision-making strategies. Resolving moral dilemmas requires an adherence to ethical guidelines, utilization of structured frameworks, and continuous professional development.

11.1 Methods for Ethical Decision-Making

Ethical decision-making is a structured approach used by forensic neuropsychologists to resolve moral dilemmas in practice. Ethical issues often arise when there are conflicting responsibilities—to the client, the legal system, and society as a whole. To make informed decisions, forensic neuropsychologists can employ several methods, including the ethical decision-making model developed by the American Psychological Association (APA) (Young & Kenny, 2022). This model outlines a step-by-step process for analyzing ethical challenges (Ameliakling, 2023).

1. **Identifying the Problem:** The first step is recognizing that an ethical issue exists. For example, a forensic neuropsychologist may be asked to disclose confidential information during a legal proceeding, which can raise concerns about the conflict between protecting client privacy and fulfilling legal obligations.
2. **Considering Relevant Guidelines:** Once the issue is identified, professionals must refer to relevant ethical guidelines, such as the **APA Ethical Principles of**

Psychologists and Code of Conduct or the **Specialty Guidelines for Forensic Psychology**. These resources provide clear guidance on professional responsibilities and how to navigate conflicting interests.
3. **Evaluating the Consequences of Various Actions:** Forensic neuropsychologists must weigh the potential outcomes of different courses of action, considering how their decisions might impact the client, the legal process, and broader societal interests.
4. **Consulting with Colleagues or Ethics Committees:** When ethical dilemmas are particularly complex, seeking peer consultation or discussing the issue with an ethics committee can provide valuable perspectives and reduce the risk of biased decision-making.
5. **Making and Implementing the Decision:** After evaluating the options, the forensic neuropsychologist must select the most ethically defensible course of action and follow through with it. Documentation of the decision-making process is crucial for ensuring accountability.

11.2 Frameworks for Analyzing Ethical Issues

Various frameworks provide structured ways to analyze and resolve ethical dilemmas in forensic neuropsychology. One widely used approach is Beauchamp and Childress's Four Principles of Biomedical Ethics, which include the following (Page, 2012).

1. Autonomy: Respecting the client's right to make informed decisions about their own care. In forensic settings, this means ensuring clients fully understand the evaluation process, possible outcomes, and limitations of confidentiality.
2. Beneficence: Acting in the best interest of the client, which may involve providing accurate assessments that can influence legal decisions such as sentencing or competency to stand trial.
3. Non-Maleficence: Avoiding harm to clients, which is particularly relevant when balancing the need for thorough evaluations against the risk of psychological distress. For example, forensic neuropsychologists must carefully consider the potential harm that might arise from disclosing sensitive information during court proceedings.
4. Justice: Ensuring fairness and equality, particularly when evaluating individuals from diverse backgrounds. Neuropsychologists must be mindful of cultural, linguistic, and socioeconomic differences to avoid biased assessments.

By applying these principles, forensic neuropsychologists can systematically evaluate ethical challenges and ensure their decisions align with both professional standards and the best interests of those involved.

12 Encouraging Ethical Behavior

Promoting ethical behavior in forensic neuropsychology requires fostering a culture of integrity and accountability. Several strategies can help neuropsychologists maintain high ethical standards in their practice.

Ethical dilemmas evolve as legal standards, societal expectations, and scientific advancements change. To remain competent and ethically grounded, forensic neuropsychologists must engage in ongoing education and training. This includes attending workshops, completing ethics courses, and staying current with developments in the field. Specialized training in forensic ethics equips professionals with the tools needed to handle complex cases and ethical challenges in diverse legal contexts.

Peer Consultation and Supervision: Regular consultation with peers and supervisors is critical for ethical decision-making. Peer consultation provides a forum for discussing challenging cases, exploring alternative perspectives, and gaining feedback on potential ethical concerns. For newer professionals, supervision from experienced forensic neuropsychologists can offer invaluable guidance. This process fosters transparency and helps prevent ethical blind spots that may arise from personal biases or overconfidence.

Adherence to Professional Standards: The ethical practice of forensic neuropsychology is grounded in adherence to professional standards, such as the APA Ethical Code and the National Academy of Neuropsychology's guidelines. These codes provide clear directives on issues like confidentiality, informed consent, and the limits of competence. Strict adherence to these standards is essential to avoid legal repercussions and protect the rights of individuals undergoing forensic evaluations. Moreover, professionals must document their adherence to ethical guidelines, ensuring that every step in the evaluation process is transparent and defensible.

13 Importance of Ongoing Compliance with Ethical Guidelines

Ethical guidelines serve as the foundation for forensic neuropsychology, helping professionals navigate the complex moral dilemmas they encounter in practice. However, adherence to these guidelines is not a one-time task—it requires ongoing compliance. As the legal system evolves and new ethical challenges emerge, forensic neuropsychologists must continuously reassess their practices to ensure they meet current standards. For example, with the growing use of neuroimaging and other advanced technologies in forensic evaluations, professionals must consider how these tools affect issues of confidentiality, informed consent, and fairness. Additionally, new court rulings may establish precedents that influence the ethical boundaries of forensic neuropsychology. Regularly reviewing ethical guidelines, attending legal workshops, and engaging with updated research are all critical to maintaining compliance.

Resolving moral dilemmas in forensic neuropsychology requires a multifaceted approach that includes ethical decision-making models, structured frameworks for analyzing dilemmas, and a commitment to professional development. By applying decision-making methods, consulting ethical guidelines, and seeking peer input, forensic neuropsychologists can navigate challenging cases while maintaining their professional integrity. Encouraging ethical behavior through continuing education, peer consultation, and adherence to professional standards helps foster a culture of accountability in forensic neuropsychology. Most importantly, compliance with ethical guidelines is not static but requires ongoing effort. As the field of forensic neuropsychology continues to evolve, professionals must remain vigilant in their commitment to ethical practice, balancing the interests of clients, the demands of the legal system, and the broader societal impact of their work. Through continuous education and a structured approach to decision-making, forensic neuropsychologists can resolve moral dilemmas in ways that uphold their ethical responsibilities and contribute to the fairness of the judicial process.

14 Ethical Dilemmas in Assessments: Navigating Complex Situations in Forensic Neuropsychology

Forensic neuropsychologists often face complex ethical dilemmas when conducting assessments in legal settings. These dilemmas arise from conflicting interests between the client, the legal system, and societal obligations. In a forensic context, neuropsychologists must balance providing objective, accurate evaluations with ensuring their actions do not unintentionally harm the individuals they assess. The ethical challenges involved in these assessments are further complicated by issues related to informed consent, confidentiality, and the potential impact of the evaluation on legal outcomes.

14.1 Complex Ethical Situations

Forensic neuropsychologists frequently navigate difficult ethical situations due to the dual obligations they hold: to the client and to the legal system. While the primary focus of their work is to provide a scientifically grounded assessment of cognitive or mental functioning, the results of these assessments can have significant consequences for the individuals being evaluated. The legal system relies on the objectivity of neuropsychologists to inform decisions related to criminal responsibility, competency to stand trial, disability claims, and more. However, clients often do not fully comprehend the implications of a neuropsychological evaluation.

Vulnerable populations, such as individuals with cognitive impairments, mental health disorders, or limited education, may struggle to understand the nature of the evaluation or its potential consequences (National Institutes of Health (US), 2007). This can create ethical conflicts, as neuropsychologists must ensure clients are adequately informed while maintaining the neutrality needed in legal proceedings. Additionally, the legal system may demand disclosures that conflict with the neuropsychologist's duty to protect client confidentiality. These competing interests can place forensic neuropsychologists in morally ambiguous situations, requiring careful navigation of both ethical and legal frameworks (Specker et al., 2018).

One of the most common ethical dilemmas in forensic neuropsychology involves the conflict between the interests of the client and the legal system. Neuropsychologists are tasked with providing objective assessments, but the findings from these evaluations can significantly impact a client's legal standing. For example, a neuropsychological evaluation may reveal cognitive deficits that could support a claim of diminished responsibility or reduced culpability in a criminal case. However, the same findings could also be used by the legal system to argue that the client is incompetent to stand trial or unfit for certain legal defenses.Consider a case where a defendant is being evaluated for cognitive impairments as part of a criminal trial. The neuropsychologist discovers that the client suffers from significant memory deficits, which may support a claim that the individual did not fully comprehend their actions at the time of the crime (Harvey, 2012). However, revealing these findings may also limit the client's ability to present a strong legal defense, as the prosecution could argue that the deficits make the individual unfit to stand trial or incompetent to make informed decisions about their legal representation. In such situations, the neuropsychologist faces a difficult choice between protecting the client's legal interests and fulfilling their duty to provide an accurate, unbiased evaluation.

Informed consent is a critical aspect of any neuropsychological evaluation, but it is particularly challenging in forensic settings (Marcopulos et al., 2024). Neuropsychologists must ensure that clients fully understand the purpose of the evaluation, the potential outcomes, and the limitations of confidentiality. Vulnerable populations, such as individuals with intellectual disabilities, mental illness, or limited legal knowledge, may not fully grasp the implications of the evaluation, leading to ethical concerns (Shivayogi, 2013).

For instance, a client with a severe mental health disorder may not fully understand that the results of the evaluation could be used against them in court. While the neuropsychologist has a duty to ensure the client is informed, the client's impaired cognitive functioning may limit their ability to provide fully informed consent. This presents an ethical dilemma: should the neuropsychologist proceed with the evaluation, knowing that the client may not fully understand its consequences? To navigate such dilemmas, neuropsychologists must ensure that they take extra steps to explain the evaluation process clearly and assess the client's capacity to consent.

15 Balancing Client and Legal Interests

Neuropsychologists play a key role in the legal process, and their assessments can significantly impact the outcomes of criminal, civil, and family law cases. As such, they must strive to balance the ethical obligations they have toward the client with the demands of the legal system.

Neuropsychologists must maintain transparency in their reporting. Regardless of the potential impact on the client, findings must be presented objectively, avoiding any bias that could influence the outcome in favor of one side. This impartiality is critical to upholding ethical standards. Vulnerable populations present unique challenges in ensuring informed consent. In these cases, neuropsychologists may need to take additional measures, such as involving family members or legal guardians, to ensure that the client understands the process (Gordon, 2020). Neuropsychologists must also clearly communicate the limits of confidentiality in legal settings. Clients should be made aware that information shared during the evaluation could be disclosed in court, which may be contrary to their interests.

16 Encouraging Ethical Behavior

To navigate these dilemmas effectively, forensic neuropsychologists must prioritize ongoing ethical training, peer consultation, and adherence to professional standards.

Ethical issues in forensic neuropsychology evolve as legal standards and societal expectations shift. Ongoing education is essential for ensuring that practitioners remain current with new developments and challenges. Forensic neuropsychologists should participate in workshops, ethics courses, and other professional development opportunities that focus on ethical decision-making in legal contexts. In complex cases, consulting with colleagues or supervisors can provide valuable insight and help neuropsychologists navigate ethical dilemmas. Peer consultation fosters a collaborative environment for discussing challenging cases and developing strategies to resolve ethical conflicts. Adherence to ethical guidelines, such as those outlined by the American Psychological Association (APA) and other relevant bodies, is critical to maintaining professional integrity. These guidelines offer clear standards for handling confidentiality, informed consent, and the balance between client and legal interests.

17 Conclusion

Forensic neuropsychology operates at the intersection of psychology, neuroscience, and the legal system. The role of the neuropsychologist in this domain is to provide expert testimony and evaluation that can inform legal decision-making in areas such as criminal responsibility, competency, and personal injury claims. However, this unique positioning presents a range of ethical dilemmas that can complicate the practice. These challenges arise due to the conflicting demands of the legal system, the rights of the individual, and the neuropsychologist's duty to uphold ethical standards of practice. One of the primary ethical challenges in forensic neuropsychology stems from the often-competing interests between clients and the legal system. The neuropsychologist's duty is to provide objective and scientifically grounded evaluations, but this can conflict with the goals of the parties involved. For example, attorneys may seek testimony that supports their legal arguments, while clients may desire outcomes that align with their personal interests. Neuropsychologists must navigate these competing pressures while maintaining their commitment to truthfulness, objectivity, and integrity. In some cases, findings from neuropsychological assessments may have significant negative consequences for the client's legal standing. For instance, in a criminal case, an assessment that suggests the individual has cognitive impairments may limit their ability to mount a defense. While this information may be critical for the court to determine competency, it can have life-altering consequences for the defendant. Balancing the need to provide accurate and honest testimony with the potential harm to the client presents a significant ethical dilemma. Similarly, in personal injury or disability claims, a neuropsychological assessment that concludes there is no significant cognitive impairment may result in the denial of financial compensation or disability benefits. This can be particularly challenging when the client's self-reported symptoms conflict with the objective findings of the evaluation. In these instances, neuropsychologists must ensure that their conclusions are based on sound scientific evidence, even if the outcome may not align with the client's desires.

Ensuring informed consent is another area fraught with ethical challenges, particularly in forensic settings. Informed consent refers to the process by which clients are made aware of the purpose, methods, and potential consequences of the neuropsychological evaluation, and voluntarily agree to participate. However, in forensic contexts, obtaining truly informed consent can be complex. For one, clients involved in legal cases may not fully understand the implications of the evaluation. This is particularly true for vulnerable populations such as individuals with cognitive impairments, psychiatric disorders, or low levels of education. Neuropsychologists have an ethical obligation to ensure that clients understand the purpose of the assessment, the limitations of confidentiality (since results may be shared with legal stakeholders), and the potential consequences of the findings. Additionally, in some forensic cases, participation in a neuropsychological evaluation may not be entirely voluntary. For example, a court may order an evaluation as part of a legal proceeding. In these situations, the neuropsychologist must carefully explain the mandatory nature of the evaluation and the ways in which the results may be used. The challenge lies in ensuring that the client understands their rights and the potential outcomes of the assessment, while also complying with legal requirements.

To navigate the complex ethical dilemmas that arise in forensic neuropsychology, practitioners can rely on established ethical frameworks and decision-making models. Ethical decision-making models often involve a step-by-step process that encourages careful consideration of all aspects of the dilemma before reaching a resolution. Key elements of this process include identifying the ethical issue, considering the relevant ethical principles (such as beneficence, non-maleficence, autonomy, and justice), and evaluating the potential consequences of various courses of action.

One widely used approach is the principle-based ethics model, which involves applying fundamental ethical principles to the dilemma at hand. For example, the principle of autonomy requires neuropsychologists to respect the client's right to make informed decisions about their participation in the evaluation. However, this principle may conflict with the principle of justice, which requires that neuropsychologists provide accurate and unbiased information to the court, even if it negatively impacts the client. Another valuable approach is the consultation and supervision model, where neuropsychologists seek guidance from peers or supervisors when faced with particularly challenging ethical dilemmas. Peer consultation allows practitioners to benefit from the experience and insights of colleagues who may have encountered similar situations. This collaborative approach fosters ethical behavior and ensures that complex issues are addressed in a thoughtful and well-informed manner.

Adhering to professional standards is not only a matter of legal compliance but also an essential aspect of ethical practice in forensic neuropsychology. The APA's Ethical Principles of Psychologists and Code of Conduct and the Specialty Guidelines for Forensic Psychology provide specific guidance for neuropsychologists working in forensic contexts. These guidelines emphasize the importance of objectivity, competence, and maintaining the integrity of the profession. In particular, neuropsychologists must be aware of the potential for dual relationships, which can compromise their objectivity. For example, serving as both a treating clinician and an expert witness in a legal case presents a clear conflict of interest. Neuropsychologists must establish clear boundaries and ensure that their role is transparent to all parties involved.

References

Academike. (2024, September 6). Examination of the acceptability of expert testimony. *Academike*. https://www.lawctopus.com/academike/an-examination-of-the-acceptability-of-expert-testimony-under-the-indian-evidence-act/

Ameliakling. (2023, June 16). *6-step guide to ethical decision-making*. Michigan State University. https://www.michiganstateuniversityonline.com/resources/leadership/guide-to-ethical-decision-making/

Boone, K. B., Kaufmann, P. M., Sweet, J. J., Leatherberry, D., Beattey, R. A., Silva, D., Victor, T. L., Boone, R. P., Spector, J., Hebben, N., Hanks, R. A., & James, J. (2024). Attorney demands for protected psychological test information: Is access necessary for cross examination or does it lead to misinformation? An interorganizational* position paper. *The Clinical Neuropsychologist, 38*(4), 889–906. https://doi.org/10.1080/13854046.2024.2323222

Chadda, R. K. (2019). Influence of the new mental health legislation in India. *BJPsych International, 17*(1), 20–22. https://doi.org/10.1192/bji.2019.18

Darby, W. C., & Weinstock, R. (2018). The Limits of Confidentiality: Informed Consent and Psychotherapy. *FOCUS the Journal of Lifelong Learning in Psychiatry, 16*(4), 395–401. https://doi.org/10.1176/appi.focus.20180020

Ethical principles of psychologists and code of conduct. (n.d.). https://www.apa.org. https://www.apa.org/ethics/code

Foote, W. E., Goodman-Delahunty, J., & Young, G. (2020). Civil Forensic Evaluation in Psychological Injury and Law: Legal, Professional, and Ethical Considerations. *Psychological Injury and Law, 13*(4), 327–353. https://doi.org/10.1007/s12207-020-09398-3

Gordon, B. G. (2020). Vulnerability in research: Basic ethical concepts and general approach to review. *Ochsner Journal, 20*(1), 34–38. https://doi.org/10.31486/toj.19.0079

Government of India. (2020). The indian evidence act, 1872. In *arrangement of sections*. https://www.indiacode.nic.in/bitstream/123456789/15351/1/iea_1872.pdf

Gowsika. (2024, September 30). *HIPAA compliance: Ensure privacy & security (Download Free Checklist)*. Sprinto. https://sprinto.com/blog/hipaa-compliance/

Guilmette, T. J., & Hagan, L. D. (1997). Ethical considerations in forensic neuropsychological consultation. *The Clinical Neuropsychologist, 11*(3), 287–290. https://doi.org/10.1080/13854049708400457

Harvey, P. D. (2012). Clinical applications of neuropsychological assessment. *Dialogues in Clinical Neuroscience, 14*(1), 91–99. https://doi.org/10.31887/dcns.2012.14.1/pharvey

Indian Council of Medical Research, Mathur, R., & Director-General Indian Council of Medical Research. (2017). *National ethical guidelines for biomedical and health research involving human participants*. Indian Council of Medical Research. https://ethics.ncdirindia.org/asset/pdf/ICMR_National_Ethical_Guidelines.pdf

Kadam, R. (2017). Informed consent process: A step further towards making it meaningful! *Perspectives in Clinical Research, 8*(3), 107. https://doi.org/10.4103/picr.picr_147_16

Marcopulos, B. A., Kaufmann, P., & Patel, A. C. (2024). Forensic neuropsychological assessment. *Behavioral Sciences & The Law*. https://doi.org/10.1002/bsl.2656

Merkt, H., Haesen, S., Eytan, A., Habermeyer, E., Aebi, M. F., Elger, B., & Wangmo, T. (2021). Forensic mental health professionals' perceptions of their dual loyalty conflict: Findings from a qualitative study. *BMC Medical Ethics, 22*(1). https://doi.org/10.1186/s12910-021-00688-2

National Institutes of Health (US). (2007). *Information about Mental Illness and the Brain*. NIH Curriculum Supplement Series–NCBI Bookshelf. https://www.ncbi.nlm.nih.gov/books/NBK20369/

Page, K. (2012). The four principles: Can they be measured and do they predict ethical decision making? *BMC Medical Ethics, 13*(1). https://doi.org/10.1186/1472-6939-13-10

People v. Hawthorne, 293 Mich. 15 | Casetext Search + Citator. (n.d.). https://casetext.com/case/people-v-hawthorne-36

Rights, O. F. C. (2022, October 20). *Summary of the HIPAA security rule*. HHS.gov. https://www.hhs.gov/hipaa/for-professionals/security/laws-regulations/index.html

Roux, C., Bucht, R., Crispino, F., De Forest, P., Lennard, C., Margot, P., Miranda, M. D., NicDaeid, N., Ribaux, O., Ross, A., & Willis, S. (2022). The Sydney declaration—Revisiting the essence of forensic science through its fundamental principles. *Forensic Science International, 332*, 111182. https://doi.org/10.1016/j.forsciint.2022.111182

Segal, T. (2024, July 31). *What is a conflict of interest?* Investopedia. https://www.investopedia.com/terms/c/conflict-of-interest.asp

Shah, P., Thornton, I., Turrin, D., & Hipskind, J. E. (2023, June 5). *Informed consent*. StatPearls–NCBI Bookshelf. https://www.ncbi.nlm.nih.gov/books/NBK430827/

Shivayogi, P. (2013). Vulnerable population and methods for their safeguard. *Perspectives in Clinical Research, 4*(1), 53. https://doi.org/10.4103/2229-3485.106389

Specialty guidelines for forensic psychology. (n.d.). https://www.apa.org. https://www.apa.org/practice/guidelines/forensic-psychology

Specker, J., Focquaert, F., Sterckx, S., & Schermer, M. H. N. (2018). Forensic practitioners' views on stimulating moral development and moral growth in forensic psychiatric care. *Neuroethics, 13*(1), 73–85. https://doi.org/10.1007/s12152-018-9363-x

Stenclik, J. & University at Albany, State University of New York. (2013). *Effects of third party observation behind a one-way mirror on neuropsychological tests with varying conative load.* In Legacy Theses & Dissertations (2009–2024). https://scholarsarchive.library.albany.edu/cgi/viewcontent.cgi?article=2278&context=legacy-etd

Sullivan, G. M. (2011). A primer on the validity of assessment instruments. *Journal of Graduate Medical Education, 3*(2), 119–120. https://doi.org/10.4300/jgme-d-11-00075.1

Swanepoel, M. (2010). Ethical decision-making in forensic psychology. *Koers–Bulletin for Christian Scholarship, 75*(4). https://doi.org/10.4102/koers.v75i4.110

Tarasoff v. Regents of University of California, 83 A.L.R. 3d 1166, 551 P.2d 334, 17 Cal. 3d 425, 131 Cal. Rptr. 14, 1976 Cal. LEXIS 297—CourtListener.com. (n.d.). *CourtListener*. https://www.courtlistener.com/opinion/1175611/tarasoff-v-regents-of-university-of-california/

Varkey, B. (2020). Principles of clinical ethics and their application to practice. *Medical Principles and Practice, 30*(1), 17–28. https://doi.org/10.1159/000509119

Ward, T. (2022). The forensic ethics of scientific communication. *The Journal of Criminal Law, 87*(1), 3–17. https://doi.org/10.1177/00220183221143985

Yadav, P. K. (2017). Ethical issues across different fields of forensic science. *Egyptian Journal of Forensic Sciences, 7*(1). https://doi.org/10.1186/s41935-017-0010-1

Young, G., & Kenny, M. C. (2022). Focusing the APA ethics code to include development: applications to abuse. *Journal of Child & Adolescent Trauma, 16*(1), 109–122. https://doi.org/10.1007/s40653-022-00484-z

Neuroscientific Evidence in Legal Proceedings

1 Introduction to Neuroscientific Evidence in Legal Proceedings

Neuroscientific evidence refers to data derived from studying the brain and nervous system that is introduced to support claims or arguments in legal contexts (Aono et al., 2019). This type of evidence typically encompasses brain imaging techniques, neurobiological findings, and other tools used to explore the neurological basis of behavior. Brain imaging methods such as functional magnetic resonance imaging (fMRI), positron emission tomography (PET), and electroencephalography (EEG) have become central to understanding the biological underpinnings of decision-making, memory, aggression, and other psychological processes (Xue et al., 2010). Neurobiological data can also include information about neurotransmitter activity, genetic markers, or the structural integrity of brain regions, offering a window into the mental states of individuals.

Neuroscientific evidence is rooted in the premise that human behavior and cognition are closely tied to the functioning of the brain. Legal professionals and scientists alike are interested in how these biological factors influence actions, potentially mitigating responsibility or enhancing the understanding of criminal intent. For instance, brain abnormalities may be presented as evidence to argue diminished capacity or explain violent tendencies, raising complex questions about the intersection of biology and personal accountability. Over the past few decades, the relevance of neuroscientific evidence in legal proceedings has surged. This trend is most notable in criminal cases, where brain scans are often used to assess a defendant's mental state or argue for mitigating circumstances, such as cognitive impairments or emotional disturbances (Aono et al., 2019). Neuroimaging can provide insights into a defendant's capacity for self-control, impulse regulation, or ability to understand the consequences of their actions. For instance, the discovery of abnormalities in the prefrontal cortex, a brain region associated with decision-making and impulse

© The Author(s), under exclusive license to Springer Nature Switzerland AG 2025

K. J. Reddy, *Foundations of Criminal Forensic Neuropsychology*,
https://doi.org/10.1007/978-3-031-83771-5_9

control, may be used to argue that a defendant was not fully responsible for their criminal behavior.

In civil cases, neuroscientific evidence is employed to assess psychological damages, brain injuries, or disabilities (Aono et al., 2019). For example, in personal injury lawsuits, neuroimaging can provide objective proof of brain damage or cognitive decline, thereby supporting claims for compensation. Family courts may also encounter neuroscientific evidence when assessing the cognitive and emotional capacities of individuals, especially in cases concerning child custody or competency evaluations.

Neuroscientific evidence introduces a unique perspective into the legal discourse by moving beyond subjective self-reports or behavioral observations to include objective biological data. However, this has also introduced debates around its ethical implications, particularly concerning the potential to infringe on an individual's privacy or the possibility of misinterpretation by laypersons, including jurors and judges.

This chapter aims to examine the multifaceted role of neuroscientific evidence within legal proceedings, specifically exploring its admissibility, reliability, and limitations.

One of the primary objectives of this chapter is to explore how neuroscientific evidence fits within the legal framework governing the admissibility of scientific evidence. In many jurisdictions, evidence must meet specific legal standards before it can be presented in court. In the United States, for example, the Daubert standard requires that scientific evidence be based on a sound methodology, subjected to peer review, and generally accepted by the relevant scientific community. A central issue is whether neuroscientific evidence consistently meets these standards, given that brain imaging techniques and neurobiological data are still areas of active research with evolving methods and interpretations.

The discussion will also highlight the challenges of integrating cutting-edge neuroscientific findings into legal systems that may not yet be fully equipped to evaluate their relevance or reliability. Courts must decide how much weight to place on neuroimaging data when determining guilt, sentencing, or compensation. The chapter will consider landmark cases where neuroscientific evidence has played a significant role and analyze the judicial reasoning behind the inclusion or exclusion of such evidence. Beyond admissibility, the reliability of neuroscientific evidence is another core issue addressed in this chapter. Brain imaging and neurobiological data are often treated as objective and infallible in the courtroom, but this assumption is far from accurate (Shafi, & Teachers College, Columbia University, 2009). Factors such as the complexity of interpreting neuroimages, the variability of individual brain functioning, and the limitations of current technology raise questions about how reliably neuroscientific evidence can support legal arguments. For instance, functional MRI scans only show blood flow changes in the brain, which are indirect measures of neuronal activity (Radiological Society of North America (RSNA) and American College of Radiology (ACR), n.d.). There is still significant debate in the scientific community about how to accurately interpret these scans and whether they can conclusively establish mental states or predict behavior. Furthermore, neuroimaging data can be subject to overinterpretation or misrepresentation when simplified for legal audiences, including jurors who may be unfamiliar with the nuances of neuroscience.

This section will delve into the scientific limitations of neuroimaging techniques and neurobiological data, emphasizing the need for caution in drawing legal conclusions from such evidence. It will also explore the role of expert witnesses in interpreting and presenting neuroscientific findings in court, highlighting the importance of balancing technical complexity with clarity.

Lastly, this chapter will address the ethical and practical limitations of using neuroscientific evidence in legal proceedings. While such evidence has the potential to enhance fairness and precision in legal decision-making, it also presents new challenges. One major concern is the risk of neuro-determinism—the idea that people's behavior is entirely dictated by their brain biology, potentially reducing personal accountability (Ochang et al., 2022). This notion could conflict with legal principles that emphasize individual responsibility for actions.

Additionally, the introduction of neuroscientific evidence may raise privacy concerns, as individuals' brain scans or genetic information could be used to predict future behaviors or determine predispositions for criminality. The potential for such information to be misused or overemphasized in legal decisions is significant, necessitating a careful consideration of both the benefits and the drawbacks of incorporating neuroscience into the legal arena. Neuroscientific evidence represents a burgeoning frontier in legal proceedings, promising to shed light on complex human behaviors and mental states. However, as this chapter will explore in depth, the use of such evidence is not without its challenges. By examining its admissibility, reliability, and limitations, this chapter aims to provide a nuanced understanding of the implications of introducing neuroscientific evidence into the legal system.

2 Historical Background

Evolution in the Courtroom

- Historical milestones in the integration of neuroscience in legal settings.

  Key Milestones

- Important developments that shaped current practices.

  Landmark Cases

- Overview of significant cases influencing admissibility standards.

3 Historical Background

The introduction of neuroscientific evidence into the courtroom has prompted debates over its reliability, ethical implications, and the extent to which it should influence legal decisions. This section explores the historical milestones that shaped the integration of neuroscience into legal proceedings, focusing on the evolution of imaging techniques from early electroencephalograms (EEGs) to modern neuroimaging. Additionally, the section examines the historical background, key legal cases, and the admissibility standards that have shaped current practices.

3.1 Evolution of Neuroscience in the Courtroom

The use of scientific evidence in legal contexts is not new, but the application of neuroscience in the courtroom is a relatively recent phenomenon. Neuroscience, as a field, has made vast strides over the past century, with advances in technology playing a crucial role in how brain activity is observed and understood. The integration of neuroscientific evidence into legal proceedings has evolved in parallel with the technological advancements in brain imaging and electrophysiology, moving from rudimentary methods like early EEGs to highly sophisticated tools such as functional magnetic resonance imaging (fMRI) and positron emission tomography (PET).

The earliest attempts to bring neuroscientific evidence into legal contexts were tied to the advent of the Electroencephalogram (EEG) in the 1920s. Developed by German psychiatrist Hans Berger, the EEG provided a non-invasive method to record electrical activity in the brain by placing electrodes on the scalp (St Louis et al., 2016). Although rudimentary by today's standards, early EEGs offered new insights into brain disorders, particularly epilepsy, and were quickly adopted in clinical settings. As early as the 1940s and 1950s, EEGs were occasionally introduced as evidence in criminal trials, particularly in cases where defendants sought to prove diminished capacity or mental illness (Brown et al., 2022).

However, the integration of EEGs into legal proceedings was often met with skepticism. Early EEG readings were crude, making them difficult for juries and judges to interpret reliably. Moreover, the legal standards for the admissibility of scientific evidence—established in the early twentieth century—were strict, requiring that evidence be both scientifically accepted and relevant to the case (Niso et al., 2022). Despite these hurdles, EEGs marked the beginning of neuroscience‘s relationship with the law, laying the groundwork for future developments.

3.2 *Advances in Imaging Techniques*

While EEGs focused on electrical activity in the brain, subsequent technological advances provided the means to visualize the brain itself. In the 1970s, the invention of computed tomography (CT) scanning allowed clinicians to create cross-sectional images of the brain. CT scans provided the first detailed views of brain structures, making it possible to detect tumors, hemorrhages, and other abnormalities (Computed Tomography (CT), n.d.). Although CT scans were initially developed for medical diagnostics, they soon found their way into legal cases where brain injuries or abnormalities were relevant to a defendant's behavior or mental state.

A significant leap came in the 1980s with the development of magnetic resonance imaging (MRI) (Grover et al., 2015). Unlike CT scans, which use X-rays, MRIs use magnetic fields to create detailed images of soft tissues, including the brain. The ability to visualize brain structures with unprecedented clarity opened new doors for neuroscientific evidence in courtrooms. For example, defense attorneys could now argue that structural abnormalities in a defendant's brain—such as lesions or developmental abnormalities—might mitigate responsibility for criminal behavior.

In the late 1990s and early 2000s, functional magnetic resonance imaging (fMRI) revolutionized both neuroscience and its legal applications. Unlike structural MRI, which provides static images, fMRI allows researchers to observe brain activity in real time by measuring blood flow to different brain regions. This functional approach offered the potential to directly correlate brain activity with behavior, making it a powerful tool for understanding mental states, intentions, and cognitive capacities—key issues in legal cases. Alongside fMRI, other functional imaging techniques, such as positron emission tomography (PET) and single photon emission computed tomography (SPECT), became valuable tools in forensic settings, providing additional ways to link brain function with behavior.

Electrophysiology: Beyond EEG

While imaging techniques like MRI and fMRI have captured the public's imagination, electrophysiological methods remain relevant in legal settings. Modern EEGs, now refined with greater sensitivity and more sophisticated analytic techniques, continue to be used in cases involving epilepsy and other neurological disorders (Grover et al., 2015). Event-related potentials (ERPs)—a technique derived from EEG that measures the brain's electrical response to specific stimuli—have also seen limited use in courtrooms (Sur & Sinha, 2009). ERPs have been used in cases where cognitive function is questioned, such as in determining whether a person is conscious or aware.

The Present: Neuroscience's Legal Relevance Today

Today, the combination of neuroimaging and electrophysiological techniques has transformed the legal landscape. Neuroscientific evidence is increasingly introduced in criminal cases to support claims related to mental illness, diminished capacity, and brain injury. Additionally, neuroscience is playing a growing role in civil cases, such as those involving personal injury, where brain imaging can be used to demonstrate the extent of trauma or damage. However, while the legal system has embraced some aspects of neuroscience, it remains cautious, particularly regarding claims that neuroscience can definitively answer questions about intent, responsibility, or guilt.

3.3 Key Milestones in the Integration of Neuroscience in Legal Settings

Several key developments have shaped the current use of neuroscientific evidence in legal proceedings. These milestones mark important moments in the evolution of how brain science interacts with law.

One of the earliest milestones in the admissibility of scientific evidence, including neuroscientific evidence, was the Frye v. United States (1923) case (Albright, 2023). The ruling established the "general acceptance" test, which held that scientific evidence must be widely accepted within the relevant scientific community to be admissible in court. Early EEG evidence, for example, was often challenged under the Frye standard, as it was not yet widely accepted within the broader scientific and legal communities.

The Daubert v. Merrell Dow Pharmaceuticals (1993) case is perhaps the most important milestone in the admissibility of scientific evidence, including neuroscientific evidence, in courtrooms (Daubert V. Merrell Dow Pharmaceuticals, Inc., 509 U.S. *579 (1993)*, n.d.). The ruling replaced the Frye standard with a new set of criteria, giving judges the role of "gatekeepers" who must determine whether the scientific evidence is relevant, reliable, and based on sound methodology. Under Daubert, scientific evidence must be testable, peer-reviewed, have a known error rate, and be generally accepted in the field. This shift allowed for more flexibility in introducing neuroscientific evidence, as long as it met these criteria.

Current Applications and Challenges

Despite the promise of neuroscientific evidence in legal settings, its use remains controversial. While techniques like fMRI and EEG have clear clinical applications, their forensic use is more complex. One major challenge is the interpretation of neuroscientific evidence: brain scans can show abnormalities, but proving a direct link between these abnormalities and criminal behavior is difficult. Additionally, the potential for over-reliance on neuroscientific evidence—a phenomenon known as "brain overclaim syndrome"—poses ethical and practical challenges. Lawyers and juries may place undue weight on brain scans without fully understanding the limitations of the technology. Another ongoing debate concerns free will and responsibility. Some legal scholars and neuroscientists argue that if brain activity can influence behavior in ways beyond a person's control, the legal system may need to reconsider traditional notions of guilt and punishment. However, others caution against undermining personal responsibility, emphasizing that neuroscience does not negate the fact that most people can still make moral and legal choices.

The integration of neuroscientific evidence in legal proceedings has evolved dramatically over the past century, from early EEGs to modern neuroimaging techniques like fMRI and PET scans. Key legal cases, such as Daubert, Roper, and Miller, have shaped the standards by which neuroscientific evidence is introduced in courtrooms, paving the way for more sophisticated arguments about brain function, responsibility, and mental illness. While neuroscience offers powerful tools to better understand human behavior, its use in legal settings must be approached with caution to ensure that it complements, rather than distorts, the pursuit of justice.

4 Types of Neuroscientific Evidence

In recent years, neuroscientific evidence has increasingly found its way into legal proceedings, influencing cases ranging from criminal trials to civil litigation. Advances in brain imaging techniques and neurobiological data applications have provided new insights into human behavior, decision-making, and mental states. These developments have raised profound questions about responsibility, intent, and the extent to which individuals can be held accountable for their actions. In this section, we will explore the primary types of neuroscientific evidence used in the legal context, including brain imaging techniques such as functional magnetic resonance imaging (fMRI), positron emission tomography (PET) scans, and electroencephalography (EEG). We will also examine the applications of neurobiological data in the legal system, comparing neuroscientific evidence with traditional legal evidence, and discussing how neuroscientific data can complement or challenge conventional methods of establishing facts in courtrooms.

4.1 Brain Imaging Techniques

The introduction of advanced brain imaging techniques into legal proceedings has fundamentally changed how courts evaluate issues related to cognition, behavior, and mental health. These technologies allow for non-invasive visualization of the brain's structure and function, offering potential insights into whether a person's brain might be impaired or functioning in ways that could affect their behavior or decision-making.

Functional magnetic resonance imaging (fMRI) is one of the most widely recognized and utilized brain imaging techniques in both neuroscience research and legal settings. Unlike traditional MRI, which provides static images of brain structures, fMRI measures brain activity in real time by detecting changes in blood oxygenation (Glover, 2011). When a specific area of the brain becomes more active, it consumes more oxygen, and the fMRI machine can detect this by measuring the associated changes in blood flow. This process, known as the blood oxygen level-dependent (BOLD) response, allows researchers to infer which brain regions are involved in specific cognitive tasks.

In the legal context, fMRI has been used in several ways. fMRI can help determine whether a defendant was in a particular mental state during the commission of a crime, such as whether they had the intent to commit the crime (mens rea) or were acting impulsively due to diminished cognitive control (Mens Rea, n.d.). There has been significant interest in using fMRI for lie detection, as certain brain regions, such as the prefrontal cortex, are thought to be involved in the process of deception (Monteleone et al., 2008). However, the use of fMRI for lie detection remains controversial due to concerns about its reliability and accuracy. In some cases, fMRI has been used to show that a defendant has brain abnormalities that could impact their behavior, such as damage to the prefrontal cortex or abnormalities in the amygdala, which are associated with impulse control and aggression (Siever, 2008).

Despite its potential, fMRI also has limitations. For one, it provides only indirect measures of neural activity by measuring blood flow rather than electrical activity. Additionally, interpreting fMRI data can be complex, and there is a risk that juries might overestimate the accuracy and reliability of brain scans due to their visual and seemingly objective nature.

Positron emission tomography (PET) is another imaging technique used to study brain function. PET scans work by injecting a radioactive tracer into the bloodstream, which travels to areas of the brain that are metabolically active (Positron Emission Tomography Scan–Mayo Clinic, n.d.). The scanner then detects the emitted positrons from the tracer and creates a visual representation of brain activity.

PET scans are especially useful for assessing neurochemical processes in the brain, such as the activity of neurotransmitters like dopamine and serotonin. This makes PET scans particularly valuable in legal cases involving mental illness, where an understanding of neurotransmitter function may be relevant to determining whether a defendant's behavior was influenced by a psychiatric condition, such as schizophrenia or bipolar disorder.

In legal contexts, PET scans have been used to assess brain damage. PET scans can reveal metabolic changes associated with traumatic brain injury (TBI), which can be a critical factor in cases where a defendant claims that brain damage has impaired their cognitive or emotional functioning (Byrnes et al., 2014). PET scans can provide evidence of abnormal brain activity in individuals with certain mental disorders, offering potential explanations for behaviors that might otherwise seem irrational or inexplicable (Kapoor & Kasi, 2022).

However, like fMRI, PET scans have limitations. The use of radioactive tracers means that PET is more invasive than other imaging techniques, and its resolution is not as high as that of MRI or fMRI. Furthermore, the results of PET scans are open to interpretation, and the presence of abnormal brain activity does not necessarily imply a direct link to criminal behavior.

Electroencephalography (EEG) is one of the oldest and most well-established methods of measuring brain activity. EEG involves placing electrodes on the scalp to record electrical activity in the brain (Light et al., 2010). Unlike fMRI and PET, which provide information about blood flow or metabolic activity, EEG directly measures the brain's electrical signals, providing a much more immediate view of neural activity.

In legal contexts, EEG has been used primarily in cases involving epilepsy or other neurological disorders that are characterized by abnormal electrical activity in the brain (Stafstrom & Carmant, 2015). EEG can be used to demonstrate that a defendant has a seizure disorder that may have contributed to a loss of control or awareness during the commission of a crime. EEG has also been used in cases where the determination of brain death is relevant, such as in disputes over end-of-life decisions.

More recently, techniques derived from EEG, such as event-related potentials (ERPs), have been used in legal settings. ERPs measure the brain's electrical response to specific stimuli and have been used to assess cognitive functions, such as attention, memory, and awareness.

4.2 Neurobiological Data Applications in Legal Contexts

Neurobiological data, including information from brain imaging techniques, has a range of applications in legal proceedings. The potential of these data lies in their ability to provide objective evidence about a person's brain function, mental state, or capacity for control over their actions. This section explores some of the key ways neurobiological data are used in legal contexts.

1. Assessing Competence and Responsibility

One of the primary uses of neuroscientific evidence in legal proceedings is to assess a defendant's mental competence and responsibility. In criminal cases, this often involves determining whether the defendant had the mens rea, or intent, to commit the crime. Brain imaging can be used to show that a defendant has a neurological condition, such as damage to the prefrontal cortex, that impairs their ability to make rational decisions or control impulses (Aono et al., 2019). This kind of evidence can be used to support claims of diminished capacity or insanity defenses.

In civil cases, neuroscientific evidence can be used to assess competence in legal decision-making, such as in cases where an individual's mental fitness to stand trial, enter a contract, or make end-of-life decisions is in question (Aono et al., 2019). By providing objective data on brain function, neurobiological evidence can complement psychological evaluations, offering additional information to judges and juries.

2. Sentencing and Mitigation

In some cases, neuroscientific evidence is used not to absolve a defendant of responsibility, but to mitigate the severity of their sentence. For example, brain imaging might show that a defendant has a brain abnormality or psychiatric condition that reduces their moral culpability for the crime. This evidence might not eliminate legal responsibility, but it could persuade a judge or jury to impose a lesser sentence, such as life imprisonment instead of the death penalty.

One notable area where neurobiological data has had a significant impact is in the context of **juvenile justice**. Neuroscientific research has shown that the brains of adolescents are not fully developed, particularly in regions involved in impulse control and decision-making. This research has influenced several U.S. Supreme Court rulings, including Roper v. Simmons (2005), which abolished the death penalty for juveniles (Amy, 2019), and Miller v. Alabama (2012), which banned mandatory life without parole for juvenile offenders (Miller V. Alabama, 2022).

3. Personal Injury and Compensation Cases

In civil litigation, particularly in personal injury cases, neuroscientific evidence is often used to demonstrate the extent of damage or impairment caused by an injury (Aono et al., 2019). Brain scans can provide visual proof of traumatic brain injury (TBI) or other neurological damage that might not be immediately apparent through traditional physical examinations. This evidence can be crucial in determining the appropriate amount of compensation for damages.

Additionally, neurobiological evidence is sometimes used in cases involving workers' compensation or disability claims, where the claimant's mental or neurological capacity is in question. By providing objective data on brain function, neuroscientific evidence can support claims of cognitive impairment or mental illness.

Comparison to Traditional Evidence

The introduction of neuroscientific evidence into legal proceedings has raised important questions about how this new form of evidence compares to more traditional forms of legal evidence, such as eyewitness testimony, forensic evidence, or psychological evaluations.

1. Objectivity and Reliability

One of the main advantages of neuroscientific evidence, such as brain imaging or EEG data, is its objectivity. Unlike eyewitness testimony or psychological evaluations, which can be subjective or prone to bias, neurobiological data is based on physical measurements of brain activity or structure. This gives neuroscientific evidence an aura of scientific reliability that can be compelling to judges and juries. However, it is important to recognize that neuroscientific evidence is not infallible. Brain scans and EEG readings require interpretation, and the meaning of the results is not always straightforward. Moreover, the connection between abnormal brain activity and behavior is often complex and not fully understood (Light et al., 2010). Just because a person has an abnormal brain scan does not necessarily mean that they will engage in criminal behavior or that their actions are beyond their control.

To further expand on the role of objectivity in neuroscientific evidence, it is crucial to explore the implications and challenges that arise when such evidence is presented in legal proceedings. The allure of neurobiological data stems from its grounding in quantifiable, scientific measurements. Unlike traditional forms of evidence—such as eyewitness testimony, which is notoriously unreliable, or psychological evaluations that often rely on subjective interpretation—neuroscientific data appears more concrete and difficult to refute. These measurements are grounded in the physical structure and functioning of the brain, something that juries and judges may view as offering objective insights into a defendant's mental state or behavior. However, the perception of objectivity in neuroscientific evidence can be misleading. Although neuroimaging techniques like fMRI, PET scans, and EEG offer valuable data, the interpretation of these images and recordings still involves a significant degree of subjectivity. For instance, fMRI scans show changes in blood flow and oxygen levels in the brain, which are then inferred to represent specific cognitive or emotional states. This is not a direct observation of thoughts or intentions, but rather an indirect measure that requires interpretation by neuroscientists (Glover, 2011). Similarly, EEG data reflects electrical activity in the brain, but the complexity of brain function means that drawing direct conclusions about behavior or intent from these readings can be fraught with difficulty.

The interpretation of neuroscientific data is one of the most significant challenges in the courtroom. Brain scans or EEG readings alone do not definitively explain behavior; rather, they must be contextualized within a broader understanding of how brain structures and neural activity relate to actions (Taylorpoulos., 2019). This is especially complicated because the brain is a dynamic system. Different areas of the brain work together in complex networks, and a single brain region might be involved in multiple cognitive functions. For example, abnormalities in the prefrontal cortex could suggest impairments in impulse control or decision-making, but this does not necessarily explain why a person would engage in a specific behavior, such as committing a crime.

Another issue is that correlation does not imply causation. Just because a brain scan reveals an abnormality does not automatically mean that the abnormality caused a particular behavior or action (Siddiqi et al., 2022). For instance, someone with a structural abnormality in the brain, such as damage to the prefrontal cortex, might exhibit impulsive behavior. However, it is important to consider that many people with similar brain abnormalities do not engage in criminal or violent actions. Neuroscientific evidence must therefore be understood within the broader context of a person's life experiences, environment, mental health, and behavioral history. Without this contextual understanding, there's a risk that the evidence could be misinterpreted, leading to biased or unjust conclusions in legal cases.

False objectivity can arise when brain imaging data is treated as an infallible indicator of truth in legal proceedings (Murphy & Rissman, 2020). In reality, brain imaging techniques are not designed to provide direct insights into legal concepts like responsibility or intent. These scans show how the brain functions in response to stimuli or reveal structural abnormalities, but they cannot tell us whether a person has the capacity to understand the consequences of their actions at a specific moment. A key example of this limitation is the use of fMRI in lie detection. While some studies suggest that certain brain areas are more active when a person is lying (such as the prefrontal cortex and anterior cingulate cortex), the reliability of fMRI for lie detection is highly debated. The assumption that specific patterns of brain activity can reliably indicate dishonesty is oversimplified because lying involves many complex cognitive processes, including memory, self-control, and emotional regulation, all of which vary across individuals. Moreover, the brain's response to lying can be influenced by factors such as stress, anxiety, or fear of being caught, which could create similar patterns of brain activity even when the person is telling the truth.

Additionally, there is the risk that jurors and judges may place undue emphasis on neuroscientific evidence due to its apparent scientific rigor and visual appeal. Brain images, particularly those produced by fMRI, are often presented in a colorful, easily digestible format, which can make them appear more definitive or persuasive than they truly are. This phenomenon is sometimes referred to as the "neurorealism" effect, where scientific data is given more weight simply because it appears to be grounded in complex technology or is visually impressive (Schweitzer et al., 2013). This can lead to a bias known as the "seductive allure" of neuroscience, where jurors might be more inclined to believe neuroscientific evidence, even if it is scientifically questionable or irrelevant to the legal question at hand.

Another important issue is the risk of overreach in the use of neuroscientific evidence. As neuroscience continues to evolve, there is a danger that the legal system might place too much reliance on these technologies, potentially leading to unjust outcomes (Aono et al., 2019). While brain scans can provide valuable information about brain function, they are not yet sophisticated enough to make definitive legal judgments about a person's intent, guilt, or mental state. Neuroscientific evidence should be seen as one tool among many, rather than the definitive answer to legal questions about behavior and responsibility. The use of neuroscience in the legal context must also be tempered by the fact that brain science is still a relatively young field, and many of its findings are preliminary or incomplete. For instance, while we know a great deal about how certain brain regions are involved in cognition and behavior, our understanding of how these regions work together as a system is still limited. Similarly, there are many aspects of human behavior that cannot be explained solely by brain activity, such as the influence of social, environmental, and cultural factors. These complexities suggest that neuroscientific evidence should be used cautiously and in conjunction with other forms of legal evidence, rather than as a standalone or definitive source of information.

2. Admissibility in Court

Another key difference between neuroscientific evidence and traditional legal evidence is its admissibility in court. Traditional evidence, such as eyewitness testimony or physical evidence, has a long history of being used in legal proceedings and is generally well-understood by judges and juries. In contrast, neuroscientific evidence is still relatively new, and its admissibility can be more contentious. In the U.S. legal system, the admissibility of scientific evidence is governed by the Daubert standard, which requires that expert testimony be based on scientifically valid reasoning or methodology (Daubert Standard, n.d.). Neuroscientific evidence has passed the Daubert standard in some cases, but courts have also rejected it when they deem it too speculative or unreliable. For example, the use of fMRI for lie detection has been widely criticized as insufficiently reliable for courtroom use.

3. Impact on Jurors

One of the key differences between neuroscientific evidence and traditional evidence is the impact it can have on jurors. Brain imaging evidence, in particular, is often presented in the form of vivid, color-coded images that show areas of the brain "lighting up" in response to different stimuli. These images can be highly persuasive, potentially leading jurors to place undue weight on neuroscientific evidence, even when its scientific validity is questionable. This phenomenon, sometimes referred to as the "seductive allure" of neuroscience, raises concerns about the potential for bias or misinterpretation of scientific data in legal contexts (Weisberg et al., 2015).

The use of neuroscientific evidence in legal proceedings has opened up new possibilities for understanding human behavior and assessing mental states in ways that were not previously possible. Brain imaging techniques such as fMRI, PET scans, and EEG provide valuable insights into brain function and have been used in cases ranging from determining mental competence to mitigating sentences. However, neuroscientific evidence also raises important challenges, particularly in terms of its admissibility, reliability, and potential impact on jurors. While neurobiological data can offer objective, scientific insights that complement traditional legal evidence, courts must carefully weigh the limitations and potential biases associated with this new form of evidence.

5 The Role of Expert Testimony

The use of expert testimony is a critical component in modern legal systems, particularly in cases where complex scientific or technical information must be presented to jurors and judges who lack the specialized knowledge necessary to interpret such data. In the context of neuroscience, expert witnesses have played an increasingly pivotal role, helping courts understand the implications of neuroscientific evidence, such as brain imaging, neuropsychological evaluations, and other biological markers. These experts are responsible for explaining the nuances of brain function, mental health, and their potential relevance to issues like culpability, mental competency, and even sentencing.

5.1 The Importance of Expert Witnesses in Legal Proceedings

The significance of expert witnesses in legal proceedings is multifaceted, especially when the case involves neuroscientific evidence. The legal system relies on expert testimony to bridge the gap between the scientific world and the legal system, which is designed to address issues of culpability, responsibility, and justice, rather than complex scientific analysis. Neuroscience experts, in particular, can shed light on how brain abnormalities, injuries, or mental disorders might affect behavior, decision-making, and responsibility.

Expert witnesses in neuroscience must translate highly technical concepts into understandable terms for legal professionals, who often have little to no training in science or medicine. Neuroscientific evidence can include brain scans (like fMRI or PET), electrical brain activity data (such as EEG), and the results of neuropsychological assessments. These types of data require thorough explanation, not just of how they are collected, but also of what they mean in the context of human behavior and legal culpability.

For instance, an expert witness might be asked to explain how a traumatic brain injury (TBI) could affect impulse control or how damage to the prefrontal cortex might impair a person's ability to understand the consequences of their actions. Such testimony can be crucial in cases where a defendant's mental state is in question, as it helps the court determine whether the individual was capable of forming the intent required to commit a crime or whether their behavior was the result of a neurological disorder.

In many criminal cases, expert witnesses are called upon to address mens rea, or the defendant's mental state at the time of the crime. Neuroscientific evidence can be used to support claims of diminished responsibility, insanity, or mitigating circumstances, especially when a brain injury or disorder can be linked to impaired judgment or decision-making abilities. Expert witnesses are essential in providing the court with the context needed to interpret these scientific findings within a legal framework.

6 The Gatekeeping Role of Judges

Judges rely heavily on expert witnesses to determine the admissibility of scientific evidence. In U.S. courts, this responsibility is guided by the Daubert Standard or the Frye Standard, which require judges to assess whether the expert's methods and conclusions are scientifically valid and relevant to the case. Expert witnesses in neuroscience must often provide testimony on both the validity of the techniques they use (e.g., whether fMRI is a reliable method for assessing brain function) and the relevance of their findings to the legal questions at hand (e.g., whether a brain abnormality could explain a defendant's behavior). Judges, acting as gatekeepers of scientific evidence, must rely on expert witnesses to help them navigate the scientific validity and legal relevance of complex data. Without expert testimony, judges and jurors might be left to make decisions based on incomplete or misunderstood information, leading to potentially unjust outcomes.

Effective Communication Strategies for Expert Witnesses

Given the complexity of neuroscientific evidence, expert witnesses must employ a variety of strategies to effectively communicate their findings in ways that are understandable and persuasive to legal professionals. Poor communication can lead to confusion, misinterpretation, or even the dismissal of valid scientific evidence. Therefore, one of the key challenges for neuroscientific experts is to present their testimony in a manner that is both scientifically accurate and accessible.

1. Simplification Without Oversimplification

One of the most critical skills for expert witnesses is the ability to simplify complex scientific concepts without oversimplifying them to the point of distortion. Neuroscience is a highly specialized field, and much of the evidence presented in court can be technically dense and difficult for non-experts to grasp. For example, explaining how functional MRI scans measure brain activity through changes in blood flow requires a careful balance of technical detail and layman's terms. The expert must convey the basic principle—that increased blood flow is correlated with brain activity in specific regions—without overwhelming the jury or judge with excessive jargon or technical minutiae.

However, there is a fine line between simplification and oversimplification. Neuroscientific concepts, like the brain-behavior relationship, are inherently complex, and oversimplifying them can lead to misunderstandings or incorrect conclusions. For instance, an expert might explain that abnormalities in the prefrontal cortex are associated with impulsive behavior, but they must also emphasize that such abnormalities do not always result in criminal actions. Simplifying the testimony to the point where it suggests a direct cause-and-effect relationship between brain abnormalities and criminal behavior would be misleading and scientifically inaccurate.

2. Use of Visual Aids

Visual aids, such as brain scans and charts, are commonly used by neuroscientific experts to enhance their testimony (Aono et al., 2019). These aids can be particularly effective in helping jurors and judges visualize the evidence, making abstract concepts more concrete. For example, showing a color-coded fMRI scan of a defendant's brain can help illustrate areas of reduced activity or structural abnormalities that are relevant to the case. However, experts must ensure that these visual aids are accompanied by clear, accurate explanations, as there is a risk that jurors might place too much weight on visually striking but scientifically limited data. This phenomenon, sometimes referred to as the "seductive allure of neuroscience," can lead jurors to believe that brain scans are definitive proof of a defendant's mental state, even when the scientific evidence is not so clear-cut (Hopkins et al., 2016).

To mitigate this, expert witnesses often use multiple forms of evidence to support their claims, integrating brain scans with other types of data, such as neuropsychological test results or behavioral assessments. By providing a more holistic picture of the defendant's cognitive and mental state, experts can help ensure that their testimony is both accurate and persuasive.

3. Tailoring Testimony to the Audience

Effective expert witnesses tailor their testimony to the specific needs and understanding of their audience. In some cases, this might mean adjusting the level of detail depending on whether the testimony is directed at a judge or a jury. Judges, who may be more familiar with legal standards of evidence, might require a more technical explanation of the methods used to collect neuroscientific data, whereas jurors, who likely have little scientific training, might need a broader overview of how brain function relates to behavior. Experts also need to be aware of cognitive biases that might affect how their testimony is received. For example, research has shown that jurors can be heavily influenced by the "CSI effect," (an American crime drama show),) where exposure to crime dramas leads them to expect high-tech, definitive forensic evidence in every case. Neuroscientific experts must be careful to manage these expectations, emphasizing the limitations of their methods and the tentative nature of some scientific conclusions. This honesty can help build credibility with the jury and prevent the overinterpretation of scientific data.

The Influence of Expert Testimony on Legal Outcomes

Expert testimony, particularly in fields like neuroscience, can have a profound impact on the outcome of legal cases. The introduction of neuroscientific evidence, when explained by a credible expert witness, can sway the decisions of jurors and judges by providing insights into the defendant's mental state, the nature of their behavior, and the possible mitigating factors that should be considered in sentencing.

1. Impact on Jury Decisions

Jurors tend to be particularly influenced by expert testimony because they often see scientific evidence as objective and impartial. In cases where neuroscientific evidence is used to explain a defendant's behavior, expert witnesses can play a crucial role in shaping the jury's perception of guilt, innocence, or culpability. For example, if an expert can demonstrate that a defendant has a neurological condition that impairs their ability to control impulsive behavior, the jury might be more inclined to accept a defense of diminished responsibility or insanity. However, the influence of expert testimony is not always straightforward. Research has shown that jurors are sometimes overly influenced by neuroscientific jargon or impressive-sounding terms, even when they do not fully understand the evidence being presented (Aono et al., 2019). This underscores the importance of clear communication and ensuring that jurors have the necessary information to critically evaluate the expert's testimony.

The power of neuroscientific evidence to influence juror decision-making is also seen in cases involving the death penalty. In capital cases, the use of neuroscientific evidence to demonstrate brain damage or cognitive impairments can be a key factor in persuading jurors to impose a sentence of life imprisonment rather than death (Du, n.d.). For instance, brain scans showing damage to the prefrontal cortex, which is associated with impulse control and decision-making, have been used to argue that defendants were less culpable for their actions due to diminished capacity.

2. Judicial Decisions and Sentencing

Judges, like jurors, are not immune to the influence of neuroscientific expert testimony. In cases where neuroscientific evidence is admitted, judges must often decide how much weight to give this evidence when determining issues like competency to stand trial, mental illness, and sentencing. Neuroscientific evidence has been used to argue for reduced sentences in cases where a defendant's brain abnormalities or cognitive impairments are shown to have contributed to their criminal behavior. One area where neuroscientific evidence has had a significant impact is in the sentencing of juvenile offenders (Manupatra, 2021). Neuroscience research showing that the adolescent brain is still developing, particularly in areas related to impulse control and decision-making, has been cited in several U.S. Supreme Court cases, including Roper v. Simmons (2005), which ruled that the death penalty for juveniles is unconstitutional. In this case, expert testimony on the neurodevelopmental differences between juvenile and adult brains was critical in shaping the court's decision. In other cases, judges have used neuroscientific evidence to mitigate sentences, arguing that a defendant's neurological impairments should be taken into account when determining their culpability and the appropriate punishment. However, the use of this evidence can also be controversial, as some legal scholars argue that neuroscience should not be used to excuse criminal behavior, particularly in cases involving violent crimes.

3. Ethical Considerations and the Risk of Over-Reliance

The increasing use of neuroscientific expert testimony in legal cases raises several ethical questions (Gkotsi et al., 2018). One concern is the potential for over-reliance on neuroscientific evidence, particularly in cases where the scientific data is still evolving or where the relationship between brain function and behavior is not fully understood. Experts must be careful not to overstate the certainty of their findings or to present neuroscientific evidence as more conclusive than it really is. Additionally, there is the risk that neuroscientific evidence could be used to diminish personal responsibility inappropriately. While neuroscience can provide valuable insights into the biological factors that contribute to behavior, it is important to remember that criminal behavior is influenced by a complex interplay of biological, psychological, and environmental factors. Expert witnesses must therefore ensure that their testimony is balanced, acknowledging the limitations of neuroscientific evidence while still presenting its potential relevance to the case (Jones et al., 2013).

Expert testimony plays an essential role in bridging the gap between the scientific community and the legal system, particularly in cases where complex neuroscientific evidence must be interpreted and understood by judges and jurors. Expert witnesses not only provide courts with the technical knowledge needed to assess the validity of scientific evidence, but they also help explain how this evidence relates to broader legal questions of responsibility, culpability, and intent (Kovera, 2001). Through effective communication strategies, including the simplification of complex concepts, the use of visual aids, and tailoring testimony to the audience, expert witnesses can ensure that their testimony is both accessible and persuasive. However, experts must also be mindful of the ethical challenges they face, including the potential for over-reliance on neuroscientific evidence and the need to avoid oversimplifying the brain-behavior relationship. Ultimately, the influence of expert testimony on legal outcomes cannot be overstated. Whether helping jurors understand the neurological basis of a defendant's behavior or guiding judges in determining appropriate sentences, expert witnesses play a pivotal role in ensuring that the legal system can accurately and fairly assess the impact of neuroscientific evidence on justice.

7 Interdisciplinary Collaboration

In recent years, there has been an increasing recognition of the importance of interdisciplinary collaboration between neuroscience and the legal profession. As neuroscience advances our understanding of brain structure, function, and behavior, the legal system is presented with both opportunities and challenges in integrating this knowledge. Cases involving criminal responsibility, competency to stand trial, sentencing, and even civil litigation benefit from neuroscientific insights. However, to ensure that this complex information is correctly understood and applied in legal settings, collaboration between neuroscientists, neuropsychologists, and legal professionals is critical. This section will explore the need for such interdisciplinary collaboration, highlight successful initiatives that have effectively bridged the gap between neuroscience and law, and provide recommendations for fostering better partnerships in the future.

The legal system and the field of neuroscience operate on vastly different principles. While law focuses on determining culpability, responsibility, and fairness, neuroscience is grounded in understanding brain function and behavior from a biological perspective. The legal system seeks to attribute responsibility and intent, often in binary terms (guilty or not guilty), whereas neuroscience recognizes that behavior is influenced by a complex interplay of neural, psychological, and environmental factors. The need for collaboration arises from the fact that legal decisions can have profound consequences, not only for defendants but also for society. With the introduction of neuroscientific evidence—such as brain scans, neuropsychological assessments, and neurobiological data—there is a growing need for legal professionals to accurately interpret and apply this evidence within the legal framework (Harvey, 2012). For instance, understanding how brain damage affects impulse control or how neurodevelopmental disorders may mitigate culpability requires specialized knowledge that legal professionals typically do not possess.

Moreover, neuroscience can shed light on issues of mental competency and diminished responsibility, offering nuanced perspectives that traditional legal frameworks may not consider. Judges and jurors, however, may lack the expertise to assess the validity or implications of neuroscientific findings. In such cases, interdisciplinary collaboration is essential to prevent the misuse or misinterpretation of scientific evidence. Effective partnerships between neuroscience and the legal profession can improve the fairness and accuracy of legal decisions, ensuring that scientific insights are appropriately considered without distorting their significance (Jones et al., 2013).

7.1 *Successful Initiatives: Bridging the Gap*

Several initiatives have successfully bridged the gap between neuroscience and the legal profession, demonstrating the power of interdisciplinary collaboration.

1. The MacArthur Foundation Research Network on Law and Neuroscience

One of the most prominent examples of effective interdisciplinary collaboration is the MacArthur Foundation Research Network on Law and Neuroscience, which has brought together neuroscientists, legal scholars, and policymakers to explore the intersection of brain science and law. This initiative aims to provide guidance on how neuroscientific findings can be appropriately used in legal contexts. It has conducted extensive research on topics like the brain development of adolescents, brain-based predictors of behavior, and the legal implications of neuroimaging. The work of the MacArthur Foundation has helped inform important legal decisions, particularly in cases involving juvenile justice (Juvenile Justice–MacArthur Foundation, n.d.). Neuroscience research showing that the adolescent brain is still developing—especially in areas related to decision-making and impulse control—has contributed to legal arguments for more lenient sentencing for juvenile offenders. This research has influenced landmark U.S. Supreme Court rulings, such as Roper v. Simmons (2005), which abolished the death penalty for juveniles, and Miller v. Alabama (2012), which ruled mandatory life sentences without parole for juveniles unconstitutional.

2. Neuro-Law Programs in Academia

Several academic institutions have developed neuro-law programs that foster interdisciplinary collaboration between neuroscience and law. For example, the Center for Neuroscience & Society at the University of Pennsylvania (Center for Neuroscience & Society—University of Pennsylvania, n.d.) and the Law and Neuroscience Project at Vanderbilt University (Archive | Law and Neuroscience Project Vanderbilt University, n.d.) focus on training both legal professionals and neuroscientists in the intersections of their fields. These programs offer coursework, seminars, and research opportunities that enable students and professionals from both disciplines to better understand the challenges and opportunities that arise when neuroscience is introduced into legal settings.

By creating formal training programs that bring together experts from both fields, these academic initiatives are helping to develop a generation of legal professionals who are well-versed in neuroscientific concepts and neuroscientists who understand the legal implications of their work.

3. Forensic Neuropsychology in the Courtroom

Another area where collaboration has proven effective is in the use of forensic neuropsychology to assess defendants' cognitive and neurological functioning (Marcopulos et al., 2024). In cases involving traumatic brain injuries (TBI), dementia, or other cognitive disorders, forensic neuropsychologists often provide expert testimony that can influence the outcome of a case. By collaborating with legal professionals, neuropsychologists help ensure that defendants receive fair trials by providing insights into their mental and cognitive state.

One notable example is the increasing use of neuroimaging and neuropsychological assessments to determine competency to stand trial. In cases where a defendant's mental competency is questioned, collaboration between neuroscientists, neuropsychologists, and legal professionals is essential to ensure that the individual receives appropriate legal representation and that the court makes an informed decision.

7.2 *Recommendations for Fostering Better Collaboration*

While there have been successful examples of interdisciplinary collaboration, there are still significant challenges to be addressed. Moving forward, several strategies can help improve partnerships between neuroscience and the legal profession.

To foster effective collaboration, there must be a greater emphasis on cross-disciplinary education. Legal professionals, including judges, lawyers, and policymakers, should have access to training that provides a foundational understanding of neuroscience. This could be achieved through continuing education programs, seminars, and workshops that focus on key concepts in brain science and their relevance to legal proceedings. Similarly, neuroscientists should receive training in the legal system and the specific legal questions that may arise in cases involving brain-based evidence. This dual education will enable both professions to communicate more effectively and collaborate more meaningfully.

One of the challenges in introducing neuroscientific evidence into the courtroom is the lack of standardized guidelines for its admissibility. Establishing clear criteria for the use of neuroscientific evidence—similar to the Daubert Standard used for general scientific evidence—would help ensure that only scientifically valid and legally relevant evidence is introduced in court. Developing these standards will require collaboration between legal professionals, neuroscientists, and policymakers. By working together, these experts can create a framework that ensures neuroscientific evidence is used appropriately and responsibly in legal proceedings.

Finally, promoting ongoing interdisciplinary research and dialogue is essential for improving collaboration between neuroscience and the law. Conferences, symposia, and joint publications can facilitate the exchange of ideas and encourage professionals from both fields to collaborate on research projects that explore the implications of neuroscience for the legal system. Organizations such as the Society for Neuroscience and the American Bar Association could play a leading role in fostering these collaborations by hosting events that bring together experts from both fields to discuss emerging issues at the intersection of neuroscience and law.

8 Case Studies and Precedent-Setting Decisions

The integration of neuroscientific evidence into legal proceedings has shaped many key cases, influencing how courts assess culpability, intent, and sentencing. Neuroscience, with its ability to provide insights into brain structure and function, has introduced novel dimensions into criminal and civil litigation, especially when questions of mental health, brain damage, or cognitive impairments arise. These cases have set important precedents in how such evidence is admitted and understood by courts, contributing to an evolving legal framework that grapples with the complexities of brain science. This section will explore notable cases that utilized neuroscientific evidence, analyze the impact these cases had on legal interpretations, and extract key lessons learned from both successful and cautionary examples.

1. Roper v. Simmons (2005)

One of the most significant cases to use neuroscientific evidence was Roper v. Simmons, which resulted in the U.S. Supreme Court ruling that imposing the death penalty on individuals who committed crimes as juveniles was unconstitutional. The court's decision was heavily influenced by neuroscience, particularly research demonstrating that adolescent brains are not fully developed, particularly in areas related to impulse control, judgment, and decision-making. Neuroscientific testimony, in this case, argued that juveniles should be treated differently from adults because their still-developing brains made them less capable of foreseeing the consequences of their actions and more susceptible to peer pressure. The ruling set a precedent in recognizing the developmental differences between adolescent and adult brains, reshaping how juvenile offenders are treated within the legal system (Center, 2024).

2. Miller v. Alabama (2012)

In Miller v. Alabama, the U.S. Supreme Court ruled that mandatory life sentences without parole for juveniles violated the Eighth Amendment's prohibition on cruel and unusual punishment. Like Roper, this decision was heavily influenced by neuroscientific research that showed the immature state of adolescent brains, particularly regarding their ability to regulate emotions and make long-term decisions. Neuroscientific evidence provided during this case emphasized that juveniles are more capable of change and rehabilitation than adults, suggesting that mandatory life sentences without the possibility of parole are disproportionately harsh for this population. This case further solidified the legal system's recognition of brain development as a critical factor in determining appropriate sentencing for juveniles (Juvenile Life Without Parole, n.d.).

3. People v. Weinstein (1992)

A groundbreaking case that introduced neuroscientific evidence into the courtroom was People v. Weinstein, where Herbert Weinstein was charged with murder after throwing his wife out of a window. Weinstein's defense team presented brain scans showing that he had a large cyst in his brain, suggesting that this brain abnormality may have contributed to his violent behavior. While the court ultimately allowed the neuroscientific evidence, the case raised important questions about the extent to which brain abnormalities should affect culpability. The jury in this case was presented with neuroscientific evidence that may have influenced their understanding of Weinstein's responsibility for his actions. Though Weinstein eventually pled guilty to a lesser charge, the case set a precedent for the admissibility of neuroscientific evidence in assessing criminal behavior (Rosen, 2007).

Impact on Legal Interpretations: Shaping Judicial Outcomes

The cases highlighted above demonstrate how neuroscientific evidence has shaped judicial outcomes by introducing new dimensions into the understanding of culpability, responsibility, and sentencing.

1. Roper and Miller: Expanding Protections for Juveniles

The decisions in Roper v. Simmons and Miller v. Alabama reshaped juvenile justice by incorporating neuroscientific research into the interpretation of the Eighth Amendment. By recognizing the developmental differences between adolescents and adults, the courts in these cases set a precedent for more lenient treatment of juvenile offenders. The recognition that adolescents are neurologically less capable of mature decision-making than adults has led to changes in sentencing practices, where juveniles are now given the opportunity for parole or rehabilitation rather than facing life without parole or the death penalty.

In People v. Weinstein, the introduction of brain scans as mitigating evidence opened the door for the use of neuroscientific findings in criminal defense. While Weinstein ultimately pleaded guilty, the case established that brain abnormalities can be considered as evidence that may affect a defendant's level of culpability. This precedent has since been used in other cases where defendants claim that brain damage or neurological impairments contributed to their criminal behavior.

The Hinckley trial demonstrated the potential for neuroscientific evidence to profoundly influence the outcome of cases involving the insanity defense. Hinckley's acquittal by reason of insanity prompted widespread debate over the use of mental illness as a defense, leading to changes in the Insanity Defense Reform Act of 1984, which made it more difficult for defendants to succeed with an insanity defense in federal cases. This case illustrates the fine line between using neuroscience to explain behavior and the legal system's need to balance accountability with compassion for mental illness.

The use of neuroscientific evidence in the legal system offers valuable lessons, both from successful and cautionary examples. Cases like Roper v. Simmons and Miller v. Alabama show how neuroscience can improve legal outcomes by providing a more nuanced understanding of brain development and behavior. These cases highlight the potential for neuroscientific evidence to create more equitable justice systems, particularly for vulnerable populations like juveniles. The success of these cases suggests that neuroscience can play a pivotal role in shaping sentencing and policy decisions that reflect scientific knowledge about the brain.

However, cases like People v. Weinstein and the Hinckley trial also illustrate the risks of over-reliance on neuroscientific evidence. In these cases, neuroscientific findings were used to mitigate culpability, raising concerns about whether such evidence could be misused to excuse criminal behavior. The insanity defense in particular demonstrates the need for caution when using neuroscience to explain behavior, as it can lead to contentious outcomes and public backlash. The use of neuroscientific evidence in legal proceedings has significantly impacted how courts interpret culpability, responsibility, and sentencing, especially in cases involving juveniles, brain abnormalities, or mental illness. Key cases like Roper v. Simmons, Miller v. Alabama, and People v. Weinstein have set important precedents, demonstrating both the potential benefits and risks of incorporating neuroscience into the legal system. As the field of neuroscience continues to evolve, legal professionals will need to carefully consider how best to integrate this evidence to ensure just and fair outcomes in future cases.

9 Conclusion

The integration of neuroscientific evidence into the legal system represents one of the most significant developments in modern legal practice. As this section has highlighted, the introduction of tools such as functional MRI (fMRI), PET scans, EEG, and other neuroimaging techniques has provided courts with new methods of understanding human behavior, particularly in relation to criminal responsibility, competency to stand trial, and sentencing. This evidence offers valuable insights into brain abnormalities, cognitive impairments, and neurodevelopmental factors that can influence behavior, allowing for a more nuanced approach to justice.

Historically, the relationship between neuroscience and the law has evolved significantly. Early efforts focused on rudimentary brain scans and paper EEG readings, whereas modern techniques allow for far more precise measurements of brain activity. These advancements have been pivotal in cases involving mental health, brain injuries, and the developmental stages of individuals such as juveniles. Notable legal decisions, such as Roper v. Simmons (2005) and Miller v. Alabama (2012), have incorporated neuroscientific evidence to argue for the more compassionate treatment of individuals whose brain development or cognitive functions affect their legal culpability. In contrast to traditional legal evidence, which often focuses on physical evidence, witness testimony, and behavioral analysis, neuroscientific evidence delves deeper into the biological basis of behavior. By presenting a scientific framework for understanding decision-making processes, impulse control, and cognitive deficits, neuroscientific findings can offer legal professionals more context for the actions of individuals involved in criminal behavior. However, this evidence is not without its controversies, as there remains the risk of over-reliance on biological determinism, as well as ethical concerns regarding the limitations of current neuroscience in explaining complex human behaviors.

Looking ahead, the evolving role of neuroscience in legal proceedings is poised to have profound implications for criminal and civil justice systems. As neuroscientific techniques become more sophisticated, courts will likely see a growing body of evidence that explains human behavior in increasingly precise ways. However, with this development comes the need for greater interdisciplinary collaboration. Legal professionals must receive the training necessary to interpret neuroscientific data accurately, while neuroscientists must engage with legal principles to ensure that their findings are relevant to the issues at hand.

Furthermore, the potential for neuroscience to influence legal standards surrounding culpability, sentencing, and even rehabilitation is considerable. Neuroscience may challenge traditional views of free will and personal responsibility, pushing the legal system to reconsider how it assesses criminal intent and moral blame. In particular, developments in neurodevelopmental research are likely to shape how juveniles and individuals with cognitive impairments are treated by the justice system in the future. The relationship between neuroscience and law is one of mutual influence, with each field shaping the understanding and practices of the other. As neuroscience advances, it provides the legal system with tools to interpret complex questions about human behavior, responsibility, and cognition. At the same time, the legal system challenges neuroscience to consider the broader societal and ethical implications of its findings.

Ultimately, neuroscientific evidence in legal contexts offers the potential for a more scientifically informed approach to justice. However, the successful integration of this evidence depends on maintaining a balanced view of its capabilities and limitations. As neuroscience continues to develop, its contributions to the legal system will likely become even more integral, potentially leading to more just and equitable outcomes, while also raising important ethical considerations that society will need to address.

References

Albright, T. D. (2023). A scientist's take on scientific evidence in the courtroom. *Proceedings of the National Academy of Sciences, 120*(41), e2301839120. https://doi.org/10.1073/pnas.2301839120

Amy. (2019, July 10). *Roper v. Simmons (2005)–Campaign for the fair sentencing of youth | CFSY*. Campaign for the Fair Sentencing of Youth | CFSY. https://cfsy.org/court-case/roper-v-simmons-2005/

Aono, D., Yaffe, G., & Kober, H. (2019). Neuroscientific evidence in the courtroom: A review. *Cognitive Research Principles and Implications, 4*(1), 40. https://doi.org/10.1186/s41235-019-0179-y

Archive | Law and Neuroscience Project | Vanderbilt University. (n.d.). https://news.vanderbilt.edu/tag/law-and-neuroscience-project/

Brown, P., Bakolis, I., Appiah-Kusi, E., Hallett, N., Hotopf, M., & Blackwood, N. (2022). Prevalence of mental disorders in defendants at criminal court. *BJPsych Open, 8*(3), e92. https://doi.org/10.1192/bjo.2022.63

Byrnes, K. R., Wilson, C. M., Brabazon, F., Von Leden, R., Jurgens, J. S., Oakes, T. R., & Selwyn, R. G. (2014). FDG-PET imaging in mild traumatic brain injury: A critical review. *Frontiers in Neuroenergetics, 5*. https://doi.org/10.3389/fnene.2013.00013

Center, D. P. I. (2024, September 25). Roper v. Simmons Resource Page. *Death penalty information center*. https://deathpenaltyinfo.org/facts-and-research/united-states-supreme-court/significant-supreme-court-opinions/roper-v-simmons-resource-page

Center for Neuroscience & Society–University of Pennsylvania. (n.d.). https://neuroethics.upenn.edu/

Computed Tomography (CT). (n.d.). *National institute of biomedical imaging and bioengineering*. https://www.nibib.nih.gov/science-education/science-topics/computed-tomography-ct

Daubert Standard. (n.d.). *LII/Legal Information Institute*. https://www.law.cornell.edu/wex/daubert_standard

Daubert v. Merrell Dow Pharmaceuticals, Inc., 509 U.S. 579 (1993). (n.d.). *Justia law*. https://supreme.justia.com/cases/federal/us/509/579/

Du, Y. (n.d.). *The application of neuroscience evidence on court sentencing decisions: Suggesting a guideline for neuro-evidence*. Seattle University School of Law Digital Commons. https://digitalcommons.law.seattleu.edu/sjsj/vol18/iss2/19/?utm_source=digitalcommons.law.seattleu.edu%2Fsjsj%2Fvol18%2Fiss2%2F19&utm_medium=PDF&utm_campaign=PDFCoverPages

Gkotsi, G. M., Gasser, J., & Moulin, V. (2018). Neuroimaging in criminal trials and the role of psychiatrists expert witnesses: A case study. *International Journal of Law and Psychiatry, 65*, 101359. https://doi.org/10.1016/j.ijlp.2018.05.007

Glover, G. H. (2011). Overview of functional magnetic resonance imaging. *Neurosurgery Clinics of North America, 22*(2), 133–139. https://doi.org/10.1016/j.nec.2010.11.001

Grover, V. P. B., Tognarelli, J. M., Crossey, M. M. E., Cox, I. J., Taylor-Robinson, S. D., & McPhail, M. J. W. (2015). Magnetic resonance imaging: Principles and techniques: Lessons for clinicians. *Journal of Clinical and Experimental Hepatology, 5*(3), 246–255. https://doi.org/10.1016/j.jceh.2015.08.001

Harvey, P. D. (2012). Clinical applications of neuropsychological assessment. *Dialogues in Clinical Neuroscience, 14*(1), 91–99. https://doi.org/10.31887/dcns.2012.14.1/pharvey

Hopkins, E. J., Weisberg, D. S., & Taylor, J. C. (2016). The seductive allure is a reductive allure: People prefer scientific explanations that contain logically irrelevant reductive information. *Cognition, 155*, 67–76. https://doi.org/10.1016/j.cognition.2016.06.011

Jones, O. D., Marois, R., Farah, M. J., & Greely, H. T. (2013). Law and neuroscience. *Journal of Neuroscience, 33*(45), 17624–17630. https://doi.org/10.1523/jneurosci.3254-13.2013

Juvenile Justice–MacArthur Foundation. (n.d.). *MacArthur foundation*. https://www.macfound.org/programs/pastwork/juvenile_justice/

Juvenile Life Without Parole. (n.d.). https://www.ncsl.org/civil-and-criminal-justice/juvenile-life-without-parole

Kapoor, M., & Kasi, A. (2022). *October 3*. StatPearls–NCBI Bookshelf. https://www.ncbi.nlm.nih.gov/books/NBK559089/

Kovera, M. (2001). Expert testimony. In *Elsevier eBooks* (pp. 5139–5141). https://doi.org/10.1016/b0-08-043076-7/02820-5.

Light, G. A., Williams, L. E., Minow, F., Sprock, J., Rissling, A., Sharp, R., Swerdlow, N. R., & Braff, D. L. (2010). Electroencephalography (EEG) and event-related potentials (ERPs) with human participants. *Current Protocols in Neuroscience, 52*(1), Unit 6.25.1. https://doi.org/10.1002/0471142301.ns0625s52

Manupatra. (2021, May 17). *MyApp*. https://articles.manupatra.com/article-details/The-Intersection-of-Law-and-Neuroscience-Implications-On-Law-of-Evidence

Marcopulos, B. A., Kaufmann, P., & Patel, A. C. (2024). Forensic neuropsychological assessment. *Behavioral Sciences & the Law, 42*, 265. https://doi.org/10.1002/bsl.2656

mens rea. (n.d.). *LII/Legal Information Institute*. https://www.law.cornell.edu/wex/mens_rea

Miller v. Alabama. (2022, June 21). *Equal justice initiative*. https://eji.org/cases/miller-v-alabama/

Monteleone, G. T., Phan, K. L., Nusbaum, H. C., Fitzgerald, D., Irick, J., Fienberg, S. E., & Cacioppo, J. T. (2008). Detection of deception using fMRI: Better than chance, but well below perfection. *Social Neuroscience, 4*(6), 528–538. https://doi.org/10.1080/17470910801903530

Murphy, E. R. D., & Rissman, J. (2020). Evidence of memory from brain data. *Journal of Law and the Biosciences, 7*(1). https://doi.org/10.1093/jlb/lsaa078

Niso, G., Krol, L. R., Combrisson, E., Dubarry, A. S., Elliott, M. A., François, C., Héjja-Brichard, Y., Herbst, S. K., Jerbi, K., Kovic, V., Lehongre, K., Luck, S. J., Mercier, M., Mosher, J. C., Pavlov, Y. G., Puce, A., Schettino, A., Schön, D., Sinnott-Armstrong, W., et al. (2022). Good scientific practice in EEG and MEG research: Progress and perspectives. *NeuroImage, 257*, 119056. https://doi.org/10.1016/j.neuroimage.2022.119056

Ochang, P., Stahl, B. C., & Eke, D. (2022). The ethical and legal landscape of brain data governance. *PLoS One, 17*(12), e0273473. https://doi.org/10.1371/journal.pone.0273473

Positron emission tomography scan–Mayo Clinic. (n.d.). https://www.mayoclinic.org/tests-procedures/pet-scan/about/pac-20385078

Radiological Society of North America (RSNA) and American College of Radiology (ACR). (n.d.). *Functional MRI (fMRI)*. Radiologyinfo.org. https://www.radiologyinfo.org/en/info/fmribrain

Rosen, J. (2007, March 6). Neuroscience–law–the brain on the stand–Jeffrey Rosen. *The New York Times*. https://www.nytimes.com/2007/03/11/magazine/11Neurolaw.t.html

Schweitzer, N., Baker, D., & Risko, E. F. (2013). Fooled by the brain: Re-examining the influence of neuroimages. *Cognition, 129*(3), 501–511. https://doi.org/10.1016/j.cognition.2013.08.009

Shafi, N., & Teachers College, Columbia University. (2009). Neuroscience and law: The evidentiary value of brain imaging. *Graduate Student Journal of Psychology, 11*. [Journal-article]. Department of Counseling & Clinical Psychology. http://www.antoniocasella.eu/archipsy/Shafi_2009.pdf

Siddiqi, S. H., Kording, K. P., Parvizi, J., & Fox, M. D. (2022). Causal mapping of human brain function. *Nature Reviews. Neuroscience, 23*(6), 361–375. https://doi.org/10.1038/s41583-022-00583-8

Siever, L. J. (2008). Neurobiology of aggression and violence. *American Journal of Psychiatry, 165*(4), 429–442. https://doi.org/10.1176/appi.ajp.2008.07111774

St Louis, E. K., Frey, L. C., Britton, J. W., Frey, L. C., Hopp, J. L., Korb, P., Koubeissi, M. Z., Lievens, W. E., Pestana-Knight, E. M., & St Louis, E. K. (2016). *Introduction. Electroencephalography (EEG): An introductory text and atlas of normal and abnormal findings in adults, children, and infants–NCBI Bookshelf.* https://www.ncbi.nlm.nih.gov/books/NBK390346/

Stafstrom, C. E., & Carmant, L. (2015). Seizures and epilepsy: An overview for neuroscientists. *Cold Spring Harbor Perspectives in Medicine, 5*(6), a022426. https://doi.org/10.1101/cshperspect.a022426

Sur, S., & Sinha, V. (2009). Event-related potential: An overview. *Industrial Psychiatry Journal, 18*(1), 70. https://doi.org/10.4103/0972-6748.57865

Taylorpoulos. (2019, October 30). Scanning for justice: Using neuroscience to create a more inclusive legal system–*Columbia Human Rights Law Review*. Columbia Human Rights Law Review. https://hrlr.law.columbia.edu/hrlr/scanning-for-justice-using-neuroscience-to-create-a-more-inclusive-legal-system/

Weisberg, D. S., Taylor, J. C. V., & Hopkins, E. J. (2015). Deconstructing the seductive allure of neuroscience explanations. *Judgment and Decision making, 10*(5), 429–441. https://doi.org/10.1017/s193029750000557x

Xue, G., Chen, C., Lu, Z., & Dong, Q. (2010). Brain imaging techniques and their applications in decision-making research. *Acta Psychologica Sinica, 42*(1), 120–137. https://doi.org/10.3724/sp.j.1041.2010.00120

Psychopathy and Criminal Behavior

1 Introduction to Psychopathy and Criminal Behavior

Psychopathy is a personality disorder characterized by a specific constellation of traits that set individuals apart from the general population, especially in how they perceive and engage with social norms, moral boundaries, and the emotions of others. This disorder has fascinated psychologists, criminologists, and legal professionals for decades, as individuals diagnosed with psychopathy are disproportionately represented in criminal populations. The relationship between psychopathy and criminal behavior is complex, encompassing biological, psychological, and environmental factors that shape the actions of those exhibiting psychopathic traits. Understanding psychopathy is critical for various fields, particularly forensic psychology, because individuals with psychopathy frequently engage in behaviors that harm others without experiencing guilt, remorse, or emotional distress. These behaviors often violate legal and moral codes, leading to criminal activity ranging from minor offenses to violent, premeditated acts. Exploring the definitions, key traits, and social implications of psychopathy can shed light on its connection to criminal behavior.

2 Definition of Psychopathy

Psychopathy is broadly defined as a personality disorder characterized by persistent antisocial behavior, impaired empathy and remorse, and bold, disinhibited, and egotistical traits (Anderson & Kiehl, 2014). The term "psychopathy" was first introduced by German psychiatrist Julius Koch in 1888, but it gained prominence in the twentieth century, primarily through the work of American psychologist Hervey Cleckley and Canadian criminal psychologist Robert Hare. Cleckley's seminal

© The Author(s), under exclusive license to Springer Nature Switzerland AG 2025

K. J. Reddy, *Foundations of Criminal Forensic Neuropsychology*,
https://doi.org/10.1007/978-3-031-83771-5_10

book, *The Mask of Sanity* (1941), laid the groundwork for understanding psychopathy as a condition in which individuals appear superficially normal but possess profound emotional and moral deficits (The Mask of Sanity (Cleckley fifth Ed*)*, 2024).

Robert Hare later developed the *Psychopathy Checklist-Revised* (PCL-R), a clinical assessment tool used to diagnose psychopathy. According to Hare, psychopathy consists of two major factors:

1. **Interpersonal and affective traits**, such as superficial charm, grandiosity, and lack of empathy, and.
2. **Lifestyle and antisocial traits**, including impulsivity, irresponsibility, and a tendency to violate societal rules.

While psychopathy is not formally recognized as a disorder in the Diagnostic and Statistical Manual of Mental Disorders, Fifth Edition (DSM-5), it is considered part of the broader category of antisocial personality disorder (ASPD) (DSM, n.d.). However, not all individuals with ASPD are psychopaths. Psychopathy represents a more severe and distinct subset of ASPD, involving both interpersonal and affective deficits.

Key Traits of Psychopathy

Individuals with psychopathy exhibit a unique set of traits that differentiate them from other antisocial or criminal personalities. These traits include superficial charm, manipulativeness, a lack of empathy, impulsivity, and a disregard for social norms. Each of these characteristics plays a crucial role in understanding the connection between psychopathy and criminal behavior.

1. Superficial Charm

One of the hallmark traits of psychopathy is superficial charm, often described as a charismatic and engaging demeanor that masks the underlying emotional deficits of the individual (Anderson & Kiehl, 2014). Psychopaths can be incredibly persuasive, socially skilled, and capable of making a positive impression, especially in short-term interactions. This superficial charm enables them to manipulate others, gain trust, and exploit relationships without arousing suspicion. Psychopaths use their charm to disarm and deceive others, often portraying themselves as likable, intelligent, and competent. In criminal contexts, this ability to manipulate others can manifest as the psychopath's capacity to coerce or deceive victims, accomplices, or even law enforcement officials. Their outward confidence and charm can make it difficult for others to detect their true intentions, which may be self-serving or harmful.

2. Manipulativeness

Closely related to superficial charm is the trait of manipulativeness. Psychopaths are skilled at controlling and exploiting others to achieve their goals, often without concern for the well-being or rights of those they manipulate. Manipulativeness in psychopaths is not limited to overt deception; it also includes subtle forms of influence, such as playing on others' emotions, lying convincingly, or using others as pawns in their personal agendas ((PDF) Pathological Lying and Deception in Psychopathic Personalities: Facial Expressions Analysis, n.d.). Manipulativeness plays a central role in the criminal activities of psychopaths, as they are often able to coerce others into illegal or unethical behavior without bearing the direct consequences themselves. In some cases, psychopaths manipulate their way into positions of power or influence, where they can carry out criminal schemes without immediate detection.

3. Lack of Empathy

One of the defining features of psychopathy is a lack of empathy or an inability to understand or share the feelings of others. This emotional deficit is perhaps the most significant contributor to the criminal behavior associated with psychopathy. While most people are deterred from harming others by feelings of guilt, compassion, or concern, psychopaths lack these emotional restraints (Gonzalez-Tapia et al., 2017). They may be able to intellectually recognize that their actions cause harm, but they do not experience the emotional discomfort that usually accompanies such recognition. The absence of empathy allows psychopaths to engage in a wide range of harmful behaviors, including violence, theft, and exploitation, without experiencing remorse or regret. This emotional detachment can lead to heinous acts, such as serial killing, where the individual feels no moral or emotional conflict about their crimes.

4. Impulsivity

Psychopaths are often characterized by impulsivity, meaning they act without considering the potential consequences of their actions. Impulsivity can manifest in reckless behavior, poor decision-making, and a disregard for personal or societal risks. This impulsivity contributes to the high rates of criminal behavior observed in individuals with psychopathy, as they may engage in risky or illegal activities without fear of repercussions (Tharshini et al., 2021). Impulsivity in psychopaths is often linked to their need for immediate gratification or stimulation. They may commit crimes such as theft, assault, or drug-related offenses in pursuit of excitement or personal gain, with little regard for long-term consequences. This impulsive behavior can escalate into more serious criminal activity as they seek greater thrills or rewards.

5. Disregard for Social Norms

A pervasive disregard for social norms and moral boundaries is another key trait of psychopathy. Psychopaths do not internalize societal rules or laws, nor do they adhere to the ethical standards that govern most people's behavior. This disregard for social norms enables them to engage in criminal behavior with ease, as they see no inherent value in following rules or respecting the rights of others (Simons & Burt, 2011). Psychopaths view social norms as obstacles to be bypassed rather than principles to be respected. This trait makes them particularly dangerous in criminal contexts, as they are willing to violate laws and commit harmful acts without experiencing the psychological restraints that deter most individuals.

Psychopathy, with its defining traits of superficial charm, manipulativeness, lack of empathy, impulsivity, and disregard for social norms, is closely linked to criminal behavior. Individuals with psychopathy are often involved in criminal activities because their emotional deficits and moral indifference allow them to harm others without experiencing guilt or fear of consequences. Understanding these traits provides valuable insight into how psychopathy contributes to criminal behavior and highlights the need for targeted interventions in legal and clinical settings.

3 Cognitive Traits of Psychopathy

The cognitive traits of psychopathy contribute to the distinctive behaviors of those diagnosed with this condition, particularly their manipulation of others and the ways in which they plan and execute criminal activities. By understanding the cognitive aspects of psychopathy, including deficits in emotional processing and the ability to manipulate and plan actions, we can better grasp how psychopathic individuals differ from non-psychopathic offenders, especially in terms of their mental approach to crime and social interaction.

3.1 Deficits in Emotional Processing

One of the central cognitive deficits in psychopathy is the impairment in emotional processing, particularly with regard to recognizing and responding to emotions in others. Psychopaths show a marked reduction in their ability to understand or experience emotions like fear, sadness, and guilt (Blair, 2013). This deficit in emotional processing is linked to specific areas of brain dysfunction, most notably in the amygdala and the ventromedial prefrontal cortex, regions responsible for emotional learning and regulation.

Studies using neuroimaging techniques have demonstrated that psychopaths have reduced activation in these brain areas when exposed to emotionally charged stimuli, such as images of fearful faces or scenes depicting suffering. This neural under-activation explains why individuals with psychopathy struggle to experience empathy or remorse, as they are neurologically impaired in their ability to process the emotional states of others (Blair, 2013).

This emotional deficit has significant implications for behavior. While most people are deterred from harmful actions by feelings of guilt or distress at the suffering of others, psychopaths are not similarly inhibited (Blair, 2013). Their reduced ability to process emotional cues leaves them free to engage in harmful or exploitative actions without the emotional feedback mechanisms that guide normal social behavior. This emotional blunting can result in cold, calculated criminal behavior where the psychopath is unaffected by the pain or distress they cause.

Moreover, psychopaths often fail to anticipate the emotional consequences of their actions for themselves (Perez, 2012). While most individuals can project how they might feel after committing a morally reprehensible act, such as regret or shame, psychopaths lack this anticipatory emotional insight. They may recognize that their actions violate social norms but are unable to fully grasp the emotional weight of such violations.

3.2 Ability to Manipulate and Plan Actions

Despite their emotional deficits, psychopaths are often highly skilled at manipulating others and planning actions in a way that maximizes their personal gain. This cognitive ability to plan, strategize, and manipulate is a key characteristic that differentiates psychopathic individuals from other offenders.

Psychopaths possess what can be described as a "cold" form of cognition, where they can think rationally and logically about situations without being influenced by emotional factors (Maiese, 2013). This allows them to engage in goal-oriented behavior that is often highly calculated. Unlike individuals who may act impulsively out of emotional distress, psychopaths tend to approach situations with a dispassionate mindset, focusing on how they can control and influence outcomes to their advantage.

The ability to manipulate others is one of the hallmarks of psychopathy. Psychopaths are adept at using their charm, intelligence, and social skills to deceive and exploit those around them (Rijnders et al., 2021). Because they lack emotional empathy, they can easily manipulate people's emotions without feeling guilty or conflicted. This cognitive ability to read others' emotional states and use that information to their own advantage is a key feature of their manipulative behavior.

For example, a psychopath may feign affection or sympathy in order to gain someone's trust, only to later exploit that trust for personal gain, whether financially, socially, or otherwise. This ability to manipulate others without emotional interference is a significant cognitive advantage that allows psychopaths to thrive in certain contexts, such as in positions of power or in criminal enterprises where deception and exploitation are necessary for success (Glass & Newman, 2009).

In addition to their manipulative skills, psychopaths are often skilled at planning and executing actions with precision. Their cognitive style is characterized by an ability to remain calm and composed even in high-pressure situations. This trait enables them to plan crimes methodically, thinking through the steps and potential obstacles in advance. In contrast to impulsive criminals who may act without foresight, psychopaths often engage in premeditated behavior that reflects careful consideration of risks and rewards (Anderson & Kiehl, 2014).

This cognitive ability to plan and execute actions without being influenced by fear or guilt also explains why psychopaths are often successful in evading capture. They can carefully manage their image, lie convincingly, and maintain control over their emotional responses, which help them deceive law enforcement or avoid detection. In some cases, psychopaths may engage in long-term criminal schemes that require sustained planning and execution, showcasing their cognitive flexibility and ability to adapt to changing circumstances.

3.3 Contrast with Non-psychopathic Offenders

While both psychopathic and non-psychopathic offenders may engage in criminal behavior, their cognitive traits and motivations are markedly different. Non-psychopathic offenders often commit crimes impulsively or in response to emotional triggers, such as anger, jealousy, or desperation (Saladino et al., 2021). Their criminal actions are more likely to be influenced by emotional states, and they may experience guilt, remorse, or regret after the fact. These emotional responses can sometimes lead to confessions or efforts at restitution, as non-psychopathic offenders are more likely to be affected by their conscience and the social consequences of their actions.

In contrast, psychopathic offenders are less likely to be driven by emotional states and more likely to engage in calculated, premeditated crimes. Their lack of emotional involvement means that they are less likely to feel remorse or regret, even after committing serious offenses (Tangney et al., 2011). Psychopaths are also more likely to engage in repeated criminal behavior, as they are not deterred by the emotional or social costs of their actions. This cognitive detachment from emotional consequences makes them particularly dangerous, as they can continue to harm others without experiencing the psychological inhibitions that typically restrain criminal behavior.

Additionally, non-psychopathic offenders often struggle with impulse control and may act without considering the long-term consequences of their actions. In contrast, psychopaths demonstrate a higher level of cognitive control over their actions, allowing them to plan and execute crimes in a deliberate and methodical manner (Martin et al., 2019). This ability to remain calm and rational, even in the midst of criminal activity, sets them apart from more impulsive offenders and contributes to their ability to evade detection.

The cognitive traits of psychopathy, including deficits in emotional processing, a high capacity for manipulation, and the ability to plan actions without emotional interference, play a crucial role in shaping the behavior of psychopathic individuals. These cognitive traits differentiate psychopaths from non-psychopathic offenders, particularly in terms of their calculated and often premeditated approach to crime. Understanding these cognitive characteristics is essential for comprehending the unique threat posed by psychopathic individuals, both within criminal contexts and in broader social interactions. Their cold, detached cognitive style allows them to exploit and harm others without being hindered by the emotional barriers that regulate most human behavior, making them especially challenging for law enforcement and mental health professionals to manage.

4 Emotional Traits of Psychopathy

Among these traits, the emotional deficiencies exhibited by psychopathic individuals are some of the most pronounced and have profound implications for their behavior, especially in social and criminal contexts. While psychopathy is often studied for its links to criminal behavior, the emotional traits of psychopathy—such as a lack of guilt and remorse, emotional detachment, and shallow affect—are critical to understanding why psychopathic individuals engage in harmful behaviors without experiencing the emotional consequences that typically deter such actions.

4.1 Lack of Guilt and Remorse

One of the most defining emotional traits of psychopathy is the profound absence of guilt and remorse (Viding, 2019). Unlike most people who feel guilt when they have wronged others, psychopaths are largely immune to these emotional experiences. This absence of guilt is closely tied to deficits in empathy and the inability to emotionally connect with the suffering of others.

The lack of guilt or remorse in psychopathic individuals can be attributed to deficits in emotional processing, particularly involving brain regions such as the amygdala and the ventromedial prefrontal cortex, which are responsible for regulating emotional responses and moral decision-making (Koenigs, 2012). These deficits prevent the psychopath from experiencing the emotional discomfort that typically follows harmful or immoral actions. For most individuals, guilt serves as a form of self-regulation, encouraging moral behavior and discouraging acts that harm others. Without guilt, psychopathic individuals are free to engage in behaviors that violate societal and moral standards without any internal emotional consequences.

In criminal contexts, this lack of guilt is especially dangerous. Psychopaths can commit violent or harmful acts, such as theft, fraud, or even murder, without experiencing the moral distress that would typically prevent such behaviors (Baskin-Sommers, n.d.). They are not deterred by the emotional toll their actions might take on others, nor do they suffer any psychological discomfort afterward. For instance, a psychopathic individual might manipulate someone for financial gain or commit an act of violence yet feel no sense of moral wrongdoing or personal responsibility. This absence of guilt allows them to continue harmful behaviors without being weighed down by the emotional burden of their actions. Moreover, this emotional trait extends beyond criminal activity into personal relationships. Psychopaths can exploit and harm close relationships—be it friends, family, or romantic partners—without any remorse. They may lie, cheat, or manipulate without ever reflecting on how their actions hurt others, thus reinforcing a pattern of self-centered behavior that prioritizes personal gain over any sense of moral obligation or emotional accountability.

4.2 Emotional Detachment and Shallow Responses

Another key emotional trait of psychopathy is emotional detachment and a shallow affect. Emotional detachment refers to the psychopath's limited capacity to experience deep emotions or connect emotionally with others. Shallow affect means that while psychopaths may exhibit emotions on the surface, these emotional responses are often fleeting, superficial, and not as deeply felt as they are by others (Anderson & Kiehl, 2014). For instance, a psychopath may show brief anger, sadness, or affection in a given situation, but these emotions quickly dissipate and do not resonate deeply within the individual.

Emotional detachment in psychopathy is often evident in their interpersonal relationships, where psychopaths fail to form genuine emotional bonds. While they may appear charming or affectionate when it serves their interests, these emotional displays are typically manipulative rather than authentic (Simon., 2014). They lack the ability to truly connect with others on an emotional level, making their relationships transactional rather than emotionally meaningful. This detachment is one reason why psychopaths are able to exploit and harm those close to them without feeling emotional repercussions.

Shallow affect, in particular, plays a significant role in the psychopath's inability to respond emotionally to situations that would typically evoke strong feelings. For example, when faced with situations that would provoke fear, guilt, or empathy in others, psychopaths exhibit a muted emotional response. This emotional blunting is part of the reason why they can engage in risky or harmful behaviors without experiencing the anxiety or stress that might otherwise deter such actions. Neuroimaging studies have shown that psychopaths have lower levels of activity in brain regions associated with fear and emotional regulation, which accounts for their shallow affect and emotional detachment.

This emotional detachment allows psychopaths to remain calm and composed even in high-stress or dangerous situations, such as when committing crimes or facing potential punishment (Kiehl & Hoffman, n.d.). Their ability to dissociate emotionally from their actions makes them difficult to predict or manage, as they do not exhibit the typical emotional cues that would indicate distress or internal conflict. While most people would exhibit fear, guilt, or regret when caught in wrongdoing, psychopaths often remain cold, indifferent, and unflustered, which can make them appear especially dangerous and calculating.

4.3 Implications for Engaging in Harmful Behaviors

The emotional traits of psychopathy—namely, the lack of guilt and remorse, emotional detachment, and shallow affect—have profound implications for the types of behaviors psychopathic individuals are likely to engage in, particularly harmful or criminal behaviors (Martens, 2021). Without the emotional brakes that most people experience when considering actions that harm others, psychopaths are free to act in ways that serve their own interests, regardless of the negative impact on others.

One of the most direct implications of these emotional deficits is the psychopath's tendency to engage in criminal or antisocial behavior. Since they do not feel guilt or remorse for their actions, psychopaths are more likely to commit acts that violate the law or societal norms. This includes violent crimes, such as assault or murder, as well as nonviolent offenses like fraud, theft, or manipulation. In some cases, psychopaths engage in crimes purely for personal gain, while in others, they may commit harmful acts for the thrill or excitement that comes with risk-taking.

The emotional detachment characteristic of psychopathy also enables individuals to engage in harm without experiencing the emotional fallout that would typically follow. For instance, a psychopath may commit a violent crime or manipulate someone into financial ruin without feeling any emotional connection to the victim or the harm caused. This emotional distance allows them to act without internal conflict, making it easier to engage in repeat offenses or escalate their harmful behaviors over time.

Another implication is the psychopath's ability to maintain composure and avoid detection, even in situations where others might show signs of stress or guilt. In legal contexts, psychopaths are often able to deceive law enforcement officers, judges, or juries due to their calm, emotionally detached demeanor (Kiehl & Hoffman, n.d.). They may lie convincingly, maintain a facade of innocence, or manipulate those around them to evade punishment. This emotional resilience and lack of guilt make it difficult to hold psychopaths accountable for their actions, as they are often able to exploit legal or social systems for their own benefit. Furthermore, the lack of emotional depth in psychopathy means that these individuals are not deterred by the long-term consequences of their actions. Most people learn from their mistakes due to the emotional consequences of guilt, shame, or fear of punishment. However, psychopaths are unaffected by these emotions, allowing them to repeatedly engage in harmful behaviors without learning from past experiences. This creates a cycle in which psychopaths continue to commit harmful acts because they are not emotionally deterred from doing so.

The emotional traits of psychopathy—specifically, the lack of guilt and remorse, emotional detachment, and shallow affect—are central to understanding why psychopathic individuals are capable of engaging in harmful behaviors without experiencing the emotional consequences that typically deter such actions. These emotional deficiencies allow psychopaths to exploit, manipulate, and harm others without feeling personal responsibility or distress. The absence of guilt and the ability to remain emotionally detached from their actions make psychopaths particularly dangerous, both in personal relationships and in broader criminal contexts. Understanding these emotional traits is essential for developing strategies to manage and mitigate the harmful behaviors associated with psychopathy.

5 Interpersonal Traits of Psychopathy

One of the most striking aspects of psychopathy is how it affects interpersonal relationships. Psychopathic individuals exhibit several unique interpersonal traits that enable them to manipulate and exploit others for personal gain. These traits, which include exploitative behavior, superficial charm, and the ability to navigate social interactions to avoid detection, make psychopathy particularly dangerous in social and criminal contexts. Understanding these traits is key to recognizing how psychopathic individuals manipulate their environment and escape accountability for their harmful behaviors.

5.1 Exploitation and Manipulation Skills

One of the hallmark interpersonal traits of psychopathy is the ability to exploit others with skillful manipulation. Psychopathic individuals are highly adept at reading social situations and understanding the vulnerabilities of those around them. They use this awareness to exploit people's weaknesses, often with little regard for the emotional or physical harm they may cause. Psychopaths are able to manipulate others because they lack emotional empathy, allowing them to act without concern for how their actions affect others (Viding, 2019). This emotional detachment frees them to treat people as mere objects or tools to be used for personal gain. For instance, a psychopathic individual might manipulate a colleague at work to take the blame for their own mistake, or they might exploit a romantic partner for financial or emotional resources without feeling guilty about the deception. Psychopaths frequently use manipulative tactics such as lying, feigning affection, or creating complex schemes to achieve their goals. Because they are not burdened by emotional responses like guilt, they can convincingly lie and deceive others without revealing telltale signs of dishonesty, such as nervousness or remorse. This makes it difficult for others to detect their true motives, allowing them to continue exploiting individuals or systems over long periods.

The manipulative skills of psychopaths are not only applied in one-on-one relationships but also in broader social systems (Wallace et al., 2022). Psychopathic individuals can exploit organizational structures, legal systems, and even entire communities. For instance, in a corporate setting, a psychopathic manager might manipulate subordinates to maintain control or achieve higher status without regard for ethical boundaries. In more extreme cases, psychopaths involved in criminal enterprises may use manipulation to avoid detection by law enforcement or to orchestrate complex criminal schemes that benefit them at the expense of others.

5.2 *Superficial Charm as a Tool for Deception*

Another prominent interpersonal trait of psychopathy is superficial charm. Psychopaths often present themselves as confident, charismatic, and personable individuals. They can be highly likable upon first meeting, which helps them deceive others into believing they are trustworthy or benign. This superficial charm is a carefully constructed facade designed to mask their true intentions, allowing them to manipulate others more effectively. Psychopaths use charm to create favorable impressions and build rapport with their targets (Owens et al., 2017). They are often skilled conversationalists, able to engage people in ways that make them feel special or understood. However, this charm is not genuine; it is a manipulative tool that psychopaths use to gain trust or access to resources. Because they are adept at reading social cues, psychopaths can quickly identify what others want to hear and say exactly what is needed to achieve their goals.

For instance, a psychopathic individual might present themselves as a caring and attentive romantic partner early in a relationship, only to later exploit their partner's trust for financial or emotional gain. In professional settings, they might use their charm to impress superiors or colleagues, only to engage in dishonest or unethical behavior once they have secured a position of power.

Superficial charm allows psychopaths to hide their emotional deficits, such as their lack of empathy or guilt, from others (Rijnders et al., 2021). By presenting themselves as likable and charismatic, they divert attention away from their true nature, making it more difficult for others to recognize their manipulative behavior. This charm also allows them to blend into social groups and environments where their exploitative tendencies might otherwise raise suspicion.

The ability to be charming and persuasive also contributes to the psychopath's success in criminal enterprises (Kiehl & Hoffman, n.d.). In criminal contexts, psychopaths may use their charm to manipulate victims, gain the trust of coconspirators, or deceive law enforcement officials. Their ability to appear calm, composed, and confident, even in high-stress situations, enhances their capacity for deception and allows them to continue engaging in harmful behavior without immediate repercussions.

5.3 *Navigating Social Interactions to Avoid Detection*

One of the most dangerous aspects of psychopathy is the ability of individuals with this disorder to navigate social interactions in a way that avoids detection. Psychopaths are experts at controlling how they are perceived by others, carefully managing their behavior to maintain a facade of normalcy. This skill allows them to engage in harmful or criminal behavior while minimizing the risk of being caught or held accountable.

A key factor in a psychopath's ability to avoid detection is their understanding of social norms and expectations. Although psychopaths may not internalize these norms emotionally, they are keenly aware of how others expect them to behave (Anderson & Kiehl, 2014). They can mimic appropriate emotional responses when necessary, such as displaying concern or empathy, to maintain the illusion that they are emotionally connected to others. This makes it difficult for even close friends, family members, or colleagues to recognize the psychopath's true intentions.

For instance, in a work environment, a psychopathic individual might maintain a friendly and professional demeanor, all the while engaging in unethical or exploitative behavior behind the scenes. Because they know how to act the part of a responsible and likable colleague, they are able to evade suspicion or accusations, often deflecting blame onto others when their actions are questioned. Psychopaths also excel at compartmentalizing their behavior, presenting different versions of themselves depending on the social context (Sadeh & Verona, 2008). They may appear as model citizens in one aspect of their lives while engaging in illegal or unethical activities in another. This ability to compartmentalize allows them to navigate multiple social roles without arousing suspicion.

In criminal contexts, psychopaths are particularly skilled at avoiding detection by law enforcement (Kiehl & Hoffman, n.d.). They may use their charm and manipulation skills to deceive investigators, creating alibis or deflecting blame onto others. Because they lack the emotional responses that typically betray guilt, such as anxiety or fear, psychopaths can maintain a calm and convincing demeanor even when questioned about their involvement in a crime. This ability to remain composed under pressure makes them particularly difficult to interrogate or prosecute.

Furthermore, psychopaths often exploit social structures to their advantage, manipulating legal systems, corporate hierarchies, or interpersonal networks to protect themselves from accountability. For example, a psychopathic criminal might use their knowledge of legal loopholes to evade prosecution or manipulate witnesses to avoid conviction. This strategic manipulation of social systems allows them to continue engaging in harmful behavior while minimizing personal risk.

The interpersonal traits of psychopathy—exploitative behavior, superficial charm, and the ability to navigate social interactions without detection—are central to understanding how psychopathic individuals manipulate and harm others. Their lack of emotional empathy allows them to exploit relationships and social systems without guilt or remorse, while their charm enables them to deceive others and avoid suspicion. Psychopaths are particularly dangerous in social and criminal contexts because they are adept at presenting a facade of normalcy while engaging in harmful or unethical behavior behind the scenes. Recognizing these interpersonal traits is essential for identifying and managing psychopathic individuals, whether in personal relationships, professional settings, or legal contexts.

6 Neuropsychological Insights

While much of the focus has been on behavioral and psychological traits, recent advancements in neuropsychology have provided valuable insights into the biological underpinnings of psychopathy. This growing body of research has shown that psychopathy is associated with structural and functional abnormalities in specific brain regions, particularly the prefrontal cortex and the amygdala. These regions play critical roles in impulse control, emotional processing, and moral decision-making, and their dysfunction helps explain the distinctive behavioral patterns observed in psychopathic individuals.

6.1 Brain Regions Involved in Psychopathy

The two most widely studied brain regions associated with psychopathy are the prefrontal cortex and the amygdala. These regions are integral to emotional regulation, impulse control, and decision-making, all areas where psychopathic individuals exhibit significant deficits.

1. Prefrontal Cortex: The prefrontal cortex (PFC) is located at the front of the brain and is responsible for higher-order cognitive functions, including decision-making, impulse control, planning, and the regulation of social behavior. It plays a crucial role in enabling individuals to consider the consequences of their actions and to make decisions based on long-term goals rather than immediate gratification.
2. Amygdala: The amygdala is a small, almond-shaped structure located deep within the brain. It is critical for emotional processing, especially in generating and interpreting emotional responses such as fear, empathy, and guilt. The amygdala helps individuals understand the emotional significance of events and regulate their emotional reactions accordingly.

6.2 The Prefrontal Cortex and Psychopathy

The prefrontal cortex is often referred to as the brain's executive center, responsible for overseeing rational thinking and controlling impulsive behaviors. In individuals with psychopathy, abnormalities in the prefrontal cortex are common and are thought to contribute to many of the hallmark traits of the disorder, such as impulsivity, poor decision-making, and a lack of forethought about the consequences of one's actions.

Research using neuroimaging techniques, such as functional magnetic resonance imaging (fMRI), has shown that individuals with psychopathy often have reduced gray matter volume and abnormal activity in the prefrontal cortex (Johanson et al., 2020). This reduction in prefrontal cortex function impairs the individual's ability to plan effectively, regulate their impulses, and make moral decisions based on the consideration of others' emotions or societal norms.

In terms of impulse control, the prefrontal cortex is responsible for inhibiting immediate urges in favor of more considered actions. For instance, when faced with a decision that might benefit oneself at the expense of others, a normally functioning prefrontal cortex would weigh the ethical implications and potential consequences of the action. However, in psychopathic individuals, the impaired prefrontal cortex fails to impose these moral brakes (Koenigs, 2012). This dysfunction may explain why psychopaths frequently engage in risky, impulsive, and often criminal behavior without regard for the potential consequences, either for themselves or their victims.

Moreover, the prefrontal cortex's involvement in planning and goal-directed behavior is also compromised in psychopathy (Koenigs, 2012). Psychopathic individuals often exhibit reckless and short-sighted behaviors, acting on immediate desires rather than long-term goals. This lack of foresight is characteristic of the disorder, where decisions are often driven by self-serving motives, with little consideration for future repercussions. This also aligns with the impulsive nature of psychopaths, as they frequently act without sufficient planning or evaluation of potential negative outcomes.

6.3 *The Amygdala and Psychopathy*

The amygdala plays a central role in processing emotions, particularly fear, empathy, and guilt—emotions that are typically underdeveloped or absent in psychopathic individuals. Neuroimaging studies have consistently demonstrated that the amygdala is structurally and functionally abnormal in people with psychopathy. Specifically, the amygdala in psychopathic individuals tends to show reduced volume and diminished activity when processing emotional stimuli. This underactivity in the amygdala explains why psychopaths exhibit a diminished capacity for empathy and emotional understanding (Deming et al., 2022). In most individuals, the amygdala helps generate emotional responses to the suffering of others, leading to feelings of guilt or compassion. In contrast, psychopathic individuals often lack these emotional responses, enabling them to engage in harmful or manipulative behavior without feeling the emotional weight of their actions. For example, the amygdala would typically activate in response to seeing someone in pain, prompting a feeling of distress or a desire to help. However, in psychopaths, the reduced functionality of the amygdala means that such emotional cues do not evoke the same empathetic responses, allowing them to act without concern for the suffering of others (Schultz et al., 2016).

Additionally, the amygdala is involved in fear processing, and its dysfunction in psychopathy may explain why psychopathic individuals are often fearless and resistant to punishment. Fear is a powerful emotion that typically serves to inhibit risky or dangerous behaviors. The amygdala helps individuals assess the potential threat or negative consequences of an action, triggering fear or anxiety that discourages harmful behaviors. In psychopaths, however, the blunted fear response associated with amygdala dysfunction allows them to engage in reckless or violent actions without the fear of punishment or the long-term consequences that would normally deter such behaviors.

6.4 The Role of these Regions in Impulse Control and Emotional Processing

Together, the prefrontal cortex and the amygdala form a critical network responsible for regulating behavior, controlling impulses, and processing emotions. In psychopathic individuals, dysfunction in these brain regions leads to the characteristic traits of the disorder, such as impulsivity, emotional detachment, and a disregard for social and moral norms. The prefrontal cortex is vital for inhibiting impulsive behaviors and guiding decision-making based on future consequences. Its dysfunction in psychopathy results in poor impulse control and an inability to plan effectively, contributing to the disorder's hallmark risk-taking and reckless behaviors. Psychopaths often act impulsively, engaging in criminal or harmful actions without considering the long-term consequences. This lack of impulse control is a direct result of impaired prefrontal cortex function, which prevents them from weighing the potential costs and benefits of their actions (Kim & Lee, 2010).

The amygdala, on the other hand, is crucial for emotional processing and empathy. Its dysfunction in psychopathy leads to a reduced ability to experience fear, guilt, or empathy, making it easier for psychopathic individuals to engage in harmful behaviors without experiencing the emotional consequences that would typically deter such actions. The underactivity of the amygdala means that psychopaths are less responsive to the emotional cues that would typically trigger guilt or fear, allowing them to manipulate, deceive, and harm others without emotional inhibition (Šimić et al., 2021).

Neuropsychological research has significantly advanced our understanding of the biological underpinnings of psychopathy. The prefrontal cortex and the amygdala, two key regions involved in impulse control and emotional processing, are consistently implicated in the disorder. Dysfunction in these areas contributes to many of the core traits of psychopathy, including impulsivity, emotional detachment, and a disregard for societal norms. By understanding the role of these brain regions, researchers and clinicians can better grasp the neurobiological foundations of psychopathy and work toward more effective interventions to manage and mitigate the harmful behaviors associated with the disorder.

7 Assessment Techniques

Assessing psychopathy is a complex process that requires a combination of neuroimaging techniques and personality assessments to capture the cognitive, emotional, and behavioral dimensions of the disorder. Psychopathy is a personality disorder that is not only characterized by emotional deficits, lack of empathy, and impulsivity, but also by distinct neurological anomalies. These characteristics manifest in specific brain regions such as the prefrontal cortex and the amygdala. Therefore, neuroimaging modalities like functional magnetic resonance imaging (fMRI) and positron emission tomography (PET) scans are increasingly used to examine the neurobiological correlates of psychopathy. Simultaneously, personality assessment tools like the Hare Psychopathy Checklist-Revised (PCL-R) and the Minnesota Multiphasic Personality Inventory (MMPI) provide important insights into the behavioral and personality traits associated with psychopathy. Together, these methods offer a comprehensive understanding of psychopathy from both biological and psychological perspectives.

7.1 Neuroimaging Modalities

Neuroimaging has revolutionized the study of psychopathy by allowing researchers to directly observe the structural and functional abnormalities in the brains of individuals with the disorder. Two of the most commonly used neuroimaging techniques in psychopathy research are functional magnetic resonance imaging (fMRI) and positron emission tomography (PET) scans. These methods offer insights into how brain activity and structure are altered in individuals with psychopathy, particularly in areas responsible for emotional processing and impulse control.

Functional Magnetic Resonance Imaging (fMRI)

Functional magnetic resonance imaging (fMRI) is a noninvasive imaging technique that measures brain activity by detecting changes in blood flow. This method relies on the fact that when a brain region is more active, it consumes more oxygen, leading to an increase in blood flow to that region (Gore, 2003). fMRI allows researchers to identify which brain areas are involved in specific cognitive and emotional processes by measuring the neural activity in real time.

In individuals with psychopathy, fMRI studies have consistently shown reduced activity in the prefrontal cortex and amygdala, two regions crucial for regulating emotions and controlling impulsive behavior (Koenigs, 2012). The prefrontal cortex is responsible for executive functions such as decision-making, moral reasoning, and impulse control, while the amygdala is involved in emotional processing, including the recognition of fear and empathy. Individuals with psychopathy often exhibit reduced activity in these areas, which correlates with their impaired ability to process emotions and make socially appropriate decisions. For instance, they may show diminished amygdala responses when exposed to fearful or distressing stimuli, indicating an impaired emotional response that may contribute to their lack of empathy and remorse.

fMRI has also been useful in studying the connections between different brain regions. In psychopathic individuals, the connectivity between the prefrontal cortex and the amygdala is often impaired, suggesting that these regions do not communicate effectively (Johanson et al., 2020). This dysfunctional connectivity may explain why individuals with psychopathy struggle to regulate their emotions and impulses, as the prefrontal cortex fails to adequately control the emotional responses generated by the amygdala.

Positron Emission Tomography (PET) Scans

Positron emission tomography (PET) scans are another valuable neuroimaging tool used to assess psychopathy. PET scans measure the metabolic activity of the brain by tracking the distribution of radioactive tracers injected into the bloodstream. These tracers attach to glucose, the brain's primary source of energy, allowing researchers to measure the levels of brain activity based on how much glucose different areas of the brain consume.

PET scans have revealed that individuals with psychopathy often exhibit lower levels of metabolic activity in the ventromedial prefrontal cortex (vmPFC), a region involved in emotional regulation, decision-making, and impulse control (Koenigs, 2012). This reduced activity is consistent with the behavioral traits of psychopathy, such as impulsivity and a lack of regard for the consequences of one's actions. PET scans have also shown abnormalities in the orbitofrontal cortex (OFC), another region associated with decision-making and moral judgment. These findings suggest that the structural and functional impairments in these brain regions may contribute to the psychopathic individual's inability to control their impulses and engage in moral reasoning.

7.2 *Personality Assessment Tests*

While neuroimaging provides insight into the biological basis of psychopathy, personality assessment tools are essential for evaluating the behavioral and emotional traits that define the disorder. Two of the most widely used personality assessments in the study and diagnosis of psychopathy are the Hare Psychopathy Checklist-Revised (PCL-R) and the Minnesota Multiphasic Personality Inventory (MMPI).

Hare Psychopathy Checklist-Revised (PCL-R)

The Hare Psychopathy Checklist-Revised (PCL-R) is considered the gold standard for assessing psychopathy in clinical and forensic settings (De Melo, 2024). Developed by Dr. Robert Hare, the PCL-R is a 20-item clinical tool that measures psychopathic traits in two major domains: interpersonal/affective traits and behavioral/social deviance. Each item is rated on a three-point scale, with a maximum score of 40, and individuals who score 30 or higher are typically classified as psychopathic.

The PCL-R assesses interpersonal traits such as glibness, superficial charm, manipulativeness, and pathological lying, as well as affective traits like lack of guilt or remorse, shallow emotions, and callousness. Additionally, the PCL-R evaluates behavioral tendencies like impulsivity, irresponsibility, and a parasitic lifestyle. These traits are observed through interviews and a review of an individual's criminal, social, and psychiatric history.

The PCL-R has been highly reliable in identifying individuals with psychopathy in both clinical and forensic populations, making it an indispensable tool for evaluating the risk of re-offending, particularly in violent crimes. Individuals who score high on the PCL-R are more likely to engage in criminal and antisocial behavior, making the checklist critical for parole and risk assessment in criminal justice settings.

Minnesota Multiphasic Personality Inventory (MMPI)

The Minnesota Multiphasic Personality Inventory (MMPI) is another widely used tool for assessing personality traits associated with psychopathy (Floyd & Gupta, 2023). The MMPI is a comprehensive psychological test designed to assess a broad range of personality traits and psychopathologies. The MMPI includes scales that measure antisocial behavior, narcissism, impulsivity, and emotional detachment, all traits commonly associated with psychopathy.

One of the key advantages of the MMPI is its ability to assess both conscious and unconscious traits. Psychopathic individuals often present themselves in a socially desirable manner, attempting to hide their more deviant tendencies. The MMPI's validity scales are designed to detect such dissimulation, making it an effective tool for assessing individuals who may be attempting to manipulate their test results. The MMPI also includes a Psychopathic Deviate (Pd) scale, which specifically measures tendencies toward antisocial behavior, impulsivity, and disregard for social norms. Individuals with high scores on the Pd scale are more likely to exhibit behaviors characteristic of psychopathy, such as manipulativeness, lack of empathy, and criminal tendencies.

The assessment of psychopathy requires a multidisciplinary approach that integrates both neuroimaging techniques and personality assessment tools. Neuroimaging modalities like fMRI and PET scans provide critical insights into the structural and functional abnormalities in brain regions such as the prefrontal cortex and the amygdala, which are involved in impulse control, emotional processing, and moral decision-making. Meanwhile, personality assessments like the Hare Psychopathy Checklist-Revised (PCL-R) and the Minnesota Multiphasic Personality Inventory (MMPI) help clinicians evaluate the behavioral and emotional traits that define psychopathy. Together, these tools offer a comprehensive framework for understanding psychopathy, guiding diagnosis, treatment, and risk assessment in both clinical and forensic contexts.

8 Risk Factors and Criminal Behavior

Criminal behavior is a complex phenomenon influenced by a combination of biological, psychological, and environmental factors. While no single factor can fully explain why individuals engage in criminal acts, certain risk factors consistently appear in research, including early trauma, environmental influences, genetic predispositions, and neurological deficits. Each of these elements plays a role in shaping an individual's likelihood of committing criminal acts. Understanding these risk factors can inform prevention strategies and interventions aimed at reducing criminal behavior.

8.1 Early Trauma and Environmental Influences

Early trauma, particularly during childhood, is one of the most significant risk factors for criminal behavior. Traumatic experiences, such as physical or emotional abuse, neglect, and witnessing violence, can have a profound impact on a child's emotional and psychological development. Adverse childhood experiences (ACEs) disrupt normal brain development, often leading to emotional dysregulation, impaired social skills, and difficulty forming secure attachments with others. These deficits increase the likelihood of engaging in criminal behavior later in life (Silva et al., 2024).

Children exposed to trauma may develop a heightened sense of fear, anger, or mistrust of others, which can manifest in antisocial behaviors as they grow older (Danese et al., 2020) For instance, a child who has experienced physical abuse may learn to resolve conflicts through aggression, while a child who has been neglected might engage in criminal activities as a means of seeking attention or fulfilling unmet needs. Research has shown that individuals with high ACE scores are significantly more likely to exhibit violent or criminal behavior in adulthood, particularly if they have not received appropriate therapeutic interventions during childhood.

Environmental factors such as poverty, family dysfunction, and exposure to crime within the community further exacerbate the risk of criminal behavior (Piquero & Lawton, 2002). Growing up in impoverished neighborhoods where crime rates are high can normalize illegal activities and reduce the perceived consequences of criminal behavior. Additionally, children raised in homes with inconsistent or harsh discipline are more likely to internalize patterns of aggression or impulsivity, which can later translate into criminal conduct. The absence of positive role models or stable caregivers deprives children of essential guidance and emotional support, making it more difficult for them to develop the social and cognitive skills necessary to navigate life's challenges in a lawful manner.

8.2 *Genetic Predispositions*

While environmental factors are crucial in shaping behavior, research has also demonstrated that genetic predispositions play an important role in determining an individual's propensity for criminal behavior. Twin and adoption studies have consistently shown that individuals with a family history of criminality or antisocial behavior are more likely to engage in such activities themselves, suggesting a heritable component to criminal behavior. One of the most widely studied genetic markers linked to criminality is the **MAOA gene**, often referred to as the "warrior gene" (McDermott et al., 2009). This gene is responsible for regulating the metabolism of neurotransmitters like dopamine, norepinephrine, and serotonin—chemicals that are critical for mood regulation and impulse control. Variants of the MAOA gene, particularly those that result in lower levels of enzyme activity, have been associated with increased aggression and impulsive behavior, especially in individuals who have experienced childhood trauma.

The interaction between genes and environment is crucial in understanding criminal behavior. Individuals who inherit genetic predispositions for aggression or impulsivity may be more likely to engage in criminal behavior if they are also exposed to negative environmental factors such as abuse or neglect (Baker et al., 2006). In contrast, those with the same genetic vulnerabilities but who grow up in supportive, nurturing environments may not exhibit criminal tendencies, highlighting the complex interplay between nature and nurture.

Additionally, research into dopamine and serotonin systems has suggested that individuals with genetic variations affecting these neurotransmitter pathways may be more prone to risk-taking and sensation-seeking behaviors (Seo et al., 2008). These traits can lead to engagement in criminal activities, particularly when combined with poor impulse control and environmental stressors.

8.3 *Neurological Deficits Linked to Criminal Behavior*

Neuropsychological research has identified several brain regions that are implicated in criminal behavior, particularly those involved in emotional regulation, impulse control, and moral reasoning. Neurological deficits in these areas are often linked to an increased likelihood of engaging in criminal activities, as the brain's ability to inhibit harmful or socially inappropriate actions is compromised. The prefrontal cortex is one of the most critical brain regions involved in regulating behavior and decision-making. It is responsible for executive functions, including planning, impulse control, and moral reasoning (Kim & Lee, 2010). Individuals with damage or dysfunction in the prefrontal cortex often exhibit poor judgment, reduced empathy, and an inability to foresee the consequences of their actions—traits that are frequently associated with criminal behavior. For example, studies of violent offenders have shown that many have lower activity levels in the prefrontal cortex, impairing their ability to control aggressive impulses and make rational decisions in high-stress situations.

The amygdala, another key brain structure, plays a central role in processing emotions, particularly fear and empathy (Šimić et al., 2021). Dysfunction in the amygdala has been linked to reduced emotional responses, making it more difficult for individuals to feel guilt or remorse for their actions. Psychopathic individuals, who often exhibit shallow emotional responses and a lack of empathy, tend to have smaller or underactive amygdala. This emotional detachment allows them to engage in harmful or violent behaviors without experiencing the emotional consequences that typically deter such actions.

Further, deficits in the ventromedial prefrontal cortex (vmPFC) and orbitofrontal cortex (OFC) are associated with impaired moral reasoning and poor decision-making (Manohar et al., 2021). These brain regions are crucial for integrating emotional and cognitive processes, allowing individuals to make decisions that consider both immediate desires and long-term consequences. In individuals with criminal tendencies, dysfunction in these areas may lead to a preference for immediate gratification, despite the potential negative outcomes, contributing to impulsive and often harmful behavior.

Studies using neuroimaging techniques, such as functional magnetic resonance imaging (fMRI) and positron emission tomography (PET) scans, have provided valuable insights into the neural mechanisms underlying criminal behavior (Whitten, 2012). These scans allow researchers to observe brain activity in real time, revealing how specific regions of the brain respond to emotional, cognitive, and social stimuli. For example, fMRI studies have shown that violent offenders often have reduced connectivity between the prefrontal cortex and the amygdala, impairing their ability to regulate emotions and control aggressive impulses. PET scans have similarly revealed lower levels of metabolic activity in brain regions responsible for impulse control and moral reasoning in individuals who engage in criminal behavior.

8.4 *Interaction of Risk Factors*

It is essential to recognize that these risk factors—early trauma, genetic predispositions, and neurological deficits—do not operate in isolation. Instead, they interact in complex ways to increase the likelihood of criminal behavior. For instance, an individual with a genetic predisposition for impulsivity may not exhibit criminal tendencies unless they are also exposed to environmental stressors such as abuse or neglect. Conversely, a person who experiences early trauma but lacks the genetic or neurological vulnerabilities associated with criminal behavior may still develop into a well-adjusted adult if they receive appropriate support and intervention.

Understanding the interaction between these risk factors is critical for developing effective prevention and intervention strategies. Early intervention programs that target at-risk children, particularly those who have experienced trauma, can help mitigate the effects of environmental and genetic risk factors. Similarly, therapeutic interventions aimed at improving emotional regulation and impulse control may reduce the likelihood of criminal behavior in individuals with neurological deficits.

Criminal behavior is influenced by a complex interplay of early trauma, environmental factors, genetic predispositions, and neurological deficits. While no single factor can fully explain why individuals engage in criminal acts, understanding these risk factors provides valuable insights into the development of criminal tendencies. By recognizing the role of both nature and nurture in shaping behavior, researchers and clinicians can work toward more effective prevention and intervention strategies that reduce the risk of criminality and promote prosocial behavior.

9 Challenges in Diagnosis and Treatment

Despite its profound impact on individuals and society, diagnosing and treating psychopathy presents numerous challenges. These challenges stem from the disorder's elusive nature, the ethical dilemmas it poses in legal contexts, and the difficulties inherent in treating individuals who often lack the motivation or willingness to change. This section will explore the unique challenges in diagnosing psychopathy, the ethical dilemmas associated with legal considerations, and the barriers to effective treatment due to the core traits of psychopathy.

9.1 Unique Challenges in Diagnosing Psychopathy

Diagnosing psychopathy is particularly difficult because it is not classified as a standalone disorder in major diagnostic manuals like the Diagnostic and Statistical Manual of Mental Disorders, Fifth Edition (DSM-5) or the International Classification of Diseases, 11th Revision (ICD-11). Instead, psychopathy overlaps with antisocial personality disorder (ASPD) and narcissistic personality disorder (NPD), making it challenging to distinguish psychopathic traits from those of other personality disorders. The widely used Hare Psychopathy Checklist-Revised (PCL-R) is considered the gold standard for assessing psychopathy, but even this tool faces limitations in accurately capturing the multifaceted nature of the disorder.

One of the primary challenges in diagnosing psychopathy is that individuals with the disorder often present with a superficial charm and an ability to manipulate their surroundings, including mental health professionals (Martens, 2021). Psychopaths are adept at mimicking normal emotions and behaviors, which can make it difficult to identify their true motives and underlying pathology. In clinical settings, they may engage in deceptive behaviors to present themselves as more stable or less dangerous than they actually are. This ability to mask their traits poses a significant challenge to accurate diagnosis, as traditional diagnostic approaches that rely on self-reporting or clinical observation may fail to detect the core features of psychopathy.

Furthermore, psychopathy exists on a continuum, with individuals exhibiting varying degrees of psychopathic traits. Some individuals may display only a few traits of psychopathy, while others exhibit a full spectrum of characteristics. This variation complicates the diagnostic process, as not all individuals who exhibit psychopathic traits meet the criteria for full-blown psychopathy. The lack of a clear, universally accepted diagnostic threshold makes it difficult for clinicians to differentiate between individuals who are psychopathic and those who merely exhibit antisocial behaviors or other personality disorder symptoms (British Psychological Society (UK), 2009).

Ethical Dilemmas in Legal Contexts

Diagnosing psychopathy in legal contexts presents unique ethical dilemmas, particularly regarding the use of psychopathy assessments in criminal proceedings. One of the main concerns is the potential for stigma and bias associated with a psychopathy diagnosis. Labeling an individual as a psychopath can influence legal decisions in ways that may not always be fair or justified (Anderson & Kiehl, 2014). For example, a diagnosis of psychopathy is often associated with increased perceptions of dangerousness and recidivism risk, which can lead to harsher sentencing, reduced chances of parole, or even preventive detention.

Moreover, there is the issue of moral responsibility. Psychopaths often have deficits in emotional processing and moral reasoning, raising the question of whether they should be held fully accountable for their actions. If an individual is unable to feel guilt or remorse due to neurological or emotional deficits, some argue that they may not have the same capacity for moral judgment as a non-psychopathic individual. This has led to debates about whether psychopathy should be considered a mitigating factor in criminal sentencing, similar to mental illness or intellectual disability. However, reducing criminal responsibility based on psychopathy can create a slippery slope in the legal system. While psychopathy may impair an individual's ability to empathize with others, it does not necessarily impede their understanding of right and wrong or their ability to control their actions. As such, the legal system faces the ethical challenge of balancing the need for justice with the understanding of psychopathy as a disorder that affects emotional and moral capacities. Additionally, there is the risk of misuse of psychopathy assessments. The Hare PCL-R, while a valuable tool, was developed for clinical and research purposes, not for determining legal outcomes. However, it is frequently used in courtrooms to assess the risk of future violence or recidivism despite concerns about its predictive accuracy in such contexts. This raises questions about the ethical use of psychopathy assessments in legal settings and the potential for these tools to be misapplied in ways that unfairly impact individuals' legal rights.

Treatment Difficulties Due to Manipulation and Lack of Motivation

Treating psychopathy poses significant challenges due to the core traits of the disorder, particularly manipulativeness, lack of empathy, and lack of motivation to change. Traditional therapeutic approaches rely on an individual's willingness to engage in the treatment process, develop insight into their behavior, and work toward personal growth. However, psychopaths often lack the intrinsic motivation to change, and their manipulative tendencies can undermine the effectiveness of treatment interventions.

Psychopaths may enter treatment not out of a genuine desire for personal change but rather to achieve a secondary gain, such as avoiding legal consequences or gaining social approval. In therapeutic settings, they may feign progress or manipulate their therapists, making it difficult to assess their true level of engagement or improvement. This manipulative behavior often leads to treatment resistance, where individuals appear to comply with therapy but fail to make meaningful changes in their behavior or emotional functioning.

Moreover, traditional cognitive behavioral therapy (CBT) and empathy training programs, which are effective for many other disorders, tend to be less successful for individuals with psychopathy (Institute for Quality and Efficiency in Health Care (IQWiG), 2022). Since psychopathy involves a fundamental deficit in empathy, efforts to teach empathy or emotional regulation may not resonate with individuals who lack the capacity to experience these emotions fully. This can create frustration for therapists and a lack of progress for patients, further complicating the treatment process.

There is also the issue of recidivism. Psychopaths have high rates of criminal recidivism, particularly violent recidivism, even after undergoing treatment (Kiehl & Hoffman, n.d.). This suggests that traditional therapeutic interventions may not be sufficient to address the underlying traits of psychopathy that contribute to criminal behavior. Researchers and clinicians are exploring alternative approaches, such as neurological interventions or pharmacological treatments, to target the brain regions involved in emotional processing and impulse control. However, these methods are still in the early stages of development, and their long-term efficacy remains uncertain.

Diagnosing and treating psychopathy is fraught with challenges due to the disorder's complex nature, its ethical implications in legal contexts, and the inherent difficulties in motivating individuals with psychopathy to engage in meaningful treatment. The manipulative and emotionally detached traits of psychopaths make it difficult to accurately diagnose the disorder and pose significant barriers to effective intervention. In legal settings, the diagnosis of psychopathy raises ethical concerns about bias, moral responsibility, and the appropriate use of psychopathy assessments. Treatment efforts, while ongoing, face considerable hurdles due to the lack of empathy and motivation exhibited by individuals with psychopathy. As research into the neurobiological and psychological underpinnings of psychopathy continues, new approaches to both diagnosis and treatment may emerge, offering hope for better management of this challenging disorder.

10 Case Studies Overview

Case studies play a critical role in advancing our understanding of psychopathy by providing detailed, real-world examples of how the disorder manifests across different individuals. These studies offer insights into the cognitive, emotional, and neuropsychological traits of psychopathic individuals that are often missed in broader epidemiological or theoretical studies. By examining case studies, researchers and clinicians can observe the complexities and nuances of psychopathy, understand how different factors like neurological deficits or early trauma contribute to the development of the disorder, and explore the effectiveness of targeted interventions. This section will highlight the importance of case studies in understanding psychopathy and present two case examples that illustrate key neuropsychological and intervention-focused aspects.

10.1 The Importance of Case Studies in Understanding Psychopathy

Psychopathy is a multifaceted disorder with significant individual variation in how it presents itself. While psychopathy is often discussed in terms of general traits such as lack of empathy, impulsivity, and manipulativeness, case studies reveal the unique ways in which these traits can combine and influence behavior. Case studies allow researchers to move beyond statistical correlations and diagnostic criteria to understand the real-world impact of psychopathy on an individual's life and social interactions. These in-depth examinations provide a more holistic view of the disorder, illustrating how psychopathic traits interact with an individual's environment, brain structure, and personality.

Furthermore, case studies are instrumental in highlighting the neuropsychological underpinnings of psychopathy. Advances in neuroimaging techniques, such as functional magnetic resonance imaging (fMRI) and positron emission tomography (PET) scans, have made it possible to observe how abnormalities in brain regions, particularly the prefrontal cortex and amygdala, contribute to the emotional and behavioral dysfunctions seen in psychopathy. Studying individuals with these abnormalities can offer insights into the biological basis of psychopathic behaviors, such as their inability to process emotions or control impulses effectively.

Case studies are also crucial for developing and refining treatment approaches for psychopathy. Given that psychopathy is notoriously difficult to treat, documenting the effects of various therapeutic interventions on specific individuals allows clinicians to identify which methods are most promising. Additionally, case studies that incorporate neuropsychological profiling can guide more tailored, individualized treatment plans, leading to potentially better outcomes than one-size-fits-all approaches.

Case Study 1: High PCL-R Scores and Prefrontal Cortex Abnormalities
In this first case, we examine an individual with high scores on the Hare Psychopathy Checklist-Revised (PCL-R), a diagnostic tool used to assess the presence of psychopathic traits. The PCL-R is a 20-item assessment that rates individuals on a scale of 0–40, with higher scores indicating a greater likelihood of psychopathy. The subject of this case, "John," scored 35 on the PCL-R, indicating a high level of psychopathic traits. John displayed the characteristic superficial charm, manipulativeness, and lack of remorse often associated with psychopathy. He had a history of criminal behavior, including repeated violent offenses, and was noted for his callous treatment of others.

Neuroimaging studies conducted as part of John's case revealed significant abnormalities in the prefrontal cortex, a region of the brain involved in impulse control, decision-making, and emotional regulation. Specifically, John had reduced activation in the ventromedial prefrontal cortex (vmPFC), an area crucial for evaluating the consequences of one's actions and integrating emotional and cognitive information. These findings were consistent with the view that deficits in the prefrontal cortex may contribute to the impulsivity and emotional detachment characteristic of psychopathy.

John's case highlights the importance of neurobiological factors in understanding psychopathy. While John's behavioral traits clearly fit the profile of a psychopath, the neuroimaging data provided a deeper understanding of why he struggled with self-regulation and empathy. His prefrontal cortex abnormalities likely impaired his ability to weigh the moral implications of his actions, making it easier for him to engage in harmful behaviors without guilt or remorse. This case also underscores the value of combining traditional diagnostic tools like the PCL-R with neuroimaging techniques to obtain a more comprehensive picture of psychopathy.

Case Study 2: Targeted Interventions Based on Neuropsychological Profiles
The second case focuses on an individual, "Lisa," who underwent targeted interventions based on her neuropsychological profile. Lisa had been diagnosed with antisocial personality disorder (ASPD), a diagnosis often used interchangeably with psychopathy in clinical settings, though they are distinct. Lisa exhibited many psychopathic traits, including emotional detachment, a lack of empathy, and a tendency to manipulate those around her. However, unlike John, Lisa had not engaged in violent criminal behavior and had shown some responsiveness to previous treatment attempts.

Neuropsychological testing revealed that Lisa had deficits in her amygdala, a brain region involved in processing emotional stimuli, particularly fear and empathy. Amygdala dysfunction is commonly observed in psychopathic individuals and is thought to contribute to their inability to form emotional connections with others or experience fear in response to potential punishment. However, Lisa also demonstrated relatively intact functioning in her dorsolateral prefrontal cortex (dlPFC), which is associated with cognitive control and planning.

Given these findings, Lisa's treatment team decided to implement a more targeted intervention that focused on strengthening her emotional processing abilities while leveraging her relatively intact cognitive control. Lisa participated in cognitive behavioral therapy (CBT), with an emphasis on emotional recognition and empathy training. In addition, she underwent mindfulness-based therapy designed to enhance her awareness of emotional and physical states, with the hope that this would improve her ability to regulate her emotions.

While the results were mixed, Lisa did show some improvement in her ability to recognize and respond to emotional cues, particularly in structured, low-stress environments. However, her lack of emotional depth and manipulative tendencies persisted in social interactions, suggesting that while targeted interventions based on neuropsychological profiles can be helpful, they may not fully overcome the entrenched emotional deficits seen in psychopathy.

These two case studies demonstrate the critical role that detailed, individualized assessments play in understanding and managing psychopathy. In the case of John, the combination of high PCL-R scores and prefrontal cortex abnormalities provided a clear neurobiological explanation for his impulsive and emotionally detached behavior. For Lisa, neuropsychological profiling allowed for a more tailored treatment approach that focused on her specific brain deficits, offering a more nuanced understanding of how psychopathy might be managed, if not entirely treated. Case studies are indispensable in unraveling the complexities of psychopathy. They provide not only a deeper understanding of the disorder's cognitive and neurobiological underpinnings but also insights into how interventions can be tailored to individual profiles. As research continues to advance, these detailed accounts will remain a cornerstone of both clinical practice and scientific inquiry into one of the most challenging personality disorders known to psychology.

11 Conclusion

Psychopathy is a complex and multifaceted personality disorder characterized by a pervasive pattern of manipulative, deceitful, and antisocial behavior. Its relationship with criminal behavior has garnered significant attention in both psychological research and the criminal justice system. Understanding this relationship is crucial for developing effective prevention and intervention strategies.

Individuals with psychopathy often exhibit a distinct emotional and interpersonal style marked by superficial charm, lack of empathy, and shallow affect. These traits enable them to manipulate others and evade accountability for their actions, which can facilitate criminal behavior. The emotional detachment associated with psychopathy contributes to an increased likelihood of engaging in violent and predatory crimes, as these individuals may view their victims as mere objects to exploit. This lack of emotional connection not only makes it easier for psychopaths to commit crimes but also complicates the process of rehabilitation, as traditional therapeutic approaches may be less effective with individuals who lack genuine remorse.

Research has shown that psychopathy is not merely a result of environmental factors but is also influenced by genetic predispositions and neurobiological abnormalities. Studies utilizing neuroimaging techniques have identified structural and functional differences in the brains of individuals with psychopathic traits, particularly in areas related to emotional processing and impulse control. These findings suggest that psychopathy may have a biological underpinning, which emphasizes the need for a nuanced understanding of the disorder in the context of criminal behavior.

Moreover, the criminal justice system often grapples with the challenges posed by psychopathic offenders. These individuals frequently possess an exceptional ability to manipulate the legal system, presenting themselves in ways that may mask their true nature. Consequently, they may evade appropriate consequences for their actions or exploit legal loopholes to their advantage. This capacity for deceit raises ethical dilemmas regarding the assessment and treatment of psychopathic individuals within correctional settings. There is an urgent need for comprehensive risk assessment tools that can effectively identify psychopathic traits in offenders, allowing for tailored interventions that address their unique needs while prioritizing public safety.

Preventing the emergence of psychopathy and its associated criminal behavior requires a multifaceted approach. Early intervention strategies, including parenting programs and educational initiatives, can help mitigate risk factors associated with the development of psychopathic traits in children and adolescents. These preventive measures should focus on fostering emotional intelligence, empathy, and prosocial behavior, laying the groundwork for healthier interpersonal relationships and reducing the likelihood of future criminal involvement.

In conclusion, the interplay between psychopathy and criminal behavior is intricate and demands careful consideration from researchers, clinicians, and legal professionals. Understanding the underlying psychological and biological mechanisms of psychopathy can lead to more effective treatment and management strategies for individuals exhibiting these traits. Furthermore, addressing the societal and environmental factors that contribute to the development of psychopathic tendencies is crucial for preventing criminal behavior. Ultimately, a comprehensive approach that combines research, clinical practice, and legal considerations will enhance our ability to address the challenges posed by psychopathy within the context of criminal behavior. Through collaborative efforts, we can aspire to create a safer society while supporting the mental health needs of individuals affected by this disorder.

References

Anderson, N. E., & Kiehl, K. A. (2014). Psychopathy: Developmental perspectives and their implications for treatment. *Restorative Neurology and Neuroscience, 32*(1), 103–117. https://doi.org/10.3233/rnn-139001

Baker, L. A., Bezdjian, S., & Raine, A. (2006). *Behavioral genetics: The science of antisocial behavior*. https://pmc.ncbi.nlm.nih.gov/articles/PMC2174903/

Baskin-Sommers, A. (n.d.). *Psychopaths can feel emotions and can be treated—don't believe what you see on crime shows*. The Conversation. https://theconversation.com/psychopaths-can-feel-emotions-and-can-be-treated-dont-believe-what-you-see-on-crime-shows-181446

Blair, R. J. R. (2013). Psychopathy: Cognitive and neural dysfunction. *Dialogues in Clinical Neuroscience, 15*(2), 181–190. https://doi.org/10.31887/dcns.2013.15.2/rblair

British Psychological Society (UK). (2009). *Borderline personality disorder*. Borderline Personality Disorder–NCBI Bookshelf. https://www.ncbi.nlm.nih.gov/books/NBK55415/

Danese, A., McLaughlin, K. A., Samara, M., & Stover, C. S. (2020). Psychopathology in children exposed to trauma: Detection and intervention needed to reduce downstream burden. *BMJ, m3073*. https://doi.org/10.1136/bmj.m3073

De Melo, T. (2024, September 30). *Exploring the hare psychopathy checklist-revised: 2nd edition. Multi-Health Systems (MHS)*. https://mhs.com/blog/exploring-the-hare-psychopathy-checklist-revised-2nd-edition/

Deming, P., Heilicher, M., & Koenigs, M. (2022). How reliable are amygdala findings in psychopathy? A systematic review of MRI studies. *Neuroscience & Biobehavioral Reviews, 142*, 104875. https://doi.org/10.1016/j.neubiorev.2022.104875

DSM. (n.d.). https://www.psychiatry.org/psychiatrists/practice/dsm

Floyd, A. E., & Gupta, V. (2023, April 24). *Minnesota multiphasic personality inventory*. StatPearls–NCBI Bookshelf. https://www.ncbi.nlm.nih.gov/books/NBK557525/

Glass, S. J., & Newman, J. P. (2009). Emotion processing in the criminal psychopath: The role of attention in emotion-facilitated memory. *Journal of Abnormal Psychology, 118*(1), 229–234. https://doi.org/10.1037/a0014866

Gonzalez-Tapia, M. I., Obsuth, I., & Heeds, R. (2017). A new legal treatment for psychopaths? Perplexities for legal thinkers. *International Journal of Law and Psychiatry, 54*, 46–60. https://doi.org/10.1016/j.ijlp.2017.04.004

Gore, J. C. (2003). Principles and practice of functional MRI of the human brain. *Journal of Clinical Investigation, 112*(1), 4–9. https://doi.org/10.1172/jci19010

Institute for Quality and Efficiency in Health Care (IQWiG). (2022, June 2). *In brief: Cognitive behavioral therapy (CBT)*. InformedHealth.org–NCBI Bookshelf. https://www.ncbi.nlm.nih.gov/books/NBK279297/

Johanson, M., Vaurio, O., Tiihonen, J., & Lähteenvuo, M. (2020). A systematic literature review of neuroimaging of psychopathic traits. *Frontiers in Psychiatry, 10*. https://doi.org/10.3389/fpsyt.2019.01027

Kiehl, K. A., & Hoffman, M. B. (n.d.). *The criminal psychopath: History, neuroscience, treatment, and economics*. https://pmc.ncbi.nlm.nih.gov/articles/PMC4059069/

Kim, S., & Lee, D. (2010). Prefrontal cortex and impulsive decision making. *Biological Psychiatry, 69*(12), 1140–1146. https://doi.org/10.1016/j.biopsych.2010.07.005

Koenigs, M. (2012). The role of prefrontal cortex in psychopathy. *Reviews in the Neurosciences, 23*(3), 253. https://doi.org/10.1515/revneuro-2012-0036

Maiese, M. (2013). Moral cognition, affect, and psychopathy. *Philosophical Psychology, 27*(6), 807–828. https://doi.org/10.1080/09515089.2013.793916

Manohar, S., Lockwood, P., Drew, D., Fallon, S. J., Chong, T. T., Jeyaretna, D. S., Baker, I., & Husain, M. (2021). Reduced decision bias and more rational decision making following ventromedial prefrontal cortex damage. *Cortex, 138*, 24–37. https://doi.org/10.1016/j.cortex.2021.01.015

Martens, W. H. J.. (2021, June 29). *The hidden suffering of the psychopath*. Psychiatric Times. https://www.psychiatrictimes.com/view/hidden-suffering-psychopath

Martin, S., Zabala, C., Del-Monte, J., Graziani, P., Aizpurua, E., Barry, T. J., & Ricarte, J. (2019). Examining the relationships between impulsivity, aggression, and recidivism for prisoners with antisocial personality disorder. *Aggression and Violent Behavior, 49*, 101314. https://doi.org/10.1016/j.avb.2019.07.009

McDermott, R., Tingley, D., Cowden, J., Frazzetto, G., & Johnson, D. D. P. (2009). Monoamine oxidase a gene (MAOA) predicts behavioral aggression following provocation. *Proceedings of the National Academy of Sciences, 106*(7), 2118–2123. https://doi.org/10.1073/pnas.0808376106

Owens, E. S., McPharlin, F. W. H., Brooks, N., & Fritzon, K. (2017). The effects of empathy, emotional intelligence and psychopathy on interpersonal interactions. *Psychiatry Psychology and Law, 25*(1), 1–18. https://doi.org/10.1080/13218719.2017.1347936

(PDF) Pathological lying and deception in psychopathic personalities: Facial expressions analysis. (n.d.). *ResearchGate*. https://www.researchgate.net/publication/301636951_Pathological_lying_and_deception_in_psychopathic_personalities_Facial_expressions_analysis

Perez, P. R. (2012). The etiology of psychopathy: A neuropsychological perspective. *Aggression and Violent Behavior, 17*(6), 519–522. https://doi.org/10.1016/j.avb.2012.07.006

Piquero, A. R., & Lawton, B. (2002). Individual risk for crime is exacerbated in poor familial and neighborhood contexts: The contribution of low birth weight, family adversity, and neighborhood disadvantage to life course-persistent offending. *Advances in Life Course Research, 7*, 263–295. https://doi.org/10.1016/s1040-2608(02)80037-5

Rijnders, R. J., Terburg, D., Bos, P. A., Kempes, M. M., & Van Honk, J. (2021). Unzipping empathy in psychopathy: Empathy and facial affect processing in psychopaths. *Neuroscience & Biobehavioral Reviews, 131*, 1116–1126. https://doi.org/10.1016/j.neubiorev.2021.10.020

Sadeh, N., & Verona, E. (2008). Psychopathic personality traits associated with abnormal selective attention and impaired cognitive control. *Neuropsychology, 22*(5), 669–680. https://doi.org/10.1037/a0012692

Saladino, V., Lin, H., Zamparelli, E., & Verrastro, V. (2021). Neuroscience, empathy, and violent crime in an incarcerated population: A narrative review. *Frontiers in Psychology, 12*. https://doi.org/10.3389/fpsyg.2021.694212

Schultz, D. H., Balderston, N. L., Baskin-Sommers, A. R., Larson, C. L., & Helmstetter, F. J. (2016). Psychopaths show enhanced amygdala activation during fear conditioning. *Frontiers in Psychology, 7*. https://doi.org/10.3389/fpsyg.2016.00348

Seo, D., Patrick, C. J., & Kennealy, P. J. (2008). Role of serotonin and dopamine system interactions in the neurobiology of impulsive aggression and its comorbidity with other clinical disorders. *Aggression and Violent Behavior, 13*(5), 383–395. https://doi.org/10.1016/j.avb.2008.06.003

Silva, C., Moreira, P., Moreira, D. S., Rafael, F., Rodrigues, A., Leite, Â., Lopes, S., & Moreira, D. (2024). Impact of Adverse childhood experiences in young adults and adults: A systematic literature review. *Pediatric Reports, 16*(2), 461–481. https://doi.org/10.3390/pediatric16020040

Šimić, G., Tkalčić, M., Vukić, V., Mulc, D., Španić, E., Šagud, M., Olucha-Bordonau, F. E., Vukšić, M., & Hof, P. R. (2021). Understanding emotions: Origins and roles of the amygdala. *Biomolecules, 11*(6), 823. https://doi.org/10.3390/biom11060823

Simon. (2014, June 13). *Manipulators and charm–character matters*. Character Matters. https://www.drgeorgesimon.com/manipulators-and-charm/

Simons, R. L., & Burt, C. H. (2011). Learning to be bad: Adverse social conditions, social schemas, and crime*. *Criminology, 49*(2), 553–598. https://doi.org/10.1111/j.1745-9125.2011.00231.x

Tangney, J. P., Stuewig, J., & Hafez, L. (2011). Shame, guilt, and remorse: Implications for offender populations. *Journal of Forensic Psychiatry and Psychology, 22*(5), 706–723. https://doi.org/10.1080/14789949.2011.617541

Tharshini, N. K., Ibrahim, F., Kamaluddin, M. R., Rathakrishnan, B., & Nasir, N. C. M. (2021). The link between individual personality traits and criminality: A systematic review. *International Journal of Environmental Research and Public Health, 18*(16), 8663. https://doi.org/10.3390/ijerph18168663

The Mask of Sanity (Cleckley 5th Ed). (2024, March 8). *EBEN Ireland*. https://ebeni.wordpress.com/unethical-leaders/cleckley-the-mask-of-sanity/

Viding, E. (2019). 2. Explaining the lack of empathy. In *Oxford University Press eBooks* (pp. 21–42). https://doi.org/10.1093/actrade/9780198802266.003.0002.

Wallace, L., Fido, D., Sumich, A. L., & Heym, N. (2022). A systematic review on the current conceptualisations of successful psychopathy. *Forensic Science International Mind and Law, 3*, 100076. https://doi.org/10.1016/j.fsiml.2022.100076

Whitten, L. (2012). Functional magnetic resonance imaging (fMRI): An invaluable tool in translational Neuroscience. https://doi.org/10.3768/rtipress.2012.op.0010.1212.

Traumatic Brain Injury and Criminal Justice

1 Introduction

Traumatic brain injury (TBI) is a complex and often debilitating condition that occurs when an external physical force injures the brain, resulting in a wide array of symptoms affecting cognition, emotions, and behavior. As a significant public health issue, TBI can have profound and long-lasting consequences for individuals, their families, and society. Not only does it impact a person's ability to function in daily life, but it is also associated with various complications, including an increased risk of engaging in criminal behavior. In fact, a disproportionate number of incarcerated individuals have histories of brain injury, making TBI a critical issue within the criminal justice system. This introduction explores what TBI is, the common symptoms associated with it, and its prevalence in the criminal justice system, highlighting its role as a potential risk factor for criminal behavior. Traumatic brain injury is defined as damage to the brain caused by an external mechanical force, such as a blow to the head, rapid acceleration or deceleration, or penetration by a foreign object. This force disrupts normal brain function, potentially resulting in temporary or permanent impairment. TBI can range in severity from mild—often referred to as concussions, where symptoms might resolve with time—to severe injuries that cause long-term disability or death. The brain, being a highly sensitive and intricate organ, is vulnerable to external forces that can damage its delicate structures. In a TBI, physical damage to brain cells and the disruption of neural networks may impair the brain's ability to process information, regulate emotions, or control behaviors. Depending on the location and extent of the injury, TBI can manifest in various ways, affecting virtually every aspect of an individual's life.

© The Author(s), under exclusive license to Springer Nature Switzerland AG 2025
K. J. Reddy, *Foundations of Criminal Forensic Neuropsychology*,
https://doi.org/10.1007/978-3-031-83771-5_11

2 Neurobiological and Cognitive Consequences of TBI

Traumatic brain injury (TBI) is a complex neurological condition resulting from an external mechanical force to the brain, leading to structural and functional impairments. It has far-reaching consequences, both neurobiological and cognitive, which can significantly alter an individual's quality of life. In this section, we explore the neurobiological effects of TBI, focusing on damage to specific brain regions and disruptions in neural networks. Following that, we examine the cognitive impairments commonly associated with TBI, such as deficits in executive functioning, memory, attention, and emotional regulation.

2.1 Damage to Brain Regions Affecting Behavior

One of the primary neurobiological consequences of TBI is direct damage to various brain regions, which, in turn, impacts behavior and cognition. Notably, certain areas of the brain are more vulnerable to injury due to their location and functional significance.

The prefrontal cortex (PFC), located in the frontal lobe, is the most susceptible to damage in TBI (Nolan et al., 2018). This vulnerability arises from its position at the front of the brain, making it prone to injuries caused by sudden acceleration and deceleration forces. The PFC is critically involved in higher-order cognitive processes, including decision-making, impulse control, planning, and social behavior. Damage to this area often results in impairments in these functions, leading to challenges in self-regulation, goal-directed behavior, and maintaining social norms (Heatherton, 2010).

Following the prefrontal cortex, the occipital lobe, situated at the back of the brain, is another region that frequently sustains damage. Although this area is primarily responsible for visual processing, TBI-related injuries to the occipital lobe can lead to visual deficits, including problems with visual perception, spatial orientation, and even visual field loss.

The temporal lobe is also commonly affected by TBI, especially in cases of lateral or rotational injuries. The temporal lobe plays a crucial role in memory formation, auditory processing, and emotional regulation (Taing et al., 2023). When this region is compromised, individuals may experience difficulties with memory retention, language comprehension, and the modulation of emotions. Given that the temporal lobe houses structures like the hippocampus and amygdala, TBI-related damage to these areas can lead to profound memory impairments and heightened emotional reactivity.

2.2 Disruptions in Neural Networks

In addition to direct damage to brain regions, TBI also causes disruptions in the neural networks that facilitate communication between different parts of the brain. These disruptions can be especially pronounced in the prefrontal cortex, where the intricate connections responsible for impulse control and decision-making are often compromised.

The PFC is highly interconnected with other brain regions, including the limbic system, which governs emotional processing, and the basal ganglia, which is involved in motor control and habit formation (Arnsten, 2009). Damage to these networks leads to deficits in impulse control and decision-making, as the brain's ability to integrate emotional and cognitive information becomes impaired (Šimić et al., 2021). As a result, individuals with TBI may struggle to inhibit inappropriate behaviors, exhibit poor judgment, and engage in risky decision-making.

Moreover, TBI-induced disruptions in the default mode network (DMN), a network involved in self-referential thinking and internal mental processes, can exacerbate difficulties in concentration, attention, and maintaining social interactions (Zhou et al., 2012). These neural disruptions contribute to the cognitive and emotional impairments frequently observed in individuals with TBI.

2.3 Cognitive Impairments in TBI

Cognitive impairments are a hallmark of TBI, affecting multiple domains of functioning. The severity and nature of these impairments depend on the extent of the injury and the regions of the brain that have been damaged. Common cognitive deficits associated with TBI include impairments in executive functioning, memory, attention, emotional regulation, and social interactions.

2.4 Executive Functioning Deficits

Executive functioning refers to a set of higher-order cognitive processes that enable individuals to plan, organize, initiate, and monitor goal-directed behavior. Damage to the prefrontal cortex, which is critical for executive functions, often results in significant difficulties in these areas. Individuals with TBI may find it challenging to engage in tasks that require planning and organization. They may struggle with setting realistic goals, developing strategies to achieve those goals, and adjusting their behavior in response to feedback. Additionally, deficits in cognitive flexibility, the ability to adapt to changing situations, can hinder their capacity to switch between tasks or modify plans in response to new information.

2.5 *Impaired Memory, Attention, and Affective Regulation*

Memory impairments are another common consequence of TBI, particularly when the temporal lobe and hippocampus are affected. Individuals may experience difficulties with working memory, which involves holding and manipulating information over short periods, as well as long-term memory, particularly in the consolidation and retrieval of information. In addition to memory deficits, TBI often results in impairments in attention. The ability to sustain attention, divide attention across tasks, and filter out irrelevant information is compromised, making it difficult for individuals to focus on complex tasks or maintain attention over prolonged periods. Affective regulation, or the ability to manage and modulate emotions, is also frequently affected by TBI. Damage to the limbic system, including the amygdala and prefrontal connections, leads to heightened emotional reactivity and difficulties in controlling emotional responses. Individuals with TBI may exhibit mood swings, irritability, and even aggression, particularly when faced with stressful or frustrating situations (Šimić et al., 2021).

2.6 *Challenges with Emotional Regulation and Social Interactions*

Emotional regulation deficits following TBI can significantly impact social interactions. Individuals with TBI may have difficulty interpreting social cues, understanding the emotional states of others, and responding appropriately in social situations. These challenges are often linked to damage in the prefrontal cortex and its connections to the limbic system, which are responsible for the integration of emotional and cognitive information. Moreover, disruptions in the theory of mind—the ability to understand and predict the thoughts, feelings, and intentions of others—are commonly observed in individuals with TBI (Dennis et al., 2012). This can result in difficulties with empathy, perspective-taking, and maintaining positive social relationships. Impairments in emotional regulation and social cognition can lead to social isolation and difficulties in maintaining interpersonal relationships. These challenges are further compounded by deficits in communication skills, including language comprehension and expression, which may arise from damage to the temporal lobes and associated neural networks.

TBI has profound neurobiological and cognitive consequences that can disrupt an individual's daily functioning and quality of life. Damage to specific brain regions, such as the prefrontal cortex, occipital lobe, and temporal lobe, along with disruptions in neural networks, contributes to deficits in impulse control, decision-making, memory, attention, emotional regulation, and social interactions (Dennis et al., 2012). Understanding the neurobiological underpinnings of these impairments is essential for developing targeted interventions to support individuals with TBI in their recovery and rehabilitation.

3 TBI and Criminal Behavior

Over the years, research has explored the potential link between TBI and criminal behavior, shedding light on how neurobiological damage caused by TBI can increase the likelihood of antisocial behavior, aggression, and criminal activity. This section delves into the connection between TBI and criminal conduct, focusing on how deficits in impulse control, emotional regulation, and executive functioning may predispose individuals to engage in criminal activities. Additionally, we will review empirical data that supports this association.

3.1 The Link Between TBI and Criminal Conduct

Impulse Control Deficits

One of the key neurobiological consequences of TBI is impaired impulse control, which can have profound implications for behavior. The prefrontal cortex (PFC), the region of the brain most commonly affected by TBI, plays a critical role in regulating impulsivity and decision-making. Damage to the PFC often leads to impulse control deficits, where individuals may struggle to inhibit inappropriate behaviors or actions (Szczepanski & Knight, 2014).

In the context of criminal behavior, this lack of impulse control can manifest as increased aggression or engagement in risky and socially unacceptable activities. For example, individuals with TBI may find it difficult to suppress urges to act aggressively when provoked or in stressful situations. Their reduced ability to evaluate the consequences of their actions may lead to violent outbursts, physical altercations, or other forms of antisocial conduct that put them at risk of criminal involvement. Aggression and violent behavior are common among individuals with TBI, particularly when the injury affects regions involved in emotional regulation, such as the PFC and the limbic system.

Affective Dysregulation

Affective dysregulation refers to difficulties in managing and modulating emotions, and it is another major consequence of TBI. The injury often disrupts the brain circuits responsible for controlling emotions, particularly connections between the prefrontal cortex and the limbic system, which includes the amygdala. As a result, individuals with TBI may experience heightened emotional reactivity, mood swings, and difficulty regulating negative emotions like anger, frustration, or sadness (Weis et al., 2021).

This impaired emotional regulation can contribute to violent behavior or antisocial tendencies. Individuals with TBI may react disproportionately to minor frustrations or challenges, leading to aggressive or hostile responses. In the criminal justice context, these emotional regulation difficulties can manifest as domestic violence, assault, or other acts of violence. Additionally, individuals with TBI may struggle to form healthy interpersonal relationships, exacerbating their vulnerability to social isolation, substance abuse, and subsequent involvement in criminal activities (Matney et al., 2022).

Affective dysregulation can also contribute to antisocial behavior, which involves disregard for societal norms and the rights of others. Individuals with TBI may become less empathetic or have difficulty understanding the emotional cues of others, leading to behaviors that are more self-serving and less concerned with social consequences (De Sousa et al., 2010). This detachment from social norms can increase the risk of engaging in criminal conduct, including theft, vandalism, or more serious offenses like assault or murder.

Executive Dysfunction and Decision-Making

Executive dysfunction is one of the most significant cognitive deficits following TBI, especially when the prefrontal cortex is damaged. Executive functions refer to a range of higher-order cognitive processes, such as planning, problem-solving, inhibitory control, and decision-making. Damage to these processes can impair an individual's ability to evaluate risks, predict consequences, and make rational decisions (De Sousa et al., 2010).

For individuals with TBI, the inability to make sound judgments can lead to poor decision-making in various aspects of life, including interactions with others, choices about substance use, or participation in criminal activity. They may engage in behaviors that they might otherwise avoid if their executive functioning were intact. For example, a person with TBI may impulsively decide to steal or engage in physical violence without fully considering the legal or personal consequences of their actions. The lack of foresight and planning, combined with emotional instability, can increase their likelihood of committing crimes (Burt, 2019).

In addition, individuals with TBI may have difficulties with self-monitoring and correcting their behavior after making poor choices. This can lead to a higher risk of recidivism—the tendency to re-offend after being involved in the criminal justice system. Without the cognitive capacity to reflect on past mistakes and adjust future behavior, individuals with TBI may find themselves repeatedly engaging in criminal acts, further entrenching them in the criminal justice system (Chan et al., 2022).

3.2 Empirical Data on TBI and Criminal Behavior

Over the years, numerous studies have explored the relationship between TBI and criminal behavior, consistently demonstrating a correlation between the two. One of the most striking findings is the high prevalence of individuals with a history of TBI within the criminal justice system.

For instance, research has shown that 60%–80% of incarcerated individuals have a history of TBI, significantly higher than the prevalence of TBI in the general population. This overrepresentation of individuals with TBI in the prison population suggests a clear link between brain injury and engagement in criminal activities.

A 2014 study published in the journal *Neuropsychology Review* examined the cognitive and behavioral impairments in offenders with TBI and found that impulse control deficits, poor decision-making, and emotional dysregulation were common among this population (Kocka & Gagnon, 2014). These impairments were strongly associated with their involvement in violent and nonviolent criminal activities. The study also highlighted that individuals with TBI were more likely to engage in repetitive criminal behavior, further emphasizing the role of executive dysfunction in recidivism.

Another significant study, conducted by Fazel et al. (2011) and published in PLOS Medicine, revealed that individuals with TBI were significantly more likely to engage in violent criminal behavior compared to those without a history of TBI. The study suggested that the cognitive and emotional consequences of TBI contribute to an increased risk of violence, with particular emphasis on affective dysregulation and impulsivity as driving factors.

Furthermore, research has indicated that individuals with TBI are more prone to substance abuse, which is also a significant risk factor for criminal behavior. The combination of cognitive impairments from TBI and substance abuse can further impair judgment and increase impulsivity, creating a dangerous cycle of behavior that increases the likelihood of criminal acts.

Impulse control deficits, emotional dysregulation, and executive dysfunction—common outcomes of TBI—can contribute to aggressive or antisocial behavior, poor decision-making, and a higher risk of recidivism. Empirical data consistently shows a strong correlation between TBI and criminal involvement, particularly in violent offenses. Understanding the link between TBI and criminal behavior is critical for developing effective interventions, rehabilitation programs, and legal policies that take into account the neurological and psychological challenges faced by individuals with TBI.

4 Legal Implications of Traumatic Brain Injury (TBI)

Traumatic brain injury (TBI) is a significant condition that not only affects individuals physically, cognitively, and emotionally but also has profound legal implications. Given its potential to impair decision-making, impulse control, and emotional regulation, TBI can complicate legal proceedings, especially when determining culpability and appropriate sentencing for those who commit crimes. The impact of TBI on legal responsibility, sentencing outcomes, and the broader justice system raises critical questions about fairness and rehabilitation. This section will explore the legal consequences of TBI, focusing on how it affects legal responsibility, sentencing, and judicial decisions, as well as the potential for wrongful convictions or inappropriate sentencing due to undiagnosed or mismanaged TBI.

4.1 TBI and Legal Responsibility

One of the most significant legal questions raised by TBI is the issue of culpability—whether individuals with TBI should be held fully accountable for their actions. TBI can cause a range of cognitive and behavioral impairments, including difficulties with impulse control, decision-making, emotional regulation, and social judgment. These impairments may reduce an individual's ability to understand the consequences of their actions, leading to behaviors that are more impulsive, irrational, or even violent.

Determining the degree to which a person with TBI is culpable for their actions becomes a complex task for the legal system. In criminal cases, individuals with severe cognitive impairments may struggle to differentiate between right and wrong or to fully comprehend the nature of their behavior (Chan et al., 2022). This raises questions about their moral and legal responsibility and whether traditional standards of guilt and punishment should apply to individuals whose behavior is significantly shaped by neurological damage.

The concept of diminished responsibility or reduced capacity is often debated in legal cases involving individuals with TBI (Stevens, 2020). Diminished responsibility refers to a legal defense in which the defendant acknowledges committing the offense but argues that their mental state or cognitive impairments, due to TBI, reduced their ability to control their actions or understand their consequences. In such cases, courts may be asked to consider whether the individual's TBI affected their intent, premeditation, or awareness of their actions, potentially reducing their culpability. However, assessing the extent to which TBI impairs an individual's mental capacity can be challenging. Cognitive impairments vary widely depending on the location and severity of the injury. For instance, damage to the prefrontal cortex, which governs executive functioning and impulse control, may lead to significant behavioral changes that can directly contribute to criminal conduct. In contrast, damage to other areas, such as the temporal lobe, may lead to memory and emotional regulation problems that indirectly influence behavior.

Given these complexities, legal professionals and forensic experts must carefully evaluate the cognitive and neuropsychological impact of TBI on defendants to determine the extent of their responsibility for their actions.

4.2 Sentencing Outcomes and Judicial Decisions

The effects of TBI on cognitive functioning and behavior also influence judicial decisions related to sentencing. Courts are increasingly recognizing that individuals with TBI may require different approaches to punishment and rehabilitation compared to offenders without such impairments. The concept of sentencing mitigation—the reduction of a sentence based on extenuating circumstances—can play a critical role in cases involving TBI.

Judges may consider a defendant's cognitive impairments as a mitigating factor when determining the appropriate sentence (Thomaidou & Berryessa, 2024). For example, if an individual's TBI led to impulse control deficits or affective dysregulation, making them more prone to violent outbursts, the court may reduce their sentence on the grounds that their neurological condition played a significant role in their criminal behavior. In such cases, courts may also explore alternative sentencing options, such as rehabilitation programs, rather than imposing harsh prison terms. These alternatives may focus on mental health treatment, cognitive rehabilitation, and interventions aimed at improving impulse control and emotional regulation (Nakao et al., 2021).

Moreover, the recognition of TBI as a factor influencing criminal behavior has led to the development of specialized programs within the criminal justice system, including mental health courts and diversion programs that offer rehabilitation rather than incarceration. These programs aim to address the underlying neurological and psychological issues contributing to criminal behavior, offering individuals with TBI a pathway to recovery and reintegration into society rather than subjecting them to punitive measures that may not address the root causes of their behavior (Chan et al., 2022).

However, despite these mitigating approaches, there are ongoing debates within the legal community regarding how much responsibility individuals with TBI should bear for their actions. While some argue that significant cognitive impairments should lead to reduced sentences or alternative rehabilitation, others contend that even with a TBI, individuals should be held fully accountable if they were capable of understanding the consequences of their actions to some extent. This debate is particularly contentious in cases involving violent offenses, where the consequences of criminal behavior are severe. Courts must weigh the need to protect public safety with the recognition that cognitive impairments, particularly those related to TBI, may limit an individual's ability to control their behavior. Striking this balance can be particularly difficult in high-stakes cases involving serious crimes such as assault, murder, or sexual offenses.

4.3 Potential for Wrongful Convictions and Harsh Sentencing

One of the most troubling legal implications of TBI is the potential for wrongful conviction or harsh sentencing due to undiagnosed or mismanaged brain injuries. Many individuals with TBI may not be aware of the full extent of their cognitive impairments or may not have access to the appropriate diagnostic and legal support to address their condition. As a result, they may be treated as fully culpable for actions that were significantly influenced by their neurological impairments.

In cases where TBI is undiagnosed or not properly considered during legal proceedings, defendants may be unfairly sentenced to long prison terms or subjected to legal penalties that do not account for their cognitive limitations (Ezer et al., 2020). This is especially problematic in the case of recidivism, where individuals with undiagnosed TBI may repeatedly engage in criminal behavior without receiving the treatment or rehabilitation needed to address their underlying neurological issues. Additionally, individuals with TBI may be more susceptible to coercion, false confessions, or misunderstanding of legal proceedings, which can increase the risk of wrongful convictions. Cognitive impairments may affect their ability to communicate effectively with their legal counsel, understand the charges against them, or navigate complex legal processes.

The legal implications of TBI are profound, raising important questions about culpability, sentencing, and justice for individuals affected by cognitive impairments (Maas et al., 2022). As research continues to highlight the significant role that TBI plays in influencing behavior, it is crucial for the legal system to adapt and recognize the need for alternative sentencing, rehabilitation options, and comprehensive evaluations of cognitive impairments in defendants. Ensuring that individuals with TBI receive fair treatment within the justice system requires collaboration between legal professionals, forensic experts, and healthcare providers to ensure that justice is served in a manner that considers the complex interplay between neurological damage and criminal behavior. Without these considerations, there is a risk of wrongful convictions, harsh sentencing, and a failure to address the root causes of criminal conduct among individuals with TBI.

5 Case Studies: TBI in Legal Contexts

The case of Phineas Gage is one of the most famous and significant incidents in the history of neuroscience, offering profound insights into the relationship between brain injury, behavior, and personality. Gage, a railroad construction foreman in the nineteenth century, survived a severe traumatic brain injury (TBI) when a large iron rod was driven completely through his skull, causing extensive damage to his prefrontal cortex (PFC). This injury resulted in significant personality changes, which have since shaped our understanding of the role the prefrontal cortex plays in decision-making, impulse control, and emotional regulation. In the modern legal context, Gage's case provides a framework for understanding how damage to the PFC can impact behavior, responsibility, and culpability in criminal cases involving TBI.

5.1 Phineas Gage: The Iconic Case of Prefrontal Cortex Damage

On September 13, 1848, Phineas Gage was working on a railroad in Vermont when an accidental explosion of blasting powder propelled a 3-foot-long, 1-inch-thick iron rod through his skull. The rod entered under his left cheekbone, passed behind his left eye, and exited through the top of his skull, severely damaging the prefrontal cortex of his brain. Remarkably, Gage survived the injury and was able to speak, walk, and function physically in many ways similar to his pre-injury self.

However, those who knew Gage reported that his personality had dramatically changed. Prior to the accident, Gage was described as responsible, hardworking, and a capable leader. After the injury, he became impulsive, emotionally volatile, and prone to inappropriate social behaviors. His physician, Dr. John Harlow, famously remarked that Gage was "no longer Gage," highlighting the extent of the personality transformation. This drastic change in behavior underscored the critical role of the prefrontal cortex in governing higher-order cognitive functions such as impulse control, social behavior, and emotional regulation.

Gage's injury and its subsequent effects on his behavior were among the first pieces of evidence that specific regions of the brain, particularly the PFC, play a pivotal role in modulating personality and executive functioning. His case became a landmark in the study of neuroscience, and its lessons continue to be relevant in modern discussions of TBI and its legal implications.

5.2 The Role of the Prefrontal Cortex in Behavior and Decision-Making

The prefrontal cortex is one of the most evolutionarily advanced regions of the brain, responsible for executive functions such as decision-making, planning, problem-solving, emotional regulation, and impulse control. Damage to this region can result in significant impairments in a person's ability to behave appropriately in social contexts, make rational decisions, and control impulses (Kim & Lee, 2010).

Gage's injury is a classic example of how damage to the prefrontal cortex can result in disinhibition, which refers to a lack of restraint and the inability to suppress socially inappropriate behaviors. In Gage's case, he became more prone to impulsive actions, displayed poor judgment, and had difficulty adhering to social norms. This type of behavior is often seen in individuals with TBI that affects the prefrontal cortex.

In modern forensic psychology and neuropsychology, these symptoms are critical when assessing individuals with TBI in legal contexts. Damage to the prefrontal cortex can impair an individual's ability to make rational decisions, control aggressive impulses, and foresee the consequences of their actions, which has significant implications for culpability in criminal cases.

5.3 TBI and the Legal Context: Applying Gage's Lessons

Phineas Gage's case offers a lens through which to view the legal challenges posed by TBI, particularly in cases involving violent or criminal behavior. When the prefrontal cortex is damaged, as in Gage's case, individuals may exhibit impulsive behaviors, poor decision-making, and emotional instability, all of which can contribute to criminal conduct.

One of the key legal questions surrounding TBI, particularly involving damage to the prefrontal cortex, is the issue of culpability. How responsible is an individual for their actions if their brain injury significantly impairs their ability to make rational decisions or control their impulses? In many legal systems, there are provisions for diminished responsibility or diminished capacity defenses, where an individual acknowledges committing a crime but argues that their mental or cognitive state, due to factors like TBI, reduced their ability to control their actions or understand the consequences.

In cases of prefrontal cortex damage, such as those involving TBI, the argument for diminished responsibility is based on the understanding that executive functions like impulse control and decision-making are compromised. As seen in Gage's case, individuals with prefrontal cortex damage may struggle to inhibit inappropriate behaviors, leading to actions that they might not have committed had their cognitive functioning been intact. For example, impulsive acts of violence or criminal conduct may result from an individual's inability to regulate emotions or foresee the consequences of their behavior.

The case of Phineas Gage also raises important considerations for sentencing in criminal cases involving TBI. Judges may consider the extent of an individual's brain injury and its impact on their behavior when determining appropriate punishment. In such cases, courts may opt for sentencing mitigation, where the severity of the punishment is reduced due to the recognition that the defendant's cognitive impairments played a significant role in their criminal behavior.

For individuals with prefrontal cortex damage, courts may also consider alternative sentencing options focused on rehabilitation rather than punishment. Programs that offer cognitive rehabilitation, mental health treatment, and impulse control therapy may be more appropriate for individuals with TBI, particularly if their criminal behavior is directly related to their neurological impairments. The goal of such programs would be to address the underlying cognitive deficits that contributed to the criminal behavior, thereby reducing the likelihood of recidivism.

Gage's case also highlights the potential for miscarriage of justice in cases involving undiagnosed or untreated TBI. Many individuals with TBI may not receive proper neurological evaluations, leading to situations where they are convicted and sentenced without adequate consideration of their cognitive impairments. This can result in wrongful convictions or overly harsh sentences for individuals whose actions were significantly influenced by their brain injuries.

In the case of undiagnosed prefrontal cortex damage, individuals may be held to the same legal standards as those without such impairments, even though their ability to control their behavior is compromised. This underscores the importance of comprehensive neurological assessments in criminal cases, particularly for individuals with a history of head trauma or behavioral changes following an injury.

The case of Phineas Gage remains a cornerstone in understanding the relationship between brain injury and behavior, particularly the role of the prefrontal cortex in affecting impulse control, decision-making, and emotional regulation. In the legal context, Gage's case offers valuable insights into how TBI, especially involving the prefrontal cortex, can complicate questions of culpability, sentencing, and justice. By applying the lessons learned from Gage's injury, modern legal systems can better navigate the complexities of cases involving TBI, ensuring that individuals with cognitive impairments receive fair treatment and appropriate rehabilitation within the justice system.

6 Challenges in Legal Settings

Traumatic brain injury (TBI) presents significant challenges in legal settings, both in the diagnosis and recognition of the condition among criminal defendants and in the provision of appropriate treatment and rehabilitation. TBI can result in a wide range of cognitive, emotional, and behavioral impairments that directly influence an individual's capacity to make rational decisions, regulate emotions, and control impulses—factors that can contribute to criminal behavior. However, due to the complexities of diagnosing TBI and the often limited understanding of its neuropsychological impacts, many individuals with TBI are not properly assessed or treated within the criminal justice system. This section will explore the key challenges associated with TBI in legal settings, including difficulties in diagnosis and recognition, as well as the intervention and treatment issues faced by offenders with TBI.

6.1 Difficulties in Diagnosis and Recognition

One of the most significant challenges in legal contexts involving TBI is the misdiagnosis or late diagnosis of brain injuries in criminal defendants. TBI can have both immediate and long-term effects on cognitive functioning and behavior, but these effects are not always immediately apparent. Mild-to-moderate TBIs, in particular, may not present obvious physical symptoms and can go undetected for years. As a result, many individuals who suffer from TBI may enter the criminal justice system without a clear understanding of the ways in which their injury has affected their behavior (Bertozzi et al., 2019).

In cases where a defendant's TBI is not diagnosed early, they may be treated as though they are fully responsible for their actions, even though their cognitive impairments may have significantly influenced their behavior. Misdiagnosis can lead to wrongful convictions or inappropriate sentencing decisions, particularly in cases where impulsivity, poor decision-making, or aggressive behavior—common symptoms of TBI—played a central role in the criminal act.

For example, damage to the prefrontal cortex, which is responsible for executive functions such as impulse control and decision-making, can lead to increased risk-taking, emotional dysregulation, and aggression. Individuals with such damage may commit crimes as a direct result of their inability to regulate their emotions or control their impulses, yet without a proper diagnosis, their behavior may be misunderstood by the legal system. This raises concerns about fairness and justice, as defendants may be convicted and sentenced without the mitigating factor of their brain injury being properly considered.

Another major challenge in legal settings is the limited understanding of neuropsychological impacts by legal professionals, including judges, attorneys, and jurors. While advances in neuroscience have deepened our understanding of the relationship between brain injuries and behavior, this knowledge has not always been integrated into the legal system. Many legal professionals lack the training or expertise necessary to recognize the signs of TBI or to understand how cognitive impairments may influence behavior (Pernu & Elzein, 2020).

This gap in knowledge can lead to biased assessments of defendants with TBI, with their actions being judged based on standard legal frameworks that do not account for the cognitive and behavioral effects of brain injury. For instance, the legal system often operates under the assumption that individuals are fully capable of making rational decisions and understanding the consequences of their actions. However, in the case of individuals with TBI, these assumptions may not hold true, particularly when the injury affects areas of the brain responsible for judgment, impulse control, or emotional regulation (Weis et al., 2021).

Moreover, expert testimony regarding the effects of TBI can be difficult to present in court. The complex nature of neuropsychological impairments often requires specialized medical and psychological evaluations, which may not always be available or admissible in legal proceedings. Even when such evidence is presented, it may be misunderstood or undervalued by legal professionals who are unfamiliar with the nuances of TBI and its effects on behavior.

6.2 Intervention and Treatment Issues

Once a defendant with TBI is convicted, another significant challenge arises: the lack of specialized treatment programs for offenders with brain injuries. TBI requires tailored interventions that address the cognitive, emotional, and behavioral impairments associated with the injury. However, most criminal justice systems do not have the resources or programs necessary to provide comprehensive care for individuals with TBI. Instead, offenders with TBI are often placed in standard correctional facilities, where their cognitive impairments may not be properly addressed (Chan et al., 2022).

Without proper treatment, individuals with TBI are at higher risk of recidivism, as their cognitive and behavioral impairments may continue to influence their actions. For example, individuals with damage to the prefrontal cortex may struggle with impulse control, making them more likely to engage in risky or criminal behavior even after incarceration. Moreover, individuals with TBI may face additional challenges in prison settings, such as difficulty following rules, understanding instructions, or regulating their emotions. These challenges can lead to further disciplinary issues within the prison system, potentially exacerbating their legal and personal problems.

Specialized rehabilitation programs that address the unique needs of individuals with TBI, such as cognitive behavioral therapy, neurofeedback, or occupational therapy, could help reduce recidivism and improve outcomes for offenders. However, such programs are often unavailable or underfunded in many legal systems, leaving individuals with TBI without the support they need to successfully reintegrate into society.

In addition to the lack of specialized programs, there are numerous barriers to accessing appropriate rehabilitation for individuals with TBI in prison settings. These barriers include limited availability of medical care, a lack of trained staff, and the stigma associated with mental health and cognitive impairments within the criminal justice system. Many prisons do not have the resources to provide individualized treatment plans for offenders with TBI, and those with brain injuries may not receive the attention they need (Chan et al., 2022).

Prison environments are often not conducive to the rehabilitation of individuals with cognitive impairments. The stress, isolation, and rigid routines of prison life can exacerbate the symptoms of TBI, particularly emotional dysregulation and behavioral outbursts. Moreover, individuals with TBI may have difficulty understanding or complying with prison rules, leading to additional punishment or isolation, which further hinders their rehabilitation.

Furthermore, continuity of care is a major issue for individuals with TBI in the criminal justice system. Upon release, many offenders with brain injuries do not have access to the medical or psychological support necessary to maintain their rehabilitation, increasing the likelihood of re-offending. This lack of post-release care underscores the need for more comprehensive and sustained interventions that address the long-term effects of TBI.

7 Importance of Interdisciplinary Collaboration

The significance of interdisciplinary collaboration has grown in recent years, particularly in the exploration of the intricate connections between traumatic brain injury (TBI) and criminal behavior. TBI, defined as an external force–induced injury to the brain, can lead to substantial impacts on cognitive function, behavioral patterns, and emotional regulation. Consequently, these impacts may play a role in the manifestation of criminal behavior, underscoring the necessity for the convergence of neurology, psychology, and legal studies for thorough evaluation and intervention. Understanding these relationships will enable one to make truer assessments in terms of criminal responsibility, risk management, and rehabilitation and, indeed, open up and continue the pursuit of a just and fair legal process. Thus, the following section discusses the importance of interdisciplinary collaboration among neurologists, psychologists, and legal experts in handling complex problems of TBI and criminal behavior.

The field of traumatic brain injury (TBI) presents unique challenges that demand a multidisciplinary approach. TBIs often result in cognitive, emotional, and behavioral impairments, which can complicate both the clinical and legal understanding of an individual's actions. Neurologists bring expertise in identifying the extent and impact of brain damage through neuroimaging and other diagnostic tools. Psychologists, particularly neuropsychologists, contribute to understanding how such injuries affect cognitive function, emotional regulation, and behavior. Finally, legal professionals require this information to assess the individual's culpability, make informed legal judgments, and devise appropriate interventions.

In cases where TBI is implicated in criminal behavior, the consequences of inadequate collaboration between disciplines can be dire. A neurologist's understanding of the physiological effects of brain injury may be insufficient without a psychologist's insight into how these effects translate into behavioral patterns. Similarly, a legal professional may struggle to interpret the impact of a TBI on a defendant's behavior without input from both medical and psychological experts. By integrating these fields, professionals can offer a more comprehensive understanding of the factors contributing to criminal behavior, leading to more nuanced legal decisions that balance the need for justice with considerations of medical and psychological factors.

7.1 The Neurology–Psychology–Law Interface

Neurology's Role

Neurologists play a critical role in diagnosing and assessing the severity of TBIs. Using neuroimaging techniques such as MRI and CT scans, neurologists can visualize damage to brain structures and identify areas that are likely to affect behavior. For example, injuries to the frontal lobe—the part of the brain responsible for impulse control, decision-making, and emotional regulation—are frequently associated with increased aggression and impulsive behaviors, both of which can contribute to criminal acts. The neurologist's findings can help establish a biological basis for changes in the individual's behavior, providing crucial information for the legal system when determining criminal responsibility. In many cases, TBI victims may not have full control over their actions due to impairments in brain function. For example, if a defendant has suffered damage to the frontal cortex, they may struggle with impulse control and decision-making, leading to actions that are out of character or socially inappropriate. However, these findings alone are not enough to make legal determinations, which is where psychology comes into play.

Psychology's Role

Psychologists, particularly neuropsychologists, assess the cognitive and behavioral impact of TBIs on individuals. Through neuropsychological testing, they can measure cognitive deficits in areas such as memory, attention, and executive function. These assessments provide insights into how the brain injury is influencing behavior and how these impairments might relate to criminal acts. Psychologists also explore the emotional and social consequences of brain injuries. TBIs can lead to emotional dysregulation, increased irritability, depression, and anxiety, all of which can increase the likelihood of criminal behavior (Maresca et al., 2023). Additionally, preexisting personality traits or psychiatric conditions may interact with the effects of a TBI, creating a complex profile that demands psychological expertise to unravel. By interpreting these cognitive and behavioral changes in light of the neurological data, psychologists offer a crucial context for the legal system. This collaboration helps distinguish between deliberate criminal actions and those that may be the result of impaired cognitive control or emotional regulation, assisting legal professionals in making more informed decisions about culpability and sentencing (Maxwell, 2023).

The Role of Law
Legal professionals are tasked with interpreting the medical and psychological evidence presented by neurologists and psychologists in cases involving TBI. Their role is to balance the need for justice with an understanding of the potential mitigating effects of brain injury on behavior. This requires a nuanced understanding of both the law and the medical complexities of TBI, emphasizing the importance of collaboration across disciplines. Lawyers rely on the expertise of neurologists and psychologists to present a comprehensive picture of the defendant's mental and physical state. For example, in cases where a defendant has committed a violent crime, the presence of a TBI might warrant a diminished capacity defense, arguing that the defendant was not fully responsible for their actions due to brain damage. Similarly, expert testimony from medical professionals may influence the type of sentencing or rehabilitation options offered, focusing on treatment and rehabilitation rather than punitive measures alone. Moreover, legal professionals work closely with medical and psychological experts to ensure that the rights of defendants with TBIs are protected. This collaboration is essential for addressing ethical issues, such as whether an individual with severe cognitive impairments is competent to stand trial or make informed decisions about their legal defense. In such cases, interdisciplinary teamwork ensures that the legal process is both just and compassionate, taking into account the defendant's neurological and psychological state.

7.2 Comprehensive Assessment and Intervention

Interdisciplinary collaboration allows for more comprehensive assessments and interventions in cases involving TBI and criminal behavior. By integrating the perspectives of neurologists, psychologists, and legal professionals, it becomes possible to develop a holistic understanding of how brain injuries impact behavior and decision-making. This, in turn, leads to more informed legal decisions that consider the complexities of brain injury while ensuring public safety. For instance, when assessing a defendant with a TBI, neurologists can provide evidence of brain damage, psychologists can interpret how this damage affects behavior, and legal professionals can incorporate this information into their case strategies. This integrated approach can also extend to treatment and rehabilitation. Rather than simply punishing offenders with TBIs, an interdisciplinary team can develop targeted interventions, such as cognitive rehabilitation or behavioral therapy, to address the underlying causes of criminal behavior and reduce the risk of recidivism.

The intersection of traumatic brain injury and criminal behavior is a complex and multifaceted issue that requires the combined expertise of neurologists, psychologists, and legal professionals. Interdisciplinary collaboration is essential for developing a comprehensive understanding of how TBIs affect behavior and for ensuring that individuals with brain injuries receive fair and just treatment in the legal system. By integrating the knowledge and skills of these diverse fields, professionals can better assess criminal responsibility, devise appropriate interventions, and promote both justice and rehabilitation.

8 Addressing TBI in the Criminal Justice System

TBI can lead to cognitive, emotional, and behavioral changes that contribute to criminal actions, making it essential to conduct comprehensive assessments when offenders have a history of brain injury. These assessments, particularly early neuropsychological evaluations, are crucial in legal proceedings as they provide insight into the offender's mental state and behavior. By tailoring intervention strategies to consider both legal and neurological aspects and focusing on rehabilitation rather than punishment, the justice system can adopt more humane and effective approaches. This section looks into the need for comprehensive assessment in cases involving TBI and criminal behavior, emphasizing the importance of neuropsychological evaluations, rehabilitation over punishment, and exploring alternatives to incarceration to reduce recidivism.

8.1 Importance of Early Neuropsychological Evaluations in Legal Proceedings

Early neuropsychological evaluations play a vital role in understanding the connection between TBI and criminal behavior. These evaluations provide detailed information about cognitive deficits, emotional regulation issues, and behavioral changes that are often associated with brain injuries. In many cases, individuals with TBIs may exhibit impulsivity, aggression, or poor decision-making skills due to impairments in executive functioning. Without proper assessment, these behaviors may be misinterpreted as deliberate criminal intent rather than a consequence of brain injury.

Neuropsychological evaluations allow legal professionals to gain a deeper understanding of an offender's mental state. By identifying specific cognitive impairments, these assessments can inform the court about the defendant's ability to understand their actions and the consequences. For example, damage to the prefrontal cortex, which is responsible for impulse control and judgment, can impair an individual's ability to control aggressive or impulsive behavior. A neuropsychological assessment would reveal this deficit, helping legal professionals determine the extent to which the injury affected the offender's behavior.

Additionally, early evaluations are essential for assessing competency to stand trial. Defendants with severe cognitive impairments may not fully understand the legal process or be able to participate in their defense, raising ethical concerns about their ability to receive a fair trial. Neuropsychological assessments can provide the necessary evidence to determine whether an individual is competent to stand trial or whether they require special accommodations, such as modified legal procedures or the appointment of a legal guardian to assist with their defense.

8.2 Tailored Intervention Strategies Considering both Legal and Neurological Aspects

Once a TBI is identified, tailored intervention strategies that consider both legal and neurological aspects are necessary. Traditional legal approaches may not adequately address the needs of TBI-affected offenders, as they often focus solely on punishment without considering the underlying causes of criminal behavior. A comprehensive assessment allows for the development of interventions that target the specific cognitive and behavioral deficits associated with the brain injury, leading to more effective and just outcomes.

For example, cognitive rehabilitation programs designed to improve executive functioning and impulse control can be incorporated into an offender's rehabilitation plan. These programs may include cognitive behavioral therapy (CBT), which helps individuals recognize and change problematic behavior patterns, or occupational therapy, which focuses on improving daily functioning and decision-making skills (Nakao et al., 2021). By addressing the neurological aspects of the offender's behavior, these interventions can reduce the likelihood of future criminal actions, ultimately promoting public safety. Legal professionals can also consider alternative sentencing options that focus on treatment and rehabilitation rather than incarceration (Martínez-Garay, 2023). In cases where the offender's behavior is directly linked to a TBI, sentencing may involve placement in a specialized treatment facility where they can receive both medical care and psychological support. This approach acknowledges the impact of the brain injury while ensuring that the offender is held accountable in a way that promotes recovery rather than simply punishing them for behavior that may be beyond their control.

8.3 Rehabilitation over Punishment

The traditional punitive model of the criminal justice system may not be appropriate for individuals with TBIs, whose cognitive impairments and behavioral changes are often a direct result of their injury. Incarcerating individuals with TBI without addressing the root cause of their criminal behavior does little to prevent recidivism and can exacerbate their condition by placing them in environments that lack proper medical and psychological care (Chan et al., 2022). Rehabilitation, on the other hand, offers a more effective solution by focusing on addressing the underlying neurological and psychological issues that contribute to criminal behavior. Individuals with TBIs can benefit from rehabilitation programs that aim to improve cognitive functioning, emotional regulation, and social skills (Barman et al., 2016). These programs are designed to help offenders manage their symptoms and develop strategies to cope with the challenges posed by their brain injury, reducing the risk of future criminal behavior. Furthermore, rehabilitation programs can be tailored to the individual's specific needs. For instance, offenders with memory deficits may participate in memory enhancement training, while those with impulse control issues may benefit from programs that focus on improving self-regulation skills (Peckham & Johnson, 2018). By offering targeted rehabilitation, the justice system can provide more meaningful interventions that address the root causes of criminal behavior and promote long-term recovery.

8.4 Exploring Alternatives to Incarceration for TBI-Affected Offenders

Incarceration is often not the most appropriate solution for offenders with TBI. Prisons are typically ill-equipped to handle the complex medical and psychological needs of individuals with brain injuries, and incarceration can exacerbate the symptoms of TBI, leading to further cognitive and behavioral decline. Instead, the justice system should explore alternatives to incarceration that focus on rehabilitation and treatment.

One such alternative are diversion programs, which redirect offenders with TBIs away from the criminal justice system and into treatment programs. These programs allow individuals to receive the medical and psychological care they need while remaining under supervision. Diversion programs often include structured environments where individuals can work on improving their cognitive and emotional functioning, reducing the likelihood of re-offending. By focusing on treatment rather than punishment, diversion programs offer a more humane and effective approach to dealing with TBI-affected offenders.

Community-based rehabilitation programs are another alternative to incarceration. These programs provide offenders with the opportunity to receive treatment while remaining in their communities, allowing them to maintain social support networks and access local resources. Community-based programs often include therapy, vocational training, and social services, all of which help offenders reintegrate into society and reduce the risk of recidivism.

8.5 Emphasis on Rehabilitation to Reduce Recidivism

Rehabilitation-focused approaches are essential for reducing recidivism among TBI-affected offenders. Research has shown that individuals with TBIs are more likely to re-offend if their cognitive and behavioral issues are not addressed. By focusing on rehabilitation rather than punishment, the justice system can break the cycle of re-offending by providing individuals with the tools they need to manage their symptoms and lead law-abiding lives. In addition to reducing recidivism, rehabilitation can improve the overall well-being of individuals with TBIs. By addressing the neurological and psychological effects of brain injury, rehabilitation programs can help offenders regain control over their lives and make positive contributions to society (Matney et al., 2022). This not only benefits the individual but also reduces the burden on the criminal justice system and promotes public safety.

Comprehensive assessment and early neuropsychological evaluations are critical in addressing the complex relationship between TBI and criminal behavior. By tailoring intervention strategies to consider both legal and neurological aspects, the justice system can adopt more humane and effective approaches that prioritize rehabilitation over punishment (Baker et al., 2015). Exploring alternatives to incarceration and focusing on rehabilitation can reduce recidivism and improve outcomes for TBI-affected offenders, ultimately promoting a more just and compassionate legal system.

9 Key Takeaways

Over the past few decades, research has increasingly shed light on the relationship between TBI and criminal behavior. Individuals who suffer from TBIs often exhibit behavioral and cognitive impairments that may increase their likelihood of engaging in criminal activity. Understanding this complex relationship is critical for the development of more informed, compassionate, and effective legal interventions. This section highlights key takeaways regarding the influence of TBI on criminal behavior, critical lessons learned from the intersection of neuroscience and criminal justice, and a call to action for early diagnosis, interdisciplinary collaboration, and legal reforms to address TBI-related issues in the criminal justice system.

10 TBI Significantly Influences Behavior and Criminal Outcomes

Research consistently shows that individuals with a history of TBI are disproportionately represented in criminal populations. Studies estimate that between 25% and 87% of incarcerated individuals have sustained at least one TBI in their lifetime, a much higher rate than in the general population (Schneider et al., 2021). TBIs, particularly those affecting the frontal lobes—regions responsible for executive functions, impulse control, and decision-making—can lead to changes in behavior that may contribute to criminal conduct.

Key behavioral symptoms of TBI that may increase the likelihood of criminal behavior include impulsivity, aggression, emotional dysregulation, and poor problem-solving abilities (Maresca et al., 2023). These cognitive and behavioral impairments can make it difficult for individuals with TBI to control their emotions, assess the consequences of their actions, or conform to social and legal expectations. In addition, TBIs can exacerbate preexisting psychiatric conditions such as depression, anxiety, or substance abuse, further complicating an individual's ability to make sound decisions (Ahmed et al., 2017).

Importantly, the relationship between TBI and criminal behavior does not imply that individuals with TBI are inherently criminal. Rather, the impairments caused by brain injuries may make certain individuals more vulnerable to circumstances that can lead to criminal behavior. Socioeconomic factors, poor access to medical care, and lack of social support often intersect with the effects of TBI, creating a perfect storm of vulnerability for those affected (Haines et al., 2018).

11 Early Diagnosis and Intervention Are Crucial

Early diagnosis and intervention for individuals who have sustained a TBI are critical to improving both legal and personal outcomes. Timely diagnosis can help mitigate the negative consequences of TBI-related cognitive and behavioral impairments. However, TBIs often go unrecognized in many criminal justice settings, particularly among individuals from marginalized or disadvantaged backgrounds. Many incarcerated individuals may have sustained a brain injury without ever receiving a formal diagnosis or adequate medical treatment (Brain Injury Association of America, 2022).

Intervention can take several forms, including medical treatment, cognitive rehabilitation, and behavioral therapy. Providing these individuals with appropriate support systems and interventions can significantly reduce the likelihood of recidivism (Beaudry et al., 2021). Cognitive–behavioral interventions, for instance, can help individuals improve their impulse control, emotional regulation, and problem-solving skills, which can reduce the risk of future criminal behavior.

Additionally, the earlier these interventions occur—whether in the context of legal proceedings, incarceration, or probation—the better the outcomes for both the individual and society (Young et al., 2017). Legal professionals, mental health experts, and healthcare providers should be trained to recognize the signs of TBI and advocate for early screening in criminal justice populations.

12 Interdisciplinary Collaboration Is Essential for Effective Assessment and Treatment

Given the complex and multifaceted nature of TBI, an interdisciplinary approach is essential for the effective assessment and treatment of individuals with brain injuries, particularly within legal contexts. Neuropsychologists, forensic psychologists, neurologists, psychiatrists, and legal professionals must work together to develop comprehensive strategies that address the needs of individuals with TBI who become involved in the criminal justice system.

- **Assessment**: Neuropsychological assessments can help evaluate the cognitive and behavioral impairments associated with TBI. These assessments provide crucial information about how a brain injury may have contributed to a defendant's actions or mental state at the time of the offense (Traumatic Brain Injury (TBI), n.d.). Legal professionals should be trained to incorporate neuropsychological evaluations into their decision-making processes, ensuring that brain injuries are considered in criminal proceedings, sentencing, and rehabilitation plans.
- **Treatment**: Incarceration alone is unlikely to address the underlying issues related to TBI. Instead, a rehabilitation-focused approach that includes medical treatment, cognitive rehabilitation, and behavioral therapy is necessary (Matney et al., 2022). Interdisciplinary teams can collaborate to create individualized treatment plans that address both the neurological and behavioral aspects of TBI, aiming to reduce recidivism and promote rehabilitation.

4. **Need for Legal Reforms and Greater Awareness of TBI in Criminal Justice.**

Despite growing awareness of the impact of TBI on criminal behavior, the legal system often fails to adequately consider TBI in criminal proceedings. There is a need for legal reforms that recognize the significance of TBI as a mitigating factor in both sentencing and rehabilitation efforts (Matney et al., 2022).

For example, courts could mandate the use of neuropsychological assessments for individuals with known histories of TBI, particularly in cases involving violent or impulsive crimes (Torregrossa et al., 2023). Additionally, legal reforms could promote alternatives to incarceration for individuals with TBI, focusing on rehabilitation and treatment rather than punishment. This approach would be more aligned with the goals of justice and public safety, as untreated brain injuries may contribute to further criminal behavior upon release (Maresca et al., 2023).

Awareness campaigns within the criminal justice system—targeting judges, attorneys, police officers, and corrections personnel—are also necessary. These campaigns would emphasize the importance of understanding the cognitive and behavioral consequences of TBI and how they may influence criminal behavior (Williams et al., 2018). By increasing awareness and education, the criminal justice system can become better equipped to handle cases involving individuals with TBI in a fair, informed, and humane manner.

Critical Lessons

Behavioral consequences of TBI can contribute to criminal behavior, particularly when cognitive impairments related to impulse control and emotional regulation are present. Early diagnosis and intervention are crucial for improving outcomes in individuals with TBI who become involved in the criminal justice system (Maresca et al., 2023). Interdisciplinary collaboration among neuropsychologists, medical professionals, and legal experts is necessary for comprehensive assessment and rehabilitation. Legal reforms and awareness are essential for ensuring that the justice system recognizes and appropriately addresses the impact of TBI on behavior and criminal proceedings (Matney et al., 2022).

Call to Action

As the understanding of TBI and its role in criminal behavior continues to grow, it is imperative that society takes proactive steps to integrate this knowledge into legal practices, healthcare, and criminal justice policies (Williams et al., 2018). Early intervention, comprehensive assessment, and interdisciplinary collaboration are key to helping individuals with TBI lead more productive lives, reduce recidivism, and improve public safety (Maresca et al., 2023). Legal reforms that recognize the complexities of TBI and emphasize rehabilitation over punishment can contribute to a more just and effective criminal justice system, ultimately benefiting both affected individuals and society at large.

13 Conclusion

The link between traumatic brain injury (TBI) and criminal behavior is a complex and significant issue in forensic psychology and criminal justice. TBI can result in profound cognitive, emotional, and behavioral changes, which, depending on the severity and location of the injury, may increase the likelihood of impulsive, aggressive, or otherwise antisocial behaviors. The neurobiological and cognitive consequences of TBI often undermine impulse control, affect emotional regulation, and impair executive functioning, creating unique challenges in addressing culpability, recidivism, and rehabilitation for individuals with TBI within the criminal justice system. As we deepen our understanding of TBI and its impact on behavior, there is a pressing need for the legal system to adapt to better assess, accommodate, and address the needs of individuals affected by brain injuries. One of the critical insights from research on TBI and criminal behavior is the role of specific brain regions in governing behavior. The prefrontal cortex (PFC) is essential for regulating impulse control, decision-making, and social behavior. When this region is damaged, often as a result of a TBI, individuals may struggle to restrain impulsive actions, regulate their emotions, and make sound judgments. These impairments can directly lead to behaviors that are considered criminal, such as assault or theft, particularly in situations where the individual acts on impulse without considering the consequences. Damage to other areas, such as the temporal lobes, which are involved in processing emotions and social cues, can further exacerbate these behavioral challenges.

This neurobiological perspective helps explain why individuals with TBIs are at a higher risk of engaging in criminal activities. Studies show that individuals with TBIs, particularly those with prefrontal cortex damage, display higher rates of aggression, impulsivity, and risk-taking behaviors compared to the general population. This connection between brain injury and criminal behavior underscores the importance of recognizing TBI as a factor that can impair individuals' behavioral regulation and increase their vulnerability to criminal conduct.

The cognitive deficits resulting from TBI contribute significantly to the observed link between brain injury and criminal behavior. Executive dysfunction, a common consequence of TBI, affects individuals' ability to plan, make decisions, and control impulses. Individuals with impaired executive functioning may struggle to weigh the consequences of their actions, which can lead to poor decision-making in high-stress or high-stakes situations. Additionally, memory impairments can affect an individual's ability to recall information relevant to making responsible decisions, further increasing the risk of engaging in criminal behavior due to momentary lapses in judgment. These cognitive impairments do not merely increase the likelihood of criminal behavior; they also complicate the legal process. A person with TBI may have difficulty understanding the legal proceedings or may be unable to recall events accurately, which can lead to unfair assessments of their culpability and intent. Moreover, impairments in affective regulation—the ability to control emotions—may contribute to violent outbursts or aggressive behavior, which can result in charges that might not have occurred had the individual been able to regulate their emotions effectively. These cognitive and emotional impairments illustrate the urgent need for the legal system to consider TBI as a critical factor in assessing an individual's behavior and criminal responsibility.

In legal settings, the presence of TBI raises complex questions about culpability and responsibility. The traditional legal system often operates on the assumption that individuals have the mental capacity to understand and control their actions. However, for individuals with TBI, this assumption may not hold true. The neurobiological and cognitive impairments resulting from TBI can limit an individual's ability to make rational choices or inhibit impulsive behavior, thereby complicating the question of criminal intent.

Some legal systems have introduced concepts such as diminished responsibility or reduced capacity to address situations where an individual's mental or cognitive state influenced their actions. These defenses acknowledge that, due to TBI, the defendant may not have had full control over their behavior or a complete understanding of their actions' consequences. In such cases, the legal system may opt for sentencing mitigation or alternative forms of rehabilitation rather than traditional punitive measures. This approach aligns with principles of fairness and justice, recognizing that individuals with TBI may not be fully culpable for actions driven by their brain injury–related impairments.

The question of recidivism is also relevant when considering individuals with TBI in the criminal justice system. Without adequate treatment and support, these individuals are at a higher risk of repeated involvement in criminal activities. Sentencing alternatives that focus on rehabilitation and cognitive therapy could be instrumental in reducing recidivism among individuals with TBI, offering them a path to managing their impairments and reintegrating into society.

Providing access to neuropsychological assessments and cognitive rehabilitation programs in correctional settings could help address this treatment gap. Rehabilitation efforts could include cognitive behavioral therapy, neurofeedback, and anger management programs designed to help individuals with TBI improve their decision-making, impulse control, and emotional regulation. Specialized programs that target the cognitive and emotional challenges associated with TBI could reduce recidivism rates and improve long-term outcomes for affected individuals. Furthermore, it is essential to establish protocols for screening and diagnosing TBI among individuals entering the criminal justice system. Early identification of TBI can ensure that individuals receive appropriate interventions and that their cognitive impairments are considered during legal proceedings. This approach promotes a more just and equitable treatment of individuals with TBI, recognizing the impact of their injuries on their behavior and potential criminal actions.

The relationship between TBI and criminal behavior presents a unique challenge for the criminal justice system. The cognitive, emotional, and behavioral impairments associated with TBI can contribute to criminal conduct, complicate assessments of responsibility, and hinder rehabilitation efforts. Addressing this issue requires a shift in how the legal system understands and accommodates individuals with brain injuries, particularly those who have experienced damage to areas like the prefrontal cortex, which are critical for impulse control, decision-making, and emotional regulation. Incorporating neuropsychological insights into legal decision-making processes and providing specialized treatment programs within correctional facilities are crucial steps toward a more informed and just legal system. By recognizing the impact of TBI on behavior and offering appropriate support, the criminal justice system can promote fairer outcomes, reduce recidivism, and provide individuals with TBI the opportunity to rehabilitate and reintegrate into society. The legacy of cases like Phineas Gage reminds us of the profound influence that brain injuries can have on behavior and underscores the importance of addressing TBI in criminal behavior with both compassion and scientific understanding.

References

Ahmed, S., Venigalla, H., Mekala, H. M., Dar, S., Hassan, M., & Ayub, S. (2017). Traumatic brain injury and neuropsychiatric complications. *Indian Journal of Psychological Medicine, 39*(2), 114–121. https://doi.org/10.4103/0253-7176.203129

Arnsten, A. F. T. (2009). Stress signalling pathways that impair prefrontal cortex structure and function. *Nature Reviews. Neuroscience, 10*(6), 410–422. https://doi.org/10.1038/nrn2648

Baker, R., Camosso-Stefinovic, J., Gillies, C., Shaw, E. J., Cheater, F., Flottorp, S., Robertson, N., Wensing, M., Fiander, M., Eccles, M. P., Godycki-Cwirko, M., Van Lieshout, J., & Jäger, C. (2015). Tailored interventions to address determinants of practice. *Cochrane Library., 2015*, CD005470. https://doi.org/10.1002/14651858.cd005470.pub3

Barman, A., Chatterjee, A., & Bhide, R. (2016). Cognitive impairment and rehabilitation strategies after traumatic brain injury. *Indian Journal of Psychological Medicine, 38*(3), 172–181. https://doi.org/10.4103/0253-7176.183086

Beaudry, G., Yu, R., Perry, A. E., & Fazel, S. (2021). Effectiveness of psychological interventions in prison to reduce recidivism: A systematic review and meta-analysis of randomised controlled trials. *The Lancet Psychiatry, 8*(9), 759–773. https://doi.org/10.1016/s2215-0366(21)00170-x

Bertozzi, G., Maglietta, F., Sessa, F., Scoto, E., Cipolloni, L., Di Mizio, G., Salerno, M., & Pomara, C. (2019). Traumatic brain injury: a forensic approach: A literature review. *Current Neuropharmacology, 18*(6), 538–550. https://doi.org/10.2174/1570159x17666191101123145

Brain Injury Association of America. (2022, July 22). *Traumatic brain injury in corrections*. https://www.biausa.org/public-affairs/media/traumatic-brain-injury-in-corrections

Burt, C. H. (2019). Self-Control and crime: Beyond Gottfredson & Hirschi's Theory. *Annual Review of Criminology, 3*(1), 43–73. https://doi.org/10.1146/annurev-criminol-011419-041344

Chan, V., Estrella, M. J., Beaulieu-Dearman, Z., Babineau, J., & Colantonio, A. (2022). Protocol for a scoping review on rehabilitation among individuals with traumatic brain injury who intersect with the criminal justice system. *PLoS One, 17*(6), e0269696. https://doi.org/10.1371/journal.pone.0269696

De Sousa, A., McDonald, S., Rushby, J., Li, S., Dimoska, A., & James, C. (2010). Understanding deficits in empathy after traumatic brain injury: The role of affective responsivity. *Cortex, 47*(5), 526–535. https://doi.org/10.1016/j.cortex.2010.02.004

Dennis, M., Simic, N., Taylor, H. G., Bigler, E. D., Rubin, K., Vannatta, K., Gerhardt, C. A., Stancin, T., Roncadin, C., & Yeates, K. O. (2012). Theory of mind in children with traumatic brain injury. *Journal of the International Neuropsychological Society, 18*(5), 908–916. https://doi.org/10.1017/s1355617712000756

Ezer, T., Wright, M. S., & Fins, J. J. (2020, June 1). The neglect of persons with severe brain injury in the united states: An international human rights analysis. https://pmc.ncbi.nlm.nih.gov/articles/PMC7348445/

Fazel, S., Lichtenstein, P., Grann, M., & Långström, N. (2011). Risk of violent crime in individuals with epilepsy and traumatic brain injury: A 35-year swedish population study. *PLoS Medicine, 8*(12), e1001150. https://doi.org/10.1371/journal.pmed.1001150

Haines, K. L., Nguyen, B. P., Vatsaas, C., Alger, A., Brooks, K., & Agarwal, S. K. (2018). Socioeconomic status affects outcomes after severity-stratified traumatic brain injury. *Journal of Surgical Research, 235*, 131–140. https://doi.org/10.1016/j.jss.2018.09.072

Heatherton, T. F. (2010). Neuroscience of self and self-regulation. *Annual Review of Psychology, 62*(1), 363–390. https://doi.org/10.1146/annurev.psych.121208.131616

Kim, S., & Lee, D. (2010). Prefrontal cortex and impulsive decision making. *Biological Psychiatry, 69*(12), 1140–1146. https://doi.org/10.1016/j.biopsych.2010.07.005

Kocka, A., & Gagnon, J. (2014). Definition of impulsivity and related terms following traumatic brain injury: A review of the different concepts and measures used to assess impulsivity, disinhibition and other related concepts. *Behavioral Sciences, 4*(4), 352–370. https://doi.org/10.3390/bs4040352

Maresca, G., Lo Buono, V., Anselmo, A., Cardile, D., Formica, C., Latella, D., Quartarone, A., & Corallo, F. (2023). Traumatic brain injury and related antisocial behavioral outcomes: A systematic review. *Medicina, 59*(8), 1377. https://doi.org/10.3390/medicina59081377

Martínez-Garay, L. (2023). Evidence-based sentencing and scientific evidence. *Frontiers in Psychology, 14*. https://doi.org/10.3389/fpsyg.2023.1309141

Maas, A. I. R., Menon, D. K., Manley, G. T., Abrams, M., Åkerlund, C., Andelic, N., Aries, M., Bashford, T., Bell, M. J., Bodien, Y. G., Brett, B. L., Büki, A., Chesnut, R. M., Citerio, G., Clark, D., Clasby, B., Cooper, D. J., Czeiter, E., Czosnyka, M., . . . Zemek, R. (2022). Traumatic brain injury: progress and challenges in prevention, clinical care, and research. *The Lancet Neurology, 21*(11), 1004–1060. https://doi.org/10.1016/s1474-4422(22)00309-x

Matney, C., Bowman, K., & Berwick, D. (2022, February 1). *Rehabilitation and long-term care needs after traumatic brain injury*. Traumatic Brain Injury–NCBI Bookshelf. https://www.ncbi.nlm.nih.gov/books/NBK580075/

Maxwell, C. (2023). Criminal responsibility and human capacity: why impaired mental functioning affects moral culpability. *Psychiatry Psychology and Law, 30*(1), 4–11. https://doi.org/10.1080/13218719.2022.2114122

Nakao, M., Shirotsuki, K., & Sugaya, N. (2021). Cognitive–behavioral therapy for management of mental health and stress-related disorders: Recent advances in techniques and technologies. *BioPsychoSocial Medicine, 15*(1), 16. https://doi.org/10.1186/s13030-021-00219-w

Nolan, A., Hennessy, E., Krukowski, K., Guglielmetti, C., Chaumeil, M. M., Sohal, V. S., & Rosi, S. (2018). Repeated mild head injury leads to wide-ranging deficits in higher-order cognitive functions associated with the prefrontal cortex. *Journal of Neurotrauma, 35*(20), 2425–2434. https://doi.org/10.1089/neu.2018.5731

Peckham, A. D., & Johnson, S. L. (2018). Cognitive control training for emotion-related impulsivity. *Behaviour Research and Therapy, 105*, 17–26. https://doi.org/10.1016/j.brat.2018.03.009

Pernu, T. K., & Elzein, N. (2020). From neuroscience to law: Bridging the gap. *Frontiers in Psychology, 11*. https://doi.org/10.3389/fpsyg.2020.01862

Schneider, B. S., Arciniegas, D. B., Harenski, C., Clarke, G. J. B., Kiehl, K. A., & Koenigs, M. (2021). The prevalence, characteristics, and psychiatric correlates of traumatic brain injury in incarcerated individuals: An examination in two independent samples. *Brain Injury, 35*(14), 1690–1701. https://doi.org/10.1080/02699052.2021.2013534

Šimić, G., Tkalčić, M., Vukić, V., Mulc, D., Španić, E., Šagud, M., Olucha-Bordonau, F. E., Vukšić, M., & Hof, P. R. (2021). Understanding emotions: Origins and roles of the amygdala. *Biomolecules, 11*(6), 823. https://doi.org/10.3390/biom11060823

Stevens, G. P. (2020). 'My Brain Made Me Do It?' Reflections on the Role of Neuroscience in Assessing Criminal Responsibility – A South African Medico-legal Perspective. *Psychiatry Psychology and Law, 27*(2), 202–213. https://doi.org/10.1080/13218719.2019.1688131

Szczepanski, S. M., & Knight, R. T. (2014). Insights into Human Behavior from Lesions to the Prefrontal Cortex. *Neuron, 83*(5), 1002–1018. https://doi.org/10.1016/j.neuron.2014.08.011

Taing, A. S., Mundy, M. E., Ponsford, J. L., & Spitz, G. (2023). Traumatic brain injury alters the relationship between brain structure and episodic memory. *Brain and Behavior, 13*(6), e3012. https://doi.org/10.1002/brb3.3012

Thomaidou, M. A., & Berryessa, C. M. (2024). Bio-behavioral scientific evidence alters judges' sentencing decisionmaking: A quantitative analysis. *International Journal of Law and Psychiatry, 95*, 102007. https://doi.org/10.1016/j.ijlp.2024.102007

Torregrossa, W., Torrisi, M., De Luca, R., Casella, C., Rifici, C., Bonanno, M., & Calabrò, R. S. (2023). Neuropsychological assessment in patients with traumatic brain injury: A comprehensive review with clinical recommendations. *Biomedicine, 11*(7), 1991. https://doi.org/10.3390/biomedicines11071991

Traumatic Brain Injury (TBI). (n.d.). *National institute of neurological disorders and stroke*. https://www.ninds.nih.gov/health-information/disorders/traumatic-brain-injury-tbi

Weis, C. N., Webb, E. K., deRoon-Cassini, T. A., & Larson, C. L. (2021). Emotion dysregulation following trauma: shared neurocircuitry of traumatic brain injury and trauma-related psychiatric disorders. *Biological Psychiatry, 91*(5), 470–477. https://doi.org/10.1016/j.biopsych.2021.07.023

Williams, W. H., Chitsabesan, P., Fazel, S., McMillan, T., Hughes, N., Parsonage, M., & Tonks, J. (2018). Traumatic brain injury: A potential cause of violent crime? *The Lancet Psychiatry, 5*(10), 836–844. https://doi.org/10.1016/s2215-0366(18)30062-2

Young, S., Greer, B., & Church, R. (2017). Juvenile delinquency, welfare, justice and therapeutic interventions: A global perspective. *BJPsych Bulletin, 41*(1), 21–29. https://doi.org/10.1192/pb.bp.115.052274

Zhou, Y., Milham, M. P., Lui, Y. W., Miles, L., Reaume, J., Sodickson, D. K., Grossman, R. I., & Ge, Y. (2012). Default-mode network disruption in mild traumatic brain injury. *Radiology, 265*(3), 882–892. https://doi.org/10.1148/radiol.12120748

Neuropsychological Evaluation of Competency to Stand Trial

1 Introduction

Competency to stand trial (CST) is a fundamental principle in legal systems that ensures an individual's capacity to participate in their defense during court proceedings. The concept of CST rests on the belief that an accused must be able to understand the nature of the charges, comprehend the court process, and communicate effectively with legal counsel. This requirement safeguards the fairness of judicial proceedings, aligning with due process principles. However, determining competency is often complex, particularly when an individual exhibits cognitive impairments or psychiatric conditions that may undermine their ability to fulfill these responsibilities. This is where neuropsychological evaluations play a crucial role in providing an objective and comprehensive assessment of the individual's mental and cognitive faculties.

The neuropsychological evaluation of CST has become an essential component of forensic practice, particularly in cases where cognitive deficits or neurological disorders may interfere with the accused's ability to participate in legal proceedings. Neuropsychologists contribute valuable expertise in evaluating the cognitive, emotional, and behavioral functions that underlie competency. By integrating clinical procedures with legal standards, neuropsychologists assess reasoning abilities, factual understanding of legal concepts, and cognitive capacities that are critical for trial participation.

This chapter provides an in-depth exploration of the neuropsychological assessment of competency to stand trial, examining the criteria, procedures, and challenges associated with this complex forensic evaluation. It outlines the legal and psychological frameworks that guide CST determinations and illustrates the multifaceted role neuropsychologists play in evaluating competency in diverse clinical populations. Through case studies and an analysis of the tools and techniques used in CST evaluations, the chapter underscores the interdisciplinary nature of these

© The Author(s), under exclusive license to Springer Nature Switzerland AG 2025

K. J. Reddy, *Foundations of Criminal Forensic Neuropsychology*,
https://doi.org/10.1007/978-3-031-83771-5_12

assessments and the importance of incorporating neuropsychological data into legal decision-making processes.

1.1 Legal Foundations and Criteria for Competency to Stand Trial

The concept of competency to stand trial has its roots in both legal and psychological principles. Legally, CST is derived from the landmark US Supreme Court case *Dusky v. United States* (1960), which established the basic criteria for competency. According to the *Dusky* standard, an individual must have "sufficient present ability to consult with his lawyer with a reasonable degree of rational understanding" and "a rational as well as factual understanding of the proceedings against him." These criteria form the cornerstone of CST evaluations and are applicable across various legal jurisdictions, though specific standards may vary.

The legal criteria for CST require an evaluation of two primary domains: (1) the individual's capacity to comprehend and engage in the legal process, including an understanding of the roles of court personnel, the nature of charges, and potential consequences; and (2) the individual's ability to assist in their defense, which includes the capacity for logical reasoning, decision-making, and effective communication with legal counsel. A CST evaluation, therefore, must address both cognitive and emotional aspects of functioning to determine whether the accused meets these legal requirements.

1.2 Neuropsychological Concepts Underlying Competency

Cognitive functioning is central to CST evaluations, as competency depends on the individual's ability to understand and participate in legal proceedings. Neuropsychological assessments focus on specific cognitive domains that are critical for competency, including attention, memory, executive functioning, and reasoning abilities. Each of these cognitive functions plays a pivotal role in ensuring that an individual can grasp legal concepts and engage meaningfully in their defense.

For example, attention is essential for following courtroom proceedings and sustaining focus during legal consultations. Memory, particularly working memory, is crucial for retaining information about legal processes and past events that may be pertinent to the case. Executive functions, including planning, impulse control, and cognitive flexibility, are key for managing complex legal decisions and understanding consequences. Reasoning and problem-solving abilities are necessary for evaluating legal options and making informed choices.

In addition to cognitive abilities, neuropsychologists must also consider emotional and behavioral factors that may influence CST. Psychiatric conditions such as schizophrenia, mood disorders, and anxiety can impair judgment, insight, and communication skills, further complicating the assessment of competency. As such, a comprehensive neuropsychological evaluation of CST encompasses both cognitive testing and a thorough examination of the individual's emotional and psychological state.

1.3 Assessment Procedures and Tools

Neuropsychological evaluations of CST typically involve a combination of cognitive tests, structured interviews, and specific instruments designed to measure legal knowledge and reasoning abilities. Cognitive tests are used to assess core domains such as attention, memory, language, and executive functioning. These tests provide objective measures of an individual's cognitive strengths and weaknesses, which are then interpreted within the context of legal competency.

Structured interviews are used to gather information about the individual's understanding of the legal process, including their knowledge of court procedures, the roles of legal personnel, and the potential outcomes of their case. These interviews also assess the individual's capacity for rational decision-making and their ability to communicate effectively with their attorney.

In addition to cognitive and clinical interviews, specialized tools have been developed to assess legal knowledge and reasoning in CST evaluations. Instruments such as the Competence Assessment for Standing Trial for Defendants with Mental Retardation (CAST-MR) and the MacArthur Competence Assessment Tool—Criminal Adjudication (MacCAT-CA) are frequently used in forensic settings. These tools are designed to evaluate specific legal competencies, such as the individual's understanding of the charges, the potential penalties, and their ability to weigh legal options.

1.4 Challenges in Evaluating Competency

Evaluating competency to stand trial presents several challenges, particularly when dealing with individuals who have neurological or psychiatric impairments. One of the primary difficulties is differentiating between cognitive deficits that genuinely impair legal competency and those that may be exaggerated or feigned. The issue of malingering—deliberate fabrication or exaggeration of symptoms—can complicate the assessment process, requiring neuropsychologists to carefully interpret test results and clinical observations.

Moreover, neuropsychological evaluations must account for cultural, educational, and linguistic differences that may affect an individual's performance on standardized tests. These factors can influence cognitive functioning and legal understanding, making it essential for neuropsychologists to use culturally sensitive assessment tools and procedures.

The neuropsychological evaluation of competency to stand trial is a complex and interdisciplinary process that integrates cognitive, emotional, and legal considerations. By providing detailed assessments of an individual's cognitive and psychological functioning, neuropsychologists play a critical role in ensuring that competency determinations are made fairly and accurately. The integration of neuropsychological data into legal evaluations helps ensure that individuals with cognitive or psychiatric impairments receive appropriate accommodations and that the legal process remains just and equitable. Through case studies and empirical evidence, this chapter demonstrates the value of neuropsychological assessments in CST determinations and highlights the importance of interdisciplinary collaboration in forensic settings.

2 Legal and Clinical Foundations of CST

The concept of competency to stand trial (CST) is a cornerstone of criminal law, aiming to protect the rights of defendants by ensuring they have the cognitive and emotional capacities to participate in their defense. This concept was most notably defined in the landmark US Supreme Court case *Dusky v. United States* (1960), which set forth the foundational criteria for CST. According to the *Dusky* standard, a defendant must possess both a factual understanding of court procedures and a rational ability to assist in their defense. These criteria highlight the dual nature of CST determinations, which require both a clinical evaluation of cognitive and emotional functioning and a legal framework for defining competency. In this section, we explore the legal and clinical foundations of CST, emphasizing the intersection of law and neuropsychology and the crucial role neuropsychologists play in forensic competency evaluations.

2.1 Legal Foundation of Competency to Stand Trial

The *Dusky* case established the modern legal standard for CST by requiring defendants to demonstrate a certain level of understanding and reasoning ability to be deemed competent. Specifically, the *Dusky* standard mandates that a defendant should be able to comprehend the nature and objectives of the trial, including the charges against them, the roles of court personnel, and the potential outcomes of the proceedings (Fortunati et al., 2006). Additionally, the defendant must possess the capacity to communicate effectively with their legal counsel, weigh legal options, and make decisions in their own best interest. These criteria are integral to ensuring that defendants have a fair opportunity to participate in their defense and that the legal process maintains its integrity.

Legal standards for CST are intended to strike a balance between respecting the rights of the defendant and upholding the interests of the judicial system. CST evaluations seek to prevent situations where individuals with cognitive impairments or severe psychiatric symptoms are unfairly subjected to the rigors of a trial (Murrie et al., 2020). However, the application of CST standards can vary significantly across legal jurisdictions, with some regions adopting slightly modified criteria or additional requirements based on local laws. For instance, certain jurisdictions may include specific provisions for assessing defendants with intellectual disabilities or evaluating the risk of malingering—deliberate feigning of cognitive impairment for secondary gain. Despite these variations, the *Dusky* standard remains the most widely accepted guideline for CST assessments in the United States and has influenced similar standards internationally.

2.2 Role of Neuropsychologists in CST Assessments

The integration of neuropsychological expertise into CST evaluations reflects the complex nature of competency determinations, which require a thorough understanding of both cognitive processes and legal requirements. Neuropsychologists are uniquely qualified to assess the cognitive, emotional, and behavioral capacities underlying CST, as their training enables them to evaluate how brain function relates to behavior and legal competency (Hokkanen et al., 2020). Neuropsychological evaluations provide detailed insights into the specific cognitive abilities that are crucial for CST, such as memory, attention, executive functioning, and reasoning.

Memory and attention are fundamental to a defendant's ability to follow courtroom procedures, recall relevant details about the case, and engage in conversations with their legal team. Executive functions, including impulse control, planning, and flexibility in thinking, are necessary for making sound legal decisions and responding to complex questions during trial. Furthermore, neuropsychologists are skilled in assessing reasoning and problem-solving abilities, which are essential for a defendant to weigh legal options and collaborate with counsel effectively. By evaluating these cognitive domains, neuropsychologists contribute valuable data that inform the court's decision on CST, ensuring that competency determinations are based on objective, clinically sound evidence (Harvey, 2019). In addition to cognitive assessments, neuropsychologists consider emotional and behavioral factors that may impact CST. Psychiatric conditions such as schizophrenia, mood disorders, and personality disorders can significantly impair a defendant's insight, judgment, and ability to communicate. Neuropsychologists also assess for malingering using specialized tools to determine whether defendants may be exaggerating or fabricating symptoms. Given the high stakes involved in CST evaluations, the role of neuropsychologists in detecting malingering and differentiating genuine cognitive deficits from intentional misrepresentation is crucial to maintaining the accuracy and fairness of the evaluation process (Bosso et al., 2022).

2.3 Clinical Evaluation and Legal Standards in CST Determinations

CST evaluations exemplify the interdisciplinary nature of forensic neuropsychology, merging clinical assessments with legal standards to provide a comprehensive picture of a defendant's competency (Pirelli et al., 2011). Clinically, neuropsychologists use a range of assessment tools, including cognitive tests, structured interviews, and standardized competency measures, to evaluate the defendant's understanding and rational abilities. Cognitive tests assess specific domains such as memory, attention, language, and executive functions, while structured interviews gather information about the defendant's legal knowledge, ability to reason, and understanding of court procedures.

In addition to cognitive testing, neuropsychologists employ structured interviews that probe the defendant's understanding of key legal concepts, such as the charges against them, the roles of legal personnel, and the potential penalties they may face. These interviews are particularly useful for assessing the defendant's ability to make informed decisions and communicate effectively with their attorney, as they simulate the interactions and decision-making processes that the defendant will encounter in court. Specialized CST assessment tools, such as the MacArthur Competence Assessment Tool—Criminal Adjudication (MacCAT-CA), are commonly used to measure the defendant's factual understanding of legal processes, rational abilities, and capacity to weigh legal options (Pinals et al., 2006).

Legal standards, such as the *Dusky* criteria, provide a framework within which these clinical assessments are interpreted (Adjorlolo & Chan, 2016). Neuropsychologists must carefully evaluate how the defendant's cognitive and emotional capacities align with the legal requirements for competency, often translating clinical findings into language that is accessible to legal professionals. This process requires neuropsychologists to balance clinical rigor with the practical considerations of the legal system, ensuring that their findings are both scientifically valid and legally relevant. The collaboration between clinical and legal professionals in CST assessments underscores the importance of cross-disciplinary communication in forensic settings, as neuropsychologists and attorneys work together to ensure that competency determinations are informed, accurate, and just (Gbadebo-Goyea et al., 2012).

The legal and clinical foundations of CST reflect the complex interplay between law and neuropsychology in forensic practice. Rooted in the *Dusky* standard, CST determinations require defendants to demonstrate both a factual and rational understanding of court proceedings, ensuring that they are able to participate meaningfully in their defense. Neuropsychologists contribute to CST evaluations by assessing the cognitive and emotional capacities that underpin competency, providing courts with objective data on the defendant's ability to understand and engage in legal processes. Through clinical evaluations that include cognitive tests, structured interviews, and specialized competency tools, neuropsychologists bridge the gap between legal standards and individual cognitive functioning, ultimately supporting fair and equitable legal proceedings. The collaboration between neuropsychologists and legal professionals in CST assessments highlights the interdisciplinary nature of forensic neuropsychology and underscores the importance of integrating clinical expertise into the legal process.

3 Neuropsychological Concepts Underlying CST

Competency to stand trial (CST) is not simply a legal requirement but is grounded in cognitive and neuropsychological processes essential for fair and just legal proceedings. To fulfill the legal criteria for CST, defendants must possess the cognitive capacity to understand court proceedings, rationally assess information, and communicate effectively with their counsel. These requirements encompass multiple cognitive domains, including memory, attention, reasoning, and executive functioning (Adjorlolo & Chan, 2016). Each of these areas contributes uniquely to a defendant's ability to engage in and comprehend the legal process. This section delves into the neuropsychological foundations of CST, examining the cognitive domains most relevant to competency determinations and highlighting how deficits in these areas can compromise a defendant's ability to participate effectively in trial proceedings.

3.1 Reasoning and Decision-Making

Reasoning and decision-making are central to CST, as they enable a defendant to evaluate evidence, understand the implications of different legal options, and make informed choices. Reasoning allows defendants to understand abstract legal concepts, weigh information objectively, and assess potential outcomes based on logic rather than impulse. Neuropsychologically, reasoning is closely related to functions within the prefrontal cortex, particularly in areas associated with executive control and problem-solving. These regions help in organizing thoughts, forming judgments, and adapting to complex social situations like legal proceedings.

Decision-making, a related but distinct process, involves selecting from multiple options based on reasoning and understanding potential consequences. In CST assessments, decision-making is often evaluated through hypothetical scenarios, where defendants must choose between legal strategies or express preferences regarding court procedures (Adjorlolo & Chan, 2016). Deficits in these areas can severely compromise a defendant's capacity to stand trial. For instance, a defendant who struggles with decision-making may be unable to choose between a plea deal and going to trial, impacting their defense strategy and potentially altering the trial's outcome.

Cognitive impairments that affect reasoning and decision-making can stem from a range of neurological and psychiatric conditions. Traumatic brain injury (TBI), for example, often results in impaired reasoning, particularly when the prefrontal cortex is damaged (McAllister, 2011). Similarly, psychiatric disorders like schizophrenia can disrupt reasoning by introducing cognitive distortions or delusions, leading defendants to make irrational choices. Neuropsychological assessments are instrumental in identifying these deficits, using tests such as the Wisconsin Card Sorting Test (WCST) to assess abstract reasoning and adaptability. This information provides courts with critical insights into the defendant's capacity for rational decision-making and can inform judgments about their competency (Kopp et al., 2019).

3.2 Memory and Comprehension of Legal Concepts

Memory, particularly working memory, is essential for CST because it enables defendants to retain and process relevant information during legal proceedings. Memory deficits can compromise a defendant's ability to remember legal advice, recall events related to their case, and understand the progression of courtroom procedures. Working memory, a subset of memory related to the temporary holding and manipulation of information, is especially pertinent, as it allows defendants to keep track of details during trial sessions, apply advice from their counsel, and remember legal terminology (Cowan, 2013).

Deficits in memory can arise from various conditions, including Alzheimer's disease, dementia, and amnestic disorders. Defendants with impaired working memory may struggle to recall their own testimony or fail to remember key advice from their attorneys, impacting their ability to assist in their defense. Memory impairments are also common in individuals with substance use disorders, where memory retrieval and retention are compromised due to chronic neurochemical changes in the brain (Cascella & Khalili, 2024).

In CST evaluations, neuropsychologists assess memory through tests that measure both short-term recall and long-term memory storage. The Wechsler Memory Scale (WMS), for instance, is a widely used tool that evaluates verbal and visual memory, allowing clinicians to assess whether a defendant's memory capacity is sufficient to engage with legal processes. If significant deficits are identified, the neuropsychologist may consider how these impairments impact the defendant's understanding of court procedures and their ability to recall and communicate relevant facts (Soble et al., 2014). These findings are then presented to the court to help determine whether memory deficits impact CST.

3.3 Attention and Focus in Courtroom Settings

Attention and focus are critical for CST, as they enable defendants to follow courtroom discussions, absorb information, and respond appropriately. Attention is a complex cognitive function encompassing various components, such as sustained attention (the ability to maintain focus over time), selective attention (the ability to concentrate on relevant information while ignoring distractions), and divided attention (the capacity to process multiple sources of information simultaneously). Each of these aspects is relevant in a courtroom context, where defendants must listen to arguments, observe the proceedings, and consult with their legal team.

Attention impairments are common in several neurological conditions, including attention deficit hyperactivity disorder (ADHD), stroke, and certain forms of dementia. Additionally, psychiatric conditions such as anxiety and depression can impair attention by diverting cognitive resources toward distressing thoughts or emotions. In CST evaluations, neuropsychologists use tasks like the Continuous Performance Test (CPT) to assess sustained and selective attention, observing whether the defendant can maintain focus and filter out irrelevant stimuli (Roebuck et al., 2016).

Inadequate attention and focus may hinder a defendant's ability to follow complex legal arguments or respond to questions in a coherent manner, impacting their ability to assist in their defense. If a defendant frequently loses focus, forgets critical information, or becomes easily distracted, it may indicate an attention deficit that compromises CST. Neuropsychologists provide detailed assessments of attention and focus, informing courts about whether these deficits are significant enough to affect trial participation (Harvey, 2012).

3.4 Executive Functioning and Behavioral Regulation

Executive functioning encompasses a range of high-level cognitive processes, including planning, impulse control, self-monitoring, and cognitive flexibility. These skills are indispensable for CST, as they allow defendants to organize their thoughts, monitor their behavior, and respond adaptively to changing circumstances in court. Cognitive flexibility, for example, is essential for processing new information and adjusting one's perspective based on feedback, while impulse control helps defendants respond appropriately to challenging situations in court.

Deficits in executive functioning are prevalent in conditions such as TBI, frontal lobe lesions, and various psychiatric disorders. Individuals with impaired executive functioning may exhibit poor behavioral regulation, difficulty controlling emotional responses, or an inability to anticipate the consequences of their actions. In court, this can manifest as impulsive outbursts, poor decision-making, or a lack of situational awareness, all of which undermine a defendant's ability to engage appropriately with legal counsel and the court.

Neuropsychologists evaluate executive functioning using assessments like the Stroop Test, which measures cognitive flexibility and impulse control, and the Tower of London, which assesses planning and problem-solving abilities (De Assis Faria et al., 2015). Findings from these tests can provide insight into whether the defendant has the self-regulatory capacities needed for CST. If significant executive deficits are identified, the neuropsychologist may conclude that the defendant's impulsivity or lack of cognitive control compromises their ability to stand trial.

3.5 Implications for Neuropsychological Assessments in CST

Neuropsychological evaluations for CST require a comprehensive assessment of cognitive domains, each of which contributes to a defendant's ability to understand, engage in, and participate in court proceedings. By examining reasoning, memory, attention, and executive functioning, neuropsychologists provide objective data that reflects a defendant's capacity to stand trial (Nestor et al., 1999). Each cognitive domain plays a unique role in competency, and deficits in any of these areas can impair a defendant's ability to assist in their defense and engage meaningfully in the legal process.

Moreover, these assessments are critical for distinguishing between genuine cognitive impairments and malingering. Forensic settings often present incentives for defendants to feign cognitive deficits to avoid trial, and neuropsychologists play a key role in detecting such attempts. Specialized measures, such as symptom validity tests, are used alongside traditional cognitive tests to differentiate genuine impairments from feigned conditions. This ensures that CST evaluations remain objective and that the legal system can make informed decisions about defendants' competency (Determinations, 2015).

Through detailed neuropsychological assessments, clinicians contribute essential information to the legal system, helping ensure that CST determinations are based on empirical evidence. The comprehensive nature of these evaluations not only supports the fairness of legal proceedings but also underscores the importance of cross-disciplinary collaboration between neuropsychologists and legal professionals. By merging clinical insights with legal requirements, neuropsychological assessments uphold the integrity of CST evaluations and safeguard the rights of defendants with cognitive impairments (Schaefer et al., 2023).

4 Key Cognitive Abilities in CST

Competency to stand trial (CST) is built on the premise that a defendant possesses specific cognitive abilities that enable them to participate meaningfully in their legal defense. Central to CST are the capacities to reason, understand factual details of the judicial process, and perform basic cognitive tasks that support effective courtroom engagement. Neuropsychologists play a vital role in evaluating these cognitive domains, as deficits in any of these areas can compromise a defendant's ability to engage with their attorney, make informed decisions, and follow the proceedings. In this section, we examine the core cognitive abilities relevant to CST, exploring how reasoning ability, factual understanding, and general cognitive skills like attention, memory, and verbal comprehension support a defendant's competency in legal contexts.

4.1 *Reasoning Ability: Weighing Legal Options and Making Rational Decisions*

Reasoning ability is fundamental to CST, as it allows defendants to evaluate legal strategies, consider advice from counsel, and make informed decisions about their case. A competent defendant should be able to understand the potential consequences of different legal choices, such as entering a plea versus going to trial, and make decisions based on logic and comprehension of their situation (Helm et al., 2018). This capacity for reasoning encompasses both abstract thinking—understanding broader implications of decisions—and concrete thinking, such as grasping specific legal options and evaluating short-term consequences.

Neuropsychologically, reasoning is rooted in executive functioning processes that engage areas of the prefrontal cortex responsible for planning, judgment, and impulse control. Deficits in these areas, often due to traumatic brain injury, neurodegenerative disorders, or psychiatric conditions like schizophrenia, can result in impaired judgment and flawed decision-making (Rabinovici et al., 2015). A defendant with limited reasoning ability may struggle to understand complex legal concepts, weigh the risks and benefits of potential outcomes, or consider their lawyer's advice in a balanced manner. This can lead to impulsive or irrational decisions that jeopardize their case and, ultimately, the fairness of the trial.

Neuropsychological assessments of reasoning ability typically employ tests that evaluate judgment, problem-solving, and planning skills. Tools like the Wisconsin Card Sorting Test (WCST) assess cognitive flexibility, while the Iowa Gambling Task (IGT) evaluates decision-making under uncertainty. Through these assessments, neuropsychologists can identify whether a defendant's reasoning abilities meet the standard for CST, providing valuable information to the court regarding the defendant's capability to navigate their legal situation (Kirkish & Sreenivasan, 1999).

4.2 *Factual Understanding of Court Proceedings*

In addition to reasoning, CST requires a basic factual understanding of the legal process, enabling defendants to recognize the roles of key figures in the courtroom and comprehend the charges against them. This knowledge includes an understanding of the functions of the judge, jury, prosecutor, and defense attorney, as well as a grasp of legal terms and procedures. Without this foundational knowledge, defendants cannot engage meaningfully with their attorney or follow courtroom discussions, which are essential for fair trial participation.

A lack of factual understanding may result from cognitive impairments, developmental disabilities, or psychiatric conditions that limit a defendant's comprehension (Viljoen et al., 2002). For instance, individuals with intellectual disabilities may find it difficult to understand complex legal language or the roles of courtroom personnel. Similarly, individuals with severe mental illnesses may have distorted perceptions of the judicial process, impairing their understanding of courtroom dynamics and leading to misinterpretations of interactions with legal professionals.

To assess a defendant's factual understanding, neuropsychologists may use structured interviews and competency-specific tools like the MacArthur Competence Assessment Tool—Criminal Adjudication (MacCAT-CA). The MacCAT-CA, for example, is designed to assess a defendant's understanding of legal procedures, knowledge of courtroom roles, and ability to interpret relevant legal concepts. In cases where significant impairments are detected, neuropsychologists may conclude that the defendant's factual understanding is insufficient to meet CST standards, informing the court's decision about competency.

4.3 Basic Cognitive Talents: Attention, Verbal Comprehension, and Memory

Beyond reasoning and factual understanding, CST requires general cognitive talents, including attention, memory, and verbal comprehension, which support a defendant's ability to follow and engage in court proceedings. These basic cognitive skills form the foundation of effective courtroom participation, as they allow defendants to track courtroom discussions, respond appropriately to questions, and recall details about their cases. Neuropsychologists assess these skills to determine whether a defendant's cognitive abilities are adequate for CST.

Attention is a multifaceted cognitive process that enables defendants to concentrate on relevant information, filter out distractions, and maintain focus over extended periods. In courtroom settings, sustained attention is critical for following legal arguments, observing witness testimonies, and engaging in dialogues with counsel (Stevens & Bavelier, 2011). Deficits in attention, common in disorders like attention deficit hyperactivity disorder (ADHD) and schizophrenia, can impair a defendant's ability to follow lengthy court proceedings or respond appropriately during questioning.

To evaluate attention, neuropsychologists may use tests like the Continuous Performance Test (CPT), which assesses sustained focus and the ability to ignore irrelevant stimuli. Findings from attention assessments are important for determining whether a defendant can remain engaged throughout the trial process. If significant attention deficits are found, these may contribute to a determination that the defendant lacks the cognitive skills necessary for CST, particularly if the inability to focus impairs their understanding of court discussions or interactions with their attorney (Attention-Deficit/Hyperactivity Disorder, n.d.).

Verbal comprehension, or the ability to understand and interpret spoken language, is another crucial aspect of CST. Defendants must comprehend courtroom language, legal terms, and questions posed by the judge or attorney to effectively engage in their defense. Verbal comprehension is especially relevant in cases where complex legal terminology is used, as defendants need to understand their rights, the charges they face, and any plea offers or judicial instructions (Redlich et al., 2017).

Language deficits can hinder a defendant's ability to communicate with their legal team, respond to questions in court, and comprehend procedural instructions. Such deficits may stem from developmental language disorders, aphasia due to brain injury or stroke, or psychiatric conditions that affect the cognitive processing of language. Neuropsychologists assess verbal comprehension through tools like the Peabody Picture Vocabulary Test (PPVT) or the Wechsler Adult Intelligence Scale (WAIS) vocabulary subtests (Bell et al., 2001). If verbal comprehension impairments are identified, these may impact the defendant's competency, especially if communication challenges prevent effective collaboration with counsel.

Memory is essential for CST, as defendants need to recall details about their case, retain information from legal discussions, and remember courtroom instructions. Working memory, which involves temporarily holding and manipulating information, is particularly relevant, as it enables defendants to follow sequences of events in court, remember legal advice, and apply information in real time. Long-term memory is also important, as defendants may need to recall events that are pertinent to the case or their own prior statements.

Memory impairments are common in conditions like Alzheimer's disease, amnestic disorders, and TBI. Defendants with memory deficits may forget key information discussed with their lawyer or struggle to remember court dates, impacting their ability to assist in their defense. Neuropsychologists assess memory through standardized tests like the Wechsler Memory Scale (WMS), which evaluates both immediate and delayed recall, and tests that measure specific types of memory, such as verbal and visual recall. Memory assessment results are critical for determining whether a defendant has the retention capacity to engage effectively in trial, especially if memory impairments affect their ability to recall critical legal information (Ozer et al., 2016).

The cognitive abilities assessed in CST evaluations—reasoning, factual understanding, attention, verbal comprehension, and memory—are all vital for ensuring a defendant's competency to stand trial. Deficits in any of these areas can limit a defendant's capacity to understand their legal options, follow court proceedings, and communicate effectively with their counsel, leading to potential violations of their right to a fair trial (Redlich et al., 2017). By evaluating these key cognitive abilities, neuropsychologists provide courts with data that support informed, accurate competency determinations.

These assessments not only aid in understanding a defendant's cognitive capacity but also help identify accommodations that may facilitate participation in legal proceedings. For example, if a defendant has difficulty with memory retention, frequent breaks or simplified explanations may enhance their understanding of court processes. Neuropsychologists' findings are thus integral to supporting CST determinations that account for individual cognitive profiles, promoting fairness and equity within the legal system. Ultimately, the role of neuropsychologists in evaluating key cognitive abilities emphasizes the importance of aligning clinical insights with legal standards, ensuring that competency evaluations uphold the rights of defendants while respecting the principles of justice.

5 Neurological Impairments and CST

The intersection of neurology and forensic neuropsychology becomes particularly significant when assessing competency to stand trial (CST), as neurological impairments can fundamentally alter a defendant's ability to engage with the judicial process. Competency to stand trial requires that individuals possess adequate cognitive capacities to comprehend court proceedings, make rational decisions, and assist in their defense. However, various neurological and psychiatric conditions can impair these capacities, making CST evaluations challenging. This section examines how conditions such as dementia, traumatic brain injury (TBI), intellectual disabilities, and severe psychiatric disorders like schizophrenia and bipolar disorder influence CST. By understanding the specific cognitive deficits linked to these conditions, neuropsychologists and legal professionals can work together to ensure that CST evaluations are conducted with accuracy, fairness, and sensitivity to each defendant's neurological profile.

5.1 Dementia and CST

Dementia, characterized by progressive cognitive decline, is a common neurological condition impacting CST, particularly among older defendants (Emmady et al., 2022). As dementia advances, it impairs multiple cognitive functions essential for courtroom engagement, including memory, attention, reasoning, and language abilities (Emmady et al., 2022). These impairments affect a defendant's ability to understand legal proceedings, recall critical case details, and make rational decisions, all of which are foundational for CST. For instance, memory deficits associated with dementia may prevent a defendant from recalling the specifics of their case, recent conversations with counsel, or even recognizing courtroom personnel, all of which can impair courtroom engagement. Additionally, dementia-related difficulties in executive functioning compromise judgment and decision-making (Emmady et al., 2022). Such individuals may struggle to evaluate legal options, comprehend plea agreements, or follow instructions from their attorney. Advanced stages of dementia further exacerbate these impairments, leading to disorientation, confusion, and an overall inability to participate effectively in trial proceedings (Fong & Inouye, 2022).

Neuropsychological assessments in CST evaluations for defendants with dementia typically involve cognitive tests that assess memory, attention, language, and executive functioning. Tools like the Mini-Mental State Examination (MMSE) or the Montreal Cognitive Assessment (MoCA) are commonly used to gauge cognitive decline (Jia et al., 2021). By examining the extent and specific nature of the cognitive impairments, neuropsychologists can provide valuable insight into whether the defendant's dementia-related deficits render them incompetent to stand trial.

5.2 *Traumatic Brain Injury and CST*

Traumatic brain injury (TBI) can cause a wide range of cognitive impairments that impact CST, depending on the severity and location of the injury (Traumatic Brain Injury (TBI), n.d.). Individuals with TBIs may experience difficulties in memory, attention, processing speed, and executive functioning, all of which can influence their capacity to engage in courtroom proceedings effectively. The effects of TBI are often variable and can range from mild cognitive impairments to severe deficits that render a defendant unable to assist in their defense.

One of the most challenging aspects of TBI in CST evaluations is the presence of executive dysfunction, which affects judgment, planning, and reasoning abilities. Defendants with TBIs may struggle to understand legal strategies, make informed decisions, or predict the consequences of their actions (Legal and Medical Considerations in Traumatic Brain Injury Litigation–John Winer Site, 2021). In cases where TBI affects frontal lobe functions, the individual may display impulsivity or emotional instability, which can further complicate their ability to engage with counsel and interact appropriately in a courtroom setting.

Memory deficits, another common effect of TBI, can also undermine a defendant's competency. Impaired memory retention can lead to difficulties in recalling important details about the case or prior discussions with legal counsel, while deficits in working memory may prevent the individual from following complex courtroom dialogues (Whiting et al., 2006). Neuropsychological assessments for TBI-related CST evaluations often use a range of tests, including the Wechsler Memory Scale (WMS) and the Wisconsin Card Sorting Test (WCST), to determine the impact of TBI on memory and executive functioning. Findings from these assessments help inform CST determinations by clarifying the extent of cognitive impairment and its implications for courtroom participation (Kelso & Tadi, 2022).

5.3 *Intellectual Disabilities and CST*

Intellectual disabilities, characterized by limitations in intellectual functioning and adaptive behavior, present unique challenges in CST evaluations. Individuals with intellectual disabilities may have deficits in understanding legal concepts, communicating effectively with counsel, and comprehending the implications of various legal strategies. These limitations are especially critical when the defendant's intellectual functioning falls well below average, as cognitive impairments can hinder factual understanding and decision-making abilities (Boat et al., 2015).

For instance, defendants with intellectual disabilities may struggle to grasp complex legal terminology, understand their rights, or appreciate the roles of different courtroom participants. Their limited cognitive abilities can prevent them from comprehending plea bargains or following the chronological sequence of courtroom events, all of which are essential for CST. Additionally, defendants with intellectual disabilities may be highly suggestible, making them more vulnerable to influence from attorneys or other parties in ways that can compromise their defense.

In CST evaluations, neuropsychologists assess intellectual functioning through standardized intelligence tests, such as the Wechsler Adult Intelligence Scale (WAIS), as well as assessments of adaptive behavior. These evaluations provide a comprehensive view of a defendant's cognitive limitations, enabling the court to consider whether the defendant's intellectual disabilities preclude them from meeting CST criteria.

5.4 *Psychiatric Disorders and CST*

In addition to neurological conditions, severe psychiatric disorders, including schizophrenia and bipolar disorder, can significantly impact CST evaluations. These disorders often present with symptoms that impair rational thinking, perception, and emotional stability, which are crucial for courtroom engagement and decision-making.

Schizophrenia, for example, can impair CST through symptoms like delusions, hallucinations, and disorganized thought processes. A defendant experiencing persecutory delusions may believe that the court is conspiring against them, preventing them from cooperating with counsel or following courtroom procedures. Similarly, auditory hallucinations can distract defendants, making it difficult for them to concentrate during the trial or communicate effectively with their attorney. Disorganized thinking, another common symptom, can impair the defendant's ability to understand legal options, process information, and respond coherently to questions.

Bipolar disorder, especially during manic or depressive episodes, can also impair CST. Manic symptoms, such as grandiosity, impulsivity, and distractibility, may prevent defendants from participating in their defense constructively. For example, a defendant in a manic state may disregard legal advice, make impulsive decisions, or behave erratically in court. During depressive episodes, symptoms like low energy, concentration difficulties, and hopelessness may hinder the defendant's engagement with counsel and understanding of legal proceedings.

Neuropsychological assessments of psychiatric disorders in CST cases focus on evaluating cognitive and emotional stability, often using tools like the Brief Psychiatric Rating Scale (BPRS) or the Positive and Negative Syndrome Scale (PANSS) for schizophrenia. These assessments help determine whether the severity of psychiatric symptoms interferes with CST, guiding courts on how to proceed with defendants whose mental health conditions may impair their competency.

5.5 The Combined Impact of Neurological and Psychiatric Impairments on CST

Defendants with co-occurring neurological and psychiatric conditions may face compounded challenges in CST evaluations. For instance, a defendant with both TBI and bipolar disorder may experience severe cognitive deficits alongside mood instability, further complicating their ability to participate in court proceedings. Similarly, dementia patients with concurrent psychotic symptoms may struggle with both cognitive decline and altered perceptions of reality, making it challenging to engage in rational decision-making.

In such cases, neuropsychologists conduct comprehensive assessments that consider the combined effects of neurological and psychiatric impairments on CST. These evaluations may involve multiple testing sessions, interviews, and observations to capture the full scope of the defendant's cognitive and psychological functioning. By understanding the unique ways in which neurological and psychiatric conditions interact, neuropsychologists provide courts with nuanced insights into CST, promoting fair and accurate competency determinations.

Neurological and psychiatric impairments present unique challenges in CST evaluations, as deficits in memory, attention, reasoning, and emotional stability can interfere with a defendant's ability to participate meaningfully in their trial. Through comprehensive neuropsychological assessments, the impact of conditions like dementia, TBI, intellectual disabilities, schizophrenia, and bipolar disorder on CST can be systematically evaluated, ensuring that defendants with cognitive impairments are treated fairly within the legal system. By accounting for these impairments, courts and neuropsychologists work collaboratively to uphold the principles of justice, promoting a balanced approach to CST evaluations.

6 Common Assessment Techniques for CST

In the context of forensic neuropsychology, evaluations for competency to stand trial (CST) require carefully designed assessment techniques that can capture a defendant's cognitive and psychological readiness to participate in court proceedings. Neuropsychologists employ a mix of standardized cognitive tests, structured interviews, and specialized tools that gauge both general cognitive functioning and specific legal comprehension. These tools are instrumental in determining a defendant's ability to engage in their defense, understand legal procedures, and make informed decisions. This section outlines some of the primary methods and tools used to assess CST, emphasizing their relevance and application within the legal context.

6.1 Cognitive and Memory Tests

Cognitive assessments are a cornerstone of CST evaluations, offering objective measures of essential cognitive abilities like memory, attention, language, and executive functioning. These domains are crucial for understanding and engaging with court proceedings. Several widely accepted cognitive tests are employed in CST evaluations to gain insight into a defendant's mental functioning and capabilities.

Wechsler Adult Intelligence Scale (WAIS): The WAIS is a comprehensive test that evaluates multiple areas of cognitive functioning, including verbal comprehension, perceptual reasoning, working memory, and processing speed (O'Connor & Ammen, 2013). The WAIS is particularly useful for CST evaluations as it offers a thorough profile of a defendant's intellectual abilities. For example, lower scores in working memory and processing speed can suggest difficulties in following and retaining complex legal information, while challenges in verbal comprehension might indicate problems with understanding legal terminology or instructions from legal counsel.

Mini-Mental State Examination (MMSE): The MMSE is a brief screening tool that assesses general cognitive functioning across areas like orientation, memory, attention, language, and visual–spatial skills (Arevalo-Rodriguez et al., 2015). In CST contexts, the MMSE helps screen for cognitive impairments, such as those associated with dementia or intellectual disabilities, that might interfere with a defendant's ability to stand trial. Scores on the MMSE provide a quick overview of cognitive status, allowing neuropsychologists to determine if more extensive testing is warranted.

Wechsler Memory Scale (WMS): Given the centrality of memory in recalling details, events, and legal instructions, the WMS is often administered in CST evaluations. It assesses various aspects of memory, including immediate, delayed, and working memory (Towse et al., 2008). Deficits on the WMS can suggest difficulties in recalling prior conversations with counsel or retaining critical information discussed in court, which are essential for effective trial participation.

Trail Making Test (TMT): The TMT assesses attention, processing speed, and cognitive flexibility, skills vital for CST (Tsiakiri et al., 2024). Part A of the TMT requires the defendant to connect numbered dots sequentially, assessing processing speed and attention. Part B is more complex, involving alternation between numbers and letters, and measures cognitive flexibility and executive functioning. Poor performance on the TMT may indicate issues with focusing on court proceedings or shifting between different types of information, both essential for interacting with legal processes.

These cognitive and memory tests provide foundational insights into a defendant's cognitive strengths and weaknesses, informing whether their impairments may impact CST. Neuropsychologists interpret the results in conjunction with clinical observations, adding depth to the understanding of the defendant's cognitive functioning.

6.2 Structured Interviews

Structured interviews offer a qualitative approach to CST assessments by evaluating a defendant's understanding of legal processes and their ability to engage with counsel and court proceedings. These interviews are standardized yet allow for flexibility in response, helping neuropsychologists gain insight into both cognitive and emotional readiness for trial.

1. **MacArthur Competence Assessment Tool—Criminal Adjudication (MacCAT-CA)**: The MacCAT-CA is a widely used tool that assesses understanding, reasoning, and appreciation of legal issues (Bolt & Van Summeren, 2014). This structured interview evaluates the defendant's ability to understand the court proceedings, weigh the pros and cons of legal decisions, and appreciate the significance of their involvement in the trial. The MacCAT-CA includes scenarios where defendants are asked to interpret hypothetical legal situations, providing neuropsychologists with insights into reasoning abilities and how they may apply to real-life legal contexts.
2. **Fitness Interview Test-Revised (FIT-R)**: The FIT-R focuses on assessing three core aspects of CST: factual knowledge of court proceedings, understanding the nature and purpose of the trial, and the ability to engage with counsel (Roesch, 2016). This interview is tailored for defendants who may have limited legal knowledge, such as those with intellectual disabilities, and aims to identify whether they meet the minimum standards for CST. By probing specific aspects of courtroom roles and processes, the FIT-R ensures that neuropsychologists can clearly delineate any gaps in a defendant's legal understanding and readiness.

Structured interviews allow neuropsychologists to explore a defendant's cognitive and emotional responses in real time, providing valuable information on their ability to engage meaningfully with their defense team and the court.

6.3 Specialized Tools for Legal Understanding and Competency

Beyond standard cognitive tests and structured interviews, specialized tools have been developed to assess specific competencies related to legal understanding and reasoning. These tools delve into the intricacies of legal knowledge, decision-making, and comprehension that are particularly relevant for CST.

1. **Georgia Court Competency Test (GCCT)**: The GCCT is a specialized tool used to assess a defendant's knowledge of courtroom procedures, including the role of each courtroom participant, the charges faced, and possible consequences (Roesch, 2016). This test is particularly useful for defendants who may lack formal education or have cognitive limitations that impact legal comprehension. The GCCT scores a defendant's responses based on their factual understanding, helping neuropsychologists assess whether this knowledge meets the requirements for CST.
2. **Evaluation of Competency to Stand Trial-Revised (ECST-R)**: The ECST-R evaluates CST by examining a defendant's factual and rational understanding of court procedures and their ability to consult with counsel. It is unique in that it uses structured questions designed to minimize leading responses and maximize the accuracy of the defendant's answers (Evaluation of Competency to Stand Trial TM Revised, n.d.). The ECST-R also includes a malingering scale, helping neuropsychologists detect any exaggeration of symptoms or intentional deception, which is crucial in cases where a defendant may be attempting to feign incompetency.
3. **Inventory of Legal Knowledge (ILK)**: This assessment tool is designed specifically to identify malingering in CST evaluations. The ILK presents defendants with questions about legal processes, some of which are intentionally misleading or contain false information ("A Literature Analysis of the Inventory of Legal Knowledge.," 2021). A defendant answering these questions incorrectly at a high rate may indicate an attempt to feign incompetency, as genuinely competent individuals are likely to catch the misleading questions. By identifying malingering, the ILK allows for a more accurate assessment of CST.

6.4 Combining Results for Comprehensive CST Evaluations

Neuropsychological evaluations for CST rely on integrating information from cognitive tests, structured interviews, and specialized tools to create a comprehensive picture of a defendant's capabilities. The combination of these techniques helps neuropsychologists assess both general cognitive functioning and specific legal competencies while also identifying any inconsistencies in responses or indications of malingering.

For instance, if cognitive tests reveal deficits in memory and attention, but structured interviews show the defendant understands legal concepts well, this could suggest that the individual's cognitive impairments are not severe enough to impact CST. Conversely, if both cognitive tests and interviews indicate significant deficits, this may be a strong indicator of incompetency.

CST evaluations require a nuanced understanding of cognitive and psychological functions, and neuropsychologists play an essential role in using assessment tools to bridge the gap between legal standards and clinical insight. By employing cognitive tests, structured interviews, and specialized tools, neuropsychologists provide courts with reliable information on a defendant's competency. These assessments not only ensure a fair legal process but also uphold the integrity of the judicial system by preventing the trial of individuals who may lack the capacity to engage meaningfully in their defense.

7 The Role of Neuropsychologists in CST Evaluations

Neuropsychologists play a vital role in competency to stand trial (CST) evaluations by serving as a bridge between clinical insights and legal standards. Their expertise allows them to assess cognitive impairments and analyze psychological conditions that might impact a defendant's capacity to participate in legal proceedings. By offering comprehensive assessments, neuropsychologists provide courts with essential information about a defendant's mental state and cognitive abilities, which are critical in determining CST. This section delves into the specific roles and responsibilities of neuropsychologists in CST evaluations, the techniques they use, and the impact of their expert testimonies in court.

7.1 Neuropsychologists as a Bridge Between Clinical and Legal Standards

In CST evaluations, neuropsychologists are responsible for interpreting and applying clinical knowledge within a legal context. They utilize clinical assessments and tools to evaluate a defendant's cognitive and emotional readiness for trial, translating their findings into terms that align with legal requirements. CST evaluations typically hinge on a few core questions: Can the defendant understand the charges against them? Are they able to comprehend and respond to courtroom proceedings? And can they consult rationally with their legal counsel? By addressing these questions, neuropsychologists help clarify the defendant's current mental state and whether any psychological or cognitive impairments hinder their ability to stand trial.

The ability of neuropsychologists to bridge these domains is invaluable to the legal system, which relies on objective and clinically sound assessments to determine whether a defendant can participate in their defense meaningfully. This integration of clinical and legal standards ensures that CST determinations are comprehensive, taking into account both cognitive and psychological factors that might influence trial competency.

7.2 *Assessing Cognitive Impairments*

One of the primary responsibilities of neuropsychologists in CST evaluations is assessing cognitive impairments that may affect a defendant's competency. Key cognitive domains—such as memory, attention, reasoning, and executive functioning—are all essential to understanding courtroom proceedings and making informed decisions. Neuropsychologists utilize standardized cognitive tests, such as the Wechsler Adult Intelligence Scale (WAIS) or the Wechsler Memory Scale (WMS), to gauge a defendant's cognitive strengths and weaknesses. The results from these tests allow neuropsychologists to pinpoint specific impairments and evaluate their potential impact on CST.

For instance, deficits in memory could impair a defendant's ability to recall details about the incident or instructions from their attorney (Go, 2017). Similarly, problems with attention and processing speed might prevent them from following court proceedings closely or responding appropriately to questions. In cases where cognitive impairments are severe, neuropsychologists may recommend additional accommodations or adjustments in the trial process to ensure the defendant's rights are upheld. Ultimately, by identifying these impairments, neuropsychologists contribute to a clearer understanding of a defendant's capacity to participate in the legal process.

7.3 *Analyzing Psychological Conditions*

Psychological conditions, including mental illnesses and mood disorders, can also play a significant role in CST determinations. Disorders such as schizophrenia, bipolar disorder, major depressive disorder, and anxiety disorders can impact a defendant's ability to rationally engage in their defense. Neuropsychologists assess whether these conditions—especially when they involve symptoms like delusions, hallucinations, or severe mood dysregulation—may interfere with a defendant's understanding of court proceedings (Schaefer et al., 2023).

For example, a defendant with schizophrenia might experience hallucinations or paranoia, which can impede their ability to communicate effectively with their attorney or distinguish between real and imagined events. Bipolar disorder, particularly in its manic phase, may lead to impulsivity and poor judgment, affecting the defendant's capacity to make rational legal decisions (Mason et al., 2014). By understanding the psychological underpinnings of these conditions, neuropsychologists can make informed judgments about the defendant's state of mind and provide recommendations for treatment or medication that could improve their competency.

7.4 Providing Expert Testimony in Court

In addition to conducting CST evaluations, neuropsychologists often serve as expert witnesses, presenting their findings in court. Their expert testimony can provide judges and juries with a clearer understanding of the defendant's mental and cognitive status, often directly influencing legal decisions regarding CST (Ryan & Westera, 2018). This role as an expert witness requires neuropsychologists to translate complex clinical information into accessible, legally relevant terms that can be understood by nonexperts.

When testifying, neuropsychologists are typically asked to explain the results of their evaluations, detailing the cognitive or psychological impairments that may affect competency. They may also respond to questions from the prosecution or defense, clarifying how these impairments might impact the defendant's ability to understand the proceedings, communicate effectively with counsel, or make informed decisions. In some cases, neuropsychologists are asked to provide recommendations, such as treatment plans, competency restoration programs, or adjustments to courtroom procedures, that could help improve the defendant's capacity for trial participation (Denney & Wynkoop, 2000).

Through expert testimony, neuropsychologists not only support their evaluation findings but also advocate for fair treatment of defendants who may be unable to participate fully in their defense due to mental or cognitive impairments. Their testimony can be pivotal in cases where competency is contested, as it provides an objective, scientifically grounded perspective on the defendant's readiness for trial.

7.5 Supporting or Challenging Competency Claims

In the legal system, neuropsychologists' evaluations are used to either support or challenge claims of competency. In cases where the defense argues that a defendant is incompetent to stand trial, the neuropsychologist's findings may substantiate this claim by highlighting significant cognitive or psychological impairments. Conversely, if the prosecution questions a defendant's claim of incompetency, a neuropsychologist's assessment may reveal malingering or feigned symptoms, indicating that the defendant possesses the necessary abilities to stand trial (Sherman et al., 2020).

The role of neuropsychologists in detecting malingering is particularly important. Specialized tools, such as the Miller Forensic Assessment of Symptoms Test (M-FAST) or the Inventory of Legal Knowledge (ILK), help determine if a defendant might be exaggerating symptoms to avoid trial. Neuropsychologists interpret these test results in the broader context of the defendant's cognitive and psychological profile, offering courts a comprehensive assessment that can expose attempts at deception (Schaefer et al., 2023). This capacity to assess and identify malingering adds an important layer of credibility to the neuropsychologist's role, ensuring that defendants who attempt to evade trial through feigned incompetency are accurately identified.

7.6 *Influence on Legal Proceedings and Sentencing*

Neuropsychologists' assessments and testimonies often have a profound influence on the course of legal proceedings. When a defendant is found incompetent, they may be diverted to a competency restoration program, typically involving psychiatric treatment or cognitive training aimed at improving their mental state and readiness for trial. Neuropsychologists may also be involved in reassessing competency after these programs to determine whether the defendant has achieved sufficient improvement (Schaefer et al., 2023).

In some cases, a neuropsychologist's assessment can impact sentencing outcomes. For example, a defendant with significant cognitive impairments due to a neurological disorder, such as traumatic brain injury or dementia, may receive a reduced sentence or alternative sentencing focused on treatment rather than punishment. This reflects the understanding that defendants with severe cognitive or psychological impairments may lack full responsibility for their actions and require specialized interventions rather than traditional sentencing. By contributing nuanced, individualized assessments, neuropsychologists ensure that sentencing decisions consider the defendant's mental and cognitive status.

7.7 *Ethical Considerations for Neuropsychologists in CST Evaluations*

Neuropsychologists involved in CST evaluations must adhere to strict ethical guidelines to ensure that their assessments are objective, unbiased, and scientifically valid. This includes the careful selection of assessment tools, accurate interpretation of results, and clear communication of findings. Neuropsychologists must also consider the potential impact of their evaluations on the defendant's legal outcomes, remaining mindful of the ethical responsibility to provide fair and impartial assessments (Casaletto & Heaton, 2017).

Additionally, neuropsychologists face the ethical challenge of balancing their duty to the court with their obligations to the defendant. While they must provide an objective evaluation, they are also responsible for ensuring that the defendant's rights are protected throughout the process. This includes recognizing the defendant's vulnerabilities and advocating for fair treatment, especially in cases involving significant cognitive or psychological impairments (Moberg & Kniele, 2006).

Neuropsychologists serve a critical function in CST evaluations, combining clinical expertise with legal insight to assess a defendant's mental readiness for trial. Through cognitive assessments, psychological evaluations, and expert testimonies, they provide the legal system with reliable, scientifically grounded information that influences decisions on competency, treatment, and sentencing. Their role not only ensures a fair and just legal process for defendants with cognitive or psychological impairments but also reinforces the integrity of the judicial system by preventing trials that might otherwise violate defendants' rights. As the field of forensic neuropsychology continues to evolve, the role of neuropsychologists in CST assessments will remain indispensable to the intersection of law and mental health.

8 Challenges in CST Evaluations

Evaluating competency to stand trial (CST) is inherently complex and presents unique challenges, particularly when defendants exhibit intricate neurological or psychiatric conditions. Neuropsychologists must navigate these complexities to determine whether a defendant is capable of understanding and participating in their defense. This process requires a careful balance between clinical rigor and legal standards, and the challenges they encounter range from dealing with co-occurring conditions to identifying malingering, or feigned incompetency. This section delves into the multifaceted difficulties faced by neuropsychologists in CST evaluations, exploring specific clinical, ethical, and procedural hurdles that arise in these assessments.

8.1 Complex Neurological and Psychiatric Conditions

One of the primary challenges in CST evaluations is dealing with defendants who present with intricate neurological or psychiatric disorders (Freedman & Zaami, 2019). Many of these conditions, such as traumatic brain injuries (TBI), dementia, intellectual disabilities, schizophrenia, and bipolar disorder, significantly impair cognitive abilities that are essential for trial competency. Neuropsychologists must assess how these conditions impact a defendant's comprehension of legal proceedings, reasoning skills, and ability to consult with legal counsel.

1. **Traumatic Brain Injury (TBI)**: Defendants with TBIs may suffer from cognitive impairments, including memory deficits, impulsivity, and poor attention spans (Rabinowitz & Levin, 2014). These impairments can severely limit their ability to retain and understand information about court processes, posing a major obstacle in CST assessments. In some cases, TBI can also cause behavioral issues that make communication with counsel difficult, further complicating the determination of CST.
2. **Dementia**: Dementia-related cognitive decline presents another challenge, as defendants may struggle with memory retention, orientation, and decision-making. These deficits can fluctuate daily, making it difficult for neuropsychologists to assess competency consistently. Determining whether dementia significantly impairs CST often requires repeated assessments and careful documentation of cognitive changes over time (Assessing Cognitive Impairment in Older Patients, 2023).
3. **Schizophrenia and Bipolar Disorder**: Severe psychiatric disorders, such as schizophrenia or bipolar disorder, present unique difficulties in CST evaluations, especially when symptoms like delusions or hallucinations interfere with reality testing (Wy & Saadabadi, 2023). Defendants with schizophrenia, for instance, might hold delusional beliefs about the legal system or their attorneys, leading to mistrust or misunderstanding of court processes. In such cases, neuropsychologists must determine whether symptoms can be managed or if they represent a permanent barrier to competency.

8.2 Co-occurring Conditions and Dual Diagnoses

In many cases, defendants undergoing CST evaluations have co-occurring mental health conditions, such as intellectual disabilities combined with substance abuse disorders, or PTSD coexisting with TBI (National Institutes on Drug Abuse (US), 2020). Dual diagnoses introduce layers of complexity, as neuropsychologists must identify which condition contributes most significantly to competency issues. Additionally, substance use disorders can exacerbate cognitive impairments, influencing mood stability, memory, and overall comprehension of legal concepts. Addressing dual diagnoses requires neuropsychologists to adopt a comprehensive approach that evaluates the combined impact of these conditions on CST rather than examining each disorder in isolation.

Assessing CST in individuals with dual diagnoses can also present practical challenges, such as determining whether substance-induced symptoms are temporary or reflect a more permanent impairment. For example, a defendant may exhibit cognitive deficits due to recent substance use, which might improve with detoxification. Neuropsychologists must evaluate whether these impairments persist beyond acute withdrawal periods, as temporary symptoms do not necessarily impact long-term CST.

8.3 Identifying Malingering or Feigned Incompetency

Malingering, or the deliberate exaggeration of symptoms to avoid standing trial, is a significant challenge in CST evaluations. Some defendants may attempt to feign cognitive or psychological impairments to create the impression of incompetency, hoping this will exempt them from trial proceedings. Neuropsychologists are tasked with discerning between genuine impairments and deliberate deception, which requires specialized assessment tools, clinical expertise, and a thorough understanding of malingering tactics.

1. **Assessment Tools for Detecting Malingering**: Neuropsychologists use specific tools to detect feigned incompetency, including the Miller Forensic Assessment of Symptoms Test (M-FAST), which is designed to assess whether symptoms are exaggerated or fabricated (Miller Forensic Assessment of Symptoms Test TM, n.d.). The Test of Memory Malingering (TOMM) is another widely used tool that evaluates defendants' efforts in memory tests to determine the presence of malingering. These tools help neuropsychologists identify inconsistencies in responses, allowing them to differentiate between actual cognitive impairments and deceptive behaviors.
2. **Interpreting Behavioral Cues**: Beyond standardized tests, neuropsychologists observe behavioral cues that may suggest malingering. For example, defendants who exaggerate symptoms may display inconsistencies in behavior, such as claiming memory impairments yet recalling specific details with ease when questioned differently. Neuropsychologists analyze these behavioral patterns, cross-referencing test results to identify signs of deception (Casaletto & Heaton, 2017).
3. **Challenges in Confirming Malingering**: Despite these tools and techniques, confirming malingering remains challenging. Defendants may be well-versed in feigning symptoms, making it difficult to detect inconsistencies. Neuropsychologists must exercise caution, as falsely identifying malingering can lead to ethical concerns, especially if defendants actually suffer from cognitive or psychological impairments (Sherman et al., 2020). In cases where malin-

gering is suspected but not confirmed, neuropsychologists might recommend a period of observation or repeated assessments to gather additional evidence.

Balancing Ethical Responsibilities

CST evaluations also pose ethical challenges for neuropsychologists, who must balance their duty to the court with their ethical obligation to provide fair and accurate assessments. Neuropsychologists are ethically bound to consider the defendant's well-being, which means ensuring that assessments do not harm the defendant or exacerbate existing conditions. This responsibility requires them to conduct evaluations with respect and sensitivity, taking into account any vulnerabilities that might impact CST.

1. **Avoiding Bias**: Ensuring objectivity is crucial in CST evaluations. Neuropsychologists must avoid personal biases that could influence their assessment, particularly when they encounter challenging defendants who may not cooperate fully. They must adhere to evidence-based practices, maintaining impartiality to uphold the integrity of their findings.
2. **Protecting Defendant Rights**: Neuropsychologists are also responsible for safeguarding defendants' rights throughout the evaluation process. This involves explaining the purpose of assessments clearly and ensuring that defendants understand how the results will be used in court. In cases where defendants exhibit severe impairments, neuropsychologists may advocate for accommodations or alternative arrangements that respect the defendant's limitations.
3. **Informed Consent and Confidentiality**: Obtaining informed consent is another ethical consideration in CST evaluations. Defendants must be informed of the nature and purpose of the evaluation, and neuropsychologists must obtain consent before proceeding. Confidentiality is also critical, although limitations exist in forensic contexts where findings are shared with the court. Neuropsychologists must clarify these limitations to defendants, ensuring transparency throughout the assessment.

Procedural and Logistical Challenges

Neuropsychologists face various procedural challenges in CST evaluations, including limited access to prior medical records, insufficient time for assessments, and environmental factors that may interfere with evaluations. In many cases, defendants may not have complete medical histories, which limits neuropsychologists' ability to evaluate their cognitive and psychological conditions accurately. Without comprehensive records, neuropsychologists must rely heavily on observation and standardized assessments, which may not fully capture a defendant's mental state.

1. **Time Constraints**: Courts often impose strict timelines on CST evaluations, which can restrict the time neuropsychologists have for comprehensive assessments. This is particularly challenging when dealing with complex cases involving co-occurring conditions or suspected malingering. Neuropsychologists must work within these constraints while ensuring that their assessments remain thorough and accurate.

2. **Environmental Factors**: Evaluations conducted in correctional facilities or other nonclinical settings can be affected by environmental factors that disrupt the assessment process. For instance, noise levels, lack of privacy, and the presence of security personnel may distract defendants, influencing their responses. Neuropsychologists must account for these variables and adjust their evaluation techniques to mitigate the impact of environmental disruptions.

CST evaluations involve numerous challenges that require neuropsychologists to exercise clinical expertise, ethical judgment, and procedural flexibility. From dealing with complex neurological and psychiatric conditions to identifying malingering and balancing ethical considerations, neuropsychologists must navigate a host of obstacles to ensure that CST determinations are accurate and fair. The importance of these evaluations cannot be understated, as they ensure that defendants receive a just trial process that respects their cognitive and psychological limitations. As the field of forensic neuropsychology continues to advance, so too will the methods and strategies that neuropsychologists employ to overcome these challenges, ensuring that CST evaluations remain a reliable and integral part of the legal system.

9 Case Studies in CST Evaluations

Competency to stand trial (CST) assessments illustrate the critical role of neuropsychological evaluations in determining whether defendants possess the necessary cognitive and psychological abilities to participate in court proceedings. Below are three case studies that highlight different neurological and psychiatric conditions affecting CST. Each case study explores a specific scenario, details neuropsychological findings, and explains the legal outcomes to underscore how neuropsychologists contribute to informed and just decisions within the legal system.

Case Study 1: Traumatic Brain Injury (TBI) and CST
Scenario.

The defendant, a 35-year-old male, was involved in a physical altercation outside a bar, where he reportedly acted aggressively, causing injuries to another individual. Witnesses described him as appearing confused and highly reactive during the incident. This behavior was consistent with the cognitive and emotional difficulties he had experienced since a severe car accident 5 years earlier, which left him with a traumatic brain injury (TBI). The accident resulted in a prolonged hospitalization, followed by extensive rehabilitation to address his memory, impulse control, and attention issues. Despite this treatment, his recovery plateaued, leaving him with chronic cognitive and emotional challenges.

Since the TBI, the defendant has struggled to maintain stable employment and relationships, often forgetting important responsibilities and responding impulsively in social situations. Family members reported that he has exhibited mood swings and episodes of disorientation, further complicating his daily functioning.

His deficits in executive functioning, specifically around impulse control and emotional regulation, have led to several encounters with law enforcement, though none had previously escalated to formal charges.

During the CST evaluation, his neuropsychologist observed considerable difficulty in his ability to comprehend the charges against him. He frequently lost track of the conversation, sometimes responding to unrelated details and failing to remember key information, such as his attorney's advice or the procedural aspects of his trial. When asked to recount the events of the incident, he offered fragmented recollections, missing critical details and sometimes inserting events that may not have occurred. These cognitive lapses suggested impairments in both his working memory and long-term memory consolidation.

Additionally, when discussing his legal options, the defendant displayed a limited understanding of the potential consequences. His reasoning skills appeared compromised, with a tendency to simplify complex decisions and an inability to weigh long-term outcomes against immediate impulses. He reacted defensively to certain questions, and his short attention span hindered his ability to engage in sustained, logical conversation.

Neuropsychological Findings

Neuropsychological assessments reveal significant deficits in working memory, attention, and executive functioning, which play pivotal roles in a defendant's capacity to engage in legal proceedings. Specifically, with working memory, attention, and executive functioning. The defendant exhibited reduced working memory capabilities, shown by difficulties retaining information about his legal rights and the charges he faced. Sustained attention was notably poor, with frequent lapses during the evaluation that limited his ability to process information and understand complex legal terms. Executive dysfunction was evident in his inability to organize his thoughts logically or consider alternative viewpoints, impacting his potential responses to legal counsel. The neuropsychologist conducted the Wechsler Adult Intelligence Scale (WAIS) and the Continuous Performance Test (CPT) to assess these domains further. Results confirmed substantial cognitive impairments that hindered the defendant's ability to participate in his defense or comprehend key aspects of the legal process. Observations during structured interviews also revealed that his behavior could be erratic, with frequent memory lapses and impulsive responses.

Based on the neuropsychological findings, the court determined that the defendant was not competent to stand trial. The neuropsychologist's report indicated that his cognitive impairments severely limited his ability to understand the proceedings, communicate effectively with his attorney, or make informed decisions regarding his defense. The court ordered temporary guardianship and recommended cognitive rehabilitation and psychotherapy to address the TBI-related deficits. Further evaluations were scheduled to reassess his competency posttreatment.

Case Study 2: Schizophrenia and CST

Scenario.

The defendant, a 27-year-old male with a history of schizophrenia, was arrested after being found trespassing on private property and allegedly vandalizing several structures on the premises. The arresting officers noted that he appeared disoriented and highly agitated, speaking incoherently about being "followed" and "watched by unseen forces." He repeatedly referenced "hidden messages" in the buildings he vandalized, believing they held clues to an ongoing conspiracy involving government officials. Witnesses reported that he had spent hours wandering the property, making erratic gestures, and muttering to himself before the vandalism incident occurred.

Following his arrest, the defendant exhibited significant challenges in engaging with the legal process. During CST evaluations, he displayed symptoms typical of his diagnosis, including disorganized thinking, where his thoughts were fragmented and often disconnected from the questions asked. Attempts by his defense attorney to explain the charges and potential legal options were repeatedly interrupted by the defendant's paranoid delusions. He expressed a pervasive belief that his attorney was complicit in a conspiracy against him, interpreting even benign actions—such as note-taking or whispered conversations—as evidence of betrayal.

The defendant's paranoid ideation extended to all legal personnel involved in his case, including the judge and prosecutor. He maintained that they were part of a coordinated effort to punish him for "uncovering" secret information. This mistrust made it nearly impossible for him to effectively participate in his defense, as he refused to consider his attorney's advice and responded erratically to questions about the charges. His delusions appeared so ingrained that he struggled to distinguish reality from his beliefs, often weaving complex narratives about hidden messages and surveillance.

In addition, the defendant's cognitive symptoms included difficulties with sustained attention and logical reasoning. When asked about the events leading up to his arrest, his account shifted frequently, with factual inconsistencies and abrupt topic changes. He found it challenging to stay on topic, frequently diverting to discuss unrelated details or perceived threats. His impaired attention span further limited his ability to follow legal conversations, and he often seemed overwhelmed or lost when complex legal terms were used.

Given his compromised mental state, the neuropsychological assessment indicated significant impairments in his ability to understand and participate in the legal proceedings, suggesting that his competency to stand trial was deeply affected by his schizophrenia symptoms.

Neuropsychological Findings

The neuropsychological assessment focused on evaluating the defendant's reasoning, reality testing, and comprehension abilities. Findings included disorganized thinking, paranoid delusions, and impaired thinking and comprehension abilities. Interviews with the defendant revealed a pattern of thought fragmentation, characterized by incoherent speech and difficulty maintaining coherent ideas about his legal situation. Paranoid delusions significantly impacted his perception of the legal process and his attorney's role, leading him to believe that he could not trust legal advice. These symptoms hindered his ability to engage in rational discussions about his defense. Standardized tests, such as the MacArthur Competence Assessment

Tool—Criminal Adjudication (MacCAT-CA), showed profound deficits in his ability to rationally weigh legal options and understand the proceedings. The neuropsychologist concluded that the defendant's psychotic symptoms substantially impaired his ability to understand legal concepts and the consequences of his actions. Despite medication, his symptoms persisted, undermining his competency to engage effectively in his defense.

Following the neuropsychologist's recommendation, the court declared the defendant incompetent to stand trial, acknowledging the severity of his mental health condition. The court ordered a competency restoration program, including psychiatric treatment to stabilize his symptoms and reduce delusional thinking. The defendant was transferred to a mental health facility, where he received medication and therapeutic interventions aimed at restoring his capacity to participate in future legal proceedings. The case underscored the importance of mental health treatment in CST, with the court prioritizing therapeutic measures over immediate prosecution.

Case Study 3: Dementia and CST

Scenario.

An 80-year-old defendant with advanced dementia faced charges of financial exploitation. During CST evaluations, he struggled to recall basic details about the charges, his lawyer's name, or court processes. He repeatedly exhibited confusion about his surroundings, becoming visibly agitated when questioned about his legal responsibilities. His family history indicated progressive cognitive decline, suggesting a diagnosis of Alzheimer's disease.

Neuropsychological Findings

Cognitive assessments revealed pervasive deficits across several domains crucial for CST, specifically memory, attention and focus, decision-making, and comprehension.

Tests like the Mini-Mental State Examination (MMSE) showed substantial impairment in short-term memory, with the defendant frequently forgetting recent information about his case and his role in the legal process. The defendant displayed minimal attention span, struggling to follow instructions or maintain a conversation without becoming distracted or confused. Evaluations also demonstrated impaired judgment and decision-making, with the defendant failing to grasp the seriousness of the legal charges or the potential outcomes. His responses to simple legal questions indicated an inability to retain and process new information, thereby severely limiting his participation in his defense. Neuropsychological tests confirmed significant impairments, with the neuropsychologist concluding that the defendant's cognitive decline compromised his competency. The structured interview results were consistent with advanced dementia, indicating a likelihood of permanent cognitive limitations.

Based on the neuropsychologist's findings, the court determined that the defendant was permanently incompetent to stand trial. Given his age and the degenerative nature of his dementia, the court ruled that he would likely never regain competency. As a result, alternative legal measures were pursued, such as appointing a guardian to manage his affairs and considering case dismissal on humanitarian grounds. This case illustrated the challenges courts face with elderly defendants and emphasized the need for alternative resolutions in cases involving irreversible cognitive decline.

10 Interdisciplinary Collaboration in CST Evaluations

In the field of forensic neuropsychology, evaluating a defendant's competency to stand trial (CST) is a complex process requiring collaboration across various professional domains. CST evaluations are designed to determine whether a defendant possesses the cognitive, emotional, and psychological capacities necessary to engage in legal proceedings effectively. Given the multidimensional nature of these evaluations, an interdisciplinary approach is essential, involving professionals such as neuropsychologists, legal experts, medical practitioners, and social workers. This collaboration not only strengthens the validity of CST determinations but also upholds the principles of justice, ensuring defendants receive fair, equitable, and comprehensive assessments.

10.1 The Role of Neuropsychologists in CST Evaluations

Neuropsychologists serve as the primary experts in assessing the cognitive and psychological capacities of defendants in CST evaluations. They conduct detailed assessments of the defendant's cognitive functions, such as attention, memory, reasoning, and executive functioning, all of which are critical for understanding legal proceedings and participating in one's defense. Neuropsychologists employ standardized cognitive tests, clinical interviews, and observation to evaluate cognitive impairments, neurological conditions, or psychiatric disorders that may hinder a defendant's ability to comprehend and navigate the legal process.

In addition to evaluating cognitive capacities, neuropsychologists must also interpret their findings within a legal context, often collaborating with attorneys and judges to explain how specific impairments may impact CST. Their assessments provide insights into the defendant's ability to consult effectively with legal counsel, understand the roles of court personnel, and grasp the implications of charges and potential sentences. However, since neuropsychologists typically lack formal legal training, they rely on legal professionals to translate their findings into applicable legal standards, ensuring that their expert opinions align with jurisdictional requirements for competency.

10.2 Contributions of Legal Professionals

Attorneys and judges play a pivotal role in CST evaluations, as they bring the legal expertise necessary to frame neuropsychological findings within the bounds of legal requirements. Attorneys, especially defense counsel, advocate for a thorough competency evaluation when they suspect their client may lack the capacity to stand trial. They provide neuropsychologists with important background information, such as the defendant's prior criminal history, current charges, and any observed behaviors that may indicate cognitive or psychological impairments. Defense attorneys work closely with neuropsychologists to clarify legal questions and align assessments with court procedures, thereby ensuring that CST evaluations fulfill the specific needs of each case.

Judges, on the other hand, are responsible for making final determinations regarding competency based on expert evaluations. They interpret the neuropsychological findings provided by expert witnesses, often in consultation with additional professional insights, to make informed decisions that balance the rights of the defendant with the demands of justice. When defendants are found incompetent, judges may also seek recommendations from medical professionals on suitable treatments to restore competency, such as psychiatric care or cognitive rehabilitation. This legal oversight ensures that CST evaluations remain impartial, rooted in expert knowledge, and reflective of both clinical and legal standards.

10.3 The Medical and Psychiatric Perspective

Medical practitioners, particularly psychiatrists and neurologists, contribute vital insights into CST evaluations, especially in cases involving complex neurological or psychiatric conditions (Trapp et al., 2022). Many defendants present with medical histories of brain injury, dementia, intellectual disabilities, or psychiatric disorders like schizophrenia, which can significantly impair cognitive and emotional functioning. Medical experts assess these conditions, determine the severity of symptoms, and provide diagnoses that may influence competency determinations (Balogh et al., 2015). For instance, in cases involving schizophrenia, a psychiatrist's evaluation can identify specific symptoms such as hallucinations, delusions, or disorganized thinking that impact the defendant's understanding of court proceedings and ability to assist in their defense.

The involvement of medical professionals also extends to treatment recommendations when defendants are found incompetent to stand trial. Restoration of competency often involves a combination of psychiatric medication, cognitive therapy, and other rehabilitative treatments to address underlying impairments. Medical professionals work alongside neuropsychologists to monitor the progress of such interventions, reassessing competency as treatment proceeds. This partnership enhances the accuracy of CST evaluations, ensuring that defendants receive appropriate medical care aimed at restoring their legal capacities whenever possible.

10.4 Social Workers and their Contributions to CST Evaluations

Social workers play an invaluable role in CST evaluations by providing a holistic perspective on the defendant's social history, family background, and current living conditions (Cjesse, 2024). Social workers are often tasked with gathering collateral information, interviewing family members, and investigating the defendant's history of mental health treatment, substance abuse, or socioeconomic challenges. Their insights contribute to a comprehensive understanding of the defendant's life circumstances, which can help contextualize their cognitive and psychological impairments within broader social and environmental factors.

In cases where defendants require additional support, such as placement in a mental health facility or assistance in managing daily tasks, social workers advocate for their well-being, ensuring that evaluations address not only cognitive abilities but also the resources available for rehabilitation. Their involvement is especially crucial for defendants with intellectual disabilities or those experiencing severe socioeconomic disadvantages, as they help bridge gaps between the legal system and community support services (Lee et al., 2023). By collaborating with neuropsychologists, medical professionals, and legal representatives, social workers help create a more inclusive and equitable approach to CST evaluations.

10.5 Benefits of an Interdisciplinary Approach in CST Evaluations

The collaborative, cross-disciplinary approach to CST evaluations provides several key benefits. First, it allows for a comprehensive assessment of the defendant's capabilities, integrating cognitive, medical, social, and legal insights into a cohesive evaluation. Such an approach reduces the risk of oversight and ensures that each aspect of the defendant's functioning is considered, leading to more informed and accurate competency determinations. This is particularly important in cases where defendants present with complex conditions, as no single professional can assess the full spectrum of cognitive, emotional, and social factors affecting competency (Lee et al., 2023).

Interdisciplinary collaboration also enhances fairness and equity in CST evaluations. By bringing together diverse expertise, the evaluation process becomes more impartial and balanced, with each professional offering unique insights that collectively contribute to a well-rounded understanding of the defendant (Bendowska & Baum, 2023). This approach minimizes the likelihood of biased or incomplete assessments, ensuring that defendants' rights are protected and that justice is served in a manner consistent with ethical and legal standards.

Finally, collaboration fosters ongoing learning and adaptation within the field of forensic neuropsychology. As professionals from different disciplines work together, they exchange knowledge and develop a deeper understanding of each other's methodologies and challenges. This continuous learning process not only improves the quality of CST evaluations but also informs best practices, allowing professionals to refine their techniques and adopt new approaches to address evolving legal and clinical needs.

Interdisciplinary collaboration in CST evaluations is fundamental to ensuring accurate, fair, and thorough assessments of defendants' competency. By uniting the expertise of neuropsychologists, legal professionals, medical practitioners, and social workers, the evaluation process gains a comprehensive perspective that considers the full scope of the defendant's abilities and challenges. This cross-disciplinary approach not only strengthens CST determinations but also reinforces the values of justice and equity, ensuring that defendants are treated with dignity and respect throughout the legal process. As CST evaluations continue to evolve, the importance of interdisciplinary collaboration will only grow, fostering a system that upholds both the scientific integrity of neuropsychological insights and the ethical standards of the legal profession.

11 Conclusion

Neuropsychological evaluations play a crucial role in ensuring that the legal system treats defendants with fairness and accuracy, particularly when issues of competency to stand trial (CST) are involved. These evaluations bridge the fields of law and science, offering detailed insights into a defendant's cognitive and psychological functioning to determine their ability to participate meaningfully in legal proceedings. When defendants present with cognitive impairments or psychiatric conditions that could limit their understanding or engagement, neuropsychological assessments become indispensable. They help ascertain whether a defendant possesses the capacity to comprehend charges, navigate court proceedings, and effectively communicate with counsel—the foundational requirements for a fair and just trial.

These assessments operate at a unique intersection, combining clinical expertise with legal standards to create an evidence-based foundation for CST determinations. Neuropsychologists evaluate critical cognitive domains such as memory, attention, executive functioning, reasoning, and factual understanding, all of which are essential for legal competency. By aligning their findings with legal benchmarks, neuropsychologists ensure that defendants are evaluated on their actual cognitive and emotional capacities rather than assumptions or biases. Through this intersection of disciplines, CST evaluations help uphold the legal principles of due process, emphasizing that trials should be conducted only when defendants are equipped to understand and engage in their defense.

Neuropsychological evaluations are also instrumental in identifying and addressing specific cognitive and psychological impairments, which may include neurological conditions like traumatic brain injury, dementia, or intellectual disabilities, as well as psychiatric disorders such as schizophrenia or bipolar disorder. Recognizing the nuanced impacts of these conditions on competency, neuropsychologists provide courts with accurate, individualized insights into each defendant's capacities and limitations. This comprehensive approach allows for tailored recommendations, such as therapeutic interventions aimed at competency restoration or alternative legal measures for those deemed permanently incompetent. In doing so, neuropsychological assessments reinforce the court's obligation to conduct fair proceedings that take into account the full spectrum of a defendant's cognitive health.

As neuropsychology continues to evolve, advancements in research and technology hold significant promise for improving the accuracy and effectiveness of CST evaluations. Emerging tools, such as neuroimaging and digital cognitive assessments, may allow for more precise identification of cognitive impairments and more efficient competency evaluations. Additionally, expanding research on the neural underpinnings of legal decision-making and cognitive functioning will deepen our understanding of competency, potentially leading to new guidelines and frameworks that better align with evolving scientific knowledge. These advancements will likely enhance the reliability of CST assessments, ensuring that competency determinations are based on the most current scientific insights.

Ultimately, the integration of neuropsychological expertise in CST evaluations upholds the ideals of justice, equity, and accuracy in the courtroom. By providing objective assessments of defendants' mental and cognitive capacities, neuropsychologists help prevent wrongful trials of individuals unable to fully engage in their defense. Their contributions promote a legal system that respects the rights of all individuals, particularly those facing cognitive or psychiatric challenges. As forensic neuropsychology continues to advance, CST evaluations will not only refine legal outcomes but also contribute to a more just and humane approach to law, one that respects the cognitive realities of each defendant while preserving the integrity of the judicial process. In this way, neuropsychological evaluations remain essential for both protecting individual rights and ensuring the ethical administration of justice.

References

A literature analysis of the inventory of legal Knowledge. (2021). *The Journal of the American Academy of Psychiatry and the Law, 49*(1), 87–95. https://doi.org/10.29158/jaapl.200042-20

Adjorlolo, S., & Chan, H. C. (2016). Determination of competency to stand trial (fitness to plead): An exploratory study in Hong Kong. *Psychiatry Psychology and Law, 24*(2), 205–222. https://doi.org/10.1080/13218719.2016.1247417

Arevalo-Rodriguez, I., Smailagic, N., Figuls, M. R. I., Ciapponi, A., Sanchez-Perez, E., Giannakou, A., Pedraza, O. L., Cosp, X. B., & Cullum, S. (2015). Mini-mental state examination (MMSE) for the detection of Alzheimer's disease and other dementias in people with mild cognitive impairment (MCI). *Cochrane Library*. https://doi.org/10.1002/14651858.cd010783.pub2

Assessing Cognitive Impairment in Older Patients. (2023, April 16). *National institute on aging*. https://www.nia.nih.gov/health/health-care-professionals-information/assessing-cognitive-impairment-older-patients

Attention-Deficit/Hyperactivity Disorder. (n.d.). *National institute of mental health (NIMH)*. https://www.nimh.nih.gov/health/topics/attention-deficit-hyperactivity-disorder-adhd

Balogh, E. P., Miller, B. T., & Ball, J. R. (2015, December 29). *The diagnostic process*. Improving Diagnosis in Health Care–NCBI Bookshelf. https://www.ncbi.nlm.nih.gov/books/NBK338593/

Bell, N. L., Lassiter, K. S., Matthews, T. D., & Hutchinson, M. B. (2001). Comparison of the Peabody picture vocabulary test—Third edition and Wechsler adult intelligence scale—Third edition with university students. *Journal of Clinical Psychology, 57*(3), 417–422. https://doi.org/10.1002/jclp.1024

Bendowska, A., & Baum, E. (2023). The significance of cooperation in interdisciplinary health care teams as perceived by polish medical students. *International Journal of Environmental Research and Public Health, 20*(2), 954. https://doi.org/10.3390/ijerph20020954

Boat, T. F., Wu, J. T., Disorders, C. T. E. T. S. S. I. D. P. F. C. W. M., Families, B. O. C. Y. A., & Education, D. O. B. a. S. S. A. (2015, October 28). *Clinical characteristics of intellectual disabilities*. Mental Disorders and Disabilities Among Low-Income Children–NCBI Bookshelf. https://www.ncbi.nlm.nih.gov/books/NBK332877/

Bolt, I. L. L. E., & Van Summeren, M. J. H. (2014). Competence assessment in minors, illustrated by the case of bariatric surgery for morbidly obese children. *Best Practice & Research Clinical Gastroenterology, 28*(2), 293–302. https://doi.org/10.1016/j.bpg.2014.02.006

Bosso, T., Vischia, F., Keller, R., Vai, D., Imperiale, D., & Vercelli, A. (2022). A case report and literature review of cognitive malingering and psychopathology. *Frontiers in Psychiatry, 13*. https://doi.org/10.3389/fpsyt.2022.981475

Casaletto, K. B., & Heaton, R. K. (2017). Neuropsychological assessment: Past and future. *Journal of the International Neuropsychological Society, 23*(9–10), 778–790. https://doi.org/10.1017/s1355617717001060

Cascella, M., & Khalili, Y. A. (2024, June 8). *Short-term memory impairment*. StatPearls–NCBI Bookshelf. https://www.ncbi.nlm.nih.gov/books/NBK545136/

Cjesse. (2024, June 21). Social work and social justice: The role of social workers. *VCU school of social work online master of social work program format*. https://onlinesocialwork.vcu.edu/blog/social-work-and-social-justice/

Cowan, N. (2013). Working memory underpins cognitive development, learning, and education. *Educational Psychology Review, 26*(2), 197–223. https://doi.org/10.1007/s10648-013-9246-y

De Assis Faria, C., Alves, H. V. D., & Charchat-Fichman, H. (2015). The most frequently used tests for assessing executive functions in aging. *Dementia & Neuropsychologia, 9*(2), 149–155. https://doi.org/10.1590/1980-57642015dn92000009

Denney, R. L., & Wynkoop, T. F. (2000). Clinical neuropsychology in the criminal forensic setting. *Journal of Head Trauma Rehabilitation, 15*(2), 804–828. https://doi.org/10.1097/00001199-200004000-00005

Determinations, C. O. P. T. I. V. T. F. S. S. a. D. (2015, June 29). *Cognitive tests and performance validity tests*. Psychological Testing in the Service of Disability Determination–NCBI Bookshelf. https://www.ncbi.nlm.nih.gov/books/NBK305230/

Emmady, P. D., Schoo, C., & Tadi, P. (2022, November 19). Major Neurocognitive Disorder (Dementia). StatPearls – NCBI Bookshelf. https://www.ncbi.nlm.nih.gov/books/NBK557444/

Evaluation of Competency to Stand Trial ™ Revised. (n.d.). PAR Inc. https://www.parinc.com/products/ECST-R

Fong, T. G., & Inouye, S. K. (2022). The inter-relationship between delirium and dementia: The importance of delirium prevention. *Nature Reviews Neurology, 18*(10), 579–596. https://doi.org/10.1038/s41582-022-00698-7

Fortunati, F., Morgan, C. A., Temporini, H., Southwick, S., Coric, V., & Feuerstein, S. (2006, March 1). *Juveniles and competency to stand trial*. https://pmc.ncbi.nlm.nih.gov/articles/PMC2990555/

Freedman, D., & Zaami, S. (2019). Neuroscience and mental state issues in forensic assessment. *International Journal of Law and Psychiatry, 65*, 101437. https://doi.org/10.1016/j.ijlp.2019.03.006

Gbadebo-Goyea, E. A., Akpudo, H., Jackson, C. D., Wassef, T., Barker, N. C., Cunningham-Burley, R., Ali, S. A., Jabeen, S., & Bailey, R. K. (2012). Collaboration: The paradigm of practice approach between the forensic psychiatrist and the forensic psychologist. *Frontiers in Psychiatry, 3*. https://doi.org/10.3389/fpsyt.2012.00089

Go, G. (2017). Amnesia and criminal responsibility. *Journal of Law and the Biosciences, 4*(1), 194–204. https://doi.org/10.1093/jlb/lsx003

Harvey, P. D. (2012). Clinical applications of neuropsychological assessment. *Dialogues in Clinical Neuroscience, 14*(1), 91–99. https://doi.org/10.31887/dcns.2012.14.1/pharvey

Harvey, P. D. (2019). Domains of cognition and their assessment. *Dialogues in Clinical Neuroscience, 21*(3), 227–237. https://doi.org/10.31887/dcns.2019.21.3/pharvey

Helm, R. K., Reyna, V. F., Franz, A. A., Novick, R. Z., Dincin, S., & Cort, A. E. (2018). Limitations on the ability to negotiate justice: Attorney perspectives on guilt, innocence, and legal advice in the current plea system. *Psychology Crime and Law, 24*(9), 915–934. https://doi.org/10.1080/1068316x.2018.1457672

Hokkanen, L., Barbosa, F., Ponchel, A., Constantinou, M., Kosmidis, M. H., Varako, N., Kasten, E., Mondini, S., Lettner, S., Baker, G., Persson, B. A., & Hessen, E. (2020). Clinical neuropsychology as a specialist profession in European health care: Developing a benchmark for training standards and competencies using the Europsy model? *Frontiers in Psychology, 11*. https://doi.org/10.3389/fpsyg.2020.559134

Jia, X., Wang, Z., Huang, F., Su, C., Du, W., Jiang, H., Wang, H., Wang, J., Wang, F., Su, W., Xiao, H., Wang, Y., & Zhang, B. (2021). A comparison of the mini-mental state examination (MMSE) with the Montreal cognitive assessment (MoCA) for mild cognitive impairment screening in Chinese middle-aged and older population: a cross-sectional study. *BMC Psychiatry, 21*(1), 485. https://doi.org/10.1186/s12888-021-03495-6

Kelso, I. G., & Tadi, P. (2022, November 7). *Cognitive assessment*. StatPearls–NCBI Bookshelf. https://www.ncbi.nlm.nih.gov/books/NBK556049/

Kirkish, P., & Sreenivasan, S. (1999). Neuropsychological assessment of competency to stand trial evaluations: a practical conceptual model. *PubMed, 27*(1), 101–113. https://pubmed.ncbi.nlm.nih.gov/10212030

Kopp, B., Maldonado, N., Scheffels, J. F., Hendel, M., & Lange, F. (2019). A meta-analysis of relationships between measures of Wisconsin card sorting and intelligence. *Brain Sciences, 9*(12), 349. https://doi.org/10.3390/brainsci9120349

Lee, K., Cascella, M., & Marwaha, R. (2023, June 4). *Intellectual disability*. StatPearls–NCBI Bookshelf. https://www.ncbi.nlm.nih.gov/books/NBK547654/

Legal and Medical Considerations in Traumatic Brain Injury Litigation–John Winer Site. (2021, August 26). *John Winer Site*. https://www.wmlawyers.com/firm-highlights/publications/legal-and-medical-considerations-in-traumatic-brain-injury-litigation/

Mason, L., O'Sullivan, N., Montaldi, D., Bentall, R. P., & El-Deredy, W. (2014). Decision-making and trait impulsivity in bipolar disorder are associated with reduced prefrontal regulation of striatal reward valuation. *Brain, 137*(8), 2346–2355. https://doi.org/10.1093/brain/awu152

McAllister, T. W. (2011). Neurobiological consequences of traumatic brain injury. *Dialogues in Clinical Neuroscience, 13*(3), 287–300. https://doi.org/10.31887/dcns.2011.13.2/tmcallister

Miller Forensic Assessment of Symptoms Test ™. (n.d.). PAR Inc. https://www.parinc.com/products/MFAST

Moberg, P. J., & Kniele, K. (2006). Evaluation of competency: Ethical considerations for neuropsychologists. *Applied Neuropsychology, 13*(2), 101–114. https://doi.org/10.1207/s15324826an1302_5

Murrie, D. C., Gardner, B. O., & Torres, A. N. (2020). Competency to stand trial evaluations: A state-wide review of court-ordered reports. *Behavioral Sciences & the Law, 38*(1), 32–50. https://doi.org/10.1002/bsl.2436

National Institutes on Drug Abuse (US). (2020). *Common comorbidities with substance use Disorders research report*. NCBI Bookshelf. https://www.ncbi.nlm.nih.gov/books/NBK571451/

Nestor, P. G., Daggett, D., Haycock, J., & Price, M. (1999). Competence to stand trial: A neuropsychological inquiry. *Law and Human Behavior, 23*(4), 397–412. https://doi.org/10.1023/a:1022339130582

O'Connor, K. J., & Ammen, S. (2013). Assessment. In *Elsevier eBooks* (pp. 89–104). https://doi.org/10.1016/b978-0-12-373652-9.00005-4.

Ozer, S., Noonan, K., Burke, M., Young, J., Barber, S., Forster, A., & Jones, R. (2016). The validity of the memory alteration test and the test your memory test for community-based identification of amnestic mild cognitive impairment. *Alzheimer S & Dementia, 12*(9), 987–995. https://doi.org/10.1016/j.jalz.2016.03.014

Pinals, D. A., Tillbrook, C. E., & Mumley, D. L. (2006). Practical application of the MacArthur competence assessment tool-criminal adjudication (MacCAT-CA) in a public sector forensic setting. *PubMed, 34*(2), 179–188. https://pubmed.ncbi.nlm.nih.gov/16844797

Pirelli, G., Gottdiener, W. H., & Zapf, P. A. (2011). A meta-analytic review of competency to stand trial research. *Psychology Public Policy and Law, 17*(1), 1–53. https://doi.org/10.1037/a0021713

Rabinovici, G. D., Stephens, M. L., & Possin, K. L. (2015). Executive dysfunction. *CONTINUUM Lifelong Learning in Neurology, 21*, 646–659. https://doi.org/10.1212/01.con.0000466658.05156.54

Rabinowitz, A. R., & Levin, H. S. (2014). Cognitive sequelae of traumatic brain injury. *Psychiatric Clinics of North America, 37*(1), 1–11. https://doi.org/10.1016/j.psc.2013.11.004

Redlich, A. D., Bibas, S., Edkins, V. A., & Madon, S. (2017). The psychology of defendant plea decision making. *American Psychologist, 72*(4), 339–352. https://doi.org/10.1037/a0040436

Roebuck, H., Freigang, C., & Barry, J. G. (2016). Continuous performance tasks: Not just about sustaining attention. *Journal of Speech Language and Hearing Research, 59*(3), 501–510. https://doi.org/10.1044/2015_jslhr-l-15-0068

Roesch, R. (2016). Competency to stand trial in the American legal system. *Oxford Research Encyclopedia of Psychology*. https://doi.org/10.1093/acrefore/9780190236557.013.80

Ryan, N., & Westera, N. (2018). The effect of expert witness testimony and complainant cognitive statements on mock jurors' perceptions of rape trial testimony. *Psychiatry Psychology and Law, 25*(5), 693–705. https://doi.org/10.1080/13218719.2018.1474815

Schaefer, L. A., Thakur, T., & Meager, M. R. (2023). *Neuropsychological assessment*. StatPearls–NCBI Bookshelf. https://www.ncbi.nlm.nih.gov/books/NBK513310/

Sherman, E. M. S., Slick, D. J., & Iverson, G. L. (2020). Multidimensional malingering criteria for neuropsychological assessment: A 20-year update of the malingered neuropsychological dysfunction criteria. *Archives of Clinical Neuropsychology, 35*(6), 735–764. https://doi.org/10.1093/arclin/acaa019

Soble, J. R., Eichstaedt, K. E., Waseem, H., Mattingly, M. L., Benbadis, S. R., Bozorg, A. M., Vale, F. L., & Schoenberg, M. R. (2014). Clinical utility of the Wechsler memory scale—Fourth edition (WMS-IV) in predicting laterality of temporal lobe epilepsy among surgical candidates. *Epilepsy & Behavior, 41*, 232–237. https://doi.org/10.1016/j.yebeh.2014.10.014

Stevens, C., & Bavelier, D. (2011). The role of selective attention on academic foundations: A cognitive neuroscience perspective. *Developmental Cognitive Neuroscience, 2*, S30–S48. https://doi.org/10.1016/j.dcn.2011.11.001

Towse, J. N., Cowan, N., Hitch, G. J., & Horton, N. J. (2008). The recall of information from working memory. *Experimental Psychology (Formerly Zeitschrift Für Experimentelle Psychologie), 55*(6), 371–383. https://doi.org/10.1027/1618-3169.55.6.371

Trapp, N. T., Martyna, M. R., Siddiqi, S. H., & Bajestan, S. N. (2022). The neuropsychiatric approach to the assessment of patients in neurology. *Seminars in Neurology, 42*(02), 088–106. https://doi.org/10.1055/s-0042-1745741

Traumatic Brain Injury (TBI). (n.d.). *National institute of neurological disorders and stroke*. https://www.ninds.nih.gov/health-information/disorders/traumatic-brain-injury-tbi

Tsiakiri, A., Christidi, F., Tsiptsios, D., Vlotinou, P., Kitmeridou, S., Bebeletsi, P., Kokkotis, C., Serdari, A., Tsamakis, K., Aggelousis, N., & Vadikolias, K. (2024). Processing speed and attentional shift/mental flexibility in patients with stroke: A comprehensive review on the trail making test in stroke studies. *Neurology International, 16*(1), 210–225. https://doi.org/10.3390/neurolint16010014

Viljoen, J. L., Roesch, R., & Zapf, P. A. (2002). An examination of the relationship between competency to stand trial, competency to waive interrogation rights, and psychopathology. *Law and Human Behavior, 26*(5), 481–506. https://doi.org/10.1023/a:1020299804821

Whiting, M. D., Baranova, A. I., & Hamm, R. J. (2006). *Cognitive impairment following traumatic brain injury*. Animal Models of Cognitive Impairment–NCBI Bookshelf. https://www.ncbi.nlm.nih.gov/books/NBK2521/

Wy, T. J. P., & Saadabadi, A. (2023, March 27). *Schizoaffective disorder*. StatPearls–NCBI Bookshelf. https://www.ncbi.nlm.nih.gov/books/NBK541012/

Mitigation and Sentencing in Criminal Cases

1 Introduction

Mitigation and sentencing represent two critical components in the criminal justice process, particularly when neuropsychological evidence is involved. In criminal cases, the sentencing phase determines the severity and type of punishment for convicted individuals, and it often considers not only the nature of the offense but also the unique characteristics and circumstances of the offender. Mitigation, on the other hand, refers to the process of presenting information and arguments to lessen the severity of the sentence. When skillfully integrated, these factors can help the court impose a sentence that aligns with justice, proportionality, and rehabilitation rather than mere retribution.

In recent years, there has been growing recognition of the relevance of neuropsychological evidence in this domain. Neuropsychological assessments can provide insight into an offender's cognitive and psychological functioning, potentially illuminating impairments that contribute to criminal behavior. For example, a history of traumatic brain injury (TBI), neurodevelopmental disorders, or mental health conditions can affect decision-making, impulse control, and risk assessment. In such cases, the court can take these mitigating factors into account, weighing them against the standard expectations of culpability and intent. This chapter explores how neuropsychological data can influence the mitigation and sentencing processes, focusing on how it supports more equitable decisions grounded in an understanding of individual capacity and circumstance.

To understand the relevance of neuropsychological evidence in mitigation and sentencing, it is important to examine the role of expert testimony and forensic reports in court proceedings. Expert witnesses in neuropsychology play a pivotal role in interpreting complex cognitive data for the court, offering insights into how neuropsychological impairments may have influenced the defendant's behavior. Through clear and accessible testimony, these experts can help the court recognize

© The Author(s), under exclusive license to Springer Nature Switzerland AG 2025

K. J. Reddy, *Foundations of Criminal Forensic Neuropsychology*,
https://doi.org/10.1007/978-3-031-83771-5_13

that certain behaviors may not stem solely from criminal intent but could be influenced by neurological or psychological factors. This approach promotes a more nuanced view of criminal responsibility, allowing juries and judges to consider how brain dysfunctions or mental health issues might impact culpability. Importantly, forensic reports backed by empirical research offer a scientific basis for understanding these conditions, lending credibility to the argument that sentencing should account for an offender's neuropsychological profile (Alimardani, 2023).

Furthermore, case law illustrates how courts have increasingly integrated neuropsychological data in determining fair and appropriate sentences. In some jurisdictions, the courts have considered conditions such as TBI, intellectual disabilities, schizophrenia, and even specific genetic predispositions when assessing an offender's culpability. This shift aligns with broader principles of justice and rehabilitation, emphasizing that sentences should be proportionate not only to the crime but also to the offender's mental state and capacity. Cases involving juvenile offenders highlight this point: courts frequently recognize that young offenders are more susceptible to cognitive and emotional immaturity and may also be more responsive to rehabilitative interventions. As a result, neuropsychological evaluations have become an essential tool for defense teams advocating for sentences that prioritize rehabilitation over punishment, particularly in cases where cognitive impairments may have contributed to criminal behavior.

Professional obligations and ethical considerations are key components when presenting neuropsychological evidence in court. Neuropsychologists and other mental health professionals must adhere to stringent ethical guidelines to maintain objectivity, avoid bias, and uphold the integrity of their testimony. The American Psychological Association (APA) and other professional bodies provide clear standards to help forensic practitioners navigate potential conflicts, such as dual roles or confidentiality breaches. While the defense may seek a mitigated sentence, forensic neuropsychologists must ensure that their evaluations and testimony remain impartial, aiming to clarify the offender's cognitive profile without exaggerating or minimizing findings. This ethical stance supports the credibility of neuropsychological evidence in court, promoting fairness and objectivity in judicial outcomes.

Ethical considerations also intersect with professional responsibilities, particularly in cases involving individuals with cognitive impairments or psychiatric disorders. Neuropsychologists must carefully balance their duty to present evidence that advocates for fair punishment with their role in promoting justice. In cases where the offender's neurological impairments are significant, practitioners may need to advocate for sentencing options that emphasize treatment or rehabilitation rather than incarceration. This advocacy aligns with the broader goal of the criminal justice system to ensure that sentences reflect both the severity of the offense and the unique circumstances of the offender. However, this approach may lead to ethical dilemmas, especially in cases involving serious offenses where public safety is a concern. Balancing these competing interests requires forensic experts to communicate clearly with the court, emphasizing that equitable sentencing can achieve justice without compromising public safety.

The application of neuropsychological evidence in mitigation and sentencing is illustrated through numerous case studies, which demonstrate how this data can influence judicial decisions. For example, in cases involving individuals with intellectual disabilities or severe mental health disorders, neuropsychological evidence has been successfully used to argue for alternative sentencing options, such as treatment programs or community-based rehabilitation. These case studies highlight the practical challenges and opportunities associated with using neuropsychological evidence to affect sentencing outcomes. For instance, expert witnesses may need to explain the limitations of an individual's executive functioning in a way that resonates with both legal professionals and lay juries. By linking neuropsychological impairments to specific behaviors or deficits in decision-making, experts can provide compelling arguments for mitigation that address the unique needs of the offender without disregarding the impact of their actions on victims and society.

In conclusion, neuropsychological evidence offers an invaluable perspective in the mitigation and sentencing phases of criminal cases, promoting fairness and proportionality in sentencing decisions. This approach allows courts to consider not only the offense but also the unique characteristics of the offender, fostering a legal system that values justice and rehabilitation. Neuropsychologists and forensic experts play a critical role in this process, bridging the gap between scientific evidence and legal principles to ensure that defendants receive sentences that accurately reflect their cognitive and emotional capacities. At the same time, ethical and professional standards guide practitioners in delivering objective and effective testimony that supports equitable judicial outcomes. By understanding the nuances of mitigation and sentencing, legal professionals can make informed decisions that acknowledge both the complexities of human behavior and the overarching goal of the justice system: to promote accountability, fairness, and rehabilitation within a framework that respects individual differences and societal values.

Through a careful consideration of neuropsychological evidence, courts can tailor sentences that reflect the offender's unique profile, thereby upholding the principles of fair punishment and fostering opportunities for rehabilitation. This balanced approach underscores the importance of neuropsychological data in fostering a more compassionate and effective criminal justice system, one that is attuned to the individual needs of offenders while safeguarding the rights and safety of the broader community.

2 Role of Mitigation in Sentencing

Mitigation plays an essential role in sentencing by providing courts with evidence that may reduce a defendant's culpability, often leading to adjusted or reduced punishments. Traditionally, sentencing serves as a way to deter crime, ensure retribution, protect society, and rehabilitate offenders. However, when a defendant's mental health issues or cognitive impairments have contributed to their criminal behavior, a purely punitive approach may be inappropriate or unjust. Mitigating evidence allows the court to weigh the unique circumstances surrounding the defendant, including any mental health disorders, neurodevelopmental disorders, trauma, or cognitive limitations. This ensures a fairer sentencing process, one that recognizes the role of underlying psychological factors in criminal behavior. By examining the role of mitigation in sentencing, we can better understand its legal, ethical, and rehabilitative dimensions in the pursuit of justice.

2.1 Defining Mitigation and its Legal Context

Mitigation in the legal context refers to evidence or circumstances that may lessen the severity of a defendant's culpability (Aggravating and Mitigating Factors in Criminal Sentencing Law, 2024). Unlike exculpatory evidence, which may absolve a defendant of guilt entirely, mitigating evidence aims to contextualize the defendant's actions, helping the court understand factors that might have diminished the individual's control or decision-making capacity. The premise is that while the defendant may indeed be guilty of the offense, the punishment should be proportionate to their mental and psychological condition at the time of the crime. The inclusion of mitigating evidence in sentencing is intended to reflect the complexity of human behavior, acknowledging that individuals with cognitive impairments or mental illness may not bear full responsibility in the same way as defendants who are free from such impairments (De Vel-Palumbo et al., 2022).

The use of mitigating evidence has grown in significance, particularly with advancements in psychology and neuroscience, which have enhanced our understanding of mental illness and cognitive impairments. Today, it is increasingly common for defendants in serious cases to be evaluated by mental health professionals, whose assessments may reveal significant psychological or cognitive factors relevant to sentencing. The court then considers this information in conjunction with legal standards to determine an appropriate sentence that reflects both the defendant's culpability and their rehabilitative needs.

2.2 Mental Health and Cognitive Impairments as Mitigating Factors

Mental health issues and cognitive impairments are among the most compelling mitigating factors in criminal sentencing. Mental illnesses, such as schizophrenia, bipolar disorder, depression, and post-traumatic stress disorder (PTSD), can profoundly affect an individual's behavior, judgment, and impulse control. For example, a person experiencing severe psychosis may not be fully aware of their actions or the consequences of those actions. Similarly, individuals with cognitive impairments, such as intellectual disabilities or brain injuries, may struggle with impulse control, risk assessment, and understanding the moral implications of their behavior.

In cases where a defendant's mental health condition played a significant role in their actions, mitigating evidence can be presented to argue for an adjusted sentence. For example, a defendant with bipolar disorder who committed a crime during a manic episode may not have had the same degree of control over their behavior as someone without the disorder. Cognitive impairments also introduce questions about the defendant's capacity to comprehend the consequences of their actions or control impulsive behavior, making a traditional punitive approach less fitting.

Studies show that mental health disorders and cognitive impairments are disproportionately prevalent in criminal populations (Moore et al., 2019). Recognizing these impairments as mitigating factors enables courts to address root causes rather than simply imposing punitive measures. By doing so, the justice system can better serve its rehabilitative goals, giving individuals the resources to address underlying psychological issues that may contribute to recidivism.

2.3 The Role of Mitigating Evidence in Adjusting Sentences

Mitigating evidence can lead to adjusted sentences in several ways. In cases involving severe mental illness or cognitive impairment, the court may decide to impose a sentence that incorporates treatment options, such as mental health counseling, rather than simply focusing on incarceration (De Vel-Palumbo et al., 2022). In certain cases, mitigating evidence may also result in reduced sentences or the possibility of probation rather than prison time, especially when the offense was nonviolent and the defendant's condition has a substantial impact on their behavior.

Neuropsychological evaluations, mental health assessments, and psychiatric testimony often play a central role in presenting mitigating evidence. These assessments provide the court with objective information about the defendant's psychological state, history of trauma, or brain functioning. By examining factors such as intelligence, memory, executive function, and emotional regulation, experts can help courts determine the extent to which these impairments may have influenced the defendant's actions. For instance, an individual with a history of head trauma may exhibit poor impulse control, resulting in behaviors that, while illegal, may have been outside their full control. This nuanced understanding can help judges and juries arrive at sentencing decisions that better reflect the individual's culpability and likelihood of rehabilitation.

2.4 Ethical and Social Considerations in Mitigation

While mitigating evidence provides an important means of ensuring fairness, it also raises ethical and social considerations. On one hand, mental health professionals face the challenge of delivering impartial assessments, even when hired by the defense or prosecution. This can be difficult in emotionally charged cases where the findings may have significant consequences for the defendant. Ensuring that mental health assessments are objective and based on sound scientific evidence is essential to maintain the integrity of the mitigation process (Iltis et al., 2013).

Another ethical consideration is public safety. Adjusting a sentence due to mitigating factors may, in some cases, result in public concerns about recidivism, especially if the defendant's mental health condition could potentially lead to further criminal behavior (Lamberti, 2016). It is the court's responsibility to weigh the needs of society against the rights and rehabilitative needs of the defendant, and this balance can be complex, particularly when the defendant poses a potential risk.

Moreover, the use of mental health and cognitive impairments in mitigation invites a larger discussion about the social responsibility to address mental illness and cognitive impairment before they lead to criminal behavior. Defendants who present with such issues often come from backgrounds with limited access to mental health resources, raising questions about the societal role in preventing criminal behavior through better access to mental health care, education, and support services.

Mitigation serves as a vital component of the sentencing process, allowing courts to consider evidence that might reduce a defendant's culpability and, by extension, their sentence. Mental health issues and cognitive impairments are among the most significant mitigating factors, highlighting how psychological and neurological dysfunctions can influence behavior in ways that diminish moral and legal culpability. By incorporating neuropsychological and psychiatric assessments into sentencing, the justice system can provide a more accurate, just, and rehabilitative approach, tailoring punishment to individual needs and circumstances. However, the use of mitigating evidence is not without ethical and social challenges. Mental health professionals must provide objective evaluations, and courts must consider both the rehabilitative potential of defendants and the safety of the public. Ultimately, mitigation represents a more humane approach to sentencing, one that recognizes the complexities of human behavior and seeks to balance justice with compassion.

3 Legal Standards and Precedents

Legal standards and precedents play a fundamental role in shaping the application of mitigation in criminal sentencing. Over time, the judiciary has established numerous precedents that support the use of mitigating factors, particularly when cognitive impairments, mental health issues, or other extenuating circumstances influence a defendant's actions. These precedents underscore the recognition of individual circumstances, fostering an approach to justice that balances retribution with the potential for rehabilitation. While punitive measures remain central to criminal law, recent legal trends emphasize a more compassionate view of justice, particularly for defendants whose mental or cognitive conditions diminish their culpability. This section explores key legal precedents that support mitigation, examines the recognition of cognitive impairments as grounds for alternative sentencing, and analyzes the shift toward rehabilitative approaches in certain cases.

3.1 Legal Precedents Supporting Mitigation in Sentencing

Mitigation, defined as the consideration of circumstances that might lessen a defendant's culpability, has long been recognized in legal standards. Numerous precedents support the use of mitigating factors, particularly in cases where defendants are influenced by mental illness, trauma, or cognitive impairments. These precedents set the foundation for an evolving understanding of justice that considers both individual circumstances and societal interests.

One of the landmark cases highlighting mitigation is *Woodson v. North Carolina* (1976) (Woodson V. North Carolina *(1976)*, n.d.), in which the US Supreme Court ruled that mandatory death sentences violated the Eighth and Fourteenth Amendments. The court argued that sentencing procedures must consider each defendant's unique circumstances to avoid cruel and unusual punishment. This case established the principle that sentencing must account for individual factors, creating a foundation for the use of mitigating evidence. Similarly, *Lockett v. Ohio* (1978) (Lockett V. Ohio, 438 U.S. *586 (1978)*, n.d.) extended this principle, ruling that courts must consider a wide range of mitigating factors—including psychological and emotional state—when determining sentences in capital cases. These cases underscore the judiciary's recognition that justice requires nuanced decision-making, especially in cases involving severe penalties.

In *Atkins v. Virginia* (2002) (Oyez, n.d.), the Supreme Court ruled that executing individuals with intellectual disabilities was unconstitutional, as it violated the Eighth Amendment's prohibition on cruel and unusual punishment. This case marked a significant milestone in recognizing cognitive impairments as legitimate grounds for mitigation, especially in the context of capital punishment. By distinguishing between defendants with intellectual disabilities and those without, the court emphasized that certain cognitive impairments reduce moral culpability and require alternative sentencing approaches.

Another important case, *Roper v. Simmons* (2005) (Roper V. Simmons, 543 U.S. *551 (2005)*, n.d.), ruled that executing juveniles was unconstitutional due to their lack of maturity, underdeveloped sense of responsibility, and susceptibility to external influences. While not specifically about cognitive impairment, this case sets a precedent for recognizing developmental factors as grounds for mitigation. It highlighted that young offenders, like those with cognitive impairments, may lack full understanding or control over their actions, warranting leniency or rehabilitative measures.

3.2 *Recognizing Cognitive Impairments as Grounds for Alternative Sentencing*

Legal standards increasingly acknowledge cognitive impairments as a valid basis for alternative sentencing. Cognitive impairments, such as intellectual disabilities, traumatic brain injuries, and neurodevelopmental disorders, can significantly influence a defendant's behavior, judgment, and impulse control. Courts are increasingly receptive to expert testimony and neuropsychological evaluations that demonstrate how these impairments reduce a defendant's capacity to fully comprehend or control their actions.

The recognition of cognitive impairments as mitigating factors aligns with the principle that justice must consider the defendant's mental state and capacity for decision-making. In *Hall v. Florida* (2014) (Hall V. Florida, n.d.), the Supreme Court ruled that states must consider a broader range of evidence when evaluating intellectual disabilities in death penalty cases, including clinical standards and professional evaluations. This case emphasized that rigid definitions of cognitive impairments are insufficient in legal contexts, advocating for a comprehensive understanding that incorporates clinical findings. *Hall* reinforced the legal standing of cognitive impairments as grounds for alternative sentencing, encouraging courts to view defendants through a clinical, evidence-based lens.

Additionally, courts are increasingly considering cognitive impairments in noncapital cases, particularly when cognitive dysfunction significantly influences the defendant's criminal behavior. Cognitive impairments are often cited in requests for reduced sentences, probation, or diversion into mental health treatment programs. Such cases emphasize rehabilitation and address the underlying cognitive limitations that contributed to the crime. In the case of People v. Patterson (2001) (People V. Patterson, 2001), a California appeals court upheld the reduction of a sentence based on the defendant's cognitive impairment due to a traumatic brain injury, affirming the importance of individualized sentencing considerations.

These precedents demonstrate that the legal system is increasingly recognizing the need for a compassionate and individualized approach to sentencing. By acknowledging cognitive impairments, courts can pursue justice in ways that promote rehabilitation and reduce recidivism, offering alternative sentencing that better reflects the defendant's capacities and challenges.

3.3 *Shift from Punishment to Rehabilitation in Sentencing*

In recent years, there has been a noticeable shift in certain areas of criminal law from punishment toward rehabilitation, particularly for defendants whose actions are influenced by cognitive impairments or mental health issues. This shift reflects an evolving understanding of criminal justice, emphasizing that punishment alone may be ineffective for individuals who, due to psychological or cognitive limitations, require specialized interventions.

Rehabilitation-oriented sentencing recognizes that individuals with mental health conditions or cognitive impairments may benefit more from treatment than from incarceration. Programs that combine therapy, skills training, and community support can help address the root causes of criminal behavior, reducing the likelihood of re-offending. Many courts now have mental health or specialty courts specifically designed to provide alternative sentencing options for individuals with psychiatric or cognitive conditions. These courts aim to divert defendants from traditional punitive systems and into treatment programs that foster recovery and behavioral change.

Rehabilitation-focused sentencing also acknowledges that some defendants may lack the cognitive capacity to respond to punishment in the same way as fully competent individuals. Individuals with severe mental illness or cognitive deficits may not benefit from punitive sentences, as their cognitive limitations impede their ability to understand the consequences of their actions or modify behavior based on punishment alone. For example, programs in many jurisdictions allow for the diversion of offenders with cognitive impairments into rehabilitative and therapeutic programs, as seen in the increasing use of competency-to-stand-trial evaluations.

However, the shift to rehabilitation is not without challenges, as courts must balance public safety with the defendant's needs. Public opinion often favors punitive approaches, particularly in serious cases. Nevertheless, many judges and policymakers are advocating for rehabilitation in appropriate cases, arguing that it offers a more sustainable and humane path toward justice. Rehabilitation-oriented sentencing has been shown to reduce recidivism, enhance community safety, and promote social reintegration, making it a valuable approach for cases involving cognitive and psychological impairments.

Legal standards and precedents play a critical role in ensuring justice that reflects individual circumstances, particularly when mental health issues or cognitive impairments reduce a defendant's culpability. Key legal precedents, such as *Atkins v. Virginia* and *Hall v. Florida*, support the use of mitigation and alternative sentencing for individuals with cognitive impairments, underscoring the judiciary's commitment to nuanced justice. The growing acknowledgment of cognitive impairments as grounds for alternative sentencing marks a significant shift in criminal justice, balancing retribution with rehabilitation. The shift from punishment to rehabilitation reflects a broader understanding of justice as a mechanism for both accountability and compassion. By incorporating rehabilitative approaches, the legal system can address the root causes of criminal behavior, offering defendants with cognitive impairments the opportunity for growth and societal reintegration. As these trends continue, legal standards and precedents will likely evolve further, fostering a justice system that is equitable, evidence-based, and compassionate.

4 Neuropsychological Foundations of Mitigation

The neuropsychological foundations of mitigation in criminal cases revolve around understanding how cognitive, emotional, and behavioral impairments can influence behavior and, consequently, impact legal responsibility. In criminal law, mitigation refers to presenting evidence that can lessen the severity of a sentence based on factors that reduce the defendant's culpability. Neuropsychology, the study of the brain–behavior relationship, plays a critical role in determining whether brain disorders, developmental delays, or other cognitive impairments might have contributed to criminal actions. By assessing the degree to which a defendant's mental state may have influenced their decision-making, impulse control, or understanding of consequences, neuropsychologists provide critical insights that can guide sentencing decisions toward more equitable outcomes. This section examines how cognitive, emotional, and behavioral impairments impact criminal behavior, the role of brain disorders and developmental delays in reducing responsibility, and the neuropsychological assessment process used to evaluate these impairments in criminal cases.

4.1 Cognitive, Emotional, and Behavioral Impairments Affecting Criminal Behavior

In criminal cases, the understanding that cognitive, emotional, and behavioral impairments can affect a defendant's behavior has significant implications for mitigation (De Vel-Palumbo et al., 2022). Cognitive impairments, such as deficits in memory, judgment, executive functioning, or attention, can impair an individual's ability to make informed decisions. For instance, impairments in executive functioning, the mental processes that allow planning, impulse control, and goal-directed behavior, can lead individuals to act impulsively without fully understanding the consequences of their actions.

Emotional impairments, including conditions like severe depression, anxiety, or personality disorders, can also contribute to criminal behavior by distorting perception, increasing emotional reactivity, or reducing empathy (Compare et al., 2014). Individuals with severe emotional impairments may struggle with regulating their emotional responses, which can lead to actions driven by intense emotional states rather than rational thought. For example, someone with borderline personality disorder might experience intense emotional swings and act impulsively in response to perceived threats or rejections, which could influence their actions during the commission of a crime.

Behavioral impairments, often associated with impulse control disorders, substance use disorders, or neurodevelopmental conditions, further contribute to diminished culpability in certain cases. These impairments often limit an individual's ability to regulate behaviors, resist urges, or make decisions in line with societal norms. For example, someone with a substance use disorder might engage in theft to support their addiction or exhibit aggression due to impaired judgment and impulse control. These cognitive, emotional, and behavioral impairments are increasingly recognized as factors that can reduce an individual's moral culpability and influence sentencing decisions.

4.2 Brain Disorders and Developmental Delays as Grounds for Mitigation

Brain disorders and developmental delays are often central to arguments for mitigation in criminal cases, as they can substantially influence an individual's understanding, decision-making, and self-control. Neurological conditions like traumatic brain injury (TBI), epilepsy, and neurodegenerative disorders, as well as neurodevelopmental disorders such as autism spectrum disorder (ASD) or intellectual disability, can impair cognitive functions and reduce a person's responsibility for their actions.

Traumatic brain injury, for example, is frequently associated with changes in personality, aggression, and impulse control. Individuals with TBI may experience difficulty regulating emotions, controlling impulses, and understanding social cues, which can contribute to socially inappropriate or even criminal behaviors. In cases where a defendant has a history of TBI, a neuropsychological assessment can provide valuable insight into how the injury might have contributed to diminished capacity for self-regulation, potentially supporting mitigation.

Neurodevelopmental disorders, such as intellectual disability and autism spectrum disorder, are also significant grounds for mitigation due to their impact on cognitive abilities, social understanding, and behavioral control. Intellectual disability, characterized by limitations in intellectual functioning and adaptive behavior, can reduce a person's ability to understand complex legal proceedings or the consequences of their actions. Consequently, courts often consider intellectual disability as a mitigating factor, with precedents such as *Atkins v. Virginia* (2002) emphasizing that individuals with intellectual disabilities should not be subjected to the death penalty due to their diminished culpability.

Autism spectrum disorder can also influence behavior in ways that may affect culpability. Some individuals with ASD may struggle with social interactions, have difficulty understanding others' intentions, or exhibit repetitive behaviors that can lead to misunderstandings or legal conflicts. For example, an individual with ASD might exhibit rigid thinking patterns or reduced social awareness, which can impact their ability to interpret or respond to social cues in ways that align with societal expectations. These characteristics can be important in mitigation, as they illustrate how neurodevelopmental differences may influence actions and limit culpability.

4.3 The Role of Neuropsychological Assessments in Evaluating Impairments

Neuropsychological assessments are essential tools for evaluating the presence and impact of cognitive, emotional, and behavioral impairments in criminal cases. Neuropsychologists conduct these assessments to determine how a defendant's impairments might have contributed to their criminal behavior and to provide evidence that can be used in sentencing considerations. These assessments typically involve a combination of clinical interviews, standardized tests, and observations designed to evaluate cognitive functioning, emotional regulation, behavioral control, and social understanding.

For instance, tests of executive functioning, such as the Wisconsin Card Sorting Test, can provide insight into an individual's problem-solving abilities, cognitive flexibility, and impulse control. Memory assessments, like the Wechsler Memory Scale, help determine if a defendant has deficits that could impair their recall of events or decision-making processes. Neuropsychologists may also use tools like the Minnesota Multiphasic Personality Inventory (MMPI) to assess emotional functioning, identifying factors like anxiety, depression, or impulsivity that may have influenced behavior.

When assessing individuals with suspected brain injuries, neuropsychologists may conduct tests like the Trail Making Test to evaluate cognitive processing speed and executive functioning, as these abilities are commonly impaired after TBI. By understanding the specific nature and severity of these impairments, neuropsychologists can determine whether a defendant's capacity to control their actions or understand consequences was compromised, potentially supporting arguments for mitigation.

Moreover, neuropsychologists consider how developmental or neurodegenerative conditions, like ASD or dementia, influence behavior over time. For individuals with ASD, assessments might focus on social cognition, empathy, and impulse control, highlighting difficulties that could reduce culpability. For elderly defendants with dementia, assessments can reveal cognitive decline, impaired memory, and limited understanding of their actions. These findings contribute to the argument for alternative sentencing that prioritizes treatment and rehabilitation over punishment.

The neuropsychological foundations of mitigation in criminal cases highlight the importance of understanding how cognitive, emotional, and behavioral impairments influence behavior and reduce culpability. By assessing factors such as traumatic brain injury, neurodevelopmental disorders, and mental health conditions, neuropsychologists provide insights that can lead to fairer sentencing outcomes. These assessments reveal how impairments affect decision-making, impulse control, and social understanding, supporting arguments for mitigation based on the defendant's mental and neurological state. In considering brain disorders and developmental delays as grounds for mitigation, the legal system increasingly recognizes the complexity of human behavior and the need for a justice approach that balances accountability with compassion. The role of neuropsychological assessment in these cases emphasizes a commitment to individualized justice, where defendants are judged not only by their actions but also by their capacities and limitations. By providing evidence of diminished culpability, neuropsychology contributes to a more nuanced and equitable legal system, offering pathways to rehabilitation and support for those whose impairments may have contributed to their criminal actions.

5 Cognitive and Emotional Impairments in Sentencing

The impact of cognitive and emotional impairments in sentencing is a critical topic in criminal law, as these impairments can influence an individual's decision-making, impulse control, and emotional regulation, thereby affecting their level of culpability. In recent years, legal systems worldwide have increasingly considered how conditions like traumatic brain injury (TBI), dementia, and schizophrenia may mitigate sentences by highlighting diminished responsibility. This section explores how cognitive and emotional impairments shape criminal behavior, examines how conditions like TBI, dementia, and schizophrenia are considered mitigating factors, and discusses the role of neuropsychological assessments in guiding sentencing decisions to achieve fairer outcomes.

5.1 Cognitive Impairments and their Impact on Decision-Making and Impulse Control

Cognitive impairments can significantly affect decision-making processes, impulse control, and the ability to understand and foresee the consequences of actions. Cognitive functions such as memory, attention, planning, problem-solving, and executive functioning allow individuals to make thoughtful choices, regulate impulses, and respond to situations with appropriate behavior. However, when these cognitive processes are compromised, an individual's capacity to make reasoned decisions and control impulses is often diminished, potentially leading to criminal behavior.

For example, individuals with traumatic brain injury (TBI) commonly exhibit deficits in executive functioning, which is the cognitive process responsible for planning, regulating behavior, and controlling impulses. Damage to the frontal lobe, often seen in TBI cases, can reduce a person's ability to exercise good judgment or resist impulsive actions, resulting in behavior that may be socially inappropriate or even criminal. In cases where TBI is identified, courts may view these cognitive impairments as a mitigating factor, as they suggest that the individual may not have had the full cognitive capacity to understand or control their actions.

Another cognitive impairment that affects criminal behavior is dementia, a progressive condition characterized by cognitive decline that affects memory, language, and executive functioning. Individuals with dementia may struggle with memory retention, impulse control, and social norms, which can lead to misunderstandings, aggression, or unintentional criminal behavior. For example, a person with dementia might exhibit socially inappropriate behavior due to their reduced understanding of social context or act in a way that violates laws without comprehending the consequences. In these instances, cognitive impairments related to dementia are taken into consideration by the legal system, often leading to alternative sentencing focused on care and management rather than punishment.

In cases of schizophrenia, cognitive impairments often include deficits in attention, working memory, and executive functioning, all of which impact decision-making. Schizophrenia-related cognitive deficits can interfere with an individual's ability to organize thoughts, make logical decisions, and interpret social cues accurately. These cognitive impairments are further compounded by symptoms such as delusions or hallucinations, which can distort perception and judgment. In cases where schizophrenia is a contributing factor to criminal behavior, courts may consider these cognitive deficits during sentencing, often opting for mental health interventions and rehabilitative sentencing.

5.2 Emotional Dysregulation and its Link to Criminal Behavior

Emotional dysregulation, or the inability to manage and respond to emotional experiences in an adaptive manner, is another factor that can contribute to criminal behavior. Emotional regulation allows individuals to respond to emotional triggers in ways that align with social norms and legal expectations. However, when emotional regulation is impaired, individuals may act impulsively, aggressively, or irrationally in response to emotional stimuli. Emotional dysregulation is commonly observed in conditions like TBI, schizophrenia, and certain personality disorders, where the ability to manage intense emotional responses is diminished.

Traumatic brain injury, especially when it involves damage to the prefrontal cortex or limbic system, can severely impair an individual's ability to regulate emotions. This can lead to heightened aggression, irritability, and impulsivity, often manifesting as a reduced ability to manage anger or frustration. In criminal cases where TBI is a contributing factor, emotional dysregulation can be cited as a mitigating factor, as it suggests that the defendant may have been unable to control their emotional responses in the same way as an unimpaired individual. Such evidence may influence courts to impose a less punitive sentence or consider alternative forms of intervention.

Schizophrenia is another condition associated with emotional dysregulation. Individuals with schizophrenia may experience heightened emotional responses due to delusions or hallucinations, leading them to act in ways that are disconnected from reality. For instance, an individual experiencing a paranoid delusion might perceive a nonthreatening situation as dangerous and respond aggressively. This disconnect from reality, compounded by emotional dysregulation, can be taken into account during sentencing, as it indicates that the defendant's actions were influenced by an impaired perception of the situation rather than criminal intent.

Personality disorders, especially borderline personality disorder (BPD) and antisocial personality disorder (ASPD), are also closely associated with emotional dysregulation. BPD, in particular, is characterized by intense and rapidly fluctuating emotions, which can lead to impulsive and sometimes aggressive behavior. Emotional dysregulation in individuals with BPD may contribute to self-destructive actions, interpersonal conflicts, or reactive aggression. While ASPD involves a disregard for the rights of others, emotional dysregulation in BPD often stems from sensitivity to rejection or abandonment. In cases involving individuals with BPD, courts may consider the role of emotional dysregulation in the behavior, often opting for mental health treatment over punitive measures.

5.3 *Disorders like TBI, Dementia, and Schizophrenia as Mitigating Factors*

In criminal cases, the presence of cognitive and emotional impairments can serve as grounds for mitigation by demonstrating that the defendant's condition affected their responsibility for their actions. Conditions like TBI, dementia, and schizophrenia are widely recognized as impairments that reduce culpability because they can limit the ability to make reasoned decisions, control impulses, and respond appropriately to emotional stimuli.

In cases involving TBI, for instance, courts often acknowledge that the cognitive and emotional impairments resulting from the injury may have influenced the defendant's behavior. For example, a defendant with TBI who exhibits impulsive aggression due to frontal lobe damage may receive a reduced sentence, with an emphasis on treatment and rehabilitation rather than incarceration. The legal system recognizes that while TBI does not absolve individuals of responsibility, it does mitigate their level of culpability.

Similarly, dementia cases often prompt courts to consider alternative sentencing options. Given that dementia is a progressive and debilitating condition, individuals with dementia are unlikely to benefit from punitive measures. Instead, courts may focus on finding care-focused or medical interventions that address the needs of the individual while ensuring public safety.

In cases of schizophrenia, the cognitive and emotional impairments associated with the condition can influence sentencing decisions, especially when symptoms such as delusions or hallucinations play a role in the criminal behavior. Courts may opt for mental health treatment rather than incarceration, recognizing that the defendant's actions were influenced by factors beyond their control. This shift in sentencing reflects a broader understanding of how mental health conditions impact behavior and the importance of rehabilitation over punishment in cases involving severe cognitive and emotional impairments.

Cognitive and emotional impairments play a critical role in the sentencing process, as they highlight the ways in which conditions like TBI, dementia, and schizophrenia can reduce an individual's culpability. By affecting decision-making, impulse control, and emotional regulation, these impairments contribute to criminal behavior in ways that are often beyond the individual's control. Legal systems that recognize cognitive and emotional impairments as mitigating factors help ensure that sentencing reflects a balanced understanding of justice, one that acknowledges the importance of rehabilitation over punishment in cases involving diminished responsibility. Through neuropsychological assessments and careful consideration of mental health conditions, courts can achieve more equitable outcomes that prioritize treatment and support for individuals with cognitive and emotional impairments, promoting a justice system that is both fair and humane.

6 Neuropsychological Assessment Tools

Neuropsychological assessments are essential in both clinical and forensic contexts, providing insights into an individual's cognitive, emotional, and psychological functioning. These assessments are often used to evaluate brain function, identify cognitive impairments, and guide treatment decisions, especially in cases where cognitive and psychological factors may influence legal outcomes. Among the most commonly used tools in neuropsychological assessment are the Wechsler Adult Intelligence Scale (WAIS) for cognitive assessment, the Neuropsychological Assessment Battery (NAB), and the Minnesota Multiphasic Personality Inventory (MMPI) for mental health evaluation. Each of these tools serves a unique purpose and offers a comprehensive look at various aspects of neuropsychological functioning, playing a crucial role in understanding an individual's mental state and cognitive abilities.

6.1 The Wechsler Adult Intelligence Scale (WAIS) for Cognitive Assessment

The Wechsler Adult Intelligence Scale (WAIS) is one of the most widely recognized tools for assessing adult intelligence and cognitive function. Developed by David Wechsler, the WAIS is designed to evaluate an individual's general intellectual ability and specific cognitive domains, including verbal comprehension, perceptual reasoning, working memory, and processing speed. Currently, the WAIS-IV is the most recent version and is widely used in both clinical and forensic settings. Its subtests provide a detailed profile of cognitive strengths and weaknesses, offering insights into areas where an individual may experience difficulties that impact everyday functioning.

The WAIS-IV is divided into several primary and supplemental subtests, with each assessing different cognitive skills. For example, the Verbal Comprehension Index (VCI) assesses an individual's understanding of verbal information, vocabulary, and general knowledge, which can offer insights into verbal learning and language processing abilities. The Perceptual Reasoning Index (PRI) focuses on nonverbal reasoning, problem-solving, and visual–motor coordination, which is essential in assessing spatial awareness and the ability to manipulate visual information. The Working Memory Index (WMI) measures the capacity to hold and manipulate information over short periods, and the Processing Speed Index (PSI) examines the ability to perform cognitive tasks quickly and accurately. Together, these indices provide a holistic view of an individual's cognitive functioning, allowing neuropsychologists to identify deficits that may impact daily life or decision-making abilities.

In forensic contexts, the WAIS-IV is particularly valuable in assessing cognitive impairments that may influence criminal behavior or an individual's capacity to understand legal proceedings. For instance, low scores in working memory and processing speed might indicate challenges in following complex instructions or recalling detailed information, which can impact a defendant's ability to participate in their defense effectively. Similarly, deficits in perceptual reasoning and problem-solving can be relevant in understanding impulsivity or poor decision-making, potentially serving as mitigating factors in criminal sentencing. Overall, the WAIS-IV is a versatile and comprehensive tool that provides valuable insights into an individual's cognitive profile, contributing to more informed legal and clinical decisions.

6.2 *The Neuropsychological Assessment Battery (NAB)*

The Neuropsychological Assessment Battery (NAB) is a comprehensive set of tests designed to evaluate various domains of cognitive functioning, including attention, memory, language, spatial processing, and executive functioning (Buczylowska & Petermann, 2018). Developed to assess both global cognitive functioning and specific cognitive skills, the NAB is widely used in clinical neuropsychology to diagnose cognitive disorders, assess the impact of neurological injuries, and guide rehabilitation plans. It consists of five primary modules, each targeting a different area of cognitive functioning: Attention, Language, Memory, Spatial, and Executive Functioning. These modules provide a thorough assessment of cognitive strengths and weaknesses, making the NAB a highly reliable tool for both clinical and research applications.

The Attention module, for instance, measures an individual's capacity to sustain focus, shift attention, and process information accurately, which is essential in evaluating attention deficits and disorders such as attention deficit hyperactivity disorder (ADHD). The Memory module assesses both immediate and delayed recall abilities, examining verbal and visual memory processes that may be affected by conditions like Alzheimer's disease or traumatic brain injury (TBI). The Language module explores language production and comprehension skills, which are crucial in identifying language-related deficits or disorders. The Spatial module evaluates visual–spatial processing abilities, and the Executive Functioning module assesses higher-order cognitive skills such as planning, problem-solving, and self-monitoring.

In forensic settings, the NAB is particularly valuable in cases involving brain injuries or cognitive impairments that might affect an individual's behavior, decision-making, or capacity to understand legal proceedings. For example, deficits in the Executive Functioning module can suggest difficulties with impulse control, planning, and risk assessment, which are relevant in cases where impulsivity or poor judgment contributed to criminal behavior. Similarly, impairments in the Memory module might indicate challenges in recalling events or details, potentially impacting witness testimony or the ability to recall legal instructions accurately. By providing a detailed assessment of cognitive functioning across multiple domains, the NAB offers insights into how neurological impairments may contribute to an individual's behavior, helping courts make more informed decisions regarding culpability and sentencing.

6.3 The Minnesota Multiphasic Personality Inventory (MMPI) for Mental Health Evaluation

The Minnesota Multiphasic Personality Inventory (MMPI) is one of the most widely used and researched psychological assessment tools for evaluating mental health and personality traits (Floyd & Gupta, 2023). Originally developed in the 1940s and currently available in its most recent version, the MMPI-2, this assessment measures a broad range of psychological conditions, including anxiety, depression, paranoia, and psychotic disorders. The MMPI-2 is structured to identify patterns of thought, behavior, and emotional regulation, making it invaluable for clinical diagnosis, treatment planning, and forensic assessments.

The MMPI-2 includes several validity scales designed to assess the test-taker's approach to the assessment, such as whether they are overreporting symptoms, underreporting symptoms, or responding inconsistently. This is particularly useful in forensic contexts, where individuals may have motivations to exaggerate or minimize psychological symptoms. The assessment also includes several clinical scales that measure a range of mental health conditions. For example, the Depression (D) scale evaluates symptoms of low mood, hopelessness, and fatigue, while the Paranoia (Pa) scale assesses suspiciousness and mistrust, which may contribute to an individual's perceptions and reactions to others.

In forensic cases, the MMPI-2 is invaluable in assessing the mental health of defendants, particularly when questions of competency to stand trial or criminal responsibility arise. For example, an individual with high scores on the Psychopathic Deviate (Pd) scale may exhibit behavioral patterns indicative of impulsivity, disregard for societal norms, or difficulty forming attachments. These traits can be relevant in understanding criminal behavior and informing sentencing decisions. Similarly, high scores on the Paranoia (Pa) scale may suggest a predisposition to interpret interactions as threatening, potentially explaining aggressive or defensive behavior in certain situations. The MMPI-2 can also help identify conditions like schizophrenia or bipolar disorder, which might serve as mitigating factors in sentencing by demonstrating that the defendant's mental health influenced their actions.

The MMPI-2 is also commonly used in competency evaluations, where it assesses whether a defendant has the psychological stability and cognitive function necessary to understand court proceedings and assist in their defense. For instance, elevated scores on the Schizophrenia (Sc) scale can indicate severe impairments in reality testing, which may suggest that the defendant is not capable of comprehending the charges against them or consulting with their attorney effectively. In such cases, the MMPI-2 provides a psychological profile that can guide the court in determining the most appropriate course of action, whether that involves treatment, rehabilitation, or alternative sentencing.

Neuropsychological assessment tools such as the WAIS, NAB, and MMPI provide critical insights into cognitive and psychological functioning, allowing clinicians and legal professionals to make more informed decisions about diagnosis, treatment, and sentencing. The WAIS assesses cognitive abilities that influence decision-making and impulse control, the NAB offers a comprehensive evaluation of various cognitive domains relevant in cases involving brain injury, and the MMPI provides a detailed profile of mental health, crucial for understanding the psychological underpinnings of behavior. Together, these tools play a vital role in identifying cognitive and emotional impairments that may mitigate responsibility in legal cases, promoting a more nuanced approach to justice and rehabilitation for individuals whose behavior is shaped by cognitive and psychological factors. Through the application of these assessments, courts are better equipped to consider the complexities of mental health and cognitive function in sentencing, aiming for fair and individualized outcomes that address the needs of both the individual and society.

7 Neuroimaging Techniques in Sentencing

Neuroimaging techniques have increasingly become valuable tools in the criminal justice system, particularly in sentencing decisions where the mental state and cognitive functioning of a defendant are in question. Techniques like magnetic resonance imaging (MRI) and positron emission tomography (PET) scans offer insights into brain structure and function, allowing for a deeper understanding of the relationship between neurological impairments and behavior. Neuroimaging evidence can provide compelling visual information that highlights structural or functional abnormalities, especially in areas of the brain like the frontal lobe, which is associated with impulse control and decision-making. These visual demonstrations of brain impairments can powerfully impact judges and juries, contributing to decisions regarding culpability, mitigation, and appropriate sentencing.

7.1 Neuroimaging Techniques in Criminal Cases: MRI and PET Scans

MRI and PET scans are two of the most prominent neuroimaging techniques used to assess brain function and structure. MRI is particularly effective at providing high-resolution images of brain anatomy, enabling clinicians to detect structural abnormalities such as brain atrophy, tumors, or lesions. In the context of criminal cases, MRI scans are often used to assess structural damage that might contribute to behavioral or cognitive impairments, which could in turn influence a defendant's actions and decisions. For example, damage to the prefrontal cortex, commonly detected through MRI, has been linked to problems with impulse control, social behavior, and decision-making, all of which can play significant roles in criminal behavior.

PET scans, on the other hand, focus on measuring brain function. By tracking the distribution of a radioactive tracer, PET scans reveal areas of high or low metabolic activity, providing insights into how different brain regions are functioning. In criminal cases, PET scans can be particularly informative when examining functional impairments that are not visible on MRI scans. For example, PET scans may reveal underactivity in the prefrontal cortex or abnormalities in the amygdala—areas linked to emotional regulation and aggression—indicating potential difficulties in managing impulses or responding to emotional stimuli appropriately. These functional insights can aid in understanding whether a defendant's neurological impairments played a role in their criminal behavior.

7.2 The Role of the Frontal Lobe in Impulse Control and Decision-Making

One of the primary brain regions of interest in neuroimaging assessments of criminal behavior is the frontal lobe, particularly the prefrontal cortex. The prefrontal cortex plays a crucial role in executive functioning, including impulse control, judgment, and decision-making. Individuals with damage to this region often struggle with controlling aggressive impulses, planning, and making rational decisions—all factors that can significantly impact behavior in high-stakes or emotionally charged situations.

For example, individuals with frontal lobe damage may act impulsively or without fully considering the consequences of their actions. Neuroimaging studies have shown that damage or dysfunction in this area can lead to disinhibited behavior, meaning that individuals may fail to suppress socially or legally unacceptable impulses (Knutson et al., 2015). In criminal cases, this type of impairment can serve as a mitigating factor during sentencing. When an MRI or PET scan demonstrates frontal lobe dysfunction, it provides tangible evidence that the defendant may have been less able to regulate their behavior, potentially reducing their level of culpability.

Such impairments are particularly relevant in cases involving violent crimes, where impulsivity and poor judgment are often contributing factors. A defendant with documented frontal lobe damage may be less capable of premeditating or controlling violent impulses, supporting arguments for mitigation in sentencing. In such cases, the defense may argue that the neurological impairment reduced the defendant's capacity to act with full responsibility, suggesting that they may benefit from rehabilitation rather than purely punitive sentencing.

7.3 Neuroimaging as a Tool for Visual Evidence in Court

In courtrooms, neuroimaging evidence is not only valuable for its scientific insights but also for its visual impact. MRI and PET scans provide concrete, visual representations of brain abnormalities, which can be highly persuasive for judges and juries who may not have extensive scientific backgrounds. This visual evidence can make the abstract concept of brain impairment more accessible and understandable, reinforcing arguments that the defendant's actions were influenced by neurological deficits beyond their control.

For instance, in cases where a defendant has been shown to have reduced prefrontal cortex activity, defense attorneys can use neuroimaging to illustrate the biological basis of impaired impulse control or decision-making. By presenting these images alongside expert testimony that explains the link between brain function and behavior, attorneys can strengthen their arguments for leniency or alternative sentencing options, such as mental health treatment. The ability of neuroimaging evidence to visually demonstrate brain impairments gives it a unique power in the courtroom, often making it more compelling than verbal testimony alone.

Neuroimaging evidence has been used successfully in several high-profile cases to argue for reduced sentences based on brain impairments. In some cases, courts have accepted neuroimaging findings as evidence that the defendant lacked full control over their actions or that their cognitive impairments contributed to their criminal behavior. This type of evidence can be particularly impactful in cases involving mental health disorders, brain injuries, or developmental disorders that affect cognitive and emotional regulation. While neuroimaging cannot directly prove causation between brain impairments and criminal actions, it provides a biological context that can support arguments for mitigation, especially when combined with behavioral assessments and expert testimony.

7.4 Challenges and Ethical Considerations in Using Neuroimaging Evidence

While neuroimaging provides valuable insights into brain function and structure, there are several challenges and ethical considerations associated with its use in sentencing. One major challenge is the risk of overinterpretation; while neuroimaging can reveal abnormalities, it does not necessarily predict behavior with certainty. Courts and juries may misinterpret brain scans as definitive evidence of reduced responsibility, even though neuroimaging findings are often only one part of a complex behavioral and psychological profile. As a result, neuroimaging experts must take care to explain the limitations of brain imaging, ensuring that the court does not place undue weight on these findings alone.

Another ethical consideration is the potential for bias, as neuroimaging evidence may unfairly influence the jury's perception of the defendant. Studies have shown that juries tend to find scientific evidence, particularly visual evidence like brain scans, to be more persuasive than other forms of evidence (Helm, 2021). This raises the risk of bias in cases where the neuroimaging findings are ambiguous or where the correlation between brain impairment and behavior is not well-established. For this reason, neuroimaging evidence should always be presented alongside comprehensive assessments that include psychological evaluations and behavioral observations.

Moreover, the use of neuroimaging in sentencing raises questions about privacy and the defendant's right to autonomy. Brain scans can reveal sensitive information about mental health conditions, personality traits, and other aspects of cognitive functioning that may extend beyond the scope of the crime in question. This information could be used unfairly against the defendant, potentially influencing sentencing decisions in ways that do not directly relate to their criminal behavior.

Neuroimaging techniques like MRI and PET scans have revolutionized the ability to assess brain function and structure, providing valuable insights that can inform sentencing decisions in criminal cases. By identifying brain abnormalities, particularly in the frontal lobe, neuroimaging can highlight impairments in impulse control, decision-making, and emotional regulation, all of which are relevant in understanding criminal behavior. The visual impact of neuroimaging evidence adds a powerful dimension to court proceedings, helping judges and juries to appreciate the neurological factors that may mitigate responsibility. However, while neuroimaging evidence can play a crucial role in advocating for more nuanced sentencing, it must be presented carefully and ethically to avoid overreliance or misinterpretation. Neuroimaging findings should be considered alongside other assessments, ensuring that they are used to support, rather than replace, a holistic understanding of the defendant's mental state. As neuroimaging technology continues to advance, its role in the justice system will likely grow, emphasizing the importance of ethical standards and careful interpretation in using brain imaging to inform fair and just sentencing outcomes.

8 Expert Testimony in Sentencing Hearings

Expert testimony in sentencing hearings plays a critical role in bridging the often complex world of neuropsychology with the legal standards that guide court decisions. Neuropsychologists are increasingly called upon to provide expert testimony that explains how cognitive impairments or psychological conditions may have influenced a defendant's actions. These expert witnesses translate technical assessments and neuropsychological data into understandable terms, helping judges and juries appreciate the extent of the defendant's mental state and its potential role in the crime. In cases where the defendant's responsibility or level of culpability is in question, neuropsychologists provide essential insights that may affect sentencing, often leading to mitigation or alternative sentencing if significant impairments are demonstrated.

8.1 The Role of Neuropsychologists in Sentencing Hearings

At sentencing hearings, neuropsychologists serve as expert witnesses tasked with explaining complex data about a defendant's cognitive or emotional impairments in ways that resonate with legal standards and objectives. Neuropsychological assessments, which may include tests of memory, attention, executive function, and emotional regulation, provide a profile of the defendant's mental functioning. However, translating this data into practical information about the defendant's culpability requires a clear explanation of how specific impairments affected the defendant's capacity to control behavior, understand consequences, or make reasoned decisions at the time of the offense.

For example, in cases involving defendants with traumatic brain injuries (TBI), neuropsychologists can testify about how specific cognitive impairments related to the injury—such as impulsivity, poor judgment, or emotional dysregulation—may have limited the individual's control over their actions. Similarly, for defendants with severe psychiatric conditions, such as schizophrenia, neuropsychologists might testify about how symptoms like hallucinations or delusions could have clouded the individual's perception of reality, impacting their ability to recognize the wrongfulness of their actions. The neuropsychologist's role in these hearings is to present data-based, scientific insights in a manner that aligns with the legal standards governing mitigation and culpability.

8.2 *Explaining Cognitive Impairments to the Court*

One of the primary responsibilities of neuropsychologists in court is to explain the impact of cognitive impairments on behavior in an accessible way. Because cognitive impairments can be highly technical, effective expert testimony requires that the neuropsychologist simplify these concepts without sacrificing scientific accuracy. Terms such as "executive dysfunction" or "impulse control deficits," for instance, need to be framed in ways that nonexperts can understand, often using analogies or concrete examples to illustrate how such impairments manifest in daily life.

For instance, when explaining executive dysfunction, a neuropsychologist might describe it as a set of mental skills that allow individuals to organize their actions, plan ahead, and control impulses. A person with executive dysfunction due to frontal lobe impairment may struggle to foresee the consequences of actions or suppress impulsive behaviors, leading to problematic decision-making. In presenting this information, neuropsychologists often underscore that cognitive impairments are not a choice or a flaw in character but are instead the result of neurological conditions that limit one's ability to function normally. By highlighting these points, neuropsychologists aid the court in understanding the difference between willful criminal behavior and actions driven by uncontrollable impairments.

8.3 *Bridging Neuropsychological Data with Legal Standards*

The intersection of neuropsychology and law requires that expert testimony meet legal standards concerning responsibility, intent, and capacity. Neuropsychologists must navigate this intersection by tailoring their testimony to address legal concepts such as "mens rea," or the mental state of the defendant at the time of the crime. Mens rea, which speaks to the intent or knowledge of wrongdoing, is a cornerstone of many criminal cases, and cognitive or emotional impairments may impact whether an individual fully understood or intended the consequences of their actions.

When addressing mens rea, neuropsychologists can use evidence from neuropsychological assessments to argue that a defendant's impaired mental state reduced their capacity to form intent. For example, in cases where cognitive impairments limit the defendant's ability to foresee the outcome of actions or differentiate between right and wrong, expert testimony can establish that the individual's mental state was not conducive to fully intentional behavior. A person with a significant cognitive disorder, such as dementia, may lack the awareness or judgment required for understanding the implications of their actions, rendering them less culpable than someone with intact cognitive functioning.

8.4 Focus: The Impact of Impairments on the Defendant's Mental State

In determining culpability, sentencing hearings often focus on how impairments affected the defendant's mental state and behavioral control at the time of the offense. Neuropsychologists may provide insights into how specific impairments—such as reduced impulse control, lack of foresight, or emotional dysregulation—shaped the defendant's reactions and actions. Such testimony can help clarify that the criminal act was not solely a product of free will but was instead influenced by neurological or psychological constraints that the defendant could not entirely control.

Consider the case of a defendant with severe emotional dysregulation stemming from a mood disorder, such as bipolar disorder, or brain injury affecting the limbic system. Neuropsychologists might testify that the defendant's heightened emotional reactivity or impaired impulse control, as a symptom of their condition, contributed significantly to their behavior during the incident. By presenting detailed examples of how emotional dysregulation manifests in daily scenarios, expert witnesses can help the court recognize that the defendant's actions may have been driven by factors outside of conscious control. This understanding of the defendant's impaired mental state may support arguments for mitigated sentencing, acknowledging that while the defendant committed a crime, their ability to control or understand their actions was compromised.

8.5 Ethical Considerations in Neuropsychological Testimony

While neuropsychological testimony offers valuable insights, it is essential to address the ethical considerations involved in presenting such evidence. Neuropsychologists must ensure that their testimony remains scientifically accurate, unbiased, and respectful of the legal process. One ethical concern is the risk of overgeneralization; while cognitive impairments can influence behavior, not every individual with an impairment will act in the same way. Neuropsychologists must avoid drawing overly deterministic conclusions, instead presenting the nuances of how impairments might interact with other situational or personal factors.

Additionally, neuropsychologists must be mindful of how their testimony may affect public perception of individuals with mental health conditions or cognitive impairments. By emphasizing that these impairments do not eliminate responsibility but rather mitigate it under specific circumstances, neuropsychologists can help promote a more balanced understanding of mental health and criminal behavior.

Expert testimony by neuropsychologists plays a vital role in sentencing hearings, providing courts with the necessary insights to make informed, compassionate decisions about culpability and punishment. By explaining the impact of cognitive and emotional impairments on behavior, neuropsychologists support arguments for more rehabilitative approaches when appropriate, promoting justice while acknowledging the complexities of human behavior. As the field of neuropsychology continues to evolve, expert testimony will remain an essential element in the pursuit of fair, equitable sentencing.

9 Forensic Reports and Legal Advocacy

Forensic reports play a crucial role in legal advocacy during sentencing, especially in cases where mental health and cognitive functioning impact a defendant's responsibility or culpability. These reports serve as a bridge between the scientific findings of neuropsychological assessments and the legal arguments made by the defense, providing the court with a comprehensive and objective evaluation of the defendant's mental state, cognitive abilities, and any mitigating factors that may warrant alternative sentencing. In preparing forensic reports, neuropsychologists must balance the rigorous requirements of scientific analysis with the need for accessible, legally relevant communication that can support defense arguments effectively. Detailed forensic reports, therefore, are invaluable tools in the pursuit of fair sentencing, enabling courts to consider the full picture of a defendant's mental health and cognitive functioning.

9.1 Structure and Purpose of Forensic Reports in Sentencing Advocacy

A well-prepared forensic report provides a systematic, evidence-based analysis of the defendant's cognitive and psychological profile. Forensic reports typically begin with a clear statement of the referral question—often focusing on the defendant's mental health, decision-making capacity, or specific cognitive impairments relevant to the case. This clarity of purpose ensures that all parties involved in the sentencing hearing understand the scope and relevance of the neuropsychologist's evaluation from the outset.

To address the referral question effectively, forensic reports must include a summary of background information, such as the defendant's medical history, social background, and any history of psychological or psychiatric conditions. The report then provides details of the neuropsychological assessments used, test results, and an interpretation of these results in the context of the defendant's functioning. This process includes assessing domains such as executive functioning, memory, and emotional regulation, which are often directly relevant to questions of culpability and behavioral control. By systematically presenting these findings, forensic reports allow legal advocates to draw on scientific evidence when arguing for mitigated or alternative sentencing.

Beyond providing raw data, forensic reports translate these findings into practical conclusions about the defendant's mental state and functioning at the time of the crime. For example, a forensic report might conclude that a defendant with a traumatic brain injury (TBI) experienced significant impulse control issues, which could have contributed to their criminal behavior. By highlighting such factors in an organized, objective way, forensic reports serve as foundational documents that defense attorneys can use to advocate for appropriate sentencing, whether through rehabilitation programs, mental health treatment, or other alternatives to traditional punishment.

9.2 Balancing Scientific Analysis and Legal Arguments

Creating an effective forensic report for legal advocacy requires a careful balance between scientific rigor and legal applicability. While neuropsychologists must adhere to objective standards in testing and analysis, their findings must also be relevant to the legal questions at hand. In the context of sentencing, this often means interpreting test results in light of concepts like intent, culpability, or capacity for self-regulation. Neuropsychologists are therefore tasked with presenting their data in ways that are both scientifically valid and aligned with legal considerations.

One challenge in balancing scientific analysis with legal arguments is ensuring that the report remains impartial. Neuropsychologists must avoid any tendency to advocate directly for the defendant, as this would compromise the report's credibility. Instead, they present findings in an objective manner that supports informed legal advocacy. Defense attorneys can then draw on these findings to argue that the defendant's cognitive or emotional impairments limit their responsibility, reduce their level of intent, or warrant a rehabilitative approach rather than strict punishment. This balance allows the forensic report to function as a reliable, unbiased document that serves both the scientific and legal communities.

To further support legal arguments, forensic reports may also include a discussion of how specific impairments influenced the defendant's behavior in the context of the crime. For example, if a defendant with a history of severe mood disorder acted impulsively during a heated confrontation, the neuropsychologist might conclude that this behavior aligns with symptoms of emotional dysregulation commonly associated with mood disorders. Such explanations give defense attorneys a scientific basis for arguing that the defendant's behavior was influenced by mental health factors, potentially justifying alternative sentencing options.

9.3 Importance of Clear and Objective Communication in Forensic Reports

Forensic reports are often presented in court and are scrutinized by judges, attorneys, and jurors who may lack scientific or psychological training. Therefore, clarity is paramount. Neuropsychologists must avoid jargon and provide explanations of technical terms, presenting findings in a straightforward manner that makes their significance clear to a lay audience. This approach ensures that the report's conclusions are accessible to all parties, facilitating an informed understanding of the defendant's mental state and its impact on their actions.

Clear communication in forensic reports involves more than just avoiding technical terms; it also means structuring the report in a logical, readable format. This often includes breaking down complex findings into subcategories—such as cognitive impairments, emotional regulation issues, and behavioral impacts—allowing readers to understand the full scope of the defendant's condition and its relevance to sentencing. The inclusion of case examples or analogies can also help make abstract concepts more relatable. For instance, when discussing a defendant's executive functioning deficits, the neuropsychologist might compare these impairments to difficulties in "mental organization," similar to navigating a maze with numerous dead ends. Such explanations make the cognitive and emotional limitations concrete for readers.

An objective tone further reinforces the report's reliability. Neuropsychologists must ensure that their conclusions are backed by data rather than subjective opinions, maintaining impartiality throughout the report. For example, rather than stating that a defendant "could not control their actions," a more objective approach might involve stating that "impulse control assessments indicate a significant deficit in behavioral regulation, which may have impaired the defendant's capacity to inhibit impulsive responses." By presenting findings in a clear, unbiased manner, forensic reports enhance the credibility of the neuropsychologist's conclusions, providing a strong basis for the defense's legal arguments.

9.4 Ethical Considerations in Forensic Reporting

Producing forensic reports for legal advocacy involves ethical responsibilities, as neuropsychologists must prioritize accuracy and impartiality to maintain the integrity of the legal process. Neuropsychologists are required to uphold confidentiality, reporting only relevant findings without bias. They must also ensure that their conclusions are based on sound data, avoiding overgeneralizations that might misrepresent the defendant's condition.

Ethical guidelines emphasize the importance of objectivity; while the report may support the defense's argument, it should not act as an instrument of advocacy. By adhering to ethical standards, neuropsychologists reinforce the credibility of their reports, ensuring that courts receive accurate and reliable insights to guide sentencing.

Forensic reports are essential tools for legal advocacy, helping shape sentencing by providing objective, scientifically grounded insights into a defendant's mental health and cognitive functioning. By balancing detailed analysis with clear communication, neuropsychologists produce reports that courts can rely on to make informed decisions. Through careful attention to both ethical standards and the needs of legal advocates, forensic reports support fair sentencing, offering courts a deeper understanding of the defendant's condition and its relevance to justice and rehabilitation.

10 Case Study 1: Mitigation in Traumatic Brain Injury (TBI)

In criminal cases involving defendants with neuropsychological impairments, a comprehensive assessment can play a crucial role in determining appropriate sentencing. A particularly compelling example of this is a case where a defendant, charged with assault, was found to have suffered from a traumatic brain injury (TBI) that severely impacted his impulse control. This case illustrates how neuropsychological evaluations can highlight mitigating factors that influence behavior, ultimately leading the court to consider rehabilitative alternatives to incarceration.

The defendant, a 32-year-old male, was charged with assault following a physical altercation at a local establishment. Witnesses reported that the defendant reacted suddenly and violently after a minor disagreement escalated, leading to injuries for the other individual involved. Upon further investigation, the defense argued that the defendant's behavior was influenced by a prior TBI that had significantly affected his cognitive and behavioral functioning. The defense team requested a neuropsychological evaluation to assess whether the defendant's actions could have stemmed from impairments related to his brain injury, thereby introducing TBI as a potential mitigating factor.

10.1 Neuropsychological Evaluation: Impulse Control Deficits

The neuropsychological evaluation revealed substantial deficits in impulse control and emotional regulation, two cognitive domains often impacted by TBI. Through cognitive and behavioral testing, the neuropsychologist found that the defendant had impairments in executive functions, which include planning, decision-making, and inhibition control. These impairments frequently manifest as difficulties in managing emotions and controlling impulsive reactions, especially under stress or in heated situations.

Several tests were administered to assess these deficits more precisely. The Wisconsin Card Sorting Test (WCST), used to assess cognitive flexibility and executive functioning, indicated significant challenges in adapting to changing rules and situations. Additionally, the Stroop Test, which measures the ability to inhibit cognitive interference, revealed that the defendant struggled to suppress impulsive reactions. Together, these findings supported the hypothesis that the defendant's TBI had left him with compromised impulse control and limited capacity for self-regulation in high-stress situations.

The neuropsychologist's report provided crucial insights into how the defendant's TBI-related impairments affected his behavior during the incident in question. Specifically, it was concluded that the defendant's impulse control deficits likely played a central role in his aggressive response, as he lacked the cognitive tools necessary to assess the situation calmly and avoid escalation. This conclusion was backed by scientific literature indicating that individuals with TBI often experience challenges in emotional regulation and impulse control, especially in contexts where social stressors or confrontations are present.

10.2 Sentencing Outcome: Rehabilitative Sentence

The court's understanding of the neuropsychological assessment findings was pivotal in the final sentencing decision. Rather than imposing a standard prison sentence, the court opted for a rehabilitative approach focused on cognitive and behavioral therapy, recognizing that the defendant's actions were, to a significant extent, influenced by his TBI-related impairments. This alternative sentence included participation in programs aimed at improving impulse control, emotional regulation, and social skills training. The defendant was also required to attend regular sessions with a neuropsychologist to monitor his progress and adapt his treatment plan as necessary.

This case illustrates the power of neuropsychological evidence in shaping sentencing outcomes. The rehabilitation-focused sentence acknowledged the role of the defendant's TBI in his behavior, balancing accountability with a recognition of his cognitive limitations. It underscores the importance of understanding neuropsychological impairments in criminal cases and highlights the potential for alternative sentencing options that prioritize rehabilitation over punishment.

11 Case Study 2: Schizophrenia and Sentencing

Another notable case involves a defendant with schizophrenia, convicted of a violent crime in which neuropsychological assessment played a key role in advocating for mental health treatment instead of a long-term prison sentence. In this case, the defendant, a 27-year-old man, was involved in a violent altercation that left another individual seriously injured. The court proceedings revealed a history of mental illness, with schizophrenia diagnosed several years before the incident. Given the nature of his symptoms, the defense argued that the defendant's criminal behavior was directly related to his impaired reality testing and delusional thinking, both of which are hallmark features of schizophrenia.

11.1 Neuropsychological Assessment: Delusional Thinking and Impaired Reality Testing

To better understand the influence of the defendant's schizophrenia on his actions, a neuropsychological assessment was conducted, focusing on his cognitive functioning, symptom severity, and insight into his condition. The assessment revealed severe impairments in reality testing and the presence of persistent delusions, which significantly distorted the defendant's understanding of the world around him.

Among the assessment tools used was the Positive and Negative Syndrome Scale (PANSS), which evaluates symptoms specific to schizophrenia, including hallucinations, delusions, and disorganized thought processes. The defendant scored high on items related to delusions and paranoid ideation, supporting the assertion that he experienced substantial distortions in reality perception. Additionally, his performance on the Neuropsychological Assessment Battery (NAB) showed deficits in executive functioning, further illustrating his limited capacity to process information logically and assess social situations accurately.

The neuropsychologist's findings concluded that at the time of the offense, the defendant likely believed he was acting out of self-preservation or responding to a perceived threat, consistent with his delusional thinking. The assessment highlighted that the defendant's actions were not motivated by malicious intent but were instead a consequence of his impaired mental state and inability to distinguish between real and imagined threats.

11.2 Sentencing Outcome: Mental Health Treatment

The neuropsychological evidence presented during the sentencing phase had a significant impact on the final outcome. Rather than sentencing the defendant to an extended prison term, the court ordered him to undergo long-term mental health treatment in a secure psychiatric facility. This sentence reflected an understanding that the defendant's schizophrenia played a fundamental role in his criminal behavior and that traditional incarceration would neither address his mental health needs nor reduce the risk of recidivism.

The court's decision to prioritize mental health treatment over punishment was grounded in a recognition of the defendant's diminished responsibility due to his severe mental illness. By assigning the defendant to a treatment facility rather than prison, the court aimed to provide a supportive environment where he could receive the medical and therapeutic interventions necessary to manage his symptoms effectively. Additionally, the structured environment of a psychiatric facility offered safeguards to ensure public safety while addressing the root causes of the defendant's behavior.

Both of these case studies illustrate the essential role of neuropsychological evaluations in shaping sentencing decisions for defendants with cognitive or mental health impairments. In the first case, the defendant's TBI-related impulse control deficits were recognized as mitigating factors that justified a rehabilitative sentence. This decision underscored the importance of understanding the cognitive limitations associated with brain injuries and their impact on behavior in high-stress situations.

In the second case, the defendant's schizophrenia, marked by delusional thinking and impaired reality testing, was found to have significantly influenced his criminal behavior. The court's decision to prioritize mental health treatment over incarceration acknowledged the defendant's diminished capacity and highlighted a shift toward rehabilitation rather than punishment for individuals with severe mental illnesses.

These cases exemplify the potential of neuropsychological assessments to provide courts with critical insights into the mental state and cognitive functioning of defendants. By incorporating such evaluations into sentencing considerations, the legal system can achieve a more nuanced approach that addresses the underlying causes of criminal behavior, promotes rehabilitation, and ultimately supports fairer, more compassionate sentencing practices. Through these examples, we see how the principles of justice can be upheld by integrating scientific evidence with a focus on individualized, context-sensitive outcomes for defendants with neuropsychological impairments.

12 Ethical and Professional Challenges in Forensic Assessments

Forensic neuropsychology is a critical intersection of psychology and the legal system, wherein neuropsychologists assess individuals involved in legal proceedings to provide insights into their cognitive, emotional, and behavioral functioning. These assessments play a vital role in informing court decisions, particularly in mitigation and sentencing. However, the practice is fraught with ethical and professional challenges that demand rigorous attention to ensure that evaluations are conducted with integrity, validity, and fairness. This section explores the challenges of maintaining objectivity in forensic assessments, ensuring valid and reliable assessments for the court, and the ethical considerations that arise when recommending sentencing outcomes.

12.1 Maintaining Objectivity in Forensic Assessments

One of the primary challenges in forensic assessments is maintaining objectivity. Forensic neuropsychologists often find themselves in a complex position, balancing the scientific aspects of their assessments with the legal demands of the cases they are involved in. This duality can lead to potential biases, where the desire to advocate for a client may inadvertently influence the objectivity of the assessment. Neuropsychologists must be acutely aware of their own biases, beliefs, and values, as these factors can color their interpretation of findings.

To combat bias, neuropsychologists are encouraged to adopt standardized assessment protocols and evidence-based practices. Using validated assessment tools, such as the Wechsler Adult Intelligence Scale (WAIS) or the Minnesota Multiphasic Personality Inventory (MMPI), can provide a more objective basis for evaluations. Furthermore, employing multiple assessment methods, including interviews, behavioral observations, and collateral information, can enhance the reliability of the findings. Despite these measures, the subjectivity inherent in interpreting neuropsychological data remains a challenge. Neuropsychologists must strive to separate their clinical impressions from the legal context to uphold the integrity of their assessments.

Additionally, the pressure from legal teams or clients to produce favorable results can further complicate the objectivity of the assessment process. Neuropsychologists may face ethical dilemmas when defense attorneys or clients attempt to influence the evaluation process or outcomes. To mitigate these challenges, it is essential for neuropsychologists to adhere strictly to ethical guidelines established by organizations such as the American Psychological Association (APA) and the American Academy of Forensic Psychology. These guidelines emphasize the importance of professional integrity, objectivity, and impartiality in forensic assessments.

12.2 Ensuring Valid and Reliable Assessments for Court

The validity and reliability of forensic assessments are paramount for their acceptance in court. Neuropsychologists must ensure that their assessments provide an accurate and comprehensive picture of the individual's cognitive and emotional functioning. Validity refers to the degree to which an assessment measures what it claims to measure, while reliability refers to the consistency of the results obtained.

To ensure valid and reliable assessments, neuropsychologists should employ standardized procedures and norm-referenced tests, which provide a benchmark for interpreting scores relative to a defined population. Additionally, ongoing training and professional development are crucial for neuropsychologists to stay informed about advancements in assessment techniques and tools. This commitment to continuous learning enhances the quality of assessments and reinforces the credibility of the findings presented in court.

Moreover, neuropsychologists must be diligent in documenting their assessment processes and results. Clear, detailed reports that outline the methods used, the rationale for selected tests, and a comprehensive interpretation of the findings not only bolster the reliability of the assessments but also enhance their defensibility in legal contexts. Accurate documentation serves as a crucial safeguard against potential challenges to the validity of the assessments.

However, neuropsychologists may encounter situations where the assessments yield ambiguous or conflicting results. In such cases, it becomes essential to communicate these complexities to the court transparently. Failing to do so can lead to misunderstandings regarding the individual's cognitive and emotional capacities, which may significantly impact sentencing decisions. Therefore, effective communication and transparency regarding the assessment process and its limitations are fundamental to ensuring that courts make informed decisions based on the best available evidence.

12.3 Ethical Considerations in Recommending Sentencing Outcomes

The ethical considerations surrounding the recommendation of sentencing outcomes are among the most profound challenges faced by forensic neuropsychologists. When evaluating defendants, neuropsychologists may uncover information about cognitive and emotional impairments that significantly impact the individual's culpability and capacity for rehabilitation. The question of how this information should influence sentencing recommendations is ethically complex.

Neuropsychologists have a professional responsibility to present their findings honestly and impartially, regardless of the potential implications for sentencing. However, the nature of forensic work often necessitates a consideration of how impairments may warrant mitigating circumstances. In cases where a defendant's mental health issues or cognitive impairments significantly influence their behavior, the neuropsychologist may advocate for alternative sentencing options, such as mental health treatment or rehabilitation, rather than incarceration.

The ethical challenge arises in ensuring that such recommendations are grounded in scientific evidence and clinical judgment rather than personal biases or advocacy for leniency. Neuropsychologists must balance their roles as evaluators with their potential influence on legal outcomes, which can create tension between advocating for the individual's best interests and fulfilling their professional obligations to the court.

Moreover, the implications of sentencing outcomes can extend beyond the individual defendant to impact broader societal issues, such as public safety and perceptions of justice. Neuropsychologists must grapple with the ethical ramifications of their recommendations, considering not only the needs of the defendant but also the potential effects on victims and the community. This holistic perspective underscores the importance of ethical decision-making in forensic neuropsychology.

The field of forensic neuropsychology presents a myriad of ethical and professional challenges that require careful navigation. Maintaining objectivity in assessments, ensuring valid and reliable evaluations, and addressing the ethical considerations surrounding sentencing recommendations are paramount for neuropsychologists working within the legal system. By adhering to established ethical guidelines, employing standardized assessment protocols, and committing to ongoing professional development, neuropsychologists can enhance the integrity of their work and contribute meaningfully to the legal process. Ultimately, the role of forensic neuropsychologists is not only to provide insight into individual cases but also to uphold the principles of justice, equity, and rehabilitation within the legal system.

13 Conclusion

The chapter on mitigation and sentencing highlights the critical role that neuropsychological evidence plays in promoting fair and individualized sentencing outcomes within the criminal justice system. As the understanding of cognitive and emotional impairments evolves, the integration of neuropsychological assessments into legal proceedings offers a pathway toward more just and compassionate resolutions for defendants. By recognizing the nuances of individual circumstances, the legal system can shift toward a more rehabilitative approach that considers not only the crime committed but also the underlying factors contributing to a defendant's behavior.

Neuropsychological evidence serves as a powerful tool in advocating for mitigating circumstances that influence sentencing outcomes. Cognitive and emotional impairments, such as traumatic brain injury, mental health disorders, or developmental delays, can significantly impact an individual's decision-making processes and impulse control. These conditions often play a pivotal role in understanding the context of a defendant's actions and their ability to navigate social and legal norms. By incorporating this evidence into sentencing deliberations, the justice system acknowledges that not all defendants possess equal culpability and that their experiences and challenges must be considered when determining appropriate consequences.

The importance of individualized sentencing cannot be overstated. Traditional punitive approaches to justice often fail to account for the complexities of human behavior, leading to one-size-fits-all sentences that may not adequately address the root causes of criminal conduct. Neuropsychological assessments provide a nuanced understanding of a defendant's mental state at the time of the offense, offering insights that can inform the court's decisions. This individualized approach not only promotes fairness but also facilitates the possibility of rehabilitation, allowing individuals to receive the support and treatment they need to reintegrate into society successfully.

Moreover, the chapter underscores the potential for neuropsychological assessments to enable a more rehabilitative justice system. By prioritizing treatment and rehabilitation over punitive measures, the legal system can address the underlying issues that contribute to criminal behavior. For example, defendants with mental health disorders may benefit from targeted therapeutic interventions rather than lengthy prison sentences. This shift toward rehabilitation not only enhances the well-being of the individual but also contributes to broader societal goals of reducing recidivism and promoting public safety.

In conclusion, the integration of neuropsychological evidence into mitigation and sentencing processes represents a significant advancement in the pursuit of justice. By acknowledging the influence of cognitive and emotional impairments on behavior and decision-making, the legal system can embrace a more compassionate and individualized approach to sentencing. This paradigm shift not only promotes fairness and equity in legal outcomes but also aligns with the broader goals of rehabilitation and societal reintegration. As the field of neuropsychology continues to advance, it holds the promise of transforming how the criminal justice system understands and responds to human behavior, ultimately leading to a more just and humane society.

References

Aggravating and Mitigating Factors in Criminal Sentencing Law. (2024, October 15). *Justia*. https://www.justia.com/criminal/aggravating-mitigating-factors/

Alimardani, A. (2023). An empirical study of the use of neuroscience in sentencing in New South Wales, Australia. *Frontiers in Psychology, 14*. https://doi.org/10.3389/fpsyg.2023.1228354

Buczylowska, D., & Petermann, F. (2018). Intraindividual variability in executive function performance in healthy adults: Cross-sectional analysis of the NAB executive functions module. *Frontiers in Psychology, 9*. https://doi.org/10.3389/fpsyg.2018.00329

Compare, A., Zarbo, C., Shonin, E., Van Gordon, W., & Marconi, C. (2014). Emotional regulation and depression: A potential mediator between heart and mind. *Cardiovascular Psychiatry and Neurology, 2014*, 1–10. https://doi.org/10.1155/2014/324374

De Vel-Palumbo, M., Ferguson, R., Schein, C., Chang, M. X., & Bastian, B. (2022). Morally excused but socially excluded: Denying agency through the defense of mental impairment. *PLoS One, 17*(7), e0272061. https://doi.org/10.1371/journal.pone.0272061

Floyd, A. E., & Gupta, V. (2023). *April 24*. StatPearls–NCBI Bookshelf. https://www.ncbi.nlm.nih.gov/books/NBK557525/

Hall v. Florida. (n.d.). https://www.apa.org. https://www.apa.org/about/offices/ogc/amicus/hall

Helm, R. K. (2021). Evaluating witness testimony: Juror knowledge, false memory, and the utility of evidence-based directions. *The International Journal of Evidence & Proof, 25*(4), 264–285. https://doi.org/10.1177/13657127211031018

Iltis, A. S., Misra, S., Dunn, L. B., Brown, G. K., Campbell, A., Earll, S. A., Glowinski, A., Hadley, W. B., Pies, R., & DuBois, J. M. (2013). Addressing risks to advance mental Health research. *JAMA Psychiatry, 70*(12), 1363. https://doi.org/10.1001/jamapsychiatry.2013.2105

Knutson, K. M., Monte, O. D., Schintu, S., Wassermann, E. M., Raymont, V., Grafman, J., & Krueger, F. (2015). Areas of brain damage underlying increased reports of behavioral disinhibition. *Journal of Neuropsychiatry, 27*(3), 193–198. https://doi.org/10.1176/appi.neuropsych.14060126

Lamberti, J. S. (2016). Preventing criminal recidivism through mental health and criminal justice collaboration. *Psychiatric Services, 67*(11), 1206–1212. https://doi.org/10.1176/appi.ps.201500384

Lockett v. Ohio, 438 U.S. 586 (1978). (n.d.). *Justia law*. https://supreme.justia.com/cases/federal/us/438/586/

Moore, K. E., Oberleitner, L. M. S., Zonana, H. V., Buchanan, A. W., Pittman, B. P., Verplaetse, T. L., Angarita, G. A., Roberts, W., & McKee, S. A. (2019). Psychiatric disorders and crime in the US population. *The Journal of Clinical Psychiatry, 80*(2). https://doi.org/10.4088/jcp.18m12317

Oyez. (n.d.). *Oyez*. https://www.oyez.org/cases/2001/00-8452

People v. Patterson. (2001, December 2). *Justia law*. https://law.justia.com/cases/california/supreme-court/2017/s225193.html

Roper v. Simmons, 543 U.S. 551 (2005). (n.d.). *Justia law*. https://supreme.justia.com/cases/federal/us/543/551/

Woodson v. North Carolina (1976). (n.d.). *LII/Legal information institute*. https://www.law.cornell.edu/wex/woodson_v_north_carolina_(1976)

Witness Testimony and Memory

1 Introduction

Witness testimony, often regarded as a cornerstone of legal evidence, holds significant influence in judicial decisions. The reliability of witness accounts, particularly their memory recall, can greatly impact the outcome of cases, making it critical to understand the psychological and neurobiological mechanisms that influence these testimonies. Neuropsychology, the field that explores the intricate relationships between brain function, cognition, and behavior, provides invaluable insights into how memory operates, how it can falter, and the factors that may enhance or hinder its reliability in a legal setting.

The processes underpinning witness memory are complex and can be subject to vulnerabilities that may reduce accuracy. Factors like cognitive biases, emotional distress, stress, suggestibility, and the passage of time can all influence how accurately a witness remembers and reports events. These influences may lead to distorted or even completely erroneous recollections, a phenomenon that raises important questions about the fairness of legal proceedings that depend on eyewitness accounts. Neuropsychologists play a critical role in examining the integrity of witness testimony and addressing potential issues of reliability through the lens of cognitive and memory science. By analyzing how memory is affected by various internal and external factors, neuropsychologists contribute to a more nuanced understanding of witness credibility and help establish protocols that mitigate risks associated with unreliable testimony.

© The Author(s), under exclusive license to Springer Nature Switzerland AG 2025

K. J. Reddy, *Foundations of Criminal Forensic Neuropsychology*,
https://doi.org/10.1007/978-3-031-83771-5_14

1.1 Cognitive Processes Underlying Witness Testimony

Memory, a complex cognitive process, involves three main stages: encoding, storage, and retrieval. At each stage, errors or biases can arise, shaping the reliability of what is later remembered and reported. Encoding, the process by which an experience is initially perceived and registered, is heavily influenced by attention, perceptual factors, and stress levels. For instance, a person who witnesses a traumatic event may focus on certain details while ignoring others, often due to the brain's prioritization of survival-relevant information over peripheral details. This prioritization can cause gaps or distortions in memory, a concept sometimes referred to as "weapon focus" in cases involving a weapon present during a crime scene.

The storage phase, where memories are consolidated, can also be vulnerable to distortion. Memory consolidation relies on neural processes that stabilize and integrate encoded information into long-term memory, yet this stage is prone to decay and interference from other information. Over time, stored memories may fade or become altered by subsequent experiences, discussions, or exposure to misinformation. Neuroimaging studies suggest that brain regions such as the hippocampus, prefrontal cortex (PFC), and amygdala are central to the consolidation of emotional and factual memory, but they are not infallible and may be influenced by sleep quality, stress hormones, and neural plasticity, all of which can affect how memories are stored over time.

The retrieval phase, when an individual recalls stored information, is also susceptible to error, especially under suggestive questioning or leading prompts. Research has shown that suggestibility—the tendency to be influenced by misleading information—can lead to false memories or confabulations, especially in situations where a witness is questioned repeatedly. The phenomenon of "source monitoring error," in which individuals misattribute the origin of a memory, can further complicate witness recall, causing witnesses to confuse their own recollections with external suggestions. Neuropsychology has identified certain conditions, such as sleep deprivation, intoxication, or high levels of stress, that can exacerbate retrieval errors, leading to memories that may feel accurate but are distorted or entirely fabricated.

1.2 Vulnerabilities and Influencing Factors in Eyewitness Memory

Eyewitness memory is particularly sensitive to various vulnerabilities that can compromise accuracy. These include emotional stress, social pressures, and suggestibility. Emotional stress, especially in traumatic situations, is known to impact the way memories are encoded and later recalled. The "flashbulb memory" phenomenon, for example, describes the vivid and seemingly accurate recollection of emotionally charged events; however, these memories are not immune to distortion and can change over time. Studies show that stress hormones such as cortisol affect memory by altering activity in the amygdala and hippocampus, which may prioritize certain aspects of the event while discarding others (Merz & Wolf, 2022).

Social pressures also play a role in shaping witness testimony. A witness may feel compelled to conform to social expectations, especially if they believe that certain responses will be viewed as more acceptable or favorable in the eyes of the legal system. This phenomenon is often exacerbated by the questioning techniques employed by law enforcement or attorneys, as repeated or suggestive questioning can introduce doubt or foster misinterpretation. Studies in social psychology demonstrate that witnesses may experience "conformity bias" when exposed to the testimonies of others, sometimes unintentionally modifying their recollections to match those of other witnesses or align with perceived expectations (Bhadra, 2021).

Suggestibility is a critical factor in memory distortion, particularly in younger witnesses or individuals with certain cognitive vulnerabilities. Research on "memory implantation" shows that it is possible to create false memories in individuals through repeated suggestion or exposure to misleading information (Muschalla & Schönborn, 2021). In legal contexts, this has profound implications, as it suggests that suggestive interrogation techniques can result in witnesses developing "memories" of events that did not actually occur. Neuroimaging research indicates that certain brain regions, such as the prefrontal cortex, are implicated in resisting suggestibility, but these regions may be compromised in younger individuals, older adults, or those with preexisting cognitive impairments.

1.3 The Role of Neuropsychology in Assessing Eyewitness Reliability

Given the complexities and vulnerabilities in memory recall, neuropsychologists play a pivotal role in evaluating the reliability of witness testimony. They can help identify when memory may be compromised due to factors like trauma, cognitive biases, or neurobiological deficits. For instance, neuropsychological assessments can measure cognitive functions related to memory, attention, and executive function, which may indicate whether a witness is prone to suggestibility or impaired recall. By providing objective, evidence-based insights into a witness's cognitive profile, neuropsychologists offer valuable information that can guide judicial decision-making and inform cross-examinations.

Moreover, advancements in neuroimaging techniques, such as functional MRI (fMRI) and electroencephalography (EEG), have allowed researchers to observe the brain mechanisms involved in memory encoding, storage, and retrieval. These technologies offer insights into how specific brain structures contribute to memory accuracy and can be used to detect patterns associated with false memories or susceptibility to suggestion. Although such technology is still in the early stages of application within the courtroom, it holds promise for more accurately assessing the reliability of witness testimony in the future.

Understanding the neuropsychological mechanisms that underpin memory is essential to enhancing the accuracy of witness testimony and safeguarding the justice process. Witness memory, while crucial, is inherently vulnerable to various cognitive, social, and biological influences that can affect its reliability. Neuropsychology offers the tools and methodologies to assess these vulnerabilities, providing a scientific basis for understanding the limitations of human memory in the legal context. By integrating neuropsychological insights into the judicial process, legal professionals can work toward minimizing wrongful convictions and fostering a more accurate and fair legal system.

2 The Importance of Witness Testimony in Legal Proceedings

In legal contexts, witness testimony has long been regarded as a key source of evidence, with juries and judges frequently relying on eyewitness accounts to make judgments in criminal and civil cases. Witness statements are often viewed as credible because they come from individuals who have directly observed the events in question, adding a layer of human insight that is both compelling and persuasive (Bex et al., 2003). However, the human memory is not an infallible recorder of past events; it is, rather, a complex cognitive process that is vulnerable to various influences and errors. These can range from external pressures and environmental factors to internal psychological dynamics that affect how information is encoded, stored, and later recalled. Integrating neuropsychological insights into the legal process allows for a more nuanced and scientifically grounded assessment of witness reliability, ultimately promoting fairer judicial outcomes.

2.1 The Persuasive Power of Eyewitness Testimony

Eyewitness testimony holds a unique status in legal proceedings, as it is often perceived as credible, direct, and straightforward. Studies in forensic psychology show that juries tend to assign high value to eyewitness accounts, considering them compelling and trustworthy (Helm, 2021). Witnesses are frequently expected to recount specific details about an event, including the people, objects, and actions involved. In many cases, these accounts can sway the direction of a trial, making witness testimony particularly influential in cases where other forms of physical evidence, like DNA or fingerprints, are lacking.

The persuasive power of eyewitness testimony stems from its apparent immediacy and the trust society places in human perception and recall. People tend to believe that memory functions like a video recording, accurately storing and playing back information when needed. This belief is especially prevalent in cases involving emotional or violent events, where witnesses may be viewed as experiencing "flashbulb memories," vivid recollections triggered by significant moments (Howe & Knott, 2015). However, psychological research suggests that these assumptions about memory accuracy are often unfounded. Memory is a reconstructive process rather than a perfect representation, and it is shaped by a range of internal and external factors (Lacy & Stark, 2013).

2.2 *The Fallibility of Memory Recall*

While eyewitness accounts are influential, research consistently shows that memory is inherently fallible. Cognitive psychologists have documented how memory recall can be affected by stress, misinformation, suggestibility, time delay, and even biases in questioning techniques (Lacy & Stark, 2013). Each of these factors can introduce errors in what a witness remembers, often without the witness being aware of the distortions. A witness may feel highly confident in their recollection, but confidence is not always an accurate indicator of reliability. Studies reveal that memory confidence and accuracy can diverge, particularly under stress or when a significant amount of time has passed since the event (Marr et al., 2020).

One of the most well-documented phenomena affecting memory is suggestibility, the tendency to be influenced by external information or leading questions (Otgaar et al., 2018). Studies show that when witnesses are asked suggestive questions or presented with misleading information after an event, they may incorporate this misinformation into their memory, effectively altering their recall (Challies et al., 2011). This is especially concerning in legal settings, where police interrogations or attorney cross-examinations may unintentionally or intentionally shape a witness's recollection.

Stress and emotional arousal also play significant roles in memory distortion. While moderate stress may enhance certain aspects of memory, extreme stress can impair both encoding and retrieval processes, especially for peripheral details (Challies et al., 2011). For example, the presence of a weapon in a violent crime can cause "weapon focus," where witnesses concentrate on the weapon itself rather than other critical details, such as the appearance of the perpetrator. Memory distortions are further exacerbated by time delay; as time passes, memories fade, and the brain may fill in gaps with plausible, but inaccurate, information.

2.3 *The Role of Neuropsychology in Evaluating Eyewitness Testimony*

Given the vulnerabilities in memory recall, neuropsychology offers critical tools for understanding the processes underlying eyewitness testimony and for evaluating its reliability. Neuropsychologists, by studying the brain mechanisms that contribute to memory formation and retrieval, provide insights that can be directly applied to the legal field. Cognitive assessments, for example, allow neuropsychologists to measure a witness's susceptibility to suggestibility, cognitive biases, and the effects of stress or trauma on memory recall. This information can guide legal professionals in distinguishing between reliable and potentially unreliable testimony.

Neuroimaging techniques, such as functional MRI (fMRI) and electroencephalography (EEG), allow researchers to observe brain activity associated with memory formation and recall. Although these tools are still in their early stages of courtroom application, they hold promise for assessing when a memory is likely to be accurate or distorted. For instance, neuroimaging studies have identified specific brain areas, like the hippocampus and prefrontal cortex, that are involved in memory recall and error detection (Dahlgren et al., 2020). Understanding how these areas function, particularly in high-stress situations, can help legal professionals determine when a witness's recollection may be compromised. Neuropsychology thus provides a scientifically grounded approach to evaluating the cognitive processes that underlie witness testimony, adding an important layer of scrutiny to the reliability of eyewitness accounts (Wise et al., 2014).

2.4 *Legal Implications and the Risk of Wrongful Convictions*

The fallibility of witness memory has serious implications for the legal system, particularly regarding wrongful convictions. Cases of wrongful conviction based on inaccurate eyewitness testimony have highlighted the need for a more informed approach to evaluating witness statements. Studies of exoneration cases, such as those reviewed by organizations like the Innocence Project, reveal that mistaken witness identification is one of the leading causes of wrongful convictions, particularly in cases lacking other corroborative evidence (DuGan et al., n.d.). These cases underscore the risks inherent in over-relying on eyewitness accounts without considering the psychological and neurobiological factors that can affect memory accuracy.

The integration of neuropsychological insights into legal proceedings offers a solution to mitigate these risks. By training legal professionals to recognize the limitations of memory and by including expert testimony from neuropsychologists, courts can develop a more realistic understanding of witness testimony (Parsey & Schmitter-Edgecombe, 2013). For instance, a neuropsychologist might explain how stress impacts memory or why certain questioning techniques may inadvertently introduce inaccuracies into a witness's account. This education can prevent overreliance on flawed memory evidence and contribute to a more balanced approach to evaluating witness credibility.

2.5 *Moving toward Evidence-Based Legal Procedures*

The incorporation of neuropsychology into the courtroom signifies a shift toward evidence-based legal procedures, where scientific insights are used to assess the credibility of witness testimony. Developing protocols that account for the known limitations of human memory can improve the justice system's ability to evaluate evidence fairly and accurately. For example, implementing standardized procedures for police lineups, avoiding leading questions, and allowing expert testimony on memory's fallibility can all contribute to reducing the risk of wrongful convictions based on unreliable witness accounts.

Additionally, neuropsychology's contribution to legal reform includes advocating for training law enforcement and legal professionals in the science of memory. Understanding that eyewitness confidence is not necessarily indicative of accuracy, for instance, can help jurors and judges make more informed decisions when weighing witness statements (Jones et al., 2020). This evidence-based approach respects the complexity of human cognition and promotes a fairer legal process by incorporating scientific principles into legal practice.

While eyewitness testimony remains a powerful and influential element of legal proceedings, its reliability cannot be taken at face value (Louw, 2015). Memory recall is an intricate, fallible process that is shaped by numerous factors, from stress to suggestion, which can distort or alter what a witness believes they have observed. Neuropsychology provides critical insights into these vulnerabilities, offering tools to assess witness reliability more accurately. By integrating these scientific findings into legal procedures, the justice system can better evaluate witness testimony, reduce wrongful convictions, and work toward a fairer and more evidence-based approach to assessing human memory in the courtroom.

3 Cognitive Processes Involved in Memory Recall

Memory recall, a vital cognitive function, enables individuals to retrieve past experiences, knowledge, and information. In everyday life, we rely on memory for learning, decision-making, and interacting with others. However, memory recall is not merely a matter of straightforward retrieval from a mental archive; it is an intricate process involving multiple stages and numerous factors that can influence its accuracy. This is especially critical in legal contexts, where the reliability of witness memory can determine the course of justice. Memory recall consists of three primary stages: encoding, storage, and retrieval (Mujawar et al., 2021). Each of these stages plays a pivotal role in shaping what is remembered and recalled and is susceptible to both external and internal influences that may lead to inaccuracies. Cognitive biases, emotional states, social pressures, and suggestive questioning can all affect how memories are formed, maintained, and ultimately recalled, making it essential to understand these processes to gauge the reliability of memory in high-stakes situations (Kaneko et al., 2021).

3.1 Encoding: The Initial Stage of Memory Formation

Encoding is the first stage of memory, where information from our sensory experiences is processed and converted into a format that can be stored. This process is influenced by factors such as attention, perceptual processing, and emotional state, all of which determine which details of an experience are recorded in memory. When we encode information, we do not capture every element of an experience; rather, we focus on particular details that seem significant at the time (Roediger, 2001). For example, in an emergency situation, a witness might focus on the face of a perpetrator, while peripheral details, like background scenery, are likely to be overlooked.

One well-documented effect during encoding is weapon focus, where witnesses to a crime involving a weapon tend to concentrate on the weapon itself, often at the expense of other crucial details like the perpetrator's face or clothing (Pickel et al., 2006). This phenomenon illustrates how the brain prioritizes encoding certain aspects over others, potentially leading to gaps or distortions in the memory of the event. Emotional states also play a substantial role in encoding; research shows that moderate levels of arousal can enhance memory encoding, while extreme stress can impair it (Schwabe et al., 2022). Neuroimaging studies have identified the amygdala, a brain region responsible for processing emotions, as a key player in encoding emotionally charged events (Šimić et al., 2021). The amygdala works in concert with the hippocampus to consolidate emotional memories, but under intense stress, this process can be disrupted, leading to fragmented or biased memories that may not accurately reflect the original event.

Encoding is also subject to cognitive biases that can affect which information is encoded and how it is interpreted (Sharif & Oppenheimer, 2020). For instance, confirmation bias, the tendency to favor information that confirms preexisting beliefs, can influence how an event is perceived and encoded. A witness with preconceived notions about a person or group may unknowingly focus on details that confirm these biases while overlooking or misinterpreting other information (Lewis, n.d.). These initial biases at the encoding stage can create lasting distortions in memory recall.

3.2 Storage: Consolidating and Maintaining Memory

The second stage of memory is storage, where encoded information is maintained over time. Storage relies on a process called consolidation, in which the brain stabilizes and integrates new memories into long-term storage (Sridhar et al., 2023). The hippocampus plays a central role in memory consolidation, but consolidation is not an instantaneous process; it unfolds over time and can be vulnerable to interference from other memories and experiences.

One of the major challenges in the storage phase is memory decay, where details fade or weaken over time. In some cases, stored memories are altered by subsequent experiences, a phenomenon known as "retroactive interference" (Mercer & Hinton, 2024). For instance, a witness may struggle to differentiate between the details of two similar events, resulting in confusion or blending of memories from separate occurrences. Furthermore, stored memories are malleable and can be reshaped through reconsolidation, a process where retrieving a memory temporarily destabilizes it, making it susceptible to modification. If a witness is repeatedly questioned about a particular event, the act of recalling the memory may alter its contents, especially if the questioning introduces suggestive or misleading information (Kloft et al., 2021).

Another influence on memory storage is the impact of social interactions and exposure to other people's accounts. Research has shown that discussing an event with others can lead to memory conformity, where individuals unconsciously adjust their memories to align with what others have said (Fischer & O'Mara, 2022). This phenomenon is particularly relevant in group settings, such as when witnesses discuss details of an event before testifying. Studies indicate that memory conformity is most likely to occur when the witness lacks confidence in their own recollection or perceives the other person as an authority (Anakwah et al., 2024). Thus, memory storage is not static; it is a dynamic process that can be reshaped by subsequent experiences, interactions, and biases.

3.3 Retrieval: Recalling and Reconstructing Memories

The final stage of memory is retrieval, where stored information is accessed and brought back into conscious awareness. Retrieval is perhaps the most vulnerable stage in the memory process, as it is influenced by various cognitive and environmental factors (Kensinger & Ford, 2019). Unlike a simple playback of recorded information, retrieval is a reconstructive process, meaning that the brain actively pieces together fragments of stored information to create a coherent recollection. This reconstruction is influenced by both the witness's internal cognitive state and external cues present at the time of recall.

One critical issue in the retrieval phase is suggestibility, the tendency to be influenced by external suggestions or leading questions. Research in forensic psychology has shown that when witnesses are exposed to suggestive questioning, they may incorporate false details into their memory (Vagni et al., 2024). This is particularly evident in the misinformation effect, where misleading information presented after an event alters a witness's memory. For instance, if a witness is asked, "Did you see the man in the blue jacket running away?" they may later recall seeing a blue jacket, even if no such detail was present. This susceptibility to suggestion during retrieval underscores the importance of careful and unbiased questioning techniques in legal settings (Bhave et al., 2023).

Another influence on retrieval is source monitoring error, where individuals misattribute the source of a memory (Kuhlmann et al., 2021). Witnesses may confuse details they imagined or were told with details they actually observed. This can result in confabulations, where individuals unknowingly insert inaccurate information into their recollection, believing it to be true. Neuropsychological studies indicate that the prefrontal cortex, a region associated with executive functions, plays a key role in source monitoring (Friedman & Robbins, 2021). However, individuals under stress, fatigue, or those with cognitive impairments may have reduced source monitoring abilities, increasing the risk of memory distortion during retrieval (Malloggi et al., 2022).

3.4 *External Influences and Internal Cognitive Biases in Memory Distortion*

Memory recall is not an isolated cognitive process; it is embedded within a web of external influences and internal cognitive biases (refer to Fig. 1). External influences include the social environment, the questioning techniques used, and the presence of misleading information (Balarezo et al., 2023). Internal cognitive biases, such as confirmation bias and overconfidence, can also distort memory. For instance, individuals often feel certain about the accuracy of their recollection, even when it is incorrect. This overconfidence can lead witnesses to assert details with high

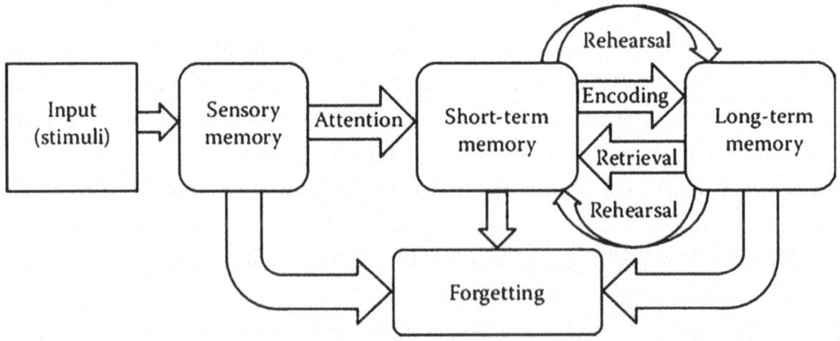

Fig. 1 The Atkinson and Shiffrin model of memory (Atkinson & Shiffrin, 1968)

certainty, potentially misleading legal professionals who equate confidence with accuracy (Giacona, n.d.).

The combined effects of external influences and internal biases mean that memory recall is inherently fallible. Neuropsychological research highlights that memory is not a perfect reflection of reality but a reconstruction shaped by numerous factors (Wang, 2020). For legal contexts, understanding these cognitive processes is essential to assess the reliability of witness testimony accurately and minimize the risk of wrongful convictions based on inaccurate recollections.

The cognitive processes involved in memory recall—encoding, storage, and retrieval—each play a vital role in shaping what individuals remember and report. Witnesses may experience disruptions at any stage, leading to inaccuracies in their recollection (Principe & London, 2022). Moreover, memory is not immune to external influences, such as suggestive questioning, or internal biases, like overconfidence, that can distort recall. Understanding these cognitive dynamics provides essential insights into the complexities of memory and its limitations, underscoring the importance of a cautious approach to interpreting witness testimony in legal proceedings (Bakhtiar, 2023).

4 Memory Retrieval and its Vulnerabilities

Memory retrieval is a complex and dynamic process that allows individuals to access and recall past experiences. While it serves as a foundation for learning, decision-making, and personal identity, memory retrieval is far from flawless. In high-stakes situations, such as legal proceedings, the accuracy of memory retrieval becomes critically important, as the reliability of eyewitness recall can profoundly impact the course of justice. However, memory is susceptible to distortion over time and is influenced by a range of cognitive and social factors (Mazerolle et al., 2021). In legal contexts, eyewitness recall is particularly vulnerable to suggestion, misinformation, and the influence of leading questions. Additionally, the longer the delay between an event and the testimony, the greater the risk of memory contamination (Dalton & Milne, 2021). Understanding these vulnerabilities is essential to mitigate the risk of wrongful convictions and develop effective legal practices that take the inherent fallibility of memory into account.

4.1 The Process of Memory Retrieval

Memory retrieval refers to the process of accessing and reconstructing information stored in the brain. Unlike a simple playback of past events, memory retrieval is an active and reconstructive process, where fragments of stored information are pieced together to form a coherent recollection. During retrieval, the brain relies on cues—such as sights, sounds, or contextual reminders—to access relevant information

(Anderson, 2020). These cues can facilitate the recall of specific memories, but they can also introduce distortions, particularly when memories are incomplete or ambiguous.

Memory retrieval depends on various cognitive processes, including the brain's ability to distinguish between real and imagined details. This function, known as source monitoring, is essential to accurately attribute the origin of a memory, such as whether it was personally experienced or learned from another source. Source monitoring can be compromised under certain conditions, leading to source misattributions where individuals confuse memories of actual events with information encountered elsewhere, such as in discussions with others or through suggestive questioning (Brown et al., 2021). This vulnerability underscores the malleable nature of memory and highlights how retrieval is a reconstructive process that is highly susceptible to external influences.

4.2 Vulnerability to Suggestion and Misinformation

One of the most well-documented vulnerabilities in memory retrieval is its susceptibility to suggestion. Research has shown that when individuals are exposed to suggestive information—whether through leading questions or misleading statements—they may unknowingly incorporate these suggestions into their memory (Kloft et al., 2021). For example, if a witness is asked, "Did you see the blue car speed away?" they might recall seeing a blue car, even if the actual car was a different color. This phenomenon, known as the misinformation effect, demonstrates how post-event information can alter an individual's memory of an event, sometimes creating entirely false details that the witness believes to be accurate.

Studies in cognitive psychology have revealed that memory is not a fixed recording but is instead subject to change every time it is recalled (Oberauer, 2022). The process of reconsolidation occurs when a memory is recalled and temporarily becomes malleable before being re-stored in a modified form. This makes memories highly vulnerable to external influences at the time of recall, especially in situations where witnesses are repeatedly questioned. Repeated questioning, especially with leading or suggestive language, can lead to the incorporation of false information into a witness's memory. In legal contexts, suggestive questioning is particularly problematic, as it can lead to false memories—instances where individuals confidently remember events or details that did not occur (Muschalla & Schönborn, 2021).

4.3 The Influence of Delay on Memory Contamination

The accuracy of memory retrieval is also highly dependent on the timing of the recall. Memory decay, or the natural fading of details over time, makes memories less vivid and precise, increasing the likelihood of distortion. In legal contexts, a significant delay between the occurrence of an event and the recall of that event (such as during a trial) can have a profound effect on memory accuracy. Forgetting curves, as described by Hermann Ebbinghaus, demonstrate that memory retention decreases rapidly after the initial encoding of information, stabilizing at a lower level over time (Radvansky et al., 2022). This natural decay means that as time passes, individuals are less likely to recall specific details and may unknowingly fill in the gaps with plausible but inaccurate information.

With the passage of time, memory is also more likely to be contaminated by interference from subsequent experiences (Lacy & Stark, 2013). For example, if a witness discusses an event with others or reads about it in the news, details from these sources may blend with their original memory, making it difficult to differentiate between firsthand experience and outside information. This effect is especially pronounced when individuals are exposed to misleading post-event information, such as media reports or other witnesses' accounts that may differ from their own (Wulff, n.d.). The social contagion effect is another factor that can lead to memory contamination; in group settings, individuals may adjust their memories to align with what others remember, believing that others' accounts may be more accurate. This phenomenon illustrates how social and environmental factors can shape and distort memory over time, often without the individual's awareness (Cikara et al., 2022).

4.4 Cognitive Biases and Memory Distortion

Memory retrieval is also subject to various cognitive biases that can distort recollection. One prominent example is confirmation bias, where individuals selectively focus on information that confirms their existing beliefs or expectations. In a legal setting, a witness might unconsciously shape their memory to align with preconceptions about a person or situation, leading to a biased or incomplete recall. Confirmation bias can be particularly insidious because it may give the witness a false sense of confidence in the accuracy of their memory, even when the memory is flawed (Pataranutaporn et al., 2024).

Overconfidence is another cognitive bias that affects memory retrieval. Studies have shown that individuals often overestimate the accuracy of their memories, particularly when they recall vivid or emotionally charged events (Diamond et al., 2020). This can be problematic in legal contexts, where the confidence of a witness is often equated with credibility by jurors and legal professionals. However, research has consistently demonstrated that confidence does not reliably correlate with accuracy; individuals can be highly confident about incorrect details, leading to false testimony that may be persuasive to others (Salovich et al., 2020).

4.5 The Role of Neuropsychology in Understanding Memory Vulnerabilities

Neuropsychology has provided valuable insights into the mechanisms underlying memory vulnerabilities, particularly through neuroimaging studies that explore the brain regions involved in memory recall. Research indicates that the prefrontal cortex and hippocampus are key areas involved in source monitoring, attention, and memory retrieval (Takehara-Nishiuchi, 2020a, 2020b). When these areas are compromised, either through stress, trauma, or cognitive fatigue, individuals may be more susceptible to memory distortion and misattribution. This knowledge has practical implications for the legal field, as it suggests that certain individuals—such as those with cognitive impairments, stress-induced memory deficits, or mental health conditions—may be at heightened risk for memory contamination (Di Nota et al., 2020).

Understanding the neural basis of memory vulnerabilities also underscores the importance of careful and ethical interviewing techniques in legal proceedings. By avoiding suggestive questioning and allowing sufficient time for witnesses to recall events without pressure, legal professionals can help reduce the risk of memory distortion and ensure that the recollections presented in court are as accurate as possible.

Memory retrieval, while fundamental to our ability to learn and navigate the world, is far from a flawless process. Eyewitness recall, particularly in legal settings, is vulnerable to a range of factors that can lead to distortion and inaccuracies. Suggestions, misinformation, delay, and cognitive biases can all influence memory recall, potentially leading witnesses to misremember or fabricate details of an event. The dynamic nature of memory, which reconstructs rather than merely retrieves information, makes it susceptible to external influences, especially under conditions of stress or repeated questioning (Fivush & Grysman, 2022). Integrating neuropsychological insights into legal practices can help identify these vulnerabilities and develop strategies to mitigate their impact, ensuring that memory recall is used judiciously and with an awareness of its inherent limitations. By acknowledging the complexities of memory retrieval and its vulnerabilities, legal systems can better safeguard the accuracy and integrity of witness testimony, minimizing the risk of wrongful convictions based on flawed memories (Bhave et al., 2023).

5 The Neurological Basis of Memory

Memory, a fundamental cognitive process, enables individuals to encode, store, and retrieve information from past experiences. This capacity is critical not only for personal identity and learning but also for effective functioning in society. The neurological basis of memory lies in complex neural networks that involve several key brain regions, notably the hippocampus and prefrontal cortex. These structures play integral roles in memory formation and retrieval, and their interactions provide the foundation for our ability to recall events and experiences. However, these neural networks are not infallible; traumatic events, cognitive biases, and environmental influences can disrupt memory processing, leading to fragmented or distorted recollections. Understanding the neurological underpinnings of memory offers valuable insights into the variability observed in eyewitness accounts, particularly in legal settings, and highlights the importance of these mechanisms in shaping reliable memory recall.

5.1 Neural Networks Involved in Memory Formation and Retrieval

The brain processes memory through interconnected networks that engage specific structures and pathways during different stages: encoding, storage, and retrieval. Encoding occurs when sensory information is transformed into a neural code that the brain can store. The hippocampus, a small, seahorse-shaped region in the medial temporal lobe, is crucial for encoding new declarative memories, such as facts and experiences (Adedayo et al., 2023). The prefrontal cortex (PFC), located at the front of the brain, is involved in higher-order functions such as attention, decision-making, and working memory, which are essential for organizing and retrieving memories (Funahashi, 2022).

The hippocampus and PFC work together to consolidate and retrieve information. During memory consolidation, the hippocampus helps stabilize newly formed memories, transferring them to the cortex for long-term storage (Takehara-Nishiuchi, 2020a, 2020b). This process is particularly active during sleep, which allows for the integration of new information with preexisting knowledge, strengthening the neural connections that make memories accessible in the future. Once memories are consolidated, the prefrontal cortex coordinates their retrieval, filtering relevant details while suppressing irrelevant information. By doing so, the brain constructs a coherent and meaningful recollection from stored fragments (Prezioso & Alessandroni, 2022).

The amygdala, an almond-shaped structure near the hippocampus, also plays an essential role in memory, particularly for emotionally charged events. Research has shown that the amygdala enhances memory encoding and consolidation for emotional experiences, which explains why memories associated with strong emotions are often more vivid and accessible (Qasim et al., 2023). However, this heightened emotional engagement can sometimes make memories less accurate, as the amygdala's involvement may prioritize emotional aspects over objective details.

5.2 Impact of Trauma on Memory Processing

While the brain's memory system is highly adaptive, it is also vulnerable to disruption, particularly in response to traumatic events. Trauma can impair the neural circuits responsible for memory encoding and retrieval, leading to fragmented or distorted memories (Solinski, 2022). For example, individuals who experience traumatic incidents often report intrusive, disorganized, or incomplete recollections of the event. This phenomenon is linked to how the brain responds to stress and high-arousal situations, which can impair the hippocampus and prefrontal cortex, thus affecting memory formation.

Under extreme stress, the hypothalamic–pituitary–adrenal (HPA) axis activates the release of cortisol, a stress hormone that prepares the body for fight or flight responses (Chu et al., 2024). While moderate levels of cortisol can enhance memory formation, particularly for emotionally significant information, chronic or acute exposure to high levels of cortisol can impair hippocampal function (Bermejo et al., 2022). This can result in memory deficits, as the hippocampus may fail to encode certain details accurately, leading to fragmented memories where individuals remember specific details but lack a coherent narrative. In legal contexts, such trauma-induced memory fragmentation can complicate the reliability of eyewitness testimony, as individuals may struggle to recall the full sequence of events or misinterpret their recollections (Dalenberg et al., 2020).

The prefrontal cortex, which plays a role in organizing and retrieving memories, is also susceptible to stress-related impairment (Klier & Buratto, 2020). When the PFC is compromised due to trauma, individuals may experience difficulty in accurately reconstructing memories or distinguishing between real and imagined details. This impaired ability to filter and organize memories contributes to the variability often seen in eyewitness accounts, where some details are recalled vividly while others are distorted or forgotten (PeConga et al., 2022). Additionally, repeated exposure to reminders of trauma can lead to reconsolidation of memories, where each recollection reopens and potentially alters the memory, adding new distortions with each retrieval.

5.3 The Role of Reconsolidation and Memory Malleability

Memory is not a static record of past events but is instead highly malleable, undergoing changes each time it is retrieved. This process, known as reconsolidation, allows memories to be updated and modified based on new experiences or information. During reconsolidation, a memory temporarily becomes malleable and can incorporate new details before it is re-stored (Prats, n.d.). While this process allows for adaptive learning, it also introduces a vulnerability: external influences can distort memories during recall.

In legal contexts, reconsolidation explains why eyewitness accounts may change over time, particularly when witnesses are exposed to suggestive information. If a witness repeatedly recalls an event and is subjected to suggestive questioning or external input, their memory of the event may incorporate this new information, leading to memory distortion (Dodier et al., 2023). For example, if an individual is questioned with leading questions or exposed to inaccurate details about an event, they may unintentionally integrate these inaccuracies into their memory during reconsolidation. This susceptibility underscores the importance of careful interviewing techniques in legal contexts to minimize the risk of memory contamination.

5.4 *Cognitive Biases and Memory Distortion*

Memory retrieval is further influenced by cognitive biases that can distort an individual's recollection of events (Colombo et al., 2020). Confirmation bias, for instance, can shape memory recall by leading individuals to focus on details that confirm their preexisting beliefs or expectations. In a courtroom setting, witnesses might unintentionally emphasize or exaggerate aspects of an event that align with their understanding of the situation, affecting the accuracy of their testimony. This bias can be exacerbated by the involvement of the prefrontal cortex, which is responsible for filtering information and reconstructing memory; if the PFC is guided by biased expectations, it may selectively recall details that fit a specific narrative (Faul, n.d.).

Confidence in memory, while often equated with accuracy, does not reliably reflect the factual accuracy of a memory. In fact, research has shown that individuals can be highly confident in their memories even when they are incorrect (Murphy & Flynn, 2022). The PFC's role in organizing and rehearsing memories may reinforce confidence, yet this confidence may mask subtle inaccuracies that have emerged through reconsolidation or cognitive biases. This disconnect between confidence and accuracy presents a significant challenge in legal contexts, where juries and judges may weigh witness confidence heavily when evaluating testimony reliability (Chalmers et al., 2022).

5.5 *Implications for Legal and Clinical Practice*

Understanding the neurological basis of memory, particularly the roles of the hippocampus, prefrontal cortex, and amygdala, provides critical insights into the variability of eyewitness testimony. It underscores the importance of using ethical, unsuggestive interviewing techniques that minimize the risk of memory distortion (Korkman et al., 2024). In legal contexts, training law enforcement and legal professionals on the fallibility of memory can help prevent wrongful convictions by promoting awareness of memory's reconstructive nature and the effects of trauma on recall.

Clinically, awareness of the impact of trauma on memory has informed therapeutic approaches such as trauma-focused cognitive behavioral therapy (TF-CBT), which helps individuals process traumatic memories in a safe and supportive environment (Yadav et al., 2024). Understanding how trauma affects the hippocampus and prefrontal cortex can aid clinicians in identifying the causes of fragmented or disorganized memories, enabling them to help clients reconstruct coherent narratives that promote healing and resilience (Jayne, n.d.).

The neurological underpinnings of memory offer a framework for understanding the inherent variability and vulnerability of memory retrieval, particularly in contexts where accuracy is paramount, such as the courtroom (Shmikler, n.d.). By examining the roles of the hippocampus, prefrontal cortex, and amygdala, researchers have revealed how encoding, storage, and retrieval are shaped by neural interactions and are influenced by trauma, reconsolidation, and cognitive biases. Integrating this knowledge into legal and clinical practices can help mitigate memory distortion, leading to more reliable eyewitness testimony and better outcomes for individuals who have experienced trauma (Williams, n.d.). The brain's memory networks, while remarkably adaptive, require careful handling to ensure the accuracy and integrity of recollections in critical situations.

6 Stress, Trauma, and Memory in Witness Testimony

Memory plays a crucial role in legal proceedings, as it allows witnesses to recount past events, offering a narrative of what transpired during a crime. However, memory is not a flawless mechanism. The effects of stress and trauma, particularly in high-stress situations like witnessing a crime, can significantly impact both memory encoding and retrieval, leading to inaccuracies and inconsistencies in witness testimony. While some memories of traumatic events may seem vivid and detailed, these "flashbulb memories" are not immune to distortion (Curci et al., 2020). Understanding how stress and trauma shape memory processes is essential for evaluating the reliability of eyewitness testimony, as well as for fostering more accurate legal outcomes.

6.1 The Effect of Stress on Memory Encoding

Memory encoding is the initial stage of memory formation, during which information is transformed into a construct that the brain can store and retrieve later (Josselyn & Tonegawa, 2020). Stressful situations activate the hypothalamic–pituitary–adrenal (HPA) axis, leading to the release of cortisol and adrenaline, which prepare the body for a "fight or flight" response. While this reaction enhances short-term survival, it can disrupt memory encoding. Research indicates that moderate levels of stress hormones can improve memory encoding, particularly for emotionally significant information, but extreme or prolonged stress often has the opposite effect, impairing the accuracy and coherence of the encoded memory (Grob et al., 2023).

Under high-stress conditions, individuals may struggle to encode specific details accurately. In eyewitness situations, this may result in fragmented or incomplete memories where certain aspects of an event—such as the perpetrator's facial features or specific actions—may be poorly remembered or entirely omitted. The hippocampus, a brain region crucial for memory formation, is especially vulnerable to the effects of cortisol (De Kloet & Joëls, 2023). High levels of cortisol can interfere with hippocampal function, making it challenging to encode events in a coherent and organized manner. Consequently, witnesses may remember key emotional moments but lack critical details that could corroborate or clarify their testimony (Nahleen et al., 2020).

Moreover, stress tends to narrow attention, leading individuals to focus intensely on certain details while ignoring others. This phenomenon, often referred to as "weapon focus," is particularly evident when a weapon is present during a crime (Lockamyeir, n.d.). Witnesses may fixate on the weapon itself, impairing their ability to recall other aspects of the event, such as the appearance of the perpetrator. As a result, high-stress situations can lead to selective attention, which affects what is encoded into memory and, ultimately, what can be recalled later (Simeon et al., 2022).

6.2 The Impact of Trauma on Memory Retrieval

While stress influences memory encoding, trauma significantly affects memory retrieval, the process of recalling stored information. Trauma-related memories, often described as "flashbulb memories," tend to be highly vivid and detailed, yet research shows they are not necessarily more accurate than other types of memories. Flashbulb memories are typically formed during intensely emotional or shocking experiences, and they often include vivid sensory details and a strong sense of "reliving" the event (Anderson, 2020). However, this vividness can be misleading; studies have found that flashbulb memories are susceptible to distortion over time, despite the confidence individuals often place in their accuracy (Curci et al., 2020).

The amygdala, a brain region involved in processing emotions, particularly fear, plays a significant role in trauma-related memory (Kredlow et al., 2021). When a traumatic event occurs, the amygdala enhances the encoding of emotional aspects of the experience, leading to memories that are rich in emotional content but may lack objective details. For instance, a witness to a violent crime may vividly remember the fear and panic they felt, but struggle to recall specific facts about the event. This selective encoding can result in incomplete or biased recollections that may undermine the reliability of the testimony (Davis et al., 2024).

Trauma also disrupts the functioning of the prefrontal cortex (PFC), which is involved in organizing memories and distinguishing between relevant and irrelevant details. Trauma-related stress can impair the PFC, making it difficult for witnesses to accurately reconstruct memories without adding or omitting details. This is especially problematic in legal contexts where witnesses may be expected to provide precise and consistent accounts of what they observed (Hope et al., 2021). Inconsistent or fragmented testimonies may be perceived as unreliable, even though these inconsistencies often reflect the natural effects of trauma on memory processing rather than intentional deception.

6.3 The Malleability of Trauma-Related Memories

One of the most challenging aspects of trauma-related memories is their malleability. Memory is not a static record of past events; rather, it is a dynamic process that is reconstructed each time it is recalled. This reconstruction is vulnerable to external influences, including suggestions and leading questions. In forensic settings, repeated questioning, suggestive interviewing techniques, or exposure to information about the crime through the media can lead to memory contamination. When witnesses recall an event multiple times, particularly under the influence of suggestion, their memories may incorporate new information that was not originally part of the experience (Bull & Milne, 2020). This process, known as reconsolidation, occurs when a memory is "reopened" for retrieval and then re-stored with potential modifications.

A phenomenon that highlights the malleability of memory in traumatic events is post-event misinformation (Sharma et al., 2024). If a witness is exposed to misleading information after the event, they may incorporate this misinformation into their memory, even if it conflicts with the original experience. This effect has been well-documented in legal research, with studies showing that witnesses can recall events inaccurately after being exposed to misleading suggestions (McCroy, n.d.). For example, if a witness is informed that the suspect was wearing a red shirt, they may later remember the suspect as wearing red, even if this detail is incorrect. In high-stakes legal proceedings, such memory distortions can have serious consequences, potentially leading to wrongful convictions or the exclusion of valuable testimony (Weir, 2023).

6.4 Legal Implications of Stress and Trauma on Memory

The complex effects of stress and trauma on memory encoding and retrieval raise important questions about the reliability of witness testimony. In many cases, juries and judges may perceive a witness's confidence or the vividness of their recollection as indicators of accuracy, yet research demonstrates that memory confidence and accuracy are not always aligned. Witnesses may be highly confident in their memories, particularly flashbulb memories, yet still recall details inaccurately due to the influence of stress, trauma, and suggestion (Curci et al., 2020).

Legal professionals are increasingly aware of the potential pitfalls in relying solely on eyewitness testimony, particularly in cases involving high-stress or traumatic events. Courts in some jurisdictions have adopted cautionary instructions to inform juries of the potential for memory distortion in traumatic circumstances. These instructions aim to reduce the weight placed on eyewitness testimony and encourage juries to consider the limitations of memory under stress (Jones et al., 2020). Furthermore, training law enforcement officers and forensic interviewers in trauma-informed practices can help minimize the risk of memory contamination. Techniques such as the cognitive interview, which allows witnesses to recall events in a supportive and unsuggestive environment, can aid in obtaining more accurate accounts (Crossland et al., 2020).

In clinical contexts, trauma-informed therapies are essential for individuals affected by traumatic memories. Techniques like trauma-focused cognitive behavioral therapy (TF-CBT) offer a structured approach to help individuals process and integrate traumatic memories in a way that reduces distress and enhances clarity. By providing individuals with a safe environment to reconstruct their memories, therapists can help reduce the emotional and cognitive distortions that arise from trauma (Shanks, n.d.).

The effects of stress and trauma on memory encoding and retrieval highlight the complexity and fallibility of memory in high-stress situations. Witnesses to traumatic events may struggle with fragmented, selective, or distorted recollections due to the impacts of stress hormones on the hippocampus, prefrontal cortex, and amygdala. Although flashbulb memories may appear vivid and precise, their accuracy is often compromised by the emotional intensity of the experience and subsequent influences (Fernández-Pérez et al., 2024). In legal contexts, understanding the vulnerabilities of memory under stress and trauma is essential to evaluating the reliability of witness testimony and ensuring fair outcomes. Integrating trauma-informed practices in both forensic and clinical settings can help improve the accuracy of memory recall and reduce the potential for memory distortion, benefiting both the individuals involved and the integrity of the legal process (Fernández-Pérez et al., 2024).

7 Post-Event Information and Suggestibility in Eyewitness Testimony

In legal settings, eyewitness testimony holds substantial weight. However, memory is not infallible; it is a reconstructive process subject to various influences, especially after the event has occurred. Post-event information, such as media reports, conversations with others, or police questioning, can lead to memory distortions in eyewitnesses. One of the primary mechanisms by which memory is affected in this way is through suggestibility—a cognitive phenomenon where an individual's memory can be altered by external cues or information. This suggestibility can lead to the unintentional embedding of misinformation into a witness's memory, sometimes resulting in misidentifications or inaccuracies that can significantly impact legal outcomes. Understanding how post-event information and suggestibility operate in eyewitness contexts is essential for ensuring fair and reliable judicial processes.

7.1 Memory as a Reconstructive Process

Contrary to the idea that memory is akin to a recording device that accurately captures events, memory is, in fact, a reconstructive process. When recalling an event, individuals piece together fragmented information stored in their memory to construct a coherent narrative. This process is susceptible to interference, especially when new information is introduced after the event (Bailey & Smith, 2024). The reconsolidation theory of memory suggests that every time a memory is recalled, it becomes temporarily unstable and is subject to modification. Consequently, any new information encountered during this "reopened" memory state can become incorporated into the memory, making it difficult to distinguish between what was originally experienced and what was subsequently learned.

For eyewitnesses, post-event information can easily become part of the reconstructed memory. For instance, if a witness to a crime overhears a news report describing the suspect's appearance or actions, these details may become unintentionally incorporated into their own memory of the event. Later, the witness may recall the news report's details as part of their original memory, leading to inaccuracies that can influence the investigation or court proceedings.

7.2 The Influence of Suggestibility on Eyewitness Memory

Suggestibility refers to the extent to which people's recollections can be influenced by external suggestions. Research in cognitive psychology shows that suggestibility is particularly pronounced in situations where individuals are uncertain or lack confidence in their own memories (Szpitalak & Polczyk, 2020). This makes eyewitnesses especially vulnerable, as memory for stressful or traumatic events is often incomplete or unclear. Studies have demonstrated that even subtle cues—such as the wording of questions—can lead witnesses to recall events differently (Deck, 2021).

One of the most well-known studies on suggestibility was conducted by Elizabeth Loftus and John Palmer, who examined the impact of question phrasing on memory recall (Ceci & Bruck, 1993). They showed participants a video of a car accident and then asked questions about what they had seen, using varying language to describe the event. For example, when asked how fast the cars were going when they "smashed" into each other versus when they "hit" each other, participants reported higher speeds for the "smashed" condition and even recalled seeing broken glass, which was not present in the video. This demonstrates how suggestive questioning can lead to false memories or distorted perceptions of the event. Such effects have profound implications for legal contexts, as police questioning techniques or attorney cross-examinations can unintentionally shape a witness's recollection, potentially leading to misidentifications or false testimony.

7.3 *The Role of Post-Event Information in Memory Distortion*

Post-event information—details introduced after the original event—can alter an eyewitness's memory by embedding misleading or incorrect information into their recollections. Sources of post-event information can include conversations with other witnesses, media coverage, and repeated interactions with law enforcement or legal representatives. This misinformation effect is especially concerning in cases where witnesses encounter details they did not initially notice or remember, as they may incorporate these new elements into their own memories.

For example, a witness to a robbery might have only seen a brief glimpse of the perpetrator but later overhears that the suspect was wearing a red jacket. Even if this detail was not part of the original memory, it can be incorporated into the witness's recollection during retrieval, especially if they are repeatedly exposed to it. In the context of media coverage, witnesses may absorb descriptions of a suspect's appearance or behavior that become embedded in their own recollections. This contamination can alter the witness's testimony, potentially creating inconsistencies or false statements that complicate the legal process.

7.4 *Mechanisms of Misinformation and Memory Integration*

The process by which misinformation becomes integrated into memory is complex and involves several cognitive mechanisms. One key mechanism is source confusion, where individuals struggle to distinguish the origin of a particular detail—whether it was part of their original experience or introduced through post-event information. This confusion can occur because memories are often stored in a way that prioritizes the content of the information over its source. Consequently, a witness may recall a piece of information but incorrectly attribute it to the original event, even if it was actually introduced through an external source, such as a conversation or news report.

Another mechanism is memory blending, where fragments of different memories or sources of information are combined to form a new, cohesive memory. This can occur when post-event information fills in gaps in the original memory, creating a false sense of completeness. Memory blending is particularly problematic because it leads to high confidence in the altered memory, making witnesses less likely to question their own recollections. This heightened confidence can make it challenging for legal professionals to detect potential inaccuracies in the testimony.

7.5 Implications for Legal Proceedings

The susceptibility of memory to post-event information and suggestibility presents significant challenges for the legal system. Eyewitness testimony, despite its known vulnerabilities, is often seen as compelling evidence in court. However, if a witness's memory has been altered by post-event information or suggestive questioning, their testimony may be unreliable. Misidentifications due to suggestibility and memory distortion have contributed to wrongful convictions, as confirmed by DNA exoneration cases analyzed by the Innocence Project, which found that a substantial proportion of wrongful convictions involved mistaken eyewitness identifications.

Legal procedures can exacerbate the problem when law enforcement officials inadvertently influence witnesses during questioning. To mitigate these risks, some jurisdictions have implemented guidelines and protocols designed to reduce suggestive influences on witnesses. For example, the cognitive interview technique minimizes leading questions and encourages witnesses to recall events from multiple perspectives, which can help produce more accurate testimonies. Additionally, some courts have introduced expert testimony on memory to educate juries about the fallibility of eyewitness memory, highlighting how factors such as suggestibility and post-event information can impact recall accuracy.

7.6 Practical Considerations for Law Enforcement Officers and Legal Professionals

Given the impact of suggestibility and post-event information on memory, law enforcement and legal professionals must adopt practices that safeguard the integrity of witness recollections. Interview techniques that emphasize open-ended questions and minimize the introduction of new information are essential. For instance, asking "What did you see?" rather than "Did you see the man in the red jacket?" reduces the likelihood of introducing suggestive cues that might alter the witness's memory.

Moreover, educating jurors and judges about the limitations of memory can help prevent overreliance on eyewitness testimony. Expert witnesses in psychology or neuropsychology can provide insights into how suggestibility and memory distortion work, helping juries critically evaluate the accuracy of witness statements. By fostering a more informed understanding of memory processes in the legal system, these measures can reduce the likelihood of wrongful convictions and enhance the fairness of legal outcomes.

The influence of post-event information and suggestibility on eyewitness memory underscores the need for caution when relying on witness testimony in legal proceedings. Memory is not a static, objective record but a dynamic and malleable process subject to distortion from external cues and misinformation. In high-stakes legal contexts, where the accuracy of testimony can determine a person's guilt or innocence, understanding the vulnerabilities of memory is essential. By adopting interview techniques that minimize suggestive influences and incorporating expert insights on memory processes, legal professionals can work toward more accurate and just outcomes. Through these efforts, the legal system can better account for the complexities of human memory, ultimately leading to fairer and more reliable verdicts.

8 Neuropsychological Evaluations of Witness Testimony: Enhancing Reliability and Reducing Memory Contamination

In legal proceedings, the reliability of witness testimony is often pivotal in establishing the events of a crime. Eyewitness accounts can profoundly influence jury decisions, yet they are not immune to error. Memory is a complex, reconstructive process that is susceptible to numerous influences, including cognitive biases, stress, and external suggestions. Neuropsychological assessments, which explore the cognitive functioning behind memory and recall, are therefore crucial for evaluating the reliability of eyewitness testimony. By integrating cognitive interview techniques, carefully constructed lineup procedures, and specialized methods like the enhanced cognitive interview, these evaluations seek to preserve the accuracy of memory recall and minimize the risk of contamination or suggestion.

8.1 The Role of Neuropsychological Assessments in Evaluating Witness Testimony

Neuropsychological evaluations aim to assess various cognitive functions, such as attention, memory, and perception, which are essential for accurate eyewitness recall. When applied to legal contexts, these assessments can shed light on a witness's ability to encode, store, and retrieve information effectively. Factors such as attention to detail, susceptibility to suggestion, and working memory capacity are often considered, as they can impact how reliably a witness recalls events.

Witnesses who experience high stress during a crime may have difficulty accurately encoding details, while those with certain cognitive vulnerabilities may be more prone to suggestion or post-event misinformation. Neuropsychological tools—such as cognitive tests assessing recall, recognition, and source monitoring—provide critical insights into these issues, offering a scientific basis to gauge the credibility of a witness's memory.

8.2 Memory Contamination and Suggestibility: Risks in Eyewitness Testimony

One of the key challenges in eyewitness testimony is memory contamination. Due to the reconstructive nature of memory, individuals are susceptible to incorporating external information, whether it be from media coverage, conversations with others, or police questioning. This phenomenon is often referred to as the misinformation effect, where misleading information introduced post-event becomes embedded in the memory, distorting the witness's original perception of the incident.

Another significant risk in eyewitness testimony is suggestibility, or the tendency for memory to be influenced by external suggestions. Suggestibility can be heightened during investigative procedures, especially if leading questions or suggestive cues are used. Neuropsychological evaluations consider these vulnerabilities, as individuals vary in their susceptibility to suggestion. For instance, research has shown that factors such as age, stress, and cognitive impairments can increase a person's likelihood of adopting false information into their memory (Oi & Frazier, 2024).

8.3 Cognitive Interviews: A Technique to Enhance Accuracy

Cognitive interviews are structured techniques developed to elicit more accurate memories from witnesses by enhancing the natural memory retrieval process. Unlike standard police interviews, which may rely on direct and leading questions, cognitive interviews are based on principles of cognitive psychology. They emphasize open-ended questioning and encourage the witness to recall details in a manner that aligns with their mental reconstruction of the event.

The cognitive interview (CI) includes techniques such as context reinstatement, which involves asking the witness to mentally return to the time and place of the incident. By imagining the sights, sounds, and feelings they experienced, witnesses can improve their access to sensory and emotional cues, which helps enhance recall. Additionally, witnesses are encouraged to recount the event from multiple perspectives or in reverse order, which helps reduce the likelihood of following a narrative template and instead focuses on retrieving genuine memories. This method has been shown to increase the accuracy of recalled information by reducing the impact of leading questions and minimizing memory distortions.

8.4 *Enhanced Cognitive Interview: Minimizing Contamination and Bias*

The enhanced cognitive interview (ECI) builds upon the original cognitive interview by incorporating additional elements to improve witness recall accuracy and reliability. The ECI introduces specific measures designed to minimize contamination and suggestive influences, making it particularly useful in high-stakes legal cases where witness testimony may be pivotal.

In the ECI, interviewers are trained to avoid leading questions and to employ open-ended prompts. This strategy not only prevents the introduction of new information but also reduces the likelihood of unintentional suggestions. For example, instead of asking a witness, "Did the suspect have a weapon?" the interviewer might ask, "Describe anything you noticed in the suspect's hands." By avoiding specific language that could imply details, the ECI allows witnesses to describe events as they remember them, promoting memory accuracy.

The ECI also emphasizes building rapport with the witness and creating a comfortable, nonthreatening environment. Establishing a sense of trust helps reduce the witness's anxiety and stress, which can improve recall and reduce susceptibility to suggestion. This approach aligns with neuropsychological findings that stress and anxiety can impair memory retrieval, particularly for details that are central to the event.

8.5 *Lineup Procedures: Reducing Suggestion in Identification*

Lineup procedures are another critical area where neuropsychological insights have influenced practices to minimize suggestibility and enhance the accuracy of eyewitness identifications. Traditional lineups, which often involve multiple individuals standing in front of the witness, have been criticized for potentially leading the witness to make assumptions based on lineup composition or subtle cues from law enforcement.

To address these issues, many legal systems have adopted double-blind procedures, where neither the witness nor the officer conducting the lineup knows the suspect's identity. This method minimizes unintentional suggestions from the officer, as they cannot unknowingly influence the witness's choice.

Additionally, sequential lineups—where suspects are presented to the witness one at a time—have been found to reduce misidentifications compared to simultaneous lineups. The sequential format encourages witnesses to evaluate each individual independently, rather than comparing all lineup members to one another. This approach aligns with cognitive psychology research, which suggests that sequential viewing helps reduce relative judgment, a process in which the witness may select the person who looks most like the suspect relative to others in the lineup, rather than relying on actual memory (Ditto et al., 2024).

8.6 The Importance of Neuropsychological Evaluation in Legal Contexts

Neuropsychological evaluations offer invaluable insights into the cognitive and psychological factors that affect memory reliability, helping legal professionals understand and account for the limitations of eyewitness testimony. By examining a witness's cognitive abilities, susceptibility to suggestion, and ability to recall details accurately, neuropsychologists can provide an informed assessment of the reliability of their testimony.

In cases involving vulnerable witnesses—such as children, individuals with cognitive impairments, or those who have experienced trauma—these evaluations are especially crucial. For example, trauma can impair memory encoding, making certain details difficult to recall or potentially altering the way memories are stored. Neuropsychologists can assess the impact of trauma on memory and offer guidance on the reliability of specific testimony.

8.7 Implications for Legal Practice

The integration of neuropsychological evaluation into legal proceedings has several important implications. First, it underscores the need for caution when relying on eyewitness testimony, particularly in high-stress or complex cases where witnesses may be more susceptible to memory contamination. Second, it highlights the role of evidence-based practices—such as cognitive and enhanced cognitive interviews, lineup reforms, and neuropsychological assessments—in improving the accuracy of witness recall.

Furthermore, courts can benefit from allowing expert testimony from neuropsychologists who can explain memory processes, suggestibility, and the impact of external influences on recall. Such testimony can help jurors and judges make more informed decisions by providing a scientific perspective on the limitations of memory, reducing the likelihood of wrongful convictions based on flawed testimony.

The reliability of witness testimony is essential for fair and just legal proceedings. Neuropsychological evaluations play a vital role in assessing and enhancing the credibility of eyewitness recall, helping prevent memory contamination and reduce suggestibility. Techniques such as the cognitive interview, enhanced cognitive interview, and refined lineup procedures are effective tools in minimizing external influences on memory, promoting accurate recall, and ultimately contributing to a more reliable judicial process. By understanding the cognitive and neurological underpinnings of memory, legal professionals can better navigate the complexities of eyewitness testimony and foster a more accurate and equitable legal system.

9 Lineup Procedures and Identification: Reducing Biases and Enhancing Reliability

In criminal investigations, lineup procedures are a common tool used to identify suspects, allowing witnesses to select individuals who resemble the person they saw during the crime. However, lineup identification is not as straightforward as it seems; it is highly vulnerable to biases and can be influenced by subtle suggestive cues from administrators, which often lead to misidentification and even wrongful convictions. Research in psychology has shown that lineup procedures need careful consideration in both design and execution to ensure fair, unbiased identifications. Techniques such as double-blind administration and well-constructed lineups have been shown to significantly reduce the potential for error, providing more reliable evidence for the judicial system.

9.1 The Psychology behind Lineup Identification and Bias

Eyewitness identifications can be easily influenced by cognitive biases and errors in perception. Human memory is not an exact record of events but rather a reconstructive process, which makes it susceptible to outside influences. Witnesses may not accurately recall facial features, especially if they viewed the perpetrator only briefly or under stressful conditions, such as during a crime. Moreover, cognitive biases, such as the tendency to pick the person who looks most like the perpetrator rather than being certain of an exact match, can result in errors.

Another significant factor influencing identification is the expectation bias that occurs when witnesses believe that the actual suspect is present in the lineup, leading them to make a selection based on assumption rather than certainty. This effect is exacerbated when lineup administrators inadvertently provide nonverbal cues or encourage particular choices, even unintentionally. These factors make it crucial to adopt procedures that minimize suggestibility and error.

9.2 The Double-Blind Lineup: Reducing Suggestive Influences

A key reform in lineup administration is the double-blind lineup procedure, in which neither the witness nor the administrator knows which person in the lineup is the suspect. The double-blind setup is widely recognized as an essential safeguard against unintentional influence. If an administrator knows who the suspect is, even unintentional gestures, pauses, or verbal prompts may communicate information to the witness, potentially leading to biased selections. Double-blind procedures eliminate this risk by ensuring that the administrator cannot influence the witness's decision.

In double-blind lineups, witnesses are typically shown the lineup members one at a time, which further reduces comparison-based decisions. This sequential lineup method contrasts with the traditional simultaneous lineup, where all individuals are presented at once, which can lead to relative judgments. Witnesses in a sequential lineup are encouraged to rely on their actual memory of the perpetrator, rather than comparing each face to the others to determine who looks "closest" to their memory of the suspect. Research has shown that double-blind, sequential lineups reduce false identifications significantly, making them a more reliable option for suspect identification (Kovera & Evelo, 2020).

9.3 Lineup Construction: Minimizing Bias through Proper Design

Proper lineup construction is another critical factor in ensuring the fairness and accuracy of identification. A poorly designed lineup can lead witnesses to select an innocent individual simply because they stand out more than the other members in the lineup. To minimize this risk, lineups must include "fillers"—individuals who fit the general description of the perpetrator but are not suspects. This ensures that the suspect does not unduly stand out and allows the witness to make a choice based on genuine recognition rather than elimination.

Lineup fairness is achieved when each member in the lineup has an equal likelihood of being chosen, which makes it harder for a witness to pick someone based solely on standout features. For example, if a lineup includes one person with facial hair and the witness recalls that the perpetrator had a beard, then a lineup where only one member has facial hair unfairly biases the selection. A fair lineup requires all individuals to share similar distinguishing characteristics, reducing the chances of misidentification based on non-crime-related traits.

Additionally, law enforcement officers should avoid giving feedback or confirming the witness's choice, as this can reinforce a potentially incorrect identification. Research has shown that post-identification feedback increases witnesses' confidence in their choice, even if it is wrong, which can bias their testimony in court (Greenspan & Loftus, 2020). By maintaining neutral interactions, law enforcement officers can help ensure that the witness's identification remains as unbiased as possible.

9.4 Sequential Vs. Simultaneous Lineups: Pros and Cons

There are two main types of lineups: sequential and simultaneous. In simultaneous lineups, the witness views all members at once, while in sequential lineups, each member is presented one at a time. Studies have shown that sequential lineups reduce false identifications, as witnesses must rely on memory rather than relative judgment (Mansour et al., 2012).

In sequential lineups, witnesses evaluate each individual separately, which discourages the tendency to choose the person who most closely resembles the perpetrator among the group, regardless of absolute accuracy. However, simultaneous lineups may sometimes be more effective for identifying actual suspects, as they give witnesses a broader context and may facilitate a stronger, immediate recognition. The choice between sequential and simultaneous lineups is context-dependent, with sequential lineups generally preferred for reducing bias, especially in high-stakes cases where misidentification risks are significant.

9.5 Cognitive Effects on Identification Accuracy

Eyewitness identification accuracy is also influenced by various cognitive and situational factors. Memory decay, stress at the time of the incident, and the presence of weapon focus (where attention is drawn to a weapon rather than the perpetrator's face) are all known to impair accurate recall. Time delays between the crime and lineup further degrade memory, increasing the likelihood of misidentification.

Neuropsychological research has highlighted that stress hormones like cortisol can disrupt memory consolidation (James et al., 2023), particularly for peripheral details. While traumatic events may create vivid, "flashbulb" memories, they are often less reliable than expected. Lineup procedures must therefore account for these cognitive effects, with researchers recommending that identification be conducted as soon as possible to reduce memory decay (Wells et al., 2020).

9.6 Legal Implications of Lineup Procedures and the Role of Expert Testimony

Improper lineup procedures have serious legal implications. Misidentification can lead to wrongful convictions, which not only harm innocent people but also allow the true perpetrator to evade justice. Several high-profile cases have underscored the importance of lineup reforms, demonstrating that biased procedures can lead to devastating consequences. Legal reforms in lineup procedures are increasingly informed by psychological research, making evidence-based techniques such as double-blind, sequential lineups more common.

Courts are also more frequently relying on expert testimony from psychologists to educate juries on the potential fallibility of eyewitness identification. Experts explain the cognitive processes involved in memory and perception, highlighting how factors like stress, time delay, and lineup construction can distort witness recall.

This testimony provides juries with a scientific perspective on lineup identifications, fostering more informed decision-making.

Lineup procedures are a crucial component of criminal investigations, but they carry inherent risks of misidentification if not carefully administered. Bias, suggestibility, and improper lineup construction can all compromise the accuracy of eyewitness identifications, leading to wrongful convictions and miscarriages of justice. Implementing double-blind, sequential lineups, constructing fair lineups with appropriate fillers, and providing clear instructions to witnesses are essential steps in reducing these risks. By incorporating neuropsychological insights into lineup practices, the legal system can make significant strides in ensuring that witness identifications are as accurate and unbiased as possible. These improvements in lineup procedure, along with expert testimony on the cognitive vulnerabilities of eyewitness memory, can provide more reliable outcomes in the justice system, ultimately contributing to fairer and more trustworthy legal proceedings.

10 Case Studies: Misidentification and Wrongful Convictions

Wrongful convictions due to misidentifications underscore the complexities and vulnerabilities in human memory. Witness testimonies, often perceived as highly credible in court, can sometimes lead to grave miscarriages of justice when memory recall is flawed or affected by trauma. Notable organizations, such as the Innocence Project, have highlighted cases where DNA evidence has exonerated wrongfully convicted individuals, underscoring the need for more accurate neuropsychological evaluations and a greater understanding of memory recall dynamics. These cases, coupled with the insights from neuropsychology, emphasize the importance of evaluating how trauma, stress, and mental health conditions like post-traumatic stress disorder (PTSD) can impact memory accuracy and reliability.

10.1 The Role of Misidentification in Wrongful Convictions

Misidentifications have been one of the leading causes of wrongful convictions, as demonstrated by a vast number of exonerations over the past few decades. The Innocence Project, a nonprofit legal organization committed to overturning wrongful convictions, has reported that mistaken eyewitness identification plays a role in approximately 69% of wrongful conviction cases overturned by DNA evidence. This statistic underscores the weight the legal system places on witness testimony, even when it may be unreliable due to memory fallibility or situational influences.

Eyewitness misidentification is often the result of several factors: suggestive police procedures, lineup biases, and cognitive limitations in the witness's recall. For example, witnesses may fall victim to the "weapon focus effect," where their attention is drawn to a weapon rather than the perpetrator's face, making accurate identification difficult. Additionally, the stress of the crime and the pressure to make a selection in a lineup can lead witnesses to rely on relative judgments, choosing the person who most resembles the perpetrator instead of being certain. These biases highlight the importance of using scientifically supported lineup practices and the critical role that neuropsychological insight plays in understanding and reducing wrongful identifications.

10.2 Case Studies Highlighting Misidentification and Trauma-Related Memory Distortions

One of the most notable cases of misidentification and wrongful conviction involves Ronald Cotton, a man who was convicted of rape in 1984 based on eyewitness testimony. The victim, Jennifer Thompson, was confident in her identification of Cotton; however, DNA evidence years later conclusively proved that Cotton was innocent, and another individual was responsible. This case highlights the inherent limitations of human memory and the fallibility of eyewitness testimony, even when the witness is confident. Thompson's identification of Cotton was influenced by cognitive biases and situational factors that affected her memory recall. This tragic misidentification showcases the need for careful scrutiny of eyewitness accounts, particularly through neuropsychological evaluations.

Another compelling case involves Calvin Willis, who served 22 years in prison for a rape he did not commit. Misidentification was again a crucial factor in his conviction, as the victim's memory of the event was unclear and likely influenced by trauma. It was only after DNA testing became available that Willis was exonerated, demonstrating the need for forensic evaluations that understand the impact of trauma on memory recall.

Such cases illustrate that memory, especially under traumatic circumstances, is not always a faithful representation of events. Trauma can significantly distort perception and recall, and research has shown that memory is prone to distortion, especially when high-stress or life-threatening situations are involved (Davis et al., 2024). These instances reinforce the importance of integrating neuropsychological insights in evaluating witness testimony to better understand the impact of trauma on memory accuracy and reliability.

10.3 PTSD and Memory Recall: How Trauma Affects Eyewitness Testimony

Witnesses with PTSD often experience intrusive memories, flashbacks, or dissociative amnesia, all of which can impair their ability to accurately recall events. PTSD has been shown to impact memory retrieval by affecting how events are encoded and consolidated. For instance, trauma survivors may exhibit memory fragmentation, where details are recalled as isolated fragments rather than as a coherent narrative. This fragmentation can make it difficult to reconstruct a sequence of events accurately, leading to inconsistencies that may appear as deceptive or unreliable in court.

In addition, PTSD-related symptoms like flashbacks can distort the perception of time and sequence. A witness may struggle to differentiate between events that happened before, during, or after a traumatic event. In one case, a witness who experienced a traumatic event during a robbery recalled details of the crime but became confused about the timing and sequencing of events, resulting in misleading testimony. Understanding these effects is critical, as neuropsychological evaluations can help discern how trauma impacts the accuracy of memory recall, thereby preventing wrongful convictions based on mistaken or fragmented testimony.

Research also indicates that PTSD can impair the retrieval of specific details, while emotional aspects of the memory may remain intact, leading to what is known as a "flashbulb memory (Metternich et al., 2020)." While these memories may feel vivid and accurate to the individual, research suggests that they are not immune to distortion and are often incomplete. This phenomenon was evident in the case of a trauma survivor who confidently described the emotional atmosphere of a crime scene but struggled to remember key factual details, such as the physical appearance of the perpetrator. Such distortions highlight the need for trauma-informed approaches in witness evaluations, helping ensure that testimonial evidence is understood in its psychological context.

10.4 Neuropsychological Evaluations: Addressing Memory Vulnerabilities

To accurately assess the reliability of a witness's memory, neuropsychologists conduct comprehensive evaluations that consider cognitive processes, trauma history, and mental health. For example, standardized memory tests and trauma screenings are used to determine whether a witness may be susceptible to memory distortion. Techniques like the enhanced cognitive interview (ECI), which relies on open-ended questions and mental reinstatement of the context, are employed to improve memory recall while minimizing suggestibility.

A critical aspect of neuropsychological evaluations in legal contexts is the assessment of **suggestibility**, which is the tendency of individuals to incorporate misinformation from leading questions or external sources. Witnesses who have experienced trauma are often more suggestible, as PTSD can heighten anxiety and confusion, making them more likely to accept misleading information. In forensic settings, neuropsychologists work to minimize these influences by understanding the witness's cognitive vulnerabilities and using techniques that limit external interference.

10.5 The Role of DNA Evidence and Neuropsychology in Exoneration

The advent of DNA testing has been instrumental in exposing the limitations of eyewitness testimony and has led to hundreds of exonerations in cases of wrongful conviction. DNA evidence provides an objective means to verify the reliability of witness testimony, serving as a check against the biases and errors inherent in human memory. However, DNA testing alone is not a substitute for a thorough understanding of the neuropsychological underpinnings of memory recall, especially in cases where DNA is not available or when witness accounts provide the primary evidence.

The Innocence Project and similar organizations continue to advocate for incorporating scientific and neuropsychological insights into legal procedures to prevent wrongful convictions. By combining DNA evidence with neuropsychological assessments, the legal system can more accurately evaluate the reliability of witness testimony, especially in cases involving traumatic events.

Cases of wrongful conviction due to misidentification illustrate the urgent need for a more scientifically informed approach to witness testimony. Neuropsychological evaluations provide a framework for understanding the impact of trauma, PTSD, and cognitive biases on memory recall, helping the legal system differentiate between reliable and unreliable testimony. With the support of DNA testing and forensic neuropsychology, courts can take proactive steps to reduce wrongful convictions by critically examining the limitations of eyewitness memory. The integration of neuropsychology into legal proceedings is essential in ensuring that witness testimony serves as a reliable form of evidence, ultimately safeguarding justice and protecting the innocent.

11 Improving the Reliability of Witness Testimony

Eyewitness testimony has long been a cornerstone of the criminal justice system, often heavily influencing jury decisions. Yet decades of research show that memory is inherently fallible, subject to distortions from both internal cognitive biases and external influences (Junnarkar & Lakhani, 2021). Recognizing these vulnerabilities has led to efforts to improve the reliability of witness testimony, especially through enhancing law enforcement practices, educating jurors on memory limitations, and leveraging neuropsychologists' insights in court. These approaches aim to address issues with memory recall, reduce the likelihood of wrongful convictions, and enhance the overall fairness of legal proceedings.

11.1 Training Law Enforcement Officers on Cognitive Interviewing Techniques

One of the most effective ways to improve the accuracy of witness testimony is through training law enforcement officers in cognitive interviewing techniques. Developed in the 1980s, the cognitive interview (CI) was designed to enhance memory retrieval while minimizing the risk of introducing new, erroneous information. This technique has proven to significantly increase the amount and accuracy of information witnesses recall compared to traditional interviewing methods.

Cognitive interviewing includes several key techniques that promote more accurate recall:

- **Context reinstatement**: Witnesses are encouraged to mentally reconstruct the environment in which the event took place, including sensory details and emotional states. This helps activate context-dependent memories, making it easier to retrieve accurate details.
- **Report everything**: Witnesses are prompted to share every detail, even if it seems trivial or insignificant. Often, seemingly minor details can trigger other memories, resulting in a more complete and coherent account.
- **Change perspective**: Witnesses are sometimes asked to describe the event from different perspectives, such as another person's viewpoint. This can encourage recall of details that may otherwise be missed.
- **Reverse order**: Asking witnesses to recall events in reverse order can prevent them from reconstructing events based on preconceived narratives or filling in gaps with assumptions.

Training law enforcement officers in CI techniques can reduce the risk of memory contamination, a common problem in eyewitness testimony. Traditional interrogation methods often involve repetitive questioning, which can introduce unintended biases or assumptions that alter the witness's memory. For example, if an officer repeatedly asks if the perpetrator had a specific characteristic, the witness may start to incorporate that detail into their recollection, regardless of its accuracy. Cognitive interviewing, by contrast, relies on open-ended questions and unsuggestive prompts, helping witnesses recall information more accurately.

Studies have shown that cognitive interviewing can yield up to 35% more accurate information than traditional methods, making it a valuable tool for law enforcement (Brimbal et al., 2021). However, implementing CI consistently requires substantial training and practice, as well as a commitment to avoiding suggestive questioning. When used effectively, it can minimize the impact of false memories and lead to more reliable testimony.

11.2 Educating Jurors on the Fallibility of Memory

Another key approach to improving witness testimony reliability is educating jurors about the cognitive limitations of memory. Jurors often view eyewitness testimony as highly credible, assuming that if a witness "remembers" something, it must be accurate. However, this assumption does not account for memory's susceptibility to errors and distortions.

Memory is not a perfect recording but rather a reconstructive process influenced by emotions, biases, and external information. Misleading questions, repeated exposure to media reports, and the stress of the incident itself can all interfere with a witness's ability to recall accurately. Jurors are often unaware of these influences and may place undue weight on eyewitness accounts. Educating jurors about the fallibility of memory can help them interpret witness testimony more critically.

One effective method for this education is jury instructions that outline common memory vulnerabilities, such as the misinformation effect and the impact of stress on recall accuracy. For example, jurors can be informed that high-stress events, such as witnessing a violent crime, can impair the encoding of details, leading to fragmented or distorted memories. Similarly, they can be educated about factors that may introduce false memories, such as leading questions or post-event information from other sources.

Courts can also use expert testimony from neuropsychologists to help jurors understand the science behind memory limitations. Neuropsychologists can provide insight into how memory works, explaining that memories are often fragmented and malleable, subject to change over time. By offering scientific explanations, neuropsychologists can help jurors appreciate that even confident witnesses may misremember critical details.

Studies have shown that jurors who receive such education are less likely to rely solely on eyewitness accounts and are more likely to critically evaluate the quality of the testimony presented (Helm, 2021). This shift in perspective can lead to fairer outcomes and reduce the risk of wrongful convictions based on faulty eyewitness testimony.

11.3 The Role of Neuropsychologists in Court: Explaining Memory Limitations

Neuropsychologists play a vital role in enhancing the reliability of witness testimony through their expertise on memory processes and vulnerabilities. In court, neuropsychologists can act as expert witnesses, providing crucial context that helps judges and juries understand how memory functions and why it can sometimes be unreliable.

One key area where neuropsychologists provide valuable insight is in addressing the influence of post-event information. Misinformation, whether from media, police questioning, or interactions with others, can become embedded in a witness's memory, making it challenging to differentiate between actual events and external suggestions. Neuropsychologists can explain how suggestibility works, especially in individuals who are anxious or susceptible to social influence, and discuss how such factors could have affected a specific witness's recollection.

Additionally, neuropsychologists can clarify the effects of stress and trauma on memory. Witnesses of traumatic events often report vivid, detailed memories, which can seem highly convincing. However, as neuropsychologists explain, trauma does not guarantee accuracy. While some details may be remembered with intense clarity, others may be distorted or entirely forgotten due to the brain's response to high-stress situations. Trauma-related memory alterations, such as flashbacks or fragmented recollections, are particularly relevant in cases involving violent crimes, where eyewitness accounts often play a central role.

Neuropsychologists also emphasize the unconscious biases that can affect memory. For instance, cross-racial identifications are particularly prone to errors, as studies have shown that people are less accurate when identifying individuals of a different race (Töredi, 2024). Neuropsychologists can help the court understand this phenomenon, along with the cognitive biases that can lead witnesses to misidentify a suspect based on similarity rather than certainty.

11.4 The Future of Reliable Eyewitness Testimony

The field of forensic psychology and neuropsychology is continuously evolving, with research revealing new insights into memory processes and their implications for witness testimony (Marr et al., 2020). Future advancements may include the development of standardized guidelines for police interviews, as well as further integration of expert testimonies that address cognitive limitations in memory recall.

Additionally, technological innovations, such as virtual reality (VR) simulations, may offer ways to help witnesses mentally reconstruct crime scenes more accurately, potentially enhancing recall without the risk of suggestibility. Neuroimaging technologies, though still largely experimental in legal settings, may also one day provide objective assessments of witness recall, helping identify when memory distortions have likely occurred (Hall & Poirier, 2020).

In the meantime, focusing on effective interviewing techniques, educating jurors, and incorporating expert testimony remains the best approach for improving the reliability of witness testimony. By acknowledging the fallibility of memory and making procedural adjustments to account for these limitations, the criminal justice system can work toward more accurate and fairer trial outcomes.

12 Ethical Considerations in the Use of Neuropsychological Findings in Legal Contexts

The integration of neuropsychological findings in legal proceedings has the potential to significantly enhance the accuracy and fairness of judicial outcomes. However, the use of these findings also brings critical ethical considerations to the forefront. Neuropsychologists must navigate complex ethical responsibilities, ensuring that they provide scientifically accurate data while also upholding principles of justice and fairness. The interpretation of memory assessments, in particular, requires caution, as misinterpretation could contribute to wrongful convictions or unfair acquittals. This report discusses key ethical considerations for neuropsychologists, emphasizing the need for careful assessment, informed consent, accurate communication of findings, and an awareness of potential biases.

12.1 The Duty to Provide Accurate Scientific Data

One of the primary ethical obligations of neuropsychologists is to provide accurate, evidence-based information in court. When a neuropsychologist testifies or submits reports, they contribute to the decision-making process in significant ways. The accuracy of these contributions is crucial, as flawed data or interpretations can mislead jurors and judges, potentially impacting the fairness of the verdict. Therefore, neuropsychologists are responsible for rigorously following scientific standards when assessing memory, cognition, and psychological state in legal contexts.

To meet this duty, neuropsychologists should rely on well-validated, standardized assessments and methodologies. For example, memory assessments used in evaluations should have established reliability and validity, as well as norms for the specific population under assessment. Neuropsychologists must also be careful to acknowledge the limitations of these tools and avoid overgeneralizing their results. Even the most accurate assessments can only provide a partial picture of an individual's mental state, memory accuracy, or cognitive capabilities. In legal contexts, where consequences are severe, neuropsychologists should clearly communicate any limitations in their findings, ensuring that judges and jurors understand the scope and boundaries of the neuropsychological evidence presented.

12.2 Balancing Objectivity with Justice

Neuropsychologists working in forensic contexts must also maintain objectivity, presenting data and conclusions without bias. However, achieving objectivity is often complicated by the adversarial nature of legal proceedings, where expert witnesses may be employed by either the defense or prosecution. In such situations, there is a risk that neuropsychologists may be pressured to interpret findings in a way that aligns with their retaining party's interests. While this pressure can be subtle, it has the potential to skew expert testimony, undermining the ethical commitment to neutrality and objective science.

To balance the duty of objectivity with the goal of justice, neuropsychologists should adopt clear professional boundaries. A neuropsychologist's role is not to advocate for one side but rather to provide accurate, scientifically grounded information. By emphasizing neutrality and declining to accept cases where conflicts of interest may arise, neuropsychologists can uphold their ethical obligation to provide unbiased information.

Professional codes of ethics, such as those provided by the American Psychological Association (APA), reinforce this commitment to impartiality. These codes advise neuropsychologists to be vigilant about potential biases, consciously avoiding interpretations that may be overly favorable to one side. Maintaining objectivity is not only an ethical duty; it is essential for the credibility and reputation of neuropsychology as a field.

12.3 Informed Consent and Confidentiality

Informed consent is a cornerstone of ethical practice in psychology, and forensic neuropsychology is no exception. Witnesses, defendants, or other individuals subjected to neuropsychological evaluation must be fully informed of the purpose, scope, and potential outcomes of the assessment. Informed consent ensures that participants understand that the assessment findings may be used in court and that their confidentiality may be limited due to the legal context.

However, informed consent in forensic settings can be challenging. Individuals may not fully understand the legal implications of their participation, especially if they are not represented by legal counsel. Neuropsychologists should work to ensure that informed consent procedures are comprehensive and clear. This may involve providing additional explanations or clarifying any legal terminology involved, ensuring that the person undergoing the assessment is genuinely informed.

Confidentiality is also a critical ethical consideration. Neuropsychologists are bound by professional standards to protect the privacy of the individuals they evaluate. Yet in legal contexts, confidentiality has limitations; assessment findings often become part of the public record once they are introduced in court. Neuropsychologists must inform individuals of these limitations at the outset, explaining that certain information may need to be disclosed as part of the legal proceedings. Balancing confidentiality with the demands of the legal process requires neuropsychologists to be transparent and diligent in their handling of sensitive information.

12.4 The Ethical Use of Memory Assessments

Memory assessments are a common tool used in forensic neuropsychology to evaluate the reliability of witness testimony. However, memory is inherently complex and fallible, and neuropsychologists must be cautious in interpreting and presenting memory assessments in court. For instance, a witness may confidently recall specific details of an event, but confidence in memory does not necessarily correlate with accuracy. External factors, such as leading questions, stress, or repeated questioning, can alter memories, leading to inaccurate or distorted recollections.

Ethical considerations are especially relevant in cases where memory assessments may influence the credibility of a witness or defendant. Neuropsychologists should avoid presenting memory assessments as infallible and instead emphasize the nuanced nature of memory. By discussing potential memory distortions and acknowledging the inherent limitations of memory recall, neuropsychologists help ensure that judges and jurors do not overestimate the accuracy of testimony based on memory assessments. Careful interpretation and communication are essential to avoid contributing to wrongful convictions or unfair legal outcomes.

Additionally, neuropsychologists must be cautious when using emerging technologies, such as neuroimaging, to support memory assessments. While neuroimaging offers valuable insights into brain activity, it is not a direct measure of memory accuracy and may be misinterpreted by nonexpert audiences. Ethically, neuropsychologists should avoid overstating the capabilities of neuroimaging, ensuring that they provide a realistic view of what such technology can and cannot reveal about memory processes.

12.5 Addressing Potential Biases in Memory Assessment

Neuropsychologists must be mindful of their own biases, as well as the biases inherent in memory assessment tools and procedures. Cultural, gender, and age-related differences can all influence memory assessment results, potentially affecting the accuracy and fairness of evaluations. For instance, some memory assessments may have been normed on populations that do not represent the diversity of individuals seen in court. Applying these assessments without adjustments can lead to biased or inaccurate conclusions.

Neuropsychologists are ethically obligated to consider these factors, seeking out culturally sensitive tools and procedures when available. They should also interpret results with an awareness of potential biases, clearly noting any limitations in their assessments. By remaining vigilant about bias and striving for cultural competence, neuropsychologists can help prevent misinterpretations that may disproportionately affect certain groups.

The ethical considerations in neuropsychological evaluations of witness testimony are numerous and complex. Neuropsychologists must strive for accuracy, objectivity, and cultural sensitivity in their work, balancing their duty to provide scientifically valid information with their commitment to justice. From informed consent and confidentiality to the ethical interpretation of memory assessments, neuropsychologists play a crucial role in ensuring that neuropsychological findings are used responsibly in legal contexts. By adhering to these ethical standards, neuropsychologists contribute to a more just legal system and help protect the rights and well-being of individuals involved in forensic assessments.

13 Conclusion

Witness testimony has long held a prominent role in legal proceedings, often influencing the outcome of trials and shaping the course of justice. Despite its compelling nature, eyewitness testimony is inherently fallible, subject to the complexities and vulnerabilities of human memory. Cognitive distortions, external influences, and internal biases can all lead to inaccuracies in memory recall, potentially contributing to wrongful convictions and miscarriages of justice. Recognizing these limitations, the integration of neuropsychological insights into legal processes offers a critical pathway to enhance the reliability of witness testimony.

The field of neuropsychology provides an invaluable understanding of memory's intricacies, shedding light on why eyewitnesses may inadvertently misremember or misinterpret events. This knowledge has led to the development of tools and methodologies, such as cognitive interviews and lineup protocols, that reduce the likelihood of memory contamination and suggestive influence. By applying scientifically grounded techniques and acknowledging the inherent complexities of memory, the legal system can move toward more accurate, fairer, and more just outcomes. This conclusion explores how the integration of neuropsychological insights can help legal professionals better interpret witness testimony, improve procedural safeguards, and ultimately foster a more reliable justice system. Memory is a dynamic and reconstructive process rather than a precise record of events. Witnesses may experience disruptions or distortions at any stage, particularly in high-stress or traumatic situations like witnessing a crime. Even under optimal conditions, memory is susceptible to forgetting, blending of events, and the incorporation of post-event information. These vulnerabilities are further compounded by cognitive biases, such as confirmation bias or the misinformation effect, which can subtly but significantly alter an individual's recollection. In recognizing memory's fallibility, neuropsychologists emphasize the importance of assessing testimony through a scientifically informed lens. By understanding the psychological processes behind memory errors, the legal system can take proactive steps to mitigate their impact on justice.

Neuropsychology has contributed several methods that can help reduce the risk of cognitive distortions in witness testimony. Techniques like the enhanced cognitive interview (ECI) and double-blind lineup procedures have been developed to account for vulnerabilities of memory and encourage more accurate recall.

Double-blind lineup procedures, wherein neither the administrator nor the witness knows the identity of the suspect, are similarly valuable in reducing suggestive influence. Such methods are essential for preventing memory contamination and addressing common issues with traditional lineup formats, such as implicit pressure to identify a suspect. Incorporating neuropsychological insights into law enforcement training can also improve witness handling practices from the earliest stages of an investigation. Standardized training on the cognitive aspects of memory recall encourages law enforcement officers to consider the limitations of memory, further safeguarding the reliability of witness testimony.

Neuropsychologists play a crucial role in educating court participants about the inherent fallibility of memory. Through expert testimony, they can elucidate how cognitive biases, stress, and trauma affect memory accuracy, helping jurors and judges interpret eyewitness accounts with an informed perspective. Expert testimony is particularly valuable in cases involving highly suggestive evidence or unreliable witness recollections. Neuropsychologists can clarify the difference between confidence and accuracy, dispelling misconceptions that often arise when a witness appears confident but maybe unknowingly inaccurate.

Misidentifications stemming from flawed witness testimony are a leading cause of wrongful convictions, as highlighted by numerous exonerations facilitated by organizations like the Innocence Project. These cases serve as poignant reminders of the devastating consequences that can arise when memory is misinterpreted or overly relied upon in legal contexts. By integrating neuropsychological insights, the legal system can adopt procedural safeguards that help prevent such miscarriages of justice.

Enhanced lineup procedures, standardized interviewing techniques, and the careful handling of post-event information all represent practical applications of neuropsychological research. Such protocols address common memory distortions and create a framework that minimizes the risk of misidentification. Neuropsychological insights offer a foundation upon which these safeguards can be built, bringing the legal system closer to achieving accuracy in its reliance on witness testimony. Additionally, educating jurors about the science behind memory recall fosters a legal culture that is more cautious and critical when interpreting eyewitness accounts. By understanding that memory can be influenced by external factors, jurors may give more measured weight to witness testimony, recognizing its potential limitations. Neuropsychologists are integral in driving these shifts, ensuring that scientific knowledge shapes judicial processes.

The integration of neuropsychology in legal processes has the potential to transform how witness testimony is understood and utilized in court. Neuropsychological insights provide tools and frameworks that address these limitations, ensuring that witness testimony is contextualized and analyzed within a scientific understanding of memory. The future of a science-infused justice system will likely see further collaboration between neuropsychology and law, with increased emphasis on research-driven practices in witness testimony evaluation. As this relationship continues to evolve, the reliability of courtroom evidence will improve, minimizing wrongful convictions and promoting fairer outcomes. Ultimately, neuropsychology's role in legal proceedings underscores a commitment to achieving justice not solely through tradition but through evidence-based advancements that reflect the complexities of the human mind. Through these efforts, the legal system can better navigate the challenges of witness testimony, upholding fairness, accuracy, and integrity in the pursuit of justice.

References

Adedayo, L., Ojo, G., Umanah, S., Aitokhuehi, G., Emmanuel, I., & Bamidele, O. (2023). *Hippocampus: Its role in relational memory*. IntechOpen eBooks. https://doi.org/10.5772/intechopen.111478

Anakwah, N., Horselenberg, R., Hope, L., Amankwah-Poku, M., & Van Koppen, P. J. (2024). The effect of authority on eyewitness memory reports across cultures. *Psychiatry Psychology and Law, 1–15*, 1. https://doi.org/10.1080/13218719.2024.2362133

Anderson, M. C. (2020). *Autobiographical memory* (pp. 351–391). Routledge eBooks. https://doi.org/10.4324/9780429449642-11

Atkinson, R., & Shiffrin, R. (1968). Human memory: A proposed system and its control processes. In *The psychology of learning and motivation/the psychology of learning and motivation* (pp. 89–195). https://doi.org/10.1016/s0079-7421(08)60422-3

Bailey, H., & Smith, M. E. (2024). Event perception and event memory in real-world experience. *Nature Reviews Psychology., 3*, 754. https://doi.org/10.1038/s44159-024-00367-0

Bakhtiar, H. S. (2023). Role and nature of evidence: Forensic insight. *Jurnal Yuridis, 10*(2), 10–22. https://doi.org/10.35586/jyur.v10i2.7072

Balarezo, J. D., Foss, N. J., & Nielsen, B. B. (2023). Organizational learning: Understanding cognitive barriers and what organizations can do about them. *Management Learning., 55*, 741. https://doi.org/10.1177/13505076231210635

Bermejo, J., Valldecabres, R., Villarrasa-Sapiña, I., Monfort-Torres, G., Marco-Ahulló, A., & Couto, B. R. D. (2022). Increased cortisol levels caused by acute resistance physical exercise impair memory and learning ability. *PeerJ, 10*, e13000. https://doi.org/10.7717/peerj.13000

Bex, F., Prakken, H., Reed, C., & Walton, D. (2003). Towards a formal account of reasoning about evidence: Argumentation schemes and Generalisations. *Artificial Intelligence and Law, 11*(2/3), 125–165. https://doi.org/10.1023/b:arti.0000046007.11806.9a

Bhadra, P. (2021). *Is forensic evidence impartial? Cognitive biases in forensic analysis* (pp. 215–227). Springer eBooks. https://doi.org/10.1007/978-981-16-4570-9_14

Bhave, S. N., Kaul, L., & Isai, P. C. (2023). *Eyewitness testimony: Looking through the lens of psychology and Indian jurisprudence* (pp. 331–347). Routledge eBooks. https://doi.org/10.4324/9781032629346-22

Brimbal, L., Meissner, C. A., Kleinman, S. M., Phillips, E. L., Atkinson, D. J., Dianiska, R. E., Rothweiler, J. N., Oleszkiewicz, S., & Jones, M. S. (2021). Evaluating the benefits of a rapport-based approach to investigative interviews: A training study with law enforcement investigators. *Law and Human Behavior, 45*(1), 55–67. https://doi.org/10.1037/lhb0000437

Brown, J., Jonason, A., Asp, E., McGinn, V., Carter, M. N., Spiller, V., & Jozan, A. (2021). Fetal alcohol spectrum disorder and confabulation in psycholegal settings: A beginner's guide for criminal justice, forensic mental health, and legal interviewers. *Behavioral Sciences & the Law, 40*(1), 46–86. https://doi.org/10.1002/bsl.2540

Bull, R., & Milne, B. (2020). *Recommendations for collecting event memory evidence* (pp. 198–222). Routledge eBooks. https://doi.org/10.4324/9780429027857-8

Ceci, S. J., & Bruck, M. (1993). Suggestibility of the child witness: A historical review and synthesis. *Psychological Bulletin, 113*(3), 403–439. https://doi.org/10.1037/0033-2909.113.3.403

Challies, D. M., Hunt, M., Garry, M., & Harper, D. N. (2011). Whatever gave you that Idea? False memories following equivalence training: A behavioral account of the misinformation effect. *Journal of the Experimental Analysis of Behavior, 96*(3), 343–362. https://doi.org/10.1901/jeab.2011.96-343

Chalmers, J., Leverick, F., & Munro, V. E. (2022). Handle with care: Jury deliberation and demeanour-based assessments of witness credibility. *The International Journal of Evidence & Proof, 26*(4), 381–406. https://doi.org/10.1177/13657127221120955

Chu, B., Marwaha, K., Sanvictores, T., Awosika, A. O., & Ayers, D. (2024). *Physiology, stress reaction*. StatPearls–NCBI Bookshelf. https://www.ncbi.nlm.nih.gov/books/NBK541120/

Cikara, M., Martinez, J. E., & Lewis, N. A. (2022). Moving beyond social categories by incorporating context in social psychological theory. *Nature Reviews Psychology, 1*(9), 537–549. https://doi.org/10.1038/s44159-022-00079-3

Colombo, D., Suso-Ribera, C., Fernández-Álvarez, J., Cipresso, P., Garcia-Palacios, A., Riva, G., & Botella, C. (2020). Affect recall bias: Being resilient by distorting reality. *Cognitive Therapy and Research, 44*(5), 906–918. https://doi.org/10.1007/s10608-020-10122-3

Crossland, D., Kneller, W., & Wilcock, R. (2020). Improving intoxicated witness recall with the enhanced cognitive interview. *Psychopharmacology, 237*(7), 2213–2230. https://doi.org/10.1007/s00213-020-05531-x

Curci, A., Lanciano, T., Curtotti, D., & Sartori, G. (2020). Lessons for the courtroom from the study of flashbulb memory: An integrative review. *Memory, 28*(3), 441–449. https://doi.org/10.1080/09658211.2020.1727522

Dahlgren, K., Ferris, C., & Hamann, S. (2020). Neural correlates of successful emotional episodic encoding and retrieval: An SDM meta-analysis of neuroimaging studies. *Neuropsychologia, 143*, 107495. https://doi.org/10.1016/j.neuropsychologia.2020.107495

Dalenberg, C. J., Brand, B. L., Loewenstein, R. J., Frewen, P. A., & Spiegel, D. (2020). Inviting scientific discourse on traumatic dissociation: Progress made and obstacles to further resolution. *Psychological Injury and Law, 13*(2), 135–154. https://doi.org/10.1007/s12207-020-09376-9

Dalton, G., & Milne, R. (2021). *Investigative interviewing: Exploring the contamination timeline of witness memory* (pp. 337–356). Elsevier eBooks. https://doi.org/10.1016/b978-0-12-816544-7.00016-4

Davis, D., Hogan, A. A., & Hart, D. J. (2024). Myths of trauma memory: On the oversimplification of effects of attention narrowing under stress. *Frontiers in Psychology, 15*. https://doi.org/10.3389/fpsyg.2024.1294730

De Kloet, E. R., & Joëls, M. (2023). The cortisol switch between vulnerability and resilience. *Molecular Psychiatry, 29*(1), 20–34. https://doi.org/10.1038/s41380-022-01934-8

Deck, S. L. (2021). *An examination of the credibility of witnesses who recall a repeated event: Cognitive competence, honesty, and perceived credibility*. https://ses.library.usyd.edu.au/handle/2123/25071

Di Nota, P. M., Stoliker, B. E., Vaughan, A. D., Andersen, J. P., & Anderson, G. S. (2020). Stress and memory: A systematic state-of-the-art review with evidence-gathering recommendations for police. *Policing an International Journal, 44*(1), 1–17. https://doi.org/10.1108/pijpsm-06-2020-0093

Diamond, N. B., Armson, M. J., & Levine, B. (2020). The truth is out there: Accuracy in recall of verifiable real-world events. *Psychological Science, 31*(12), 1544–1556. https://doi.org/10.1177/0956797620954812

Ditto, P. H., Celniker, J. B., Siddiqi, S. S., Güngör, M., & Relihan, D. P. (2024). Partisan bias in political judgment. *Annual Review of Psychology., 76*, 717. https://doi.org/10.1146/annurev-psych-030424-122723

Dodier, O., Barzykowski, K., & Souchay, C. (2023). Recovered memories of trauma as a special (or not so special) form of involuntary autobiographical memories. *Frontiers in Psychology, 14*. https://doi.org/10.3389/fpsyg.2023.1268757

DuGan, G., Ellis, R., Flom, J., Grisham, J., Johnson, C., Lander, E. S., Reno, J., Rothman, M., Schulte, S., Steingart, B., Tananbaum, A. H., Taylor, J., Verkuil, P. R., & Board of Directors,

& M.K. Enterprises, Inc. (n.d.). Reevaluating lineups: Why witnesses make mistakes and how to reduce the chance of a misidentification. In N. Benjamin (Ed.), *Cardozo School Of Law*. Yeshiva University. https://www.innocenceproject.org/wp-content/uploads/2016/05/eyewitness_id_report-5.pdf

Faul, L. (n.d.). *Examining multiple routes to emotional memory Bias–ProQuest*. https://www.proquest.com/openview/79e6fe1b91d1810ce06bfcef8b5a9864/1?cbl=18750&diss=y&pq-origsite=gscholar

Fernández-Pérez, D., Gómez-Guillén, A., Talavera, I., Nieto, M., Ricarte, J. J., & Ros, L. (2024). Gender differences and the association between the phenomenological characteristics of autobiographical memories and psychopathic traits in a university student sample. *Memory, 1–12*, 19. https://doi.org/10.1080/09658211.2024.2402417

Fischer, V., & O'Mara, S. M. (2022). Neural, psychological, and social foundations of collective memory: Implications for common mnemonic processes, agency, and identity. *Progress in Brain Research, 1–30*. https://doi.org/10.1016/bs.pbr.2022.07.004

Fivush, R., & Grysman, A. (2022). Accuracy and reconstruction in autobiographical memory: (re) consolidating neuroscience and sociocultural developmental approaches. Wiley interdisciplinary reviews. *Cognitive Science, 14*(3), e1620. https://doi.org/10.1002/wcs.1620

Friedman, N. P., & Robbins, T. W. (2021). The role of prefrontal cortex in cognitive control and executive function. *Neuropsychopharmacology, 47*(1), 72–89. https://doi.org/10.1038/s41386-021-01132-0

Funahashi, S. (2022). Prefrontal cortex and working memory. In *Brain science* (pp. 515–543). https://doi.org/10.1007/978-981-19-7268-3_10

Giacona, A. M. (n.d.). *How systematically increasing estimator variables affects the confidence-accuracy relationship–ProQuest*. https://www.proquest.com/openview/84b8023650bf45dbf06efbd9ce54e3bb/1?cbl=18750&diss=y&pq-origsite=gscholar&parentSessionId=1JSxS76Vnr3PjI3VpspvQuVOCOM%2BZf1fpW9vhzrZkoQ%3D

Greenspan, R. L., & Loftus, E. F. (2020). Eyewitness confidence malleability: Misinformation as post-identification feedback. *Law and Human Behavior, 44*(3), 194–208. https://doi.org/10.1037/lhb0000369

Grob, A., Ehlers, D., & Schwabe, L. (2023). Strong but fragmented memory of a stressful episode. *eNeuro, 10*(9), ENEURO.0178-23.2023. https://doi.org/10.1523/eneuro.0178-23.2023

Hall, H. V., & Poirier, J. G. (2020). *Detecting malingering and deception*. CRC Press. eBooks. https://doi.org/10.4324/9780429423031

Helm, R. K. (2021). Evaluating witness testimony: Juror knowledge, false memory, and the utility of evidence-based directions. *The International Journal of Evidence & Proof, 25*(4), 264–285. https://doi.org/10.1177/13657127211031018

Hope, L., Anakwah, N., Antfolk, J., Brubacher, S. P., Flowe, H., Gabbert, F., Giebels, E., Kanja, W., Korkman, J., Kyo, A., Naka, M., Otgaar, H., Powell, M. B., Selim, H., Skrifvars, J., Sorkpah, I. K., Sowatey, E. A., Steele, L. C., Stevens, L., et al. (2021). Urgent issues and prospects at the intersection of culture, memory, and witness interviews: Exploring the challenges for research and practice. *Legal and Criminological Psychology, 27*(1), 1–31. https://doi.org/10.1111/lcrp.12202

Howe, M. L., & Knott, L. M. (2015). The fallibility of memory in judicial processes: Lessons from the past and their modern consequences. *Memory, 23*(5), 633–656. https://doi.org/10.1080/09658211.2015.1010709

James, K. A., Stromin, J. I., Steenkamp, N., & Combrinck, M. I. (2023). Understanding the relationships between physiological and psychosocial stress, cortisol and cognition. *Frontiers in Endocrinology, 14*. https://doi.org/10.3389/fendo.2023.1085950

Jayne, K. A. (n.d.). *Identification of the contexts and mechanisms of art psychotherapy treatment that supports healing and recovery for adults who have experienced complex trauma: The development of a treatment manual–unification neuro-informed trauma reconsolidation art psychotherapy (UNTRAP)–ProQuest*. https://www.proquest.com/docview/2778642824?pq-origsite=gscholar&fromopenview=true&sourcetype=dissertations%20&%20Theses

Jones, A. M., Bergold, A. N., & Penrod, S. (2020). Improving juror sensitivity to specific eyewitness factors: Judicial instructions fail the test. *Psychiatry Psychology and Law, 27*(3), 366–385. https://doi.org/10.1080/13218719.2020.1719379

Josselyn, S. A., & Tonegawa, S. (2020). Memory engrams: Recalling the past and imagining the future. *Science, 367*(6473). https://doi.org/10.1126/science.aaw4325

Junnarkar, M., & Lakhani, S. (2021). *Investigating the eyewitness: Accuracy and fallacies of memory* (pp. 203–213). Springer eBooks. https://doi.org/10.1007/978-981-16-4570-9_13

Kaneko, A., Asaoka, Y., Lee, Y., & Goto, Y. (2021). Cognitive and affective processes associated with social biases. *The International Journal of Neuropsychopharmacology, 24*(8), 645–655. https://doi.org/10.1093/ijnp/pyab022

Kensinger, E. A., & Ford, J. H. (2019). Retrieval of emotional events from memory. *Annual Review of Psychology, 71*(1), 251–272. https://doi.org/10.1146/annurev-psych-010419-051123

Klier, C., & Buratto, L. G. (2020). Stress and long-term memory retrieval: A systematic review. *Trends in Psychiatry and Psychotherapy, 42*(3), 284–291. https://doi.org/10.1590/2237-6089-2019-0077

Kloft, L., Monds, L. A., Blokland, A., Ramaekers, J. G., & Otgaar, H. (2021). Hazy memories in the courtroom: A review of alcohol and other drug effects on false memory and suggestibility. *Neuroscience & Biobehavioral Reviews, 124*, 291–307. https://doi.org/10.1016/j.neubiorev.2021.02.012

Korkman, J., Otgaar, H., Geven, L., Bull, R., Cyr, M., Hershkowitz, I., Mäkelä, J., Mattison, M., Milne, R., Santtila, P., Van Koppen, P., Memon, A., Danby, M., Filipovic, L., Garcia, F., Gewehr, E., Bell, O. G., Järvilehto, L., Kask, K., et al. (2024). White paper on forensic child interviewing: Research-based recommendations by the European Association of Psychology and law. *Psychology Crime and Law, 1–44*, 1. https://doi.org/10.1080/1068316x.2024.2324098

Kovera, M. B., & Evelo, A. J. (2020). Improving eyewitness-identification evidence through double-blind lineup administration. *Current Directions in Psychological Science, 29*(6), 563–568. https://doi.org/10.1177/0963721420969366

Kredlow, M. A., Fenster, R. J., Laurent, E. S., Ressler, K. J., & Phelps, E. A. (2021). Prefrontal cortex, amygdala, and threat processing: Implications for PTSD. *Neuropsychopharmacology, 47*(1), 247–259. https://doi.org/10.1038/s41386-021-01155-7

Kuhlmann, B. G., Symeonidou, N., Tanyas, H., & Wulff, L. (2021). Remembering and reconstructing episodic context: An overview of source monitoring methods and behavioral findings. In *The psychology of learning and motivation/the psychology of learning and motivation (pp. 79–124)*. https://doi.org/10.1016/bs.plm.2021.06.002

Lacy, J. W., & Stark, C. E. L. (2013). The neuroscience of memory: Implications for the courtroom. *Nature Reviews. Neuroscience, 14*(9), 649–658. https://doi.org/10.1038/nrn3563

Lewis, D. N. S. (n.d.). *Wrongful conviction: Using lived experience to explore errors in juror cognition*. ScholarWorks. https://scholarworks.waldenu.edu/dissertations/9643/

Lockamyeir, R. F. (n.d.). *Weapons at a distance: An investigation of the weapon focus effect as a function of distance–ProQuest*. https://www.proquest.com/docview/2572600008?pq-origsite=gscholar&fromopenview=true&sourcetype=Dissertations%20&%20Theses

Louw, D. (2015). *Forensic psychology* (pp. 351–356). Elsevier eBooks. https://doi.org/10.1016/b978-0-08-097086-8.21074-x

Malloggi, S., Conte, F., De Rosa, O., Cellini, N., Di Iorio, I., Ficca, G., & Giganti, F. (2022). False recalls, but not false recognitions, at the DRM paradigm are increased in subjects reporting insomnia symptoms: An online study. *Sleep Medicine, 100*, 347–353. https://doi.org/10.1016/j.sleep.2022.09.005

Mansour, J. K., Beaudry, J. L., Bertrand, M. I., Kalmet, N., Melsom, E. I., & Lindsay, R. C. L. (2012). Impact of disguise on identification decisions and confidence with simultaneous and sequential lineups. *Law and Human Behavior, 36*(6), 513–526. https://doi.org/10.1037/h0093937

Marr, C., Otgaar, H., Sauerland, M., Quaedflieg, C. W. E. M., & Hope, L. (2020). The effects of stress on eyewitness memory: A survey of memory experts and laypeople. *Memory & Cognition, 49*(3), 401–421. https://doi.org/10.3758/s13421-020-01115-4

Mazerolle, M., Smith, A., Torrance, M., & Thomas, A. (2021). Understanding older adults' memory distortion in the light of stereotype threat. *Frontiers in Psychology, 12*. https://doi.org/10.3389/fpsyg.2021.628696

McCroy, K. (n.d.). *The effects of type of recall on memory accuracy in an eyewitness case vignette*. Digital Commons@NLU. https://digitalcommons.nl.edu/diss/728/

Mercer, T., & Hinton, D. (2024). *The effect of interference and time on forgetting in visual short-term memory*. https://wlv.openrepository.com/handle/2436/625750

Merz, C. J., & Wolf, O. T. (2022). How stress hormones shape memories of fear and anxiety in humans. *Neuroscience & Biobehavioral Reviews, 142*, 104901. https://doi.org/10.1016/j.neubiorev.2022.104901

Metternich, B., Spanhel, K., Schoendube, A., Ofer, I., Geiger, M. J., Schulze-Bonhage, A., Mast, H., & Wagner, K. (2020). Flashbulb memory recall in healthy adults—A functional magnetic resonance imaging study. *Memory, 28*(4), 461–472. https://doi.org/10.1080/09658211.2020.1733022

Mujawar, S., Patil, J., Chaudhari, B., & Saldanha, D. (2021). Memory: Neurobiological mechanisms and assessment. *Industrial Psychiatry Journal, 30*(3), 311. https://doi.org/10.4103/0972-6748.328839

Murphy, G., & Flynn, E. (2022). *Deepfake false memories* (pp. 112–124). Routledge eBooks. https://doi.org/10.4324/9781003357360-10

Muschalla, B., & Schönborn, F. (2021). Induction of false beliefs and false memories in laboratory studies—A systematic review. *Clinical Psychology & Psychotherapy, 28*(5), 1194–1209. https://doi.org/10.1002/cpp.2567

Nahleen, S., Strange, D., & Takarangi, M. K. T. (2020). Does emotional or repeated misinformation increase memory distortion for a trauma analogue event? *Psychological Research, 85*(6), 2453–2465. https://doi.org/10.1007/s00426-020-01409-x

Oberauer, K. (2022). When does working memory get better with longer time? *Journal of Experimental Psychology Learning Memory and Cognition, 48*(12), 1754–1774. https://doi.org/10.1037/xlm0001199

Oi, K., & Frazier, C. (2024). Testing of significant changes in big-five personality factors over time in the presence and absence of memory impairment and life-related stress. *Scientific Reports, 14*(1), 19555. https://doi.org/10.1038/s41598-024-70388-5

Otgaar, H., Howe, M. L., Merckelbach, H., & Muris, P. (2018). Who is the better eyewitness? Sometimes adults but at other times children. *Current Directions in Psychological Science, 27*(5), 378–385. https://doi.org/10.1177/0963721418770998

Parsey, C. M., & Schmitter-Edgecombe, M. (2013). Applications of Technology in Neuropsychological Assessment. *The Clinical Neuropsychologist, 27*(8), 1328–1361. https://doi.org/10.1080/13854046.2013.834971

Pataranutaporn, P., Archiwaranguprok, C., Chan, S. W. T., Loftus, E., & Maes, P. (2024, September 13). *Synthetic human memories: AI-Edited Images and videos can implant false memories and distort recollection*. arXiv.org. https://arxiv.org/abs/2409.08895

PeConga, E., Pickrell, J. E., Bernstein, D. M., & Loftus, E. F. (2022). *Misinformation effect*. Routledge eBooks (pp. 419–435). https://doi.org/10.4324/9781003154730-30.

Pickel, K. L., Ross, S. J., & Truelove, R. S. (2006). Do weapons automatically capture attention? *Applied Cognitive Psychology, 20*(7), 871–893. https://doi.org/10.1002/acp.1235

Prats, A. (n.d.). *Implementing the reconsolidation paradigm in treating Misophonia*. CUNY Academic Works. https://academicworks.cuny.edu/hc_sas_etds/1135/

Prezioso, E., & Alessandroni, N. (2022). Enacting memories through and with things: Remembering as material engagement. *Memory Studies, 16*(4), 962–983. https://doi.org/10.1177/17506980221108475

Principe, G. F., & London, K. (2022). How parents can shape what children remember: Implications for the testimony of young witnesses. *Journal of Applied Research in Memory and Cognition, 11*(3), 289–302. https://doi.org/10.1037/mac0000059

Qasim, S. E., Mohan, U. R., Stein, J. M., & Jacobs, J. (2023). Neuronal activity in the human amygdala and hippocampus enhances emotional memory encoding. *Nature Human Behaviour, 7*(5), 754–764. https://doi.org/10.1038/s41562-022-01502-8

Radvansky, G. A., Doolen, A. C., Pettijohn, K. A., & Ritchey, M. (2022). A new look at memory retention and forgetting. *Journal of Experimental Psychology Learning Memory and Cognition, 48*(11), 1698–1723. https://doi.org/10.1037/xlm0001110

Roediger, H. (2001). *Reconstructive memory, psychology of.* Elsevier eBooks (pp. 12844–12849). https://doi.org/10.1016/b0-08-043076-7/01521-7.

Ruffini, A. a. L. D. D. I. a. R. a. S. S. D. a. G. (2014). *Quantitative EEG for brain–computer interfaces.* CRC Press eBooks (pp. 172–189). https://doi.org/10.1201/b17605-11

Salovich, N. A., Donovan, A. M., Hinze, S. R., & Rapp, D. N. (2020). Can confidence help account for and redress the effects of reading inaccurate information? *Memory & Cognition, 49*(2), 293–310. https://doi.org/10.3758/s13421-020-01096-4

Schwabe, L., Hermans, E. J., Joëls, M., & Roozendaal, B. (2022). Mechanisms of memory under stress. *Neuron, 110*(9), 1450–1467. https://doi.org/10.1016/j.neuron.2022.02.020

Shanks, J. E. (n.d.). *Relationships between shame, cognitive distortions and positive relationships with others among young adults, and changes in shame resulting from an intervention focusing on cognitive distortions.* Scholars Crossing. https://digitalcommons.liberty.edu/doctoral/5091/

Sharif, M. A., & Oppenheimer, D. M. (2020). The effect of categories on relative encoding biases in memory-based judgments. *Organizational Behavior and Human Decision Processes, 162*, 1–8. https://doi.org/10.1016/j.obhdp.2020.10.005

Sharma, P. R., Spearing, E. R., Wade, K. A., & Jobson, L. (2024). Distress reactions and susceptibility to misinformation for an analogue trauma event. *Cognitive Research Principles and Implications, 9*(1), 53. https://doi.org/10.1186/s41235-024-00582-6

Shmikler, E. C. (n.d.). *Negative memory bias and the impact of early childhood stress–ProQuest.* https://www.proquest.com/docview/2771090433?pq-origsite=gscholar&fromopenview=true&sourcetype=Dissertations%20&%20Theses

Simeon, D., Knutelska, M., Putnam, F. W., Schmeidler, J., & Smith, L. M. (2022). Attention and memory in depersonalization-Spectrum dissociative disorders: Impact of selective-divided attentional condition, stimulus emotionality, and stress. *Journal of Trauma & Dissociation, 24*(1), 42–62. https://doi.org/10.1080/15299732.2022.2079798

Šimić, G., Tkalčić, M., Vukić, V., Mulc, D., Španić, E., Šagud, M., Olucha-Bordonau, F. E., Vukšić, M., & Hof, P. R. (2021). Understanding emotions: Origins and roles of the amygdala. *Biomolecules, 11*(6), 823. https://doi.org/10.3390/biom11060823

Solinski, S. (2022). *Memory, trauma and the therapeutic encounter.* Routledge eBooks (pp. 749–769). https://doi.org/10.4324/9781003057314-57.

Sridhar, S., Khamaj, A., & Asthana, M. K. (2023). Cognitive neuroscience perspective on memory: Overview and summary. *Frontiers in Human Neuroscience, 17.* https://doi.org/10.3389/fnhum.2023.1217093

Szpitalak, M., & Polczyk, R. (2020). Reducing interrogative suggestibility: The role of self-affirmation and positive feedback. *PLoS One, 15*(7), e0236088. https://doi.org/10.1371/journal.pone.0236088

Takehara-Nishiuchi, K. (2020a). Prefrontal–hippocampal interaction during the encoding of new memories. *Brain and Neuroscience Advances, 4*, 239821282092558. https://doi.org/10.1177/2398212820925580

Takehara-Nishiuchi, K. (2020b). Neurobiology of systems memory consolidation. *European Journal of Neuroscience, 54*(8), 6850–6863. https://doi.org/10.1111/ejn.14694

Töredi, D. (2024, October 1). Reducing and measuring the cross-race effect. https://eresearch.qmu.ac.uk/handle/20.500.12289/13881

Vagni, M., Maiorano, T., & Giostra, V. (2024). *The suggestibility of child witnesses suspected victims of abuse: an overview between research and psycho-forensic implications.* ojs.pensamultimedia.it. https://doi.org/10.7347/RIC-012024-p83.

Wang, Q. (2020). The cultural foundation of human memory. *Annual Review of Psychology, 72*(1), 151–179. https://doi.org/10.1146/annurev-psych-070920-023638

Weir, E. (2023). *How do jurors evaluate memory evidence? An open-ended approach to investigating beliefs about memory that jurors bring to the courtroom.* https://doi.org/10.26686/wgtn.22396048.

Wells, G. L., Kovera, M. B., Douglass, A. B., Brewer, N., Meissner, C. A., & Wixted, J. T. (2020). Policy and procedure recommendations for the collection and preservation of eyewitness identification evidence. *Law and Human Behavior, 44*(1), 3–36. https://doi.org/10.1037/lhb0000359

Williams, K. (n.d.). *Perceptions of secondary trauma and memory accuracy in criminal justice professionals–ProQuest.* https://www.proquest.com/openview/eac8325903f465f6fbe4f1429d4eccfa/1?pq-origsite=gscholar&cbl=18750&diss=y

Wise, R. A., Sartori, G., Magnussen, S., & Safer, M. A. (2014). An examination of the causes and solutions to eyewitness error. *Frontiers in Psychiatry, 5.* https://doi.org/10.3389/fpsyt.2014.00102

Wulff, A. N. (n.d.). *Repeated retrieval impacts memory for both original event and post-event information–ProQuest.* https://www.proquest.com/openview/08554f1d65a0ce09de3ddf2fd19b73a4/1?pq-origsite=gscholar&cbl=18750&diss=y

Yadav, G., McNamara, S., & Gunturu, S. (2024). *Trauma-informed therapy.* StatPearls–NCBI Bookshelf. https://www.ncbi.nlm.nih.gov/books/NBK604200/

Neuropsychology of Juvenile Offenders

1 Introduction

Juvenile delinquency presents a complex and multifaceted issue, with young offenders demonstrating behavioral patterns that can range from minor infractions to serious crimes. In recent years, neuropsychology has offered new insights into the cognitive, neurobiological, and psychosocial underpinnings of juvenile delinquency, providing a more profound understanding of the biological, psychological, and social factors that influence adolescent criminal behavior. This perspective moves beyond the traditional criminological lens, which has historically emphasized environmental and social factors, by also investigating how brain development, cognitive deficits, and neurobiological vulnerabilities intersect with external influences to shape delinquent tendencies in youth. By focusing on the neuropsychological components that contribute to juvenile delinquency, we can explore developmental processes and individual differences that make certain adolescents more prone to engaging in criminal conduct, while others, under similar circumstances, do not.

A neuropsychological perspective on juvenile delinquency involves examining how specific brain regions, cognitive functions, and biological systems contribute to behaviors commonly observed in delinquent youth. Adolescence is a period marked by significant brain maturation, particularly in regions implicated in executive functioning, such as the prefrontal cortex (PFC). This region is crucial for impulse control, risk assessment, and decision-making—all skills that are often underdeveloped in young offenders. Additionally, emotional regulation and social cognition processes, associated with the amygdala and other limbic structures, undergo critical development during adolescence. When these systems do not mature optimally or are disrupted, either through environmental stressors or genetic predispositions, young individuals may struggle with controlling aggressive impulses, empathizing with others, and making rational decisions—deficits that contribute to the likelihood of engaging in delinquent acts.

© The Author(s), under exclusive license to Springer Nature Switzerland AG 2025

K. J. Reddy, *Foundations of Criminal Forensic Neuropsychology*,
https://doi.org/10.1007/978-3-031-83771-5_15

In exploring juvenile delinquency from a neuropsychological perspective, it is essential to consider the interplay of three major domains: cognitive, neurobiological, and psychosocial factors. Cognitive factors encompass the skills and processes involved in thinking, learning, and problem-solving. Juvenile offenders frequently exhibit deficits in areas such as attention, memory, executive function, and verbal skills. These cognitive deficits can impede academic performance, interpersonal relationships, and adaptive functioning, making it difficult for affected individuals to adhere to societal rules and expectations. Furthermore, poor executive functioning and reduced impulse control can exacerbate tendencies toward risk-taking and aggressive behavior, common traits observed in juvenile delinquents.

Neurobiological factors include the structural and functional aspects of the brain that influence behavior. Several studies have highlighted how brain regions like the PFC, amygdala, and anterior cingulate cortex (ACC) differ in function and structure in juvenile delinquents compared to nondelinquent peers (Wagels & Hernandez-Pena, 2024). The PFC, as mentioned, is essential for executive control and judgment, while the amygdala plays a significant role in emotion regulation and reactivity to stress or perceived threats. When these regions are either underdeveloped or compromised, juveniles may be more likely to react impulsively and emotionally, leading to problematic behaviors that can escalate to criminal acts. Neurotransmitter systems, such as those involving dopamine and serotonin, also play a crucial role in risk-taking, aggression, and reward sensitivity, with imbalances often linked to delinquent behaviors.

Finally, psychosocial factors provide a broader context, illustrating how environmental and social experiences shape the developmental trajectory of juvenile offenders. Adolescents are highly influenced by their social environments, and factors such as family dynamics, peer influence, socioeconomic status, and exposure to trauma or violence can significantly impact their behavior. For example, young people raised in environments with inconsistent discipline, neglect, or abuse are more likely to develop maladaptive coping mechanisms, low self-esteem, and a sense of alienation—all of which can increase the propensity toward delinquency. Additionally, exposure to peers who engage in risky behaviors or criminal activities can further reinforce antisocial tendencies, particularly in individuals already exhibiting neuropsychological vulnerabilities.

Addressing juvenile delinquency from a neuropsychological perspective underscores the importance of considering developmental factors in intervention and prevention strategies. Traditional punitive measures often overlook the root causes of delinquent behavior, focusing on punishment rather than rehabilitation. However, recognizing that many juvenile offenders have underdeveloped or impaired cognitive and emotional skills suggests that more effective interventions should target these areas directly. Programs that focus on enhancing cognitive abilities, impulse control, emotional regulation, and social skills have shown promise in helping young offenders learn healthier ways to manage their behavior and make decisions. Additionally, family-based interventions, peer counseling, and school-based programs can help address the psychosocial factors that contribute to delinquency, providing adolescents with the support and guidance they need to navigate challenges more effectively.

Developmental neuropsychology provides crucial insights into why adolescents may engage in delinquent acts, highlighting that many young offenders lack the neurological maturity and cognitive resources necessary for self-regulation and social responsibility. Adolescence is a period of ongoing development, during which individuals experience both heightened vulnerability and potential for change. Given this, addressing juvenile delinquency through a developmental lens can help identify at-risk youth before their behaviors escalate into chronic criminal patterns. Early intervention programs targeting cognitive, neurobiological, and psychosocial factors have the potential to reduce juvenile crime rates and promote healthier developmental trajectories. By addressing the neuropsychological components of delinquency, such interventions offer a promising alternative to the cycle of punishment, recidivism, and missed opportunities for rehabilitation.

In sum, the neuropsychology of juvenile offenders provides a holistic understanding of the various factors contributing to adolescent criminal behavior. Rather than viewing delinquency solely as a moral failing or a result of poor socialization, this perspective acknowledges that cognitive deficits, neurobiological immaturity, and adverse social conditions create a constellation of risk factors that predispose certain youths to delinquency. Addressing these factors through early assessment, personalized intervention, and supportive developmental strategies can not only aid in the rehabilitation of juvenile offenders but also contribute to broader crime prevention efforts. By focusing on the cognitive, neurobiological, and psychosocial roots of juvenile delinquency, society can shift from a retributive approach to one that emphasizes growth, resilience, and the potential for positive change in young lives.

2 Neurobiological and Cognitive Vulnerabilities in Juvenile Offenders

Juvenile offenders often exhibit behaviors that stem not only from environmental influences but also from neurobiological and cognitive vulnerabilities that uniquely impact adolescents. Research has shown that adolescence is a period of profound neurodevelopmental changes, which significantly influence cognitive capacities, emotional regulation, impulse control, and decision-making (Lowe et al., 2020). Juveniles in this developmental stage experience notable imbalances in brain maturation, particularly in the prefrontal cortex (PFC) and the limbic system, both of which are critical for executive functions and emotional regulation, respectively. These neurobiological factors, when coupled with cognitive vulnerabilities, increase susceptibility to impulsive and risky behaviors that can lead to delinquency. By examining how these neurological processes and cognitive deficits shape juvenile behavior, we can better understand the risk factors that predispose adolescents to criminal conduct and identify potential intervention points to aid in rehabilitation.

2.1 Adolescent Brain Development: Impulsivity and Decision-Making

During adolescence, the brain undergoes rapid development and reorganization, which lays the foundation for adult cognitive and emotional capacities. This period is marked by the maturation of various brain regions that contribute to higher-order thinking, planning, and self-regulation. However, these changes do not occur uniformly; instead, the brain's reward and emotional centers tend to mature earlier than regions associated with self-control and decision-making. As a result, adolescents are particularly susceptible to impulsive behaviors, which can often manifest as delinquency or criminal actions when compounded by environmental stressors or negative peer influences.

One key component of adolescent brain development is the gradual myelination and synaptic pruning occurring within the PFC, a process that facilitates faster, more efficient brain communication and improves cognitive control. Unfortunately, the PFC is one of the last brain regions to fully mature, and its developmental lag compared to other regions, such as the limbic system, leads to a natural imbalance. This imbalance often results in heightened impulsivity and poor decision-making abilities, as the adolescent brain struggles to weigh long-term consequences against short-term rewards. Juveniles thus experience a higher tendency toward impulsive and reckless actions, as they lack the fully developed neural mechanisms needed for impulse control and future-oriented thinking.

2.2 Prefrontal Cortex Immaturity and Executive Function Deficits

The PFC plays a crucial role in executive functions, which encompass the ability to plan, make decisions, inhibit impulses, and anticipate outcomes. In juvenile offenders, the immaturity of the PFC is closely tied to deficits in these executive functions, which increases the likelihood of engaging in criminal behavior. The underdevelopment of the PFC can result in weaker cognitive control, leading to poor impulse control and a propensity to make decisions based on immediate gratification rather than considering long-term risks. Studies have shown that juveniles with poor executive functioning are more likely to engage in risky behaviors and exhibit antisocial tendencies, as they lack the cognitive resources necessary for self-regulation and responsible decision-making (Coenen et al., 2021).

Executive function deficits in adolescents manifest as difficulties in impulse control, attention, cognitive flexibility, and working memory, which all contribute to delinquent behavior. For instance, a juvenile who struggles with attention control may have difficulty following instructions or adhering to societal norms, making them more likely to act impulsively. Impulse control deficits are especially common in juvenile offenders and are often linked to an increased likelihood of engaging in criminal activities. These adolescents may struggle to resist urges to act on aggressive impulses, which can lead to violent or antisocial behavior without consideration of the consequences. Furthermore, cognitive inflexibility and poor working memory hinder juveniles' ability to learn from past experiences, adjust their behavior, or plan for the future—traits that make it challenging to navigate complex social situations and conform to legal and societal expectations.

2.3 Limbic System: Heightened Emotional Reactivity During Adolescence

In addition to PFC immaturity, the limbic system—particularly structures like the amygdala—plays a central role in adolescent emotional processing. During adolescence, the limbic system is highly active and sensitive to emotional stimuli, which leads to greater emotional reactivity. This heightened emotional reactivity can influence behavior in ways that increase the likelihood of risky or aggressive actions. Adolescents tend to experience emotions more intensely than adults, a factor that can amplify impulsive responses and contribute to poor decision-making in high-stakes or emotionally charged situations.

The amygdala, a key component of the limbic system, is responsible for processing fear, threat perception, and emotional memories. Its heightened activity during adolescence can lead juveniles to respond more intensely to perceived threats or provocations, even in situations that might not warrant such strong reactions. This increased sensitivity to threat is associated with a greater likelihood of aggressive responses, as the adolescent brain may interpret ambiguous cues as hostile or threatening, resulting in an impulsive, defensive reaction. Such reactions can lead to violent or criminal behavior, particularly in environments where the individual perceives frequent threats or has a history of exposure to trauma.

Furthermore, the limbic system's interaction with the PFC is still developing during adolescence, meaning that juveniles may struggle to effectively regulate their emotional responses. While the PFC would typically help temper emotional impulses, its immaturity in adolescents leaves them prone to acting on intense emotions without considering the potential consequences of their actions. This disconnect between emotional reactivity and cognitive control creates a vulnerability that predisposes juveniles to criminal behavior, particularly in stressful or conflict-laden situations.

2.4 Neurobiological Vulnerabilities and Susceptibility to Criminal Behavior

The combined effects of PFC immaturity and heightened limbic activity create a neurobiological environment that makes adolescents more vulnerable to criminal conduct. These neurobiological vulnerabilities are compounded by individual differences in genetic predispositions, environmental stressors, and social influences, all of which interact to shape the likelihood of delinquent behavior. Adolescents with certain genetic markers or neurobiological traits, such as those associated with heightened reward sensitivity or aggression, may be especially susceptible to peer pressure, risky behaviors, and impulsive actions. Furthermore, environmental factors, including socioeconomic challenges, family instability, and exposure to violence, can exacerbate these vulnerabilities, making it even harder for at-risk adolescents to avoid engaging in delinquent acts.

This neurobiological susceptibility emphasizes the need for interventions that account for the unique developmental stage of juveniles. Rather than relying solely on punitive measures, which often fail to address the root causes of delinquent behavior, effective intervention strategies should focus on enhancing cognitive control, emotional regulation, and social skills. Approaches such as cognitive behavioral therapy (CBT), mindfulness training, and family-focused programs can help juveniles develop the executive functioning and coping skills needed to resist impulses and make healthier choices. Addressing neurobiological and cognitive vulnerabilities early in adolescence can also provide juveniles with the tools they need to navigate social pressures and emotional challenges in ways that promote positive development and reduce the risk of criminal behavior.

Understanding juvenile delinquency through the lens of neurobiological and cognitive vulnerabilities provides a more nuanced perspective on why adolescents are at an elevated risk for criminal behavior. The interplay between an immature PFC, heightened limbic activity, and environmental influences creates a unique set of challenges for juveniles, who often lack the cognitive and emotional tools necessary to navigate complex social situations without resorting to impulsive or aggressive behaviors. Addressing these vulnerabilities through targeted interventions offers the opportunity to reshape the developmental trajectories of at-risk youth, guiding them toward healthier, more prosocial behaviors and reducing the incidence of juvenile crime.

3 Psychosocial Factors Contributing to Delinquency

Juvenile delinquency is a complex social issue influenced by an array of psychosocial factors that shape adolescent behavior. While neurobiological vulnerabilities play a significant role in adolescent impulsivity and decision-making, the social environment in which an adolescent grows up can profoundly impact their behavior. Factors such as peer pressure, family environment, socioeconomic status, and exposure to trauma or neglect are all key contributors to delinquency. Adolescents are in a critical developmental phase, heavily influenced by their surroundings, role models, and social interactions. When positive influences are absent or negative factors predominate, the risk of delinquent behavior increases significantly. Understanding these psychosocial contributors to juvenile delinquency can help inform preventative measures and interventions that address the root causes of risky behavior in youth.

3.1 Influence of Peer Pressure on Adolescent Behavior

Peer influence is one of the strongest predictors of adolescent behavior and can significantly impact an individual's likelihood of engaging in delinquent activities. Adolescence is a developmental period marked by a heightened need for social acceptance and a strong desire to fit in with peers. Adolescents who feel isolated or lack supportive friendships are often more susceptible to negative peer influences, as they seek belonging and validation within social groups. This desire to conform to the behaviors and attitudes of peers can lead adolescents to engage in risky or illegal activities that they might otherwise avoid.

Peer pressure can encourage behaviors ranging from minor rule-breaking to serious criminal conduct. Studies have shown that juveniles are more likely to engage in delinquent acts, such as vandalism, substance abuse, or theft, when surrounded by peers who support or engage in these behaviors (Kang, 2023). The presence of peers can also amplify the thrill and perceived rewards of risky activities, as adolescents often value peer approval over long-term consequences. Furthermore, adolescents with neurobiological vulnerabilities, such as reduced impulse control or increased reward sensitivity, are particularly susceptible to peer pressure, as they may struggle to resist the immediate rewards associated with peer-approved behaviors.

Interventions aimed at mitigating the effects of negative peer pressure can play a significant role in preventing delinquency. Programs that encourage positive peer relationships, promote social skills, and foster a sense of belonging outside of risky groups can help adolescents form healthier connections and resist negative influences. Additionally, mentorship programs that connect at-risk youth with positive role models or peers who have successfully navigated similar challenges can provide valuable support and guidance.

3.2 *Family Environment and Its Role in Delinquency*

The family environment is one of the most critical factors influencing adolescent behavior, serving as the primary context in which values, behavioral norms, and emotional regulation skills are learned. Stable and supportive family dynamics can protect against delinquency by fostering a sense of security and self-worth in adolescents. Conversely, family environments characterized by conflict, neglect, inconsistent discipline, or abuse can increase the risk of delinquent behavior. Adolescents from unstable family backgrounds may lack the emotional support and guidance necessary to make healthy decisions, leading them to seek belonging and validation elsewhere, often within peer groups involved in risky or criminal activities.

Research has consistently shown that adolescents who experience negative family dynamics are more likely to exhibit externalizing behaviors, such as aggression and impulsivity, which are linked to delinquency (Bozzay et al., 2017). Inconsistent or harsh disciplinary practices, for example, can lead to confusion and resentment, resulting in defiance and rule-breaking. A lack of parental supervision is also associated with higher rates of delinquency, as adolescents with minimal parental monitoring have greater freedom to engage in unsupervised and potentially dangerous activities. Furthermore, adolescents who grow up witnessing or experiencing abuse may normalize aggressive behavior and struggle with emotional regulation, increasing their likelihood of engaging in violent or antisocial acts.

Positive family relationships, clear communication, and consistent discipline are essential for fostering healthy development in adolescents. Family-based interventions, such as family therapy or parenting programs, can equip parents with the skills needed to provide effective guidance and support. Such interventions have shown promise in reducing delinquency by improving family cohesion, enhancing parenting skills, and encouraging positive family interactions.

3.3 *The Impact of Socioeconomic Status on Adolescent Behavior*

Socioeconomic status (SES) is another powerful determinant of adolescent behavior and is closely linked to rates of juvenile delinquency. Adolescents from low SES backgrounds often face numerous stressors, including financial instability, limited access to educational resources, and neighborhood violence. These stressors can lead to a sense of powerlessness, hopelessness, and resentment, which may drive some adolescents toward delinquent behavior as a means of coping or asserting control. In disadvantaged neighborhoods, adolescents may have fewer opportunities to engage in prosocial activities, making delinquency a more accessible or appealing option.

Low SES can also lead to increased exposure to negative influences, as adolescents in impoverished areas are more likely to encounter peers engaged in criminal activities. Additionally, limited access to extracurricular programs, recreational facilities, and other prosocial outlets can restrict adolescents' options for positive engagement, increasing the likelihood that they will spend time in unsupervised and potentially risky environments. Economic hardship can also strain family relationships, contributing to stress, conflict, and reduced parental involvement, which, in turn, exacerbates the risk of delinquency.

Addressing socioeconomic factors requires a systemic approach, with policies and programs aimed at increasing access to educational and recreational resources for low-income families. Community-based initiatives, such as youth centers, mentorship programs, and after-school activities, can provide safe spaces for adolescents to develop positive relationships, learn valuable skills, and build resilience against delinquent behaviors.

3.4 Role of Trauma, Neglect, and Emotional Regulation Challenges

Adolescents who have experienced trauma or neglect often face additional barriers to emotional and behavioral regulation, increasing their risk for delinquency. Trauma, such as abuse, loss, or exposure to violence, can disrupt normal emotional development and lead to maladaptive coping mechanisms. Many adolescents who engage in delinquent behavior have histories of trauma, which may contribute to difficulties in managing anger, anxiety, or sadness. Unresolved trauma can lead to heightened emotional reactivity, impulsive behavior, and a diminished capacity for empathy, all of which are factors associated with criminal conduct.

Neglect, which includes emotional neglect and the lack of parental attention, can be equally damaging. Adolescents who feel neglected often struggle with low self-esteem, poor social skills, and a lack of trust in others, which can make it difficult to form healthy relationships. As a result, neglected adolescents may become involved in delinquent activities as a way of gaining attention or escaping from feelings of worthlessness. Additionally, neglected adolescents may not have learned effective ways to regulate their emotions, making them more likely to resort to aggression or defiance when faced with stress.

Interventions focused on trauma recovery and emotional regulation can be highly effective in addressing the root causes of delinquency among adolescents. Trauma-informed approaches, such as cognitive behavioral therapy (CBT) and dialectical behavior therapy (DBT), can help adolescents process traumatic experiences, develop coping skills, and improve emotional regulation. Additionally, social and emotional learning (SEL) programs in schools can teach adolescents essential skills for managing emotions, resolving conflicts, and making responsible decisions.

Psychosocial factors play a significant role in shaping adolescent behavior and influencing the likelihood of delinquency. The combined effects of peer pressure, family environment, socioeconomic status, and exposure to trauma or neglect create a complex web of risk factors that can predispose adolescents to engage in criminal conduct. Addressing these factors through targeted interventions, family support, and community programs can help mitigate the influence of negative psychosocial environments and promote healthier developmental trajectories. By focusing on the social context and emotional needs of at-risk youth, society can take a proactive approach to reducing juvenile delinquency and fostering resilience among adolescents.

4 Executive Functioning Deficits in Juvenile Offenders

Executive functioning refers to a set of high-level cognitive processes that enable individuals to plan, make decisions, solve problems, and control impulses. These functions are critical for navigating daily life, responding appropriately to social cues, and adhering to social norms. For adolescents, executive functions are still developing and maturing, especially within the prefrontal cortex (PFC), the brain region responsible for most executive tasks. Juvenile offenders, however, often exhibit deficits in executive functioning, which can increase susceptibility to criminal behavior by hindering their ability to control impulses, evaluate risks, and make well-considered decisions. Understanding the role of executive functioning deficits in juvenile delinquency provides insight into how cognitive weaknesses contribute to antisocial behavior and highlights the importance of targeted interventions to support at-risk youth.

4.1 Executive Functions: Planning, Decision-Making, Problem-Solving, and Impulse Control

Executive functions encompass various skills, including planning, decision-making, problem-solving, and impulse control. Planning involves the ability to think ahead, set goals, and organize actions to achieve those goals. Decision-making requires evaluating options, assessing potential consequences, and choosing the best course of action. Problem-solving includes analyzing complex situations, identifying potential solutions, and implementing effective responses. Impulse control, on the other hand, refers to the capacity to inhibit immediate responses, resist temptations, and manage emotions.

These cognitive skills are essential for adolescents to navigate complex social environments, manage interpersonal conflicts, and avoid risky behaviors. However, when executive functioning is impaired, juveniles may struggle with basic self-regulation and decision-making, making them more likely to engage in delinquent acts. A juvenile with poor planning abilities, for instance, may act on immediate impulses without considering potential consequences, such as getting caught or harming others. Similarly, deficits in problem-solving and decision-making can make it difficult for adolescents to find constructive solutions to social challenges, leading them to resort to criminal or aggressive behaviors as a coping mechanism.

4.2 Executive Functioning Deficits in Juvenile Offenders and Links to Criminal Behavior

Numerous studies have shown that juvenile offenders are more likely than their non-offending peers to exhibit deficits in executive functioning (Griffith et al., 2024). These deficits are associated with a range of criminal behaviors, including theft, violence, substance abuse, and property destruction. Impaired executive functioning reduces juveniles' ability to control impulsive actions, resist peer pressure, and manage frustration or anger. For example, a juvenile with weak impulse control may be more prone to engage in risky behaviors, such as theft or assault, without considering the consequences or moral implications of these actions.

One of the critical links between executive functioning deficits and juvenile delinquency is the inability to delay gratification. Adolescents with impulse control issues often act on immediate desires or emotions, without evaluating the long-term consequences of their actions. This tendency is particularly problematic when combined with peer influence, as juveniles with impulse control problems may be more likely to follow along with risky or illegal behaviors promoted by their social group. Additionally, poor decision-making skills can lead juveniles to make choices that increase their involvement in criminal activities. For instance, they may join gangs or engage in illegal acts as a means of gaining acceptance or social validation, unable to foresee the potential long-term consequences of such affiliations.

4.3 Neuropsychological Assessments and Executive Functioning Impairments

Neuropsychological assessments of juvenile offenders reveal significant impairments in various executive functioning domains, including attention, working memory, and impulse control. These assessments often use tests that measure specific cognitive abilities, such as the Wisconsin Card Sorting Test (WCST) for cognitive flexibility, the Stroop Test for attention and impulse control, and the Tower of London task for planning. Findings from these assessments consistently show that juvenile offenders tend to perform poorly on tasks requiring sustained attention, delayed gratification, and complex problem-solving, compared to nondelinquent peers.

1. **Attention Deficits**: Attention is a fundamental component of executive functioning, essential for maintaining focus on a task, filtering out distractions, and orga-

nizing information. Many juvenile offenders exhibit attention deficits, which can interfere with their ability to stay engaged in school, follow rules, or consider the consequences of their actions. Attention deficits can lead to impulsivity, as juveniles may struggle to sustain focus on a task long enough to assess it thoroughly or recognize potential risks. Juveniles with attention impairments often make quick, poorly considered decisions, driven by immediate impulses rather than thoughtful analysis.

2. **Working Memory Deficits**: Working memory refers to the ability to hold and manipulate information in the mind over short periods. It is a crucial element of executive functioning that underlies complex cognitive processes such as reasoning, planning, and decision-making. Juvenile offenders frequently exhibit working memory deficits, which affect their ability to process information effectively and make informed choices. A juvenile with a poor working memory may struggle to remember the consequences of past actions or consider multiple factors when making decisions, leading to hasty, unplanned behavior. Working memory deficits can also hinder learning from experience, as juveniles may fail to retain lessons from past mistakes, increasing the likelihood of repeated criminal behaviors.
3. **Impulse Control Deficits**: Impulse control is perhaps the most directly related aspect of executive functioning to juvenile delinquency, as it encompasses the ability to inhibit inappropriate responses, delay gratification, and regulate emotions. Juvenile offenders often exhibit impaired impulse control, which makes them more likely to act on immediate urges without considering the consequences. This lack of inhibition can lead to aggressive or violent responses to perceived threats, involvement in risky behaviors, and engagement in criminal activities. For example, a juvenile with poor impulse control may respond to an insult with physical aggression, rather than walking away or finding a peaceful resolution.

Impulse control deficits are particularly problematic during adolescence, a period marked by increased emotional reactivity and a heightened sensitivity to peer influence. Juveniles with impaired impulse control may find it especially difficult to resist peer pressure to engage in delinquent acts, as they are more driven by immediate rewards and social validation than by potential long-term risks.

4.4 Implications for Rehabilitation and Intervention

Understanding executive functioning deficits in juvenile offenders highlights the need for interventions that address these cognitive vulnerabilities directly. Traditional punitive approaches, such as incarceration, often fail to address the underlying cognitive and neurological issues contributing to delinquency. Instead, rehabilitation programs that focus on improving executive functioning skills can help juveniles develop the cognitive tools they need to make better decisions, manage impulses, and avoid criminal behavior.

1. **Cognitive Behavioral Therapy (CBT)**: CBT has shown effectiveness in helping juveniles identify and modify thought patterns that lead to impulsive and aggressive behavior. By working with juveniles to develop better planning, problem-solving, and impulse control skills, CBT can help them approach challenging situations in a more controlled, constructive way.
2. **Mindfulness and Self-Regulation Training**: Mindfulness techniques can help juveniles develop greater awareness of their thoughts, emotions, and impulses, which can lead to improved self-regulation. Practicing mindfulness has been shown to reduce impulsivity and improve emotional control, enabling juveniles to pause and consider their actions before reacting.
3. **Executive Skills Training**: Programs specifically designed to enhance executive functions, such as planning, working memory, and decision-making, can help juveniles develop the skills necessary to make responsible choices. Training in these areas can provide practical tools for juveniles to apply in real-world situations, promoting healthier behavioral patterns and reducing delinquency.

Executive functioning deficits are a significant factor contributing to juvenile delinquency, affecting adolescents' ability to control impulses, make sound decisions, and respond adaptively to social challenges. The underdevelopment of these skills, combined with heightened susceptibility to peer pressure and emotional reactivity, creates a unique set of cognitive vulnerabilities that predispose juveniles to criminal behavior. By addressing these deficits through targeted interventions, society can better support at-risk youth, helping them develop the cognitive tools needed to avoid delinquent behavior and foster more positive developmental trajectories. This approach not only promotes rehabilitation for individual offenders but also contributes to the broader goal of reducing juvenile crime and enhancing community safety.

5 Role of Neuropsychology in Juvenile Justice

The juvenile justice system seeks to balance accountability for criminal behavior with a rehabilitative approach that considers the unique developmental needs of young offenders. Adolescence is a critical period marked by substantial neurobiological, cognitive, and emotional development, making juveniles uniquely sensitive to interventions that can guide their development in a positive direction. In this context, neuropsychology provides valuable insights into the underlying cognitive, emotional, and neurodevelopmental capacities of young offenders. This data can inform courts, probation officers, and rehabilitation professionals about the individual's needs, allowing for decisions that align with both legal and rehabilitative goals. By identifying neuropsychological deficits, courts can customize interventions to address the specific cognitive and emotional needs of the youth, thereby reducing recidivism and promoting positive societal reintegration.

5.1 The Developmental Vulnerability of Adolescents

The adolescent brain is uniquely vulnerable to both external influences and internal dysregulation. Critical brain regions, particularly the prefrontal cortex—which governs executive functions such as decision-making, impulse control, and planning—undergo significant maturation during this period. Neurodevelopmental factors that disrupt normal cognitive functioning in young people, including trauma, brain injuries, genetic predispositions, and mental health disorders, are often contributors to antisocial behaviors that lead to juvenile offending. Neuropsychological evaluations allow for a nuanced understanding of an adolescent's cognitive profile, distinguishing deficits in impulse control or emotional regulation from a purely behavioral issue.

Adolescents with conditions such as attention deficit hyperactivity disorder (ADHD), conduct disorder, and trauma-related disorders often exhibit deficits in working memory, attentional focus, and problem-solving skills. Left untreated, these impairments can contribute to impulsive and aggressive behaviors. Neuropsychological evaluations, by identifying these deficits, can shape how courts and other stakeholders approach sentencing and rehabilitation, focusing on therapeutic interventions tailored to individual deficits instead of punitive measures that fail to address the underlying cognitive issues.

5.2 Neuropsychological Evaluations in Juvenile Courts

Neuropsychological evaluations offer a comprehensive picture of a young offender's cognitive strengths and weaknesses. They assess various domains including memory, attention, executive functioning, emotional regulation, and social cognition. These evaluations are especially valuable for assessing risk factors that may predispose adolescents to recidivism. For instance, low impulse control and poor executive functioning are linked to an increased likelihood of repeat offenses. In juvenile courts, such evaluations can help inform sentencing decisions, guiding the choice between detention and rehabilitative measures. For example, an adolescent with severe attention and executive function deficits may benefit more from targeted therapeutic interventions rather than from a punitive sentence.

Understanding an adolescent's neuropsychological profile is particularly important in cases where there may be developmental or intellectual disabilities. Youths with intellectual impairments may be vulnerable to peer pressure or have difficulties understanding the consequences of their actions, thus necessitating specific rehabilitative approaches. Courts can also leverage neuropsychological data to assess the maturity level of a young offender, particularly in relation to their capacity for criminal responsibility, competency to stand trial, and the degree of comprehension of their actions. These insights can be particularly crucial in cases involving complex legal issues, such as determining the appropriateness of a juvenile's waiver to adult court.

5.3 *Tailored Interventions and Rehabilitation*

A critical role of neuropsychology in the juvenile justice system is guiding the development of tailored interventions. Neuropsychological profiles can reveal specific cognitive and emotional deficits that, if untreated, may hinder the juvenile's ability to participate effectively in rehabilitation programs. For example, if a young offender exhibits severe deficits in attention and emotional regulation, this information can guide the selection of intervention strategies, focusing on skills such as anger management, impulse control, and improved attention to behavioral cues.

Programs like cognitive behavioral therapy (CBT), dialectical behavior therapy (DBT), and mindfulness-based interventions are often recommended for adolescents with these profiles. For instance, juveniles with heightened impulsivity and emotional dysregulation could benefit from DBT, which emphasizes emotional regulation and distress tolerance. By aligning the interventions with the neuropsychological profile of the adolescent, therapists can increase the likelihood of rehabilitation success and reduce the chances of recidivism.

5.4 *Neurodevelopmental Considerations and Ethical Implications*

Juveniles often enter the justice system with multiple layers of neurodevelopmental challenges. For example, traumatic brain injuries, substance abuse histories, and adverse childhood experiences are prevalent among young offenders and can exacerbate neuropsychological impairments. Neuropsychology enables the identification of such deficits, allowing the court to adopt a more rehabilitative perspective in sentencing decisions. When courts have a comprehensive understanding of a juvenile's neurodevelopmental status, they are better equipped to make ethical and informed decisions that prioritize the juvenile's potential for growth and positive behavioral change.

However, ethical considerations are significant, as neuropsychological assessments must be conducted with respect for the juvenile's autonomy and confidentiality. The disclosure of neuropsychological data to the courts must be carefully managed, balancing the need for informed judicial decisions with the juvenile's right to privacy and respect for developmental vulnerabilities. Legal practitioners should be trained in understanding these neuropsychological factors and how they may impact behavior, competency, and rehabilitation potential, reducing the risk of overly punitive measures that do not consider these critical developmental aspects.

5.5 *Reducing Recidivism Through Rehabilitation and Support*

Neuropsychology contributes to the long-term goal of reducing recidivism by addressing the root causes of offending behaviors. By identifying neuropsychological deficits, interventions can be tailored to support developmental growth, helping young offenders acquire the cognitive and social skills they need to reintegrate successfully into society. Neuropsychological data can also help inform post-release support strategies, such as ongoing therapeutic interventions and community-based programs. For instance, community mentorship, vocational training, and life skills development can be tailored to support the specific cognitive and emotional needs identified during the evaluation.

Research supports the efficacy of neuropsychologically informed interventions in promoting better outcomes in terms of reducing recidivism (Dumornay et al., 2022). Rehabilitation efforts that are customized to address individual neuropsychological deficits demonstrate higher rates of engagement and success, as young offenders are better able to build resilience and adaptive skills. As a result, neuropsychological assessments serve as a bridge between the justice system and rehabilitative services, enhancing the potential for meaningful change and reducing the likelihood of re-offending.

The role of neuropsychology in juvenile justice is invaluable, as it brings a deeper understanding of the cognitive and emotional capacities of young offenders. By incorporating neuropsychological evaluations, the juvenile justice system can adopt a rehabilitative approach tailored to the individual's developmental needs, cognitive capacities, and socio-emotional challenges. This neuropsychologically informed approach enables the court to make ethical, individualized decisions that prioritize both accountability and rehabilitation, thereby fostering better outcomes for youth offenders and enhancing public safety.

6 Restorative Justice Strategies for Juvenile Offenders

Restorative justice offers an alternative approach to traditional punitive measures in the juvenile justice system by focusing on healing, accountability, and the rehabilitation of young offenders. This philosophy centers on repairing the harm caused by criminal behavior and fostering a sense of social responsibility rather than relying solely on punishment. Restorative justice strategies encourage offenders to make amends, build empathy, and reintegrate as productive members of society. When applied to juveniles, these strategies hold significant promise, as adolescents are in a crucial phase of neurodevelopment, marked by heightened receptivity to rehabilitation. Integrating neuropsychological perspectives into restorative justice allows for a better understanding of young offenders' cognitive and emotional capabilities, helping shape interventions that promote empathy, accountability, and long-term behavioral change.

6.1 The Core Principles of Restorative Justice in Juvenile Offenses

Restorative justice is built upon principles that emphasize repairing harm, accountability, and active involvement of all affected parties. In the context of juvenile justice, this approach aims to address the underlying causes of criminal behavior and create opportunities for personal growth and behavioral reform. Core restorative justice practices involve dialogues, mediation, and reconciliation sessions, where offenders, victims, and community members collaboratively work toward resolution. For juveniles, restorative justice can help build a sense of empathy and social responsibility—traits that can be crucial for their development and future behavior.

The practice of restorative justice in juvenile cases often centers on three main goals: victim–offender reconciliation, offender rehabilitation, and the reintegration of the juvenile into society. This collaborative process can help the offender understand the impact of their actions on others, facilitating a sense of accountability. Research shows that these processes can be transformative for young offenders, as they are more likely to grasp the consequences of their actions and become motivated to make positive changes (Steinberg et al., 2004). Victims, too, often benefit from restorative justice, as they gain a sense of closure and are provided with an opportunity to voice their feelings and ask questions, which can be instrumental in their healing process.

6.2 Neuropsychological Perspectives on Juvenile Rehabilitation

Neuropsychology sheds light on why restorative justice approaches may be particularly effective for juvenile offenders. Adolescence is a period of ongoing brain development, especially in areas related to emotional regulation, empathy, and impulse control. The prefrontal cortex, responsible for decision-making and moral reasoning, is still maturing during adolescence, making youth especially susceptible to impulsive behaviors and social influences. At the same time, adolescents have an increased capacity for behavioral change and are more responsive to interventions aimed at empathy-building and social responsibility.

The neuropsychological perspective emphasizes the importance of fostering prosocial skills, emotional understanding, and perspective-taking, all of which are integral to restorative justice practices. Techniques such as empathy training, role-playing, and guided reflection can help juveniles recognize the emotions of others, understand the impact of their actions, and develop a sense of social responsibility. Studies indicate that these practices can have positive effects on brain structures involved in empathy, moral reasoning, and impulse control (Saladino et al., 2021). By fostering the development of these skills, restorative justice strategies tap into the adolescent's potential for growth, helping address cognitive and emotional deficits that may contribute to antisocial behaviors.

6.3 *Strategies in Restorative Justice for Juvenile Offenders*

a. **Victim–Offender Mediation**

   One of the core strategies in restorative justice is victim–offender mediation, which allows for direct dialogue between the young offender and the victim. This process offers the juvenile an opportunity to comprehend the emotional impact of their actions, often resulting in increased empathy and a stronger sense of accountability. In such sessions, a mediator facilitates the discussion, helping both parties express their feelings and work toward a mutually acceptable resolution. This can be a transformative experience for young offenders, who may otherwise struggle to appreciate the impact of their actions due to underdeveloped social cognition skills.

b. **Community Service and Reparative Work**

   Community service is another common restorative justice strategy that reinforces the importance of social responsibility. For juvenile offenders, completing community service tasks is not only a way of making amends but also a means of fostering a connection with their community. Engaging in positive activities allows juveniles to build a sense of pride and accomplishment, counteracting previous feelings of guilt or shame associated with their actions. From a neuropsychological perspective, participating in community service tasks encourages prosocial behavior and helps strengthen pathways in the brain associated with empathy, cooperation, and emotional regulation.

c. **Restorative Circles and Family Group Conferencing**

   Restorative circles and family group conferencing involve the juvenile, family members, victims, and community members in a collective discussion about the offense and its repercussions. These group sessions provide a supportive space where the young offender can acknowledge their actions, make amends, and work on rebuilding trust. Neuropsychologically, these gatherings offer juveniles a platform to practice perspective-taking and empathy, skills that are vital for moral and social development. Family group conferencing, in particular, strengthens familial bonds and creates a support system that can guide the youth through their rehabilitation journey.

d. **Empathy and Cognitive–Behavioral Interventions**

Specific neuropsychologically informed interventions, such as cognitive behavioral therapy (CBT) with an emphasis on empathy training, can complement restorative justice practices. CBT techniques help juveniles identify and challenge maladaptive thoughts, reducing aggressive or impulsive responses. Empathy training, an essential component in CBT for juveniles, can foster emotional understanding and increase prosocial behavior, making young offenders less likely to re-offend. Integrating such interventions into the restorative justice framework allows for a comprehensive approach to rehabilitation that not only focuses on amends but also addresses the cognitive and emotional factors underlying the offense.

6.4 Benefits of Restorative Justice in Reducing Recidivism

The rehabilitative nature of restorative justice holds significant potential for reducing recidivism among juvenile offenders. Unlike traditional punitive measures, which can exacerbate feelings of alienation and reinforce antisocial tendencies, restorative justice aims to foster a sense of community, empathy, and personal accountability. Studies show that juveniles who participate in restorative justice programs are less likely to re-offend than those who undergo traditional punitive measures, as they are more likely to internalize the lessons of responsibility and empathy (Livingstone et al., 2013).

The neuropsychological emphasis on empathy and moral reasoning helps juveniles develop a more nuanced understanding of right and wrong, reducing the likelihood of future offenses. Additionally, the social support embedded within restorative justice processes provides juveniles with positive role models and guidance, crucial factors in developing prosocial behavior. As such, restorative justice aligns with the neurodevelopmental needs of adolescents, supporting them in their journey toward rehabilitation and positive societal reintegration.

6.5 Challenges and Ethical Considerations

While restorative justice offers many advantages, certain challenges and ethical considerations must be addressed. Ensuring that juveniles genuinely understand the restorative process and feel empowered to participate without coercion is critical. Ethical issues also arise in cases involving severe offenses, where victims may be reluctant to engage in dialogue or may fear re-traumatization. Careful facilitation by trained mediators is necessary to ensure that the process is constructive and respectful for all participants. Additionally, a neuropsychologically informed approach should consider individual differences in cognitive and emotional maturity, adjusting the intervention techniques to suit each juvenile's developmental stage and specific needs.

Restorative justice strategies for juvenile offenders provide a compassionate and effective alternative to traditional punitive approaches by focusing on empathy, accountability, and community reintegration. Through practices such as victim–offender mediation, community service, and family group conferencing, restorative justice fosters the cognitive and emotional growth of juveniles, supporting the development of empathy, social responsibility, and moral reasoning. The neuropsychological perspective underscores the importance of these strategies, as adolescence represents a period of significant neural plasticity and growth. By promoting rehabilitation over punishment, restorative justice not only addresses the root causes of juvenile delinquency but also supports the broader goals of public safety and social cohesion.

7 Cognitive Behavioral Therapy for Juvenile Offenders

Cognitive behavioral therapy (CBT) is a widely recognized and effective intervention for addressing behavioral and psychological issues in diverse populations, including juvenile offenders. For young offenders, CBT offers a structured approach to understanding and modifying maladaptive thought patterns and behaviors, helping reduce impulsivity, improve emotional regulation, and foster problem-solving skills. By directly addressing cognitive and emotional deficits that often contribute to criminal behavior, CBT can help juveniles build healthier behavioral patterns and, ultimately, reduce the likelihood of re-offending. When integrated with other therapeutic approaches, such as family therapy or restorative justice, CBT is particularly effective in supporting the rehabilitation of juvenile offenders and promoting positive behavioral changes.

7.1 The Need for Cognitive–Behavioral Interventions in Juvenile Justice

Juveniles entering the justice system frequently exhibit a range of cognitive, emotional, and behavioral issues that contribute to their offending behavior. Adolescence is a developmental period marked by ongoing brain maturation, particularly in regions associated with impulse control, decision-making, and emotional regulation. Cognitive deficits, including poor problem-solving skills, distorted thinking patterns, and impulsivity, often underlie the actions that lead young individuals into the justice system. Additionally, many juvenile offenders have experienced adverse childhood experiences (ACEs), such as trauma, neglect, or family instability, which can exacerbate these cognitive and emotional difficulties.

CBT provides a valuable framework for helping young offenders address these issues, as it focuses on identifying and restructuring maladaptive thoughts and beliefs. This, in turn, influences emotions and behaviors in positive ways. Through CBT, juveniles can develop the skills to manage their emotions, cope with stress, and think critically about the consequences of their actions. These skills are not only essential for reducing immediate criminal behavior but also help build resilience, promoting long-term behavioral change.

7.2 The Core Principles and Techniques of CBT for Juvenile Offenders

CBT is founded on the principle that thoughts, emotions, and behaviors are interconnected and that modifying dysfunctional thoughts can lead to healthier emotional and behavioral responses. For juvenile offenders, CBT sessions are structured around teaching them to recognize and challenge cognitive distortions—faulty or exaggerated patterns of thinking that reinforce negative emotions and behaviors. Common cognitive distortions among young offenders include all-or-nothing thinking, personalization (blaming oneself for external events), and catastrophizing (expecting the worst outcome). By identifying these patterns, CBT helps juveniles build awareness of their own thought processes and reframe their responses to challenging situations.

Several key techniques are commonly used in CBT with juvenile offenders:

- **Cognitive Restructuring:** Juveniles learn to identify irrational or distorted thoughts that contribute to their emotional distress or problematic behavior. For example, a young offender who believes "Nobody cares about me" may be guided to examine the evidence against this belief and consider more balanced perspectives, such as positive interactions with family members or mentors.
- **Skill-Building for Emotional Regulation:** Adolescents are taught strategies to manage strong emotions, such as anger or frustration, in constructive ways. Techniques like deep breathing, mindfulness exercises, and self-talk can help young offenders control impulsive reactions and stay calm in triggering situations.
- **Problem-Solving Training:** Juveniles are guided through structured approaches to solve real-life problems, enhancing their capacity to make reasoned decisions. Problem-solving training encourages youths to define a problem, generate alternative solutions, weigh potential consequences, and select the best course of action.
- **Role-Playing and Modeling:** These techniques allow juveniles to practice new skills in a safe environment. For instance, role-playing scenarios that simulate peer pressure or conflict can help young offenders prepare to handle such situations more effectively in the real world.

7.3 *Impact of CBT on Emotional Regulation and Impulsivity in Juveniles*

A critical benefit of CBT for juvenile offenders is its effectiveness in improving emotional regulation and reducing impulsivity—two areas that are often underdeveloped in adolescents and contribute significantly to criminal behavior. CBT helps juveniles recognize the triggers that lead to emotional outbursts or impulsive decisions and provides tools for responding more constructively. This is particularly relevant in the context of the juvenile justice system, as impulsivity and poor emotional control are often linked to offenses like assault, theft, and vandalism.

By developing these skills, juveniles can better manage situations that previously led to aggressive or harmful actions. For example, a young offender who used to respond to frustration with physical aggression may, through CBT, learn to pause and use problem-solving techniques to address the issue or walk away if the situation becomes overwhelming. Studies show that improving emotional regulation can lead to lower rates of recidivism, as juveniles gain the tools to manage their emotions rather than acting on impulses (Salinas & Venta, 2021).

7.4 *Role of CBT in Reducing Recidivism*

CBT has proven to be highly effective in reducing recidivism among juvenile offenders, particularly when combined with other therapeutic approaches that address the complex needs of these individuals. Research indicates that juveniles who receive CBT as part of their rehabilitation are less likely to re-offend, as they develop cognitive and emotional skills that deter criminal behavior (*Preventing Future Crime With Cognitive Behavioral Therapy | National Institute of Justice*, n.d.). The long-term benefits of CBT can be attributed to its emphasis on self-awareness and self-regulation—qualities that enable young offenders to make thoughtful decisions and avoid risky behaviors.

For optimal results, CBT is often integrated with other interventions, such as family therapy, substance abuse treatment, and restorative justice practices. Family therapy complements CBT by addressing family dynamics and improving communication within the home, creating a supportive environment that reinforces positive behavioral changes. Substance abuse treatment, which is necessary for juveniles with addiction issues, helps remove barriers to effective cognitive and emotional functioning, thus enhancing the effectiveness of CBT. Restorative justice, with its emphasis on empathy and accountability, also pairs well with CBT by providing juveniles with a space to understand the impact of their actions on others.

7.5 Challenges in Implementing CBT with Juvenile Offenders

While CBT is effective, implementing it with juvenile offenders poses certain challenges. Many young offenders may initially resist CBT, as they may lack motivation or have mistrust toward authority figures. Additionally, cognitive and emotional immaturity can make it difficult for some juveniles to fully engage with the introspective components of CBT. To address these challenges, therapists often adapt CBT techniques to make them more engaging and accessible. For example, using interactive activities or simplified language can help juveniles better understand the concepts being taught.

Another challenge lies in the accessibility and consistency of therapy. Juveniles in detention centers or those who lack stable home environments may have limited access to consistent CBT sessions, which can hinder progress. For CBT to be effective, juveniles require ongoing support and practice, underscoring the need for community-based programs and resources that extend beyond detention facilities.

Cognitive behavioral therapy plays a vital role in the rehabilitation of juvenile offenders, offering a structured, evidence-based approach to address the maladaptive thought patterns and behaviors that contribute to criminal actions. By teaching juveniles skills for emotional regulation, problem-solving, and impulse control, CBT promotes self-awareness and behavioral change, helping reduce recidivism. When combined with other therapeutic interventions like family therapy and restorative justice, CBT has a powerful impact on supporting young offenders' rehabilitation and reintegration into society. Despite the challenges in implementation, the long-term benefits of CBT are well-documented, making it a cornerstone of effective juvenile justice reform aimed at fostering personal growth and reducing future offenses.

8 Intervention and Rehabilitation Techniques for Juvenile Offenders

Intervention and rehabilitation techniques are essential components in addressing juvenile delinquency, offering pathways to help young offenders develop healthier behaviors and reduce the risk of re-offending. Unlike punitive measures, rehabilitative approaches prioritize personal growth, emotional regulation, and social reintegration. Diversion programs, multisystemic therapy (MST), and functional family therapy (FFT) are prominent methods used to support juveniles in navigating away from crime, often involving collaboration with families, schools, and communities. By addressing underlying issues, such as family dynamics, peer influence, and emotional challenges, these approaches help redirect juveniles from traditional justice pathways, supporting a holistic approach to rehabilitation.

8.1 The Role of Diversion Programs in Juvenile Justice

Diversion programs aim to provide alternatives to the traditional justice system, redirecting juveniles into rehabilitative services that prioritize personal development over punishment. These programs typically focus on first-time or low-risk offenders, allowing them to avoid formal charges and detention. Diversion can take many forms, including community service, educational programs, counseling, and mentorship. The primary goal is to prevent the potentially damaging effects of formal criminal records and institutionalization, which can negatively impact a young person's future opportunities and increase the likelihood of re-offending.

For example, one common form of diversion involves educational or skill-building workshops designed to promote self-awareness, conflict resolution, and decision-making skills. By learning these skills, juveniles gain the tools to handle challenges in healthier ways and avoid actions that may lead them back into the justice system. Diversion programs often partner with schools and community organizations to ensure that juveniles receive the necessary support and supervision. These programs can be particularly effective when they integrate support for educational and vocational goals, helping young offenders establish constructive life pathways.

The impact of diversion programs is significant; studies have shown that juveniles who participate in diversion programs are less likely to re-offend compared to those who go through traditional court proceedings (Schwalbe et al., 2011). By providing a positive intervention at an early stage, diversion programs help prevent young offenders from becoming entrenched in the justice system and contribute to their long-term success.

8.2 Multisystemic Therapy: Addressing the Social Environment

Multisystemic therapy (MST) is a highly effective intervention model that focuses on the social systems influencing a juvenile's behavior, including family, peers, school, and the community. MST is designed for young offenders who display serious antisocial behavior, addressing the various environmental factors that contribute to these behaviors. Rather than isolating individuals, MST emphasizes the importance of family engagement, community involvement, and accountability.

One of the core principles of MST is empowering families to support their children's positive behavioral changes. Therapists work closely with family members to improve communication, resolve conflicts, and set appropriate boundaries. By engaging the entire family in therapy, MST helps establish a stable and supportive home environment, reducing the likelihood that juveniles will resort to crime as a means of coping with stress or seeking attention. MST therapists may also work with schools and peer groups to ensure consistent support across the juvenile's life, addressing problematic behaviors within their social networks and promoting positive peer influences.

Research has demonstrated the effectiveness of MST in reducing recidivism among juvenile offenders (Olsson et al., 2021). By involving families in the therapeutic process, MST enables juveniles to apply what they learn in therapy to real-life situations. This approach fosters long-term resilience and equips young people with the coping mechanisms they need to handle challenges more effectively. The collaborative nature of MST also strengthens community ties, as schools and local organizations are often involved in the therapeutic process, creating a network of support for juveniles.

8.3 Functional Family Therapy: Enhancing Family Dynamics

Functional family therapy (FFT) is another family-centered intervention that targets juveniles with behavioral problems, particularly those whose family environments may contribute to their challenges. FFT operates on the principle that family dynamics play a critical role in shaping behavior and that interventions aimed at improving these relationships can have a profound effect on juveniles' lives. Through FFT, families learn how to communicate more effectively, resolve conflicts, and create a supportive home environment.

FFT sessions focus on building trust and understanding within the family unit. Therapists help families recognize negative patterns, such as inconsistent discipline or hostile communication, that may fuel delinquent behavior. For instance, if a young offender's behavior stems from feelings of neglect or unresolved anger, FFT can help family members acknowledge these issues and work together to find healthier ways of interaction. FFT also involves training parents or guardians in skills like active listening, constructive feedback, and appropriate discipline techniques.

One of the key strengths of FFT is its adaptability. The therapy can be modified to address the specific needs of each family, allowing for a tailored approach that is sensitive to cultural and contextual factors. Studies show that FFT is highly effective in reducing criminal behavior and improving family functioning (Sexton & Turner, 2010). By fostering healthier relationships at home, FFT equips juveniles with a stronger support system, reducing their need to seek affirmation or camaraderie in delinquent peer groups.

8.4 Importance of Early Intervention

Early intervention is a critical factor in preventing long-term criminal trajectories for juveniles. Research indicates that the earlier an intervention occurs, the more effective it is in steering juveniles away from a future of crime (Olsson et al., 2021).

Early interventions often focus on identifying risk factors, such as exposure to violence, academic difficulties, and substance abuse, which can predispose juveniles to delinquent behavior. By addressing these issues before they escalate, early interventions can reduce the likelihood that juveniles will become repeat offenders.

One of the primary benefits of early intervention is that it allows young people to develop positive coping mechanisms and decision-making skills before they become entrenched in delinquent behaviors. For instance, school-based programs that teach social and emotional skills can help at-risk youth learn how to manage anger, set goals, and form healthy relationships. These programs not only provide juveniles with constructive outlets for their energy but also connect them to positive role models who can guide their development.

Furthermore, early intervention can reduce the need for more intensive rehabilitation measures later on, as juveniles are less likely to develop severe behavioral issues if they receive support early. Programs that focus on skill-building, academic support, and mentorship offer juveniles a sense of purpose and belonging, reducing the appeal of crime as an alternative path.

8.5 Integrating Diversion, MST, and FFT for Comprehensive Rehabilitation

While each intervention technique offers unique benefits, integrating diversion programs, MST, and FFT creates a comprehensive approach to rehabilitation. Diversion programs provide a proactive alternative to the justice system, MST addresses environmental and peer influences, and FFT enhances family dynamics. Together, these interventions create a holistic framework that addresses the varied and interconnected factors contributing to juvenile delinquency.

When implemented collaboratively, these techniques support juveniles in building self-awareness, emotional regulation, and positive social skills. By focusing on rehabilitation rather than punishment, integrated interventions emphasize the potential for growth and change in each young offender. This collaborative model also benefits communities by fostering resilience, reducing crime rates, and promoting a culture of accountability and empathy.

Intervention and rehabilitation techniques such as diversion programs, MST, and FFT play a crucial role in redirecting juveniles from the traditional justice system toward rehabilitative services. By addressing family dynamics and peer influences and providing early intervention, these approaches offer young offenders a chance to develop constructive life skills and avoid long-term criminal pathways. The integration of these techniques provides a comprehensive framework for supporting juvenile rehabilitation, emphasizing the importance of community, family, and individual growth in fostering a brighter future for young offenders. Through these strategies, the juvenile justice system can support positive, lasting changes, enabling juveniles to break free from cycles of crime and reintegrate into society as productive individuals.

9 Challenges in Addressing the Needs of Juvenile Offenders

Introduction

Addressing the needs of juvenile offenders presents unique and complex challenges for the justice system. Unlike adults, juveniles are still undergoing significant cognitive and emotional development, which requires an approach that balances accountability with rehabilitation. The juvenile justice system faces a difficult task: meeting these youths' needs while protecting public safety and encouraging positive behavioral change. Key challenges include balancing punishment with rehabilitation, addressing the often complex mental health and behavioral needs of young offenders, and tailoring interventions to fit each juvenile's cognitive and developmental profile. Understanding these challenges is essential to developing effective strategies that help juvenile offenders reintegrate into society while reducing recidivism.

9.1 Balancing Punishment with Rehabilitation: A Systemic Dilemma

The juvenile justice system has long grappled with the question of whether its primary aim should be punishment or rehabilitation. On one hand, there is a need to hold young offenders accountable for their actions and deter future delinquent behaviors. However, focusing solely on punishment risks exacerbating the challenges these juveniles face, often pushing them further into the criminal justice system and limiting their opportunities for personal growth.

The punitive approach, which emphasizes punishment over rehabilitation, can be detrimental to juveniles who are still in the formative stages of development. Studies have shown that young offenders are more likely to experience poor outcomes in adult life, including higher rates of recidivism, if they are exposed to harsh punitive measures such as detention or incarceration (Creemers et al., 2022). Incarceration, in particular, isolates juveniles from positive influences and community support, reducing their chances of successfully reintegrating upon release.

Rehabilitation-focused approaches, on the other hand, emphasize counseling, education, and social services to address the underlying issues contributing to delinquent behavior. These methods aim to guide juveniles toward productive behaviors, often with a focus on personal development, empathy, and responsibility. However, rehabilitative measures require resources, funding, and a dedicated support network, which can strain justice systems that are not adequately equipped to provide them. Finding a balance between punishment and rehabilitation is a challenging but necessary endeavor, requiring the justice system to weigh public safety and individual transformation in equal measure.

9.2 *Complex Needs of Juvenile Offenders: Emotional Dysregulation, Substance Abuse, and Mental Health Conditions*

Juvenile offenders often face a host of complex issues that extend beyond the scope of traditional delinquent behavior. Many come from backgrounds of trauma, abuse, neglect, or poverty, factors that contribute to emotional dysregulation and impulse control issues. Emotional dysregulation can lead to problems with anger, frustration, and aggression, making it difficult for juveniles to respond appropriately in stressful situations. These challenges can create a cycle of negative behaviors that reinforce criminal tendencies, particularly if juveniles do not receive the psychological support they need.

Substance abuse is another common challenge among juvenile offenders. Research shows that many young offenders use drugs or alcohol as a coping mechanism to deal with stress, anxiety, or trauma (Ayres, 2020). Substance abuse further complicates their behavior, often leading to impaired decision-making, academic struggles, and strained relationships. The justice system, however, is not always equipped to address substance abuse, and programs specifically targeting addiction are not uniformly available across juvenile facilities.

Additionally, comorbid mental health conditions such as depression, anxiety disorders, ADHD, and post-traumatic stress disorder (PTSD) are prevalent among juvenile offenders. These conditions can hinder their ability to follow instructions, communicate effectively, and build healthy relationships. Juveniles with mental health issues require tailored treatment plans that consider both their delinquent behavior and their mental health needs. Unfortunately, juvenile detention facilities often lack the mental health resources necessary to diagnose and treat these conditions effectively. The shortage of mental health professionals, coupled with an overemphasis on discipline and control, means that many juveniles do not receive the treatment they need, which can lead to worsening symptoms and an increased likelihood of recidivism.

9.3 *Tailoring Interventions to Each Juvenile's Cognitive and Developmental Profile*

A significant challenge in rehabilitating juvenile offenders is that each young person has a unique cognitive and developmental profile, influenced by factors such as age, upbringing, trauma history, and mental health status. Adolescents are at a stage of life characterized by impulsivity, susceptibility to peer pressure, and a limited capacity for long-term planning and understanding of consequences. Traditional intervention models often fail to account for these developmental differences, instead treating juveniles as though they possess the same cognitive maturity and decision-making capacity as adults.

Tailoring interventions to individual needs requires a nuanced understanding of adolescent brain development and behavior. Cognitive behavioral therapy (CBT) is one approach that has proven effective with juveniles, as it addresses maladaptive thought patterns and behaviors and provides tools for self-regulation and problem-solving. However, for interventions like CBT to be successful, they must be adapted to the developmental stage of the juvenile. Younger offenders may require simpler language and visual aids, while older adolescents might benefit from more advanced discussions about responsibility and self-awareness.

Neuropsychological assessments can also play a valuable role in determining the specific needs of juvenile offenders. These assessments provide insights into cognitive deficits, attention and memory issues, and executive function impairments, which can inform tailored interventions. For example, a juvenile with a history of impulsive behavior and poor decision-making might benefit from interventions focused on impulse control and decision-making skills. By understanding the cognitive and developmental profiles of juvenile offenders, therapists and educators can design interventions that resonate with each individual, increasing the likelihood of positive behavioral change.

9.4 Resource Limitations and Systemic Barriers

Despite the benefits of tailored and rehabilitative approaches, many juvenile justice systems face resource limitations and systemic barriers that hinder their ability to meet the needs of young offenders. Juvenile facilities are often underfunded and understaffed, lacking the necessary mental health professionals, social workers, and educational resources to provide comprehensive care. In many cases, facilities prioritize security and control over individualized support, which can prevent juveniles from accessing the services they need.

Furthermore, the transient nature of juvenile detention complicates treatment continuity. Juveniles may be released from detention before completing a treatment program or transferred between facilities, disrupting their progress. In addition, many families lack the financial means to support continued therapy or counseling after a juvenile is released. Without continued support, juveniles may struggle to apply the skills they learned during rehabilitation, increasing the risk of recidivism.

9.5 The Need for Community-Based Programs and Continued Support

To address these challenges, it is crucial for juvenile justice systems to invest in community-based programs and provide continued support after a juvenile is released. Community programs, such as mentorship initiatives, vocational training, and substance abuse treatment, can help juveniles transition back into society. These programs offer continuity of care, reinforcing the skills juveniles learn in detention and helping them establish positive social connections and life goals.

Continued support is also vital for addressing issues related to mental health and substance abuse. Juveniles who receive ongoing counseling, family support, and community mentorship are more likely to stay on track and avoid re-offending. Additionally, community-based programs offer a rehabilitative alternative to detention, enabling juveniles to serve their sentences in environments that foster growth and accountability rather than isolation and punishment.

Addressing the needs of juvenile offenders requires a holistic approach that considers their developmental stages, mental health needs, and social environments. Balancing punishment with rehabilitation, understanding complex mental health challenges, and tailoring interventions to each juvenile's cognitive profile are essential steps in supporting positive change. Overcoming resource limitations and promoting community-based alternatives can improve outcomes for young offenders, helping them reintegrate into society and reducing recidivism. By acknowledging the unique challenges these juveniles face and providing appropriate support, the justice system can fulfill its role in nurturing a healthier, more constructive future for young people.

10 Case Studies: Neuropsychological Interventions for Juvenile Offenders

Neuropsychological interventions have proven effective in addressing the unique needs of juvenile offenders, especially those who struggle with conditions like ADHD, impulsivity, and traumatic brain injuries (TBIs). These interventions aim to enhance cognitive functions, improve emotional regulation, and reduce recidivism, ultimately offering juveniles a chance for positive rehabilitation. By examining two specific cases—a juvenile with ADHD and impulsivity issues and another with TBI—this report explores how targeted neuropsychological interventions have facilitated successful behavioral changes, thereby underscoring the value of such approaches in juvenile justice.

10.1 Case 1: Addressing ADHD and Impulsivity in a Juvenile Offender

Background In the first case, the 15-year-old male juvenile offender had long struggled with attention deficit hyperactivity disorder (ADHD), a neurodevelopmental condition that profoundly affected his academic performance, social interactions, and overall behavior. ADHD in his case was primarily characterized by symptoms of impulsivity, inattention, and hyperactivity, creating challenges across multiple areas of his life. From an early age, he exhibited difficulties with maintaining focus in school, listening to instructions, and completing tasks that required sustained mental effort, which often led to feelings of frustration and alienation from his peers and authority figures.

Over time, his inability to control impulsive behavior began manifesting in more problematic ways. For instance, his impulsivity led to poor decision-making in social situations, often resulting in misunderstandings or conflicts with peers and adults. These impulsive actions escalated into repeated minor offenses, including theft and minor assault, typically occurring in situations where he struggled to process and manage his emotions effectively. For example, in situations where he felt provoked, he would act out without fully understanding or considering the consequences of his actions, leading to disciplinary issues both at school and home. The absence of well-developed coping mechanisms for handling frustration and anger exacerbated his tendency to react impulsively in challenging situations.

In addition to his impulsive tendencies, he had difficulty with emotional self-regulation. Emotions, especially frustration and anger, would quickly intensify, often overwhelming him. This limited emotional control contributed significantly to his confrontational behavior and repeated behavioral issues. His inability to focus, follow rules, or maintain positive social relationships led to a cycle of punitive measures and suspensions, which further alienated him and reinforced his sense of isolation from peers and authority figures. Despite attempts to address his behavior through disciplinary action, these efforts were ineffective and only fueled his underlying issues.

As his involvement with the justice system increased, it became clear that his ADHD-related challenges played a central role in his recurrent behavioral issues. With each encounter, his frustration, impulsivity, and defiance compounded, and he began to adopt a negative self-image shaped by the constant cycle of punishment and failure. Recognizing the importance of a tailored intervention that addressed his ADHD and impulse control directly, a neuropsychological evaluation was conducted to gain deeper insight into the cognitive and emotional aspects influencing his behavior. This evaluation formed the basis for a structured intervention plan focused on improving his executive functioning, emotional self-regulation, and social skills, ultimately aiming to break the cycle of impulsivity and poor decision-making that had led him into the juvenile justice system.

Neuropsychological Assessment and Intervention Following his assessment, a neuropsychological evaluation was conducted to better understand his cognitive deficits, focusing on executive functions, attention span, and emotional regulation. Results indicated severe deficits in impulse control, attentional focus, and working memory—areas crucial for decision-making and behavioral self-regulation.

The intervention program was structured around cognitive training to strengthen executive functions, impulse control, and emotional self-regulation. Cognitive behavioral therapy (CBT) formed a core component of the treatment, with additional support through computerized cognitive training exercises that focused on enhancing attention and working memory. Specific techniques included:

1. **Cognitive Behavioral Therapy (CBT):** Tailored to address the juvenile's impulsive tendencies, CBT helped him become aware of his automatic, impulsive responses and taught him strategies for pausing before acting. Role-playing exercises, combined with real-life scenarios, provided opportunities to practice these skills in controlled settings.
2. **Computerized Cognitive Training:** This intervention used a series of games and tasks targeting working memory and attention control. Over time, the training improved his ability to stay focused and reduced his need to react impulsively in high-stakes situations.
3. **Mindfulness-Based Techniques:** Mindfulness practices, particularly guided breathing exercises, were introduced to support emotional regulation. These techniques provided him with tools to calm his mind and body, thereby increasing his capacity for emotional awareness and reducing stress-related impulsivity.

Outcome and Success Factors The neuropsychological intervention achieved significant improvements in the juvenile's behavioral patterns. He exhibited reduced impulsivity, better focus, and increased self-control. His teachers and caregivers noted a marked improvement in his behavior, including fewer disruptive outbursts in class and a noticeable willingness to follow instructions. Moreover, his recidivism risk reduced as he became more reflective and able to anticipate the consequences of his actions, a key outcome attributed to the CBT and cognitive training.

This case highlights how neuropsychological interventions tailored to ADHD can mitigate criminal tendencies among juvenile offenders. By strengthening cognitive and emotional regulation, the intervention enabled the juvenile to manage his behavior more effectively, improving his long-term prospects for rehabilitation.

10.2 Case 2: Neuropsychological Intervention for a Young Offender with Traumatic Brain Injury

Background In the second case, the 17-year-old male juvenile offender had sustained a traumatic brain injury (TBI) during a high-impact sports accident while playing football. The injury had a profound impact on his cognitive and emotional functioning, causing changes that drastically altered his personality and behavior. Before the accident, he was known among his family and peers as a friendly, cooperative individual with no significant behavioral issues. He had a stable academic record and participated actively in school and social activities, generally demonstrating resilience, empathy, and impulse control. However, the TBI marked a turning point, fundamentally reshaping his personality and ability to regulate emotions.

Following the TBI, his family and school began to notice a stark shift in his demeanor. He became more irritable, aggressive, and prone to outbursts of anger, struggling with heightened impulsivity and emotional volatility. This change puzzled those around him, as he frequently engaged in behaviors that were entirely out of character. Previously mild-mannered, he now exhibited aggression even in minor conflicts, reacting with physical or verbal hostility when frustrated. Tasks that required patience, focus, or sustained mental effort became challenging, and he often abandoned them abruptly, overwhelmed by frustration or anger.

The injury had primarily impacted areas of his brain associated with executive functioning, especially the prefrontal cortex, which plays a crucial role in regulating emotions, social behaviors, and decision-making. Damage to the prefrontal cortex can significantly impair an individual's ability to control impulses, assess risks, and manage complex social interactions—skills essential for navigating daily life without resorting to aggression. Consequently, his ability to think through the consequences of his actions was diminished, and he frequently acted on impulse, driven by emotional reactions rather than logical thought processes.

These neurocognitive deficits manifested in various ways, from difficulties with processing speed to impaired working memory and diminished problem-solving capabilities. His processing speed slowed considerably, meaning that he struggled to keep up with conversations, instructions, and environmental cues, often missing critical pieces of information that might have helped him navigate social conflicts. His memory was also affected, leading to issues with following multistep tasks and retaining key details, further complicating his ability to manage his environment effectively.

Emotionally, he found it nearly impossible to regulate his anger, leading to frequent incidents of aggression at school and home. For example, minor frustrations—such as misunderstandings with peers or disciplinary corrections from teachers—would provoke intense reactions. Instead of responding calmly or attempting to resolve the conflict, he would react impulsively, sometimes engaging in minor assaults or damaging property in anger. The cumulative impact of these behaviors led to several encounters with the juvenile justice system, as he began to be seen as a "problematic" individual by authorities, educators, and peers who were unaware of the neuropsychological challenges underpinning his actions.

The family and school reported feeling at a loss, as traditional disciplinary measures only seemed to exacerbate his anger and frustration, leading to a worsening cycle of aggression and punitive responses. They observed that he was often remorseful after incidents, suggesting an awareness of his actions and their negative consequences. However, his ability to anticipate these consequences before acting was diminished, indicating that his impulsivity was a direct result of his TBI-related deficits rather than intentional defiance.

Given the complex nature of his post-injury challenges, a comprehensive neuropsychological evaluation was conducted to determine the full extent of his cognitive and emotional impairments. The assessment revealed marked deficits in areas critical for emotional control, social decision-making, and self-regulation. Based on these findings, an intervention plan was developed to specifically target his processing speed, memory, and emotional regulation capabilities, with the goal of reducing his impulsivity, enhancing his frustration tolerance, and helping him rebuild social connections.

This background underscores the profound impact that TBI can have on juvenile behavior, particularly in cases where the injury affects the brain regions responsible for impulse control and emotional regulation. Without intervention, these changes often lead young individuals into cycles of recidivism, as their behavioral challenges are frequently misunderstood as intentional delinquency rather than neurological consequences. In this case, the neuropsychological intervention aimed to address these root causes, providing the juvenile with tools to manage his cognitive limitations and emotional responses in a way that would support his rehabilitation and reintegration into society.

Neuropsychological Assessment and Intervention After his assessment, an intensive neuropsychological intervention plan was developed, focusing on cognitive rehabilitation, emotion regulation training, and family therapy. This multifaceted approach aimed to address both the cognitive impacts of the TBI and the social–behavioral challenges that had arisen.

1. **Cognitive Rehabilitation Therapy (CRT):** CRT targeted cognitive domains affected by the TBI, such as memory, processing speed, and executive function. Exercises involved structured tasks that required planning, problem-solving, and recalling information, gradually enhancing his cognitive flexibility and reducing the cognitive frustration he often experienced in social situations.
2. **Emotion Regulation and Anger Management Training:** Given his heightened impulsivity and emotional dysregulation, the intervention incorporated emotion regulation skills training. Techniques included cognitive reappraisal, where he learned to reinterpret triggering situations to reduce emotional responses, and relaxation techniques like progressive muscle relaxation to manage physical symptoms of anger.
3. **Family Therapy:** To foster a supportive environment, family therapy sessions were integrated into his treatment. This aspect was crucial because it helped family members understand his post-injury behavior changes, taught them effective communication techniques, and provided them with strategies to support his emotional needs. Family therapy also facilitated the juvenile's emotional growth by establishing trust and consistent reinforcement of positive behaviors within the family unit.

Outcome and Success Factors The neuropsychological interventions led to significant progress in the juvenile's ability to regulate his emotions and control his aggressive impulses. Over time, he developed strategies to identify and manage feelings of frustration before they escalated. His teachers observed a decline in disruptive incidents, while his family reported fewer conflicts at home. Importantly, his rate of recidivism decreased markedly as he gained control over his aggression and improved his decision-making skills.

This case demonstrates how neuropsychological interventions can aid juvenile offenders with TBI by addressing the specific neurocognitive and emotional challenges that emerge post-injury. By enhancing cognitive flexibility, improving anger management, and strengthening family support systems, the intervention facilitated his rehabilitation and reduced his involvement with the justice system.

Key Takeaways and Implications for Juvenile Justice
These case studies illustrate the potential for neuropsychological interventions to support the rehabilitation of juvenile offenders, particularly those with conditions such as ADHD and TBI. Several themes emerge:

1. **Personalized Interventions**: Neuropsychological interventions need to be tailored to the cognitive and emotional profiles of each juvenile. For instance, interventions that target impulsivity may benefit juveniles with ADHD, while those focusing on emotion regulation may be crucial for those with TBI.
2. **Holistic Approach**: Effective intervention programs often combine multiple therapeutic techniques—such as cognitive training, CBT, and family therapy—to address the complex needs of juveniles. This integrated approach can improve both cognitive functioning and social behavior, setting a foundation for long-term behavioral change.
3. **Reduction in Recidivism**: By addressing the root causes of delinquent behavior, neuropsychological interventions reduce the likelihood of re-offending, illustrating the role of neuropsychology in fostering rehabilitation over punishment in the juvenile justice system.
4. **Role of Family Support**: Engaging family members in therapy can reinforce the positive changes facilitated by individual interventions. Family support provides a critical foundation for juveniles as they transition out of the justice system and back into society.

Neuropsychological interventions offer valuable insights and strategies for rehabilitating juvenile offenders by focusing on cognitive and emotional development. The successful applications of these interventions in cases of ADHD and TBI showcase their ability to foster meaningful behavioral changes and reduce recidivism. By adopting a neuropsychological approach, the juvenile justice system can better meet the needs of young offenders, supporting their journey toward rehabilitation and social reintegration.

11 Reducing Recidivism in Juvenile Offenders

Reducing recidivism among juvenile offenders is a complex and multifaceted challenge, with effective neuropsychological interventions emerging as a critical approach to decreasing the likelihood of re-offending. Neuropsychological interventions aim to address underlying cognitive, emotional, and social deficits that may contribute to delinquent behavior. Through early identification of risk factors and tailored intervention strategies, the juvenile justice system can take proactive steps to mitigate repeated criminal behavior and promote resilience and positive life outcomes among young offenders.

11.1 Understanding the Risk Factors

Juvenile offenders often present with a range of neuropsychological risk factors that increase their likelihood of recidivism. Common challenges include impulsivity, emotional dysregulation, learning disabilities, and difficulties with executive functioning. For example, conditions like ADHD, conduct disorder, and traumatic brain injuries (TBIs) are prevalent among juvenile offenders, with each of these conditions linked to an increased risk of criminal behavior. Impulsivity, a frequent issue in ADHD and conduct disorder, impairs the ability to think through consequences before acting, leading to behaviors that can result in conflict with the law. Additionally, deficits in emotional regulation make it challenging for some juveniles to manage anger and frustration, which can lead to aggressive or violent responses to stress.

Environmental factors, such as adverse childhood experiences (ACEs), substance abuse, and unstable family dynamics, further complicate these neuropsychological risks. ACEs, which include abuse, neglect, and household dysfunction, have been linked to higher rates of criminality and mental health challenges later in life. Substance abuse is also a significant contributor, as it can exacerbate cognitive deficits and impair judgment, making recidivism more likely. Addressing these risk factors early can help prevent juveniles from becoming entrenched in the criminal justice system.

11.2 Neuropsychological Assessments as a Foundation for Intervention

Neuropsychological assessments are instrumental in identifying the specific cognitive, emotional, and behavioral challenges faced by juvenile offenders. These assessments examine functions such as memory, attention, impulse control, and problem-solving abilities, which are essential for making sound decisions and engaging in positive social interactions. By gaining a comprehensive understanding of a juvenile's neuropsychological profile, clinicians and legal professionals can develop tailored interventions that address the unique needs of each individual.

For instance, assessments may reveal that a juvenile with a history of aggressive behavior is struggling with low frustration tolerance and poor emotional regulation. In such cases, interventions might focus on emotional regulation skills, helping the individual learn to manage their emotions without resorting to violence. Similarly, a juvenile who demonstrates impulsive decision-making may benefit from cognitive–behavioral training to enhance their executive functioning skills, such as delaying gratification, considering consequences, and practicing self-control.

These assessments also aid in identifying strengths that can be leveraged in the rehabilitation process. A juvenile who excels in a particular area, such as creative expression or sports, might be guided toward activities that provide constructive outlets for their energy and emotions. This strengths-based approach can enhance motivation for change and build a sense of self-worth, both of which are important for reducing recidivism.

11.3 Intervention Strategies to Reduce Recidivism

Effective intervention strategies for reducing recidivism among juvenile offenders often include a combination of therapeutic approaches, skill-building programs, and environmental support. Cognitive behavioral therapy (CBT) is a cornerstone intervention, as it targets maladaptive thought patterns and behaviors that contribute to delinquency. CBT helps juveniles identify and challenge cognitive distortions, such as thinking errors that justify or minimize their actions. By replacing these thoughts with more constructive beliefs, juveniles can improve their decision-making processes and reduce impulsivity.

Multisystemic therapy (MST) and functional family therapy (FFT) are other effective approaches, particularly for juveniles whose offending behavior is influenced by family dynamics and peer relationships. MST addresses the various systems in a young offender's life—family, school, peer groups, and the community—to create a supportive network that encourages positive behavior. By involving family members in therapy, MST helps families learn strategies to manage behavioral issues and support the juvenile's rehabilitation. FFT, similarly, focuses on improving communication and reducing conflict within the family unit. This approach not only benefits the juvenile but also strengthens the family as a whole, creating a more stable and supportive environment that reduces the likelihood of recidivism.

In cases where cognitive impairments are a significant factor, interventions may include cognitive training programs designed to improve attention, memory, and executive functioning. These programs, which can involve computer-based exercises or therapist-led activities, are particularly valuable for juveniles with ADHD, TBI, or learning disabilities. By strengthening cognitive skills, juveniles are better equipped to succeed academically and socially, reducing the likelihood of frustration and negative behaviors that can lead to re-offending.

11.4 Building Resilience and Promoting Positive Outcomes

Promoting resilience is a key element in reducing recidivism, as resilient juveniles are better able to cope with stress and make constructive choices. Interventions that focus on resilience-building often emphasize skill development in areas such as emotional regulation, self-efficacy, and problem-solving. By teaching juveniles how to manage their emotions and cope with adversity, these interventions foster a greater sense of agency and control over their lives, which can reduce feelings of hopelessness or aggression that contribute to recidivism.

Programs that encourage goal setting, vocational training, and educational support also play a vital role in building resilience. Many juvenile offenders have struggled in traditional educational settings, and offering alternative learning opportunities can help them develop a sense of purpose and direction. Vocational training, in particular, provides practical skills that increase employability, helping juveniles envision a positive future outside of the justice system.

Community involvement and mentorship are additional protective factors. Community programs that engage juveniles in positive social activities, such as sports, arts, or volunteer work, create opportunities for meaningful connections and a sense of belonging. Mentorship programs, which pair juveniles with positive role models, have been shown to be effective in reducing recidivism by providing guidance, support, and encouragement. A mentor who demonstrates empathy, accountability, and resilience can inspire juveniles to adopt these qualities in their own lives.

11.5 The Role of Neuropsychological Interventions in Policy and Practice

Neuropsychological interventions underscore the importance of a rehabilitation-focused approach to juvenile justice, one that prioritizes understanding and addressing the underlying causes of delinquent behavior. This approach contrasts with punitive models that emphasize retribution, as neuropsychological interventions seek to equip juveniles with the skills needed for positive change. Integrating neuropsychological insights into juvenile justice policies can lead to more effective, individualized treatment plans and reduce the risk of re-offending.

By incorporating neuropsychological assessments into the juvenile justice system, courts and clinicians can make more informed decisions about diversion, sentencing, and treatment. Young offenders who display significant neurocognitive impairments might benefit more from community-based programs and intensive therapy than from incarceration. A system that prioritizes treatment over punishment is better positioned to help juveniles reintegrate successfully into society.

In conclusion, reducing recidivism among juvenile offenders requires a comprehensive approach that combines early identification of risk factors, tailored neuropsychological assessments, and evidence-based intervention strategies. By focusing on building resilience and addressing cognitive and emotional challenges, neuropsychological interventions have the potential to break cycles of recidivism, offering juvenile offenders a chance to achieve meaningful and lasting rehabilitation. Through these measures, the juvenile justice system can support positive outcomes for young offenders, guiding them toward productive and law-abiding lives.

12 Importance of Early Intervention and Support

Early intervention during adolescence is a critical strategy for reducing the likelihood of long-term criminal behavior and promoting positive outcomes. Adolescence is a formative period characterized by rapid psychological, social, and neurological development, making it an ideal window for addressing issues that may predispose youth to criminal behavior. By identifying and supporting at-risk individuals early on, communities, schools, and families can significantly reduce the potential for future involvement in the justice system. Support systems, including mentorship and educational programs, provide a framework for positive development, resilience, and social integration.

12.1 The Impact of Early Intervention on Reducing Criminal Behavior

Research has shown that early intervention can substantially decrease the likelihood of juvenile delinquency and long-term criminal behavior (Aazami et al., 2023). Adolescents at risk of offending often exhibit behaviors or circumstances associated with risk, such as emotional dysregulation, impulsivity, substance abuse, or exposure to adverse environments like poverty, abuse, or family instability. These factors can limit youths' ability to make constructive choices, often leading to behavioral issues that, if unaddressed, may progress into criminal behavior.

Neurologically, adolescence is a time when the brain's executive functions—impulse control, planning, and judgment—are still developing. These are vital for making sound decisions, managing emotions, and establishing positive social relationships. Early intervention programs that focus on these areas help strengthen these cognitive skills, enhancing emotional regulation and social competence. For example, programs that teach problem-solving, decision-making, and emotional self-regulation can make a significant difference in how at-risk adolescents respond to challenges and stress. By instilling these skills early, youth are less likely to engage in risky behaviors that can lead to legal issues.

12.2 Role of Schools in Identifying At-Risk Youth

Schools play a pivotal role in identifying adolescents who may be at risk of engaging in criminal behavior. Teachers, school counselors, and administrators are often the first to notice signs of behavioral issues, learning disabilities, or emotional challenges. Schools are uniquely positioned to observe and address such behaviors in a structured setting, providing both the stability and support many at-risk adolescents lack in other aspects of their lives.

Implementing screening tools, regular check-ins, and social and emotional learning (SEL) programs can aid schools in identifying students who might benefit from early intervention. SEL programs, for example, focus on developing empathy, relationship skills, and emotional management, providing young people with tools to handle social and personal challenges constructively. Additionally, anti-bullying campaigns and peer support initiatives create a safer, more supportive environment for students. By creating a culture that values empathy and respect, schools can reduce negative behaviors that contribute to delinquency and provide a safe space for students to express their concerns and struggles.

Furthermore, collaboration between schools and mental health professionals can ensure that at-risk students receive appropriate support. For instance, school-based counseling services or partnerships with community mental health agencies can offer additional resources, such as family therapy, individual counseling, or group interventions. These services can address issues like anxiety, depression, and trauma, which, if left unaddressed, can contribute to negative coping mechanisms and behavioral problems.

12.3 The Role of Families and Communities in Early Intervention

Families and communities are essential to the early intervention process, providing a foundational layer of support that influences adolescents' behavioral and emotional development. Families can encourage positive behavior by establishing open lines of communication, setting clear expectations, and modeling healthy emotional regulation. When parents or caregivers are involved and supportive, adolescents are more likely to develop resilience, self-esteem, and a sense of responsibility.

Communities also contribute by fostering environments that promote healthy social interactions and provide constructive activities for young people. Community programs, such as recreational activities, youth clubs, and mentorship initiatives, offer adolescents an alternative to negative influences, such as gang involvement or substance abuse. They help fill the gaps that may be left by family or school environments and can offer stable and positive relationships with mentors or peers. Through these activities, adolescents learn social skills, teamwork, and problem-solving—all crucial for reducing risk factors associated with juvenile delinquency.

Mentorship programs, in particular, have been shown to be effective in reducing juvenile delinquency and promoting positive outcomes. A mentor can offer guidance, emotional support, and a sense of stability, which are especially important for youth who may not receive consistent support from family members. By building trust, mentors encourage adolescents to discuss their challenges and guide them toward constructive solutions, providing a model for healthy adult relationships. Moreover, mentors who have themselves overcome adversity can inspire youth to envision a positive future for themselves, showing them that it is possible to change and succeed despite past difficulties.

12.4 Educational Programs and Support Systems

Educational programs are essential components of early intervention, offering a pathway to personal and academic success for at-risk youth. Traditional educational settings do not always cater to the unique needs of every student, especially those with learning disabilities, emotional challenges, or behavioral issues. Programs designed to meet these needs—such as vocational training, alternative schooling, or individualized learning plans—help keep students engaged in their education and reduce their chances of dropping out, a risk factor strongly associated with future criminal behavior.

Programs focused on career and vocational training, for example, equip adolescents with practical skills that can lead to gainful employment, fostering self-sufficiency and reducing the allure of illegal activities as a means of income. Educational support programs that address learning disabilities or provide tutoring also play a role in enhancing self-esteem, as academic struggles are often a source of frustration and negative self-image for at-risk youth. These support systems provide alternatives to disengagement and encourage adolescents to view education as a pathway to success.

Interventions can also include therapeutic programs like cognitive behavioral therapy (CBT), which addresses maladaptive thinking patterns and promotes healthier ways of coping with stress and frustration. Adolescents who struggle with aggression, impulsivity, or negative self-concepts benefit from CBT because it helps them understand the connection between their thoughts, emotions, and behaviors, thereby fostering emotional regulation and improved decision-making. When combined with school and community support, these programs contribute to the development of well-rounded individuals less likely to engage in criminal activities.

The importance of early intervention and support for at-risk adolescents cannot be overstated. By addressing underlying issues during adolescence, the likelihood of criminal behavior and involvement with the justice system is significantly reduced. Schools, families, and communities are vital pillars in this effort, each contributing unique resources and perspectives to help guide young people toward positive futures. Schools identify and address behavioral and emotional issues, while families provide stability and model constructive behavior. Communities offer mentorship and positive activities that keep youth engaged and away from negative influences. Ultimately, successful early intervention relies on collaboration across these systems to create a cohesive support network that can respond effectively to the needs of at-risk youth. Through mentorship, educational programs, and therapeutic support, young people are given the tools to navigate challenges, build resilience, and make choices that lead to fulfilling, law-abiding lives. By investing in early intervention, society invests in a safer, healthier, and more positive future for all.

13 Promoting Resilience in Juvenile Offenders

Promoting resilience in juvenile offenders is essential for encouraging positive behavioral change and reducing recidivism. Resilience-building programs, which focus on fostering emotional strength and coping skills, provide at-risk youth with the psychological tools they need to overcome challenges and make constructive choices. By creating supportive environments that use positive reinforcement, resilience-based interventions empower young offenders to shift away from maladaptive behaviors and develop healthier coping mechanisms. Neuropsychology plays a critical role in identifying protective factors that contribute to resilience, allowing for tailored interventions that address the unique needs of juvenile offenders and increase their chances of successful rehabilitation.

13.1 The Concept of Resilience in Juvenile Offenders

Resilience is the capacity to adapt positively in the face of adversity, and it is especially relevant for juvenile offenders, many of whom have experienced difficult or traumatic backgrounds. Resilience allows individuals to overcome negative influences and make constructive decisions even when faced with significant challenges. For juvenile offenders, resilience-building involves developing emotional regulation, problem-solving skills, and social competence, all of which are essential for making better choices and avoiding criminal behaviors. Building resilience is a gradual process, but research shows that fostering resilience in at-risk youth reduces the likelihood of re-offending and facilitates their reintegration into society (Hodgkinson et al., 2020).

Juvenile offenders often come from environments that may lack supportive figures, stable family structures, or positive role models, which can make building resilience more challenging. Factors such as poverty, exposure to violence, family instability, or neglect increase vulnerability to maladaptive coping strategies, which can manifest in behavioral problems or criminal activity. By focusing on resilience, interventions aim to strengthen protective factors that empower juveniles to handle stress and adversity in constructive ways.

13.2 The Role of Resilience-Building Programs in Rehabilitation

Resilience-building programs are integral to juvenile rehabilitation, as they emphasize emotional development, self-esteem, and coping skills. Many juvenile offenders struggle with emotional regulation, impulsivity, and a limited ability to cope with stress. Programs that focus on building resilience address these issues by providing tools and techniques for handling emotions, fostering self-awareness, and teaching strategies to navigate difficult situations without resorting to aggression or criminal behavior.

These programs use a strengths-based approach that encourages young offenders to recognize their potential and focus on positive outcomes rather than past mistakes. Cognitive behavioral therapy (CBT) is commonly used in resilience-building programs, helping youth identify and modify negative thought patterns that contribute to maladaptive behaviors. For instance, if a juvenile offender tends to react aggressively when criticized, CBT can help them recognize this pattern, explore alternative responses, and develop healthier ways to express frustration.

In addition to CBT, some programs incorporate elements of mindfulness and stress management to improve emotional control and awareness. Mindfulness-based interventions encourage juveniles to focus on the present moment and develop greater control over impulsive behaviors. By practicing mindfulness, young offenders learn to recognize emotional triggers and reduce automatic responses, which is essential for managing situations that could lead to re-offending. Through resilience-building, juveniles gain greater self-efficacy, an essential factor for making constructive decisions and improving self-worth.

13.3 Positive Reinforcement and Supportive Environments

Supportive environments that emphasize positive reinforcement are crucial for promoting resilience. Many juvenile offenders have faced criticism and punitive responses throughout their lives, reinforcing negative self-perceptions and reducing their motivation to change. By contrast, resilience-building programs prioritize positive reinforcement, encouraging juveniles to view their strengths and successes as stepping stones toward a better future. Positive reinforcement is effective in enhancing motivation, as it helps juveniles feel recognized and valued, which bolsters self-esteem and confidence.

Supportive environments include settings such as group therapy sessions, mentorship programs, and peer support groups. Group therapy provides a structured space where young offenders can share their experiences, learn from each other, and feel supported. Mentorship programs, in which adult mentors provide guidance and encouragement, are also highly effective in fostering resilience. Mentors serve as positive role models, offering a stable relationship that many juvenile offenders may not have experienced before. The presence of a mentor who believes in their potential helps juveniles develop a sense of worth and motivates them to engage in constructive behaviors.

In addition to mentorship, peer support groups provide a sense of community and belonging that can help juveniles develop resilience. In these groups, individuals share similar challenges and experiences, which creates an environment of mutual support and understanding. Peer support fosters social connectedness and reduces feelings of isolation, promoting resilience by helping juveniles realize they are not alone in their struggles.

13.4 The Neuropsychology of Resilience and Protective Factors

Neuropsychology plays a vital role in understanding resilience in juvenile offenders, as it sheds light on the underlying cognitive and emotional processes that influence behavior. Protective factors—elements that enhance resilience and reduce the likelihood of maladaptive behavior—are an important focus in neuropsychological assessments of juvenile offenders. These factors include strong social connections, self-regulation skills, and problem-solving abilities, all of which are associated with reduced risk of re-offending.

Through neuropsychological assessments, professionals can identify specific areas where juveniles may lack resilience, allowing for personalized interventions. For example, if a neuropsychological assessment reveals that a juvenile offender has difficulty with impulse control or emotional regulation, targeted interventions such as cognitive–behavioral exercises can be applied to strengthen these skills. The neuropsychological insights gained from assessments help tailor resilience-building programs to address individual needs, ensuring that interventions are both relevant and effective.

Furthermore, neuropsychology highlights the importance of early interventions, as the adolescent brain is still developing, particularly in areas related to decision-making, impulse control, and emotional regulation. Early resilience-building interventions that focus on these developmental areas have a greater impact, helping juveniles develop the cognitive and emotional tools they need to resist criminal influences and adopt healthier behaviors.

13.5 Resilience-Building as a Long-Term Preventative Strategy

Promoting resilience is not only beneficial for the immediate rehabilitation of juvenile offenders but also serves as a preventative strategy for reducing recidivism in the long term. By equipping young people with coping skills, emotional regulation, and problem-solving abilities, resilience-building programs empower them to handle future stressors without resorting to criminal behavior. The skills gained through resilience-building programs are transferable to various aspects of life, including education, employment, and personal relationships, supporting overall well-being and reducing vulnerability to re-offending.

Long-term resilience is supported by continuous access to supportive networks and positive reinforcement, even after juveniles have exited the justice system. Communities play an important role in providing these ongoing resources, such as vocational training, educational support, and community service opportunities. By fostering a sense of belonging and connection, communities reinforce the resilience-building efforts initiated during rehabilitation, helping juveniles transition successfully into adulthood.

Building resilience in juvenile offenders is a powerful approach to rehabilitation, reducing the likelihood of re-offending and promoting positive outcomes. Resilience-building programs focus on developing emotional regulation, self-efficacy, and coping skills, which empower young people to make constructive choices even in challenging situations. Positive reinforcement and supportive environments, including mentorship and peer support, reinforce these efforts, encouraging juveniles to see themselves as capable of change. Neuropsychology plays a pivotal role in identifying the protective factors that enhance resilience, allowing for individualized interventions that address specific needs. By focusing on resilience, juvenile justice systems can foster long-term positive development, reducing the risk of recidivism and helping young offenders build fulfilling lives. Through continued support and engagement, resilience-building efforts extend beyond rehabilitation, enabling at-risk youth to transition successfully into adulthood and become constructive members of society.

14 Conclusion

The neuropsychology of juvenile offenders provides critical insights into how cognitive, emotional, and developmental factors contribute to delinquent behavior, emphasizing the need for tailored intervention strategies that address these specific vulnerabilities. Juvenile offenders often experience a range of developmental challenges, such as deficits in executive functioning, poor impulse control, and difficulties with emotional regulation, all of which increase their susceptibility to risky behaviors and limit their ability to make constructive choices. By understanding the neuropsychological profiles of juvenile offenders, professionals can design interventions that address these deficits directly, providing young people with the skills and support they need to avoid future criminal behavior and build healthier, more resilient lives.

One of the core findings in the neuropsychological study of juvenile offenders is that developmental vulnerabilities play a significant role in shaping behavior. Many juveniles in the justice system show impaired executive functions—such as planning, attention, impulse control, and decision-making—all of which are crucial for navigating social and personal challenges. These deficits are often compounded by psychosocial factors, including exposure to violence, family instability, and poor access to educational and mental health resources. Without early intervention, these developmental and environmental challenges can create a cycle of maladaptive behaviors, reinforcing criminal tendencies and increasing the risk of recidivism.

Effective intervention for juvenile offenders requires early, tailored rehabilitation programs that address these neuropsychological vulnerabilities. Programs that incorporate cognitive behavioral therapy (CBT), social skills training, and emotional regulation exercises are especially beneficial in promoting adaptive behaviors. Additionally, neuropsychological assessments help identify individual strengths and weaknesses, allowing clinicians and support teams to personalize interventions to suit each juvenile's unique profile. This personalized approach not only addresses specific cognitive deficits but also empowers juvenile offenders to recognize their potential for positive change. Through rehabilitative techniques that focus on building self-awareness, emotional control, and decision-making skills, these programs help juveniles develop resilience, better equipping them to face challenges and reduce future criminal behavior.

The role of support systems in rehabilitation cannot be overstated, as a strong, supportive environment is essential for sustaining the positive changes initiated in rehabilitative settings. Family, schools, and community networks are instrumental in reinforcing the skills learned in intervention programs. For instance, a supportive family can provide stability, guidance, and positive reinforcement, while schools and communities can offer educational and vocational opportunities, mentorship, and social support. Collectively, these resources enable juvenile offenders to establish constructive relationships, set goals, and envision a path forward that steers them away from crime.

Finally, neuropsychology highlights the importance of resilience as a protective factor that can prevent recidivism among juvenile offenders. By strengthening resilience, interventions reduce the likelihood of juveniles reverting to criminal behaviors even when faced with adversity. Resilience-building programs focus on fostering self-efficacy, problem-solving skills, and adaptive coping mechanisms, all of which help juveniles manage stress without turning to aggression or delinquency.

In conclusion, the neuropsychology of juvenile offenders underscores the importance of addressing developmental, cognitive, and psychosocial vulnerabilities to achieve lasting rehabilitation. Early intervention, targeted rehabilitation, and strong support systems offer juvenile offenders the chance to develop resilience and create a positive future. With these tools, juvenile justice systems can reduce recidivism, promote constructive development, and help young offenders integrate into society as responsible, capable individuals.

References

Aazami, A., Valek, R., Ponce, A. N., & Zare, H. (2023). Risk and protective factors and interventions for reducing juvenile delinquency: A systematic review. *Social Sciences, 12*(9), 474. https://doi.org/10.3390/socsci12090474

Ayres, T. C. (2020). Childhood trauma, problematic drug use and coping. *Deviant Behavior, 42*(5), 578–599. https://doi.org/10.1080/01639625.2020.1746132

Bozzay, M. L., Joy, L. N., & Verona, E. (2017). Family violence pathways and externalizing behavior in youth. *Journal of Interpersonal Violence, 35*(23–24), 5726–5752. https://doi.org/10.1177/0886260517724251

Coenen, E., Pleysier, S., & Put, J. (2021). Executive functions, self-control and juvenile delinquency. *Psychology Crime and Law, 28*(10), 1004–1023. https://doi.org/10.1080/1068316x.2021.1984480

Creemers, H. E., Van Logchem, E. K., Assink, M., & Asscher, J. J. (2022). Ramping up detention of young serious offenders: A safer future? *Trauma Violence & Abuse, 24*(4), 2863–2881. https://doi.org/10.1177/15248380221119514

Dumornay, N. M., Finegold, K. E., Chablani, A., Elkins, L., Krouch, S., Baldwin, M., Youn, S. J., Marques, L., Ressler, K. J., & Moreland-Capuia, A. (2022). Improved emotion regulation following a trauma-informed CBT-based intervention associates with reduced risk for recidivism in justice-involved emerging adults. *Frontiers in Psychiatry, 13*. https://doi.org/10.3389/fpsyt.2022.951429

Griffith, R. L., Nowalis, S., & Monroe-Gulick, A. (2024). Executive functioning and offending behavior: An updated meta-analysis. *Criminal Justice and Behavior, 51*(4), 528–551. https://doi.org/10.1177/00938548231225260

Hodgkinson, R., Beattie, S., Roberts, R., & Hardy, L. (2020). Psychological resilience interventions to reduce recidivism in young people: A systematic review. *Adolescent Research Review, 6*(4), 333–357. https://doi.org/10.1007/s40894-020-00138-x

Kang, S. (2023). *The effect of high school peers on juvenile delinquency*. ideas.repec.org. https://ideas.repec.org/a/kea/keappr/ker-20230101-39-1-05.html

Livingstone, N., Macdonald, G., & Carr, N. (2013). Restorative justice conferencing for reducing recidivism in young offenders (aged 7 to 21). *Cochrane Library, 2020*(6). https://doi.org/10.1002/14651858.cd008898.pub2

Lowe, C. J., Morton, J. B., & Reichelt, A. C. (2020). Adolescent obesity and dietary decision making—A brain-health perspective. *The Lancet Child & Adolescent Health, 4*(5), 388–396. https://doi.org/10.1016/s2352-4642(19)30404-3

Olsson, T. M., Långström, N., Skoog, T., Löfholm, C. A., Leander, L., Brolund, A., Ringborg, A., Nykänen, P., Syversson, A., & Sundell, K. (2021). Systematic review and meta-analysis of noninstitutional psychosocial interventions to prevent juvenile criminal recidivism. *Journal of Consulting and Clinical Psychology, 89*(6), 514–527. https://doi.org/10.1037/ccp0000652

Preventing Future Crime With Cognitive Behavioral Therapy | National Institute of Justice. (n.d.). National Institute of Justice. https://nij.ojp.gov/topics/articles/preventing-future-crime-cognitive-behavioral-therapy

Saladino, V., Lin, H., Zamparelli, E., & Verrastro, V. (2021). Neuroscience, empathy, and violent crime in an incarcerated population: A narrative review. *Frontiers in Psychology, 12*. https://doi.org/10.3389/fpsyg.2021.694212

Salinas, K. Z., & Venta, A. (2021). Testing the role of emotion dysregulation as a predictor of juvenile recidivism. *European Journal of Investigation in Health Psychology and Education, 11*(1), 83–95. https://doi.org/10.3390/ejihpe11010007

Schwalbe, C. S., Gearing, R. E., MacKenzie, M. J., Brewer, K. B., & Ibrahim, R. (2011). A meta-analysis of experimental studies of diversion programs for juvenile offenders. *Clinical Psychology Review, 32*(1), 26–33. https://doi.org/10.1016/j.cpr.2011.10.002

Sexton, T., & Turner, C. W. (2010). The effectiveness of functional family therapy for youth with behavioral problems in a community practice setting. *Journal of Family Psychology, 24*(3), 339–348. https://doi.org/10.1037/a0019406

Steinberg, L., Chung, H. L., & Little, M. (2004). Reentry of young offenders from the justice system. *Youth Violence and Juvenile Justice, 2*(1), 21–38. https://doi.org/10.1177/1541204003260045

Wagels, L., & Hernandez-Pena, L. (2024). Neural correlates of hostile attribution bias - A systematic review. *Aggression and Violent Behavior, 78*, 101975. https://doi.org/10.1016/j.avb.2024.101975

Neuropsychological Perspectives on Recidivism

1 Introduction

Recidivism, or the tendency of previously incarcerated individuals to reoffend, is a complex phenomenon with significant societal, economic, and psychological implications. Various psychological and social factors influence repeat offending, but increasingly, research is uncovering how neuropsychological factors play a critical role in driving recidivism. Neuropsychology examines the relationships between brain function and behavior, and this perspective offers a nuanced understanding of how cognitive deficits, neurobiological impairments, and psychosocial variables contribute to recidivism. A comprehensive neuropsychological approach can improve our ability to predict, manage, and reduce the risk of reoffending, thus contributing to more effective rehabilitation and prevention strategies within the criminal justice system.

1.1 Neuropsychological Factors and Recidivism

1. **Cognitive Impairments**

Cognitive impairments—particularly in executive functions like impulse control, decision-making, planning, and emotional regulation—are linked with higher rates of recidivism. Executive functions rely on the integrity of the prefrontal cortex, which is often compromised in individuals who display criminal behaviors. Deficits in attention, working memory, and abstract reasoning further limit an individual's capacity to assess risks, foresee consequences, and avoid impulsive behaviors that could lead to criminal activities. Studies show that individuals with pronounced cognitive impairments may struggle to conform to societal

© The Author(s), under exclusive license to Springer Nature Switzerland AG 2025

K. J. Reddy, *Foundations of Criminal Forensic Neuropsychology*,
https://doi.org/10.1007/978-3-031-83771-5_16

norms and resist engaging in illegal activities, ultimately leading to repeated interactions with the criminal justice system (Miller, 2014).

2. **Neurobiological Underpinnings**

Neurobiological impairments, particularly those related to the prefrontal cortex, limbic system, and neurotransmitter systems (such as serotonin and dopamine), are strongly associated with aggressive, impulsive, and risk-taking behaviors. Damage to the prefrontal cortex, often linked to traumatic brain injuries (TBIs), can impair the brain's capacity to process social cues, empathize with others, and regulate emotions—factors essential to social adaptation. Research on TBIs, for instance, has shown that individuals with such injuries are at a higher risk of criminal behavior and recidivism due to their compromised ability to control impulses and emotions (Ling et al., 2019). Structural abnormalities or dysfunctions in the amygdala and other limbic structures further contribute to impaired threat recognition and emotional regulation, which may increase the likelihood of violent or impulsive actions that lead to reoffending.

3. **Psychosocial Influences**

Neuropsychological factors interact with various psychosocial influences, including socioeconomic status, family history, and exposure to trauma, which can amplify the risk of recidivism. Early adverse childhood experiences, including physical or emotional abuse, have a lasting impact on brain development and can lead to maladaptive coping strategies. In environments where individuals experience chronic stress, they may develop heightened sensitivity to stressors, coupled with limited coping skills. These factors, compounded by neuropsychological impairments, increase the likelihood of reoffending, as these individuals may resort to familiar patterns of behavior, particularly under stressful conditions or social pressure.

1.2 Importance of Understanding Neuropsychological Factors in Recidivism

1. **Predictive Potential**

Incorporating neuropsychological assessments into the criminal justice system can enhance the accuracy of risk assessments, helping to identify individuals at high risk of recidivism. Assessment tools that evaluate cognitive functioning, impulse control, emotional regulation, and executive functions can inform more tailored interventions. For instance, individuals with pronounced executive function deficits may benefit from interventions that focus on impulse control and decision-making strategies, while those with emotional regulation impairments may require therapy that targets affective processing and stress management.

2. **Rehabilitation and Management Strategies**

Effective rehabilitation strategies for reducing recidivism should address neuropsychological deficits. Rehabilitation programs that include cognitive-behavioral therapy (CBT) are highly effective for individuals with cognitive impairments, as they promote behavioral modification, cognitive restructuring, and emotional regulation. Neurofeedback, a neuropsychological intervention that uses EEG to help individuals regulate brain activity, has shown promise in enhancing attention, emotional regulation, and impulse control, all of which are crucial for minimizing reoffending risk. Moreover, mindfulness-based interventions can promote self-regulation by strengthening brain networks related to attention and executive function, potentially reducing the impulsive and aggressive tendencies associated with recidivism.

3. **Improving Judicial Outcomes**

A neuropsychological perspective on recidivism can help shape judicial policies that consider individual differences in cognitive and neurobiological functioning. For instance, individuals with neuropsychological deficits may require different sentencing approaches or conditions of probation that reflect their unique rehabilitation needs. Courts and parole boards could consider neuropsychological assessments when evaluating parole eligibility, potentially granting leniency to those showing significant improvement in cognitive and emotional regulation abilities through rehabilitation. Such an approach could lead to more personalized and fair judicial outcomes that acknowledge neuropsychological variability among offenders.

1.3 The Role of Neuropsychology in Reducing Recidivism

1. **Assessment and Screening**

Neuropsychologists play an essential role in conducting assessments that identify cognitive and emotional deficits in offenders. Standardized neuropsychological tests, such as the Wisconsin Card Sorting Test (WCST) or the Tower of London Test, are effective in measuring executive function, impulse control, and planning abilities. Using these assessments as part of routine evaluations for offenders can help identify individuals at high risk of recidivism due to specific neuropsychological impairments. Additionally, neuropsychological screenings can identify offenders who would benefit from specialized interventions, improving rehabilitation outcomes and reducing the likelihood of reoffending.

2. **Developing Targeted Interventions**

With insights from neuropsychological assessments, interventions can be tailored to meet individual needs. For example, neurofeedback training has shown promise in enhancing self-regulation and reducing impulsivity. In cases where traumatic brain injury or other neurobiological impairments contribute to recidivism risk, neurorehabilitation therapies that promote neural plasticity and cognitive recovery may help restore functioning. By addressing the specific neuropsychological needs of offenders, neuropsychologists can support the development of individualized rehabilitation plans that mitigate the risk factors for reoffending.

3. **Educating Stakeholders**

Integrating neuropsychological expertise into criminal justice policy requires educating stakeholders, including judges, attorneys, and correctional officers, about the influence of neuropsychological factors on behavior. Workshops, training programs, and expert testimony in court can increase awareness of how cognitive and emotional impairments affect decision-making, impulse control, and social behavior. By fostering a more informed criminal justice environment, neuropsychologists can advocate for policies that accommodate the neuropsychological needs of offenders, promoting a more rehabilitative and less punitive approach to criminal justice.

Understanding the neuropsychological factors underlying recidivism offers a crucial avenue for addressing the challenge of repeat offending. By examining cognitive deficits, neurobiological impairments, and psychosocial influences, neuropsychology provides insights that can enhance our ability to predict, manage, and reduce recidivism. Effective assessment, intervention, and education strategies rooted in neuropsychology can transform how the criminal justice system addresses recidivism, contributing to better rehabilitation outcomes and reducing the societal and individual burdens associated with repeat offending. A neuropsychological perspective not only deepens our understanding of recidivism but also fosters a more humane, evidence-based approach to justice, where prevention and rehabilitation are prioritized over punishment.

2 Neurobiological Foundations of Recidivism

While environmental and social circumstances play significant roles in determining recidivism risk, neurobiological foundations, such as brain structure abnormalities and neurochemical imbalances, also significantly contribute to reoffending behaviors. Key neurobiological vulnerabilities include impairments in impulse control, decision-making, and emotional regulation, which are essential for pro-social behavior. Traumatic brain injuries (TBIs) and neurodevelopmental disorders further increase susceptibility to reoffending by compromising critical brain functions. Understanding these neurobiological underpinnings can pave the way for targeted interventions and preventive strategies to reduce recidivism.

2.1 *Brain Structures Associated with Impulse Control, Decision-Making, and Emotional Regulation*

1. **Prefrontal Cortex (PFC)**

The prefrontal cortex (PFC) is central to higher-order cognitive functions, including impulse control, decision-making, planning, and emotional regulation. Different regions within the PFC, particularly the dorsolateral prefrontal cortex (DLPFC) and the ventromedial prefrontal cortex (VMPFC), play distinct roles in these processes. The DLPFC is critical for executive functions like working memory and attention, which aid individuals in making reasoned decisions rather than acting impulsively. The VMPFC, on the other hand, is associated with processing emotions and evaluating the consequences of actions, which helps in making socially appropriate decisions. Damage or underdevelopment in these regions, often seen in individuals with histories of antisocial behavior, correlates with increased impulsivity, poor judgment, and heightened recidivism risk.

2. **Amygdala**

The amygdala, a key structure within the limbic system, is involved in processing emotions, especially those related to fear and aggression. In a healthy brain, the amygdala functions in conjunction with the PFC to modulate emotional responses to various situations, helping an individual respond appropriately to social cues. However, in individuals with diminished amygdala function or connectivity issues between the amygdala and the PFC, emotional responses can become dysregulated. This dysregulation often manifests as heightened aggression, reduced empathy, and impulsive decision-making, which are common traits in repeat offenders. Studies have shown that reduced amygdala volume or impaired amygdala function is associated with an increased likelihood of reoffending, as these individuals struggle to control aggressive impulses and may lack sensitivity to the emotional consequences of their actions (Willis, n.d.).

3. **Anterior Cingulate Cortex (ACC)**

The anterior cingulate cortex (ACC) is involved in error monitoring, impulse control, and decision-making. It helps individuals recognize mistakes and adjust their behavior accordingly, playing a role in learning from past experiences and adapting behavior to avoid negative consequences. Dysfunction in the ACC can lead to an impaired ability to learn from punishment or to recognize and respond to social cues that discourage reoffending. Research suggests that lower ACC activity is associated with poor impulse control and a reduced ability to modify behavior, making individuals more prone to repeat offenses even after experiencing the legal and social consequences of their actions (Ghahramani et al., 2016).

2.2 Neurochemical Imbalances Contributing to Risk-Seeking Behavior and Impulsivity

1. **Dopamine**

Dopamine, a neurotransmitter associated with reward processing, plays a pivotal role in the regulation of motivation, pleasure, and risk-seeking behavior. Elevated dopamine levels, particularly in the mesolimbic reward pathway, can increase tendencies toward impulsive and risk-taking behaviors. In the context of criminal behavior, individuals with heightened dopamine responses may be more prone to seeking immediate rewards without consideration of potential negative consequences, leading to an increased likelihood of reoffending. Additionally, research has shown that dopaminergic dysfunction is often linked with addictive behaviors, further compounding recidivism risk by making it harder for individuals to resist engaging in risky or illicit activities that provide immediate gratification (Volkow et al., 2010).

2. **Serotonin**

Serotonin is a neurotransmitter critical for regulating mood, impulse control, and aggression. Low serotonin levels have been implicated in impulsive aggression and increased vulnerability to external stressors. Individuals with serotonin imbalances may struggle with frustration tolerance, exhibit heightened aggression, and fail to control impulsive responses. Low serotonin levels are commonly observed in individuals with antisocial personality traits and are associated with an increased propensity for aggressive and impulsive behavior, both of which are linked to recidivism. Medications that help to balance serotonin levels, such as selective serotonin reuptake inhibitors (SSRIs), have been shown to reduce impulsive aggression, suggesting that therapeutic regulation of serotonin could be beneficial in reducing reoffending rates.

3. **GABA and Glutamate**

Gamma-aminobutyric acid (GABA) is the brain's primary inhibitory neurotransmitter, while glutamate is the primary excitatory neurotransmitter. A balance between GABA and glutamate is crucial for maintaining a stable emotional state and cognitive function. Imbalances in this system can lead to hyperexcitability in brain areas associated with impulse control, such as the PFC. For instance, low GABA activity or excessive glutamate can result in increased impulsivity, aggression, and susceptibility to stress, heightening the likelihood of reoffending. Given that stress often triggers maladaptive behaviors, imbalances in the GABA-glutamate system can make it more difficult for individuals to regulate their responses to stressors and avoid impulsive or aggressive actions that could lead to criminal behavior.

2.3 Neurobiological Vulnerabilities Increasing Susceptibility to Reoffending

1. **Traumatic Brain Injuries (TBI)**

Traumatic brain injuries (TBI), particularly those affecting the frontal lobe, are common among incarcerated individuals and are linked to higher rates of recidivism. TBIs can impair the PFC's capacity for impulse control, planning, and emotional regulation, making it difficult for individuals to control aggressive tendencies or resist impulsive actions. Individuals with TBIs may also experience emotional dysregulation, difficulties with social cognition, and reduced empathy, all of which increase the risk of reoffending. Studies have shown that individuals with a history of TBI have a higher likelihood of engaging in aggressive behaviors and a reduced ability to benefit from rehabilitation programs that rely on self-regulation and reflection, further compounding recidivism risk (Fournier, n.d.).

2. **Neurodevelopmental Disorders**

Neurodevelopmental disorders such as attention-deficit/hyperactivity disorder (ADHD) and conduct disorder are also associated with an increased risk of recidivism. Individuals with ADHD, for example, often struggle with impulse control, attentional regulation, and delayed gratification due to functional abnormalities in the PFC and associated networks. Conduct disorder, characterized by aggressive and antisocial behavior in childhood, is often a precursor to adult antisocial personality disorder. Both conditions are linked with heightened risk for criminal behavior and recidivism, as these individuals may lack the cognitive resources needed to avoid risky or impulsive actions and struggle to adapt to the expectations of the criminal justice system. Targeted interventions addressing these neurodevelopmental vulnerabilities, such as cognitive-behavioral therapy and medication, can help reduce reoffending rates by providing individuals with tools to better manage their impulsivity and risk-seeking tendencies.

The neurobiological foundations of recidivism underscore the role of brain structures, neurochemical imbalances, and neurobiological vulnerabilities in shaping behaviors that increase reoffending risk. Impairments in the prefrontal cortex, amygdala, and anterior cingulate cortex, along with neurotransmitter imbalances in dopamine, serotonin, and GABA/glutamate systems, contribute to impulsivity, poor decision-making, and emotional dysregulation. These neurobiological factors are further compounded by vulnerabilities arising from TBIs and neurodevelopmental disorders, making certain individuals more susceptible to reoffending. A comprehensive understanding of these neurobiological underpinnings can inform targeted rehabilitation and prevention strategies within the criminal justice system, contributing to more effective and sustainable efforts to reduce recidivism.

3 Cognitive Factors Contributing to Recidivism

While recidivism is influenced by multiple factors, cognitive aspects play a fundamental role in shaping individuals' likelihood of reoffending. Key cognitive factors associated with recidivism include deficits in executive functioning, cognitive distortions, maladaptive thinking patterns, and poor decision-making abilities. These cognitive deficits can impair individuals' ability to assess the risks of their actions, predict consequences, and regulate impulsive responses, thereby reinforcing criminal behaviors and increasing the likelihood of reoffending. Addressing these cognitive vulnerabilities is crucial for designing effective interventions aimed at reducing recidivism rates.

3.1 Deficits in Executive Functioning and Their Link to Recidivism

1. **Overview of Executive Functions**

Executive functions are a set of cognitive processes, including working memory, cognitive flexibility, and inhibitory control, that are essential for goal-directed behavior, planning, and self-regulation. These functions are predominantly governed by the prefrontal cortex, an area that is often underdeveloped or impaired in individuals who engage in criminal activities. Deficits in executive functioning can hinder one's ability to make reasoned decisions, regulate emotions, and avoid impulsive actions, all of which are crucial in resisting criminal impulses and adjusting to societal norms.

2. **Impulsivity and Inhibitory Control**

A significant number of individuals with criminal tendencies exhibit heightened impulsivity, which refers to the inability to delay gratification or resist urges that are harmful in the long run. Impaired inhibitory control, a core component of executive functioning, plays a key role in this tendency. Individuals with poor inhibitory control struggle to suppress impulsive behaviors, which can manifest in criminal actions that provide immediate rewards but come with severe consequences. Studies have shown that individuals with lower levels of inhibitory control and higher impulsivity are more likely to reoffend, as they tend to prioritize short-term gains over long-term consequences (Bell & Polaschek, 2016).

3. **Planning and Problem-Solving Deficits**

Effective planning and problem-solving are essential for adapting to everyday challenges and making constructive decisions. Individuals with deficits in these executive functions often fail to consider alternative courses of action or recognize the steps needed to achieve a goal without resorting to criminal behavior. Without adequate problem-solving skills, these individuals may rely on criminal means to meet their needs or resolve conflicts, increasing their risk of reoffending. Research indicates that recidivists commonly display deficits in these areas, which impairs their ability to follow through with rehabilitation programs or adapt to societal expectations following release (Recidivism | National Institute of Justice, n.d.).

4. **Working Memory and Attention**

Working memory and attentional control are also vital executive functions that affect one's ability to process information, hold relevant details in mind, and make informed decisions. Individuals with poor working memory may struggle to keep rules, laws, and social norms in mind when confronted with temptations or challenges. They may also have difficulty remembering past consequences, leading to repeated offending. Poor attention further exacerbates this issue by reducing focus on long-term goals and encouraging distractibility, which can lead to risky decisions.

3.2 *Cognitive Distortions and Maladaptive Thinking Patterns that Reinforce Criminal Behavior*

1. **Understanding Cognitive Distortions**

Cognitive distortions refer to biased, irrational thought patterns that individuals use to interpret reality in a way that justifies or rationalizes their behavior. In the context of criminality, cognitive distortions can include justifications for violating social norms, minimizing the impact of harmful actions on others, and perceiving oneself as a victim of circumstances. These distorted beliefs reinforce criminal behavior by allowing individuals to sidestep feelings of guilt or shame and to continue engaging in harmful activities without internal conflict.

2. **Common Cognitive Distortions in Criminal Behavior**

Among the cognitive distortions commonly found in criminal populations are externalization of blame, entitlement, minimization of harm, and hostile attribution bias. Externalization of blame involves attributing responsibility for one's actions to external factors, such as poverty, discrimination, or past trauma, rather than acknowledging personal responsibility. Entitlement allows individuals to believe they deserve certain privileges regardless of the legal or moral implications. Minimization of harm enables them to downplay the consequences of their actions on others, while hostile attribution bias leads them to interpret neutral situations or interactions as hostile, justifying aggressive responses.

3. **Reinforcement of Criminal Behavior through Distorted Thinking**

These maladaptive thinking patterns can create a self-sustaining cycle of criminal behavior. For example, individuals who believe that they have been treated unfairly by society may feel justified in breaking the law as a form of retribution. Similarly, those who minimize the harm caused by their actions are unlikely to feel remorse, reducing their motivation to change their behavior. The persistence of such distortions can contribute to recidivism, as individuals may perceive themselves as victims of circumstance rather than agents capable of change. Addressing these distortions through cognitive-behavioral interventions is critical for helping individuals adopt healthier, more realistic ways of thinking.

3.3 Poor Decision-Making Abilities and Inability to Foresee Consequences as Predictors of Reoffending

1. **The Role of Decision-Making in Criminal Behavior**

Decision-making is a complex cognitive process that involves evaluating risks and benefits, predicting outcomes, and selecting the best course of action from multiple options. In individuals prone to recidivism, decision-making processes are often impaired, leading to poor choices that prioritize immediate gains over long-term consequences. Many recidivists exhibit a "present bias," a cognitive tendency to favor immediate rewards even if they lead to adverse outcomes later on. This shortsighted approach to decision-making significantly increases the likelihood of reoffending.

2. **Inability to Foresee Consequences and Risk Assessment**

Effective decision-making relies on the ability to anticipate the consequences of one's actions, which requires intact executive functioning and future-oriented thinking. Many individuals who reoffend have difficulty with this aspect of decision-making, often acting on impulse without considering the repercussions. This inability to foresee consequences is particularly problematic in the criminal justice context, where failure to consider the legal and social consequences of one's actions can lead to repeated offenses. Furthermore, deficits in risk assessment may make individuals more prone to engaging in high-risk behaviors, as they either underestimate the potential harm or lack awareness of alternative, safer options.

3. **Behavioral and Cognitive Interventions for Enhancing Decision-Making Skills**

Cognitive-behavioral therapy (CBT) and decision-making training programs are frequently used in correctional settings to improve decision-making skills in individuals at high risk of reoffending. By addressing cognitive biases, teaching problem-solving techniques, and promoting future-oriented thinking, these interventions can help individuals better evaluate the long-term consequences of their actions and reduce impulsivity. Studies indicate that CBT-based programs focused on decision-making skills can decrease recidivism rates, as individuals learn to recognize the thought processes that lead to criminal behavior and adopt more constructive alternatives (Batastini, 2010).

Cognitive factors, including deficits in executive functioning, cognitive distortions, and poor decision-making abilities, play a significant role in recidivism. Impaired executive functions such as impulse control, planning, and working memory hinder individuals' capacity to regulate behavior, making them more likely to reoffend. Cognitive distortions and maladaptive thinking patterns provide internal justification for criminal behavior, reinforcing attitudes that sustain reoffending. Lastly, poor decision-making abilities and an inability to foresee consequences compound the likelihood of recidivism by leading individuals to prioritize immediate rewards over long-term goals. Addressing these cognitive deficits through targeted cognitive-behavioral interventions can aid in reducing recidivism, fostering healthier decision-making, and ultimately promoting successful reintegration into society.

4 Psychosocial Elements Influencing Recidivism

While cognitive and neurobiological aspects contribute significantly to recidivism, psychosocial influences also play a central role. Understanding these influences is essential for developing effective interventions that reduce the rates of reoffending. Key psychosocial factors affecting recidivism include socio-environmental influences such as poverty, lack of social support, and unstable living conditions; the impact of peer pressure and dysfunctional relationships; and the exacerbating effect of mental health issues, particularly substance abuse, on the risk of reoffending. By addressing these elements, criminal justice systems and rehabilitation programs can create more supportive environments for reintegration and reduce the social costs associated with recidivism.

4.1 Impact of Socio-Environmental Factors on Recidivism

1. **Poverty and Economic Disadvantage**

Poverty and economic insecurity are powerful predictors of criminal behavior and recidivism. Individuals released from incarceration who return to economically disadvantaged communities face limited opportunities for employment, which in turn heightens the likelihood of reoffending. Without a stable income, these individuals may resort to criminal activities as a means of survival, especially if they lack the skills or qualifications required for gainful employment. Furthermore, the stress associated with financial instability can exacerbate impulsive decision-making, which can lead to criminal behavior even when alternative options are available.

2. **Lack of Social Support**

Social support plays a critical role in the successful reintegration of formerly incarcerated individuals. People who have strong, supportive relationships with family members, friends, or community networks are better equipped to navigate post-incarceration challenges and resist returning to criminal behavior. However, many individuals released from prison lack this essential support due to strained family relationships, social stigma, or ostracization from their communities. This absence of positive social connections can lead to feelings of isolation and hopelessness, which increase the likelihood of relapse into criminal activities. Research shows that individuals who have meaningful social bonds and community connections are less likely to reoffend, highlighting the importance of social support in reducing recidivism (Mowen et al., 2018).

3. **Unstable Living Conditions**

Housing instability is another significant socio-environmental factor influencing recidivism. Formerly incarcerated individuals often encounter barriers to securing stable housing due to a lack of financial resources, legal restrictions, or societal discrimination against people with criminal records. This instability creates an environment of uncertainty, leaving individuals vulnerable to influences that may drive them back to crime. Studies indicate that stable housing arrangements reduce the likelihood of reoffending, as secure housing fosters a sense of stability and belonging that can positively affect behavior (Jacobs & Gottlieb, 2020). Conversely, homelessness or unstable living conditions can push individuals toward criminal activities for survival, increasing the risk of recidivism.

4.2 Influence of Peer Pressure and Dysfunctional Relationships on Repeated Criminal Behavior

1. **Impact of Peer Associations on Criminal Behavior**

Associating with peers who engage in criminal activities is a significant predictor of recidivism, especially for individuals who lack other forms of social support. After release, individuals who resume relationships with criminally involved peers are more likely to reengage in illegal behavior. Peer pressure exerts a strong influence on individuals, especially when combined with feelings of loyalty or a desire to belong. Studies show that former offenders who maintain close ties with pro-criminal peer groups have a higher risk of reoffending, as these relationships can reinforce criminal norms and behaviors (Rokven et al., 2016).

2. **Dysfunctional Family Relationships**

Dysfunctional family dynamics, such as domestic violence, substance abuse, or mental health issues, can contribute to the cycle of recidivism. Returning to a family environment characterized by conflict or instability can trigger stress responses and maladaptive coping mechanisms, increasing the likelihood of criminal behavior. In contrast, a supportive family environment can serve as a protective factor, helping individuals to make positive changes and avoid reoffending. Programs that focus on family therapy and rebuilding family relationships can be beneficial in addressing this risk factor by promoting healthier, more supportive home environments for individuals at risk of recidivism.

3. **Romantic Relationships and Intimate Partner Influence**

Romantic relationships also play a significant role in either supporting or undermining the reintegration process. Healthy, supportive relationships can offer emotional stability and motivation to stay on a positive path, reducing the risk of recidivism. However, relationships marked by dysfunction or codependency, especially those involving substance abuse or criminal behavior, can have the opposite effect. Studies indicate that intimate partner influence can lead to recidivism when individuals feel pressured to engage in criminal activities to maintain their relationship (Wyse et al., 2014). Rehabilitation efforts that emphasize healthy relationship dynamics and offer counseling on managing relationship stressors can help mitigate this risk factor.

4.3 Role of Mental Health Issues and Substance Abuse in Exacerbating the Risk of Recidivism

1. **Mental Health Disorders and Criminal Behavior**

Mental health disorders such as depression, anxiety, bipolar disorder, and schizophrenia can increase vulnerability to criminal behavior, particularly if left untreated. These conditions can impair judgment, reduce impulse control, and diminish individuals' capacity to make reasoned decisions. Furthermore, individuals with untreated mental health issues may experience symptoms that impair their ability to navigate social and economic challenges, heightening their risk of recidivism. Research shows that recidivism rates are significantly higher among individuals with mental health disorders, underscoring the need for accessible mental health services within the criminal justice system (Lamberti, 2016).

2. **Substance Abuse as a Recidivism Risk Factor**

Substance abuse is one of the most significant risk factors for recidivism. Addiction not only contributes directly to criminal behavior, such as drug-related offenses, but also affects cognitive functioning, including decision-making, self-control, and problem-solving skills. Substance abuse disorders are associated with impaired impulse control and risk-taking behavior, both of which contribute to the likelihood of reoffending. Furthermore, drug or alcohol dependency often leads individuals to prioritize obtaining substances over law-abiding behavior. Substance abuse treatment programs within and outside correctional facilities are critical for addressing this factor, as they help individuals develop healthier coping mechanisms and reduce dependency-related criminal behavior.

3. **Dual Diagnosis and the Impact on Recidivism**

Many individuals at risk of recidivism suffer from a dual diagnosis, meaning they experience both a mental health disorder and substance abuse disorder. This combination can be particularly challenging to address, as substance use often exacerbates mental health symptoms and vice versa. Dual-diagnosis individuals may require more intensive, integrated treatment to address the complex interactions between their mental health and addiction issues. Studies indicate that untreated dual diagnosis significantly increases recidivism risk, as individuals are left struggling with compounded challenges (Hegner, 1998). Programs that integrate mental health and substance abuse treatment show promising results in reducing reoffending rates for this population, as they address both disorders concurrently.

Psychosocial factors, including socio-environmental conditions, peer and family influences, and mental health issues, play a crucial role in influencing recidivism. Economic disadvantage, lack of social support, and unstable living situations create barriers to successful reintegration and increase the likelihood of reoffending. Peer pressure and dysfunctional relationships, particularly with criminally involved peers or family members, can reinforce criminal behavior and hinder individuals' efforts to reintegrate positively. Additionally, mental health issues, especially when accompanied by substance abuse, exacerbate the risk of recidivism by impairing judgment, impulse control, and decision-making abilities.

Addressing these psychosocial factors is essential for reducing recidivism rates and promoting successful reintegration. Effective intervention programs must consider these elements, offering mental health and substance abuse treatment, supporting stable housing, and fostering positive social relationships. By addressing the root causes and supporting individuals in overcoming psychosocial challenges, criminal justice systems can better assist individuals in breaking the cycle of reoffending and achieving lasting change.

5 Challenges in Assessing Recidivism Risk

Assessing the risk of recidivism is essential for informing decisions regarding sentencing, parole, and rehabilitation. The accuracy of these assessments holds significant implications for both public safety and the well-being of offenders. However, evaluating recidivism risk, especially from a neuropsychological perspective, presents unique challenges. The complexities involved in conducting neuropsychological evaluations, the limitations of traditional risk assessment tools in capturing neuropsychological and cognitive variables, and the need for integrating neuropsychological data into forensic assessments all contribute to the intricate landscape of recidivism risk assessment. Understanding these challenges can lead to more accurate assessments and better-informed decision-making in the criminal justice system.

5.1 Complexities of Conducting Neuropsychological Evaluations for Predicting Recidivism

1. **Diverse Neuropsychological Profiles of Offenders**

Offenders exhibit a wide range of neuropsychological profiles due to varying backgrounds, developmental histories, and experiences of trauma, substance abuse, or neurological conditions. Conducting neuropsychological assessments to predict recidivism requires careful consideration of these diverse factors. Traumatic brain injuries, neurodevelopmental disorders, or neurocognitive deficits such as poor impulse control or executive dysfunction can significantly influence behavior, including the likelihood of reoffending. However, identifying and interpreting these cognitive impairments in a way that accurately predicts future risk remains challenging. Traditional assessments may overlook nuanced variations in neuropsychological functioning that can affect recidivism, underscoring the need for specialized tools and expertise in this field.

2. **Diagnostic and Ethical Challenges**

The process of conducting neuropsychological assessments for recidivism prediction can also raise ethical concerns. Offenders undergoing evaluations may experience heightened levels of stress, which can influence their cognitive performance, leading to results that may not be entirely reflective of their typical behavior or risk level. Additionally, assessments conducted in forensic settings can introduce biases, as evaluators may consciously or unconsciously adjust their evaluations based on the offender's history or legal context. This can compromise the objectivity and validity of the assessment process. Ensuring that neuropsychological assessments are conducted ethically and with minimal external influence is essential for obtaining accurate and reliable results in recidivism prediction.

3. **Technical and Logistical Barriers**

Conducting neuropsychological evaluations requires specialized knowledge, training, and equipment that may not always be available within correctional settings. Many facilities lack access to neuropsychologists, and obtaining a comprehensive neuropsychological evaluation can be costly and time-consuming. The scarcity of resources and expertise limits the ability to conduct these assessments consistently across all offenders. Additionally, neuropsychological testing can be labor-intensive, requiring time for administering, scoring, and interpreting results. These logistical challenges hinder the widespread use of neuropsychological evaluations in routine recidivism assessments, limiting the ability to capture the full spectrum of cognitive and neurological factors relevant to reoffending.

5.2 Limitations of Traditional Risk Assessment Tools in Accounting for Neuropsychological and Cognitive Factors

1. **Over-Reliance on Historical and Demographic Data**

Many traditional risk assessment tools, such as the Level of Service Inventory-Revised (LSI-R) or the Static-99, rely heavily on historical, demographic, and behavioral data to estimate an offender's likelihood of reoffending. While these tools provide valuable insights, they often fail to account for individual differences in cognitive functioning and neurological health. Cognitive impairments, mental health conditions, and neurological disorders can affect behavior in ways that are not captured by static risk factors such as age, criminal history, or socioeconomic background. This reliance on demographic data can result in inaccurate predictions, as the tools do not fully address the neuropsychological underpinnings of criminal behavior and recidivism.

2. **Lack of Sensitivity to Cognitive Impairments and Executive Dysfunction**

Traditional tools also often lack sensitivity to cognitive impairments, such as deficits in memory, attention, or executive functioning, that are strongly associated with recidivism risk. Executive dysfunction, for example, is linked to poor impulse control and decision-making, which are critical factors in reoffending. Without accounting for these cognitive deficits, risk assessments may overlook individuals who present significant neuropsychological vulnerabilities. Consequently, individuals with neurological conditions such as traumatic brain injury (TBI), attention-deficit/hyperactivity disorder (ADHD), or neurodegenerative diseases may receive assessments that do not fully reflect their risk level, leading to either overestimation or underestimation of their propensity to reoffend.

3. **Predictive Limitations in High-Risk Populations**

For high-risk populations, such as those with histories of violence or substance abuse, traditional assessment tools may provide less reliable predictions. Neuropsychological factors, particularly those associated with aggression, impulsivity, and risk-seeking behaviors, are not adequately captured by traditional models. Additionally, individuals with high impulsivity or aggressive tendencies may display cognitive biases and distorted decision-making patterns that influence their risk profile. Traditional assessments, which are primarily designed to evaluate static and historical data, do not adequately capture these dynamic risk factors, limiting the effectiveness of predictions for individuals with complex cognitive and neuropsychological profiles.

5.3 Need for Incorporating Neuropsychological Data into Forensic Assessments to Enhance Accuracy

1. **Improving Individualized Risk Assessment**

Integrating neuropsychological data into recidivism assessments could allow for more individualized, accurate evaluations of offenders. Neuropsychological data provides insights into specific cognitive, emotional, and neurological traits that contribute to an individual's likelihood of reoffending. By including this information, assessors can better identify high-risk offenders who may not be adequately flagged by traditional tools. For example, individuals with deficits in impulse control or emotional regulation can be identified as needing targeted interventions. Including neuropsychological assessments in forensic evaluations allows for a more personalized approach that considers the full range of factors influencing criminal behavior, ultimately leading to better-informed recommendations for management, treatment, or intervention.

2. **Enhancing Predictive Validity of Assessments**

Including neuropsychological variables in risk assessments has the potential to enhance the predictive validity of these tools, especially when assessing individuals with complex behavioral and cognitive profiles. Neuropsychological data can provide additional dimensions for evaluating risk, such as impulsivity, attention deficits, or emotional dysregulation, which are directly relevant to recidivism. For instance, research shows that individuals with poor executive functioning are more likely to engage in high-risk behaviors, including criminal activities (Norman et al., 2022). By capturing these neuropsychological factors, risk assessment tools can offer a more comprehensive and accurate prediction of recidivism, helping criminal justice systems make better decisions regarding sentencing, rehabilitation, and release.

3. **Informing Targeted Interventions and Treatment Plans**

Incorporating neuropsychological data into recidivism assessments also provides valuable information for developing targeted interventions. Individuals identified with cognitive impairments, for example, could benefit from specific cognitive rehabilitation programs designed to improve executive functioning and impulse control. Offenders with emotional dysregulation may respond well to treatments focused on anger management or emotion regulation. By tailoring interventions to address specific neuropsychological vulnerabilities, practitioners can better support offenders' reintegration efforts, reducing the likelihood of recidivism. This approach not only enhances the effectiveness of rehabilitation programs but also contributes to a more efficient allocation of resources within the criminal justice system.

Assessing recidivism risk from a neuropsychological perspective presents a unique set of challenges. Neuropsychological evaluations require specialized expertise, pose ethical and logistical challenges, and can be resource-intensive. Traditional risk assessment tools, while useful, often fall short in capturing cognitive and neuropsychological factors that contribute significantly to reoffending behavior. These limitations highlight the need for integrating neuropsychological data into forensic assessments to enhance the accuracy and predictive validity of recidivism evaluations. By accounting for neuropsychological variables, criminal justice systems can make more informed decisions, allowing for targeted interventions that address specific cognitive and emotional vulnerabilities in offenders. This approach not only improves public safety by reducing reoffending rates but also promotes a fairer, more individualized assessment process that takes into account the complex, multifaceted nature of criminal behavior.

6 Neuropsychological Approaches to Risk Assessment

Risk assessment is a critical component in making decisions about sentencing, parole, and rehabilitation within the criminal justice system. Neuropsychological approaches to risk assessment introduce a valuable dimension by evaluating cognitive, emotional, and behavioral factors that traditional models often overlook. By using specialized tools and techniques, these assessments can shed light on neuropsychological risk factors such as impulsivity, executive dysfunction, and emotional dysregulation, which are often tied to recidivism. Incorporating neuropsychological data into risk prediction models allows for more accurate forecasting and individualized intervention strategies. Furthermore, real-world case studies illustrate how neuropsychological assessments have effectively informed judicial and correctional decisions.

6.1 Tools and Techniques Used to Assess Neuropsychological Risk Factors

1. **Executive Function Tests**

Executive functioning—the cognitive processes involved in planning, decision-making, impulse control, and behavioral regulation—is a crucial area of interest in neuropsychological risk assessment. Tests like the Wisconsin Card Sorting Test (WCST) and the Stroop Test are widely used to assess executive function capabilities. These tests measure cognitive flexibility, inhibition, and the ability to shift strategies, which are essential in understanding an individual's ability to conform to social norms and regulations. For instance, individuals with impairments in these areas are more likely to exhibit impulsive or risk-seeking behaviors, both of which are predictive of recidivism.

2. **Attention and Memory Assessments**

Attention and memory are foundational cognitive functions that play a role in an individual's ability to follow instructions, learn from past experiences, and foresee consequences. Tools such as the Continuous Performance Test (CPT) and the Wechsler Memory Scale (WMS) are valuable in assessing these functions. Deficits in attention and memory may lead to misunderstandings in social and legal contexts, poor impulse control, and decreased capacity for long-term goal-setting, which can heighten the risk of reoffending. Such impairments often appear in individuals with traumatic brain injury (TBI) or attention-deficit/hyperactivity disorder (ADHD), who may exhibit recidivism rates higher than those without such impairments.

3. **Emotional and Behavioral Regulation Instruments**

Emotional dysregulation, including heightened levels of anger or aggression, is often associated with reoffending. Tools like the Iowa Gambling Task (IGT) and the Emotional Stroop Test can assess an individual's ability to regulate emotions and make decisions under stress. These assessments provide insights into impulsivity and aggression, which are highly relevant to violent or impulsive offending. Additionally, behavioral checklists, like the Barratt Impulsiveness Scale, help quantify impulsivity, a core trait in offenders prone to repeated criminal behavior. Such tools are especially valuable for identifying high-risk individuals who might benefit from anger management or impulse control programs.

4. **Neuroimaging Techniques**

While neuroimaging is not routinely used in all forensic contexts due to cost and accessibility, it offers valuable insights in complex cases. Functional magnetic resonance imaging (fMRI) and positron emission tomography (PET) scans can identify abnormalities in brain structures associated with decision-making and emotional regulation, such as the prefrontal cortex, amygdala, and anterior cingulate cortex. Neuroimaging data can highlight structural or functional impairments that might not be evident through behavioral tests alone. For instance, individuals with reduced prefrontal cortex activity may struggle with impulse control, increasing their risk of reoffending. Neuroimaging thus serves as a powerful supplementary tool in cases requiring detailed neurological evaluation.

6.2 Incorporating Neuropsychological Insights into Risk Prediction Models

1. **Enhancing Predictive Validity with Neuropsychological Variables**

Traditional risk assessment tools often rely on static factors such as age, criminal history, and socioeconomic background. By incorporating neuropsychological variables like executive functioning, emotional regulation, and impulsivity, risk prediction models can become more dynamic and nuanced. Research shows that deficits in executive functioning and emotional regulation are directly linked to criminal behavior and recidivism (Meijers et al., 2015). Adding these variables to prediction models helps refine the risk level estimation, allowing for more precise risk profiles.

2. **Creating Multidimensional Risk Profiles**

Integrating neuropsychological data enables the development of multidimensional risk profiles, which are more personalized and informative than traditional models. For instance, an individual with severe impulsivity and poor decision-making skills but a low criminal history score might receive a lower risk classification under conventional assessments, potentially underestimating their recidivism risk. With neuropsychological data, assessors can identify high-risk individuals based on cognitive and behavioral vulnerabilities that traditional tools might miss. This multidimensional approach to risk profiling allows for better-targeted interventions, reducing recidivism more effectively.

3. **Improving Rehabilitation and Intervention Plans**

Neuropsychological data can inform specific, evidence-based interventions that address the individual's cognitive and emotional vulnerabilities. For example, offenders with attention and memory deficits might benefit from cognitive rehabilitation programs, while those with emotional regulation issues might require anger management or mindfulness-based interventions. By tailoring rehabilitation programs based on neuropsychological profiles, criminal justice systems can not only lower recidivism rates but also provide offenders with skills that facilitate reintegration into society. Neuropsychological insights can thus enhance the design and delivery of correctional programs, making interventions more effective and resource-efficient.

6.3 *Case Studies Showing the Role of Neuropsychological Assessments in Risk Prediction*

1. **Case Study: Use of Neuropsychological Assessment in Sentencing Decisions**

In a landmark case involving a repeat offender with a history of violent behavior, neuropsychological assessment played a crucial role in the court's sentencing decision. The offender, a 35-year-old male, exhibited significant executive dysfunction and impulsivity, as revealed by assessments like the WCST and the IGT. Neuroimaging showed reduced activity in his prefrontal cortex, consistent with poor impulse control and emotional dysregulation. These findings were presented in court, highlighting his neuropsychological vulnerabilities and his limited capacity for self-regulation. Based on this information, the court opted for a rehabilitation-focused sentence with mandatory cognitive-behavioral therapy and anger management programs instead of a purely punitive sentence, allowing for a more rehabilitative approach informed by his neuropsychological risk profile.

2. **Case Study: Predicting Recidivism with Neuropsychological Insights in Parole Decisions**

In another case, a parole board reviewed the case of a 28-year-old male with a history of substance abuse and nonviolent offenses. Neuropsychological evaluations revealed impairments in memory, attention, and decision-making, likely stemming from a history of alcohol dependence. His Continuous Performance Test scores were significantly lower than average, indicating difficulties in sustaining attention. Recognizing these cognitive impairments, the parole board decided to release him with specific conditions, including regular cognitive rehabilitation sessions and mandatory substance abuse counseling. Post-release follow-up showed that the individual's adherence to his rehabilitation plan significantly reduced his likelihood of reoffending, illustrating the value of neuropsychological insights in parole decision-making.

3. **Case Study: Informing Treatment Plans through Neuropsychological Risk Assessment**

A young adult, diagnosed with ADHD and a history of minor criminal behavior, underwent neuropsychological evaluation as part of a pre-sentencing assessment. Testing revealed that his executive functioning and attention deficits contributed to impulsive, risky behaviors. Recognizing these neuropsychological vulnerabilities, the court included targeted cognitive training and behavioral therapy in his sentence. This individualized treatment plan aimed to improve his self-control and attentional capacity, addressing the root neuropsychological contributors to his behavior. Over time, these interventions reduced his impulsivity and improved his decision-making skills, helping prevent further offenses.

Neuropsychological approaches to risk assessment represent an important advancement in predicting, managing, and reducing recidivism. Tools and techniques, such as executive function tests, memory assessments, and neuroimaging, allow practitioners to assess cognitive and emotional vulnerabilities that traditional models may overlook. By incorporating neuropsychological insights into risk prediction models, professionals in the criminal justice system can create multidimensional profiles that enhance predictive validity and support more effective interventions. Case studies demonstrate the success of these approaches in tailoring sentencing, parole decisions, and rehabilitation plans to offenders' individual neuropsychological profiles, promoting rehabilitation and reducing recidivism.

7 Intervention Strategies to Address Recidivism

Addressing recidivism requires a multifaceted approach that goes beyond punitive measures to consider the underlying cognitive, behavioral, and social factors driving criminal behavior. Intervention strategies such as cognitive-behavioral therapy (CBT), neuropsychological rehabilitation, and restorative justice initiatives target these factors and work toward the rehabilitation and reintegration of offenders. By focusing on cognitive distortions, enhancing cognitive functions, and promoting community-based support, these approaches offer a comprehensive framework to reduce recidivism and promote long-term behavioral change.

7.1 Cognitive-Behavioral Therapies for Recidivism

1. **Correcting Cognitive Distortions**

Cognitive-behavioral therapy (CBT) is widely recognized as an effective intervention for reducing recidivism by addressing cognitive distortions, such as blaming others, justifying criminal behavior, and minimizing the impact of one's actions. Offenders may develop maladaptive thinking patterns that reinforce criminal behavior, which can impede their ability to recognize the consequences of their actions or empathize with others. CBT techniques, such as cognitive restructuring, challenge these faulty beliefs and replace them with more constructive, reality-based thoughts.

For instance, cognitive restructuring exercises help offenders analyze their thought patterns, identify distortions, and reframe these thoughts in a more rational and responsible way. An individual with a history of aggression may learn to recognize triggers for anger and identify alternative, nonviolent responses. Through regular CBT sessions, offenders develop self-awareness and gain the skills needed to control impulsive behavior, enhancing their ability to make better decisions and reduce the likelihood of reoffending.

2. **Improving Problem-Solving Skills**

Many offenders struggle with problem-solving and decision-making, often leading to impulsive actions and poor choices. CBT includes training in problem-solving skills and equipping offenders with a structured approach to navigate difficult situations and make more thoughtful decisions. Problem-solving skills training typically involves learning to define problems clearly, consider multiple solutions, evaluate the consequences of each option, and choose the most constructive course of action.

This intervention strategy is particularly effective for individuals who experience frustration and conflict in social interactions, as it enables them to approach these situations calmly and thoughtfully. For example, offenders may practice resolving hypothetical disputes without resorting to aggression. By refining problem-solving skills, CBT helps offenders address challenges more effectively, reducing reliance on criminal responses and contributing to long-term behavioral change.

7.2 Neuropsychological Rehabilitation Techniques

1. **Enhancing Cognitive Functions**

Neuropsychological rehabilitation focuses on improving cognitive deficits that contribute to criminal behavior, such as impulsivity, poor attention, and memory issues. Many offenders, especially those with a history of traumatic brain injuries or neurodevelopmental disorders, exhibit impairments in executive functioning, which are linked to poor impulse control and decision-making. Neuropsychological rehabilitation techniques, including cognitive exercises and computerized training programs, target these deficits to improve attention, memory, and self-regulation.

For instance, exercises in working memory training help offenders practice holding and manipulating information, which is essential for planning and foreseeing the consequences of actions. Cognitive control training can enhance an individual's ability to inhibit impulsive responses and maintain focus on long-term goals, skills that are directly associated with a lower risk of reoffending. By addressing these cognitive vulnerabilities, neuropsychological rehabilitation helps offenders develop better self-control, making them less susceptible to impulsive, criminal acts.

2. **Addressing Emotional Regulation**

Emotional dysregulation is a common factor in recidivism, especially for individuals involved in violent offenses. Neuropsychological rehabilitation incorporates strategies to enhance emotional regulation, such as mindfulness-based training and biofeedback techniques. Mindfulness exercises teach offenders to be more aware of their emotional states, helping them recognize when they are becoming angry or stressed and take proactive steps to manage these emotions.

Biofeedback, a technique that involves monitoring physiological responses like heart rate and muscle tension, allows individuals to understand and control their physical reactions to stress. By learning to calm their bodies through relaxation techniques, offenders can better manage anger and anxiety, reducing the likelihood of aggressive behavior. Neuropsychological rehabilitation thus supports emotional resilience, enabling offenders to respond to challenging situations in healthier ways.

7.3 Restorative Justice and Community-Based Programs

1. **Restorative Justice: Promoting Accountability and Empathy**

Restorative justice (RJ) is an alternative approach to traditional punitive measures, focusing on the accountability of offenders, healing for victims, and community involvement. RJ programs create opportunities for offenders to engage in dialogue with victims and understand the impact of their actions. This process promotes empathy, encourages personal responsibility, and motivates behavioral change by helping offenders connect their actions to the harm caused.

RJ sessions often include victim-offender mediation, where offenders listen to the experiences of victims, fostering a sense of remorse and accountability. Offenders are encouraged to express genuine regret, and in some cases, agree to make reparations. This process reinforces the offenders' responsibility for their actions and strengthens their commitment to avoiding future harm. Restorative justice programs thus provide a supportive environment for behavioral change, reducing the likelihood of reoffending by nurturing empathy and accountability.

2. **Community-Based Interventions for Reintegration**

Successful reintegration into society is crucial in preventing recidivism, as social isolation, lack of support, and economic instability are significant contributors to reoffending. Community-based interventions focus on providing offenders with resources and support networks that facilitate their transition into society. Programs may include job training, housing assistance, and mentoring, which address socio-environmental factors that influence criminal behavior.

Community-based support plays an essential role in offering guidance and stability to individuals after incarceration. Mentorship programs, where former offenders are paired with community mentors, help provide structure, accountability, and encouragement, which are critical in the early stages of reintegration. Access to stable housing, employment, and social support reduces the likelihood of returning to criminal activities out of desperation or social isolation. Community-based programs thus serve as a crucial support network, promoting positive life changes and helping offenders build a sense of belonging and purpose.

7.4 Case Examples Illustrating the Effectiveness of These Approaches

1. **CBT-Based Programs in Correctional Facilities**

Studies have shown that CBT-based programs in correctional facilities reduce recidivism by addressing the cognitive distortions and problem-solving deficits that drive criminal behavior. In a meta-analysis, inmates who completed CBT programs had significantly lower recidivism rates compared to those who did not participate in such interventions (Landenberger & Lipsey, 2005). These findings suggest that CBT, targeting core cognitive and behavioral factors, is a practical and evidence-based approach to reducing repeat offenses.

2. **Neuropsychological Rehabilitation for Offenders with Cognitive Deficits**

Neuropsychological rehabilitation has proven effective in cases involving offenders with cognitive deficits, such as TBI or ADHD. One study involving juvenile offenders with ADHD found that cognitive rehabilitation improved attention and impulse control, leading to reduced behavioral issues and reoffending rates. These results highlight the importance of tailored interventions that address cognitive vulnerabilities associated with recidivism.

3. **Restorative Justice Programs as Alternatives to Traditional Sentencing**

Restorative justice programs, especially those that involve victim-offender mediation, have shown promising results in promoting behavioral change. One example involves a restorative justice program for young offenders involved in nonviolent crimes, where participants reported greater empathy for victims and a stronger commitment to avoiding future harm. This evidence supports RJ's effectiveness in addressing the emotional and relational factors that contribute to recidivism.

Addressing recidivism requires a comprehensive approach that integrates cognitive, neuropsychological, and social factors into effective intervention strategies. Cognitive-behavioral therapy, neuropsychological rehabilitation, and restorative justice programs each play a crucial role in reshaping the thought patterns, cognitive functions, and social interactions that contribute to reoffending. Through these evidence-based interventions, offenders gain the skills and support necessary for long-term behavioral change, ultimately enhancing their capacity to reintegrate successfully and reduce their likelihood of reoffending.

8 Community-Based Support Programs for Reducing Recidivism

The journey from incarceration to successful reintegration is often fraught with challenges, including stigma, limited resources, and a lack of social and psychological support. Community-based support programs are designed to help individuals navigate this path, offering resources to address socioeconomic, psychological, and educational needs. These programs play a critical role in helping individuals reintegrate effectively and reducing recidivism by equipping them with skills, confidence, and a support network to build new lives outside of the prison system. With specific attention to those with neuropsychological vulnerabilities, these programs aim to address deficits that might otherwise impede successful reintegration.

8.1 Importance of Social and Psychological Support

1. **Social Support for Reintegration**

Reintegration is a social process that requires the acceptance and inclusion of former offenders into the community. Social support networks—such as family, friends, mentors, and peers—play a critical role in this process. For individuals with neuropsychological vulnerabilities, social support is especially crucial, as they often face cognitive or emotional challenges that can impair their ability to make sound judgments, control impulses, or build trust with others. Community-based programs foster a sense of belonging and encourage former offenders to build healthy relationships, reducing feelings of isolation and promoting emotional resilience.

Support groups and mentoring programs are valuable because they provide a sense of community and accountability. Peer support, in particular, is highly effective, as individuals who have experienced similar struggles can offer empathy, understanding, and encouragement. For instance, organizations like the National Alliance on Mental Illness (NAMI) have peer-led support groups specifically for individuals with mental health issues and histories of incarceration. This structure enables former offenders to share experiences, gain coping skills, and feel less alone in their journey toward reintegration.

2. **Psychological Support for Emotional Resilience**

Former offenders often return to society with psychological scars from incarceration, such as trauma, anxiety, and depression. These mental health challenges can contribute to a sense of hopelessness or a perceived inability to change, increasing the risk of recidivism. Community-based programs that offer psychological support help address these issues by providing access to counseling, mental health services, and crisis intervention.

Cognitive-behavioral therapy (CBT) and trauma-focused interventions are commonly used to address the mental health needs of individuals post-incarceration. These therapies teach skills for managing stress, understanding personal triggers, and reinterpreting negative thought patterns. In some cases, community programs also offer psychoeducation on neuropsychological conditions like ADHD or PTSD, allowing individuals to better understand their symptoms and seek appropriate care. Psychological support services thus provide the emotional scaffolding that many former offenders need to manage stress and navigate life's challenges constructively.

8.2 Educational and Vocational Programs for Positive Change

1. **The Role of Educational Programs**

Education is one of the most significant predictors of successful reintegration and a lower risk of reoffending. Educational programs offer former offenders the opportunity to expand their knowledge, develop critical thinking skills, and build self-confidence. Research shows that individuals who engage in education while incarcerated are less likely to reoffend, as education increases employability and social adaptability (Stickle & Schuster, 2023). Educational attainment also fosters a sense of achievement and self-worth, which are key factors in breaking the cycle of criminal behavior.

Adult education programs often focus on literacy, high school equivalency (such as GED preparation), and even college-level courses. Some community-based programs partner with local colleges to provide educational support and resources post-release. For example, the Prison to College Pipeline (P2CP) initiative by John Jay College of Criminal Justice in New York connects individuals with academic and social support, allowing them to pursue higher education upon release. This kind of educational support not only enhances cognitive abilities but also equips individuals with a goal-oriented focus that counters tendencies toward criminal behavior.

2. **Vocational Training and Employment Opportunities**

Employment is a vital factor in reducing recidivism, as it provides financial stability, purpose, and social integration. Community-based programs often include vocational training and job placement services to help former offenders acquire skills and secure stable employment. Programs tailored to neuropsychological needs may offer additional support in developing soft skills, such as communication and time management, which are often challenging for individuals with cognitive impairments or mental health issues.

Job training programs can vary widely, from trade skills (such as plumbing, carpentry, or culinary arts) to professional skills (such as computer programming or customer service). For example, The Doe Fund in New York City provides comprehensive vocational training for individuals with criminal records, focusing on soft and technical skills and even offering transitional employment opportunities. Vocational training initiatives like these not only promote economic independence but also reduce the likelihood of reoffending by fostering a sense of accomplishment and stability.

8.3 Case Studies of Successful Community Programs

1. **The Fortune Society's "The Castle"**

Located in Harlem, New York, The Fortune Society operates a residential reentry program known as "The Castle." This program offers housing, employment support, substance abuse treatment, and mental health services to formerly incarcerated individuals. The Fortune Society's approach focuses on creating a supportive community that empowers participants to take responsibility for their lives and make positive choices. For individuals with neuropsychological vulnerabilities, The Castle offers tailored services such as case management, cognitive rehabilitation, and therapy for emotional regulation. Studies of The Fortune Society's programs reveal that individuals who participate in The Castle experience significantly lower rates of recidivism compared to those who lack access to similar support. For instance, a study conducted on The Castle's participants showed that those who received stable housing, psychological support, and job training were far less likely to reoffend than those without such resources. The program's success is attributed to its holistic and individualized approach, which empowers participants to make sustainable, positive changes in their lives. The reduction in recidivism rates at The Castle underscores the importance of community-based support and the value of addressing the full spectrum of needs among formerly incarcerated individuals. By providing services that help participants stabilize their lives, find employment, and build supportive relationships, The Castle fosters a sense of agency and accountability that is crucial for long-term success. The program's structure demonstrates that, with the right support systems, individuals can overcome neuropsychological and socioeconomic barriers, leading to productive lives free from criminal activity (The Fortune Society Presents "the Castle" | the Fortune Society, 2024).

2. **Pathways to Housing Program**

Pathways to Housing, initially established in New York, provides housing-first initiatives that focus on securing stable housing as a prerequisite to addressing other issues such as mental health, substance abuse, and unemployment. The program offers support to individuals with severe mental illness and histories of incarceration, recognizing that housing stability is foundational to successful reintegration.

Pathways to Housing combines housing with mental health care, case management, and vocational training. Studies have shown that providing secure housing reduces recidivism by addressing homelessness—a common barrier to reintegration (Jacobs & Gottlieb, 2020). Participants who received stable housing were more likely to engage in therapy, maintain employment, and avoid criminal activity.

3. **California's Anti-Recidivism Coalition (ARC)**

The Anti-Recidivism Coalition (ARC) in California provides mentoring, mental health support, and job training for formerly incarcerated youth and young adults. ARC's holistic approach includes community-building activities, support groups, and access to higher education programs. With its focus on building self-esteem, enhancing job skills, and encouraging positive peer relationships, ARC has demonstrated remarkable success in reducing recidivism among high-risk youth.

ARC also recognizes the importance of addressing neuropsychological vulnerabilities. The program incorporates mental health services and has formed partnerships with local universities to provide neuropsychological assessments and interventions for participants with learning disabilities or traumatic brain injuries. This tailored approach allows ARC to better support individuals with specific cognitive or emotional needs, contributing to lower reoffending rates.

Community-based support programs offer a transformative path for individuals seeking to break the cycle of criminal behavior and reintegrate successfully into society. Through social and psychological support, educational and vocational training, and comprehensive case management, these programs address the unique needs of each individual, particularly those with neuropsychological vulnerabilities. By fostering social connections, building resilience, and creating pathways for personal growth, community-based programs are instrumental in reducing recidivism and promoting sustainable behavioral change. The success of initiatives like The Fortune Society, Pathways to Housing, and ARC illustrates that, with the right support, formerly incarcerated individuals can lead productive, fulfilling lives, free from the constraints of their past actions.

9 Addressing Criminogenic Needs: Reducing Recidivism through Targeted Interventions

Recidivism, or the tendency of individuals to relapse into criminal behavior, remains a significant concern within the criminal justice system. Addressing criminogenic needs — the specific traits, behaviors, and psychological factors associated with a heightened likelihood of criminal activity — has become a cornerstone in efforts to lower recidivism rates. Criminogenic needs often encompass issues like substance abuse, impulsivity, emotional dysregulation, and other neuropsychological and behavioral factors that perpetuate criminal tendencies. By identifying and directly addressing these needs through neuropsychological interventions and targeted therapies, practitioners can create comprehensive rehabilitation programs that promote long-term behavioral change and reduce the cycle of reoffending.

9.1 Identifying Criminogenic Needs

Criminogenic needs refer to specific factors that drive individuals toward criminal behavior, and these needs vary significantly across individuals. Broadly, criminogenic needs include:

- **Substance Abuse**: Substance abuse disorders are among the most common criminogenic factors, often exacerbating impulsivity, reducing emotional control, and clouding judgment. Individuals with substance use disorders are also more likely to associate with criminal networks, reinforcing negative behaviors.
- **Poor Emotional Regulation**: Emotional dysregulation — difficulty managing or responding to emotional experiences — is another significant contributor to criminal behavior. It is commonly seen in individuals who struggle with anger, aggression, and anxiety, often resulting in impulsive and reactive actions that lead to legal conflicts.
- **Impulsivity and Poor Decision-Making**: Impulsivity is strongly linked to recidivism, as individuals who lack impulse control are more likely to engage in risky behaviors without considering long-term consequences. This tendency is particularly concerning in individuals with neurodevelopmental disorders, such as ADHD, or those who have experienced traumatic brain injuries.
- **Antisocial Cognitions and Attitudes**: Cognitive distortions that foster antisocial beliefs and attitudes can lead individuals to rationalize or justify criminal behavior. These thought patterns, which may include blaming others, minimizing the harm caused by one's actions, or harboring hostility toward authority figures, further increase the risk of reoffending.

Addressing these criminogenic needs through tailored interventions helps to create a holistic treatment plan that not only reduces criminal behavior but also enhances individuals' overall well-being, self-regulation, and interpersonal skills.

9.2 Neuropsychological Interventions for Criminogenic Needs

In recent years, neuropsychological interventions have shown promise in addressing the underlying cognitive and behavioral factors that contribute to criminal activity. These interventions, grounded in neuroscience and psychology, seek to modify neural pathways associated with impulsivity, aggression, and emotional dysregulation.

1. Therapy for Emotional Dysregulation and Impulsivity

    - **Dialectical Behavior Therapy (DBT)**: Originally developed for individuals with borderline personality disorder, DBT has been adapted to treat various forms of emotional dysregulation and impulsivity in criminal populations. This approach combines cognitive-behavioral techniques with mindfulness strategies to help individuals regulate emotions, tolerate distress, and develop healthier interpersonal relationships. DBT's focus on emotional regulation and distress tolerance makes it particularly effective for high-risk individuals prone to reactive violence or substance abuse.
    - **Cognitive Behavioral Therapy (CBT)**: CBT remains one of the most widely used and empirically supported treatments for criminal behavior. It targets cognitive distortions, such as blaming others or minimizing the consequences of one's actions, and replaces these distortions with pro-social, constructive thoughts. CBT programs specifically tailored for offenders, such as reasoning and rehabilitation (R&R), aim to enhance problem-solving skills, encourage responsible decision-making, and reduce impulsive actions.
    - **Neurofeedback Training**: Neurofeedback, a technique that trains individuals to modulate their brainwave activity, has shown potential to help individuals gain control over impulsivity and emotional responses. For instance, neurofeedback can help individuals shift from high-beta brainwaves, which are associated with hyperarousal and stress, to low-beta or alpha waves that promote calmness and focus. This technique is particularly valuable for individuals with ADHD or TBI, where impulsivity and poor regulation are common challenges.

2. Substance Abuse Treatment Programs

    - **Integrated Treatment Approaches**: Substance abuse treatment for offenders often incorporates a combination of detoxification, counseling, relapse prevention, and skills training. In neuropsychological terms, this treatment addresses the reward pathways in the brain, helping individuals manage cravings and avoid triggers. Programs like Cognitive-Behavioral Substance Abuse Treatment (CBT-SAT) specifically target the maladaptive thought patterns associated with substance use, teaching clients to replace these thoughts with healthier coping mechanisms.
    - **Medication-Assisted Treatment (MAT)**: For individuals with opioid or alcohol dependence, MAT combines behavioral therapy with medications such as methadone, buprenorphine, or naltrexone. These medications reduce cravings and withdrawal symptoms, which helps prevent relapse and facilitates engagement in counseling and cognitive-behavioral interventions.

3. Addressing Cognitive Distortions and Antisocial Thinking

    - **Moral Reconation Therapy (MRT)**: MRT focuses on increasing moral reasoning skills among offenders, helping them develop empathy, accountability, and social responsibility. This approach has been shown to reduce recidivism in various criminal populations by promoting pro-social behaviors and challenging the cognitive distortions that justify criminal actions.

- **Social Skills Training (SST)**: Many offenders struggle with interpersonal skills, which can lead to conflict and reinforce criminal behavior. SST programs teach individuals how to communicate effectively, handle criticism, and resolve conflicts without aggression, which enhances their ability to build healthy relationships and avoid hostile encounters.

9.3 Case Studies: Reducing Recidivism by Addressing Criminogenic Needs

Case studies demonstrate the success of these neuropsychological interventions in reducing recidivism, particularly when the specific criminogenic needs of high-risk populations are targeted.

- **Case Study 1 Treating Emotional Dysregulation in Violent Offenders**
- A study conducted at a maximum-security facility implemented DBT for a group of violent offenders with histories of emotional dysregulation and aggression. The program, which ran for 6 months, focused on improving emotional regulation, impulse control, and interpersonal effectiveness. Results showed a marked reduction in aggressive incidents within the facility and lower recidivism rates in the year following release. Participants reported that the skills they learned helped them manage anger and avoid reactive violence, both in prison and after reentry
- **Case Study 2 Addressing Substance Abuse and Impulsivity**
- In a community-based treatment program for individuals on probation with co-occurring substance abuse and impulsivity issues, a combination of CBT-SAT and neurofeedback training was provided. CBT helped participants understand and replace maladaptive thought patterns related to substance use, while neurofeedback improved impulse control and emotional stability. Recidivism rates for participants were significantly lower compared to a control group receiving standard probationary supervision, suggesting that this combined approach enhanced self-regulation and reduced drug-related reoffending
- **Case Study 3 Reducing Antisocial Cognitions in Repeat Offenders**
- MRT was introduced in a correctional facility housing repeat offenders with histories of theft and fraud. Through regular group sessions, participants explored the consequences of their actions, built empathy, and learned problem-solving skills. The program significantly lowered recidivism rates among participants by challenging the cognitive distortions that supported their criminal behaviors, instilling a sense of moral responsibility, and fostering positive relationships

Addressing criminogenic needs through neuropsychological interventions provides a targeted and effective strategy for reducing recidivism. By focusing on the underlying cognitive and emotional factors that contribute to criminal behavior, practitioners can help high-risk individuals develop the skills and self-regulation needed to lead productive, law-abiding lives. As these case studies illustrate, interventions that directly address issues like emotional dysregulation, substance abuse, and antisocial thinking not only improve individual outcomes but also enhance public safety by breaking the cycle of reoffending.

10 Substance Abuse and Its Role in Recidivism: A Neuropsychological Perspective

Substance abuse is a major factor in criminal recidivism, as addiction often leads to cognitive impairments, poor impulse control, and a diminished ability to make responsible decisions. These neuropsychological effects of addiction create conditions that perpetuate the cycle of reoffending, particularly when substance use is accompanied by other mental health issues. Addressing substance abuse as a criminogenic need, therefore, is essential to reduce recidivism. This report examines the neuropsychological impact of substance abuse on brain functioning, explores the challenges of treating individuals with co-occurring substance abuse and mental health disorders, and discusses integrative treatment approaches that target both addiction and cognitive deficits to help reduce the risk of reoffending.

10.1 Neuropsychological Effects of Substance Abuse on Brain Functioning

Substance abuse has significant and lasting effects on the brain, particularly in regions associated with executive functioning, impulse control, and decision-making. Chronic drug and alcohol use alters brain structure and disrupts neurotransmitter function, leading to cognitive and behavioral impairments that increase the risk of criminal behavior. The primary neuropsychological effects of substance abuse include:

1. **Impaired Decision-Making**: Substance abuse impairs the prefrontal cortex, the part of the brain responsible for complex decision-making, planning, and evaluating the consequences of actions. The prefrontal cortex governs rational thinking, and its disruption through prolonged substance abuse can lead individuals to prioritize immediate gratification over long-term consequences. This impairment makes it harder for individuals to make responsible decisions and increases the likelihood of engaging in high-risk or illegal activities.
2. **Reduced Impulse Control**: Addiction reduces self-control by weakening the function of areas like the prefrontal cortex and the anterior cingulate cortex, which regulate impulse control. This reduced control over impulses contributes

to a heightened risk of impulsive or criminal behavior. For instance, individuals struggling with addiction may find it challenging to avoid substance-related offenses or impulsive behaviors like theft or assault, particularly when faced with triggering situations.

3. **Increased Risk-Seeking Behavior**: Many addictive substances, such as stimulants, lead to increased dopamine release, reinforcing the reward-seeking behavior associated with addiction. This results in an ongoing cycle of seeking "highs" or intense experiences, often without regard for consequences. The drive for immediate reward can lead individuals toward risky behaviors that, in turn, increase their likelihood of reoffending, as they become trapped in a pattern of seeking instant gratification.
4. **Cognitive and Memory Deficits**: Long-term substance abuse often leads to structural damage in memory-related regions, such as the hippocampus. These changes impair an individual's ability to retain information, remember past consequences, and learn from mistakes. The resulting cognitive deficits make it difficult for individuals to engage in productive rehabilitation and increase the likelihood of repeating criminal behavior, as they may fail to internalize and retain lessons from previous experiences.

The impact of these neuropsychological deficits on behavior highlights the importance of addressing substance abuse as a central factor in recidivism. When addiction impairs cognitive and behavioral functioning, individuals face greater challenges in controlling impulsive behavior, making sound decisions, and adhering to societal rules.

10.2 Challenges in Treating Dual Diagnoses of Substance Abuse and Mental Health Issues

Substance abuse frequently coexists with other mental health disorders, such as depression, anxiety, or personality disorders, creating complex treatment challenges. This combination, referred to as a dual diagnosis or comorbidity, presents unique issues in rehabilitation, increasing both the risk of reoffending and the difficulty of treating the individual effectively. Key challenges include:

1. **Interaction of Symptoms**: Substance abuse and mental health disorders often exacerbate each other, creating a cycle of worsening symptoms. For example, a person with anxiety may use alcohol to self-medicate, which could worsen both the addiction and the underlying anxiety. These interactions complicate treatment efforts, as addressing one condition in isolation may inadvertently worsen the other.
2. **Increased Risk of Non-Compliance**: Individuals with dual diagnoses may struggle with treatment adherence due to impaired cognitive functioning, organizational skills, and motivation. Substance abuse and mental health disorders

can make it difficult for individuals to engage fully in therapeutic interventions, and cognitive impairments related to addiction further challenge consistent participation.

3. **Higher Risk of Relapse**: People with dual diagnoses are at a heightened risk of relapse because untreated mental health symptoms can trigger substance use, and substance use can worsen mental health symptoms. This cyclic relationship not only increases the likelihood of reoffending but also limits progress during treatment, as both conditions perpetuate each other.
4. **Stigma and Access to Care**: Stigma around both addiction and mental health conditions may prevent individuals from accessing necessary care. The social stigma associated with addiction often limits the availability of adequate treatment options, particularly for individuals involved in the criminal justice system. Without accessible, holistic treatment, individuals are more likely to return to criminal behavior.

10.3 Integrative Treatment Approaches to Reduce Recidivism Risk

To effectively reduce recidivism, treatment must address both substance abuse and the associated cognitive and psychological deficits. Integrative treatment approaches that incorporate behavioral, neuropsychological, and pharmacological methods offer a promising solution.

1. **Integrated Dual Diagnosis Treatment (IDDT)**: IDDT is a holistic approach that addresses both substance abuse and mental health conditions simultaneously, using therapeutic techniques such as cognitive-behavioral therapy (CBT) for addiction and dialectical behavior therapy (DBT) for emotional regulation. IDDT reduces relapse rates by providing a comprehensive framework that addresses all aspects of an individual's well-being, from addiction management to mental health stabilization.
2. **Medication-Assisted Treatment (MAT)**: MAT involves using medications like methadone, naltrexone, or buprenorphine to reduce cravings and manage withdrawal symptoms, particularly for opioid and alcohol dependence. When combined with behavioral therapies, MAT can stabilize individuals, reduce their dependence on substances, and enhance their capacity to engage in cognitive and emotional rehabilitation. Studies show that MAT reduces criminal behavior associated with addiction by addressing the physical dependence that drives many substance-related offenses (General, 2016).
3. **Neurofeedback and Cognitive Rehabilitation**: Neurofeedback is a technique that enables individuals to train their brain activity, promoting self-regulation and reducing impulsive behavior. Through neurofeedback, individuals can learn to manage their impulsivity, reduce stress, and strengthen executive functioning. Cognitive rehabilitation programs target specific cognitive deficits, such as

memory and attention impairments, helping individuals improve their cognitive resilience and avoid behaviors that contribute to criminal activity.

4. **Community-Based Support and Vocational Training**: Community programs play a critical role in supporting the reintegration of individuals post-incarceration, providing access to stable housing, peer support, and vocational training. By addressing the social and environmental factors that contribute to substance abuse and criminal behavior, these programs help individuals build a stable foundation for recovery. Vocational training provides a path to employment and stability, while peer support groups foster accountability and a sense of belonging.

10.4 Case Studies Highlighting Integrative Approaches

Integrative treatment models that address both addiction and mental health needs have shown promising outcomes in reducing recidivism. For instance:

- **Drug Courts with Treatment Mandates**: Drug courts provide an alternative to incarceration for individuals with substance use disorders, mandating addiction treatment as part of the legal process. Studies show that drug court participants have lower recidivism rates than those who go through the traditional criminal justice system, as the focus on rehabilitation reduces the likelihood of reoffending (Belenko et al., 2013).
- **Therapeutic Communities in Prisons**: Therapeutic communities within prison systems create a structured environment focused on rehabilitation rather than punishment. These communities use cognitive-behavioral therapies, life skills training, and peer support to address addiction and prepare individuals for reintegration into society. Research demonstrates that therapeutic communities effectively reduce recidivism rates by addressing both substance use and underlying cognitive deficits (Mitchell et al., 2012).

Substance abuse plays a central role in criminal behavior and recidivism, as addiction impairs cognitive functioning, diminishes impulse control, and exacerbates mental health issues. Reducing reoffending requires a comprehensive treatment model that addresses both addiction and cognitive vulnerabilities. By using integrated treatment methods such as IDDT, MAT, neurofeedback, and community support, it is possible to break the cycle of reoffending, helping individuals recover from addiction and make meaningful, lasting changes in their behavior. Through these holistic and evidence-based strategies, the criminal justice system can move toward a more rehabilitative approach that prioritizes recovery and reduces the risk of reoffending.

11 Promoting Desistance through Neuropsychological Approaches

Desistance, the process by which individuals cease engaging in criminal behavior and achieve long-term positive change, has become a crucial focus in modern criminology and criminal justice. For individuals with neuropsychological vulnerabilities or impairments, desistance is often complicated by cognitive and emotional challenges that perpetuate maladaptive behaviors. Neuropsychological interventions that target these underlying issues can be essential in fostering long-term behavioral change, providing individuals with the tools necessary to break the cycle of criminality. This report explores the role of neuropsychological interventions in promoting desistance, with a focus on building cognitive and emotional resilience to prevent recidivism.

11.1 Understanding Desistance in the Context of Criminal Behavior

Desistance is not merely about stopping criminal activity but involves a transformation in identity, cognition, and behavior that leads to positive, sustainable changes in an individual's life. Desistance is a gradual and often nonlinear process that can be influenced by various personal, social, and environmental factors. Research suggests that effective desistance requires addressing not only the external conditions surrounding an individual, such as employment and housing, but also the internal factors, including cognitive and emotional health, that may drive criminal behavior (Walker et al., 2014).

For individuals with a history of neuropsychological impairments—such as executive functioning deficits, impulsivity, emotional dysregulation, or impaired decision-making—the pathway to desistance can be particularly challenging. These cognitive and emotional barriers often make it difficult for individuals to adjust to societal expectations and may predispose them to situations where reoffending seems unavoidable. Neuropsychological interventions can address these issues, helping individuals achieve the resilience necessary to pursue desistance successfully.

11.2 Role of Neuropsychological Interventions in Fostering Behavioral Change

Neuropsychological interventions, particularly those targeting cognition and emotion regulation, play an essential role in promoting desistance. These interventions focus on strengthening executive functioning, improving impulse control, and teaching adaptive problem-solving skills. Key neuropsychological interventions that foster behavioral change and support desistance include:

1. **Cognitive-Behavioral Therapy (CBT)**: CBT is widely used in correctional and rehabilitative settings to help individuals recognize and alter maladaptive thoughts and behaviors. Through CBT, individuals learn to identify cognitive distortions, manage impulsive behaviors, and develop coping strategies for stressful situations. By promoting a shift in thought processes, CBT aids in addressing some of the core cognitive deficits that often accompany criminal behavior, such as poor decision-making and impulsivity. This shift is critical for individuals working toward desistance, as it helps replace criminal thought patterns with prosocial ones.
2. **Dialectical Behavior Therapy (DBT)**: Originally developed for individuals with borderline personality disorder, DBT is effective in addressing emotional dysregulation and impulsive behavior. DBT teaches skills in emotional regulation, distress tolerance, and interpersonal effectiveness, which are particularly beneficial for individuals with high emotional volatility. By providing individuals with tools to manage emotions and tolerate stress, DBT fosters resilience, making it easier for individuals to avoid criminal behaviors driven by emotional impulsivity.
3. **Neurofeedback and Biofeedback**: Neurofeedback is an emerging tool in desistance-focused interventions, as it provides individuals with real-time feedback on their brain activity, enabling them to learn self-regulation skills. Neurofeedback sessions help individuals train their brain activity, especially in regions associated with impulse control and attention. Biofeedback, on the other hand, helps individuals regulate physiological responses, such as heart rate and respiration, that are linked to stress and anxiety. These techniques support behavioral change by improving self-regulation, enhancing focus, and reducing impulsive tendencies.
4. **Cognitive Remediation Therapy (CRT)**: CRT focuses on improving cognitive skills such as memory, attention, and executive functioning, which are often compromised in individuals with neuropsychological vulnerabilities. By addressing these cognitive deficits, CRT helps individuals build the mental flexibility and focus needed to manage everyday challenges without resorting to maladaptive behaviors. Improved cognitive skills can strengthen individuals' problem-solving abilities, making them more resilient and less prone to engaging in criminal acts.
5. **Motivational Interviewing (MI)**: MI is an approach that helps individuals explore and resolve ambivalence toward change. This therapy focuses on increasing intrinsic motivation, making it particularly effective for individuals who may not initially see the value in desistance. By helping individuals understand their personal reasons for wanting to change, MI fosters a sense of agency and commitment to long-term desistance.

11.3 Building Cognitive and Emotional Resilience to Prevent Recidivism

A critical aspect of neuropsychological approaches to desistance is building resilience, both cognitive and emotional, to support individuals in navigating the challenges they face during reintegration. Cognitive resilience involves strengthening skills such as self-regulation, impulse control, and problem-solving, which are crucial in making sound decisions and avoiding high-risk behaviors. Emotional resilience, on the other hand, is the ability to manage emotions effectively, particularly during stressful or triggering situations.

1. **Cognitive Resilience**: Building cognitive resilience requires enhancing executive functioning, which includes working memory, mental flexibility, and inhibitory control. Interventions such as CRT and neurofeedback help individuals improve these cognitive skills, providing them with the tools to handle complex situations without resorting to impulsive or criminal actions. A resilient individual is better equipped to cope with triggers and resist the immediate gratification of harmful behaviors.
2. **Emotional Resilience**: Emotional resilience is developed through interventions like DBT and CBT, which teach individuals to regulate emotions, manage stress, and cope with interpersonal conflicts. Emotional resilience is particularly important in the context of desistance, as emotional dysregulation is a common driver of impulsive and violent behaviors. For example, someone who has learned to manage anger and anxiety effectively is less likely to respond with aggression or engage in impulsive crimes.
3. **Supportive Environments and Social Resilience**: Social and environmental resilience also play a vital role in desistance. Supportive environments, such as community-based rehabilitation programs, can offer a safe space for individuals to practice new skills and build healthy relationships. Positive social connections, along with vocational and educational support, reinforce cognitive and emotional resilience by providing individuals with alternative pathways and sources of support. Studies indicate that individuals who have access to social resources, such as mentors or community support groups, are more likely to sustain desistance over time (Kirkwood, 2021).

11.4 Case Studies Highlighting the Effectiveness of Neuropsychological Interventions in Promoting Desistance

Case studies demonstrate that neuropsychological interventions targeting cognitive and emotional resilience can significantly impact recidivism and promote lasting behavioral change:

- **Case of Cognitive-Behavioral Interventions in Youth Offenders**: A study involving juvenile offenders with high recidivism rates applied CBT and CRT to address cognitive distortions and executive function deficits. After a year of therapy, these youth demonstrated improved decision-making abilities and reduced impulsivity, which contributed to a substantial decrease in reoffending rates.
- **Neurofeedback for Substance-Abusing Offenders**: In a pilot program for substance-abusing individuals with a history of criminal behavior, neurofeedback was used to promote self-regulation and emotional stability. Participants reported better impulse control and emotional management, which helped reduce the frequency of criminal acts and substance use. Neurofeedback-trained individuals were also more responsive to other therapeutic interventions, indicating enhanced cognitive resilience.
- **Dialectical Behavior Therapy for Women with Borderline Personality Disorder**: DBT was used in a correctional setting for women with borderline personality disorder who exhibited repeated offenses due to emotional dysregulation. DBT reduced incidents of self-harm and aggression, allowing these individuals to reintegrate successfully with improved emotional resilience and lower recidivism rates.

Neuropsychological approaches that focus on fostering cognitive and emotional resilience are essential in promoting desistance and preventing recidivism. By addressing the underlying cognitive deficits and emotional challenges that contribute to criminal behavior, these interventions empower individuals to make lasting changes. Promoting desistance through neuropsychological interventions requires a holistic approach that not only focuses on the cessation of criminal acts but also fosters the cognitive, emotional, and social skills necessary for a fulfilling and law-abiding life. Through this comprehensive support, individuals can achieve meaningful transformation, breaking free from cycles of criminality and moving toward a more positive future.

12 The Importance of Tailored Interventions for Reducing Recidivism

Recidivism, or the tendency of individuals to reoffend after serving a sentence, remains a pressing issue in the criminal justice system. While punitive measures have traditionally been the focus, evidence increasingly supports the need for rehabilitative approaches that address the underlying factors contributing to criminal behavior. One such approach involves the use of tailored interventions—individualized treatment plans that consider the specific neuropsychological, cognitive, and social needs of offenders. By recognizing the diverse profiles of individuals in the justice system and providing comprehensive, targeted support, tailored interventions have the potential to significantly reduce recidivism rates and improve long-term outcomes.

12.1 The Need for Individualized Treatment Plans

Offenders in the criminal justice system are not a homogenous group; they present with a variety of neuropsychological vulnerabilities, mental health issues, and environmental challenges. Individualized treatment plans that address these specific profiles are critical for effective rehabilitation. Many offenders have underlying neuropsychological impairments, such as deficits in executive functioning, poor emotional regulation, or impulsivity, which can predispose them to criminal behavior. These impairments may result from traumatic brain injuries (TBIs), neurodevelopmental disorders, or adverse childhood experiences. Identifying these vulnerabilities through comprehensive assessments enables the development of targeted interventions that address the root causes of criminal behavior. For example, an individual with impaired impulse control due to a TBI may benefit from neurofeedback training to enhance self-regulation, while someone with cognitive distortions might require cognitive-behavioral therapy (CBT) to reshape maladaptive thought patterns. A one-size-fits-all approach fails to account for the unique needs of offenders. Tailored interventions prioritize the individual's specific challenges, whether related to substance abuse, emotional dysregulation, or lack of problem-solving skills. Such interventions are designed not only to address deficits but also to build strengths, foster resilience, and promote pro-social behaviors. Offenders frequently present with comorbid conditions, such as substance use disorders combined with mental health issues like depression or anxiety. Integrated treatment plans that simultaneously target these co-occurring conditions are essential for reducing recidivism. For instance, combining medication-assisted treatment for substance abuse with trauma-informed therapy can address both addiction and the psychological triggers underlying criminal behavior.

12.2 Comprehensive Interventions for Better Outcomes

Effective tailored interventions rely on a multifaceted approach that integrates cognitive rehabilitation, therapy, and social support. This holistic strategy ensures that individuals receive the necessary tools to reintegrate into society and avoid reoffending.

Cognitive rehabilitation focuses on improving cognitive functions such as memory, attention, and decision-making, which are often impaired in offenders. Techniques such as computerized cognitive training programs and neuropsychological exercises can enhance problem-solving skills and impulse control, reducing the likelihood of criminal behavior. For example, a study on individuals with executive function deficits showed significant behavioral improvements following targeted cognitive training sessions. Therapy plays a central role in addressing the psychological factors contributing to criminal behavior. CBT is particularly effective in helping individuals identify and challenge distorted thinking patterns that reinforce offending. Other therapeutic modalities, such as dialectical behavior therapy (DBT), are beneficial for individuals struggling with emotional dysregulation and impulsivity.

Additionally, trauma-focused therapies, such as eye movement desensitization and reprocessing (EMDR), are crucial for offenders with histories of trauma. By addressing the psychological scars that may drive maladaptive behaviors, these therapies provide a foundation for long-term change.

The importance of social support cannot be overstated. Community-based programs that provide access to education, vocational training, and housing assistance are instrumental in facilitating successful reintegration. These programs not only reduce the socioeconomic stressors that contribute to recidivism but also foster a sense of belonging and purpose. Vocational training programs, for instance, equip individuals with job skills that increase employability, thereby reducing financial pressures and the temptation to reoffend. Similarly, mentorship initiatives connect individuals with positive role models who can guide them through the challenges of reintegration.

12.3 Long-Term Follow-Up and Monitoring

One of the most critical aspects of tailored interventions is the provision of long-term follow-up and monitoring. Criminal behavior is often entrenched, and sustainable change requires ongoing support to prevent relapse into old patterns. Continuous evaluation of an individual's progress is essential to ensure the effectiveness of the intervention. Regular neuropsychological assessments can help identify emerging challenges and guide adjustments to the treatment plan. For instance, if an individual demonstrates improvement in impulse control but struggles with stress management, additional support in stress-reduction techniques can be incorporated.

The risk of relapse into criminal behavior is particularly high during the transition from incarceration to community life. Structured monitoring systems, such as probation services combined with therapeutic check-ins, provide accountability and support during this vulnerable period. These systems can help individuals navigate challenges, such as finding employment or rebuilding family relationships, that might otherwise lead to reoffending. Long-term success relies on building cognitive and emotional resilience. Resilience training programs teach individuals coping strategies to manage stress, regulate emotions, and make positive choices. Such programs are especially effective when combined with peer support groups, which offer a sense of community and shared experiences.

Tailored interventions are a cornerstone of effective strategies for reducing recidivism. By addressing the unique neuropsychological, cognitive, and social needs of offenders, these individualized treatment plans foster meaningful change and support successful reintegration. Comprehensive approaches that combine cognitive rehabilitation, therapy, and social support, coupled with long-term follow-up and monitoring, provide the tools necessary for sustainable behavioral transformation.

As the justice system evolves, prioritizing tailored interventions will be essential in creating a more rehabilitative and equitable framework for addressing criminal behavior.

13 Conclusion

Recidivism, the tendency of individuals to reengage in criminal behavior after intervention or incarceration, poses a significant challenge to criminal justice systems worldwide. While sociological and economic factors are often emphasized, the role of neuropsychological factors in recidivism has gained increasing recognition. Impairments in brain functioning, cognitive deficits, and emotional dysregulation are frequently observed in offender populations, influencing their likelihood of reoffending. Integrating neuropsychological insights into risk assessment and rehabilitation strategies is essential for addressing the root causes of criminal behavior and fostering long-term positive outcomes. Neuropsychological impairments contribute significantly to the development and persistence of recidivism. Many offenders exhibit deficits in executive functioning, a set of cognitive processes involved in planning, decision-making, and impulse control. These impairments can hinder an individual's ability to foresee the consequences of their actions, resist immediate temptations, or adapt to pro-social norms. For example, dysfunction in the prefrontal cortex, the brain region responsible for higher-order cognitive functions, has been linked to impulsivity and poor decision-making. Similarly, abnormalities in the amygdala and limbic system can impair emotional regulation, increasing susceptibility to aggression and reactive behavior. Individuals with such impairments are more likely to engage in criminal activities, especially under stress or in emotionally charged situations. Substance abuse, prevalent among offender populations, exacerbates these vulnerabilities by further impairing neural pathways associated with self-control and risk assessment. Chronic drug use can damage brain regions critical for regulating behavior, creating a cycle of addiction and criminality that is difficult to break without targeted intervention.

Traditional risk assessment tools in criminal justice often fail to account for the neuropsychological factors that influence behavior. Incorporating neuropsychological evaluations into these assessments can provide a more comprehensive understanding of an individual's risk profile. Assessments that evaluate cognitive functions such as memory, attention, and impulse control can identify deficits that may increase the likelihood of reoffending. These tests, combined with brain imaging techniques such as functional MRI (fMRI) or electroencephalography (EEG), offer objective data on the structural and functional health of the brain. Insights from neuropsychology can help identify maladaptive thinking patterns and emotional vulnerabilities that contribute to criminal behavior. For instance, individuals with heightened sensitivity to threat due to amygdala hyperactivity may be more prone to aggression, necessitating interventions focused on emotional regulation. Integrating neuropsychological data into predictive models can improve the accuracy of recidivism forecasts. By considering factors such as cognitive impairments, emotional dysregulation, and neurobiological vulnerabilities, these models can guide decisions regarding sentencing, parole, and rehabilitation.

To reduce recidivism, interventions must address the specific neuropsychological needs of offenders. Tailored rehabilitation programs that incorporate cognitive, behavioral, and emotional components can foster desistance—the process of ceasing criminal behavior and transitioning toward a pro-social lifestyle. Programs that focus on improving executive functions, such as decision-making and impulse control, can help offenders develop the skills needed to resist criminal behavior. Techniques like computerized cognitive training or neurofeedback are particularly effective in enhancing brain functions associated with self-regulation. Cognitive-behavioral therapy (CBT) and other evidence-based modalities address maladaptive thought patterns and emotional dysregulation. For offenders with trauma histories, trauma-focused therapies such as eye movement desensitization and reprocessing (EMDR) provide additional benefits by resolving psychological distress that may drive criminal behavior. Neuropsychological interventions are most effective when combined with social and environmental support. Community-based programs that offer vocational training, housing assistance, and mentorship help offenders reintegrate into society while reducing external pressures that contribute to recidivism.

Successful reintegration requires a long-term commitment to building resilience and pro-social behaviors. Tailored interventions should be complemented by follow-up monitoring and support to ensure sustainable change. Neuropsychological approaches play a pivotal role in this process by empowering individuals with the cognitive and emotional tools needed to navigate challenges and make positive choices. Incorporating neuropsychological perspectives into the criminal justice system not only reduces recidivism but also promotes fairness by addressing the underlying vulnerabilities that contribute to offending. By prioritizing rehabilitation over punishment, society can create opportunities for transformation and reduce the burden of crime on communities. In conclusion, understanding the neuropsychological underpinnings of recidivism is critical for developing effective interventions. Tailored approaches that integrate cognitive rehabilitation, therapy, and social support offer the best chance of fostering desistance and ensuring successful reintegration. By embracing these strategies, the criminal justice system can move toward a more rehabilitative and equitable framework that benefits both offenders and society at large.

References

Batastini, A. B. (2010). *Decision making training in a jail setting*. https://doi.org/10.17918/etd-3229.

Belenko, S., Hiller, M., & Hamilton, L. (2013). Treating substance use disorders in the criminal justice system. *Current Psychiatry Reports, 15*(11). https://doi.org/10.1007/s11920-013-0414-z

Bell, R. K., & Polaschek, D. L. L. (2016). Do high-risk prisoners entering treatment have clinically impaired cognitive impulse control? *Psychiatry Psychology and Law, 24*(4), 576–593. https://doi.org/10.1080/13218719.2016.1256016

Fournier, L. F. (n.d.). *Mental health problems, traumatic brain injury, and offending behavior among persons incarcerated in a County Jail—ProQuest*. https://www.proquest.com/docview/2564139851?pq-origsite=gscholar&fromopenview=true&sourcetype=Dissertations%20&%20Theses.

General, O. O. T. S. (2016, November 1). The neurobiology of substance use, misuse, and addiction. Facing Addiction in America - NCBI Bookshelf. https://www.ncbi.nlm.nih.gov/books/NBK424849/.

Ghahramani, M., Sohrabi, M., Kakhki, A., & Besharat, M. (2016). The effects of physical activity on impulse control, attention, decision-making and motor functions in students with high and low impulsivity. *Biosciences Biotechnology Research Asia, 13*(3), 1689–1696. https://doi.org/10.13005/bbra/2318

Hegner, R. E. (1998, April 14). *Dual diagnoses: The challenge of serving people with concurrent mental illness and substance abuse problems*. NCBI Bookshelf. https://www.ncbi.nlm.nih.gov/books/NBK559478/.

Jacobs, L. A., & Gottlieb, A. (2020). The effect of housing circumstances on recidivism: Evidence from a sample of people on probation in San Francisco. *Criminal Justice and Behavior, 47*(9), 1097–1115. https://doi.org/10.1177/0093854820942285

Kirkwood, S. (2021). 'A wee kick up the arse': Mentoring, motivation and desistance from crime. *Criminology & Criminal Justice, 23*(2), 183–199. https://doi.org/10.1177/17488958211043691

Lamberti, J. S. (2016). Preventing criminal recidivism through mental health and criminal justice collaboration. *Psychiatric Services, 67*(11), 1206–1212. https://doi.org/10.1176/appi.ps.201500384

Landenberger, N. A., & Lipsey, M. W. (2005). The positive effects of cognitive–behavioral programs for offenders: A meta-analysis of factors associated with effective treatment. *Journal of Experimental Criminology, 1*(4), 451–476. https://doi.org/10.1007/s11292-005-3541-7

Ling, S., Umbach, R., & Raine, A. (2019). Biological explanations of criminal behavior. *Psychology Crime and Law, 25*(6), 626–640. https://doi.org/10.1080/1068316x.2019.1572753

Meijers, J., Harte, J. M., Jonker, F. A., & Meynen, G. (2015). Prison brain? Executive dysfunction in prisoners. *Frontiers in Psychology, 6*. https://doi.org/10.3389/fpsyg.2015.00043

Miller, L. (2014). Juvenile crime and juvenile justice: Patterns, models, and implications for clinical and legal practice. *Aggression and Violent Behavior, 19*(2), 122–137. https://doi.org/10.1016/j.avb.2014.01.005

Mitchell, O., Wilson, D. B., & MacKenzie, D. L. (2012). The effectiveness of incarceration-based drug treatment on criminal behavior: A systematic review. *Campbell Systematic Reviews, 8*(1). https://doi.org/10.4073/csr.2012.18

Mowen, T. J., Stansfield, R., & Boman, J. H. (2018). Family matters: Moving beyond "If" family support matters to "Why" family support matters during reentry from prison. *Journal of Research in Crime and Delinquency, 56*(4), 483–523. https://doi.org/10.1177/0022427818820902

Norman, E. M., Polaschek, D. L. L., & Starkey, N. J. (2022). Executive function in individuals who are compliant and non-compliant with the conditions of a community-based sentence. *Psychiatry Psychology and Law, 30*(2), 161–176. https://doi.org/10.1080/13218719.2021.2003268

Recidivism | National Institute of Justice. (n.d.). National Institute of Justice. https://nij.ojp.gov/topics/corrections/recidivism.

Rokven, J. J., De Boer, G., Tolsma, J., & Ruiter, S. (2016). How friends' involvement in crime affects the risk of offending and victimization. *European Journal of Criminology, 14*(6), 697–719. https://doi.org/10.1177/1477370816684150

Stickle, B., & Schuster, S. S. (2023). Are schools in prison worth it? The effects and economic returns of prison education. *American Journal of Criminal Justice, 48*(6), 1263–1294. https://doi.org/10.1007/s12103-023-09747-3

The Fortune Society presents "The Castle" | The Fortune Society. (2024, April 4). The Fortune Society. https://fortunesociety.org/event-show/the-fortune-society-presents-the-castle/.

Volkow, N. D., Wang, G., Fowler, J. S., Tomasi, D., Telang, F., & Baler, R. (2010). Addiction: Decreased reward sensitivity and increased expectation sensitivity conspire to overwhelm the brain's control circuit. *BioEssays, 32*(9), 748–755. https://doi.org/10.1002/bies.201000042

Walker, K., Bowen, E., Brown, S., & Sleath, E. (2014). Desistance from intimate partner violence. *Journal of Interpersonal Violence, 30*(15), 2726–2750. https://doi.org/10.1177/0886260514553634

Willis, J. (n.d.). *The relationship between emotional intelligence and recidivism among female offenders - ProQuest*. https://www.proquest.com/openview/b7f3b4cb70dc5948ba6bf5281ef45c38/1?cbl=18750&diss=y&pq-origsite=gscholar.

Wyse, J. J. B., Harding, D. J., & Morenoff, J. D. (2014). Romantic relationships and criminal desistance: Pathways and processes. *Sociological Forum, 29*(2), 365–385. https://doi.org/10.1111/socf.12088

Cultural Considerations in Forensic Neuropsychology

1 Introduction

Forensic neuropsychology stands at the confluence of neuroscience, psychology, and the legal system, offering critical insights into the cognitive and behavioral functioning of individuals involved in legal cases. In this interdisciplinary domain, neuropsychological assessments are employed to address questions related to criminal responsibility, competence to stand trial, malingering, and the impact of brain injuries or neurological disorders on behavior. However, the increasing diversity of societies underscores the imperative need to integrate cultural considerations into these evaluations. Culture, which encompasses shared values, beliefs, practices, and behaviors within a group, significantly influences cognitive functioning, emotional expression, and interpersonal dynamics. Consequently, forensic neuropsychologists must consider the intersection of culture, ethnicity, and neuropsychological assessments to ensure accurate, fair, and equitable evaluations in legal contexts.

1.1 Culture, Ethnicity, and Neuropsychological Assessments

The assessment of cognitive and behavioral functioning is inherently influenced by cultural factors. Neuropsychological tests, traditionally developed in Western contexts, often reflect cultural norms, language structures, and educational systems that may not align with those of non-Western populations. For instance, differences in verbal expression, memory strategies, and problem-solving approaches across cultures can lead to disparate performance on standardized assessments. These variations risk the underestimation or overestimation of cognitive deficits when cultural and linguistic backgrounds are not adequately considered (Fernández & Abe, 2017).

© The Author(s), under exclusive license to Springer Nature Switzerland AG 2025
K. J. Reddy, *Foundations of Criminal Forensic Neuropsychology*,
https://doi.org/10.1007/978-3-031-83771-5_17

Ethnicity further complicates this landscape, as it intersects with systemic inequalities, socioeconomic status, and educational access, which can shape cognitive development and neuropsychological test performance (Duncan et al., 2012). In forensic settings, where assessments often inform high-stakes legal decisions, such as criminal sentencing, competence to stand trial, or eligibility for disability benefits, the consequences of cultural insensitivity are profound. Misinterpretation of results due to cultural bias can perpetuate systemic injustices, disproportionately affecting marginalized populations.

Forensic neuropsychology must also grapple with the challenge of acculturation, which refers to the process of adapting to a new cultural environment (Bekteshi & Bellamy, 2024). Acculturation levels can influence cognitive and psychological functioning, creating variability even among individuals from similar cultural backgrounds. For example, immigrants with limited proficiency in the dominant language may struggle with language-dependent neuropsychological tests, resulting in scores that misrepresent their true abilities. Similarly, individuals who identify with multiple cultural identities may experience unique stressors, such as cultural dissonance or discrimination, that impact cognitive functioning and emotional well-being (Groen et al., 2019).

1.2 Importance of Cultural Competence in Forensic Neuropsychology

Cultural competence, defined as the ability to understand, respect, and effectively respond to cultural differences, is a cornerstone of ethical and accurate neuropsychological practice. In forensic settings, the implications of cultural competence extend beyond individual evaluations, influencing the broader perception of fairness within the legal system.

Understanding cultural differences is vital for ensuring that neuropsychological assessments are both valid and reliable across diverse populations. This involves recognizing that culture shapes not only cognitive processes but also attitudes toward mental health, legal systems, and authority figures. For example, individuals from collectivist cultures may prioritize group harmony over individual expression, potentially affecting their responses during interviews or assessments. Similarly, cultural stigmas surrounding mental illness or neurological disorders may influence the extent to which individuals disclose symptoms or seek help, complicating the assessment process. Cultural competence also mitigates the risk of perpetuating biases in forensic evaluations. For instance, standardized tests often rely on normative data that may not adequately represent the cultural backgrounds of all individuals. The inappropriate application of such norms can lead to misdiagnoses, unfair legal outcomes, and the erosion of trust in forensic neuropsychological practices (Greiffenstein & Kaufmann, 2017). Moreover, cultural insensitivity in communication or assessment procedures can exacerbate the stress experienced by individuals undergoing evaluations, potentially compromising the validity of test results.

This chapter aims to illuminate the challenges and propose solutions for fostering culturally competent practice in forensic neuropsychology.

The chapter begins by exploring the cultural and ethnic factors that influence cognitive functioning and neuropsychological assessments. It examines how cultural differences manifest in test performance, behavioral patterns, and attitudes toward the legal system. Particular attention is given to the implications of acculturation, bilingualism, and socioeconomic disparities, which often intersect with cultural identity to shape neuropsychological outcomes.

A critical analysis of systemic barriers and biases in forensic neuropsychology underscores the importance of cultural competence. This section explores how the reliance on Western-centric assessment tools, normative data, and diagnostic frameworks can perpetuate inequities in forensic settings. Case studies and empirical evidence are employed to illustrate the real-world impact of cultural insensitivity, emphasizing the ethical and legal ramifications of biased evaluations.

The chapter concludes by offering evidence-based strategies to enhance cultural competence in forensic neuropsychology. These include the development of culturally adapted assessment tools, the integration of qualitative methods to supplement standardized tests, and the incorporation of cultural training for forensic neuropsychologists. Emphasis is placed on the importance of interdisciplinary collaboration, involving linguists, cultural psychologists, and legal professionals, to address the multifaceted challenges posed by cultural diversity in forensic contexts.

1.3 Toward a Culturally Inclusive Forensic Neuropsychology

The integration of cultural considerations into forensic neuropsychology is not merely a matter of ethical obligation; it is a prerequisite for achieving accuracy, fairness, and justice in legal evaluations. As societies become increasingly multicultural, forensic neuropsychologists must embrace a paradigm shift that prioritizes cultural competence as a foundational element of practice. By acknowledging and addressing the cultural dimensions of cognitive functioning, forensic neuropsychology can contribute to a more equitable legal system that respects the diversity of human experiences.

This chapter seeks to equip practitioners, researchers, and legal professionals with the knowledge and tools necessary to navigate the complexities of culture in forensic neuropsychology. Through a comprehensive exploration of challenges and solutions, it aims to foster a culturally inclusive approach that upholds the principles of fairness and integrity in forensic assessments. In doing so, it underscores the transformative potential of cultural competence in advancing the field of forensic neuropsychology and promoting justice for all individuals, irrespective of their cultural or ethnic backgrounds.

2 Theoretical Frameworks in Cultural Competence

Cultural competence is a critical skill for forensic neuropsychologists working in increasingly diverse societies. It involves the ability to understand, respect, and effectively address the cultural, linguistic, and social needs of individuals from varied backgrounds. The significance of cultural competence in forensic neuropsychology lies in its role in mitigating biases, improving the accuracy of assessments, and promoting equitable legal outcomes. This section explores the concept of cultural competence, examines key theoretical frameworks that inform culturally responsive practices, and discusses how these frameworks enable clinicians to integrate cultural factors into assessments and interventions.

Cultural competence refers to the ongoing process by which professionals acquire the knowledge, skills, and attitudes necessary to work effectively within the cultural contexts of their clients (Kolhatkar & Berkowitz, 2014). It requires an awareness of one's own cultural assumptions, an understanding of the client's cultural background, and the ability to adapt practices to meet the client's unique needs.

In forensic neuropsychology, cultural competence is particularly relevant because assessments often influence legal decisions with profound consequences, such as determining criminal responsibility, competency to stand trial (CST), or eligibility for rehabilitation programs. Without cultural competence, practitioners risk misinterpreting behaviors, misdiagnosing conditions, and perpetuating systemic inequities within the legal system.

2.1 Key Theoretical Models in Cultural Competence

2.1.1 The Cultural Formulation Interview (CFI)

The cultural formulation model, outlined in the DSM-5, provides a structured framework for understanding an individual's cultural identity and its impact on their mental health and behavior (Aggarwal, 2024). In forensic contexts, the CFI helps neuropsychologists contextualize behaviors and symptoms that might otherwise be pathologized or misunderstood. For instance, culturally specific expressions of distress, such as somatization in Southeast Asian populations, can be recognized as normative rather than indicative of a psychological disorder.

2.1.2 Ecological Systems Theory

Bronfenbrenner's ecological systems theory highlights the interconnected layers of influence on an individual's development, including microsystems (family and peers), mesosystems (interactions between microsystems), exosystems (societal structures), and macrosystems (cultural norms and values) (Tong & An, 2024).

In forensic neuropsychology, this theory emphasizes the importance of considering the broader cultural and societal context in which the individual operates. For example, understanding how systemic inequalities, such as poverty or limited access to education, shape cognitive development and behavior can prevent biased conclusions during assessments.

2.1.3 The Culturally Adapted Therapy (CAT) Model

The CAT Model focuses on tailoring therapeutic interventions to align with the client's cultural values, beliefs, and practices. This approach includes strategies such as incorporating culturally relevant metaphors, adapting communication styles, and integrating traditional healing practices (Masuda et al., 2022). While primarily applied in therapeutic settings, the CAT Model has implications for forensic neuropsychology. Culturally adapted interviews and assessments can improve the accuracy of findings by fostering trust and reducing cultural misunderstandings.

2.1.4 The Intersectionality Framework

Intersectionality, introduced by Kimberlé Crenshaw, examines how overlapping identities (e.g., race, gender, socioeconomic status) intersect to shape an individual's experiences (Bauer et al., 2021). In forensic neuropsychology, this framework helps clinicians recognize the unique challenges faced by individuals with multiple marginalized identities. For example, an African American woman with a low socioeconomic background may experience compounded effects of racism and poverty, influencing her mental health and cognitive performance. An intersectional approach ensures that assessments account for these layered experiences.

2.2 Application of Theoretical Frameworks in Practice

The integration of these frameworks into forensic neuropsychology enhances the validity and fairness of assessments.

1. Assessment Practices:
   - The CFM provides a structured approach for gathering culturally relevant information, enabling clinicians to differentiate between culturally normative behaviors and pathological conditions.
   - Ecological systems theory prompts practitioners to consider external factors, such as community violence or systemic oppression, that may influence test results.

2. Diagnostic Evaluations:
   - The CAT Model supports the adaptation of diagnostic interviews to align with the client's cultural communication style, ensuring that important information is not overlooked.
   - Intersectionality underscores the need for individualized evaluations that consider the interplay of multiple identity factors.
3. Intervention Planning:
   - The CAT Model can inform recommendations for culturally appropriate rehabilitation programs. For instance, incorporating indigenous practices into treatment plans for Native American clients may enhance their engagement and outcomes.
4. Legal Advocacy:
   - These frameworks equip neuropsychologists to advocate for systemic changes, such as the development of culturally validated assessment tools or the inclusion of cultural training in forensic settings.

2.3 Challenges in Applying Cultural Competence Frameworks

Despite their utility, implementing these frameworks in forensic settings presents challenges. Limited availability of culturally validated tools, time constraints, and systemic biases can hinder the integration of cultural competence into practice. Additionally, practitioners may struggle with their own implicit biases or a lack of cultural knowledge.

To overcome these barriers, forensic neuropsychologists must prioritize ongoing education, seek mentorship from culturally knowledgeable peers, and engage in self-reflection to uncover and address their biases. Collaboration with cultural consultants and community leaders can also enhance cultural understanding and inform practice.

Theoretical frameworks in cultural competence, such as the cultural formulation model, ecological systems theory, the CAT Model, and intersectionality, provide invaluable guidance for forensic neuropsychologists. These frameworks enable practitioners to navigate the complexities of cultural diversity, ensuring that assessments and interventions are accurate, fair, and respectful of the client's background. As societies become increasingly multicultural, the relevance of cultural competence in forensic neuropsychology will only grow. By integrating these frameworks into their work, practitioners uphold the principles of justice and equity, contributing to a legal system that truly respects the dignity and diversity of all individuals.

3 Challenges of Language Barriers in Forensic Neuropsychology

Language plays a central role in neuropsychological assessments, as many evaluation tools rely heavily on verbal instructions, comprehension, and responses. In forensic neuropsychology, language barriers can present significant challenges, particularly when individuals being assessed have limited proficiency in the language of the evaluator or the standardized testing materials. These barriers can lead to inaccurate results, misinterpretations, and biased conclusions, which may, in turn, affect legal decisions. This section examines the impact of language differences on neuropsychological testing, explores how language proficiency influences test performance and communication, and proposes strategies for overcoming these barriers to ensure fair and accurate assessments.

3.1 Impact of Language Differences on Neuropsychological Testing and Assessment Outcomes

Language barriers can profoundly affect the validity and reliability of neuropsychological assessments. Many neuropsychological tests are developed and standardized in a specific language and cultural context, often favoring monolingual speakers of the dominant language. When applied to individuals who do not share the same linguistic background, these tests may yield inaccurate or misleading results.

Standardized neuropsychological tests often assume fluency in a particular language and familiarity with its cultural references (Nielsen et al., 2024). For individuals with limited proficiency in the test language, difficulties in comprehension and expression can lead to artificially low scores, particularly in domains such as verbal fluency, working memory, and comprehension. These outcomes may not accurately reflect an individual's cognitive abilities but instead reveal language-related limitations (Lareyre et al., 2023). For example, a bilingual individual with limited proficiency in English may score poorly on a word recall task due to linguistic constraints, even though their cognitive functioning is intact. Such results could be misinterpreted as indicative of memory impairment or a cognitive disorder.

In forensic contexts, inaccurate assessments can have severe legal consequences. Misinterpreted test results may lead to unjust outcomes, such as wrongful convictions, inappropriate sentencing, or inadequate rehabilitation recommendations. Language barriers thus raise ethical concerns, as they can undermine the fairness of evaluations and perpetuate systemic inequities in the legal system.

3.2 How Language Proficiency Affects Test Performance and Communication

Language proficiency influences several aspects of neuropsychological assessment. Tests measuring verbal fluency, vocabulary, and comprehension are particularly affected by language barriers. Limited language skills may reduce performance, even when the individual's underlying cognitive abilities are intact. Many tests impose strict time limits, which can disproportionately disadvantage individuals who take longer to process and respond in a non-native language. Idiomatic expressions, culturally specific references, or unfamiliar concepts embedded in test items can confuse non-native speakers, further affecting their performance.

Effective communication between the clinician and the individual is critical in forensic neuropsychology. Language barriers can hinder rapport building, reduce the individual's comfort level, and limit their ability to provide accurate and detailed information about their experiences. Additionally, clinicians may misinterpret nonverbal cues or fail to account for cultural variations in communication styles, leading to further misunderstandings.

3.3 Strategies for Overcoming Language Barriers

Addressing language barriers in forensic neuropsychology requires a multifaceted approach, combining the use of linguistic resources, cultural adaptations, and methodological innovations. The following strategies can help mitigate the impact of language differences and enhance the fairness and accuracy of assessments:

Qualified interpreters play a crucial role in bridging language gaps during neuropsychological assessments (Casas et al., 2011). Interpreters should be trained in psychological terminology and ethical considerations, ensuring they can accurately convey technical concepts without bias. Interpreters must remain impartial, refraining from influencing the individual's responses or providing unsolicited explanations. Clinicians should brief interpreters on the goals and structure of the assessment to ensure smooth communication. While interpreters can facilitate communication, their involvement may introduce additional variables, such as slight alterations in phrasing or unintended bias. Clinicians must carefully monitor these interactions and account for their potential impact on assessment outcomes.

Providing translated versions of neuropsychological tests can improve accessibility for individuals with limited language proficiency. However, effective translation goes beyond direct linguistic conversion and requires cultural adaptation. Translated tests should undergo validation to ensure they measure the same constructs as the original version. This involves psychometric analyses to verify reliability and validity across languages. Test items should be adapted to align with the cultural context of the individual, replacing culturally specific references with more universally understood concepts. Clinicians should avoid comparing scores from translated tests to norms developed for the original language, as differences in linguistic complexity and cultural familiarity may affect performance.

Nonverbal and culturally fair tests, which minimize reliance on language and culturally specific knowledge, offer valuable alternatives for individuals with language barriers. Some examples of these tasks include the Raven's Progressive Matrices, the Wechsler Nonverbal Scale of Ability (WNV), and Cognitive Screening Tools.

- **Raven's Progressive Matrices**: A nonverbal measure of abstract reasoning and problem-solving (Bilker et al., 2012).
- **Wechsler Nonverbal Scale of Ability (WNV)**: Designed to assess cognitive abilities without relying on language (Wechsler Nonverbal Scale of Ability (WNV)—Pearson Clinical, n.d.).
- **Cognitive Screening Tools**: Instruments like the Clock Drawing Test or Trail Making Test, which require minimal verbal interaction (Clock Drawing Test (CDT)—Strokengine, n.d.).

These tools can provide a more accurate assessment of cognitive abilities while reducing the influence of language proficiency.

Incorporating qualitative methods, such as structured interviews or ethnographic approaches, allows clinicians to gather contextual information about the individual's cultural background, language history, and educational experiences. These insights can help contextualize test results and reduce the risk of misinterpretation.

Clinicians must prioritize ongoing training in cultural competence and language considerations.

One of these may be language proficiency. Learning key phrases or basic conversational skills in the languages commonly encountered in their practice. Another one is bias awareness, reflecting on their own linguistic and cultural assumptions and how these may influence their assessments. And finally, professional development, participating in workshops or courses on cross-cultural neuropsychology.

Language barriers present significant challenges in forensic neuropsychology, affecting the validity of assessments, the accuracy of interpretations, and the quality of clinician–client communication. These challenges have profound implications in forensic contexts, where assessment outcomes often carry legal weight. By employing strategies such as using qualified interpreters, translating and adapting testing materials, incorporating nonverbal tests, and conducting qualitative assessments, clinicians can address these barriers and enhance the fairness and accuracy of their evaluations. Additionally, continuous training and self-reflection are essential for fostering cultural competence and mitigating the impact of language differences. Ultimately, addressing language barriers requires a commitment to equitable practices that respect the linguistic and cultural diversity of individuals. As forensic neuropsychology continues to evolve, integrating these strategies will be critical for ensuring ethical and effective practice in an increasingly multicultural world (Sweet et al., 2022).

4 Cultural Norms and Socioeconomic Factors in Neuropsychological Assessments

In neuropsychology, cultural norms and socioeconomic factors play a critical role in shaping individuals' behavior, expression of symptoms, and responses to assessments. Forensic neuropsychologists must navigate these influences to ensure accurate, equitable, and contextually appropriate evaluations. Failing to account for cultural and socioeconomic contexts can lead to misdiagnoses, biased interpretations, and unfair legal outcomes. This section explores the impact of cultural norms on neuropsychological functioning and assessment, examines the role of socioeconomic status (SES) in psychological well-being, and highlights the importance of contextualizing evaluations within the cultural and socioeconomic background of the individual.

4.1 The Influence of Cultural Norms on Behavior, Symptoms, and Assessment Responses

Cultural norms, or the shared beliefs, practices, and values within a cultural group, significantly influence how individuals perceive, express, and respond to psychological phenomena. These norms shape behaviors and cognitive processes, including how individuals approach and engage with neuropsychological assessments. Cultural norms often dictate how psychological distress or cognitive impairments are expressed. For instance, somatic symptomatology (e.g., headaches, fatigue, or body aches) is more prevalent in some cultures as an expression of emotional or psychological distress. In contrast, others may emphasize verbal articulation of emotions. In collectivist societies, individuals might downplay symptoms or impairments to avoid stigma or preserve family reputation. Conversely, in individualist cultures, people may express symptoms more explicitly, aiming to address personal well-being. Clinicians unaware of these differences may misinterpret symptom presentations, diagnosing underreporting as denial or exaggeration as malingering.

Cultural norms also influence test-taking behavior, such as willingness to engage, confidence in responses, or attitudes toward authority figures like clinicians (Fong et al., 2016). In some cultures, individuals may give responses they believe align with the perceived expectations of the examiner, compromising the authenticity of their answers. Avoidance of eye contact, often perceived as a sign of dishonesty in Western contexts, may signify respect in other cultures (Uono & Hietanen, 2015).

Different cultures emphasize distinct cognitive styles that affect performance on neuropsychological tests. Western cultures often promote analytic thinking, focusing on individual elements, while Eastern cultures emphasize holistic thinking, considering broader contexts. These differences can affect performance on tasks requiring abstract reasoning, pattern recognition, or memory recall.

4.2 Socioeconomic Status and Its Impact on Psychological Functioning

Socioeconomic status encompasses factors such as income, education, occupation, and access to resources, profoundly influencing psychological functioning and neuropsychological assessment outcomes. SES intersects with cultural norms, shaping an individual's lived experiences and access to opportunities, which must be considered during evaluations. SES determines access to education, healthcare, and other vital resources that influence cognitive development and psychological well-being. Individuals from lower SES backgrounds may have limited access to quality education, affecting foundational skills like literacy, numeracy, and critical thinking. These disparities can skew neuropsychological test results, especially when tasks rely on educational attainment. Restricted access to medical and mental health services can exacerbate cognitive impairments or mental health conditions, further affecting assessment outcomes (Halalmeh et al., 2023).

Chronic stress, often associated with poverty, job insecurity, and housing instability, has well-documented effects on cognitive and emotional functioning. Prolonged stress triggers dysregulation in the hypothalamic-pituitary-adrenal (HPA) axis, leading to structural and functional changes in brain regions like the hippocampus, amygdala, and prefrontal cortex (Stephens & Wand, 2012). These changes manifest as impairments in memory, attention, and executive functioning. Individuals experiencing chronic stress may display irritability, fatigue, or difficulty concentrating, which can be misinterpreted as malingering or lack of effort during assessments.

In forensic settings, low-SES individuals often face additional pressures, such as limited legal representation, biases in the justice system, and higher exposure to environmental stressors (e.g., crime and discrimination). These factors can exacerbate psychological vulnerabilities, complicating the interpretation of neuropsychological test results.

To provide accurate and fair assessments, clinicians must adopt a holistic approach that integrates cultural and socioeconomic contexts into the evaluation process. This requires both an understanding of the individual's background and a willingness to adapt standard practices to meet their unique needs. Gathering a detailed history of the individual's cultural and socioeconomic background is critical. Understanding the individual's cultural values, norms, and beliefs. Assessing fluency in the test language and exposure to bilingual or multilingual environments. Identifying potential disparities that could affect test performance. Exploring experiences of discrimination, trauma, or acculturation that may influence psychological functioning.

Standardized tests should be adapted to minimize cultural and SES biases. Using culturally and socioeconomically relevant normative data ensures that test scores are interpreted within an appropriate context. Incorporating nonverbal measures, such as visual-spatial tasks, can reduce linguistic and cultural biases. Allowing breaks, modifying time limits, or using alternative formats can accommodate individuals affected by stress or fatigue. Clinicians must undergo training to enhance their cultural competence and understanding of SES-related challenges. Reflecting on implicit biases that may influence their interpretations. Staying informed about cultural and SES dynamics relevant to their practice. Ensuring that evaluations prioritize equity, respect, and understanding. Incorporating insights from other professionals, such as cultural consultants, social workers, or community leaders, can enrich the evaluation process. These collaborations provide additional perspectives on the individual's background and needs, enhancing the accuracy and fairness of assessments.

Cultural norms and socioeconomic factors profoundly influence behavior, symptom expression, and responses to neuropsychological assessments. Ignoring these factors risks perpetuating biases and inequities, particularly in forensic contexts where the stakes are high. By contextualizing evaluations within the individual's cultural and socioeconomic background, clinicians can better understand the interplay of these influences on psychological functioning. Strategies such as comprehensive history-taking, adapting testing materials, and pursuing cultural competence training are essential for fostering equitable and accurate assessments. In forensic neuropsychology, adopting a culturally and socioeconomically informed approach is not merely an ethical imperative but a professional necessity. By addressing these challenges, practitioners can ensure that their evaluations contribute to justice, fairness, and the well-being of all individuals, regardless of their background.

5 Bias in Neuropsychological Assessments

Bias in neuropsychological assessments poses significant challenges to achieving accurate, fair, and meaningful evaluations. When assessments fail to consider the cultural, linguistic, and socioeconomic contexts of the individuals being evaluated, the results can be misleading or discriminatory. This section explores potential sources of bias in neuropsychological testing, the consequences of cultural misunderstandings in interpreting results, and the need for practitioners to critically evaluate their own biases and assumptions.

5.1 Sources of Bias in Neuropsychological Assessments

Neuropsychological tests are often developed in Western contexts and standardized on populations that do not reflect the diverse cultural and linguistic backgrounds of individuals worldwide. These tools may inherently favor the cognitive styles, language skills, and educational experiences prevalent in the population on which they were normed. Tests requiring high proficiency in the test's language can disadvantage non-native speakers or those with limited formal education. For example, verbal memory or comprehension tests often reflect cultural knowledge embedded in the language, making them less valid for individuals from different linguistic backgrounds. Test content may include culturally specific concepts or references unfamiliar to individuals from other cultural groups. A memory recall test referencing objects or events uncommon in certain cultures may yield artificially low scores. Standardized tests rely on normative data sets that may not represent diverse populations. Using these norms to interpret results can lead to inaccurate conclusions about an individual's cognitive abilities.

Bias can arise not only from the tools themselves but also from the manner in which tests are administered and interpreted. Implicit biases held by examiners may affect how they perceive or interact with individuals from different cultural or socioeconomic backgrounds. For instance, an examiner may misinterpret behaviors or responses due to cultural differences in communication styles. The individual being assessed may feel anxiety about confirming negative stereotypes associated with their cultural or socioeconomic group, leading to poorer performance.

Socioeconomic disparities can also introduce bias. Individuals from low-income backgrounds may have had fewer educational opportunities or less exposure to formal testing environments, affecting their performance in ways unrelated to their true cognitive abilities.

5.2 Cultural Misunderstandings and Their Consequences

Cultural misunderstandings in neuropsychological assessments can lead to misinterpretation of results and inappropriate conclusions.

Cultural norms influence how individuals express psychological distress or cognitive challenges. Misunderstanding these expressions can result in misdiagnoses. In some cultures, emotional distress is expressed somatically (e.g., physical pain), while in others, it is verbalized. A clinician unfamiliar with these norms might mislabel somatic expressions as malingering or dismissive of underlying psychological conditions (Chafetz et al., 2019). Cultural factors can lead to the over- or underestimation of an individual's cognitive capacities. Individuals from collectivist cultures may exhibit different approaches to problem-solving compared to those from individualistic cultures, affecting performance on certain tests. Without understanding these differences, clinicians may incorrectly assess cognitive functioning.

In forensic settings, biased assessments can have dire consequences, such as wrongful convictions or inappropriate sentencing. A misunderstanding of cultural nuances can lead to erroneous evaluations of competence to stand trial, criminal responsibility, or rehabilitation potential.

5.3 The Practitioner's Role in Addressing Bias

To mitigate bias, practitioners must critically evaluate their own assumptions, adopt culturally competent practices, and ensure fairness in the assessment process. Implicit biases—automatic, unconscious attitudes or stereotypes—can influence how clinicians interpret behaviors and responses. Recognizing and addressing these biases is a critical step toward equitable practice. Engaging in cultural competence training and actively reflecting on one's biases can help practitioners reduce the influence of stereotypes. Regularly consulting with colleagues or supervisors about challenging cases can provide alternative perspectives and mitigate individual biases.

Practitioners must integrate cultural considerations into every stage of the assessment process. Collecting detailed information about the individual's cultural, linguistic, and socioeconomic background helps contextualize test results. When possible, practitioners should use tests validated for the individual's cultural or linguistic group. If such tools are unavailable, they should clearly document the limitations of the assessment. Using culture-specific norms or interpreting results within the context of the individual's cultural background ensures greater accuracy.

When faced with complex cases involving cultural or linguistic differences, consulting with cultural experts or interpreters can enhance the quality of the assessment. Employing trained interpreters ensures accurate communication and prevents misinterpretation due to language barriers. Collaborating with individuals knowledgeable about the examinee's culture can provide insights into culturally specific behaviors or norms.

5.4 Strategies for Reducing Bias in Neuropsychological Assessments

Efforts to create culturally fair assessments involve designing tasks that minimize cultural and linguistic biases. For instance, nonverbal tests that rely on visual-spatial skills rather than language comprehension can reduce barriers for individuals from diverse linguistic backgrounds. Incorporating diverse populations into normative data sets is essential for creating more representative benchmarks. Collaborations between researchers across cultures can help build databases that better reflect global populations. Practitioners should interpret test results within the broader context of the individual's background, avoiding overreliance on rigid cutoff scores or norms. Continuous professional development in cultural competence ensures that practitioners remain informed about emerging research and best practices for equitable assessments.

Bias in neuropsychological assessments arises from multiple sources, including culturally biased testing tools, examiner assumptions, and structural inequities.

These biases not only compromise the accuracy of evaluations but also risk perpetuating discrimination and inequity, particularly in forensic contexts where assessments carry significant consequences. To counteract bias, practitioners must engage in critical self-reflection, adopt culturally informed practices, and seek collaboration when necessary. By prioritizing fairness and equity, neuropsychologists can provide assessments that are not only scientifically valid but also ethically sound, contributing to just and meaningful outcomes for all individuals.

6 Culturally Appropriate Testing Tools in Neuropsychology

The use of culturally validated and appropriate neuropsychological assessments is critical to ensuring accurate, fair, and meaningful evaluations. As societies grow increasingly diverse, the limitations of standardized assessments—often developed and normed within Western populations—become evident. This section explores the importance of culturally appropriate tools, reviews existing culturally adapted tests, and underscores the necessity for ongoing research to develop methodologies that align with the cultural and linguistic diversity of global populations.

6.1 The Importance of Culturally Validated Testing Tools

Neuropsychological assessments aim to measure cognitive, emotional, and behavioral functions, often providing the foundation for diagnosis, treatment planning, and legal determinations. When tests fail to account for cultural differences, their validity diminishes. Memory, problem-solving, and reasoning can vary across cultures due to differences in educational systems, traditions, and day-to-day experiences. A test developed in one culture may not accurately measure these constructs in another. Inappropriate tools increase the risk of misdiagnosis. For instance, a low score on a verbal fluency task may reflect linguistic unfamiliarity rather than true cognitive impairment.

Cultural bias in assessments perpetuates inequities, especially in high-stakes settings like forensic neuropsychology. A culturally inappropriate tool could unfairly disadvantage individuals from marginalized groups, leading to incorrect legal or clinical outcomes. Practitioners have an ethical obligation to ensure that tools are fair and non-discriminatory. The American Psychological Association (APA) and other professional bodies emphasize cultural competence as a key component of ethical practice. In multicultural societies, tools must be adaptable for diverse populations to address the needs of immigrant and minority communities.

6.2 Existing Culturally Adapted Neuropsychological Tests

Over the years, researchers and clinicians have recognized the need for culturally adapted assessment tools. These adaptations may involve translating existing tests, modifying content, or developing entirely new instruments tailored to specific populations. The Wechsler scales, widely used in neuropsychology, have been translated and adapted for use in multiple languages and cultures. These adaptations often involve re-norming the test with culturally appropriate references and examples. The MMSE has been adapted for various cultures, with modifications to reflect linguistic and cultural norms. For example, the recall items or language components may differ in culturally specific versions.

Some tools are specifically designed for particular cultural or linguistic groups. One such tool is the African Neuropsychological Battery (Ikanga et al., 2022). This tool addresses the unique cultural and linguistic contexts of individuals in sub-Saharan Africa, emphasizing culturally relevant cognitive domains. Another such tool is the Cambridge Cognitive Examination for Older Adults in Low-Educated Populations (CAMCOG-LE) (Hon et al., 1999). This tool accommodates individuals with limited formal education, offering an equitable assessment of cognitive functioning.

Nonverbal assessments are particularly valuable for minimizing cultural and linguistic biases. One of the tools is the Raven's Progressive Matrices. This widely used nonverbal test of abstract reasoning minimizes language dependency and cultural content, making it suitable for cross-cultural contexts. Another tool is called the Test of Nonverbal Intelligence (TONI). Similarly, the TONI assesses problem-solving and reasoning without reliance on language, offering a fairer evaluation for non-native speakers or individuals with language impairments.

6.3 Challenges and Limitations of Existing Tools

Despite progress, the availability of culturally appropriate tools remains limited, and significant gaps exist in ensuring fairness across diverse populations. Culturally adapted tools often lack robust normative data from diverse populations. This limitation affects the validity and reliability of test interpretations for underrepresented groups. For example, a test adapted for a specific culture may still rely on norms from the original population, reducing its accuracy. Translation alone does not guarantee cultural appropriateness. Certain cultural nuances—such as attitudes toward authority, problem-solving styles, or social norms—may not be adequately addressed in the adapted version. Developing, validating, and standardizing culturally appropriate tools is resource-intensive, requiring collaboration among experts in neuropsychology, linguistics, and cultural studies. This process is often underfunded, particularly in low- and middle-income countries.

6.4 The Need for Ongoing Research and Development

To ensure inclusivity, ongoing research must focus on populations historically underrepresented in neuropsychological research. Collaborating with researchers in diverse regions can expand normative datasets, making tools more representative. Tools must undergo rigorous validation across multiple cultural contexts to establish their universality or limitations. Incorporating indigenous and traditional knowledge systems into neuropsychological frameworks can enrich assessments and make them more relevant to specific populations. One example of this is that cognitive domains emphasized in Western models, such as working memory or verbal fluency, which may be complemented by skills valued in other cultures, such as storytelling or navigation.

Advances in digital technology offer opportunities to create adaptable, scalable, and culturally responsive tools. Interactive, adaptive tests can adjust difficulty levels or content based on the examinee's background. Digital platforms can incorporate multiple languages and dialects, enabling broader accessibility. Equipping neuropsychologists with the skills to administer and interpret culturally adapted tools is as important as developing the tools themselves. Regular training programs on the use of culturally validated tools can enhance practitioners' competence. Encouraging collaboration among neuropsychologists worldwide can foster the exchange of knowledge and best practices.

Culturally validated and appropriate neuropsychological assessment tools are essential for ensuring accurate, fair, and meaningful evaluations. While progress has been made in developing culturally adapted tests, significant challenges remain, including limited normative data, inadequate cultural sensitivity, and resource constraints. Addressing these gaps requires ongoing research, greater representation of diverse populations, and the integration of indigenous knowledge systems. Technology can play a transformative role in creating adaptable tools, while training practitioners in culturally competent testing practices is essential for translating theory into practice. Ultimately, the development and implementation of culturally appropriate neuropsychological tools not only enhance the validity of assessments but also uphold the ethical principles of fairness, equity, and respect for cultural diversity. By prioritizing these efforts, neuropsychologists can contribute to a more inclusive and just approach to cognitive and psychological evaluation.

7 Importance of Interpretation Services in Forensic Neuropsychology

In forensic neuropsychology, effective communication between the practitioner and the client is pivotal to obtaining accurate assessments and ensuring equitable treatment. For individuals with limited proficiency in the language used during assessments, the presence of qualified interpreters becomes indispensable. This section explores the necessity of interpretation services in forensic settings, identifies challenges associated with their use, and provides best practices for maximizing their effectiveness. Furthermore, it highlights how these services contribute to accurate assessments and uphold fairness within the legal system.

7.1 The Need for Qualified Interpreters

Language proficiency significantly impacts the ability to understand instructions, respond to questions, and engage meaningfully during neuropsychological assessments. Forensic evaluations, in particular, often involve high-stakes scenarios where comprehension is critical. Interpreters bridge linguistic gaps, ensuring that the client's thoughts, concerns, and responses are conveyed accurately to the examiner. Miscommunication due to language barriers can lead to incorrect interpretations of a client’s cognitive abilities or psychological state, resulting in flawed conclusions.

Language is closely tied to culture. Interpreters not only translate words but also provide insight into cultural nuances that might otherwise be overlooked. One such example is that idiomatic expressions or culturally specific references may carry meanings that a non-native practitioner might misinterpret without context.

Forensic neuropsychologists have an ethical responsibility to ensure that language differences do not disadvantage clients. Professional guidelines, such as those from the American Psychological Association (APA), emphasize the importance of equitable treatment, which includes providing interpretation services when necessary.

7.2 Challenges of Using Interpreter Services in Forensic Settings

Despite their importance, interpretation services come with challenges that can complicate their use in forensic neuropsychology. General interpreters may lack familiarity with neuropsychological terminology, leading to potential miscommunication. Specialized training in psychological and legal contexts is often required. In linguistically diverse populations, finding an interpreter fluent in a client’s specific dialect can be difficult. Interpreters may inadvertently omit critical information or misinterpret phrases, affecting the accuracy of the assessment. An interpreter’s personal biases or assumptions could inadvertently color the interpretation, especially in emotionally charged or complex cases. High-quality interpretation services can be expensive, and availability may be limited, particularly in rural or underserved areas. The use of interpreters often extends the duration of assessments, which may increase stress for both clients and practitioners.

In forensic contexts, confidentiality is paramount. The involvement of an interpreter introduces a third party, which may raise concerns about the security of sensitive information.

7.3 *Best Practices for Using Interpretation Services*

To maximize the effectiveness of interpreter services and mitigate potential challenges, practitioners should adhere to best practices tailored to forensic settings. Use interpreters certified in forensic and psychological interpretation, with training in relevant terminology and concepts. Ensure interpreters are familiar with the client's cultural background, enabling them to provide accurate and nuanced translations. Before the assessment, practitioners should provide interpreters with context about the evaluation's purpose, the nature of the questions, and the importance of neutrality. Practitioners must establish the interpreter's role as a neutral facilitator of communication rather than an advocate or advisor for the client. Practitioners should address the client directly, rather than speaking to the interpreter, to maintain rapport and engagement. Provide clear, concise instructions to reduce the likelihood of misinterpretation.

After the session, practitioners and interpreters should review any ambiguities or challenges encountered during the process. Document the interpreter's involvement and any potential limitations it introduced in the assessment report.

7.4 *How Effective Interpretation Contributes to Accurate Assessments and Fair Treatment*

Effective interpretation ensures that the client's responses are accurately conveyed, reducing the risk of errors in scoring or interpretation. Interpreters act as conduits, ensuring that the client's thoughts and emotions are faithfully represented. Cultural nuances that might otherwise be misread are clarified through accurate interpretation. Forensic neuropsychological assessments often influence legal outcomes, such as determining competency to stand trial or assessing cognitive impairments in criminal cases. Interpretation services help uphold justice by ensuring assessments are equitable. Clients with limited language proficiency can fully participate in the evaluation process, protecting their legal rights (Martinez et al., 2021). Interpretation services mitigate the linguistic and cultural biases that could disadvantage clients in forensic contexts. A client who feels understood and respected is more likely to cooperate during assessments, enhancing the reliability of the evaluation. Effective interpretation reduces anxiety stemming from language barriers, enabling the client to focus on the task at hand.

7.5 Future Directions for Interpretation Services

As forensic neuropsychology evolves, the demand for skilled interpreters will continue to grow. Offering specialized training for interpreters in forensic and neuropsychological contexts. Incorporating tools like real-time translation software, though these should complement, not replace, human interpreters. Creating standardized protocols for the use of interpreters in forensic settings to ensure consistency and quality.

Interpretation services are indispensable in forensic neuropsychology, addressing language barriers that could otherwise undermine the validity of assessments and the fairness of legal outcomes. While challenges such as interpreter availability, accuracy, and confidentiality persist, adhering to best practices ensures that these services enhance, rather than hinder, the evaluation process. By prioritizing the integration of skilled interpreters and refining protocols for their use, practitioners can uphold ethical standards, foster equity, and contribute to the delivery of justice (Mennella et al., 2024). As cultural and linguistic diversity continues to shape forensic contexts, effective interpretation services will remain a cornerstone of culturally competent neuropsychological practice.

8 Cultural Formulations in Diagnostic Evaluations

Cultural formulations are an essential framework in clinical and forensic psychology, allowing practitioners to understand and interpret a client's mental health and behavior within the context of their cultural background. Diagnostic evaluations, especially in forensic settings, require nuanced approaches to avoid misdiagnoses and biases that could lead to unjust outcomes. By incorporating cultural formulations, clinicians can adopt a holistic perspective, accounting for the intersection of cultural, social, and personal factors that influence mental health and behavior. This section explores the definition and application of cultural formulations, their importance in providing comprehensive diagnostic assessments, and case studies that highlight their utility in forensic evaluations.

8.1 Definition and Application of Cultural Formulations

Cultural formulations refer to structured methods of assessing and integrating an individual's cultural background into clinical and diagnostic evaluations. They involve identifying cultural influences on symptoms, understanding cultural explanations for distress, and evaluating the client's cultural identity and support systems. The DSM-5 outlines the Cultural Formulation Interview (CFI) as a tool to facilitate this process, providing a structured method to gather culturally relevant information. Understanding the client's cultural background, including ethnicity, language, religion, and social affiliations. Exploring how the client interprets their symptoms through cultural beliefs and practices. Identifying stressors related to acculturation, discrimination, or socioeconomic challenges and recognizing culturally specific support systems. Addressing potential cultural biases or miscommunications in the therapeutic relationship. Integrating all cultural dimensions into a comprehensive understanding of the client's mental health and behavior.

In forensic neuropsychology, cultural formulations are applied to interpret a client's cognitive and psychological functioning within their cultural and contextual background. This is crucial for many reasons. One could be evaluating competency to stand trial or criminal responsibility. Understanding behavior patterns and symptom expression influenced by cultural norms. Providing culturally sensitive recommendations for rehabilitation or intervention.

8.2 Importance of Integrating Cultural Background into Diagnostic Assessments

Failure to consider cultural factors can lead to misinterpretation of symptoms. For instance, culturally normative behaviors may be mistakenly labeled as pathological if viewed through a Western-centric lens. One example could be how spiritual beliefs involving communication with ancestors may be misdiagnosed as delusions in cultures where such practices are common. Incorporating cultural formulations ensures that the diagnosis reflects the client's lived experiences, reducing bias and enhancing accuracy. Socioeconomic challenges, such as poverty and discrimination, often intersect with cultural identity, influencing mental health outcomes. Integrating these factors into diagnostic assessments provides a more comprehensive understanding of the client. In forensic contexts, cultural formulations ensure that assessments consider the client's cultural and social realities, reducing the likelihood of unjust legal outcomes. This aligns with ethical principles of equity and fairness in psychological practice.

8.3 Best Practices for Implementing Cultural Formulations

Cultural formulations are vital in ensuring diagnostic evaluations account for the complexities of cultural identity. When implemented effectively, they lead to more accurate assessments, fostering equity in forensic and clinical outcomes. Tools like the DSM-5 Cultural Formulation Interview can guide practitioners in gathering relevant cultural information systematically. Clinicians should undergo training to develop cultural competence, including awareness of their own biases and knowledge of diverse cultural practices. Consulting with cultural liaisons or interpreters familiar with the client's background enhances the depth and accuracy of assessments. Recognize that cultural identity is complex and multifaceted, requiring personalized approaches to each client.

8.4 Future Directions in Cultural Formulations

Ongoing research is needed to expand the understanding of cultural influences on mental health and behavior, particularly among underrepresented populations. Creating diagnostic tools validated for diverse cultural groups ensures that assessments are equitable and accurate. Embedding cultural formulation training into forensic psychology curricula equips future practitioners with the skills to apply these frameworks effectively.

Cultural formulations are indispensable for understanding the interplay of cultural, social, and psychological factors in diagnostic evaluations. By integrating a client's cultural background into assessments, practitioners can avoid misdiagnoses, enhance accuracy, and promote fairness, particularly in forensic contexts where the stakes are high. Case studies demonstrate the profound impact of cultural formulations in achieving equitable outcomes, emphasizing their critical role in modern neuropsychological practice. As the field advances, continued research, training, and tool development will ensure that cultural formulations remain a cornerstone of comprehensive and ethical forensic evaluations.

9 Case Studies

These case studies underscore the profound influence of cultural differences on forensic neuropsychological assessments and legal decisions. Language barriers, culturally specific expressions of distress, and unfamiliarity with legal systems can significantly impact outcomes if not adequately addressed. Integrating cultural competence into forensic evaluations not only enhances the accuracy of assessments but also promotes justice by ensuring that individuals are evaluated within the context of their unique cultural and personal experiences.

9.1 Case Study 1

Mr. P., a 45-year-old male of Mexican origin, was arrested for vehicular manslaughter after running a red light and causing a fatal accident. During the investigation, Mr. P. displayed significant confusion and difficulty answering questions during police interrogations and legal proceedings. This prompted concerns about his cognitive functioning and competency to stand trial (CST). Mr. P. was referred for a forensic neuropsychological assessment to determine whether cognitive impairments were impacting his ability to understand the charges against him and assist in his defense. The initial evaluation utilized standardized cognitive tests administered in English, despite Mr. P. being a native Spanish speaker with limited proficiency in English.

The results indicated severe cognitive deficits, including poor memory, executive functioning, and attention skills. Based on these results, the prosecutor argued that Mr. P. was cognitively impaired and unfit to stand trial, suggesting the need for long-term custodial care. However, a defense attorney requested a second opinion from a culturally competent forensic neuropsychologist.

The second evaluator conducted the assessment in Spanish using culturally and linguistically validated tools. Additionally, an interpreter assisted in bridging any remaining language gaps during the assessment process.

This reevaluation revealed that Mr. P.'s cognitive performance was within normal limits for his age and education level. The earlier findings of cognitive deficits were attributed to the language barrier and unfamiliarity with English-based testing materials. Furthermore, the evaluator considered Mr. P.'s educational background in rural Mexico, where formal schooling was limited, and adjusted the interpretations of the test scores accordingly. The neuropsychologist also explored cultural factors influencing Mr. P.'s behavior during legal proceedings. His apparent confusion and hesitation in answering questions were rooted in his unfamiliarity with the U.S. legal system and a cultural tendency to defer to authority figures rather than assertively advocate for oneself.

The culturally informed assessment revealed no significant cognitive impairments, enabling Mr. P. to be deemed competent to stand trial. The court acknowledged the initial errors in the evaluation and dismissed the findings of cognitive dysfunction. With the aid of cultural advocacy, the defense successfully argued that the accident was caused by mechanical failure, not negligence or impairment. Mr. P. was acquitted of criminal charges.

9.2 Case Study 2

Ms. S., a 34-year-old Somali refugee, was charged with child endangerment after leaving her 6-year-old child unattended in a public park. Witnesses reported that Ms. S. appeared disoriented and agitated when questioned by law enforcement. This prompted concerns about her mental health and ability to parent. Ms. S. was referred for a forensic psychological evaluation to determine whether mental illness influenced her behavior and whether she posed a risk to her child. Initial evaluations suggested possible psychosis due to her reported auditory hallucinations and descriptions of seeing spirits. The evaluator, unfamiliar with Somali cultural practices, diagnosed her with schizophrenia based on these accounts. Consequently, child protective services (CPS) recommended that Ms. S.'s child be placed in foster care, and criminal charges were pursued. The defense sought a second opinion from a forensic neuropsychologist with expertise in cross-cultural assessments.

The second evaluator recognized the importance of cultural beliefs in interpreting Ms. S.'s symptoms. In Somali culture, belief in spirits or "djinn" is common and not necessarily indicative of mental illness. Ms. S.'s reports of hearing her late mother's voice were reinterpreted as culturally normative expressions of grief rather than hallucinations. Furthermore, the evaluator explored Ms. S.'s refugee background, including her experiences of trauma and loss. Her disoriented behavior on the day of the incident was attributed to post-traumatic stress disorder (PTSD) exacerbated by her isolation and lack of social support in the host country. The evaluation also considered Ms. S.'s parenting practices in the context of her cultural norms. In Somali culture, communal parenting is common, and children are often left under the informal supervision of neighbors or community members. This cultural perspective provided context for her decision to leave her child in the park, which she viewed as a safe space rather than neglect.

The second evaluation prompted a reexamination of the charges. The court recognized that Ms. S.'s behavior was not rooted in psychosis but in cultural practices and trauma-related distress. She was referred for trauma-focused therapy and a community integration program to build social support. CPS worked with cultural liaisons to provide parenting education tailored to her cultural background, allowing her child to remain in her care under supervision.

These case studies underscore the profound influence of cultural differences on forensic neuropsychological assessments and legal decisions. Language barriers, culturally specific expressions of distress, and unfamiliarity with legal systems can significantly impact outcomes if not adequately addressed. Integrating cultural competence into forensic evaluations not only enhances the accuracy of assessments but also promotes justice by ensuring that individuals are evaluated within the context of their unique cultural and personal experiences.

10 Negotiating Cultural Diversity in Forensic Settings

Forensic settings bring together diverse individuals whose cultural backgrounds, beliefs, and experiences shape their behaviors, perceptions, and interactions. In such contexts, forensic practitioners face the dual responsibility of ensuring fair legal processes and delivering accurate, culturally informed assessments. The complexity of cultural diversity in legal contexts necessitates a multifaceted approach to understanding and integrating these factors into forensic practice. This chapter section explores the challenges of working with culturally diverse populations, the strategies practitioners can employ to develop cultural competence, and the vital role of advocacy and community engagement in fostering cultural understanding.

10.1 Challenges in Working with Culturally Diverse Populations

Cultural diversity introduces unique challenges into forensic neuropsychology, particularly in legal contexts where stakes are high and misunderstandings can lead to significant consequences. Cultural biases and stereotypes can inadvertently influence practitioners' perceptions and decision-making. For instance, behaviors considered abnormal in one culture might be typical in another. Without a culturally informed perspective, practitioners risk interpreting culturally normative behaviors as signs of pathology or criminal intent.

Many standardized neuropsychological assessments were developed within Western cultural contexts and may not adequately capture the cognitive, emotional, or behavioral nuances of individuals from non-Western backgrounds. This limitation can result in biased outcomes, with underperformance on culturally unfamiliar tasks being misattributed to deficits rather than contextual factors. Language differences often create obstacles in assessment, treatment, and legal processes. Miscommunications can arise when culturally specific expressions or idioms of distress are misunderstood, potentially leading to incorrect conclusions.

Forensic practitioners often face ethical challenges when navigating cultural differences. For example, respecting cultural practices while adhering to legal standards and professional ethics can be a delicate balance. This becomes particularly complex in cases where cultural norms conflict with legal or societal expectations, such as in issues related to family dynamics or gender roles. Developing cultural competence is essential for navigating the challenges of cultural diversity in forensic settings. This involves acquiring the knowledge, skills, and attitudes necessary to provide culturally responsive care and ensuring that legal and clinical processes remain fair and equitable.

Formal training in cultural competence is a critical step in preparing forensic neuropsychologists to address the complexities of cultural diversity. Training sessions that focus on understanding cultural worldviews, biases, and their impact on forensic practices. Incorporating real-world case studies into training to illustrate the role of culture in shaping behaviors and legal outcomes. Familiarizing practitioners with culturally validated tools and techniques for interpreting results within appropriate cultural contexts. Practitioners must critically examine their own cultural assumptions and biases. Structured self-reflection exercises, implicit bias tests, and peer discussions can help uncover and address these biases, enabling more objective and culturally sensitive evaluations.

Developing culturally responsive interviewing skills is crucial. Practitioners should tailor their questions and interactions to account for cultural norms and values, ensuring that the individual feels respected and understood. Consulting with cultural liaisons, anthropologists, or community representatives can provide practitioners with deeper insights into the cultural context of their clients. These collaborations are particularly valuable when assessing individuals from cultures unfamiliar to the evaluator.

Beyond individual practice, forensic neuropsychologists play a broader role in advocating for culturally inclusive practices and engaging with communities to foster mutual understanding and trust. Forensic practitioners can advocate for systemic changes that address cultural disparities in the legal and mental health systems. This includes pushing for the inclusion of culturally diverse norms in test standardization and the creation of policies that support equitable access to legal and mental health services. Building relationships with diverse communities is essential for promoting cultural understanding and reducing the stigma associated with forensic and psychological evaluations.

Practitioners can organize workshops, participate in community forums, and collaborate with local organizations to bridge cultural gaps. Experienced forensic neuropsychologists can mentor early-career professionals, emphasizing the importance of cultural competence and sharing strategies for negotiating cultural diversity in forensic settings. Additionally, they can take leadership roles in professional organizations to promote cultural diversity within the field. Effective cultural negotiation in forensic settings has a direct impact on legal outcomes, influencing everything from competency evaluations to sentencing decisions. By integrating cultural competence into their practice, forensic neuropsychologists ensure that their assessments reflect the individual's unique experiences and that legal processes uphold principles of fairness and justice.

In a criminal case involving an immigrant defendant, a culturally competent evaluation that accounts for acculturation stress, language barriers, and culturally normative behaviors might reveal mitigating circumstances. These insights can lead to alternative sentencing options, such as rehabilitation programs that address cultural factors, rather than punitive measures.

Negotiating cultural diversity in forensic settings is an ongoing and dynamic process that requires dedication, self-awareness, and a commitment to lifelong learning. By addressing the challenges of cultural diversity, developing cultural competence, and engaging in advocacy and community outreach, forensic neuropsychologists can ensure that their practices are inclusive, accurate, and just. These efforts contribute to a legal system that not only recognizes the complexity of human diversity but also actively works to uphold fairness and equity in its processes.

11 Conclusion

Cultural considerations are central to the practice of forensic neuropsychology, where the stakes of accurate and fair assessments are high. This chapter has explored the multifaceted ways in which culture intersects with neuropsychological assessments in forensic settings, underscoring the critical need for cultural competence to uphold justice and equity.

A recurring theme throughout the chapter is the profound influence of culture on cognition, behavior, and the expression of symptoms. Standardized assessment tools, often rooted in Western norms, may fail to capture the lived experiences and nuanced expressions of individuals from diverse backgrounds. This disparity can lead to misinterpretation of results, misdiagnoses, and unjust legal outcomes. Forensic neuropsychologists must critically evaluate these limitations and strive to contextualize their findings within the cultural and socioeconomic realities of the individuals they assess.

Key challenges in this domain include addressing language barriers, understanding the impact of socioeconomic factors, and overcoming inherent biases in testing tools. Language proficiency, for instance, significantly affects test performance and communication, requiring the use of interpreters and culturally validated materials to ensure fairness. Similarly, socioeconomic factors, such as access to education and healthcare, shape an individual's cognitive and psychological profile, demanding a contextualized approach to evaluation. Biases, whether explicit or implicit, can skew interpretations, making it essential for practitioners to engage in self-reflection and adopt culturally responsive methodologies.

The chapter also emphasized the value of theoretical frameworks, such as the Cultural Formulation Model, in guiding practitioners toward more inclusive practices. These frameworks encourage clinicians to move beyond surface-level cultural awareness, fostering deeper understanding and integration of cultural factors into diagnostic and therapeutic processes. Additionally, the development and use of culturally adapted testing tools represent a critical step toward addressing disparities and improving the validity of neuropsychological evaluations.

One of the chapter's core messages is the necessity for forensic neuropsychologists to engage in continuous learning and adaptation. Cultural competence is not a static skill but an ongoing process that involves staying informed about evolving cultural norms, demographic shifts, and advancements in assessment methodologies. Training programs, workshops, and mentorship opportunities are vital avenues for enhancing cultural knowledge and skills. Moreover, collaboration with cultural experts and community leaders can provide valuable insights and promote mutual understanding.

The role of advocacy and community engagement also emerged as a critical component of culturally sensitive forensic practice. By advocating for systemic changes, such as the inclusion of diverse populations in test standardization and equitable access to legal and mental health services, practitioners contribute to a more just and inclusive system. Community outreach efforts further strengthen trust between forensic professionals and the populations they serve, fostering a more collaborative and informed approach to justice.

In conclusion, the integration of cultural considerations into forensic neuropsychology is not merely an ethical obligation but a fundamental aspect of professional competence. By embracing cultural diversity, practitioners enhance the accuracy, fairness, and relevance of their work, ultimately contributing to a legal system that respects and upholds the dignity of all individuals. As the field continues to evolve, forensic neuropsychologists must remain committed to cultural sensitivity in every aspect of their practice, from assessment to advocacy. Only through such dedication can they ensure that justice is truly served in a manner that honors the rich complexity of human diversity.

References

Aggarwal, N. K. (2024). The cultural formulation interview in case formulations: A state-of-the-science review. *Behavior Therapy, 55*(6), 1130–1143. https://doi.org/10.1016/j.beth.2024.05.009

Bauer, G. R., Churchill, S. M., Mahendran, M., Walwyn, C., Lizotte, D., & Villa-Rueda, A. A. (2021). Intersectionality in quantitative research: A systematic review of its emergence and applications of theory and methods. *SSM - Population Health, 14*, 100798. https://doi.org/10.1016/j.ssmph.2021.100798

Bekteshi, V., & Bellamy, J. L. (2024). Adapting for well-being: Examining acculturation strategies and mental health among Latina immigrants. *Social Sciences, 13*(3), 138. https://doi.org/10.3390/socsci13030138

Bilker, W. B., Hansen, J. A., Brensinger, C. M., Richard, J., Gur, R. E., & Gur, R. C. (2012). Development of abbreviated nine-item forms of the Raven's standard progressive matrices test. *Assessment, 19*(3), 354–369. https://doi.org/10.1177/1073191112446655

Casas, R., Guzmán-Vélez, E., Cardona-Rodriguez, J., Rodriguez, N., Quiñones, G., Izaguirre, B., & Tranel, D. (2011). Interpreter-mediated neuropsychological testing of monolingual Spanish speakers. *The Clinical Neuropsychologist, 26*(1), 88–101. https://doi.org/10.1080/13854046.2011.640641

Chafetz, M. D., Bauer, R. M., & Haley, P. S. (2019). The other face of illness-deception: Diagnostic criteria for factitious disorder with proposed standards for clinical practice and research. *The Clinical Neuropsychologist, 34*(3), 454–476. https://doi.org/10.1080/13854046.2019.1663265

Clock Drawing Test (CDT)—Strokengine. (n.d.). https://strokengine.ca/en/assessments/clock-drawing-test-cdt/.

Duncan, A. F., Watterberg, K. L., Nolen, T. L., Vohr, B. R., Adams-Chapman, I., Das, A., & Lowe, J. (2012). Effect of ethnicity and race on cognitive and language testing at age 18-22 months in extremely preterm infants. *The Journal of Pediatrics, 160*(6), 966–971.e2. https://doi.org/10.1016/j.jpeds.2011.12.009

Fernández, A. L., & Abe, J. (2017). Bias in cross-cultural neuropsychological testing: Problems and possible solutions. *Culture and Brain, 6*(1), 1–35. https://doi.org/10.1007/s40167-017-0050-2

Fong, E. H., Catagnus, R. M., Brodhead, M. T., Quigley, S., & Field, S. (2016). Developing the cultural awareness skills of behavior analysts. *Behavior Analysis in Practice, 9*(1), 84–94. https://doi.org/10.1007/s40617-016-0111-6

Greiffenstein, M. F., & Kaufmann, P. M. (2017). *Basics of forensic neuropsychology* (pp. 887–926). Taylor & Francis eBooks. https://doi.org/10.4324/9781315271743-37

Groen, S. P., Richters, A. J., Laban, C. J., Van Busschbach, J. T., & Devillé, W. L. (2019). Cultural identity confusion and psychopathology. *The Journal of Nervous and Mental Disease, 207*(3), 162–170. https://doi.org/10.1097/nmd.0000000000000935

Halalmeh, D. R., Salama, H. Z., LeUnes, E., Feitosa, D., Ansari, Y., Sachwani-Daswani, G. R., & Moisi, M. D. (2023). The role of neuropsychology in traumatic brain injury: Comprehensive literature review. *World Neurosurgery, 183*, 128–143. https://doi.org/10.1016/j.wneu.2023.12.069

Hon, J., Huppert, F. A., Holland, A. J., & Watson, P. (1999). Neuropsychological assessment of older adults with Down's syndrome: An epidemiological study using the Cambridge cognitive examination (CAMCOG). *British Journal of Clinical Psychology, 38*(2), 155–165. https://doi.org/10.1348/014466599162719

Ikanga, J., Basterfield, C., Taiwo, Z., Bragg, P., Bartlett, A., Howard, C., Robert, S., & Stringer, A. Y. (2022). The reliability of the African neuropsychology battery in persons of African descent. *Archives of Clinical Neuropsychology, 37*(4), 839–848. https://doi.org/10.1093/arclin/acac003

Kolhatkar, G., & Berkowitz, C. (2014). Cultural considerations and child maltreatment. *Pediatric Clinics of North America, 61*(5), 1007–1022. https://doi.org/10.1016/j.pcl.2014.06.005

Lareyre, F., Nasr, B., Chaudhuri, A., Di Lorenzo, G., Carlier, M., & Raffort, J. (2023). Comprehensive review of natural language processing (NLP) in vascular surgery. *EJVES Vascular Forum, 60*, 57–63. https://doi.org/10.1016/j.ejvsvf.2023.09.002

Martinez, E. M., Carr, D. T., Mullan, P. C., Rogers, L. E., Howlett-Holley, W. L., McGehee, C. A., Mangum, C. D., & Godambe, S. A. (2021). Improving equity of care for patients with limited English proficiency using quality improvement methodology. *Pediatric Quality and Safety, 6*(6), e486. https://doi.org/10.1097/pq9.0000000000000486

Masuda, A., Morgan, L., Spencer, S. D., Qina'au, J., & Jo, D. (2022). *Cultural adaptations of acceptance and commitment therapy* (pp. 662–679). Oxford University Press eBooks. https://doi.org/10.1093/oxfordhb/9780197550076.013.30

Mennella, C., Maniscalco, U., De Pietro, G., & Esposito, M. (2024). Ethical and regulatory challenges of AI technologies in healthcare: A narrative review. *Heliyon, 10*(4), e26297. https://doi.org/10.1016/j.heliyon.2024.e26297

Nielsen, T. R., Franzen, S., Watermeyer, T., Jiang, J., Calia, C., Kjærgaard, D., Bothe, S., & Mukadam, N. (2024). Interpreter-mediated neuropsychological assessment: Clinical considerations and recommendations from the European Consortium on Cross-Cultural Neuropsychology (ECCroN). *The Clinical Neuropsychologist, 1–31.* https://doi.org/10.1080/13854046.2024.2335113

Stephens, M. A. C., & Wand, G. (2012). Stress and the HPA axis: Role of glucocorticoids in alcohol dependence. https://pmc.ncbi.nlm.nih.gov/articles/PMC3860380/.

Sweet, J. J., Boone, K. B., Denney, R. L., Hebben, N., Marcopulos, B. A., Morgan, J. E., Nelson, N. W., & Westerveld, M. (2022). Forensic neuropsychology: History and current status. *The Clinical Neuropsychologist, 37*(3), 459–474. https://doi.org/10.1080/13854046.2022.2078740

Tong, P., & An, I. S. (2024). Review of studies applying Bronfenbrenner's bioecological theory in international and intercultural education research. *Frontiers in Psychology, 14*. https://doi.org/10.3389/fpsyg.2023.1233925

Uono, S., & Hietanen, J. K. (2015). Eye contact perception in the west and east: A cross-cultural study. *PLoS One, 10*(2), e0118094. https://doi.org/10.1371/journal.pone.0118094

Wechsler Nonverbal Scale of Ability (WNV)—Pearson Clinical. (n.d.). https://pearsonclinical.in/solutions/wechsler-nonverbal-scale-of-ability-wnv-2/.

Advances in Forensic Neuropsychological Research

1 Introduction

Forensic neuropsychology represents a critical nexus of neuroscience, psychology, and the legal system. This specialized field employs neuropsychological methods to evaluate cognitive, emotional, and behavioral functioning in individuals involved in legal contexts. Whether assessing competency to stand trial (CST), responsibility in criminal cases, or cognitive impairments in civil disputes, forensic neuropsychology has evolved into an indispensable discipline. Over the past decade, rapid advancements in this field have revolutionized its methodologies, offering a deeper understanding of the brain–behavior relationship and its implications in legal decision-making. This chapter aims to provide an overview of these developments, highlight the innovative research that has shaped forensic neuropsychology, and explore potential future directions for the field.

1.1 The Rapid Evolution of Forensic Neuropsychology

The growth of forensic neuropsychology can be attributed to parallel advancements in neuroscience, neuroimaging technologies, and legal standards. Historically, the discipline relied heavily on traditional paper-and-pencil tests to assess cognitive deficits and psychological conditions. However, the advent of neuroimaging techniques like functional magnetic resonance imaging (fMRI), diffusion tensor imaging (DTI), and electroencephalography (EEG) has enabled more precise identification of structural and functional brain abnormalities. These tools have enhanced the ability of forensic neuropsychologists to link specific impairments with neurological conditions, strengthening the reliability of expert testimony.

© The Author(s), under exclusive license to Springer Nature Switzerland AG 2025
K. J. Reddy, *Foundations of Criminal Forensic Neuropsychology*,
https://doi.org/10.1007/978-3-031-83771-5_18

Recent research has also emphasized the integration of neuropsychological data with behavioral and psychosocial assessments. This multidisciplinary approach is particularly relevant in forensic contexts where cognitive impairments, mental health disorders, and environmental factors intersect. For instance, studies have examined how traumatic brain injury (TBI) affects impulse control and decision-making in criminal defendants, providing a nuanced perspective on culpability and rehabilitation potential (Wilson, 2023). Similarly, the intersection of neurodevelopmental disorders, such as autism spectrum disorder (ASD) or attention-deficit/hyperactivity disorder (ADHD), with legal outcomes has garnered significant attention, shedding light on vulnerabilities in the justice system's handling of such cases.

1.2 Significance of Recent Developments

The implications of recent advancements in forensic neuropsychology extend beyond academia, influencing real-world legal practices. Improved understanding of cognitive and neural mechanisms has led to more sophisticated evaluations of legal constructs like CST and criminal responsibility. For instance, the use of event-related potentials (ERPs) in EEG studies has provided insights into attentional control deficits in defendants, allowing for more tailored interventions and courtroom considerations (Ienca & Andorno, 2017).

One notable area of progress is the application of artificial intelligence (AI) and machine learning (ML) in forensic neuropsychology. Algorithms trained on large datasets can analyze patterns in neuropsychological test scores, brain imaging, and behavioral data to predict outcomes like recidivism risk or rehabilitation potential. This technological integration enhances the objectivity and efficiency of forensic assessments, although ethical concerns about bias and data privacy remain.

The integration of cultural and contextual factors into forensic neuropsychological research has also been a pivotal development (Bergkamp et al., 2023). Recognizing the diversity in cognitive and behavioral norms across populations, researchers have emphasized the need for culturally sensitive assessments (McIntosh et al., 2024). For example, adapting neuropsychological tests for non-Western populations ensures that conclusions drawn in forensic evaluations are accurate and equitable.

1.3 The Importance of Staying Current with Research Trends

Given the dynamic nature of forensic neuropsychology, staying abreast of emerging research is essential for professionals in the field (Bergkamp et al., 2023). Legal cases increasingly involve complex neuropsychological evidence, and outdated methodologies or interpretations can jeopardize justice. For instance, while the use of neuroimaging as evidence is growing, misinterpretation of findings can lead to either undue leniency or excessive punitive measures.

Continuous professional development is equally vital for maintaining ethical standards. Advances in understanding neuroplasticity, brain connectivity, and the interplay between cognition and emotion demand that forensic neuropsychologists refine their practices regularly. Training programs and certification processes must integrate these advancements, equipping practitioners with the tools to handle contemporary forensic challenges.

Furthermore, collaboration with interdisciplinary teams—comprising neuroscientists, legal professionals, and ethicists—ensures that forensic neuropsychological assessments remain relevant and scientifically robust. Such collaboration fosters the translation of cutting-edge research into practical applications, enhancing the accuracy of expert testimony and the fairness of legal outcomes.

1.4 Future Directions in Forensic Neuropsychology

While significant progress has been made, the future of forensic neuropsychology holds even greater potential. One promising avenue is the development of biomarkers for cognitive and emotional dysfunctions. Research on neural correlates of impulsivity, aggression, and empathy could refine the assessment of criminal behavior and inform personalized rehabilitation strategies (Al-Juhani et al., 2024).

Another frontier is the use of virtual reality (VR) and immersive technologies in forensic evaluations. VR-based tasks can simulate real-world scenarios to assess cognitive and emotional responses, offering more ecologically valid measures than traditional tests. For instance, VR environments could be used to evaluate a defendant's capacity for decision-making under stress, providing courts with nuanced insights into their mental state.

The ethical challenges posed by advancements in forensic neuropsychology also warrant exploration. As technologies like fMRI and AI become integral to assessments, questions about consent, data ownership, and the potential misuse of neuropsychological findings must be addressed (Shen et al., 2024). Establishing clear guidelines and safeguards will be crucial to preserving the integrity of the field.

Finally, greater emphasis on prevention and early intervention could transform the role of forensic neuropsychology (Sweet et al., 2022). By identifying at-risk individuals and addressing cognitive or emotional deficits before they lead to criminal behavior, the field could contribute to reducing recidivism rates and fostering rehabilitation. Programs integrating neurofeedback training, mindfulness-based interventions, and cognitive-behavioral therapies offer promising pathways for proactive engagement.

The field of forensic neuropsychology stands at the forefront of bridging science and justice, with advancements in technology and research methodologies paving the way for more precise, ethical, and impactful practices (Velloso, n.d.). Staying current with these developments is not merely an academic exercise but a professional imperative that directly influences the fairness and efficacy of legal outcomes. As this chapter will explore, the future of forensic neuropsychological research lies in its ability to adapt to emerging challenges, embrace interdisciplinary collaboration, and innovate in ways that enhance both individual lives and societal systems (Bodin et al., 2023). By doing so, forensic neuropsychology will continue to evolve as a cornerstone of modern legal practice, offering invaluable insights into the complexities of human behavior within the judicial framework.

2 State-of-the-Art Research Findings

Criminal behavior is a complex phenomenon influenced by a myriad of biological, psychological, and environmental factors. In recent years, advances in neuropsychological research have shed light on the brain-based mechanisms underpinning criminal actions, offering a nuanced understanding of the interplay between cognitive processes, neural structures, and behavior. These insights are instrumental in refining forensic assessments and interventions, bridging the gap between theoretical frameworks and clinical applications. This section examines the latest research studies contributing to our understanding of the neuropsychological aspects of criminal behavior, highlighting state-of-the-art findings, emerging trends, and the imperative of translating cutting-edge research into forensic practice.

2.1 Examination of the Latest Research Studies in the Neuropsychological Aspects of Criminal Behavior

One of the most significant advancements in understanding criminal behavior is the identification of specific neural correlates linked to aggression, impulsivity, and antisocial tendencies. Functional neuroimaging studies using tools such as functional magnetic resonance imaging (fMRI) and positron emission tomography (PET) have revealed structural and functional abnormalities in key brain regions (Ko et al., 2013). For instance, research has consistently implicated the prefrontal cortex (PFC)—responsible for executive functions like decision-making, impulse control, and moral reasoning—in individuals with a history of violent crimes (Anselmo et al., 2022). Damage or underactivity in the PFC is associated with impaired judgment and reduced ability to foresee the consequences of actions, contributing to criminal behavior.

The amygdala, a critical component of the limbic system involved in emotional regulation and threat perception, has also been a focal point of investigation (Šimić et al., 2021). Reduced amygdala volume or hyperactivity has been observed in individuals with psychopathic traits, indicating heightened emotional reactivity or blunted fear responses. These findings support theoretical models suggesting that emotional dysregulation and reduced empathy play a central role in criminal acts, particularly in cases involving interpersonal violence.

Emerging research also highlights the importance of neural connectivity in understanding criminal behavior (Saladino et al., 2021). Diffusion tensor imaging (DTI) studies have shown that disruptions in white matter tracts connecting the PFC to the amygdala impair the regulation of emotional impulses, leading to increased aggression (Waller et al., 2017). This "disconnectivity hypothesis" underscores the need to examine brain networks rather than isolated regions, reflecting a shift towards more holistic neuropsychological models.

Beyond structural and functional imaging, electroencephalography (EEG) and event-related potentials (ERPs) have provided insights into the temporal dynamics of brain activity associated with criminal tendencies. Reduced P300 amplitudes, which reflect attention and decision-making processes, have been documented in offenders, suggesting deficits in processing consequences and inhibiting inappropriate actions. These findings offer a valuable framework for integrating neurophysiological markers into forensic evaluations, particularly in assessing risk for recidivism.

2.2 *Emerging Trends in Forensic Neuropsychology*

Recent research trends in forensic neuropsychology extend beyond the identification of neural abnormalities to explore the interactions between biological predispositions, environmental influences, and psychological states (Schug et al., 2021). One such trend is the examination of adverse childhood experiences (ACEs) and their neuropsychological consequences. Studies reveal that ACEs, such as abuse, neglect, or exposure to violence, contribute to dysregulated stress responses, alterations in brain development, and increased vulnerability to criminal behavior (Cooke et al., 2021). This perspective shifts the focus from individual culpability to a broader understanding of systemic factors shaping criminality, emphasizing the importance of trauma-informed forensic practices.

Another critical area of inquiry is the role of neurodevelopmental disorders in criminal behavior. Conditions such as autism spectrum disorder (ASD), attention-deficit/hyperactivity disorder (ADHD), and fetal alcohol spectrum disorders (FASD) are disproportionately represented in forensic populations (Velloso, n.d.). Neuropsychological assessments of these individuals often reveal deficits in executive functioning, social cognition, and emotion regulation, which may predispose them to legal infractions. For example, impaired theory of mind—common in ASD—can lead to misunderstandings of social norms, while impulsivity in ADHD increases the likelihood of risk-taking behaviors.

Genetic and epigenetic research is also transforming our understanding of the neuropsychology of criminal behavior (Becker, 2023). Studies on the monoamine oxidase A (MAOA) gene, often dubbed the "warrior gene," suggest that genetic predispositions to aggression are modulated by environmental factors, such as early-life stress (Haller, 2020). These findings underscore the complexity of genetic-environment interactions and their implications for personalized forensic interventions.

Technological advancements are shaping emerging trends in forensic neuropsychology as well. Artificial intelligence (AI) and machine learning (ML) algorithms are being developed to analyze patterns in neuropsychological and behavioral data, predicting risks such as recidivism or violence. These tools not only enhance the precision of assessments but also highlight ethical considerations surrounding the use of AI in forensic contexts, such as bias and transparency.

2.3 Integrating Cutting-Edge Research into Clinical Practice

The integration of state-of-the-art research findings into clinical settings is paramount for improving forensic assessments and interventions. Translational neuropsychology bridges the gap between laboratory discoveries and real-world applications, ensuring that advancements in the understanding of criminal behavior directly inform practices within the justice system.

One practical implication of recent research is the refinement of forensic assessments. Traditional methods, while valuable, often fail to capture the complexity of brain–behavior relationships (Gunter & Judd, 2020). Incorporating neuroimaging, electrophysiological data, and genetic markers into evaluations enhances the accuracy and depth of assessments, providing courts with scientifically robust evidence. For instance, demonstrating impaired connectivity between the PFC and amygdala in a defendant could offer mitigating evidence in sentencing decisions, highlighting the neurobiological underpinnings of impulsivity.

Interventions based on cutting-edge research also promise to improve outcomes for offenders. Neurofeedback training, which targets specific brain regions or networks, has shown the potential to enhance self-regulation and reduce aggression in forensic populations. Similarly, mindfulness-based interventions have been effective in promoting emotional regulation and reducing recidivism, particularly when tailored to individuals with histories of trauma or neurodevelopmental disorders (Becker et al., 2023).

The integration of trauma-informed care into forensic settings is another critical advancement. Recognizing the long-term neuropsychological impact of ACEs on criminal behavior allows for the development of interventions that address underlying trauma rather than focusing solely on punitive measures. Such approaches not only improve individual rehabilitation outcomes but also contribute to broader systemic reforms within the justice system.

Moreover, interdisciplinary collaboration is essential for translating research into practice. Forensic neuropsychologists must work closely with legal professionals, policymakers, and neuroscientists to ensure that findings are interpreted accurately and applied ethically. This collaborative approach fosters a more comprehensive understanding of criminal behavior, enhancing the fairness and efficacy of forensic practices.

Advances in neuropsychological research have significantly deepened our understanding of the mechanisms underlying criminal behavior, offering valuable insights into brain function, development, and connectivity (Van Dongen et al., 2024). State-of-the-art findings, such as the role of the PFC, amygdala, and neural networks, are transforming forensic assessments, while emerging trends emphasize the importance of trauma, neurodevelopmental disorders, and genetic-environment interactions. Integrating these insights into clinical settings not only improves the accuracy of evaluations but also informs interventions that promote rehabilitation and reduce recidivism. As forensic neuropsychology continues to evolve, the seamless translation of cutting-edge research into practice will remain a cornerstone of its contribution to the justice system, fostering evidence-based approaches that prioritize both scientific rigor and ethical responsibility (Mulligan, 2024).

3 Neurological Bases of Criminal Behavior: Innovative Methods to Study Criminal Actions

Criminal behavior is a multifaceted phenomenon arising from the complex interplay of biological, psychological, and environmental factors. In recent years, forensic neuroscience has advanced our understanding of the neurological underpinnings of such behaviors. By integrating innovative methods such as psychophysiological measurements, neuroimaging techniques, and genetic analysis, researchers can elucidate the biological mechanisms that predispose individuals to antisocial behavior (Kempes, 2023). These approaches not only deepen theoretical insights but also enhance practical applications in forensic settings, from evaluations to interventions.

3.1 Psychophysiological Measurements

Psychophysiological measurements, including heart rate variability (HRV) and galvanic skin response (GSR), provide real-time insights into autonomic nervous system activity and emotional regulation. These techniques are pivotal for understanding how physiological processes contribute to criminal behavior, particularly in high-stress or emotionally charged situations.

HRV refers to the variation in time intervals between consecutive heartbeats, reflecting the balance between the sympathetic and parasympathetic branches of the autonomic nervous system. Reduced HRV is associated with poor emotional regulation, impulsivity, and aggressive behavior—traits often linked to criminal acts. Studies in forensic populations, particularly among individuals with antisocial personality disorder or psychopathy, have consistently reported lower HRV levels (Kavish et al., 2019). In forensic contexts, HRV can be used to assess an individual's ability to manage stress or anticipate negative outcomes. For instance, offenders with diminished HRV may struggle with impulse control or fail to consider the consequences of their actions, contributing to criminal conduct. Additionally, HRV biofeedback training has emerged as a potential rehabilitative tool, helping offenders improve their emotional regulation and decision-making capabilities.

GSR, or electrodermal activity, measures the electrical conductance of the skin, which increases with sweat gland activity. As an indicator of emotional arousal, GSR is often used to study responses to fear, stress, or threat (Petrescu et al., 2021). In forensic research, offenders with psychopathic traits have shown reduced GSR responses during fear conditioning tasks, suggesting impaired anticipatory emotional responses (Casey, 2013). This deficit may contribute to risk-taking and a lack of concern for the consequences of criminal actions.

The integration of GSR data into forensic evaluations can help identify individuals with diminished emotional reactivity or heightened stress sensitivity, providing additional context for understanding their behaviors. GSR can also complement traditional psychological assessments, offering objective physiological evidence that supports behavioral observations.

3.2 Neuroimaging Techniques

Advances in neuroimaging have revolutionized the study of criminal behavior, allowing researchers to examine brain structures and functions associated with aggression, moral reasoning, and impulse control (Pietrini & Bambini, 2009). Techniques such as magnetic resonance imaging (MRI), functional MRI (fMRI), and positron emission tomography (PET) have shed light on the neural correlates of criminal actions, enhancing both theoretical knowledge and forensic applications.

3.3 Structural Neuroimaging

Structural MRI studies have consistently identified abnormalities in brain regions implicated in decision-making and emotional regulation among offenders (Gregory, 2012). The prefrontal cortex (PFC), often referred to as the brain's executive center, plays a critical role in impulse control, moral reasoning, and planning. Reduced gray matter volume in the PFC has been observed in individuals with a history of violent offenses, suggesting impaired cognitive control over aggressive impulses.

The amygdala, a key region for processing emotions such as fear and aggression, also exhibits structural differences in offenders. Smaller amygdala volumes have been linked to reduced empathy and heightened aggression, particularly in individuals with psychopathic traits. Understanding these structural abnormalities provides a biological basis for behaviors that deviate from societal norms.

3.4 *Functional Neuroimaging*

Functional imaging techniques, such as fMRI and PET, enable researchers to study brain activity patterns during specific tasks or in response to stimuli. For example, offenders often exhibit hypoactivity in the PFC and hyperactivity in the amygdala when processing emotionally charged or threatening stimuli (Šimić et al., 2021). This imbalance between cognitive control and emotional reactivity may contribute to impulsive or violent actions.

Functional imaging has also been used to study moral reasoning in offenders. Reduced activity in the medial PFC during tasks involving ethical dilemmas suggests impaired moral judgment, which may play a role in criminal decision-making (Raine & Yang, 2006). These findings have significant implications for forensic practice, particularly in assessments of criminal responsibility or competency to stand trial.

3.5 *Emerging Imaging Techniques*

Newer techniques, such as diffusion tensor imaging (DTI), provide insights into the connectivity between brain regions. DTI studies have revealed disrupted white matter pathways between the PFC and amygdala in offenders, indicating impaired communication between areas responsible for emotion regulation and executive function (Raschle et al., 2015). This emerging field offers a more nuanced understanding of the neural networks underlying criminal behavior.

3.6 *Genetic Markers and Criminal Behavior*

The exploration of genetic markers provides an additional dimension to understanding criminal behavior, focusing on how inherited traits influence predispositions to antisocial actions. While no single "criminal gene" exists, genetic research has identified specific markers associated with aggression, impulsivity, and risk-taking (Wilson, 2015).

The MAOA gene, which encodes an enzyme responsible for breaking down neurotransmitters such as serotonin and dopamine, has been extensively studied in the context of aggression. Low-activity variants of the MAOA gene, often called the "warrior gene," have been linked to increased aggression, particularly in individuals who experienced childhood adversity. This finding underscores the importance of gene-environment interactions, where genetic predispositions manifest in response to specific environmental triggers. Recent advances in genetics have employed polygenic risk scores to assess the cumulative effect of multiple genetic variants on behavior (Xiang et al., 2024). PRS analyses have shown promise in predicting predispositions to traits like impulsivity or aggression, which are relevant to forensic evaluations. This approach allows for a more comprehensive understanding of how multiple genes interact to influence behavior. Epigenetic studies explore how environmental factors, such as trauma or chronic stress, influence gene expression without altering the underlying DNA sequence (Klengel & Binder, 2015). For instance, epigenetic modifications resulting from adverse childhood experiences can affect brain development and function, increasing the likelihood of criminal actions. These findings highlight the dynamic interplay between biology and environment, emphasizing the need for holistic approaches to understanding and addressing criminal behavior.

3.7 Implications for Forensic Practice

The integration of psychophysiological, neuroimaging, and genetic methods into forensic practice offers a multidimensional perspective on criminal behavior. These techniques provide objective data that complement traditional psychological assessments, enhancing the accuracy and reliability of evaluations.

Moreover, these innovations have potential applications in intervention and rehabilitation. For example, neurofeedback training based on HRV or functional imaging data could help offenders improve emotional regulation and decision-making. Similarly, identifying genetic or epigenetic risk factors may inform preventative strategies or individualized treatment plans.

Innovative methods such as psychophysiological measurements, neuroimaging techniques, and genetic studies are transforming the study of criminal behavior's neurological bases (Kempes, 2023). By providing objective insights into the biological mechanisms underlying antisocial actions, these approaches enhance forensic evaluations and interventions. As the field continues to advance, interdisciplinary collaboration and ethical considerations will be essential to fully realize the potential of these technologies in promoting justice and rehabilitation.

4 Novel Therapeutic Approaches in Forensic Rehabilitation

Rehabilitative efforts in the criminal justice system have historically relied on behavioral and cognitive therapies to reduce recidivism and reintegrate offenders into society. However, as the field of forensic neuropsychology advances, novel therapeutic techniques are emerging that leverage neuroscience and technology to target the underlying neurological and psychological contributors to criminal behavior. This section explores cutting-edge therapeutic approaches, including cognitive enhancement programs, virtual reality therapies, and neurofeedback training, emphasizing their potential to transform rehabilitation and promote self-regulation and emotional control among offenders.

Cognitive Enhancement Programs Cognitive enhancement programs aim to improve executive functioning, decision-making, and impulse control in individuals who exhibit criminal behavior. By targeting core cognitive deficits, these interventions seek to address the root causes of antisocial actions rather than merely mitigating symptoms.

Executive Functioning and Criminal Behavior Executive functions, including working memory, cognitive flexibility, and inhibitory control, are critical for adaptive decision-making and emotional regulation. Deficits in these areas are common among offenders, particularly those with histories of substance abuse, traumatic brain injury, or neurodevelopmental disorders. Impaired executive functioning can lead to impulsivity, poor judgment, and difficulty anticipating consequences, all of which increase the risk of recidivism.

Targeted Cognitive Training Programs such as cognitive remediation therapy (CRT) focus on enhancing specific cognitive skills through repetitive exercises and tasks. For example, computerized training programs can improve working memory and attention span by progressively increasing task difficulty. Research has shown that offenders who undergo CRT demonstrate better problem-solving abilities, reduced impulsivity, and improved adherence to rehabilitation programs (Wettermann et al., 2020).

Applications in Forensic Settings Cognitive enhancement programs are increasingly being implemented in correctional facilities as part of broader rehabilitation efforts. Tailored interventions can address individual deficits, making these programs adaptable to diverse offender populations. Additionally, combining cognitive training with traditional therapies, such as cognitive-behavioral therapy (CBT), has shown synergistic effects, further reducing the likelihood of reoffending.

4.1 *Virtual Reality Therapies*

Virtual reality (VR) therapy represents a groundbreaking approach to offender rehabilitation, offering immersive environments for therapeutic interventions that simulate real-life scenarios. This innovative method allows individuals to practice adaptive behaviors in controlled settings, bridging the gap between therapeutic exercises and real-world application.

Immersive Environments for Behavior Modification VR therapies use interactive simulations to expose offenders to situations that challenge their cognitive and emotional responses. For example, individuals with anger management issues can be placed in virtual environments that mimic conflict situations, allowing them to practice de-escalation techniques in a safe and controlled manner. Similarly, VR scenarios can simulate high-risk situations, such as opportunities for theft or substance use, enabling offenders to rehearse making prosocial decisions. One of the unique applications of VR therapy is its potential to foster empathy in individuals with psychopathic or antisocial tendencies. By immersing offenders in virtual scenarios where they experience the perspective of a victim, VR can help cultivate emotional awareness and understanding of the consequences of their actions. Studies have reported increased emotional engagement and improved social attitudes among participants who underwent empathy-focused VR interventions (Winter et al., 2022).

VR therapy can complement traditional rehabilitation methods, such as CBT or anger management programs. By providing experiential learning opportunities, VR enhances the retention and application of therapeutic concepts. Furthermore, the data collected during VR sessions, such as physiological responses and decision-making patterns, can inform personalized treatment plans.

4.2 *Neurofeedback Training*

Neurofeedback training, a noninvasive technique that helps individuals regulate brain activity, has gained traction as a therapeutic tool for offenders. By promoting self-regulation and emotional control, neurofeedback addresses key factors underlying criminal behavior, such as impulsivity, aggression, and emotional dysregulation.

Neurofeedback involves monitoring brain activity using electroencephalography (EEG) and providing real-time feedback to the individual. Participants learn to modulate their brainwave patterns to achieve desired states, such as relaxation, focus, or emotional stability. Over time, this practice enhances neural connectivity and strengthens the brain regions associated with self-regulation and decision-making. Neurofeedback training has shown promise in reducing symptoms of aggression and impulsivity among offenders. For example, individuals with histories of violent behavior often exhibit excessive activity in the amygdala, the brain's fear and aggression center, coupled with reduced activity in the prefrontal cortex, which governs impulse control. Neurofeedback can help rebalance this dynamic, improving emotional regulation and reducing the likelihood of reactive violence. Neurofeedback is also effective in managing stress and anxiety, which are common among incarcerated individuals. By teaching participants to maintain a calm and focused mental state, neurofeedback training can enhance coping skills and reduce the risk of maladaptive behaviors in high-stress situations. The benefits of neurofeedback training extend beyond the rehabilitation period, as individuals often retain their self-regulation skills long after completing the program. Additionally, advances in portable neurofeedback devices have made this intervention more accessible and scalable, enabling its integration into diverse forensic settings.

4.3 Implications for Rehabilitation

The adoption of these novel therapeutic approaches in forensic settings represents a paradigm shift in offender rehabilitation. By addressing the cognitive, emotional, and neural factors underlying criminal behavior, these methods offer a more comprehensive and individualized approach to reducing recidivism.

Combining cognitive enhancement programs, VR therapies, and neurofeedback training within a unified rehabilitation framework can maximize therapeutic outcomes. For instance, cognitive training can improve the foundational skills needed for success in VR simulations, while neurofeedback can enhance emotional readiness for engaging in therapeutic exercises. While these interventions hold significant promise, their implementation must be guided by ethical principles. Informed consent, privacy, and the potential for unintended consequences must be carefully considered to ensure that these techniques are used responsibly and effectively. Continued research is needed to refine these therapies and establish evidence-based protocols for their application in forensic contexts (Prujean et al., 2021). Collaboration between neuroscientists, psychologists, and legal professionals will be essential to advancing this field and ensuring that these innovative methods contribute meaningfully to offender rehabilitation.

Novel therapeutic approaches, including cognitive enhancement programs, virtual reality therapies, and neurofeedback training, are transforming the landscape of offender rehabilitation. By addressing the underlying neurological and psychological factors that contribute to criminal behavior, these techniques offer new avenues for reducing recidivism and promoting reintegration into society. As forensic neuropsychology continues to evolve, these innovations underscore the importance of integrating cutting-edge research into practice, fostering a more effective and humane criminal justice system (Bakhtiar, 2024).

5 Implications for Forensic Practice

The rapid advancements in forensic neuropsychology have significantly influenced how legal and psychological professionals address the complexities of criminal behavior and cognitive functioning in legal contexts. By incorporating cutting-edge research findings into forensic practice, professionals can refine assessments, interventions, and legal strategies to achieve more equitable and effective outcomes (Osborne, 2024). This section explores the practical ramifications of these advancements, highlights case studies demonstrating real-world applications, and underscores the importance of translating research knowledge into practice to improve outcomes for individuals in the legal system.

5.1 Practical Ramifications of Advancements in Forensic Neuropsychology

Recent innovations in forensic neuropsychology, including neuroimaging, psychophysiological measurements, and neurogenetic research, have reshaped how the legal system understands and evaluates criminal behavior (Newsome & Cullen, 2017). Neuropsychological research has provided critical insights into the neural and cognitive underpinnings of criminal actions, emphasizing factors such as executive dysfunction, emotional dysregulation, and impaired decision-making (Gkintoni et al., 2024). These findings have informed the development of more nuanced assessment tools that consider an individual's cognitive and emotional state in the context of their behavior. Advancements in technologies like functional magnetic resonance imaging (fMRI) and electroencephalography (EEG) have enabled forensic practitioners to identify subtle neural anomalies that might contribute to criminal behavior. For instance, identifying reduced activity in the prefrontal cortex or hyperactivity in the amygdala can help establish a link between neurobiological dysfunction and impulsive or aggressive tendencies. These tools are now being used to assess criminal culpability, competency to stand trial, and risk of recidivism with greater precision. Research-driven therapeutic interventions, such as neurofeedback training and cognitive enhancement programs, have emerged as effective tools for addressing the root causes of antisocial behavior (Villalón et al., 2023). By tailoring interventions to an individual's neurocognitive profile, forensic practitioners can promote behavioral change and reduce recidivism rates.

The integration of neuropsychological findings into forensic practice has also raised important ethical and legal questions. For instance, the admissibility of neuroimaging evidence in court remains a topic of debate, as does the potential for misuse of genetic markers in criminal cases. These challenges highlight the need for ongoing collaboration between neuroscientists, legal experts, and ethicists to establish clear guidelines for the responsible use of forensic neuropsychological tools.

5.2 Translating Research Knowledge into Practice

The effective translation of neuropsychological research into forensic practice requires an interdisciplinary approach, ongoing education, and collaboration among stakeholders in the legal and psychological fields.

Despite the wealth of innovative research, there remains a significant gap between academic findings and their application in forensic settings (Van Asten, 2013). This disconnect often stems from a lack of familiarity among legal professionals with neuropsychological concepts and tools. Bridging this gap requires comprehensive training programs that equip forensic practitioners with the knowledge and skills to integrate research findings into their work (Nilendu, 2024). To ensure consistency and reliability, standardized protocols for the use of neuropsychological tools in forensic settings are essential. For instance, establishing guidelines for the interpretation of neuroimaging data or the ethical use of genetic markers can enhance the credibility and utility of these techniques in legal contexts. Collaboration between neuropsychologists, legal professionals, and policymakers is crucial for translating research into practice. Interdisciplinary teams can work together to design interventions, develop legal strategies, and address ethical concerns, fostering a more holistic approach to forensic neuropsychology. As the field evolves, forensic practitioners must stay abreast of emerging trends and advancements. Regular workshops, conferences, and continuing education programs can help professionals remain current, ensuring that their practice reflects the latest research and technological innovations.

The practical implications of advancements in forensic neuropsychology are profound, offering new tools and insights to improve assessments, interventions, and legal outcomes. Case studies illustrate how innovative research findings are being applied in real-world settings, from competency evaluations to the design of rehabilitative programs. However, the successful integration of research knowledge into practice requires concerted efforts to bridge the gap between academia and the legal system (Bolton & Stolcis, 2003). By fostering interdisciplinary collaboration, developing standardized protocols, and promoting continuous professional development, forensic neuropsychology can continue to advance as a critical field that enhances justice and rehabilitation for individuals involved in the legal system.

6 Interdisciplinary Collaboration and Knowledge Translation in Forensic Neuropsychology

Forensic neuropsychology, at the intersection of neuroscience, psychology, and law, requires a multidisciplinary approach to address the complex issues it encompasses. Interdisciplinary collaboration enhances the field by fostering the integration of diverse perspectives, methodologies, and expertise. This section examines the role of interdisciplinary collaboration in advancing forensic neuropsychology, highlights the importance of integrating insights from psychology, neuroscience, law, and criminal justice to inform best practices, and explores opportunities for partnerships between academic researchers and practitioners to promote knowledge translation and innovation.

6.1 The Role of Interdisciplinary Collaboration

Forensic neuropsychology inherently draws upon multiple fields, including cognitive neuroscience, clinical psychology, and legal studies (Fabian, 2010). Collaboration between professionals in these areas enables the development of comprehensive frameworks for understanding and addressing criminal behavior. For instance, neuroimaging researchers can identify structural brain anomalies in offenders, while psychologists interpret these findings in the context of behavioral assessments, and legal experts determine their relevance to culpability or sentencing (Glannon, 2014). Collaboration is crucial for tackling multifaceted questions about criminal behavior. Why do some individuals with similar risk factors exhibit antisocial tendencies while others do not? How can cognitive deficits or mental health issues be considered in determining criminal responsibility? Interdisciplinary teams bring a breadth of expertise that can lead to more nuanced answers and solutions. Innovations in forensic neuropsychology often emerge from collaborative efforts. For example, the integration of psychophysiological measurements (e.g., heart rate variability and galvanic skin response) with behavioral data has been made possible through partnerships between neuroscientists and psychologists. These advances enable the creation of tools and interventions tailored to the unique needs of offenders, improving outcomes for individuals and society.

6.2 Integrating Insights from Psychology, Neuroscience, Law, and Criminal Justice

Psychologists contribute deep insights into the cognitive, emotional, and social factors underlying criminal behavior. Assessments of personality traits, cognitive abilities, and psychopathology are vital for understanding offenders' motivations and identifying rehabilitative pathways. Neuroscience provides tools to explore the neural mechanisms driving behavior. Technologies such as fMRI and EEG reveal patterns of brain activity associated with impulsivity, aggression, or diminished executive control, offering objective data to complement psychological evaluations. Legal professionals help translate scientific findings into the language of the courtroom. They ensure that evidence from neuropsychological assessments is admissible, relevant, and presented in ways that uphold justice. For example, the legal system relies on forensic neuropsychologists to explain how brain dysfunction may impact criminal responsibility or competency to stand trial. The criminal justice system plays a critical role in applying forensic insights to real-world contexts.

Corrections officers, probation officers, and rehabilitation specialists implement evidence-based practices derived from interdisciplinary research, such as cognitive training programs or neurofeedback therapy.

6.3 Opportunities for Academic-Practitioner Partnerships

Academic research in forensic neuropsychology often contains valuable insights that are underutilized in practice. Partnerships between researchers and practitioners can bridge this gap by translating complex findings into actionable strategies. For instance, academics can collaborate with law enforcement agencies to develop training programs on recognizing cognitive impairments in suspects or witnesses. Collaborative efforts can lead to the creation of standardized tools tailored to forensic contexts. For example, researchers and clinicians can co-design neuropsychological tests that assess competency to stand trial, incorporating cutting-edge neuroscience and psychometric techniques. Practitioners working in correctional facilities or rehabilitation centers often face challenges in implementing interventions that are both effective and scalable. Partnering with academics can result in the development and testing of innovative programs, such as virtual reality-based empathy training or neurofeedback for emotional regulation, ensuring these approaches are grounded in evidence. Academic-practitioner partnerships can influence policy by generating evidence to support systemic changes. For example, data on the neural correlates of recidivism risk might inform parole decisions or sentencing guidelines, promoting practices that prioritize rehabilitation over punitive measures. Creating platforms for regular interaction between academics and practitioners is essential. Conferences, workshops, and online forums facilitate the exchange of ideas, ensuring that research addresses practical needs and that practitioners stay updated on emerging findings.

6.4 Challenges and Strategies for Effective Collaboration

One of the significant challenges in interdisciplinary work is the difference in terminology and priorities across fields. Legal professionals may find neuroscientific jargon inaccessible, while scientists might struggle to grasp the nuances of legal standards. Developing shared language and goals through regular communication is critical for effective collaboration. Academic researchers often prioritize theoretical advancement, while practitioners focus on immediate application. Finding a balance between these perspectives requires mutual respect and a commitment to co-creating solutions that are both scientifically rigorous and practically viable. Interdisciplinary projects can be resource-intensive, requiring funding for technologies, training, and personnel. Advocacy for cross-sector funding initiatives and grants that support collaborative research is essential to sustain these efforts.

Interdisciplinary collaboration is pivotal to advancing forensic neuropsychology, enabling the integration of diverse expertise to address the complexities of criminal behavior and justice. By combining insights from psychology, neuroscience, law, and criminal justice, professionals can develop evidence-based practices that improve outcomes for offenders and the broader legal system. Partnerships between academic researchers and practitioners offer opportunities to translate knowledge into action, fostering innovations in assessment, intervention, and policy. As the field continues to evolve, fostering collaboration across disciplines will remain a cornerstone of progress, ensuring that forensic neuropsychology contributes meaningfully to justice and rehabilitation.

7 Future Directions in Forensic Neuropsychology

The field of forensic neuropsychology stands at the confluence of neuroscience, psychology, and the legal system, addressing the intricate relationships between brain function, behavior, and criminal responsibility. As technology and scientific understanding continue to evolve, the potential for transformative advancements grows. This section explores prospective research avenues, highlights the need for ongoing innovation in assessment and intervention strategies, and examines the ethical considerations associated with these advancements.

7.1 Potential Future Research Avenues

AI and machine learning hold promise for advancing forensic neuropsychological practices by enhancing predictive accuracy and streamlining assessments. Machine learning algorithms could analyze large datasets from neuroimaging, psychophysiological measures, and behavioral evaluations to identify patterns indicative of criminal tendencies or risk of recidivism.

While current research often focuses on cross-sectional data, longitudinal studies tracking individuals over time could provide deeper insights into how neuropsychological factors influence the trajectory of criminal behavior (Glannon, 2014). For example, monitoring changes in brain structure or function in offenders undergoing rehabilitation could inform the development of evidence-based interventions. Emerging technologies, such as functional near-infrared spectroscopy (fNIRS) and diffusion tensor imaging (DTI), offer new ways to explore brain activity and connectivity. These tools could improve our understanding of how structural and functional abnormalities contribute to criminal behavior, particularly in cases involving traumatic brain injury (TBI) or neurodevelopmental disorders. Epigenetics examines how environmental factors, such as trauma or stress, influence gene expression without altering DNA sequences. Exploring the epigenetic markers associated with criminal behavior could shed light on how biological predispositions interact with environmental triggers, enabling more nuanced risk assessments and interventions. VR could serve as a research tool to simulate real-world scenarios for offenders, helping researchers study decision-making processes and emotional responses in controlled environments (Van Gelder et al., 2019). Additionally, VR could be used for training legal professionals to recognize neuropsychological impairments in offenders.

7.2 *The Need for Ongoing Innovation in Assessment and Intervention Strategies*

Future advancements should focus on developing assessment protocols tailored to individual neurocognitive profiles. Personalized assessments could integrate data from neuroimaging, genetic testing, and psychometric evaluations to provide a comprehensive understanding of an individual's strengths and vulnerabilities. Innovative interventions like neurofeedback and BCIs could revolutionize rehabilitation efforts by providing offenders with tools to regulate their neural activity. For instance, neurofeedback training targeting the prefrontal cortex could enhance self-control and decision-making abilities. Integrating neuropsychological insights with psychosocial support could lead to holistic rehabilitation programs that address offenders' cognitive, emotional, and social needs. These programs could combine mindfulness-based practices, cognitive-behavioral therapy, and neurofeedback to foster long-term behavioral change. As forensic neuropsychology expands globally, adapting tools and interventions to different cultural contexts becomes essential. Future research should prioritize the development of culturally sensitive assessments and therapies, ensuring their relevance and effectiveness across diverse populations. Innovations in forensic neuropsychology could transform legal practices by providing objective evidence of cognitive or neural impairments. For example, brain imaging data could support arguments for diminished capacity or inform competency evaluations. However, integrating such technologies requires careful consideration of their reliability, accessibility, and legal admissibility.

7.3 *Ethical Considerations of Advancements*

The use of advanced neuroimaging, genetic testing, and AI raises concerns about privacy and informed consent. Offenders undergoing assessments must be fully informed about how their data will be used, stored, and potentially shared with legal authorities. Genetic testing for predispositions to aggression could inadvertently stigmatize individuals or be misused in legal contexts, necessitating clear ethical guidelines.

One risk of forensic neuropsychology is the potential for deterministic interpretations of behavior, where individuals are perceived as "predisposed" to criminality based on their neural or genetic profiles. Such views could undermine personal agency and lead to discriminatory practices in sentencing or rehabilitation. As forensic neuropsychology advances, courts must grapple with the admissibility of complex scientific evidence. Establishing rigorous standards for reliability, validity, and interpretability is crucial to prevent misuse or overreliance on neuropsychological findings. Bias in forensic assessments or interventions could exacerbate existing disparities in the criminal justice system. For instance, certain genetic markers or neurocognitive profiles may be overrepresented in specific racial or socioeconomic groups, leading to unintended stigmatization. Researchers and practitioners must strive to mitigate such biases through transparent practices and inclusive research. AI-driven tools must be carefully designed to avoid perpetuating biases present in historical data. Ensuring that AI systems are interpretable and subject to human oversight is essential to maintaining ethical standards in forensic practice.

The future of forensic neuropsychology lies in its ability to integrate technological innovation with interdisciplinary collaboration and ethical responsibility. Potential research avenues, such as AI integration, longitudinal studies, and advanced neuroimaging, promise to deepen our understanding of criminal behavior and improve forensic practices. Simultaneously, ongoing innovation in assessment and intervention strategies can lead to more personalized, effective, and culturally sensitive approaches to rehabilitation. However, the ethical implications of these advancements must remain at the forefront, guiding the responsible application of forensic neuropsychological tools. By balancing innovation with ethical rigor and interdisciplinary cooperation, the field can continue to evolve, contributing meaningfully to both the justice system and the broader understanding of human behavior.

8 Key Takeaways

Advances in forensic neuropsychology represent a transformative force in the intersection of neuroscience, psychology, and the legal system. This section reflects on the significance of these advancements for legal decision-making, therapeutic interventions, and the broader pursuit of justice. It emphasizes the necessity for professionals in the field to remain adaptable and informed about emerging research developments and advocates for ongoing collaboration between researchers and practitioners to ensure the efficacy and fairness of forensic practices.

8.1 The Significance of Advances in Forensic Neuropsychology

Forensic neuropsychology has emerged as an essential tool in understanding the complex interplay between brain function and behavior, particularly in the context of criminal actions and legal accountability. Technological and methodological innovations in the field have broadened its impact, influencing areas such as competency evaluations, criminal responsibility assessments, and the development of rehabilitation programs. Advancements in forensic neuropsychology provide courts with more objective and nuanced insights into defendants' cognitive and emotional functioning. This has significant implications for legal decisions involving competency to stand trial (CST), mitigation of sentences, and determinations of criminal responsibility. Neuropsychological assessments help determine whether a defendant can understand legal proceedings and assist in their defense (Marcopulos et al., 2024). For instance, the integration of neuroimaging can reveal structural abnormalities or functional deficits in brain regions critical for reasoning and decision-making. By uncovering the neurobiological underpinnings of behaviors, such as impulsivity or aggression, forensic neuropsychology can clarify the extent to which these factors influence a defendant's actions, aiding in fair adjudication.

The development of evidence-based therapeutic approaches informed by neuropsychological insights has revolutionized offender rehabilitation. Programs targeting executive dysfunction, emotional dysregulation, and impulsivity leverage tools such as cognitive enhancement strategies, neurofeedback training, and mindfulness-based interventions. These approaches improve decision-making and self-regulation, reducing the likelihood of reoffending. Innovative research methodologies, including psychophysiological measurements, neuroimaging, and genetic studies, have deepened our understanding of the neurological bases of criminal actions (Yen et al., 2023). These insights help distinguish between behaviors rooted in neurobiological impairments and those shaped by environmental or psychosocial factors, providing a holistic perspective on criminality.

8.2 The Necessity for Adaptability and Lifelong Learning

As the field evolves, professionals in forensic neuropsychology must remain adaptable and committed to lifelong learning. Rapid advancements in technology, coupled with a growing body of research, demand continuous updating of knowledge and skills to stay at the forefront of practice.

Keeping pace with developments in neuroimaging, genetic testing, and therapeutic methodologies is critical for maintaining relevance in the field. Professionals must engage with academic literature, attend conferences, and participate in workshops to integrate cutting-edge findings into their practice. Recent studies on functional near-infrared spectroscopy (fNIRS) have highlighted its potential for noninvasive assessment of brain activity. Incorporating such tools into forensic evaluations could enhance accuracy and accessibility (Rupawala et al., 2018). The integration of artificial intelligence (AI), machine learning, and virtual reality (VR) into forensic neuropsychology underscores the need for practitioners to develop proficiency in these technologies. AI-driven tools, for instance, can streamline data analysis and improve the predictive validity of assessments, while VR can provide immersive environments for both research and therapeutic interventions. Given the multidisciplinary nature of forensic neuropsychology, professionals must actively seek insights from related fields such as law, criminology, and social work. Understanding legal frameworks and societal contexts enhances the application of neuropsychological findings in real-world scenarios.

8.3 Collaboration Between Researchers and Practitioners

Collaboration between academic researchers and practitioners is pivotal in ensuring that forensic neuropsychology translates effectively from theory to practice. Such partnerships foster innovation, address practical challenges, and bridge the gap between research and application.

Academic researchers often generate insights that remain underutilized in forensic settings due to a lack of communication or applicability. Practitioners, on the other hand, possess firsthand knowledge of the challenges faced in clinical or legal contexts. Collaborative efforts can align research goals with practical needs, resulting in tools and interventions that are both scientifically rigorous and operationally feasible. Joint efforts between academic institutions and forensic organizations can improve training programs for future professionals. By integrating research findings into curricula and providing hands-on experience with emerging technologies, such initiatives prepare practitioners for the complexities of modern forensic neuropsychology. Effective knowledge translation ensures that scientific discoveries are communicated in a manner accessible to legal professionals, policymakers, and the general public. This involves simplifying technical findings, highlighting their implications, and providing clear guidelines for implementation.

8.4 Call to Action

The field of forensic neuropsychology is uniquely positioned to contribute to a more equitable and scientifically informed justice system. However, realizing its full potential requires collective action on several fronts. Governments, academic institutions, and private organizations must prioritize funding for research in forensic neuropsychology. Investments in longitudinal studies, advanced neuroimaging technologies, and intervention trials will pave the way for groundbreaking discoveries. As the field advances, ethical considerations must guide its growth. This includes safeguarding individuals' privacy, addressing biases in assessment tools, and ensuring that findings are not misused to perpetuate inequalities. Collaborative efforts between ethicists, legal professionals, and neuropsychologists are essential in this regard. Forums for interdisciplinary dialogue, such as conferences and working groups, can foster mutual understanding and innovation. These platforms provide opportunities for professionals from diverse backgrounds to share insights, challenge assumptions, and co-create solutions.

Advocacy efforts should aim to integrate neuropsychological insights into policy reforms that enhance the fairness and effectiveness of the legal system. For instance, policies that emphasize rehabilitation over punishment for neuropsychologically impaired offenders align with the principles of restorative justice.

Advances in forensic neuropsychology have redefined the possibilities for legal decision-making, offender rehabilitation, and the understanding of criminal behavior. As the field continues to evolve, professionals must remain adaptable, informed, and collaborative to harness these advancements effectively. By fostering partnerships between researchers and practitioners, investing in innovation, and prioritizing ethical responsibility, forensic neuropsychology can contribute meaningfully to a more just and humane legal system. The journey ahead is as challenging as it is promising, demanding a steadfast commitment to excellence, equity, and progress.

9 Conclusion

This chapter has traversed the significant advancements, challenges, and future directions within forensic neuropsychology, underscoring its pivotal role in the criminal justice system. By embracing innovation, interdisciplinary collaboration, and ethical responsibility, forensic neuropsychology has evolved into a transformative discipline, reshaping how criminal behavior is understood, assessed, and addressed.

One of the central themes of this chapter has been the critical importance of innovation in forensic neuropsychology. The integration of cutting-edge technologies, such as neuroimaging, virtual reality, and artificial intelligence, has significantly enhanced our ability to study brain–behavior relationships in forensic contexts. These tools have refined assessments, improving their accuracy, objectivity, and predictive validity. Emerging therapeutic interventions, such as cognitive enhancement programs, neurofeedback training, and immersive virtual reality therapies, have demonstrated promise in addressing cognitive and emotional deficits in offenders. These advances not only improve rehabilitation outcomes but also hold the potential to reduce recidivism, offering a more humane and effective approach to justice.

The exploration of genetic markers and psychophysiological measurements, such as heart rate variability and galvanic skin response, has provided a deeper understanding of the neurobiological and environmental factors contributing to criminal behavior. This knowledge equips forensic professionals with a more comprehensive perspective, enabling them to develop tailored interventions that address the root causes of criminality.

Forensic neuropsychology is inherently dynamic, evolving alongside advancements in science, technology, and societal norms. Its multidisciplinary nature ensures that it remains adaptable, drawing from psychology, neuroscience, criminology, and law to inform best practices. This adaptability is particularly crucial in addressing the complex, multifaceted nature of criminal behavior and its implications for legal decision-making. As the field progresses, ethical considerations must remain at the forefront. The application of neuropsychological findings in forensic contexts raises questions about privacy, consent, and the potential for misuse of data. Balancing scientific innovation with ethical responsibility is essential to ensure that advancements contribute to justice and equity rather than perpetuating biases or inequalities. The impact of forensic neuropsychology on the criminal justice system cannot be overstated. By providing objective insights into the cognitive and emotional states of defendants, it enhances the fairness and accuracy of legal decisions. Furthermore, its contributions to offender rehabilitation and recidivism reduction align with restorative justice principles, promoting societal reintegration over punitive measures.

The continued growth of forensic neuropsychology depends on the active engagement of its practitioners, researchers, and allied professionals. Readers are encouraged to stay abreast of the latest research, participate in professional development opportunities, and contribute to the field's expansion through innovation and collaboration. Interdisciplinary partnerships are vital in addressing the challenges that lie ahead. By fostering dialogue between researchers, clinicians, legal professionals, and policymakers, forensic neuropsychology can ensure its findings are translated into practical, impactful solutions. These collaborations not only enhance the discipline's relevance but also amplify its potential to drive meaningful change within the justice system.

Finally, aspiring professionals in forensic neuropsychology are urged to approach the field with curiosity, creativity, and a commitment to ethical practice. By embracing these principles, they can contribute to a future where forensic neuropsychology continues to illuminate the complexities of human behavior, advancing justice and rehabilitation for all.

Forensic neuropsychology stands at the intersection of science and justice, offering tools and insights that redefine our understanding of criminal behavior and its implications. As the field evolves, its professionals must remain adaptable and committed to the pursuit of knowledge, ensuring that their contributions align with the principles of equity and human dignity. By embracing innovation, fostering collaboration, and prioritizing ethical responsibility, forensic neuropsychology can continue to shape a more just and informed society, leaving a lasting legacy in both science and law.

References

Al-Juhani, A., Alzahrani, M. J., Zainab Abdullah, A., Alnefaie, A. N., Alnowaisser, L. N., Alhadi, W., Alghamdi, J. K., & Bauthman, M. S. (2024). Neuroimaging and brain-based markers identifying neurobiological markers associated with criminal behaviour, personality disorders, and mental health: A narrative review. *Cureus*. https://doi.org/10.7759/cureus.58814

Anselmo, A., Lucifora, C., Rusconi, P., Martino, G., Craparo, G., Salehinejad, M. A., & Vicario, C. M. (2022). Can we rewire criminal mind via non-invasive brain stimulation of prefrontal cortex? Insights from clinical, forensic and social cognition studies. *Current Psychology, 42*(24), 20765–20775. https://doi.org/10.1007/s12144-022-03210-y

Bakhtiar, H. S. (2024). The evolution of scientific evidence theory in criminal law: A transformative insight. *Media Iuris, 7*(2), 221–240. https://doi.org/10.20473/mi.v7i2.51095

Becker, P. (2023, July 14). *It's the brain, stupid: Neuroscience, risk, and crime*. De Gruyter. .

Becker, T. D., Ramirez, S. C., Boude, A. B., Leong, A., Ivanov, I., & Rice, T. R. (2023). Interventions for prevention and treatment of substance use in youth with traumatic childhood experiences: A systematic review and synthesis of the literature. *European Child & Adolescent Psychiatry*. https://doi.org/10.1007/s00787-023-02265-x

Bergkamp, J., McIntyre, K. A., & Hauser, M. (2023). An uncomfortable tension: Reconciling the principles of forensic psychology and cultural competency. *Law and Human Behavior, 47*(1), 233–248. https://doi.org/10.1037/lhb0000507

Bodin, D., Beebe, D. W., Fuchs, K., Lucas, J., & Marcopulos, B. (2023). The American Board of Clinical Neuropsychology (ABCN) and American Academy of Clinical Neuropsychology (AACN): Recent milestones and future goals 2014–2023. *The Clinical Neuropsychologist, 37*(4), 784–811. https://doi.org/10.1080/13854046.2023.2190538

Bolton, M. J., & Stolcis, G. B. (2003). Ties that do not bind: Musings on the specious relevance of academic research. *Public Administration Review, 63*(5), 626–630. https://doi.org/10.1111/1540-6210.00325

Casey, A. R. (2013). Investigating the relationship between psychopathy, fear conditioning, and facial affect recognition. https://doi.org/10.26686/wgtn.17005801.v1

Cooke, E. M., Connolly, E. J., Boisvert, D. L., & Hayes, B. E. (2021). A systematic review of the biological correlates and consequences of childhood maltreatment and adverse childhood experiences. *Trauma Violence & Abuse, 24*(1), 156–173. https://doi.org/10.1177/15248380211021613

Fabian, J. M. (2010). Neuropsychological and neurological correlates in violent and homicidal offenders: A legal and neuroscience perspective. *Aggression and Violent Behavior, 15*(3), 209–223. https://doi.org/10.1016/j.avb.2009.12.004

Gkintoni, E., Skokou, M., & Gourzis, P. (2024). Integrating clinical neuropsychology and psychotic spectrum disorders: A systematic analysis of cognitive dynamics, interventions, and underlying mechanisms. *Medicina, 60*(4), 645. https://doi.org/10.3390/medicina60040645

Glannon, W. (2014). The limitations and potential of neuroimaging in the criminal law. *The Journal of Ethics, 18*(2), 153–170. https://doi.org/10.1007/s10892-014-9169-y

Gregory, S. (2012). The antisocial brain: Psychopathy matters. *Archives of General Psychiatry, 69*(9), 962. https://doi.org/10.1001/archgenpsychiatry.2012.222

Gunter, T. D., & Judd, S. M. (2020). Behavioral genetics in antisocial spectrum disorders with particular attention to epigenetics. In *The Wiley International handbook on psychopathic disorders and the law* (2nd ed., pp. 189–220). https://doi.org/10.1002/9781119159322.ch8

Haller, J. (2020). *Neurogenetics, genome-wide association and candidate gene studies* (pp. 67–126). Springer eBooks. https://doi.org/10.1007/978-3-030-46331-1_3

Ienca, M., & Andorno, R. (2017). Towards new human rights in the age of neuroscience and neurotechnology. *Life Sciences Society and Policy, 13*(1). https://doi.org/10.1186/s40504-017-0050-1

Kavish, N., Bergstrøm, H., Piquero, A. R., Farrington, D. P., & Boutwell, B. B. (2019). The longitudinal association between resting heart rate and psychopathic traits from a normative personality perspective. *American Journal of Criminal Justice, 45*(3), 410–425. https://doi.org/10.1007/s12103-019-09504-5

Kempes, M. (2023). Added value of neurotechnology for forensic psychiatric and psychological assessment. *Handbook of Clinical Neurology*, 217–232. https://doi.org/10.1016/b978-0-12-821375-9.00015-3

Klengel, T., & Binder, E. B. (2015). Epigenetics of stress-related psychiatric disorders and gene × environment interactions. *Neuron, 86*(6), 1343–1357. https://doi.org/10.1016/j.neuron.2015.05.036

Ko, J. H., Tang, C. C., & Eidelberg, D. (2013). Brain stimulation and functional imaging with fMRI and PET. *Handbook of Clinical Neurology*, 77–95. https://doi.org/10.1016/b978-0-444-53497-2.00008-5

Marcopulos, B. A., Kaufmann, P., & Patel, A. C. (2024). Forensic neuropsychological assessment. *Behavioral Sciences & the Law*. https://doi.org/10.1002/bsl.2656

McIntosh, T. R., Susnjak, T., Arachchilage, N., Liu, T., Watters, P., & Halgamuge, M. N. (2024, February 15). Inadequacies of large language model benchmarks in the era of generative artificial intelligence. arXiv.org. https://arxiv.org/abs/2402.09880.

Mulligan, J. (2024). Behavioural biometrics: A novel approach to user authentication in information systems security. https://openrepository.aut.ac.nz/items/2c778099-1dc6-4111-915f-2d015dc3e1ae.

Newsome, J., & Cullen, F. T. (2017). The risk-need-responsivity model revisited: Using biosocial criminology to enhance offender rehabilitation. *Criminal Justice and Behavior, 44*(8), 1030–1049. https://doi.org/10.1177/0093854817715289

Nilendu, D. (2024). Enhancing forensic education: Exploring the importance and implementation of evidence-based education system. *Egyptian Journal of Forensic Sciences, 14*(1). https://doi.org/10.1186/s41935-023-00375-w

Osborne, N. T. (2024). Interventional pathology: Ethical implications for adapting with the evolving medical landscape. https://etd.ohiolink.edu/acprod/odb_etd/etd/r/1501/10?clear=10&p10_accession_num=neomgs171666811621986.

Petrescu, L., Petrescu, C., Oprea, A., Mitruț, O., Moise, G., Moldoveanu, A., & Moldoveanu, F. (2021). Machine learning methods for fear classification based on physiological features. *Sensors, 21*(13), 4519. https://doi.org/10.3390/s21134519

Pietrini, P., & Bambini, V. (2009). Homo ferox: The contribution of functional brain studies to understanding the neural bases of aggressive and criminal behavior. *International Journal of Law and Psychiatry, 32*(4), 259–265. https://doi.org/10.1016/j.ijlp.2009.04.005

Prujean, C., Ward, T., & Vandevelde, S. (2021). Translating science to clinical practice in correctional settings. *Aggression and Violent Behavior, 63*, 101703. https://doi.org/10.1016/j.avb.2021.101703

Raine, A., & Yang, Y. (2006). Neural foundations to moral reasoning and antisocial behavior. *Social Cognitive and Affective Neuroscience, 1*(3), 203–213. https://doi.org/10.1093/scan/nsl033

Raschle, N. M., Menks, W. M., Fehlbaum, L. V., Tshomba, E., & Stadler, C. (2015). Structural and functional alterations in right Dorsomedial prefrontal and left insular cortex co-localize in adolescents with aggressive behaviour: An ALE meta-analysis. *PLoS One, 10*(9), e0136553. https://doi.org/10.1371/journal.pone.0136553

Rupawala, M., Dehghani, H., Lucas, S. J. E., Tino, P., & Cruse, D. (2018). Shining a light on awareness: A review of functional near-infrared spectroscopy for prolonged disorders of consciousness. *Frontiers in Neurology, 9*. https://doi.org/10.3389/fneur.2018.00350

Saladino, V., Lin, H., Zamparelli, E., & Verrastro, V. (2021). Neuroscience, empathy, and violent crime in an incarcerated population: A narrative review. *Frontiers in Psychology*, 12. https://doi.org/10.3389/fpsyg.2021.694212

Schug, R. A., Gao, Y., Glenn, A. L., Huang, Y. L., Peskin, M., Yang, Y., & Raine, A. (2021). The developmental evidence base. In *Forensic psychology* (3rd ed., pp. 221–262). https://doi.org/10.1002/9781394260669.ch11

Shen, F. X., Wolf, S. M., Lawrenz, F., Comeau, D. S., Dzirasa, K., Evans, B. J., Fair, D., Farah, M. J., Han, S. D., Illes, J., Jackson, J. D., Klein, E., Rommelfanger, K. S., Rosen, M. S., Torres, E., Tuite, P., Vaughan, J. T., & Garwood, M. (2024). Ethical, legal, and policy challenges in field-based neuroimaging research using emerging portable MRI technologies: Guidance for investigators and for oversight. *Journal of Law and the Biosciences, 11*(1). https://doi.org/10.1093/jlb/lsae008

Šimić, G., Tkalčić, M., Vukić, V., Mulc, D., Španić, E., Šagud, M., Olucha-Bordonau, F. E., Vukšić, M., & Hof, P. R. (2021). Understanding emotions: Origins and roles of the amygdala. *Biomolecules, 11*(6), 823. https://doi.org/10.3390/biom11060823

Sweet, J. J., Boone, K. B., Denney, R. L., Hebben, N., Marcopulos, B. A., Morgan, J. E., Nelson, N. W., & Westerveld, M. (2022). Forensic neuropsychology: History and current status. *The Clinical Neuropsychologist, 37*(3), 459–474. https://doi.org/10.1080/13854046.2022.2078740

Van Asten, A. C. (2013). On the added value of forensic science and grand innovation challenges for the forensic community. *Science & Justice, 54*(2), 170–179. https://doi.org/10.1016/j.scijus.2013.09.003

Van Dongen, J. D., Haveman, Y., Sergiou, C. S., & Choy, O. (2024). Neuroprediction of violence and criminal behavior using neuro-imaging data: From innovation to considerations for future directions. *Aggression and Violent Behavior*, 102008. https://doi.org/10.1016/j.avb.2024.102008

Van Gelder, J., De Vries, R. E., Demetriou, A., Van Sintemaartensdijk, I., & Donker, T. (2019). The virtual reality scenario method: Moving from imagination to immersion in criminal decision-making research. *Journal of Research in Crime and Delinquency, 56*(3), 451–480. https://doi.org/10.1177/0022427818819696

Velloso, G. T. (n.d.). *A technology assessment of brain-computer interfaces: Bridging present and future with a human-centered perspective - ProQuest*. https://www.proquest.com/openview/2ae1390e8bf5d68f7451906d55cc8d70/1?cbl=2026366&diss=y&pq-origsite=gscholar.

Villalón, R., María, L. C., Martínez-Álvarez, I., & Mateos, M. (2023, August 24). Undergraduates' perceptions of an online training to integrate conflicting sources in writing. Universidad a Distancia De Madrid. https://udimundus.udima.es/handle/20.500.12226/2199

Waller, R., Dotterer, H. L., Murray, L., Maxwell, A. M., & Hyde, L. W. (2017). White-matter tract abnormalities and antisocial behavior: A systematic review of diffusion tensor imaging studies across development. *NeuroImage Clinical, 14*, 201–215. https://doi.org/10.1016/j.nicl.2017.01.014

Wettermann, A., Völlm, B., & Schläfke, D. (2020). Highly structured treatment programs for addicted offenders: Comparing the effects of the reasoning & rehabilitation program and DBT-F. *Frontiers in Psychiatry, 11*. https://doi.org/10.3389/fpsyt.2020.499241

Wilson, D. (2015). *The 'criminal gene'*. Edward Elgar Publishing eBooks. https://doi.org/10.4337/9781783478828.00008

Wilson, L. (2023). Current processes for identifying and managing traumatic brain injury (TBI) in the justicesector. https://openrepository.aut.ac.nz/items/fb25a8ce-21d5-499a-aa29-431109639159.

Winter, R., Leanage, N., Roberts, N., Norman, R. I., & Howick, J. (2022). Experiences of empathy training in healthcare: A systematic review of qualitative studies. *Patient Education and Counseling, 105*(10), 3017–3037. https://doi.org/10.1016/j.pec.2022.06.015

Xiang, R., Kelemen, M., Xu, Y., Harris, L. W., Parkinson, H., Inouye, M., & Lambert, S. A. (2024). Recent advances in polygenic scores: Translation, equitability, methods and FAIR tools. *Genome Medicine, 16*(1). https://doi.org/10.1186/s13073-024-01304-9

Yen, C., Lin, C., & Chiang, M. (2023). Exploring the Frontiers of neuroimaging: A review of recent advances in understanding brain functioning and disorders. *Life, 13*(7), 1472. https://doi.org/10.3390/life13071472

Index

© The Editor(s) (if applicable) and The Author(s), under exclusive license to Springer Nature Switzerland AG 2025
K. J. Reddy, *Foundations of Criminal Forensic Neuropsychology*,
https://doi.org/10.1007/978-3-031-83771-5

O

P

R

The manufacturer's authorised representative in the EU is Springer Nature Customer Service Centre GmbH, Europaplatz 3, 69115 Heidelberg, Germany. If you have any concerns regarding our products, please contact ProductSafety@springernature.com

Printed and bound by CPI Group (UK) Ltd, Croydon, CR0 4YY

30/09/2026

02225596-0019